An Ethnohistorical
Dictionary of China

An Ethnohistorical Dictionary of China

JAMES S. OLSON

GREENWOOD PRESS
Westport, Connecticut

Library of Congress Cataloging-in-Publication Data

Olson, James Stuart, 1946–
    An ethnohistorical dictionary of China / James S. Olson.
      p. cm.
    Includes bibliographical references and index.
    ISBN 0–313–28853–4 (alk. paper)
    1. Ethnology—China—Dictionaries. 2. China—Ethnic relations—
dictionaries. I. Title.
DS730.074   1998
305.8'00951—dc21   97–27110

British Library Cataloguing in Publication Data is available.

Library of Congress Catalog Card Number: 97–27110
ISBN: 0–313–28853–4

First published in 1998

Greenwood Press, 88 Post Road West, Westport, CT 06881
An imprint of Greenwood Publishing Group, Inc.

Printed in the United States of America

The paper used in this book complies with the
Permanent Paper Standard issued by the National
Information Standards Organization (Z39.48–1984).

10 9 8 7 6 5 4 3 2 1

Contents

Preface   vii

The Dictionary   1

Appendix A: 1990 Populations of Officially Recognized
Nationalities in the People's Republic of China   395

Appendix B: A Chronology of Chinese History   397

Appendix C: Autonomous Ethnic Political Units in the People's
Republic of China   409

Selected Bibliography of English Titles   415

Index   423

Preface

Putting together an ethnohistorical dictionary of China has proven to be a daunting task. Part of the problem, of course, is defining ethnicity. Most anthropologists argue that ethnicity is a sense of individual identity with a larger group based on any combination of racial, religious, linguistic, and class similarities. The possible number of permutations on these five factors can further be complicated by rates of acculturation and assimilation over time. At any given moment, ethnic loyalties tend to be dynamic rather than static, subject to infinite variety because of economic, demographic, political, and social change. No sooner do anthropologists publish their research than group circumstances change.

This is particularly true in the case of Chinese ethnohistory. Discussing linguistic groups in the People's Republic of China (PRC), for example, is particularly difficult because the government insists on maintaining the fiction that there is only one Chinese language, and that it is divided into a series of dialects. To argue otherwise would require government officials to recognize major ethnic divisions with the dominant Han people, something Chinese officials have been extremely reluctant to do.

Most linguists argue, however, that the definition of "dialect" means that it is mutually intelligible by users of other "dialects" of the same language. The Chinese government claims that eight dialects of the language exist within the national boundaries: Mandarin, Wu, Jin, Gan, Xiang, Hakka, Yue, and Min. The problem with that definition, of course, is that none of these so-called dialects is mutually intelligible with the other. The people who speak them may very well be united by their Han* descent and their shared eclectic mix of Buddhist, Taoist, and Confucian religious beliefs, but they cannot understand one another's spoken languages, which should render them members of different ethnic groups.

Complicating the issue even more is the fact that each of the Chinese languages possesses many dialects, and some of those dialects are not mutually intelligible to speakers of related dialects.

At the same time, however, all Chinese languages share an unusual linguistic similarity. They cannot be mutually understood by different speakers, but they all employ the same written script, which is mutually readable. Also, if an outsider asks a Wu or Mandarin speaker what language he or she speaks, the answer is invariably "Chinese." Some linguists have begun employing the term "regionalect" to describe the Chinese languages. Whether or not Mandarin, Wu, Gan, Xian, Hakka, Jin, Yue, and Min are dialects, regionalects, or languages, they divide the more than 1.1 billion Han peoples into distinguishable, individual groups whose members share loyalty and a sense of identity with one another because of language.

Political realities also complicate a description of ethnicity in China. I have endeavored here to include descriptions of all the major ethnic groups in China, but in doing so I must define just exactly what I mean by China. Is the People's Republic of China really China, or must Taiwan be included, as the Chinese Communist party insists? Or is the Republic of Taiwan on Formosa the legitimate political representative of the Chinese people? Hong Kong became part of the People's Republic of China on July 1, 1997, but Macao, until December 20, 1999, at least, will remain a part of the Portuguese empire. Tibet also poses a problem. Many Tibetan nationalists will certainly reject the notion that Tibet is part of the People's Republic of China because they feel that the Chinese invasion and occupation of Tibet are illegitimate. Indian nationalists feel the same way about the Aksai Chin region of the Kashmir, which borders Tibet. Aksai Chin was clearly under Indian control until 1959, when Chinese armies moved in and claimed the region. India protests the claim, but the matter has not yet been settled.

In an effort to be inclusive, I have therefore defined China very broadly. For the purposes of *An Ethnohistorical Dictionary of China*, China includes the People's Republic of China, the Republic of China on Taiwan, Tibet, and the Aksai Chin region of Jammu and Kashmir. Such an approach will, no doubt, offend the political assumptions of many people, especially human rights activists interested in East and Central Asia, but I decided that being as inclusive as possible rather than as exclusive as possible was the lesser of two evils.

Another problem with discussing ethnicity in China grows out of the country's recent history. With the triumph of Mao Zedong and the Chinese Communist party in 1949, China all but closed itself off to the outside world. It became nearly impossible for foreign scholars to gain access to the People's Republic of China, and opportunities to conduct fieldwork for anthropologists and archaeologists evaporated. Chinese scholars continued their work and published the results of their research in Mandarin-language journals, but access to them by Western scholars was limited by the language problem and by the all too frequent unwillingness of the central government to distribute information abroad. In the paranoia of a totalitarian state, any and all information becomes grist for foreign espionage mills. The central government has rigidly controlled the flow of information in and out of the People's Republic of China. As a result, major Western scholarly journals in anthropology, ethnology, sociology, linguistics, and archaeology carried few articles about contemporary Chinese society during the 1950s, 1960s, and 1970s. Even after the Cultural Revolution ended, when government censorship standards relaxed somewhat, it was still difficult, if not impossible, for social scientists to get into the PRC.

Finally, certain political paradigms in the People's Republic of China affect the ways in which social scientists approach the study of ethnicity. Although the vast majority of the people of the PRC and the Republic of China are of Han descent, there are tens of millions of minority peoples. Most ethnologists would agree that these minorities are divided into hundreds of ethnic groups. The central government, however, has refused to acknowledge such diversity. They have officially recognized only fifty-five minority "nationalities," even though many of those minority groups have no general sense of nationalism and are divided into dozens of subgroups based on linguistic, religious, demographic, and social differences. An asterisk (*) in the text indicates a separate entry.

I wish to express my appreciation to librarians at Sam Houston State University, Brigham Young University, Rice University, the University of Texas at Austin, the University of California at Los Angeles, and the University of California at Berkeley. I would also like to express my appreciation to Cynthia Harris, my editor at Greenwood, for her patience in seeing this project to its completion.

A

A LONG. See **NU.**

A NU. See **NU.**

A WA. The A Wa people—also known as A Wo, A Va, and A Vo—are considered by many ethnologists in the People's Republic of China (PRC) to be a subgroup of the Wa,* an officially recognized minority nationality. Most Wa live in the southwestern reaches of Yunnan Province, primarily in Ximeng, Cangyuan, Menglian, Gengma, Lancang, Shuangjiang, Yongde, and Zhenkang counties. They are concentrated demographically in Ximeng and Cangyuan counties. Most A Wa are farmers, but their farming techniques vary from village to village; some use traditional slash-and-burn methods, and others employ more modern, sophisticated techniques. They raise wet rice, dry rice, maize, millet, tubers, and wheat. Classifying them as a subgroup of the Wa, however, poses problems to ethnologists and ethnolinguists. The A Wa dialect is not mutually intelligible with most of the other Wa dialects, and because of that reality, most A Wa people view themselves more as A Wa than as Wa. The process of ethnogenesis, in which they see themselves primarily as Wa people, is not yet complete.

A YIA. See **NU.**

ABA. See **SHOR.**

ABIN. See **SHOR.**

ABOR. See **ADI.**

ABORSA. See **ADI.**

ABUIT. See **ADI.**

ACHA. See **HEZHEN.**

ACHA. See **JINGPO.**

ACHANG. The Achang people—also identified by their neighbors and Chinese and European ethnologists as Daisa, Hansa, Maingtha, Mongsha, Ngachang, Mengsa, Mengsa-shan, and Xunchuan—are one of the smaller officially recognized minority nationalities in the People's Republic of China (PRC). The 1990 national census gave them a total of 27,708 people, and today that number is probably approaching 30,000. They can be found today in far western Yunnan Province, especially in Longchuan, Lianghe, and Luxi counties. The region is today designated as the Dehong Dai-Jingpo Autonomous Prefecture. Some Achangs can also be found living across the frontier in northeastern Myanmar (Burma). In terms of their language and material culture, they are closely related to the Jingpo.* Many ethnologists consider the Achangs to be a subgroup of the Kachin* people.

Achangs prefer to live in valleys and small plains that are surrounded by mountains. They select their village sites at the foot of a mountain or at the edge of a plain, and a typical village consists of several patrilineally related groups. It is also not at all uncommon for Han,* Dai,* and Hui* peoples to live in Achang villages.

Chinese historical documents first make note of the Achangs during the Tang dynasty more than a thousand years ago, when they were known as the Xunchuan people. They originated to the north and to the east in what is today northern Myanmar and settled in western Yunnan. By the thirteenth century, the Achangs had taken up residence in their present homeland in the Dehong Dai-Jingpo Autonomous Prefecture.

Because of geographical isolation and indigenous economies, the region of far western Yunnan Province has never had a monoculture. Different ethnic groups live in close proximity to one another, even with each other in many pluralistic villages. The Achang are surrounded by a variety of other ethnic groups. Because they have adopted so much of the material culture of the surrounding groups, the Achang are hardly distinguishable any more to outsiders as a distinct ethnic identity.

Of course, they are quite distinguishable to one another. The Achang language is classified by ethnolinguists as a branch of the Tibeto-Burman* cluster in the Sino-Tibetan language family. It remains the primary language of the Achang, although many of them are also bilingual in Dai, Chinese,* Jingpo, Wa,* and/

or De'ang.* The Achang are divided into two primary subgroups based on dialect. The Fusa dialect of Achang is spoken on the Fusa plains. It has been heavily influenced by Dai, Burmese, and Jingpo. The Lianghe dialect has a complex mix of Chinese, Jingpo, and Lisu* words.

Historically, the Achang economy has revolved around subsistence levels of wet-rice agriculture. They also produce sugar cane and oil products in Lianghe and Luxi, and tobacco in the region of the Fusa plains. They have adapted their planting and harvesting to the prevailing weather patterns, particularly the arrival of the monsoon season. Tobacco, sugarcane, and oil-producing plants generate cash for the Achang economy. Achang blacksmiths are widely known regionally for their high-quality ironware. Textile production and silversmithing are also part of the local economy.

In recent decades, the Achang economy has changed. The production of wet rice, tobacco, sugarcane, and oil-producing plants continues, as does Achang ironworking and silversmithing. However, since the Communist victory in 1949, the central government has become increasingly involved in the economic life of the Achang. State programs to resettle Han people throughout the country as a means of encouraging assimilation have brought tens of thousands of immigrants to western Yunnan Province. The newcomers have succeeded in taking control—through outright seizure, legal purchase, or government condemnation—of large portions of Achang land. Instead of working as subsistence farmers on communal land, the Achang are rapidly becoming skilled workers, employed primarily by Shan businessmen. Since 1956, the Achang still engaged in agriculture have been forced by law to sell their produce to the central government at a fixed price.

Land tenure has also evolved over the years. In ancient times, land was controlled by Dai feudal lords or Achang chiefs. After the revolution, the landlords lost the land, although peasant families still had to pay rent to them. A brisk commerce in land sales took place among peasant households until 1956, when the central government mandated communal or state ownership of the land. They then experienced a steady, long-term decline in production because the peasants could no longer keep the fruits of their labor. In 1982 Chinese officials reversed their policy and redivided the communal land among the peasants, a decision that has led to substantial increases in agricultural productivity.

The Achang social structure is based on a system of patrilineal descent, in which members of a village or several villages trace their ancestry back to a common male. Individuals must marry outside their patrilineal group, and marriages are generally arranged by parents for economic advantage. The fundamental family unit of Achang society is a patriarchal family that includes two or three generations.

Religion divides the Achang into two communities. The Achang in the Fusa and Lasa regions, who received the Buddhist faith from neighboring Dai people, are followers of Theravada Buddhism. Theravada Buddhism, which came to the Achang by way of India, differs substantially from the Mahayana Buddhism common among the Han people. Archaic and conservative, Theravada Buddhism views salvation as a future state distinct from the present; individuals find nirvana by transcending the present and detaching themselves from worldy concerns. The more progressive Mahayana Buddhism, on the other hand, is comfortable with the notion that any individual, through acts of love and charity, can achieve nirvana. Mahayana Buddhism has an activist spirit; Theravada Buddhism is more passive. Some Achangs are also identified as Hinayana Buddhists.

In Lianhe, Luxi, and other regions of Achang settlement, the more traditional animist faith still prevails, although the people also practice a form of ancestor worship. In the indigenous Achang religion, animals, plants, minerals, sun, moon, stars, and the earth are alive and are imbued with a measure of knowledge, individual consciousness, and an awareness of the things around them. The people give names to every tree, animal, river, stream, meadow, mountain, hill, and valley, as well as to days, weeks, months, and seasons. All of creation has a spiritual essence, and there is a balance and solidarity to nature.

A strong element of shamanism also imbues the Achang religion. Like other indigenous, animist peoples, the Achang believe that the natural world's balance depends upon respect for nature. Disobedience and disrespect toward the natural world can easily ignite vengeance and retribution. Beyond the world of animals, objects, and natural phenomena, Achang religion functions in the world of spirits. The existence of a variety of mythological, unseen beings, such as water spirits, house ghosts, and cloud-beings, is taken for granted in Achang culture. All of these unseen beings function actively in the world according to supernatural laws, and when the events of the natural world appear disruptive or illogical, Achangs blame these invisible spirits and appeal to shamans for assistance. Rituals, ceremonies, and magical devotions are the stock-in-trade of the shamans. By seeing life in terms of magical casuality, the Achang feel more powerful in dealing with their environment.

SUGGESTED READING: Tan Leshan, "Achang," in Paul V. Hockings, ed., *The Encyclopedia of World Cultures*, vol. 6, *East and Southeast Asia*, 1991.

ADI. The Adi—also known as the Aborsa, Abuits, Aduits, and Tanis—comprise an ethnic group of approximately 40,000 people. The vast majority of them can be found today living in the Arunachal Pradesh area of India, which is located in the far northeastern region of the country, bordering southeastern Tibet and far northern Myanmar (Burma). They are divided into the following subgroups: the Aka, Padam, Minyong, Pangi, Shimong, Mimat, Ashing, Pasi, Karko, Bokar, Bori, Ramo, Pailibo, Milang, Tangam, Tangin, and Gallong. Of these, the Padam, Minyong, and Shimong are the largest in terms of population. The most dense concentration of Adi people occurs on the southern slopes of the Himalayan mountains, between the Dihing River and the Subansiri River in Arunachal Pradesh's Siang District. Scattered groups also live in northern Myanmar as well as across the border in the People's Republic of China (PRC). The PRC Adi—primarily in far southeastern Tibet, northwestern Yunnan Province, and southwestern Sichuan province—number less than a thousand and constitute one of the country's tiniest ethnic minorities.

Ethnolinguists classify the Adi language as part of the Tibeto-Burman* language family, and they are divided into a number of subgroups based upon dialect. The dialects, which are mutually intelligible, include Bori, Bomo-Janbo, Mimat, Aieng, Pasi, Minyong, Padam, Milang, Pangi, and Shimong.

Historically, the Adis were a politically dominant people in the northwest frontier region of India. They exercised a good deal of political and military influence in the mountainous regions from Tibet to Assam, and they managed to exact tribute from many of their ethnic neighbors. More than once in the eighteenth and nineteenth centuries, when Great Britain controlled the subcontinent, military expeditions were sent against the Adi to subdue them, and the foreign armies always encountered bitter resistance.

Today, the Adi people have settled down into a political accommodation with their Indian, Burmese, and Chinese neighbors. Most Adis are small-scale farmers who practice traditional slash-and-burn production techniques. Because of cycles of soil exhaustion, they relocate their villages every several years. Adi farmers raise rice, maize, tobacco, ginger, red peppers, and pumpkins; sugarcane and opium are their primary cash crops. They prefer to build their villages on hilltops, usually with a sloping incline on one side with easy access to a river, and a steep decline on the other side, which facilitates defense from enemy attacks. Houses are built on stilts and in rows.

Adi society is organized around patrilineal clans, which themselves are divided into numerous subclans. Most of these are further divided into moieties. Subclans remain strictly exogamous today, and the Adi prefer their clans to be exogamous as well. Each Adi village is considered an autonomous political unit, with a village council, known as the *kebang* and based on clan representation, responsible for community-wide decisions. Groups of villages join together to form a *bango*, which is essentially a multivillage political council.

Traditional religious animism still thrives in Adi villages. The Adi believe in a series of major deities—including Seti, the earth god, and Melo, the sky god—who are relatively independent of human affairs. They also, however, worry about Epom, the son of Robo, who is the father of all evil spirits. People who die unnatural deaths live in the world of Epom and bring harm and danger to human society. On the other hand, Benji Bama is a powerful benign spirit who can counter the powers of Epom and his angels. Only through proper personal conduct and observance of important religious ceremonies can evil spirits be held at bay.

SUGGESTED READINGS: J. N. Chowdbury, *A Comparative Study of Adi Religion*, 1971; Christoph von Fürer-Haimendorf, "Religious Beliefs and Ritual Practices of the Minyong Abors of Assam, India," *Anthropos* 49 (1954), 588–604; Parmanand Lal and Biman Kumar Das Gupta, *Lower Siang People*, 1979; Hugh R. Page, Jr., "Abor," in Paul V. Hockings, ed., *The Encyclopedia of World Cultures*, vol. 6, *East and Southeast Asia*, 1991; Sachin Roy, *Aspects of Padam-Minyong Culture*, 1960; Frederick J. Simoons and

Elizabeth S. Simoons, *A Ceremonial Ox of India: The Mithan in Nature, Culture, and History*, 1968; L. R. N. Srivastava, *The Gallongs*, 1962.

ADUIT. See **ADI.**

AHI. The Ahi are one of the subgroups of the Yi* peoples of the People's Republic of China (PRC). Although the Yi are an officially recognized minority nationality of more than seven million people, they are divided into a variety of subgroups whose sense of ethnic identity is quite parochial, based on region and dialects that are usually not mutually intelligible. The Ahi can be found living today in Yunnan and Guizhou provinces, usually in autonomous political subdivisions established by the PRC government for the Yi. They are especially concentrated near Lunan, a town located southeast of the city of Kunming. Ethnolinguists believe that the Ahi language is more closely related to Hani* and Lisu* than to Yi. The Ahi descend from the ancient Tusan people native to the Kunming region of Yunnan and the Chengdu in Sichuan. The Ahi economy is overwhelmingly agricultural. At lower elevations, Ahi farmers produce maize, potatoes, buckwheat, and oats as staples. In the highlands, they raise cattle, sheep, goats, and horses. Chickens and pigs are ubiquitous in Yi villages. Poorer Yi families supplement their diets by collecting acorns, roots, wild vegetables, and herbs, and by fishing and hunting. Most Ahi live in mountain hamlets of less than twenty households. They continue to be devoted to an eclectic religion that fuses elements of Buddhism, Daoism, and their indigenous animism, although a minority converted to Christianity in the 1920s and 1930s.

AHKA. See **AKHA.**

AHNI. See **HANI.**

AHWENKE. See **EVENK.**

AIHUI. The Aihui people constitute one of the subdivisions of the Butha,* themselves a subgroup of the Daur* people.

AJI. See **JINGPO**.

AKHA. The Akha (Ahka, Aini, Aka, Ak'a, Akaza, Ake) are one of the smaller ethnic groups living today in the People's Republic of China (PRC). They can also be found in Thailand, Myanmar (Burma), and Laos. Their self-designation is Akaza, which means Akha people. They are known to Tai*-speaking people as Ekaw (Ikaw, Ikho) or sometimes just Kaw, which the Akha consider to be an epithet. They speak a tonal language that ethnolinguists consider to be part of the large Sino-Tibetan family. More particularly, they classify Akadaw (the Akha language) as a branch of the Southern Loloish group of the Lolo-Burmese cluster of languages. The Akha language is further broken down into a number of dialects, all of which are mutually intelligible except for Akui (Akhui, Ako, Akho, Ake). Because of the regional expansion of Tai-speaking people in the last several centuries, the Akha language has adopted a number of Tai loan words. Although there is no indigenous Akha script, Christian missionaries have created an Akha written language by developing Roman-based and Thai-based alphabets.

Anthropologists and archaeologists have engaged in a vigorous debate about Akha origins. Many consider them to be a subgroup of the Hani* people. Some scholars place them near the Tibetan borderlands, while others are convinced that they come from southern and eastern Yunnan in China. Today, the Akha are distributed over a wide area of China, Myanmar, Laos, Thailand, and Vietnam. There are approximately 450,000 Akha living in the region, and perhaps 170,000 of them are located in the highlands of southern Yunnan Province. They live in hillside and mountainside villages of between one hundred and one thousand people. Their houses are built of logs, bamboo, and thatch. Small, narrow pathways through the forests connect family compounds, which are often fenced.

The Akha economy revolves around both subsistence and commercial agriculture. Their staple crop is rice, which they raise through slash-and-burn techniques. It is usually a form of dry-rice horticulture that is completely dependent upon rainfall for necessary moisture. Where water sources are predictable and geography permits, the Akha raise rice in irrigated, terraced fields. In the same fields as the dry rice, Akha farmers plant pumpkins, maize, beans, and green vegetables. As part of the transition from subsistence to more commercialized forms of economic activity, some Akha farmers have begun to produce cash crops as well, primarily corn, cotton, soybeans, chilis, and opium poppies. Akha livestock production includes chickens, hogs, ducks, goats, cattle, and water buffalo. They also supplement their diets when necessary by foraging (fruits, mushrooms, and berries), hunting (wild boar, deer, and the bamboo gopher), and fishing.

The Akha social system is based on patrilineal descent in which polygyny is permitted. Patrilineal kinship and marriage alliances provide important political and social bonds. They maintain highly egalitarian values. The traditional Akha, who have not converted to Christianity, practice an animist faith in which deceased ancestors are called upon to sustain fertility and provide protection from natural disasters. A supreme being, who gave the Akha their moral code, is recognized. They also pray to a Rice Mother to provide good harvests. The Akha who have converted to Christianity live in separate villages.

SUGGESTED READINGS: Leo Alting von Geusau, ''Dialects of Akhazan: The Interiorizations of a Perennial Minority Group,'' in John McKinnon and Wanat Bhruksasri, eds., *Highlanders of Thailand*, 1983; Cornelia Ann Kammerer, ''Akhas,'' in Paul V. Hockings, ed., *Encyclopedia of World Cultures*, vol. 6, *East and Southeast Asia*, 1991, and ''Shifting Gender Asymmetries among Akha of Northern Thailand,'' in Nancy Eberhardt, ed., *Gender, Power, and the Construction of the Moral Order: Studies from the Thai Pe-*

riphery, 1988; Paul Lewis, *Akha-English Dictionary,* 1968, and *Ethnographic Notes on the Akhas of Burma,* 1970; Paul Lewis and Elaine Lewis, ''Akha (Kaw),'' in *Peoples of the Golden Triangle: Six Tribes of Thailand,* 1984.

AKHO. The Akho people are an ethnic subgroup of the Hani* people of the People's Republic of China (PRC). Scattered numbers of Akho can also be found living in Thailand and Myanmar (Burma). The Akho people of the PRC are located in the far southeastern corner of Yunnan Province, between the Mengle and the Ailao mountain ranges. Their society is patrilineal and patriarchal, with kinship relations organized around patrilineal clans. Each clan consists of from thirty to forty households, and each clan maintains elaborate ancestral histories, which trace their origins back more than forty generations. Most of the Akho, of course, remain tied to the agricultural economy, and a few still work in a traditional subsistence economy. They raise a variety of crops, including rice, maize, beans, buckwheat, millet, tea, peanuts, sugarcane, cotton, chili peppers, ginger, and indigo. Because of recent economic development programs in southwestern Yunnan, increasing numbers of Akho men can be found working in local factories and mines.

AKHUI. See **AKHA.**

AKKA. See **AKHA.**

AKO. See **AKHA.**

AKSU. Aksu is one of the vernaculars of the Uigur* language spoken in the Xinjiang Uigur Autonomous Region of the People's Republic of China.

AKSULIK. See **UIGUR.**

AKUI. See **AKHA.**

ALBAN. The Albans are a subgroup of the Kazak* peoples of the Xinjiang Uigur Autonomous Region, Gansu Province, and Qinghai Province in the People's Republic of China.

ALISHAN. See **TSOU.**

ALSHAA. The Alshaas are a subgroup of the Mongol* peoples of the People's Republic of China. Their dialect is spoken primarily in the northwestern section of the Inner Mongolian Autonomous Region. Most Alshaa are farmers and herders, who raise barley, wheat, oats, corn, millet, potatoes, buckwheat, sorghum, apples, and a variety of vegetables. Some Alshaa also raise horses, cattle, camels, and goats, although their preferred livestock today is sheep.

ALTAI. Discussing Altai ethnicity is a difficult matter because the Altais remain highly divided in terms of subgroup loyalties. The 1989 census of the Soviet Union listed the Altai population at 71,317 people, and at least that many can be found across the border in the Mongolian People's Republic. Several thousand Altais are also located in the People's Republic of China (PRC), primarily just south of the point where the borders of Mongolia, Kazakstan, Russia, and the Xinjiang Uigur Autonomous Region meet.

A process of ethnogenesis has been at work among them for the past two centuries, but tribal loyalties remain very strong, as do linguistic differences between the various Altai subgroups. Their language belongs to the North Turkic group of languages. The Altais are divided into two well-identified groupings. The Northern Altai—also known as Chenevyy Tatar or Back Country Tatar— emerged from an on-going fusion of three tribal groups: the Tubalars, Chelkans, and Kumandins. Ethnologists surmise that the Northern Altai tribes first emerged out of a mix of ancient Samoyedic, Kettish, Ugrian, and Turkic peoples. They speak a language belonging to the Old Uigur group of the eastern division of the Turkic branch of the Uralo-Altaic linguistic family. The Tubalars are actually a group of Tofalars who broke away and mingled with Chelkans and Kumandins. The Tubalars live primarily along the left bank of the Bya River and on the northwestern coast of Lake Teletskoe. The Chelkans, who live in the Lebed' River Basin, retain only the slightest sense of separate identity, as do the Kumandins, who live along the Bya River.

The Southern Altai first emerged between the sixth and eighth centuries as descendents of the ancient Saiano-Altais, a Turkish people. From the thirteenth through the eighteenth centuries, various Mongolian tribes also joined the mix. The Southern Altai speak a language which is part of the Kipchak division of the Turkic branch of the Uralo-Altaic linguistic family. The language closely resembles Kirgiz.* Four subgroups went into the making of the Southern Altai: the Altai Kizhi, Telengit, Telesy, and Teleut. The Southern Altai have also been known historically as the Belyy, Altai, Gornyy, Porubezhny, and Biy Kalmyk. Of the Southern Altai subgroups, the Altai Kizhi and the Teleut retain a strong sense of group identity. The Altai people, southern and northern, live primarily in the Gorno-Altai Autonomous Oblast of the Altai Krai in western Siberia. The Altai Krai borders the Mongolian People's Republic and the People's Republic of China on the southeast. Other Altais live across the borders in both of those countries.

The traditional Altai economy revolved around cattle breeding and hunting. They also engaged in deer breeding and harvested the animals for their antlers for exportation to China for use in the manufacture of folk medicines. The money the Altais received from those exports provided them with the cash they needed to purchase trade goods, particularly metal tools and varieties of cloth. They lived in feudal, patriarchal societies. Those centrifugal ethnic forces were so strong that, as late as the early 1920s, the Altais identified themselves as

Tubalars, Chelkans, Kumandins, Altai Kizhis, Teleuts, Telesy, and Telengits rather than as Altais.

Although the Russians* first established contact with the Altais in the seventeenth century, the region remained under the control of the Dzungarian state until the eighteenth century. Dzungaria, also known as Sungaria, encompassed what is today northwestern China. From the eleventh to the fourteenth centuries, the region was under Mongol* control, but Tamerlane overran the area in 1389. Until 1758 it was under a Kalmuck confederation, when China incorporated Dzungaria into Xinjiang. The Altai tribes had traditionally been a very proud people, known throughout Central Asia for their ferocity and tenacity. During the first half of the eighteenth century, many of them left Dzungaria and invaded Kazakh territory, capturing Tashkent and eventually almost reaching the Ural mountains in the west. After taking control of the region in 1758, the Chinese launched a war of extermination against the Altai, and when it was over only a few thousand Altai were alive, most of whom were isolated in the Altai mountains. Russia began to assert control over the area several years later, and Russian sovereignty was finalized with the annexation of the region in 1866. The surviving Altai were under the control of ethnic Russians, except for a few thousand who found themselves surrounded by increasing numbers of Han* settlers to the east.

The expansion of Russian and Han power, however, did not wipe out Altai identity. In fact, it only intensified it. The Altai found Russian and Han culture to be heavy-handed and assimilationist, and by the early 1900s they were openly resisting it. A new religion, termed Burkhanism or White Faith, swept through the Altai tribes. It was a distinctly anti-Russian, messianic faith at whose center was the mythical Oirot Khan, supposedly a descendent of Genghis Khan who promised to liberate the Altai from Russian domination and restore them to a pre-Russian, pre-Chinese reality. Burkhanism had its formal beginnings in 1904 when Chot Chelpanov, an Altai shepherd, reported he had been visited by Oirot Khan, who was riding a white horse. The Oirot Khan told Chelpanov to pass the message that the Altai peoples were to adhere to a rigid code of behavior and avoid all contact with Russians and Chinese. Nor were they to eat from the same utensils as Christians. The religion spread through the Altai communities, forcing czarist authorities to arrest Chot Chelpanov and crush the movement. When Japan defeated Russia in the Russo-Japanese War, Burkhanism acquired a decidedly pro-Japanese flavor.

After the Bolshevik Revolution, Altai nationalism assumed a secular dimension under the leadership of B. I. Anuchin. He convened the Constituent Congress of the High Altai in February 1918 and demanded the creation of an Oirot Republic, which would also include Khakassians and Tuvinians. He expected Russia, Mongolia, and China to surrender territory for the new republic. With Russia in the middle of a civil war, the creation of such a republic appeared to be the only way of stopping a continuing process of Russification among the Altai. Many Altai leaders sided with the Mensheviks against the Bolsheviks during the conflict. By 1920 the area was under strict Soviet control. During the early 1920s, Sary-Sen Kanzychakov emerged as a new Altai nationalist leader, and he too demanded creation of a Greater Oirotia State. The People's Comissariat for Nationalities initially responded positively to the idea of an Autonomous Oirot-Khakassian Province, but the idea was stillborn. Instead, the Oirot Autonomous Oblast was created in the Altai Krai of Russia. The Soviet Union tolerated the talk of Greater Oirotia and Burkhanism until 1933, when it began to denounce the nationalist movement as a conspiracy fomented by "Chinese merchant capitalists" and the "Mongol-Lamaist bureaucracy."

During the 1920s and 1930s, Soviet authorities began to implement their socialist ideology in the Altai Krai. Altai cattle and breeding operations were collectivized, a program that inspired violent resistance among the Altais. To avoid the program, thousands of Altais took their herds across the border into Mongolia and China.

World War II hurt the Altais even more. Both the Russian and Chinese governments accused Altai nationalists of being pro-Japanese. As a result, much of the Communist party membership in the Oirot Autonomous Oblast of the Soviet Union was purged. In 1948 the Soviet Union banned use of the word Oirot, which it described as counterrevolutionary. The Oirot Autonomous Oblast was renamed the Mountainous-Altai Autonomous Oblast (Gorno-Altai Autonomous Oblast). The capital city—Oirot-Tura—was renamed Gornoaltaisk. All Soviet reference books and textbooks dropped the use of the word Oirots and called them Altais. At the time, China was in the midst of its own civil war and did little to suppress Altaian nationalism.

After the establishment of the People's Republic of China in 1949, Chinese authorities began to assert more control over the Altai. The Altai region is coveted both by Russia and China because of the wealth of its natural resources—manganese, iron ore, silver, gold, mercury, lead, wolfram, and timber. The PRC, of course, will not tolerate in the least the idea of a Greater Altaian State that includes portions of Russia, China, and Mongolia. After the collapse of the Soviet Union in 1991, some Chinese Altais moved back across the border into Russian Siberia, a demographic trend the Chinese government did not discourage. Today, the Chinese government refuses to acknowledge the reality of Altaian ethnicity or nationalism. Representatives of the three primary Altai subgroups—Kumandins, Chelkans, and Tubalars—can all be found today living in northern Xinjiang.

SUGGESTED READINGS: *The Great Soviet Encyclopedia*, vol 1, 301–4, 1973; Walter Kolarz, *The Peoples of the Soviet Far East*, 1969.

ALTAI KIJHI. See **ALTAI.**

ALTAI KIJI. See **ALTAI.**

ALTAI KIZHI. See **ALTAI.**

ALTAI KIZHI. See **KHOTON.**

ALTAIAN. See **ALTAI.**

ALTAIC. The term Altaic refers to a large family of languages that stretch from Turkey in the southwest across Central Asia and North China and on to northeastern Siberia. Practically all of the languages spoken in northern China are Altaic. They are named after the Altaic mountains in southwestern Mongolia. The Altaic language family is divided into three branches. The Turkic branch includes, in the People's Republic of China (PRC), the Kazak,* Kirgiz,* Tatar,* Uzbek,* Uigur,* Yugur,* and Salar* languages. Mongolian* (see MONGOL) is the second of the Altaic linguistic branches, and in the PRC, the following groups speak a Mongolian language: the Buryat,* the Oirat,* the Daur,* the Dongxiang,* the Bonan,* the Yugur,* and the Tu.* The third branch of Altaic is Tungus, which is the easternmost cluster. The Tungusian languages of the PRC include Evenk,* Oroqen,* Hezhen,* Xibe,* and Manchu.*
SUGGESTED READINGS: Ivan Lopatin, "The Tungus Languages," *Anthropo* 53 (1958), 427–40; Nikolaus Poppe, *Introduction to Altaic Linguistics*, 1965; S. Robert Ramsey, *The Languages of China*, 1987; Robert Underhill, *Turkish Grammar*, 1976.

ALTAY. See **ALTAI.**

ALTAY KIJI. See **ALTAI.**

ALTAYAN. See **ALTAI.**

AMDO. Amdo is one of the three primary dialects of Tibetan.* Calling it a dialect, however, is complicated by the fact that it is only marginally intelligible to speakers of Kham,* another Tibetan dialect, and is not mutually intelligible to speakers of Dbusgtsang,* the other Tibetan dialect. Speakers of the Amdo dialect are located in several autonomous prefectures in Gansu and Qinghai provinces; in Hualong Hui Autonomous County, Xunhua Salar Autonomous County, and Ledu County in Qinghai Province; and in the Aba Tibetan Autonomous Prefecture of Sichuan Province. There are four mutually intelligible Amdo dialects: Hbrogpa, Rongpa, Rongmahbroga, and Rtahu.

AMI. The Ami—also known as Amia, Moamiami, Mo-quami, and Pangtash— are one of the nine indigenous tribal peoples of Taiwan in the Republic of China. Anthropologists consider them indigenous to the east coast of the island between eastern Hualicn and northeastern Taidong. Because of the influence of Japan on the island after 1900, as well as the surrounding millions of Han* people, the Amis are in an advanced state of acculturation. Ethnolinguists today estimate that approximately 120,000 people in Taiwan speak one of five Ami dialects. Sakizaya is spoken in the northern reaches of Ami country; Northern Ami is spoken in a region located just to the south of the Sakizayas (speakers of Sak-izaya are known as the Nanshi Amis); Tavalong-Vataan is spoken by the Amis living along the Tavalong-Vataan River; Central Ami is spoken south of the Tavalong-Vataan dialect region (these people are known as Xiuguluan Amis and Coastal Amis); and Southern Ami is spoken south of the Central Ami dialect region (Southern Amis are also known as Puyuma Amis and Hengchun Amis).

Until around 1930, the Ami frequently found themselves at odds and engaged in warfare against Atayals,* Puyumas, and Bununs.* Since then those tribal conflicts have for the most part been nonviolently politicized. They prefer to live in the lowland plains and can be found scattered across a long but relatively narrow stretch of land on the coast of Taitung and Hualien counties. With a population exceeding 130,000 people, the Amis are the largest of the indigenous peoples of Taiwan. Amis speak a Austroasiatic language whose roots are in the South and Central Pacific. Ami material culture also reflects Pacific origins, although the pace of assimilation is making them more and more difficult to recognize. In recent decades, Amis have also married exogamously to Han as well as other indigenous Taiwanese people. In the process, they have increas-ingly adopted the Min language of Mandarin as their own.

Compared to other indigenous peoples on Taiwan, the Ami lifestyle is tech-nologically advanced. They live in houses made of hardwood beams and planks, bamboo, and grass thatch. Because of sophisticated agricultural techniques used in the production of maize, rice, and sweet potatoes, the Amis live in relatively large villages, some of them composed of more than one thousand people each. As a matrilineal society, the Ami recognize the most elderly woman in any household as the head of the family. In terms of village politics, councils made up of senior women preside and make major community decisions. The Amis maintain an extraordinary respect for age in their communities, and political and social authority resides in older people.

Because of their large population and their location on the eastern coast of Taiwan, the Ami people are no longer isolated from the larger society. Their indigenous neighbors are the Atayals to the north and northwest, the Bununs to the west, and the Puyumas and Paiwans* to the south. Government policies in the Republic of China are dedicated to the education and assimilation of the Ami people.

SUGGESTED READINGS: Raleigh Ferrel, *Taiwan Aboriginal Groups: Problems in Cul-tural and Linguistic Classification*, 1969; *The Republic of China Yearbook 1995*, 1996; Mei-chun Tang, "Han and Non-Han in Taiwan: A Case of Acculturation," *Bulletin of the Institute of Ethnology* (Taipei), 30 (1970); Te-hsuing Yao, *Formosan Aboriginal Culture Village*, 1988; Yvonne Yuan, "Migrate, Assimilate, or Integrate?," *Free China Review* 42 (June 1992), 4–15.

AMIA. See **AMI.**

AMOK. The Amoks are considered by many ethnologists in the People's Republic of China (PRC) to be a subgroup of the Wa,* an officially recognized minority nationality. Most Wa people live in the southwestern reaches of Yunnan Province, primarily in Ximeng, Canghyuan, Menglian, Gengma, Lancang, Shuangjiang, Yongde, and Zhenkang counties. Most Amoks are farmers who raise wet rice, dry rice, maize, millet, tubers, and wheat. Classifying them as a subgroup of the Wa, however, poses problems to ethnologists and ethnolinguists. The Amok dialect is not mutually intelligible with most of the other Wa dialects, and because of that reality, most Amoks view themselves more as Amok than as Wa.

AMULET MIAO. See **MONTENKAU.**

ANAN. See **MAONAN.**

ANG. See **DE'ANG.**

ANGKU. See **K'ALA.**

ANU. See **NU.**

ANUNG. The Anungs are a subgroup of the Lisu* people of Yunnan Province in the People's Republic of China (PRC). Along with other Lisu peoples, most Anungs are concentrated between the Sawleen River and the Mekong River in western Yunnan Province. The Anung language is not mutually intelligible with most of the other Lisu tongues, and it is closely related to Akha,* Lahu,* and Yi.* They are more likely to identify themselves as ethnic Anungs than as Lisus. They employ a social system that revolves around a variety of patrilineal, exogamous clans that exercise great political power. Most Anung live at higher elevations, usually in ridgeline villages between 3,500 and 10,000 feet in altitude. They are swidden farmers who produce maize, mountain rice, millet, and barley.

APA TANI. The Apa Tanis are a small, demographically concentrated ethnic group living today in the far northwestern extremity of Arunachal Pradesh State in India, primarily near the borders of Assam and Tibet. Ethnolinguists classify their language within the Tibeto-Burman* family. Most Apa Tanis are settled farmers who employ sophisticated irrigation techniques to produce a variety of grains and vegetables. All land is privately owned, and titles are transferable to the next generation. The Apa Tani social structure is rigidly divided into two classes—the landless and the landlords—and intermarriage between the groups is strictly prohibited. The total Apa Tani population in India is approaching 20,000 people today, and because of their proximity to Himalayan trade routes

and the border with Tibet, there may very well be, at any given time, a handful of Apa Tanis in the People's Republic of China.
SUGGESTED READING: *Atlas of Man*, 1978.

ARISAN. See **TSOU.**

ASILUMA. The Asilumas are an ethnic subgroup of the Hani* people of the People's Republic of China (PRC). Scattered clusters of Asilumas can also be found living in Thailand and Myanmar (Burma). The PRC Asilumas are located in the far southeastern corner of Yunnan Province, between the Mengle and the Ailao mountains. Their society revolves around a series of powerful patrilineal clans. Asilumas see themselves more as Asilumas than as Hanis.

ASSAMESE. Today, more than fifteen million people claim membership in the Assamese ethnic group. The vast majority of them live in Assam State in far northeastern India, although a very small number, primarily merchants and traders, can be found across the frontier in far southeastern Tibet. About two-thirds of Assamese are Hindus in their religious loyalties, while the rest are Muslims. Assamese Muslims are known as the Garia people. In India, the vast majority of Assamese are farmers who raise rice and tea.
SUGGESTED READING: Vincent Smith, *The Oxford History of India*, 1981.

ATAYAL. The Atayal people—also known regionally and in the scholarly literature as Atazans, Etalls, Taiyals, and Tayals—are one of the indigenous peoples of Taiwan in the Republic of China. Their population exceeds 70,000 people, more than 20 percent of the indigenous people of the island. Most Atayals are widely distributed in the central highlands of the northern region of Taiwan, primarily in northern Nantou County and in Yilan and Taipei counties. Some Atayals can also be found today in the counties of Taoyuan, Xinchu, Miaoli, and Taizhong.

Atayal is divided into two mutually intelligible dialects: Segoleg* and Tseole.* Although Segoleg is a relatively unified dialect spoken in the central Atayal region, Tseole has a number of vernaculars and is spoken in the eastern and western areas of Atayalic settlement. The closest aboriginal neighbors to Atayals are the Saisiyats* to the west and the Bununs* and Amis* to the south. The Atayals are divided into three subgroups: the Segolegs (Seqoleq, Sqoleqs), the Tseoles (Tsou, Tse'ole'), and the Sedegs* (Sedeqs). Some ethnologists do not consider the Sedegs an Atayal subgroup but an independent ethnic entity. Chinese demographers estimate the number of Atayal speakers today at approximately 40,000 people.

Like most people in the world still living a premodern lifestyle, the Atayals live largely in a subsistence economy characterized by the slash-and-burn cultivation of millet, rice, sweet potatoes, and taro. They supplement their fundamentally agricultural diet by hunting deer and wild boar. The Atayals have traditionally dressed themselves in tapo, a clothing made of bark, but in recent years they have begun to opt for commercially produced shirts, pants, and dresses. Also in recent years, they have largely given up their traditional iron-smithing techniques for the production of spears, knives, and axes in favor of stronger, commercially manufactured steel tools. Most Atayals living traditional lifestyles dwell in part-subterranean houses constructed of walls made of branches and cordwood topped by gabled roofs of slate, wood shingles, or thatch.

The Atayals have long been loyal to their indigenous animistic faith, in which their Taiwanese environment is alive with spirits, ghosts, and unseen forces, and in which tribal shamans must appease those forces through ritualistic ceremonies. They call these spirits *utux*. The Atayals also believe that their dead ancestors still live spiritually and can influence their lives. Atayals speak a Proto Austronesian language whose roots are in the South and Central Pacific. They have no written language. In recent years, Taiwanese government policy has worked to integrate the Atayals into modern society and modern economy through education and infrastructural improvements.

SUGGESTED READINGS: *The Republic of China Yearbook 1995*, 1996; Yvonne Yuan, "Migrate, Assimilate, or Integrate?," *Free China Review* 42 (June 1992), 4–15.

ATAYALIC. The term Atayalic is a linguistic reference to one group of languages spoken by indigenous peoples on Taiwan in the Republic of China. Included in the Atayalic group are Atayal* and Sedeg.*

SUGGESTED READING: S. A. Wurm, B. T'sou, D. Bradley, et al., eds., *Language Atlas of China*, 1987.

ATAZAN. See **ATAYAL.**

ATSA. See **ZAIWA.**

ATSI. See **ZAIWA.**

AXI. The Axi people are an ethnic group in the People's Republic of China (PRC), although the central government has never extended to them any formal recognition. Official PRC publications classify the Axi as a subgroup of the Yi* people, and, indeed, they speak a Yi language. But Axi is not mutually intelligible with the vast majority of other Yi languages, and the Axis give themselves a distinct, separate identity. They will acknowledge a certain cultural affinity with the Yi, but they insist that they are a separate people. Most Axi live today in Mile County of Yunnan Province.

The traditional Axi economy has been overwhelmingly agricultural. At lower elevations, Axi farmers produced maize, potatoes, buckwheat, and oats as staples. They also raised cattle, sheep, goats, and horses in the highlands. Chickens and pigs are ubiquitous in Axi villages. Poorer Axi families supplement their diets by collecting acorns, roots, wild vegetables, and herbs, and by fishing and hunting. Opium was an important cash crop until the Chinese government outlawed its production late in the 1930s. Although the Communist government has continued the prohibition, many Axi farmers still produce opium illegally and sell it on the black market.

After Mao Zedong's victory in 1949, traffic along the Burma Road slowed to a standstill. Government policies, which so discouraged anything resembling free enterprise capitalism, rendered southwestern China a very inhospitable place for capital investment or commerce. During the 1960s and 1970s, the Cultural Revolution, with its ideological zealotry, only made things worse. The Axi economy, as well as that of much of China, reverted to near-subsistence levels of production. In 1979, however, to lift the country out of the morass into which it had fallen, the central government began to implement economic reforms. Market economy instruments and personal profit were no longer considered evil, and an economic revival came to southeastern China in the 1980s and 1990s.

Most of the Axi today live in mountain hamlets that cannot even be considered villages. They usually average only twenty households. Axi homes are single-story constructions of wood and dirt. There are no windows. Cattle and sheep sleep indoors with family members. In recent years, more and more Axi families are building brick and tile houses similar to those used by neighboring Han* families. An eclectic mix of Daoism, Buddhism, and traditional ancestor worship characterizes Axi religious beliefs. A good number of Axis, descendents of ancestors who listened to Christian missionaries in the 1920s and 1930s, are Christians today.

SUGGESTED READINGS: Mike Edwards, "Our Man in China: Joseph Rock," *National Geographic* 191 (January 1997), 62–100; Li Ming, "Liang Mountains: Home of the Yi People," *China Today* 39 (July 1990), 34–39; Lin Yueh-Hwa (Lin Yaohua) and Naranbilik, "Yi," in Paul V. Hockings, ed., *The Encyclopedia of World Cultures*, vol. 6, *East and Southeast Asia*, 1991; Yao Aiyun, "Unique Dance of the Axi People," *China Today* 45 (June 1996), 61–62.

B

BAHENG. Baheng is a subdialect of the Bunu* language, which is part of the larger Yao* cluster of people in the People's Republic of China.

BAI. The Bais—also identified locally and by scholars as the Baihuo, Bai Man, Baini, Baizi, Baizu, Ber Deser, Ber Wa Deser, Bo Bozi, Cuan, La Bhu, Minchia, Minchia-tzu, Minjia, Pai, Paijen, Paiwan, Paiman, Pernutuu, Pertsu, Petsen, Petsu Shua Ber Ni, Po, Shua Bern Ni, and Sou—are one of the People's Republic of China's (PRC) recognized minority nationalities. In fact, they constitute the largest concentrated ethnic minority group in southwestern China. They refer to themselves as Bozi, Baini, Baihuo, or Baizi and live primarily in Yunnan Province. The Bai peoples have for centuries been scattered widely throughout Yunnan and Sichuan provinces, but today most Bais live in the Dali Baizu Autonomous Region in Yunnan. They are particularly concentrated in the region where the Chang (Yangtze) River, which closely parallels the Mekong River in Yunnan, changes course and heads east toward the South China Sea. Significantly smaller numbers of Bai can be found today in Liangshan in Sichuan Province, Sangzhi County in Hunan Province, and in the Bijie District of Guizhou Province. The 1990 national census placed the Bai population at 1,594,827, with more than two thirds of them living in the Dali Baizu Autonomous Region. Chinese demographers today place the Bai population at approximately 1,750,000 people.

Ethnolinguists are confused about how to classify the Bai language. Some of its characteristics indicate that Bai is a Tibeto-Burman* language, but equally compelling arguments can be made that it is Mon-Khmer* or Tai.* It also possesses similarities to Loloish languages. A minority of linguists even consider it a distant relative of Chinese.* They argue that Bai is a Sinitic language that broke away from Chinese more than 2,500 years ago, even before what is known as the linguistic period of "Old Chinese." Bai also contains a significant number of loan words from "Middle Chinese," the main Sinitic language of the seventh century. They have never enjoyed the use of a written language, so those who are literate read Chinese. In fact, they have adapted Chinese characters to a Bai pronunciation system. Large numbers of Bai who are bilingual also speak a Mandarin* dialect. It seems quite certain that the Bais are among the oldest inhabitants of Yunnan Province, but their origins are elusive. Bai ties to Han* people are extensive, and they are considered to be one of China's most acculturated minority nationalities.

Historians have determined that the first recorded contact between Han and Bai in Chinese history occurred during the third century B.C., when Qin armies conquered the Kingdom of Bo and took Bo people as slaves. The Bo were the ancestral parents of the Bai. In 182 B.C., large numbers of Han settlers began arriving in the Bai homeland. By the third century A.D., the Chinese were referring to the Bo as the "Sou" people. By the next century they were known as the "Cuan." In A.D. 937, a prominent, charismatic Cuan, or "Bai," man named Duan Siping managed to impose a political unity over dozens of Bai subgroups and founded the Kingdom of Dali, which survived for nearly three centuries.

During that time, the Bai people stayed in close political and social contact with China's Song dynasty. Mongol* armies conquered the Dali Kingdom in 1253, and Mongol soldiers settled permanently in the region and married Bai women. The Mongol presence lasted for more than a century, but in 1368, an army under the control of the Ming dynasty invaded southwestern China and drove out the Mongols. At that point, Bai peoples came under the Chinese civil service system and the system of county magistrates. Thousands of Han soldiers and administrators settled permanently in the region and took Bai wives. Han people then began to refer to the Bais as "Minjia," which translates as "common people," a designation that separated Bais from surrounding Han soldiers, bureaucrats, farmers, and merchants. The local culture remained far more Bai than Han, but it was the beginning of a process of acculturation that continues today.

During the late nineteenth century, the Bai joined with several other minority ethnic groups and rose up in rebellion against the Qing dynasty. In 1874 Du Wenxiu, a prominent local Hui* leader, formed a coalition of Hui, Bai, Naxi,* Yi,* Dai,* Jingpo,* and local Han peoples that attacked representatives of the local Qing administration. The uprising succeeded temporarily, but eighteen years later Qing armies showed up in force and stamped out the rebellion.

The social, cultural, and political life of the Bai people remained relatively unchanged for the next half century, but completion of the Burma Road in 1938, which linked the Bai region commercially with Burmese and Indian markets, ended forever their isolation from the outside world. Christian missionaries made their way into Bai settlements and won some converts, although most Bais refused the enticement and viewed with suspicion their countrymen who were baptized. During World War II, Chinese Nationalists occupied the region, but they were defeated in 1949 as part of the revolution. Late in 1956, the central government established the Dali Baizu Autonomous Region.

The Bai people enjoy a small measure of self-government, at least compared to many other groups in the People's Republic of China, but the Communist triumph in 1949 nevertheless had a profound impact on their lives. Before the revolution, less than 10 percent of the Bai population owned 75 percent of the land, and most Bais worked as peasant farmers, tenant farmers, or farm laborers. In the mid-1950s, the central government nationalized all of the land and forced Bai farmers into collectives. The program alienated the Bai elites, who lost much of their wealth, but it had relatively little impact on most tenant farmers and laborers. Since then, Bai farmers have seen land tenure systems evolve according to changing government policies. Beginning in the early 1980s, in order to boost agricultural productivity, the central government turned back to individual and family production systems and away from collective entities.

The traditional Bai economy has been overwhelmingly agricultural. At lower elevations, especially in high plains regions, Bai farmers have produced rice and wheat as staple crops, while at higher altitudes, maize and buckwheat have been the primary crops. Opium was traditionally an important cash crop, but the Chinese government outlawed its production late in the 1930s. Although the Communist government has continued the prohibition, many Bai farmers produce opium illegally and sell it on the black market. Other Bai cash crops include tea, sugarcane, tobacco, cotton, peanuts, and citrus. Bai villages, which traditionally are located on the Dali plain and near the shores of Lake Erhai, are also replete with pigs, chickens, horses, mules, sheep, donkeys, and water buffalo. Bai farmers also raise cattle in pastures at the bases of mountains. Most Bai homes today are still are two-story affairs consisting of mud-brick walls and tile roofs. Families sleep on the second floor and maintain the bottom floor for livestock. The Chinese government has recently encouraged industrial development in the Bai homeland, and today perhaps 10 percent of the Bai people work in chemical, textile, food-processing, paper, and leather factories.

After Mao Zedong's victory in 1949, traffic along the Burma Road slowed to a standstill. Government policies, which discouraged anything resembling free enterprise capitalism, rendered southwestern China a very inhospitable place for capital investment or commerce. During the 1960s and 1970s, the Cultural Revolution, with its ideological zealotry, only made things worse. The Bai economy, as well as that of much of China, reverted practically to subsistence levels of production. In 1979, however, to lift the country out of the morass into which it had fallen, the central government began to implement economic reforms. Market economy instruments and personal profit were no longer considered evil, and an economic revival came to southeastern China in the 1980s and 1990s.

Elements of traditional, indigenous Bai religious beliefs still survive in the community and consume the spiritual energy of the people. In the highly animistic traditional religion, the Bai endowed the objects of the natural world—plants, animals, rivers, mountains, valleys, lakes, sun, moon, wind, and stars—with consciousness and influence. Individual Bai villages maintain a pantheon of deities relevant to them. Those deities can be either benign or malignant; malignant deities must be appeased by shamanistic rituals. Bais also believe devoutly in invisible poltergeists, or ghosts, who visit them from the world of the unconscious and influence their lives. There are four categories of these spirits: spirits who created the world; spirits associated with nature worship, such as earth, sun, moon, river, or mountain spirits; national heroes or good and notable people; and Buddhist deities.

Buddhism came to the Bai in the ninth century, and Daoist influences came later. Most Bais today believe in an afterlife and in the reality of reincarnation and multiple lives before the soul reaches nirvana. From Daoism and Confucianism, the Bais have adopted rituals for ancestor worship, although unlike in Han ancestor worship, the Bai believe that they must do so in order to earn the protection of their ancestors from dangerous poltergeists. As a result of this system of religious beliefs, Bai villages contain a variety of religious practitioners, including Buddhist monks and local shamans. During the Cultural Revolution, from 1966 to 1976, when the government unleashed an ideological crusade against all manifesations of religiosity, Red Guard cadres destroyed most of the religious temples in Bai settlements. Since then, the central government has been more tolerant of Bai devotions.

SUGGESTED READINGS: Li Sen, "Back Home in a Bai Village," *China Reconstructs* 32 (October 1983), 40–42; Luo Yuheng, "The Torch Festival of the Bai People," *China Today* 45 (February 1996), 52–54; Colin Mackerras, "Aspects of Bai Culture: Change and Continuity in a Yunnan Nationality," *Modern China* 14 (January 1988), 51–84; Beth E. Notar, "Bai," in Paul Hockings, ed., *The Encyclopedia of World Cultures*, vol. 6, *East and Southeast Asia*, 1991; S. Robert Ramsey, *The Languages of China*, 1987; David Y. H. Wu, "Chinese Minority Policy and the Meaning of Minority Culture: The Example of Bai in Yunnan, China," *Human Organization* 49 (Spring 1990), 1–13.

BAI MAN. See **BAI.**

BAIHONG. See **HANI.**

BAIHUO. See **BAI.**

BAIMA. The Baimas form one of the smaller subgroups, in terms of population, of the Qiang* peoples of the People's Republic of China (PRC). Their own ethnonym is "Ben." They have also been known historically as the Baima Zangren or White Horse People. Their language is one of the Qiang dialects and is part of the Qiang branch of the Sino-Tibetan language family. No written script exists for Qiang, and a Chinese dialect is gradually becoming the native language of more and more Baimas.

The Baimas live in the mountain passes separating the Chinese lowlands in the east from the Tibetan highlands to the west. Most Baimas reside in rugged mountain villages; their homes consist of multistoried, flat-roofed houses constructed of stone. Subsistence farmers, they raise barley, buckwheat, potatoes, and beans, using slash-and-burn hoe farming as well as double-team cattle plowing. In Baima villages located below 7,000 feet in elevation, maize has become the staple product. As cash crops, Baimas produce apples, walnuts, peppers, and opium, and they collect bundles of firewood and medicinal herbs for commercial sale. Most Baimas remain loyal to their ancestral animistic religion.

Like other Qiang subgroups in the PRC, some Baimas consider themselves a distinct ethnic entity, not simply an extension or a subgroup of Qiang peoples. Following the lead of Pumi* nationalists, who in 1960 secured official recognition for the Pumis as a minority nationality, Baima leaders have requested a similar classification from the central government. With a population of as much as 40,000 people, they argue that their claim is as compelling as that of the Pumis. As of yet, the central government has not agreed with them.
SUGGESTED READING: Hong Bing, "A Day with the Baima," *China Today* 40 (July 1991), 66–72.

BAIMA ZANGREN. See BAIMA.

BAINI. See BAI.

BAISHA. The Baisha people are a subgroup of the Bendi* people, who are themselves a subgroup of the Li* ethnic group of Hainan Island in the People's Republic of China. The Baisha dialect can be heard today in the eastern half of Baisha County, where it is spoken by nearly 40,000 people.

BAIYI. The Baiyi are one of the many subgroups of the Dai* people, an officially recognized minority nationality in the People's Republic of China. The vast majority of Baiyis live in Yunnan Province, particularly in the Dehong Dai and Jingpo Autonomous Prefecture and in the Xishuangbanna Dai Autonomous Prefecture. Baiyis have been commercial farmers for more than a thousand years. They are also among the first of the rice cultivators in the region. At a time more than 1,400 years ago, when most of the inhabitants of Yunnan were hunters and foragers, the Baiyis were wet-rice farmers who cultivated large paddy fields. They employed elephants as draft animals to plow the fields. Today, most Baiyi farmland is employed in wet-rice farming. They also produce dry rice on terraced, hillside fields. Cash crops include tea, cotton, tobacco, camphor, sisal, sugarcane, coffee, bananas, mangoes, and rubber.

BAIZHUNG DAI. See DAI.

BAIZI. See BAI.

BAIZU. See **BAI.**

BANKEO. Bankeo is one of the subdialects of Lahu,* a dialect of the Yellow Lahu* language in the People's Republic of China.

BANLAN. Banlan is one of the subdialects of Lahoshi,* a dialect of the Yellow Lahu* language of the People's Republic of China.

BAOAN. See **BONAN.**

BAOCHENG. Baocheng people are a subgroup of the Qi* people, who are themselves a subgroup of the Li* minority of Hainan Island in the People's Republic of China. Baocheng speakers constitute 14 percent of the Qi people. Most Baochengs live in eastern Baoting County.

BAOXIAN. Baoxian is one of the three dialects of the Ha language, which itself is a subgroup of the Li* language of Hainan Island in the People's Republic of China. Baoxian speakers live along the Ningyuan River from Yaxian County to Ledong County. Accounting for only 16 percent of all Ha speakers, they are the smallest of the Ha dialects.

BAOZITONG. The Baozitongs are a subgroup of the Kirgiz* people. They speak a Northern Kirgiz dialect and live primarily in Wensu County in the Xinjiang Uigur Autonomous Region of the People's Republic of China.

BARATILANG. The Baratilangs are one of the four primary clans of the Burusho* people of the Hunzu Valley in Pakistan.

BARGA. The Bargas (Bargu) are a subgroup of the Mongol* people of the People's Republic of China. Their dialect, spoken primarily in the northeastern section of the Inner Mongolian Autonomous Region, is divided into two vernaculars: The so-called New Bargu vernacular is spoken by more than 50,000 people, and the Old Bargu vernacular by approximately 15,000 people. Most Bargas are farmers and herders, who raise barley, wheat, oats, corn, millet, potatoes, buckwheat, sorghum, apples, and a variety of vegetables. They also raise horses, cattle, camels, and goats, although their preferred livestock today is sheep.

BARGU. See **BARGA.**

BAYAN MANDAL. See **KHOTON.**

BAYAN-HONGOR. Bayan-Hongor is one of several vernaculars of the Ordo dialect of the Mongolian language. It is spoken primarily in the Hovd banner of southwestern Mongolia and across the immediate frontier in the Inner Mongolian Autonomous Region of the People's Republic of China. See **ORDO** and **MONGOL**.

BE. See **LIMKOU**.

BEIJINGESE. The term "Beijingese" is used here to refer to the residents of the city of Beijing, the capital city of the People's Republic of China (PRC). Beijing is located in northeastern China, within Hebei Province, 250 kilometers northwest of the Yellow Sea coastline. Ever since the Manchu* conquest in the mid-seventeenth century, China has been ruled from the north, and over the centuries, the city of Beijing has acquired an identity as the political center of the country. Nearly six million people live today in Beijing, and the vast majority of them are of Han* descent. After Mao Zedong's successful revolution in 1949, the new government decided to bring about a careful integration of the country's diverse minorities.

That challenge forced them to make some decisions about language. Nearly 90 percent of the country consisted of people of Han descent, but the government had to decide which Chinese* language would become the officially recognized national language. There were, and are today, eight different Chinese languages, none of which are mutually intelligible: Mandarin,* Wu,* Gan,* Jin,* Hakka,* Xiang,* Yue,* and Min.* Because Mandarin was spoken by more than 80 percent of ethnic Chinese, Chinese Communist party officials decided to designate Mandarin as the national language. They also claimed that all eight Chinese languages were dialects of one another. Chinese linguists identify several general clusters of Mandarin dialects. One of those clusters—Northern Mandarin—is spoken all over northeastern China. All of these Mandarin dialects are mutually intelligible, but the government selected the Beijing dialect as the standard.

As a result of these linguistic and political factors, the residents of Beijing have acquired a unique, collective identity that sets them apart from other Han Chinese, even from those who speak one of the Northern Mandarin dialects. They live in the city that is today the heartland of world communism and the center of the country, and they speak the dialect that the world now recognizes as "official" Chinese.

SUGGESTED READING: S. Robert Ramsey, *The Languages of China*, 1987.

BEINAN. Beinan, also known as Nanwang, is one of the five mutually intelligible dialects of the Puyuma* language spoken by an indigenous people living on Taiwan in the Republic of China.

BEISIJIU. Beisijiu is one of the five mutually intelligible dialects of the Puyuma* language spoken by an indigenous people living on Taiwan in the Republic of China.

BEIYI. See **DAI.**

BEN. See **BAIMA, QIANG,** or **TIBETAN.**

BENDI. The Bendi people are a subgroup of the Li* people of Hainan Island in the People's Republic of China. Most Bendis speak one of two mutually intelligible dialects: Baisha and Yuanmen. The total number of Bendi speakers exceeds 50,000 people.

BENDIREN. See **GELAO** and **MULAM.**

BENGLONG. See **DE'ANG.**

BENLONG. See **DE'ANG.**

BENREN. The Benrens are considered by many ethnologists in the People's Republic of China (PRC) to be a subgroup of the Wa,* an officially recognized minority nationality. Most Wa people live in the southwestern reaches of Yunnan Province, chiefly in Ximeng, Cangyuan, Menglian, Gengma, Lancang, Shuangjiang, Yongde, and Zhenkang counties, but primarily in Ximeng and Cangyuan counties. Most Benrens are farmers, but their techniques vary from village to village; some use traditional slash-and-burn methods and others employ more modern sophisticated techniques. They raise wet rice, dry rice, maize, millet, tubers, and wheat.

   Classifying the Benren as a subgroup of the Wa poses problems to ethnologists and ethnolinguists. The Benren dialect is not mutually intelligible with most of the other Wa dialects. Because of that reality, most Benrens view themselves more as Benren than as Wa. The process of ethnogenesis, by which they will see themselves primarily as Wa people, is not yet complete.

BENTEN. See **WA.**

BER DESER. See **BAI.**

BER WA DSER. See **BAI.**

BHAKTAPUR. The Bhaktapurs form one of the primary linguistic subgroups of the Newar* people of Nepal.

BHOTE. See **BHUTANESE.**

BHOTIA. The term "Bhotia" is used as a generic reference to people of Mongol* extraction who live today in the Himalayan region stretching from Himachal Pradesh State to Arunachal Pradesh State in India and including Bhutan.

They speak a great variety of Tibeto-Burman* dialects. See **BHUTANESE** and **TIBETAN**.

BHUTANESE. The Bhutanese—also known as the Bhote, Bhotia, and Bhutia— live in the nation of Bhutan, a region of 47,182 square kilometers bordered by Tibet to the north, Bengal to the south, Sikkim to the west, and Arunachal Pradesh to the east. Bengal, Sikkim, and Arunachal Pradesh are all regions of India. South Asian demographers placed the Bhutanese population at 1,566,000 in 1990. Another 100,000 Bhutanese people live in West Bengal, India, and in Nepal. The Bhutanese capital is Thimbu, but it is little more than a cluster of houses surrounding a small palace. Bhutan is a completely rural nation.

In lingistic terms, however, Bhutanese do not constitute a distinct ethnic group. Tibetan* is spoken in north and central Bhutan. This Tibetan language constitutes one of the larger groups of Kham* dialects spoken in southeastern Tibet. The Sangla* ethnic group, which lives in southeastern Bhutan, speak a Nepali language, as do the Rai,* Gurung,* and Limbu* peoples of Bhutan. Several thousand Nepalese Brahmins and Chhetris, who also live in Bhutan, speak Nepali as well. At any given moment, along the trade route between Tibet and Bhutan, groups of Bhutanese—Tibetans, Sanglas, Rais, Gurungs, and Limbus—can be found living in Tibet. Each of the country's fifteen political districts is characterized by its own dialect.

The Bhutanese economy is overwhelmingly agricultural, with rice, wheat, maize, and millet serving as their main crops. They also raise apples, peaches, plums, and apricots. Industrial development has been badly retarded in Bhutan. Because their villages are so often located in remote mountain retreats, the Bhutanese have developed a unique form of terraced agriculture. Because of the existence of one railroad, some timber resources can be exploited. Most of the country remains in a subsistence economic state.

The fastest growing element of the Bhutanese population are the Nepalese, because of their practice of polygamous marriage. It is not unusual for Nepalese households to consist of three or more wives and fifteen to twenty children. It is a similar story in Sikkim, where the Nepalese have become the dominant ethnic group. Many Tibetan Bhutanese fear that Bhutan is in for the same fate because of the Nepalese birthrate.

The primary religion of Bhutan is the Red-Hat Kargyupa sect of Lamaist Buddhism. In some regions of Bhutan, ethnic Tibetans still practice their animistic, shamanistic religion, known locally as Bon. Some of the Nepalese people living in Bhutan practice Hinduism or a Hindu-Lamaist mix.

SUGGESTED READINGS: Brenda Amenson-Hill, "Bhutanese," in Paul V. Hockings, ed., *The Encyclopedia of World Cultures*, vol. 3, *South Asia*, 1991; Balaram Chakaravarti, *A Cultural History of Bhutan*, 1980; William M. Jenkins, *The Himalayan Kingdoms: Bhutan, Sikkim, and Nepal*, 1963; Pradyumna P. Karan, *Bhutan: A Physical and Cultural Geography*, 1967; Blanche C. Olshak, *Bhutan: Land of Hidden Treasures*, 1971; Nari Rustomij, *Bhutan: The Dragon Kingdom in Crisis*, 1978.

BHUTIA. See **BHUTANESE.**

BIG-BOARD MIAO. See **MIAO.**

BI-KAW. The Hani* people of Yunnan Province in the southwestern reaches of the People's Republic of China, northern Myanmar (Burma), northern Laos, northern Vietnam, and northern Thailand are subdivided into three general linguistic clusters. Because the dialects are barely mutually intelligible to members of the other dialect groups, some ethnolinguists prefer to use the term "regionalect" to describe them. One of the three Hani regionalects is Bi-Kaw.

BINGZHOU. The Bingzhous are one of the linguistic subgroups of the more than 48 million Han* people who speak the Jin* Chinese language. Bingzhous today can be found in central Shaanxi Province, particularly in the Taiyuan, Qingxu, Loufan, Yuci, Taigu, Qixian, Pingyao, Jiexiu, Lingshi, Jiaocheng, Wenshui, Xiaoyi, Shouyang, Uushe, and Yuxian regions.

BIRAR. See **EVENK.**

BITSO. See **DAI.**

BIYUE. The Biyues (Byues) are an ethnic subgroup of the Hani* people of the People's Republic of China (PRC). Scattered numbers of Biyue people can also be found today living in Thailand and Myanmar (Burma). The Biyues living in the PRC are located in the far southeastern corner of Yunnan Province, between the Mengle and the Ailao mountain ranges. Hani society is patrilineal and patriarchal. Kinship relations are organized around patrilineal clans. Each of these clans consists of from thirty to forty households, and each clan maintains elaborate ancestral histories, tracing their origins back more than forty generations. Most Hanis, of course, remain tied to the agricultural economy. Some Hani farmers still work in a traditional subsistence economy. Farmers in Xishuangbanna and Lancang still practice slash-and-burn techniques, but in the Honghe area, more sophisticated techniques are used. Most Biyues work as farmers today, raising a variety of crops that include rice, maize, beans, buckwheat, millet, tea, peanuts, sugarcane, cotton, chili peppers, ginger, and indigo. Because of recent economic development programs in southwestern Yunnan, increasing numbers of Biyue men can be found working in local factories and mines.

BIZIKA. See **TUJIA.**

BIZKA. See **TUJIA.**

BLACK BENLONG. See **DE'ANG.**

BLACK BONE YI. See **YI.**

BLACK KUCONG. See **LAHU.**

BLACK LAHU. Black Lahu is one of the two major Lahu* languages in the People's Republic of China. Black Lahu has three major dialects. The Lahuna* dialect includes, in China, the Meuneu and Panai subdialects. The Nu* dialect includes the Kaishin and Namhpehn subdialects. The Shehleh* dialect in China has one subdialect: Laho Aleh.

BLACK YI. See **YI.**

B'LAI. See **LI.**

B'LI. See **LI.**

BLANG. The Blang people are one of the officially recognized national minority groups in the People's Republic of China (PRC). Most of the nearly 90,000 Chinese Blangs live today in Menghai County, which is located in the far southwestern corner of Yunnan Province, bordering Myanmar (Burma). They can also be found in Shuangjiang County as well as in Jinghong, Yongde, Yunxian, Shidian, Changning, Lancang Lahu Autonomous County, Mojiang Hani Autonomous County, Jingdong Yi Autonomous County, and Jinggu Dai-Yi Autonomous County. Several thousand Blangs live across the border in northeastern Myanmar. They live in close proximity to the Han,* Dai,* and Wa* peoples of Yunnan. Blang is a Mon-Khmer* language that ethnolinguists classify with the South Asian language family. Since there is no written Blang language, literate Blangs read and write Chinese.* Most Blangs today also speak some Chinese, Dai, or Wa, and their language is loaded with loan words and cognates from those languages.

Until the tenth century, the Blang were animists who practiced a local, environmentalist religion that would today be considered superstitious by most Blangs and Hans. Elements of that religion still exist in the folk culture, but they no longer consume much spiritual energy in Blang society. Beginning in the tenth century, a large-scale conversion of Blangs to Theravada Buddhism came at the hands of the neighboring Dai people, and most Blangs remain Theravada Buddhists today. There are also a few Christians among them. When the Burma Road was completed from India through Burma and into southwestern China in 1938, British missionaries made their way into Blang country and converted some people to the Methodist and Presbyterian denominations. They immediately tried to persuade Blang men to stop the ritual tattooing of their limbs and torsos, a characteristic of Blang culture, but the outbreak of World War II ended those efforts.

Blang villages tend to be located at higher altitudes, usually between 4,500 feet and 6,500 feet. They live in two-story bamboo homes, in which the upper floor is used by people and the lower floor is used by the livestock, which includes chickens, ducks, cattle, pigs, and sometimes water buffalo. Blang farmers produce dry rice, maize, and beans, which constitute staples in their diets, and for cash they raise tea, cotton, and sugarcane. Each Blang village may contain up to one hundred households organized into a dozen or more exogamous clans.

SUGGESTED READINGS: Paul V. Hockings, "Blang," in Paul V. Hockings, ed., *The Encyclopedia of World Cultures*, vol. 6, *East and Southeast Asia*, 1991; Ma Yin, ed., *China's Minority Nationalities*, 1989.

BLUE MIAO. See **MIAO.**

BO. See **BAI.**

BOAT PEOPLE. The term "boat people" is used to describe a unique ethnic group of approximately 15,000 people who live permanently in junks and sampans that float in Hong Kong harbor. With the official transfer of Hong Kong to the People's Republic of China (PRC) on July 1, 1997, the so-called boat people became citizens of the PRC. Most of the more than six thousand boats in the harbor are worked today by family crews. Most of the boat people are of Han* Chinese extraction, and most of them speak the Yue* or Hakka* language. But what sets the boat people apart ethnically is their economic lifestyle. They live out their entire lives on the boats and marry endogamously—other boat people—rather than landsmen. In doing so, their economic lifestyle confers upon them the status of a distinct ethnic group.

SUGGESTED READING: *Atlas of Man*, 1978.

BOD. See **TIBETAN.**

BODASH. See **TIBETAN.**

BODO. See **NAGA.**

BODPA. See **TIBETAN.**

BOGAR. The Bogar (Bokars) people are a small ethnic group of approximately 3,000 people living today in Milin, Longzi, and Medog counties in the Tibetan Autonomous Region. Although the government of the People's Republic of China (PRC) classifies them as part of the Lloba* minority nationality, the Bogars are more likely to identify themselves as Bogar than as Lloba. They have difficulty in understanding the other so-called Lloba language, which is known as Yidu.* Much larger Bogar communities can also be found scattered across the border in southeastern Tibet, northern Myanmar (Burma), the far north-western corner of Yunnan Province in the PRC, and on the banks of the Siang River and the Yamne River in Arunachal Pradesh State in northeastern India.

The Bogars were part of the southern migration which brought them, centuries ago, out of central Tibet into southern Tibet and across the Himalayan mountains into the Assam Valley of India. During the ensuing centuries after their arrival, to avoid political and economic domination by other groups, they settled in mountainous highlands, where they currently reside. They locate their villages with defense in mind. Bogars prefer to live on hilltops, with access to a river via a sloping incline, with a very steep decline on the opposite side of the village. Houses are then constructed on elevated platforms, with the rear of the home facing the hillside. They still function in a largely subsistence economy based on slash-and-burn agriculture, fishing, foraging, and hunting.

SUGGESTED READINGS: Tiley Chodag, *Tibet: The Land and the People*, 1988; Paul V. Hockings, "Lloba," in Paul V. Hockings, ed., *The Encyclopedia of World Cultures*, vol. 6, *East and Southeast Asia*, 1991; S. A. Wurm, B. T'sou, D. Bradley, et al., eds., *Language Atlas of China*, 1987.

BOKAR. See **BOGAR** and **LLOBA.**

BOLUOZU QIANG. The Boluozus are a subgroup of the Qiang* people, who are themselves a subgroup of a larger cluster of Qiang-speaking people located near the Tibetan* frontier in northern Yunnan Province and northwestern Sichuan Province in the People's Republic of China.

BON. The Bon people are considered a subgroup of Tibetans* who live today in the Kham District of southeastern Tibet or across the border in Bhutan. The Bon pursue a subsistence lifestyle in remote Himalayan villages. Although they speak a Tibetan dialect consistent with others in southeastern Tibet, they have never accepted Lamaist Buddhism. Bon people remain loyal to an animistic faith that revolves around a myriad of unseen ghost spirits and the spirits of ancestors who influence human affairs. The distinction between Bon animism and Tibetan and Bhutanese Buddhism is so sharp that it separates them into a distinct ethnic group. Several hundred Bon people live today on the Chinese side of the Tibetan-Bhutanese frontier.

SUGGESTED READINGS: Barbara Aziz, *Tibetan Frontier Families*, 1978; Tiley Chodag, *Tibet: The Land and the People*, 1988; Dalai Lama, *My Land and My People*, 1962; Rebecca French, *The Golden Yoke: The Legal System of Buddhist Tibet*, 1994; David Snelgrove and Hugh Richardson, *A Cultural History of Tibet*, 1980.

BONAN. The Bonan are one of the smaller ethnic groups in the People's Republic of China (PRC). They are also known as the Baoans, Paoans, Paongans, and Ponans. Their self-designation is Pounang K'ung. The Bonan population today comprises approximately 13,000 people, most of whom can be found living in several villages in Gansu Province in north central China. A much smaller cluster of Bonans can also be found in Qinghai Province. The Gansu Bonan reside in Dadun, Ganmei, and Gaoli villages, all in the Jishi foothills near the cities of Linxia, Dahejia, and Liuji. Other Chinese Muslims, particularly the Dongxiangs* and Salars,* can also be found living near the Gansu Bonan. Tongren County is the homeland of most Qinghai Bonan people, where they dwell in several villages on both sides of the Longwu River.

Ethnologists know very little about the origins of the Bonan people, although Bonan oral historians talk of their beginnings in the armies of Genghis Khan, which expanded across Eurasia and Asia. They were part of the great Mongol* Yuan state until 1368, when Yuan power disintegrated and most of the soldiers and administrators retreated back to Mongolia. Some of them, however, remained behind, and included within this group are the Bonan. At the time, they resided in Tongren County, Qinghai Province. They assumed a Bonan ethnic identity over the course of the next several centuries as a result of intermarriage with a complex variety of Tibetan,* Han,* Tu,* and Hui* peoples. Most Chinese ethnologists consider the Bonun to be close relatives of the Hui people.

Early in the 1800s, a small number of Bonan converted to Islam, an event that put them at odds with their Tibetan and Tu neighbors, all of whom were Buddhists. The friction between Buddhists and Muslims occasionally erupted into violence. In the late 1950s and early 1960s, the confrontation became so violent that the Islamic Bonan decided to move. They traveled first to Xunhua, where Salar Muslims welcomed them for a time, but then they gradually migrated down the Huang River into Gansu Province, where they live today. In recent years, the Salar and Bonan peoples of Xunhua in Gansu Province have worked together to plant trees in the foothills of the Jishi mountains to provide a natural geographic boundary between them. The Bonans who remained behind in Tongren County have not converted to Islam but have retained their Buddhist faith. They have been all but assimilated by surrounding Tibetan and Han peoples, although there are still several thousand people in Qinghai who are vaguely aware of their Bonan ancestry.

Among the Gansu Bonans, a profound division separates one group of Muslims from another. Some Bonans are Sunni Muslims, while others are Shiite Muslims. But regardless of their Muslim sect, they have been targeted frequently over the years by zealous Hans anxious to suppress Islam in China.

Most Bonans make their living today as farmers, raising wheat and rye as staples. Because of dramatic improvements in agricultural productivity, they enjoy substantial crop surpluses, which they sell in open, commercial markets. Bonans not engaged in wheat and rye farming can usually be found working in the logging, silversmithing, and charcoal industries. They are also highly esteemed in the Gansu and Qinghai provinces because of the so-called Bonan knife, a brass or copper cutting instrument with elaborately carved bone handles.

The Bonan language is part of the larger Altaic* family of languages. It is broken down into two distinct dialects—Dahejia* and Tongren*—which reflect the geographic and religious divisions in the Bonan community. The Dahejia-speaking Bonan are primarily Muslims who live in Gansu Province; the Tongren-speaking Bonan are mostly Buddhists who live in Qinghai Province. Because of their Muslim faith and demographic concentration, the Dahejia Bonan maintain a powerful sense of ethnic identity. Although Chinese government officials have tried to be more accommodating in the last decade to their Muslim nationalities, the Bonans, like other Islamic faithful in the PRC, have vivid memories of the tumultuous years of the Cultural Revolution of the 1960s and early 1970s. Mao Zedong unleashed an ideological crusade to purge China of its "bourgeois" tendencies, but in many areas the purging was more a form of Han oppression than political reeducation. Red Guard cadres composed of young Han zealots entered Bonan settlements in Gansu and Qinghai provinces and attacked Muslims and their mosques. Muslim clerics were often forced, under the threat of death, to eat pork, a practice strictly forbidden in Islamic religious culture. They were sometimes relocated to communal farms and forced to tend pigs. Mosques were frequently defaced when Red Guard cadres tried to suppress Islam in China. Times are better for Bonan Muslims now, but there is little love lost for the Han.

SUGGESTED READINGS: Ma Lingyu, "The Baoan People's Search for Identity," *China Reconstructs* 34 (June 1985), 43–44; Henry G. Schwarz, "Bonans," in Richard V. Weeks, ed., *Muslim Peoples*, 1984, and *The Minorities of Northern China: A Survey*, 1984.

BOPA. The Bopas constitute one of the primary subdivisions of the Tibetan* peoples.

BOUYEI. The Bouyeis—also known as the Buyi, Chungchia, Dioi, Ichia, Ijen, Joachia, Jui, Pui, Puyueh, Shuibu, Penti, Yo, and Zhongjia—are one of the larger of the officially recognized minority nationalities in the People's Republic of China (PRC). In the 1990 national census, demographers counted a total of 2,545,059 people who identified themselves as Bouyei, and today that number is probably closer to 2,700,000 people. Most of them can be found in the Yunnan-Guizhou Plateau, particularly in southern Guizhou Province and across the border in Guangxi Province. They speak a language that ethnolinguists classify as part of the Zhuang-Dong branch of the Sino-Tibetan language family. In fact, Bouyei and Zhuang* are closely enough related to give the two peoples a common ancestry. The Northern Zhuang* dialect is mutually intelligible with the Bouyei language. Most Han* people look upon the Bouyeis as a subgroup of the Zhuang. They are one of the northernmost extensions of Tai*-speaking peoples in the PRC. Most outsiders have a difficult time, linguistically and culturally, distinguishing between the Bouyei and the Zhuang. Both groups wear Han Chinese clothes, employ Han Chinese farming techniques, speak fluently a Chinese* language, and think of themselves as very close relatives of the Han Chinese. Some Bouyei and Zhuang even consider themselves to be essentially Han. In urban areas, non-Han peoples often mistakenly assume that Bouyei are Han.

Most Bouyei families live in villages located on plains or in river valleys. Like several other ethnic communities in Guizhou and Yunnan provinces, they live in two-story houses, in which the upper floor is reserved for parents and children, and the lower floor is used to protect livestock, which may include sheep, cattle, goats, chickens, ducks, pigs, and water buffalo. The soil of the Yunnan-Guizhou Plain is rich and fertile, and Guizhou farmers raise wet rice, dry rice, wheat, maize, potatoes, millet, buckwheat, beans, and sorghum, which they usually consume within their own communities. For cash crops, they produce cotton, hemp, silk, ramie, sugarcane, tea, coffee, bananas, and cocoa. Small-scale Bouyei timber operations produce pine and fir for export.

In Guizhou and northern Yunnan provinces, the Bouyei are also known for their astute business skills. For centuries, they have served as middlemen in the trade routes connecting Han and the minority groups of the region. Bouyei peddlars carried trade goods from community to community. In recent decades, as infrastructures have improved and local economies have become more complex, some Bouyei have ventured into larger-scale commercial operations. Most of these Bouyei businessmen are fluent in several languages, including Chinese. The Bouyei religion is an eclectic mix of indigenous animism, Daoism, and Christianity.

SUGGESTED READINGS: Paul V. Hockings, ''Blang,'' in Paul Hockings, ed., *The Encyclopedia of World Cultures*, vol. 6, *East and Southeast Asia*, 1991; Lu Xinglun, ''The Bouyei Nationality,'' *China Reconstructs* 31 (September 1982), 48–53; Ma Yin, ed., *China's Minority Nationalities*, 1989; Zeng Qingnan, ''The Bouyei of Guizhou Province,'' *China Today* 43 (September 1994), 36–42.

BOUYI. See **BOUYEI.**

BOYI. See **DAI.**

BOZI. See **BAI.**

BRABAW. Brabaw is one of the two dialects of the Thao* people, who live today on Taiwan in the Republic of China.

BRAO. See **WA.**

BRITISH. At the present time, there are approximately 10,000 people in Hong Kong who claim British, or Anglo, ancestry. On July 1, 1997, they officially became a new ethnic community in the People's Republic of China. See **HONG KONGESE.**

BUBAN. See **ZHUANG.**

BUDAI. See **ZHUANG.**

BUDDHIST BONAN. See **BONAN.**

BUDONG. See **ZHUANG.**

BUGALAT. The Bugalats are a subgroup of the Buryats,* a Mongol* people of Siberian Russia and the Inner Mongolian Autonomous Region in the People's Republic of China.

BUGUR. Bugur is one of the vernacular subgroups of the Uigur* language spoken in Xinjiang Uigur Autonomous Region of the People's Republic of China. Most speakers of Bugur live in and around the oasis community of Bugur.

BULA. The Bulas are a subgroup, based upon dialect, of the Zaiwa* people of Yunnan Province in the People's Republic of China.

BULANG. See **ZHUANG.**

BULONG. See **ZHUANG.**

BULONGKOL. The Bulongkols are a subgroup of the Kirgiz* people. They speak a southern Kirgiz dialect and live primarily in Akto, Yengishar, and Guma counties in the Xinjiang Uigur Autonomous Region of the People's Republic of China.

BUMAN. See **ZHUANG.**

BUMIN. See **ZHUANG.**

BUNA. See **ZHUANG.**

BUNAO. The Bunaos are a Bunn subgroup, who are part of the larger Yao* cluster of people in the People's Republic of China. Bunao itself is further divided into five subdialects: Dongnu, Nunu, Bunuo, Naogelao, and Numao.

BUNONG. See **ZHUANG.**

BUNU. The Bunus are a subgroup of the Yao* people of the People's Republic of China. Demographers place the Bunu population at nearly 500,000 people, most of whom live in remote mountainous regions of the Guangxi Zhuang Autonomous Region and in Guizhou, Hunan, and Yunnan provinces. The Bunu language is divided into five mutually intelligible dialects: Bunao,* Baheng,* Wunai,* Jiongnai,* and Younuo.* Each of these can be further broken down into a variety of subdialects.

BUNUN. The Bunun people—also known regionally and in the anthropological literature as Bunums, Vonums, and Vununs—are classified as one of the indigenous groups of Taiwan in the Republic of China. Today, they are scattered across the mountainous region of central Taiwan, where the climate is subtropical. Demographers today estimate the Bunun population at approximately 42,000 people. Several thousand Bunun have relocated to such major cities as Taipai and Taischung, but the vast majority of them remain in rural areas. Ethnolinguists classify Bunun as part of the Proto-Northern Indonesian language family, which is a branch of Proto-Austronesian. The Bunun are divided into six subgroups based on differences in dialect and culture: the Takbanuath,* the Takebaka,* the Taketodo,* the Takevatan,* the Takopulan,* and the Isibukun.* Of the six groups, the Isbukun are the largest in terms of population, and the Takopulan have all but disappeared, assimilated into the other subgroups.

Until the end of World War II, the Bunun economy was a subsistence one based on using slash-and-burn farming techniques to raise maize and sweet potatoes. During the war, Japanese occupation forces required the Bunun to raise wet rice, which they continued to do after the Japanese departed. During the 1970s, Bunun farmers gradually became integrated into the larger commercial economy of Taiwan and began to produce several cash crops. That economic integration, however, has not been without its problems. Bunun farmers and merchants often feel exploited by Han* Chinese middlemen who control the flow of goods between Bunun villages and Taiwanese producers and consumers.

In the Bunun social system, residence is patrilocal and descent is patrilineal. Over the past century, the influence of Han Chinese culture on the Bunun has strengthened the patrilineal elements of the social structure. They maintain a complex system of clans and subclans, with surnames taken from the name of an individual's subclan. They are strictly monogamous. The average size of a Bunun village is approximately 120 people.

The traditional Bunun religion, like that of most aboriginal peoples, is animistic, polytheistic, and shamanistic. Bununs believe that all plants, animals, and natural objects possess their own spirits, and that human beings need to be careful to appease and propitiate those spirits. The spirit that exists in all natural objects is called *hanido*. Evil spirits and gods must be controlled through the magic of the shaman. Human beings, the Bunun believe, possess two *hanidos*— a good *hanido* of the right shoulder and a bad *hanido* of the left shoulder. Bununs also believe in the *dehanin*, a vast spirit of the sky that controls the movement of celestial objects and the weather. In recent years, Christian missionaries have made considerable headway among the Bununs. For example, many Bununs now describe the Christian deity as *dehanin* and Satan as *hanido*.

SUGGESTED READINGS: Robert Farrell, *Taiwan Aboriginal Groups: Problems in Cultural and Linguistic Classification*, 1969; Ying-Kuei Huang, "Bunun," in Paul Hockings, ed., *Encyclopedia of World Cultures*, vol. 6, *East and Southeast Asia*, 1991, and "Conversion and Religious Change among the Bunun of Taiwan," Ph.D. diss., University of London, 1988; Mei-chun Tang, "Han and Non-Han in Taiwan: A Case of Acculturation," *Bulletin of the Institute of Ethnology* 30 (1970), 99–110.

BUPIAN. See **ZHUANG.**

BUROONG. The Buroongs are one of the four primary clans of the Burusho* people of the Hunzu Valley in Pakistan.

BURUSHO. The Burushos—also known as Hunzus, Hunzukuts, and Burushaskis—are a mountain people who live primarily in Hunza State and Nagir State in Pakistan. They live in deep valleys and gorges cut by the Hunza River and its tributaries. Currently, the population of the Burushos exceeds 60,000 people. Some live across the Pakistani-Chinese frontier in the immediate border region of Tibet. Ethnolinguists are unable to classify the Burusho language, but it is divided into two dialects that reflect Burusho locations in Hunza and Nagir.

Burusho legend claims that they descend from three European soldiers left behind when the armies of Alexander the Great began their retreat from the region. Each of these soldiers founded a village—Baltir, Ganesh, and Altit—and all Burushos claim to descend from the peoples of one of these villages.

Burushos live in heavily fortified villages constructed 9,000 or 10,000 feet in altitude and hundreds of feet above the Hunza River gorge. Most Burushos are subsistence farmers who plant their crops in carefully attended terraced fields. Their major crops are potatoes, beans, wheat, barley, millet, rye, buckwheat, rice, and a variety of fruits and vegetables. They also raise cattle, goats, sheep, and chickens, and they continue to hunt to supplement their diets.

Burusho society revolves around four major patrilineal clans, all of them located in the city of Baltit, and several minor clans distributed widely throughout the region. The four major Burusho clans are the Buroongs,* the Diramitings,* the Baratilangs,* and the Khurukuts.* In addition to the clan system, Burusho society is divided into five classes, including the Thamos, the royal family; the Uyongko and Akabirting, who fill most government posts; the Bar, Bare, and Sis groups, who farm the land; the Baldakuyos and Tsilgalashos, who are teamsters and carriers for other groups; and the Berichos, who are ethnic Indians. The Baldakuyos and Tsilgalashos are the Burushos most likely to find their way across the border into China because they help transport commodities along the Pakistanti-Chinese trade routes.

Burushos are virtually all Muslims of the Ismaili tradition. They look to the Aga Khan as their spiritual leader. They are less likely than other Pakistani Muslims to observe their daily prayers, fast during Ramadan, and regularly attend the local mosque.

For centuries, the Hunza Valley in the Karakoram Range was one of the most isolated territories of the world. In 1978, however, Chinese and Pakistani workers completed construction of the Karakoram Highway, which cut directly through the Hunza Valley, linking up the region to commercial trade routes between Pakistan and the People's Republic of China. The total Burusho population today totals only approximately 60,000 people, of which only a few hundred live at the end of the Karakoram Highway in China.

SUGGESTED READINGS: J. T. Clark, "Hunza in the Himalayas: Storied Shangri-La Undergoes Scrutiny," *Natural History* 72 (1963), 38–45; David Lorimer, *The Burushaski Language*, 1938; John McCarry, "High Road to Hunza," *National Geographic* 185 (March 1994), 114–34; Hugh R. Page, Jr., "Burushos," in Paul V. Hockings, ed., *The Encyclopedia of World Cultures*, vol. 3, *South Asia*, 1991.

BURYAT. The Buryats are one of the Mongol* people of Central Asia and Siberia. They have also been called Buryat Mongols. The vast majority of Central Asia's 450,000 Buryats are located in Russia today. Three administrative subdivisions of the Russian Federation are dedicated to the Buryats: The Buryat Autonomous Republic (Buryatia) and two lesser entities, the Ust'Orda Buryat National Okrug of Irkutsk Oblast and the Aga Buryat National Okrug of Chita Oblast. Smaller numbers of Buryats live across the frontier in the Inner Mongolian Autonomous Region (IMAR) of the People's Republic of China (PRC). The region of Central Asia that today crosses the border of Russia and the PRC is known as Buryatia.

Ever since the Bolshevik Revolution of 1917, Soviet authorities have considered Buryatia to be strategically significant. By maintaining their influence in Buryatia, the Soviets could keep a tight rein on the Mongolian People's Republic, which most political scientists considered to be little more than a sixteenth Soviet republic. The Soviets feared an independent Mongolia because of the impact it could have on Russian access to the rich natural resources of Siberia. The Buryats are also the northernmost followers of the Dalai Lama of Tibet, and the Soviets worried frequently over the years about the potential of a pan-Mongol-Tibetan nationalist movement that would threaten Central Asia and Siberia.

Buryat is a dialect of Mongolian, but it is different enough from Khalkha, the primary dialect of the Mongolian People's Republic, to render the two languages mutually understandable only with great difficulty. Buryat is also divided into five subdialects of its own—Bugalat, Khora, Ekhirit, Khongodor, and Tabunut.

Ever since the early 1900s, Buryat nationalism and a spirit of pan-Mongolism have emanated from Buryatia. Jamtsarano was an early advocate. During the Russo-Japanese War of 1904–1905, Japanese agents tried to promote a pan-Mongol spirit, much to the anger and frustration of the Russians.* During the years of the civil war in Russia between 1918 and 1922, Japanese military forays into Siberia and Buryatia only heightened Russian fears of Buryat loyalties. During the late 1930s and throughout World War II, thousands of Buryats were slaughtered by a suspicious Soviet government. Joseph Stalin's government particularly targeted Buryat Lamaist monks.

Buryat Nationalism is thriving today, and the government of the PRC is equally suspicious of Buryat loyalties in the Inner Mongolian Autonomous Region. Dashi-Nima Dondupov, one of the leading Buryat cultural and political figures of today, is a patriarchal figure who still conducts religious services and political meetings in the Lake Baikal region, and who has followers across the border in the IMAR. Chinese government officials are quick to stamp out any expressions of Buryat nationalism and pan-Mongolism among the Buryats.

SUGGESTED READINGS: Don Belt, "The World's Great Lake," *National Geographic* 181 (June 1992), 2–40; *Current Digest* 41 (March 22, 1989), 22–23; Walter Kolarz, *The Peoples of the Soviet Far East*, 1954; Ross Marlay, "Buryats," in James S. Olson, ed., *Ethnohistorical Dictionary of the Soviet Union*, 1993; William O. McCagg and Brian D. Silver, eds., *Soviet Asian Ethnic Frontiers*, 1979; Robert Rupen, *How Mongolia Is Really Ruled*, 1979, and *Mongols of the Twentieth Century*, 1964; K. V. Vyatkina, "The Buryats," in M. G. Levin and L. P. Potapov, eds., *The Peoples of Siberia*, 1964, pp. 203–42; Pyotr Zubkhov, "Buryatia: A Republic on Lake Baikal," *Soviet Life* 378 (1988), 41–46.

BUSHUANG. See **ZHUANG.**

BUTAUL. See **PAIWAN.**

BUTHA. Butha is one of the primary dialects of the Daur* language. Daur is spoken in the Molidawa Daur Autonomous Banner District of far northeastern China in the Inner Mongolian Autonomous Region and across the border in Heilongjiang Province in the People's Republic of China. The remainder of the Daur people can be found on the other side of the country, living near the city of Qiqihar in the Xinjiang Uigur Autonomous Region. Butha is spoken by approximately 40,000 Daur people. Butha is prominent in Morindawa Banner and in Nenjianng County, Nehe County, and Gannan County. There are four Butha vernaculars: Nawen, Nemor, Aihui, and Mergen. The Nawen tongue is spoken in the western Butha region. During the past several decades, speakers of the Nemor vernacular, who had long lived east of the Nonni River, have crossed the river into western Butha territory, where their language is now fusing with Nawen. The third vernacular is Aihui, also known locally as Darbin. Mergen, the fourth Butha vernacular, can be heard in Nenjiang County.

BUTU. See **ZHUANG.**

BUYI. See **BOUYEI.**

BUYUE. See **ZHUANG.**

BYAU MIN YAO. The Byau Min Yaos are currently considered by the People's Republic of China (PRC) to be a subgroup of the Yao* people, who live in Guangxi, Hunan, Guangdong, Jiangxi, Guizhou, and Yunnan provinces. The problem with classifying Byau Min Yaos with the other so-called Yao peoples is language. The government argues that there are four subgroups of the Yao people—Byau Min Yao, Kim Mun Yao,* Mien Yao,* and Yao Min*—but these are not really dialects. Although all four are classified in the Miao-Yao* linguistic family, they are not mutually intelligible. If the language spoken by Byau Min Yao people is not comprehensible to the other Yao subgroups, then the argument for separate and official ethnic status is a compelling one.

Demographers estimate that there are more than 300,000 Byau Min Yao people. Their economies vary according to ecological setting, but agriculture, hunting, and foraging are present among all of them. Their social system is based on patrilineal descent, and young people are expected to marry endogamously. Elders frown on an individual who marries somebody from another Yao group. That stigma against exogamous marriage to any other people, including other Yao, is further evidence that the Byau Min Yao constitute a distinct ethnic entity.

BYRYUGSOLI. The Byryugsoli are a subgroup of the Sarikol* people, who are themselves a subgroup of the Tajiks* in the People's Republic of China.

BYUANG. See **ZHUANG.**

BYUE. See **BIYUE** and **HANI.**

C

CANGLO MOINBA. The Canglo people constitute a relatively small ethnic group who live primarily in Medog County and in the Dongjiu region of Linzhi County in the Tibetan Autonomous Region of the People's Republic of China. Chinese demographers estimate their contemporary population at approximately 5,000 people and classify them as a subgroup of the Moinbas,* but their language is not really mutually intelligible with Cuona* and Motuo,* the other major Moinba dialects. Canglos are more likely to identify themselves as Canglos than as Moinbas.

Canglos speak a Tibeto-Burman* language, part of the Sino-Tibetan family, which is divided into several mutually intelligible dialects. Most Canglos are farmers and pastoralists who live in isolated mountainous villages and raise rice, maize, millet, buckwheat, soybeans, sesame seeds, cattle, and sheep.

SUGGESTED READINGS: Tiley Chodag, *Tibet: The Land and Its Peoples*, 1988; Paul V. Hockings, "Moinba," in Paul V. Hockings, ed., *The Encyclopedia of World Cultures*, vol. 6, *East and Southeast Asia*, 1991; Ma Yin, ed., *China's Minority Nationalities*, 1989; S. A. Wurm, B. T'sou, D. Bradley, et al., eds., *Language Atlas of China*, 1987.

CANTONESE. See **UANGZHOUESE** and **YUE.**

CENTRAL AMI. Central Ami is one of the five primary dialects of the Ami* language, which is spoken by the Ami people, an indigenous group living on Taiwan in the Republic of China. They are also known as Coastal Amis* and Xiuguluan Amis.*

CENTRAL DE'ANG. Ethnolinguists group the many De'ang* dialects in three clusters, one of which is known as Central De'ang. Since so many of the De'ang dialects are not mutually intelligible, it might be more appropriate to describe them as separate languages.

CENTRAL MIAO. See **QIAN DONG.**

CHAKHAR. The Chakhars are a subgroup of the Mongol* people of the People's Republic of China. Their dialect, spoken primarily in the central section of the Inner Mongolian Autonomous Region, is closely related to the Shiliingol* dialect. Both Chakhar and Shiliingol bear a close resemblance to Khalkha, the primary Mongolian dialect of the Mongolian People's Republic. Most Chakhars are farmers and herders, who raise barley, wheat, oats, corn, millet, potatoes, buckwheat, sorghum, apples, and a variety of vegetables. Mongols also raise horses, cattle, camels, and goats, although their preferred livestock today is sheep.

CHAM. More than a thousand years ago, the Cham people migrated out of India and settled in the Red River Delta and the Mekong River Delta in Vietnam, as well as on the island of Hainan in the South China Sea. They were a warlike, seafaring people. Chams were highly Indianized, and their religious beliefs reflected a syncretic mix of Buddhism, Hinduism, and their own animism. They made their living in trade and in piracy they conducted throughout the maritime channels of Southeast Asia. Today, the Cham language is no longer spoken on the island of Hainan in the People's Republic of China, but hundreds of residents there are at least aware of their Cham ancestry.
SUGGESTED READING: P. K. Benedict, "A Cham Colony on the Island of Hainan," *Harvard Journal of Asiatic Studies* 6 (1941), 129–34.

CHANG. The Chang people are considered to be a subgroup of the Naga,* a group of more than one million people who live primarily in the state of Nagaland in northeastern India. A few Nagas can also be found across the border in northern Myanmar (Burma) and in the far southern reaches of Yunnan Province in the People's Republic of China. Most of them are farmers who raise crops in terraced, hillside fields. They also raise cattle, sheep, pigs, and dogs for food.

CHANGGAN. The Changgan people are a subgroup of the Qiongwen people, who are themselves a linguistic subgroup of the Min* language of Chinese in the People's Republic of China and the Republic of China on Taiwan. Changgan speakers can be found today in Dongfang and Changjiang counties in Hainan Province. See **HAN** and **MINNAN.**

CHANGJING. The Changjing people are a subgroup of the Gan*-speaking Han* Chinese of the People's Republic of China. Most Changjing speakers can be found today in Pingjiang County in Hunan Province and in the Nanchang, Xin-jian, Anyi, Yongxiu, Xiushui, De'an, Xingzi, Duchang, Hukou, Gao'an, Fengxin, Jing'an, Wuning, and Tonggu regions of Jiangxi Province. See **HAN**.

CHANGYI. The Changyi people are a subgroup of the Xiang*-speaking Han* Chinese of the People's Republic of China. Most Changyis live today in thirty-two cities and counties of Hunan Province. See **GAN** and **XIANG**.

CHAOBOOBOL. See **PAIWAN**.

CH'AOHSIEN. See **KOREAN**.

CHAOSHAN. The Chaoshan people are a subgroup of the Minnan* people, themselves a linguistic subgroup of the Min* language of Chinese in the People's Republic of China and the Republic of China on Taiwan. Chaoshan speakers can be found today in the Chaozhou, Shantou, Nan'ao, Chenghai, Raoping, Jieyang, Jiexi, Chaoyang, Puning, Huilai, Haifeng, and Lufleng regions of eastern Guangdong Province.

CHASHAN. See **JINGPO**.

CHELKAN. The Chelkans are one of the primary subgroups of the Altai,* a minority ethnic group living today in the far northern region of the Xinjiang Uigur Autonomous Region in the People's Republic of China.

CHE-NUNG. The Che-nungs are a subgroup of the Lisu* people of Yunnan Province in the People's Republic of China. Along with other Lisu peoples, most Che-nungs are concentrated between the Sawleen River and the Mekong River in western Yunnan Province. Their language is not mutually intelligible with most of the other Lisu tongues; it is closely related to Akha,* Lahu,* and Yi.* They are more likely to identify themselves as ethnic Che-nungs than as Lisus, and they employ a social system that revolves around a variety of patrilineal, exogamous clans that exercise great political power. Most Che-nungs live at higher elevations, usually in ridgeline villages between 3,500 and 10,000 feet in altitude. They are swidden farmers who cultivate maize, mountain rice, millet, and barley.

CHIANG. See **QIANG**.

CH'IANG. See **QIANG**.

CHIEH-PANTO. See **TAJIK**.

CH'I-LAO. See **GELAO**.

CHILIN. See **OROQEN.**

CHIN. See **JING.**

CHINESE. In addition to referring to people around the world who are of ethnic Han* descent, the term "Chinese" is a linguistic reference. Discussing the Chinese language, however, is an extremely complicated matter, both linguistically and politically. In the People's Republic of China (PRC), for example, it is particularly difficult because the government continues to insist that there is only one Chinese language, and that it is divided into a series of dialects. To argue otherwise would require government officials to recognize major ethnic divisions within the dominant Han people, something Chinese officials have been extremely reluctant to do.

Most linguists argue, however, that the definition of the term "dialect" means that it is mutually intelligible with other dialects of the same language. The Chinese government claims that eight dialects of the language exist within the national boundaries: Mandarin,* Wu,* Gan,* Jin,* Xiang,* Hakka,* Yue,* and Min.* The problem with that definition, of course, is that none of these so-called dialects is mutually intelligible with the other. The people who speak them may very well be united by their Han descent and their shared eclectic mix of Buddhist, Daoist, Confucian, and folk religious beliefs, but they cannot understand one another's spoken languages, which should render them members of different ethnic groups. Complicating the issue even more is the fact that each of the eight Chinese languages possesses many dialects, and some of those dialects are not mutually intelligible to speakers of related dialects.

At the same time, however, Chinese speakers share an unusual linguistic similarity. The spoken Chinese languages cannot be mutually understood to different speakers, but they all employ the same written script, which can be read by all. Also, if an outsider asks a Wu or Mandarin speaker what language he or she is speaking, the answer is invariably "Chinese." Some linguists have begun employing the term "regionalect" to describe the eight Chinese languages. Whether or not Mandarin, Wu, Gan, Jin, Xiang, Hakka, Yue, and Min are dialects, regionalects, or languages, they divide the more than 1.1 billion Han people into distinguishable, individual groups whose members share loyalty and a sense of identity with one another because of language.

The question of establishing a standard national Chinese language became a political football in the nineteenth and twentieth centuries. It is an issue important to national security. The Chinese government has long addressed the issue of linguistic diversity in an attempt to blunt the centrifugal forces of ethnicity. They have long feared the possibility that minority nationalities, particularly those who possess a territorial concentration, might seek independence. For centuries, a succession of Chinese governments have viewed the Xinjiang region in the far west as a buffer against Russian* expansion, Tibet as a buffer to intrusions from British* India, and Yunnan as a buffer from the Vietnamese. In order to prevent ethnic rebellions, the government adopted a conciliatory policy toward the larger minorities, extending to them a good deal of political autonomy. So far, the PRC has managed to avoid the political cataclysm that destroyed the Soviet Union in 1991.

Recognizing the minority languages, however, was a relatively simple matter compared to determining which of the Chinese dialects would become the national standard. Demographically, the vast majority of Han people spoke Mandarin, but Han people in southern and southeastern China often associated Mandarin with the despised Qing (Manchu*) dynasty. There were also profound political ramifications. Leftist intellectuals resisted the notion of a national language altogether, primarily because they believed it would become the domain of the bourgeoisie and because it would render illiterate the rest of the population. Eventually, demographic reality won out, and Mandarin received political recognition as the standard Chinese dialect.

After Mao Zedong's 1949 victory and the flight of non-Communists to Taiwan, the new Republic of China had to make the same decision. Most of the native Han residents of Taiwan spoke the Min language, although Hakka was also spoken. During the flight from the mainland, large numbers of Yue (Cantonese) and Mandarin speakers went to Taiwan. The government of the Republic of China designated Mandarin as its official language.

SUGGESTED READINGS: R. A. D. Forrest, *The Chinese Language*, 1948; Chad Hansen, *Language and Logic in Ancient China*, 1983; Tao-tai Hsia, *China's Language Reform*, 1956; Hsu Ying and J. Marvin Brown, *Speaking Chinese in China*, 1983; Paul Kratochvil, *The Chinese Language Today*, 1968; Winfred P. Lehmann, ed., *Language and Linguistics in the People's Republic of China*, 1975; Fang-Kuei Li, "Languages and Dialects," *Journal of Chinese Linguistics* 1 (1974), 1–13; S. Robert Ramsey, *The Languages of China*, 1987; S. A. Wurm, B. T'sou, D. Bradley, et al., eds., *Language Atlas of China*, 1987.

CHINESE SHAN. See **DAI.**

CHING. See **JING.**

CHINGPAW. See **JINGPO.**

CHINGPO. See **JINGPO.**

CHON. The Chon people constitute a tiny ethnic group who may or may not still have a handful of representatives living in the People's Republic of China. They speak a Mon-Khmer* language in the Austroasiatic linguistic family. Beginning in the eighteenth century, the expansion of Tai*-speaking people into northern Laos displaced the Chons, pushing them into far northern Laos, across the border into China, and into Thailand. Chons have not been seen in southern

Yunnan Province for years now, but there remains a strong likelihood that at least a few people there are aware of their Chon origins.

Traditionally, Chons lived in relatively small households, and their villages were located on mountain ridges at lower elevations in tropical rain forests. They were farmers who raised dry rice, maize, legumes, taro, yams, pigs, chickens, and goats.

SUGGESTED READINGS: Kristina Lindell, Hakan Lundstrom, Jan-Olof Svantesson, and Damrong Tayanin, *The Kammu Year: Its Lore and Music*, 1982; Robert Parkin, *A Guide to Austroasiatic Speakers and Their Languages*, 1991.

CHONG'ANJIANG MIAO. The Chong'anjiang Miaos are an ethnic group of approximately 40,000 people who live in Guizhou Province, particularly in Huangping, Kaili, Qianxi, and Zhijin counties. The Chong'anjiang language is divided into four mutually intelligible dialects. Although demographers and ethnologists in the People's Republic of China classify them as a Miao* subgroup, the Chong'anjiangs have a distinct sense of identity.

CHRISTIAN. Describing Christians as an ethnic group in the People's Republic of China (PRC) and the Republic of China may pose difficulties for some, but when ethnicity is defined as a sense of individual loyalty to a group based on racial, linguistic, religious, national origin, or class affinities, it becomes possible to see the Christian minority in China as an ethnic group.

Jesuit missionaries from Spain and Portugal first took Roman Catholicism to China in the sixteenth century, where they established a small Christian foothold along the coast in Guangdong Province. In the nineteenth century, when British influence in China increased, Protestant missionaries representing the Anglican, Presbyterian, and Methodist denominations began making converts in China. These Protestant missionaries worked among the minority nationalities in Yunnan Province as well as among Han peoples throughout the country. At the same time, Roman Catholic missionary priests and nuns, usually from Ireland, came to China to run the Catholic parishes and parochial schools. During the twentieth century, a variety of additional Christian groups established missions in Taiwan, Hong Kong, and Macao, including Pentecostals, Mormons, and Jehovah's Witnesses.

Since Mao Zedong's victory in 1949 and the rise to power of the Chinese Communist party, Christians in the PRC have often found themselves the object of official persecution. During the years of the Cultural Revolution in the late 1960s and early 1970s, that persecution became violent, and Christian ministers and priests frequently found themselves in prison or in "reeducation camps" and their churches razed. Today, although the PRC is still officially atheistic, government officials are somewhat more circumspect in their approach to the Christian community.

Determining the exact number of Christians in China is a difficult matter, primarily because persecution in the past has made many people reluctant to declare themselves as Christians when asked by PRC census takers. According to recent estimates, there are as many as 500,000 Christians in Hong Kong, equally divided between Catholics and Protestants. Macao has perhaps 35,000 Christians, most of whom are Roman Catholics. There are more than one million Christians in the Republic of China on Taiwan, and they represent a great variety of denominations. There are approximately six million avowed Christians in the PRC, of which about 60 percent are Catholics and the remainder Protestants.

SUGGESTED READINGS: Chan Kim-Kwong and Alan Hunter, "Religion and Society in Mainland China in the 1990s," *Issues and Studies* 30 (August 1994), 52–68; *Christian Science Monitor*, August 7, 1996, and January 21, 1997; Judy Polumbaum, "Beijing Catholics Enjoy Renewed Freedom of Belief," *China Reconstructs* 31 (July 1982), 58–59; K. H. Ting, "Chinese Protestants Today," *China Reconstructs* 32 (May 1983), 36–37.

CHUAN QIAN DIAN. Chuan Qian Dian, also known as Western Miao and Sichuan-Guizhou-Yunnan Miao, is one of the three major dialects spoken by the Miao* people in the People's Republic of China (PRC). It is spoken by more than 1.7 million people in Sichuan, Guizhou, and Yunnan provinces. Sichuan-Guizhou-Yunnan Miao is divided into seven dialects, each of which possessses its own subdialects. The primary dialect has two subdialects. Northeastern Yunnan Miao is spoken by 200,000 people in the cities of Yunming and Zhaotong and Wuding, Luquan, Yiliang, Daguan, and Yongshan counties in Yunnan Province and in Weining and Hezhang counties in the Shuicheng Special Region of Guizhou Province. The Giuyang Miao dialect has four of its own subdialects. So does the Huishui Miao dialect, which is spoken in Huishui and Changshun counties in Guizhou. The Mashan dialect is spoken by more than 100,000 people in Changshun, Luodian, Huishui, Ziyun, and Wangmo counties in Guizhou Province. Mashan possesses four primary subdialects of its own. Luopohe Miao is spoken by nearly 50,000 people in Fuquan, Weng'an, Guiding, Longli, Kaili, and Kaiyang counties in Guizhou Province. Finally, nearly 50,000 Miaos speak the Chong'anjiang dialect and live in Huangping, Kaili, Qianxi, and Zhijin counties in Guizhou Province.

CHUANG. See **ZHUANG.**

CHUNGCHIA. See **BOUYEI.**

CHUQU. The Chuqu people are a linguistic subgroup of Wu*-speaking Han* people in the People's Republic of China (PRC). Chugu speakers total nearly seven million people and live in Zhejiang, Jiangxi, and Fujian provinces in the PRC. Chuqu can also be divided into two distinctive dialects of its own: Chuzhou and Longqu.

CHUZHOU. The Chuzhou people are a linguistic subgroup of the Chuqu* people, who themselves speak a dialect of the Wu*-speaking Han* people in the People's Republic of China. More than 1.5 million people speak the Chuzhou dialect, and most of them live in Lishui, Jinyun, Yunhe, Qingtian, Taishun, Wengcheng, Wuyi, Qingyuan, and Jingning She Autonomous counties in Zhejiang Province.

CHYSH. See **SHOR.**

CO SUNG. See **LAHU.**

CO XUNG. See **LAHU.**

COASTAL AMI. The Coastal Ami are one of the five primary subgroups of the Ami* people of Taiwan in the Republic of China. Most Coastal Amis live in the strip of Taidong County that stretches up the coast next to Hualien County. They are also known as Central Amis and as Xiuguluan Amis.

COOKED MIAO. The term "Cooked Miao" has been used in the People's Republic of China to describe Miao* people in Yunnan and Guizhou provinces who have acculturated successfully to Han* institutions.

COWRIE-SHELL MIAO. See **MIAO.**

CUAN. See **BAI.**

CUN. The Cun people are an ethnic group of approximately 60,000 people who live on Hainan Island in the People's Republic of China (PRC). They are concentrated in northern Dongfang County on the south bank of the Changhuajiang River in the Sigeng, Xinjie, Hongjhiang, and Baoban communities. Other Cuns can be found living today on the north bank of the Changhuajiang River near the Changhuajiang community in Changjiang County. They are not an officially recognized minority nationality in the PRC because government officials classify Cuns as a subgroup of the Han* majority. The Cun language is a curious mixture of Li* and Chinese,* although the Li roots predominate. The vast majority of Cuns also speak a Mandarin* dialect. Most Cuns are farmers who raise coconuts, coffee, cocoa, sisal, rubber, cashews, pineapples, mangoes, and bananas. Rice is their staple, and because of the tropical climate of Hainan and its fertile soil, they are able to produce three rice crops a year.
SUGGESTED READING: S. A. Wurm, B. T'sou, D. Bradley, et al., eds., *Language Atlas of China*, 1987.

CUONA. The Cuona people are a relatively small ethnic group who live today in the Tibetan Autonomous Region of the People's Republic of China (PRC).

Chinese demographers estimate their current population at approximately 35,000 people. Cuonas are classified as part of the officially recognized Moinba* minority nationality, but their language is not really mutually intelligible with the other major Moinba language, which is known as Motuo.* Although the central government of the PRC does not consider them to be a distinct ethnic entity, most Cuonas identify themselves as Cuonas rather than as Moinbas, although they acknowledge Moinba kinship. The vast majority of the Cuona population today lives in Cuona County of Lebu Prefecture and Medog County in Dexing Prefecture of the Tibetan Autonomous Region.

Cuonas speak a Tibeto-Burman* language, part of the Sino-Tibetan family, which is divided into dozens of mutually intelligible dialects. Most Cuona families are farmers and pastoralists. Because of persecution from ethnic Tibetans* over the years, they live in isolated, forested, mountainous, or deep gorge areas of southern Tibet. Their local climate is subtropical and the soil is fertile. Cuona farmers produce rice, maize, millet, buckwheat, soybeans, and sesame seeds, and Cuona pastoralists herd cattle and sheep. Hunting remains important as a source of protein and male bonding.

SUGGESTED READINGS: Tiley Chodag, *Tibet: The Land and Its Peoples*, 1988; Paul V. Hockings, "Moinba," in Paul V. Hockings, ed., *The Encyclopedia of World Cultures*, vol. 6, *East and Southeast Asia*, 1991; Ma Yin, ed., *China's Minority Nationalities*, 1989; S. A. Wurm, B. T'sou, D. Bradley, et al., eds., *Language Atlas of China*, 1987.

D

DA KA VA. The Da Ka Vas are considered by many ethnologists in the People's Republic of China to be a subgroup of the Wa,* an officially recognized minority nationality. Most Wa people live in the southwestern reaches of Yunnan Province, primarily in Ximeng, Canghyuan, Menglian, Gengma, Lancang, Yongde, Shuangjiang, and Zhenkang counties, where they work as farmers. They raise wet rice, dry rice, maize, millet, tubers, and wheat. Classifying them as a subgroup of the Wa, however, poses problems to ethnologists. The Da Ka Va dialect is not mutually intelligible with most of the other Wa dialects; therefore, most Da Ka Va people tend to view themselves more as Da Ka Va than as Wa. The process of ethnogenesis, by which they may come to regard themselves primarily as Wa people, is not yet complete.

DABAO. The Dabao make up one of the linguistic subgroups of the more than 48 million Han* people who speak the Jin* Chinese* language. Most Dabaos can be found living today in thirty cities, counties, and banners in central and northern Shanxi Province, northern Shaanxi Province, and the western region of the Inner Mongolian Autonomous Region in the People's Republic of China.

DAENG. See DE'ANG.

DAFLA. The Daflas are a small ethnic group whose homeland today can be found in the far northern reaches of Arunachal Pradesh State in India. Because of their proximity to the Himalayan trade routes and the border of the People's Republic of China (PRC), there are probably, at any given time, some Daflas living in the PRC. The isolation caused by their geographically rugged homeland has insulated Daflas from most outside influences.

In terms of their ethnic and linguistic roots, they are of Mongol* stock, with their origins in northern Central Asia. Daflas speak a Tibeto-Burman* language. Dafla society is characterized by high levels of political decentralization. They live in longhouses, which house from sixty to eighty people, all of whom are related. Each of the longhouses essentially constitutes an independent political unit. Daflas are swidden farmers who continue today to hunt, fish, and forage to supplement their diets. Their total population today is approaching 20,000, of whom only a handful are residents of the PRC.
SUGGESTED READING: *Atlas of Man*, 1978.

DAFULU. The Dafulus are one of the most prominent clans of the Lisu* people of the People's Republic of China.

DAGHOR. See **DAUR.**

DAGUER. See **DAUR.**

DAGUR. See **DAUR.**

DAHEJIA. The Dahejias are one of the principal subgroups of the Bonan* people. The Dahejias, who are overwhelmingly Muslim, live in Gansu Province of the People's Republic of China.

DAHUER. See **DAUR.**

DAI. The Dai are one of the fifty-five officially recognized minority nationalities of the People's Republic of China (PRC). Until 1953 government officials identified them as the Tai or Thai people. They have also been known as Ngios, Ngiaws, Taina, Taini, Taili, Taipeng, Taiya, Tehung Tai, Chinese Shan, Hsi-Shuang Panna Tai, and Pai-Is. Among their minority neighbors, which include the Lahu,* Hani,* Jingpo,* Benlong, Wa,* Bulang, and Achang,* the Dai are identified as Bitsos, Siams, or La Siams. Virtually all of the 1,025,128 Dai identified in the 1990 Chinese national census live in Yunnan Province, particularly in the Dehong Dai and Jingpo Autonomous Prefecture and in the Xishuangbanna Dai Autonomous Prefecture, which are located in far southern Yunnan. Another substantial Dai cluster can be found in Lincang Prefecture, very close to the border with Myanmar (Burma). Together, these groups constitute nearly two-thirds of the Dai population. The remaining ethnic Dai people are scattered widely throughout southern and southwestern Yunnan Province. Several thousand Dai are also living today in southern Sichuan Province. The total Dai population today is approaching 1.2 million people.

The Dai language is classified as one of the Zhuang-Dong cluster of the Tai* linguistic family. Closely related to the Thai people of Thailand, most Dai employ one of several variants of the Siamese written language; they are not nearly as sinicized as the Zhuang.* In fact, ethnologists consider the Dai to be more of a southeast Asian people than a Chinese people.

The Dai people have long been an important ethnic group in southwest China and southeastern Asia. They have their origins more than three thousand years ago south of the Yangtze River in what is today south-central China. Han* Chinese* expansionism over the millenia gradually pushed them southward, which explains why Dai and Dai-related peoples can also be found in Myanmar, Thailand, Laos, and Vietnam, where they are known as Shans, Tais, or Thais. Over the millenia, Dais have exercised a great deal of power in the region.

During the tenth century, Dais established political sovereignty over the region now identified by historians as the Mong Mao Kingdom. It was succeeded in the eleventh century by another Dai imperial entity known as the Kocambi Kingdom. The Mong Mao and Kocambi kingdoms were the dominant political power in the Dehong region. At the same time, the Dai operated the Yonaga (Xienrun) Kindgom in Xishuangbanna. It was in the thirteenth century that Marco Polo, the great European traveler, encountered the Dai people on his way to northern China. He commented on their practice of ritualistic tattooing.

From the thirteenth to the eighteenth centuries, the Lanna (Babai Xifu) Kingdom in northern Thailand was a Dai political entity. The local groups who historically found themselves under Dai control were the De'ang,* Blang,* Hani, Lahu, Achang, and Jingpo.

In the fourteenth century, the southwestern expansion of Han political power finally reached southwestern Yunnan, and the Dai soon found themselves under Chinese political control. Hundreds of thousands of Han soldiers representing the Ming dynasty came to Yunnan and remained there as military colonists. Astutely observing that it would be better to work through the Dai than against them, the Chinese imperial government established what soon became known as the *tusi* system. Existing Dai kings and nobility received appointment as official *tusi* lords, and the Chinese dynasties extended official political recognition to their Dai administrations, giving them suzerainty over other ethnic minorities in the region.

The typical *tusi* leader enjoyed absolute legislative, judicial, administrative, and military power within his regional domain as long as he obeyed the mandates of the imperial government and met his quota payments of tribute, taxes, and forced labor. Because all land was also owned by the *tusi*, he functioned not only as an official governmental unit but also as a landlord. The fusion of political and economic authority essentially created a feudal order in Dai country. Between the fourteenth and the twentieth centuries, the *tusi* system gradually weakened and was incrementally replaced by regular Han administrative systems. In 1956 the current administrative system of district, county, autonomous prefecture, autonomous region, and province was imposed. Not surprisingly, the central dynamic of recent Dai history has been a struggle for power between Dai and the minority nationalities they governed as well as between Dai and Han peoples.

Chinese ethnolinguists classify the Dai language and its dialects as part of the Zhuang-Dong (Kam-Tai) cluster of the Sino-Tibetan language family. Some ethnolinguists in Europe and the United States disagree, arguing that Dai is part of the Thai-Austronesian language family. There are six versions of written Dai: Dailu, Daina Daipeng, Dehong Dai, Jinping Dai, Xinping Dai, and Xishuang-banna Dai. Of those, Dehong Dai and Xishuangbanna Dai are the most widely used.

The Dai are divided into three major subgroups based on dialect and geographical location. With a current population of as many as 675,000 people, the Dailu constitute the largest of those subgroups. Dailus reside in the Xishuang-banna region, and many of them are literate in the Xishuangbanna written script. The Daina people are the second largest of the subgroups, with their population today approaching 480,000 people. Most Daina Dai are concentrated in Dehong and Lincang. The smallest of the Dai subgroups is the Daija, whose current population numbers approximately 75,000 people. Most Daija Dai people live in Yuanjiang County, Xinping County, and in the Red River Valley of Yunnan. The Dailu, Daina, and Daija groups are themselves divided into dozens of subgroups based on geographical location and dialect.

Some of the Daina subgroups, for example, are the Daide, Daipeng, Daila, Dailian, and Pudai. Dais are able to distinguish between the various subgroups by dialect and by the characteristic color of the blouses worn by Dai women. Other Dai subgroups include the Baiyis, Lus, and Nuas. Because the various Dai subgroups are closely related culturally and linguistically, because their dialects are often mutually intelligible, and because they all identify themselves by some variant of the name Tai, most ethnobiologists are comfortable with designating them as a single ethnic group.

The Dai homeland typically exists in river valleys or flatlands of the area, usually between 1,500 feet and 4,000 feet of elevation. The climate is tropical or semitropical depending upon the altitude. Heavy annual rainfall has produced thick tropical and semitropical monsoon forests. Dai villages contain anywhere from forty to one hundred households, and their homes vary in construction. The Xishuangbanna Dai live in two-story bamboo homes, in which the second story is reserved for the family and the first floor is used for livestock. Daina Dai homes, on the other hand, are more like those of their Han neighbors, with wood frames, mud-brick walls, and tile roofs. Livestock pens are built inside a family compound but at some distance from the house.

Unlike most of the other minority nationalities in Yunnan Province, the Dai have been commercial farmers for more than a thousand years. They are also the first to cultivate rice in the region. At a time more than 1,400 years ago when most of the inhabitants of Yunnan were hunters and foragers, the Dai were wet-rice farmers cultivating large paddy fields. They used elephants as draft animals to plow the fields. When large numbers of ethnic Han began arriving in Dai country, more sophisticated production techniques dramatically enhanced yields. Today, more than two-thirds of all Dai farmland is employed in wet-rice farming. They also produce dry rice on terraced, hillside fields. Cash crops include tea, cotton, tobacco, camphor, sisal, sugarcane, coffee, bananas, mangoes, and rubber. The Dai are not known for their skills as merchants or industrialists. They simply sell their produce to state-run stores who purchase it at fixed prices. Ethnic Han, Hui,* Naxi,* and Bai* peoples have traditionally served as middlemen in the commercial activities of Dai country.

The rise of the Communist party to power in China after 1949 brought significant changes to Dai farmers. The government encouraged the production of sugarcane and rubber over other products, and many Dai farmers made the transition. Central government economic and ideological planners also implemented dramatic changes in land tenure arrangements. For centuries in Dai regions, all land had been owned by *tusi* landlords. In what was essentially a feudal arangement, Dai farmers received land from *tusi* landlords and, in return for its use, pledged percentages of revenues, labor, and even military loyalty. Late in the nineteenth century, a number of *tusi* landlords sold their property to Han settlers, who then used Dai farmers as sharecroppers and tenants. In 1957 the Chinese collectivized agriculture in much of Yunnan Province and organized Dai farmers into cooperatives and then into communes. The collective approach to farming was misguided and mismanaged, and yields dropped steadily over the next two decades. In 1981, after the ideological fervor of the Cultural Revolution had subsided, the Chinese Communist party reformed collective agriculture by contracting paddy fields for wet-rice farming to individual households while keeping the dry lands communal. Each household was required pay a grain tax to the central government and sell its yields at state-mandated prices, but they could make their own economic decisions about resource allocation and keep the profits when they exceed production quotas. Since 1981 the reforms have accounted for substantial gains in Dai agricultural productivity.

The traditional Dai society was divided into two groups based on family origins. The aristocracy was composed of three levels: the *mong* and his lineal descendents were upper-class landlords; the *wung* were his collateral relatives; and the *lulangdaopa* were distant relatives of both *wung* and *mong*. The second major group in the Dai social structure included commoners, who were also divided into three stratified clusters: the *daimong* who were natives to the region; the *gunghengchao* who were individuals born into the servant families of the *mong*; and the *kachao* who were slaves owned by *mong* families. Although the Chinese government formally abolished all class divisions in 1949, the Dai still remain conscious of their individual origins.

Although elements of indigenous Dai animism survive in the superstitions of less-educated people, most Dai today are Buddhists, primarily of the Hinayana tradition. Buddhism, both Theravada and Hinayana, first came to Dai country in the seventh century, but the religion did not make significant inroads until the sixteenth century. In the early nineteenth century, Dao Yin Mong, a prominent Dai *tusi* in Xishuangbanna, married a Burmese princess, after which Buddhism became the official religion and quickly became the faith of the Dai aristocracy. By the twentieth century, it was common for most aristocatic Dai men to spend several years in a Buddhist monastery. Dai Buddhism demands that individuals follow the so-called Middle Way, achieving balance in life by avoiding extremes and by pursuing the Four Noble Truths, which claim that existence is synonymous with suffering, that suffering springs from desire, that suppression of desire will eliminate suffering, and that desire is eliminated only by controlling individual conduct and thought. Only then can the spirit of the dead achieve the state of nirvana, or eternal peace. The vast majority of Dai Buddhists adhere to one of four sects: Ruen, Baizhhung, Dolie, or Zodi.

Dai animism still exists among illiterate commoners. They believe that after death, a Dai adult becomes a benign spirit, while an individual who dies violently becomes an evil spirit. Rituals performed by Buddhist monks are employed to rid one's home of evil spirits, to expiate the sins of the deceased, and to release the spirit of the deceased from purgatory. Individuals who die as children do not become spirits at all.

SUGGESTED READINGS: William Clifton Dodd, *The Dai Race*, 1923; Lucien M. Hanks, *Rice and Man*, 1972; Hu Yue, "Tattooing of the Dai People," *China Today* 44 (November 1995), 34–36; Peng Jianqun, "Working for the Welfare of the Dai People," *China Today* 43 (August 1994), 56–57; T'ien Ju-k'ang, "Pai Cults and Social Age in the Tai Tribes of the Yunnan-Burmese Frontier," *American Anthropologist* 51 (1949), and *Religious Cults of the Pai-I along the Burma-Yunnan Border*, 1985; Wang Zhusheng, "Dai," in Paul V. Hockings, ed., *The Encyclopedia of World Cultures*, vol. 6, *East and Southeast Asia*, 1991; Yu Jiao, "Bamboo Houses by the Lancang River," *China Reconstructs* 32 (February 1983), 50–52.

DAI DLI. See **LI.**

DAIJA. The Daijas are one of the primary subgroups of the Dai* people of Yunnan Province in southwestern China.

DAILU. In southwestern China and the northern reaches of southeast Asia, the term "Dailu" is a synonym for the Dai* people. It is also one of the several written versions of the Dai language.

DAINA. The Dainas are one of the primary subgroups of the Dai* people of Yunnan Province in southwestern China.

DAINA DAIPENG. Daina Daipeng is one of the several written versions of the Dai* language of Yunnan Province in southwestern China.

DAISA. See **ACHANG.**

DAKPA. See **MOINBA.**

DANG. See **DE'ANG.**

DARANG. See **TARANG.**

DARBIN. See **DAUR.**

DARD. The term "Dard" has been used for centuries to describe the residents of the Hindu Kush region of northern Pakistan and Afghanistan, but it is more accurate today to speak of the "Dardic" languages, which are classified in the Indo-Aryan family of languages. Included in the Dardic cluster are Kashmiri. The term "Dardistan" describes the Gilgit, Hunza, Chitral, Yasin, Nagar, Panyal, Kohistan, and Astore regions of northern Pakistan. The only Dardic peoples that could be part of the People's Republic of China (PRC) today are the handful of Burushos* of the Hunza Valley who periodically make their way into the PRC on business.
SUGGESTED READING: Paul V. Hockings, "Dard," in Paul V. Hockings, ed., *The Encyclopedia of World Cultures*, vol. 3; *South Asia*, 1991.

DASHAN. See **JINGPO.**

DATIAN. The Datian people are a subgroup of Minnan peoples, themselves a linguistic subgroup of the Min* language of Chinese* in the People's Republic of China (PRC) and the Republic of China on Taiwan. Datian speakers can be found today in Datian County in southern Fujian Province of the PRC. See **HAN** and **MINNAN.**

DATONG. The Datong people are a subgroup of the Gan*-speaking Han* Chinese* of the People's Republic of China. Most Datongs today live in the Daye, Xianning, Jiayu, Puqi, Chongyang, Tongcheng, Tongshan, Yangxin, and Jianli regions of Hubei Province and the Linxiang, Yueyang, and Huarong regions of Hunan Province.

DAUR. The Daur people—also known in China and Kazakstan as the Daghor, Dagur, Daguer, Dahhuer, Dayur, Dawoer, Takanerh, Takuanerb, and Tahuerh— are one of China's smaller officially recognized minority nationalities. The 1990 census of the People's Republic of China (PRC) put their population at 121,627, and today it is probably closer to 130,000 people. The majority of the Daur people live in the Molidawa Daur Autonomous Banner District of far northeastern China in the Inner Mongolian Autonomous Region (IMAR). As many as 30,000 of them are located deep in the Greater Hinggan Mountains in the eastern reaches of the IMAR. Perhaps a third of the Daurs reside in Heilongjiang Province. The remainder of the Daurs can be found on the other side of the country, living in Tacheng County of the Xinjiang Uigur Autonomous Region. Some are also located across the border in far southeastern Kazakstan.

Until the seventeenth century, most Daurs resided in the Amur River Valley, but the expansion of Russian* settlement all the way to the Pacific Ocean disturbed Chinese authorities. In 1682 the Russian government dispatched Russian Orthodox missionaries to work among the Daurs and convert them to Christianity. Alarmed Manchu* government authorities decided to relocate the Daur people rather than have them fall under Russian influence. The Daur migrants were placed in settlements scattered widely throughout northwestern Manchuria in what is today the northeastern section of the IMAR. Some were also relocated across Mongolia in northern Xinjiang. Today, the greatest concentration of Daurs can be found in the Nonni River Valley near Qiqihar Province in Heilongjiang Province.

During the twentieth century, ethnolinguists have debated the origins of the Daur language and how to classify it. Some scholars have argued that it is a Tungus (see **TUNGISIC PEOPLE**) language; others have claimed that it is an unusual mix of Tungus and Mongolian (see **MONGOL**). More recently, however, scholars have begun to agree that Daur is a Mongolian language with four distinct dialects. The dialects are mutually intelligible but nevertheless serve to divide the Daurs into recognizable subgroups. Approximately 40,000 Daurs speak the Qiqihar dialect, which can be heard in and around Qiqihar City, Fuyu County, Longjiang County, Araong Banner, and Vutha Banner. Qiqihar itself is divided into three distinct vernaculars. Jiangdong is spoken in Fuyu County, especially east of the Nonni River. Jiangxi is spoken in the area north of Meilisi and west of the Nonni River and in Fularji.

The second major Daur dialect is Butha, which is spoken by approximately 40,000 Daur people. Butha is prominent in Morindawa Banner and in Nenjiang County, Nehe Couunty, and Gannan County. There are four Butha vernaculars. The Nawen tongue is spoken in the western Butha region, Nemor, Aihui, and Mergen. During the past several decades, speakers of the Nemor vernacular, who had long lived east of the Nonni River, have crossed the river into western Butha territory, where their language is now fusing with Nemor. The third vernacular is Aihui, also known locally as Darbin. Mergen, the fourth Butha vernacular, can be heard in Nenjiang County.

Hailar, the third Daur dialect, is spoken by 15,500 speakers. It is different enough from Qiqihar and Butha to be understood by those groups only with great difficulty. It has two vernaculars of its own: Nantun, which is spoken in Hailar City and in Nantun, the seat of the Evenk Autonomous Banner; and Mokertu, which is spoken in and around the towns of Bayintala and Mokertu in the Evenk Autonomous Banner.

The fourth Daur dialect is known as Ili. Approximately 5,000 people speak the Ili dialect, which can be heard today in Xinjiang. Ili reflects the long interaction between the Daur and Kazaks in Xinjiang. Like Hailar, many Ilis consider themselves ethnically distinct from other Daur subgroups. Because of their proximity to Manchus, Mongols, and Hezhens* in Heilongjiang Province, the Daur dialects are loaded with Mongol, Manchu, and Hezhen words. The presence of so many Manchu words in the Daur dialects can also be explained by the fact that during the Qing dynasty in Chinese history, from 1644 to 1911, the Daurs employed the Manchu system of writing. Substantial numbers of Daurs are bilingual, speaking their own dialect as well as Chinese,* Uigur,* Mongolian, Hezhen, Kirgiz,* or Kazak.*

In terms of their economic history, the Daurs once served, during the seventeenth, eighteenth, and nineteenth centuries, as important commercial middlemen in trade between the Chinese interior and the vast plains north of the Great Wall. Gold, furs, skins, metal tools, and medicinal herbs were transported through Daur territory. The Daur also engaged in commercial fishing on the rivers of the homeland and in lumber operations. Most Daur, however, made their livings as farmers, pastoralists, and hunters. Their societies were egalitarian and lineage based.

Much of that has changed since the 1950s because of Communist party-driven economic planning. Instead of the subsistence, small-scale farming of their past, the Daur have been encouraged by government agricultural advisers to plant much larger fields and to plant soybeans, maize, and sorghum for distribution throughout the country. For their own diets, the Daur still raise millet, oats, and buckwheat, to which they add milk, butter, and sugar and consume as a porridge. Daur pastoralists raise horses, sheep, and cattle, although they do it on a much larger scale today because of the encouragement of the central government. A large number of Daur men work for wages in the logging industry. Hunting remains an important element of Daur society, although it is less significant as a dimension of their economy than it was before 1949. Nevertheless, Daur men still hunt in order to supplement their diets with protein from wild fowl and venison.

Daur society, in spite of pressure from the central government to assimilate Han* social systems, continues to function around localized patrilineages, which the Daur call *mokan*. The members of each *mokan* live in the same village and share the same surname. Above the level of the *mokan*, the fundamental social unit is the *hala*, which consists of people who share a surname but live in a different village. Young men and women may not marry an individual from the same *hala*. In spite of government dictates to the contrary, Daur marriages are arranged, although the practices of arranging such marriages before birth and having the bride raised in her future husband's household are dying out. The Daur still maintain a strong preference that marriages occur between matrilateral cross-cousins. Each man is expected to maintain a lifelong interest in the welfare of his sister's children, even to the point of protecting them and assisting them socially and economically.

Although a few Daur have converted to Lamaist Buddhism, most remain faithful to a syncretic mix of their indigenous, animist religion and elements of Hinayana Buddhism and Han ancestor worship. The Daur view the natural world as a cosmic whole. Animals, plants, minerals, sun, moon, stars, and the earth are alive, imbued with a measure of knowledge, individual consciousness, and awareness of the things around them. They name every tree, animal, river, stream, meadow, mountain, hill, and valley, as well as days, weeks, months, and seasons. All of creation has a spiritual essence, and there is a balance and solidarity to nature. The Daur are particularly concerned with sky gods, whom they call *tenger*. Annual sacrifices are made to appease the *tenger*.

Over the centuries, ancestor worship has made the jump from Han culture to Daur religion. Each Daur *mokan* and *hala* has a designated ancestral deity, usually a female, who is worshipped by all the people of the village and the surname cluster. The Daur also accept an element of Buddhism, for they believe that upon death, the soul of every living creature departs the body and undergoes reincarnation. The most exemplary people can become gods, while the worst people are assigned permanently to hell.

A strong element of shamanism also imbues the Daur religion. Like other indigenous, animist peoples, the Daur believe that the natural world's balance depends upon respect for nature. Disobedience and disrespect toward the natural world can easily ignite vengeance and retribution. On the other hand, careful observation of the behavior of plants, animals, and the elements can assist the Daur in predicting the future, avoiding danger and tragedy, and controlling the fear, decay, sickness, and misery leading to death. For the Daur, the sacred and the profane, the spiritual and the temporal, are one and the same.

Beyond the world of animals, objects, and natural phenomena, the Daur religion functions in the world of spirits. The existence of a variety of mythological, unseen beings, such as water spirits, house ghosts, and cloud-beings, is taken for granted in Daur culture. All of these unseen beings function actively in the world according to supernatural laws, and when the events of the natural world appear disruptive or illogical, the Daur blame these invisible spirits and appeal to their female shamans for assistance. Rituals, ceremonies, and magical devotions are the stock-in-trade of the shamans, who are usually specially selected women who pass on their knowledge, powers, and skills to their descendents. By seeing life in terms of magical casuality, the Daur learn to deal with their environment and avoid a fatalistic surrender to outside forces often spawned by political oppression and economic poverty.

SUGGESTED READINGS: Mark Bender and Su Huana, *Folktales of the Daur Nationality*, 1971; Paul V. Hockings, "Daur," in Paul V. Hockings, ed., *The Encyclopedia of World Cultures*, vol. 6, *East and Southeast Asia*, 1991; Peng Jianqun, "The Hockey-Playing Daur," *China Today* 41 (November 1992), 60–62; Henry G. Schwarz, *The Minorities of Northern China: A Survey*, 1984.

DAWOER. See **DAUR.**

DAYUR. See **DAUR.**

DBU. The Dbu people are ethnic Tibetans* who speak the Dbu vernacular of the Dbusgtsang* dialect. Most Dbu speakers live in Llasa City and Shannan Prefecture.

DBUSGTSANG. Dbusgtsang is one of the three primary dialects of Tibetan.* Calling it a dialect, however, is complicated by the fact that it is only marginally intelligible to speakers of Kham,* another Dbusgtsang dialect, and is not mutually intelligible to speakers of Amdo,* the other Tibetan dialect. Dbusgtsang, spoken widely throughout the Tibetan Autonomous Region, is divided into four mutually intelligible dialects: Dbus, Gtsang, Mngahri, and Sherpa.

DE'ANG. The De'ang people—also known by neighbors and scholars as the Ang, Benglong, Benlong, Black Benlong, Daeng, Dang, Humai, Kunlois, La'eng, Liang, Niang, Palaung, Ra-ang, Red Benlong, Rumai, and Ta-ang—make up one of the People's Republic of China's smallest recognized national minorities. Their population was approximately 6,000 people in 1949 and had grown to 12,275 by the time of the 1982 national census. Today, Chinese demographers estimate that the De'ang population is approaching 15,000 people. The De'angs can be found distributed unevenly throughout the frontier area between southwestern Yunnan Province in the People's Republic of China (PRC) and northeastern Myanmar (Burma). Most Yunnan De'angs reside today in the Dehong Dai and Jingpo Autonomous Prefecture. They are especially concentrated in the Santaishan region of Luxi County and in the Junnong region of Zhenkang County. Other De'angs can be found in the Lincang Administration Area and in the Baoshan Administration Area.

The De'ang language is classified by most ethnolinguists in the Mon-Khmer* cluster of the Austroasiatic linguistic family. It is broken down into three dialects that serve to divide the De'ang into ethnic subgroups. The dialects are regionally based on the De'ang clusters in Santaishan region of Luxi County, the Junnong region in Zhenkang County, and in the Lincang Administration region. Because of the proximity of large numbers of Han,* Dai,* and Jingpo* peoples, most De'angs are bilingual or trilingual. Many Chinese linguists consider the De'angs to be close relatives of the Wa* people.

Chinese historians and archaeologists believe that the De'ang are relatively direct descendents of the first settlers of the Dehong region of Yunnan Province. These ancestors, called the ''Pu'' people, first appear in Chinese historical documents dated more than two thousand years ago. Other Mon-Khmer-speaking people in Yunnan can also trace their ancestry to the Pu, although not quite as directly as the De'ang. During the Qing dynasty, Chinese records refer to the De'ang as the Benlong people. Since around 1200 A.D., the De'ang have lived in close association with Tai*-speaking peoples, particularly the Dai.

The De'ang economy remains overwhelmingly agricultural. The people of the Dehong region engage in wet-rice farming, while in Lincang, De'ang farmers are more likely to produce dry rice, maize, and tubers. For more than a century, tea has served as the primary De'ang cash crop. To acquire metal tools, cloth, and salt, the De'angs trade their bamboo-woven handicrafts with Dai and Han merchants.

For centuries, land tenure in De'ang society was communal; the villages owned the property and leased it out to individual families. During the nineteenth century, private property arrangements began to appear, and when large numbers of Han and Dai settlers arrived in De'ang villages, alienation of the land began. By 1949 Han and Dai settlers had purchased approximately 90 percent of the land formerly owned by the De'ang villages. Most De'angs became tenant farmers who rented land from the new Dai and Han owners. Even that arrangement began to change in 1956, when the PRC's agrarian reform movement nationalized all farmland and introduced collective forms of production. The Han and Dai owners lost their individual property, but it made relatively little difference to the De'ang, who were already laboring as tenants.

De'ang society is organized patrilineally. Each village contains several patrilineal clusters of people, and each cluster is composed of anywhere from thirty to forty nuclear families. De'ang surnames have mostly been sinicized. De'angs require marriages to be within the village but outside the patrilineal group, and they prefer what anthropologists describe as asymmetrical cross-cousin unions, in which a man marries a daughter of his mother's brothers. After marriage, the couple moves into the groom's father's household until they can afford a home of their own.

The De'ang people were converted to Theravada Buddhism under the influence of their Dai neighbors. Most De'ang villages support a Buddhist temple and a Buddhist monk, who sees to their spiritual needs. Like other Buddhists, the De'angs look forward to achieving nirvana—an otherwordly state of eternal peace and balance—as a reward for meritorious spiritual achievements in this life. Most elements of the ancient De'ang indigenous animist faith have disappeared.

SUGGESTED READINGS: Tan Leshan, "De'ang," in Paul V. Hockings, ed., *The Encyclopedia of World Cultures*, vol. 6, *East and Southeast Asia*, 1991; Ma Yin, ed., *China's Minority Nationalities*, 1984; Guo Mingong, "A Benglong Nationality Village," *China Reconstructs* 34 (March 1985), 54–55.

DEED. See OIRAT.

DEHONG DAI. The term "Dehong Dai" refers to one of the six written versions of the Dai* language of southwestern China. It is one of the more popular and widely used of those languages today and is especially prominent in the Dehong region of Yunnan Province.

DEJING. Dejings are a subgroup of the Zhuang* people of the People's Republic of China. The Dejing language is classified as one of the Southern

Zhuang* dialects, and most of its speakers live today in Debao, Jingxi, and Napo counties in the Guangxi Zhuang Autonomous Region.

DENG. The Deng people—also known as the Dengpa, Teng, and Tengpa— account for a tiny ethnic minority of the People's Republic of China (PRC). They live today in the far southeastern tip of Tibet, in the densely populated, agriculturally fertile Kham District. Most of them can be found in the Zayul Region along the Ngachu, Zayulchu, Gedochu, and Dolegchu rivers. Zayul is characterized by densely forested high mountains, deep gorges, and rapidly flow- ing rivers. Wildlife is abundant.

Dengs speak a language that is part of the Sino-Tibetan linguistic family, but it is divided into two dialects which are barely mutually intelligible, with enough differences to give the speakers of each a distinct ethnic identity. Approximately 6,000 people speak the Tarang* (Darang) language, while 8,000 speak the Ka- man* (Geman) language.

Like most Tibetans,* the Deng are small farmers who raise pigs, goats, wheat, millet, rice, and a variety of vegetables. They also engage in commercial activ- ities along the Tsangpo River, Tibet's economic lifeline. Their religion is an eclectic mix of Deng animism and Lamaist Buddhism. Most Dengs live in wooden homes. Maize is the staple of their diet.

In the southeastern region of Tibet, Deng men and women are readily iden- tifiable by their costumes. Sleeveless gowns, short pants, and bamboo hats char- acterize the dress of Deng men; the Deng women wear short-sleeved blouses and long dresses. Their midriffs are typically bare. Women bind their hair up into a bun in the back. Silver beads and ornaments also adorn Deng women.

The Dengs view themselves as a distinct people, quite different from other Tibetans and from Han* Chinese.* Their own religious traditions claim that long ago, a golden god named Achani married a female monkey. They had three sons—Tongka, Tongma, and Tongde—who became the ancestors of the Han, Tibetan, and Deng peoples. Tongde, according to the legend, decided to move away from his brothers and go up into the mountains. From him came the Deng people.

After the PRC assumed military and political control of Tibet, Deng leaders applied for official recognition as a minority nationality. Because of the small size of the Deng population and their integration into the commercial economy of southeastern Tibet, Chinese authorities were not sympathetic and denied the application. Tibetan authorities did not help the situation. Tibetan nationalists have never accepted the idea of Chinese sovereignty, and they insisted that all Tibetans were members of a single ethic group. They feared that official rec- ognition of any Tibetan group as a ''Chinese'' nationality would weaken their hopes for eventual national liberation. In 1990 Deng leaders began to threaten secession from Tibet and from the PRC unless their demands for official rec- ognition were met.

SUGGESTED READINGS: Tiley Chodag, *Tibet: The Land and the People*, 1988; Fei

Hsiao Tung, *Toward a People's Anthropology*, 1981; David Y. H. Wu, ed., *National Policy and Minority Cultures in Asia*, 1988; Graham Young, ed., *China: Dilemmas of Modernisation*, 1985.

DENGPA. See DENG.

DEORI. The Deoris are a Tibetan* people whose primary homeland today is in Assam and Aranunchal Pradesh states in India. They speak Tibetan, primarily one of the Kham* dialects of southwestern Tibet, which is part of the Tibeto-Burman* family. Although the vast majority of the more than 40,000 Deori people live in India, several hundred of them make their way into Tibet on trade routes. What sets them apart from other Tibetans, however, is their religion. Whereas most Tibetans are Lamaist Buddhists, the Deori are Hindus. They are a riverine people who raise rice as their staple.
SUGGESTED READINGS: Barbara Aziz, *Tibetan Frontier Families*, 1978; Tiley Chodag, *Tibet: The Land and the People*, 1988; Dalai Lama, *My Land and My People*, 1962; Rebecca French, *The Golden Yoke: The Legal System of Buddhist Tibet*, 1994.

DERUNG. See DRUNG.

DI. See QING.

DIOI. See BOUYEI.

DIRAMITING. The Diramitings are one of the four primary clans of the Burusho* people of the Hunzu Valley in Pakistan.

DIVERGENT LAHU. Divergent Lahu is a linguistic term for one of the primary Lahu* languages of the People's Republic of China. It includes two key dialects: Lahu Lawmeh and Lahu Velon.

DOG-MOUTH MIAO. See MONNDAUKLE.

DOLAKHA. The Dolakhas are one of the primary linguistic subgroups of the Newar* people of Nepal.

DOLIE DAI. See DAI.

DONG. The Dong people—sometimes known as the Kams, Tongs, Tungs, Tung-jens, and Tong-chias—are one of the officially recognized minority nationalities of the People's Republic of China (PRC). They call themselves Kams. With a population today that is approaching 2.7 million people, the Dong are one of the most visible ethnic groups in the foothills where the frontiers of Hunan, Guizhou, and Guangxi provinces come together. They especially straddle the frontier of Guizhou and Hunan provinces and the Guangxi-Zhuang Autonomous Region. Scattered groups of Dong people can also be found in other regions of these three provinces. Anthropologists recognize the Dongs as the northeastern-most extension of the Tai*-speaking people of Southeast Asia.

Ethnolinguists place the Dong language within the Zhuang-Dong branch of the Sino-Tibetan linguistic family. The structural and morphological similarities between Zhuang* and Dong clearly indicate that the two peoples share a common ethnic ancestry, even though today that common history is in the distant past. There was no written language for Dong until after the establishment of the PRC. Because Dong possesses more than fifteen different tones, it is considered one of the most complex languages in the world. Dong is divided into two primary dialects—southern and northern—and each of them can be broken down into three subdialects. Approximately 62 percent of Dongs speak the southern dialect and 38 percent the northern dialect.

As part of its program to improve relations with the larger of the recognized minority nationalities, the central Chinese government assigned linguists to develop a Dong written language using romanized letters. The romanized version of Dong was completed in 1958, but it has made only modest inroads as the written language of the Dong people. The vast majority of literate Dongs employ Chinese* ideographs to communicate in writing. The northernmost Dongs have become highly sinicized in recent years, mixing with Han* people and losing their language and cultural distinctiveness. To the south, however, are Dong people who retain a strong sense of group identity.

Chinese historians and archaeologists believe that the Dongs first appeared in the historical record as an identifiable ethnic group in the tenth century during the Sung dynasty. In the thirteenth century, pressured by Mongol* expansion, the Dongs began their southern migration, which eventually brought them to their present homes in Guizhou, Hunan, and Guanxi provinces.

Although a few Dong towns number in excess of seven hundred households of up to 3,500 people, most Dongs prefer smaller arrangements, in which twenty to thirty households constitute a village. When a child is born, the parents plant dozens of fir saplings, known as eighteen-year trees, which will provide the child with building materials to construct a home after marriage. Those homes are typically two-story affairs, in which families keep firewood and livestock—chickens, ducks, pigs, cattle, and water buffalo—on the ground floor and reserve the second story for family gatherings and sleeping arrangements. Dong settlements are recognizable by ubiquitous drum towers, which may reach as high as thirteen stories, around which villagers gather for town meetings and festivals. Covered bridges with complicated stone arches and tile roofs are also characteristic of Dong regions.

The Dong economy, blessed by fertile soil and more than fifty inches of rainfall a year, is primarily agricultural. Most Dongs are valley-dwelling farmers. On nearby mountainous hillsides, farms are worked primarily by Miao* people. Tobacco, cotton, rapeseed, and soybeans are raised commercially and sold for cash in order for the Dong to be able to purchase metal tools, firearms, ammunition, cloth, and other manufactured goods. For their own consumption as staples, Dong farmers raise rice, wheat, millet, maize, and sweet potatoes. Only in the last fifteen years has the central government invested industrial capital in the Dong region.

Most of the Dong people remain faithful to their ancestral, animistic religion. They are a polytheistic people who endow the local environment—including animals, plants, insects, rivers, caves, mountains, lakes, valleys, sun, moon, and stars—with individual consciousness and real power. These spirits and deities must be acknowledged ceremonially and occasionally appeased in order to maintain peace and balance. The pantheon of Dong deities also includes a particularly important ''saint mother'' who has become the object of worship and veneration in most Dong temples and altars. For a time in the early 1950s and again during the Cultural Revolution of the late 1960s and early 1970s, Chinese goverment officials tried to suppress the Dong religion, but as soon as political pressure was relaxed, traditional ceremonialism and worship returned to the Dong communities.

SUGGESTED READINGS: Paul V. Hockings, ''Dong,'' in Paul V. Hockings, ed., *The Encyclopedia of World Cultures*, vol. 6, *East and Southeast Asia*, 1991; Ma Yin, ed., *China's Minority Nationalities*, 1989; Siria Mitchell, ''Defining Success in a Dong Village,'' *China Today* 43 (February 1994), 50–52; Peng Jianqun, ''Dong Customs in Song and Dance,'' *China Reconstructs* 36 (June 1987), 66–72; You Yuwen, ''With the Dong People of Guangxi,'' *China Reconstructs* 28 (July 1979), 21–23.

DONGGAN REN. See **HUI**.

DONGLIAO. See **SHE**.

DONGMAN. See **SHE**.

DONG-SHUI. The term ''Dong-Shui,'' or ''Kam-Sui,'' is employed by ethnolinguists to refer to a branch of the Tai* languages spoken in southwestern China. Included in the Dong-Shui cluster are Dong,* Shui,* Mulam,* Maonan,* Mak,* and Then.*

SUGGESTED READING: S. Robert Ramsey, *The Language of China*, 1987.

DONGSUI. The Dongsui people are a subgroup of the Gan*-speaking Han* Chinese* of the People's Republic of China. Most Dongsuis today live in Dongkou, Suining, and Longhui counties in Hunan Province.

DONGXIANG. The Dongxiang—also known as Tonghsiang, Tunghsiang, Dongxiang Hui and Mongolian Huihui—are one of the People's Republic of China's (PRC) Muslim minority groups. Ethnic Russians* have long referred to them as the Shirongol Mongols. Dongxiangs call themselves Santa. Dongxiang is actually a Chinese word, which translates as "people of eastern villages," because the Dongxiang settlements are located east of the Han* settlement patterns. Demographers place their current population at nearly 400,000 people, based on the PRC's 1990 census that numbered them at 373,872. The vast majority of Dongxiangs can be found in north central China. Their homeland is the Dongxiang Autonomous County, a political subdivision created in 1950 in Gansu Province. It is south of the Yellow River and high in the mountains east of the city of Linxia. Dongxiang Autonomous County is located in the Linxia Hui Autonomous Prefecture and is bordered by the Tao River to the east, the Daxia River to the West, and the Huang River to the north. Their villages and small towns hug the rivers flowing out of the Qilian mountains. The major towns in Dongxiang country are Hezheng and Sonoba. Other clusters of Dongxiang—in which they live in consolidated neighborhoods—can be found today in Hezheng County and in the city of Linxia, which are also in Gansu Province. Finally, a few thousand Dongxiang live in Dingxi District and in the Ningxia Hui Autonomous Region.

Although "Dongxiang" means "people of the eastern villages," in Gansu Province, it is not uncommon for outsiders to use the term to refer to any faithful Muslim. Inside the Muslim community, the term has a more specific meaning. Gansu Province is also home to several other Muslim ethnic groups, including the Salar,* Hui,* and Bonan,* but the groups, because of linguistic differences, are not related, although their common devotion to Islam is a powerful bond.

Dongxiang is part of the Altaic* linguistic family and one of the Mongolian group of languages. It is divided into three mutually intelligible dialects. The Sonoba dialect, spoken by approximately 50 percent of the Dongxiang, can be heard in Sonan, Chuntai, Pingzhuang, Mianguchi, Dashu, Yanling, Dabankong, Dongyuan, and Baihe in Dongxiang Autonomous County. Sonoba is also spoken in portions of Linxia County and Hezheng County. The Wangjiaji dialect is spoken in the townships of Guoyan, Nalesi, and Daban in Dongxiang Autonomous County. About 30 percent of the Dongxiang speak Wangjiaji. Wangjiaji can also be heard in parts of Guanghe County and Kangle County. Finally, about 20 percent of the Dongxiang speak Sijiaji, primarily in the townships of Sijia, Tangang, and Kaole, as well as in Yongjing County.

There is considerable debate among historians and anthropologists about the origins of the Dongxiang people. One theory suggests that the Dongxiang, like the Salar and Bonan, are the descendents of Mongol* garrison soldiers. During the great age of Ghenghis Khan in the thirteenth century, the Mongol empire stretched across Asia. The Hezhou region of Gansu Province became a military staging area for the Mongol assault on Tibet. In the fourteenth century, when the Mongol empire began to retract, several thousand troops remained behind and became permanent residents. The current Dongxiang population descends from those soldiers.

Another group of scholars, however, argues that the Dongxiang were part of the ancient Chagatai Khanate, a powerful political empire in what is today Xinjiang Province. They converted to Islam during the Yuan period of Chinese history. When other Mongols refused to convert, the Muslims migrated to what is today Minqin County in Gansu Province because they were considered traitors by the Mongolian Buddhists. These migrants eventually split into two groups. One group traversed the Helan Mountains and settled in Hetao. Today, their descendents are Muslim Mongols living in the Alashan Left Banner in the Inner Mongolian Autonomous Region. The second group moved to the south, crossed the Huang River, and settled in the Hezhou region. The complex history of the Dongxiang people is reflected by the fact that their family surnames are of Mongol, Han, Hui, and even Tibetan* origin.

The Dongxiang economy is overwhelmingly agricultural, although in the past two decades, because of infrastructural improvements and capital investment, factories manufacturing electrical generators, farm implements, cement, and bricks have been constructed there. Most Dongxiang farmers raise potatoes, wheat, barley, millet, and corn. Dongxiang potato mash, used in the production of Chinese snack foods, vinegar noodles, and liquor, is prized among Han Chinese and other ethnic groups in Gansu and Qinghai provinces. Dongxiang farmers also produce broad beans, hemp, sesame seeds, and rapeseeds, and melon and fruit farms can be found along the Tao and Daxia rivers.

The Dongxiang are an extremely devout Muslim people. Before Mao Zedong's victory in China in 1949, there were nearly six hundred mosques and thousands of Dongxiang religious professionals. At that time, approximately two-thirds of all the Dongxiang were Sunni Muslims, while one-third were Shiites. A very small number were loyal to the Wahhabiyaa sect. The Dongxiang became objects of political repression during the years of the Cultural Revolution in the mid-1960s, when cadres of Red Guards defiled mosques and often forced Dongxiang leaders to eat pork, which is forbidden by the Koran. The experience dramatically sharpened the Dongxiang sense of ethnic identity, particuarly in terms of how they viewed Han people.

In recent years, central government authorities have been more circumspect toward the Muslims of Gansu and Qinghai provinces, working discreetly with them through the government-sponsored Chinese Islamic Association. The Islamic fundamentalist movement, which has had such a profound effect on politics in the Middle East, Iran, and former Soviet Central Asia, is a source of deep concern to Chinese officials, who worry today that any attempt to suppress Dongxiang religious practices might backfire into an Islamic uprising.

SUGGESTED READINGS: Ma Yin, ed., *China's Minority Nationalities*, 1989; Henry G. Schwarz, "Dongxiang," in Richard V. Weekes, ed., *Muslim Peoples*, 1984, *The Minorities of Northern China: A Survey*, 1984, and "A Script for the Dongxiang," *Zentralasiatische Studien* 16 (1982), 153–64.

DONGXIANG HUI. See DONGXIANG.

DONI. The Donis are an ethnic subgroup of the Hani* people of the People's Republic of China (PRC). Scattered groups of Doni can also be found living in

Thailand and Myanmar (Burma). The PRC Donis are located in the far south-eastern corner of Yunnan Province, between the Mengle and the Ailao mountain ranges. Their society is patrilineal and patriarchal, with kinship relations organized around patrilineal clans. Each clan consists of from thirty to forty households, and each clan maintains elaborate ancestral histories. Their group identity is based more on a sense of being Doni than on being Hani. Most Doni, of course, remain tied to the agricultural economy, and some still work in a traditional subsistence economy. They raise a variety of crops, including rice, maize, beans, buckwheat, millet, tea, peanuts, sugarcane, cotton, chili peppers, ginger, and indigo. Because of recent economic development programs in southwestern Yunnan, increasing numbers of Doni men can be found working in local factories and mines.

DRABA. The Draba people are a recently discovered minority nationality in the People's Republic of China (PRC). PRC social scientists are currently conducting ethnographic research into Draba origins, trying to determine how to classify them, and until that research is completed, the process of extending them official recognition will be postponed. The Draba language has not yet been classified. PRC demographers estimate the Draba population at approximately 15,000 people, the vast majority of whom live in the Ganzhi Tibetan Autonomous Prefecture in Sichuan Province. Most Drabas live in highland villages where they raise rice, maize, millet, pigs, poultry, and wheat.
SUGGESTED READING: S. A. Wurm, B. T'sou, D. Bradley, et al., eds., *Language Atlas of China*, 1987.

DROKPA. See **TIBETAN.**

DRUKPA. See **TIBETAN.**

DRUNG. With a 1990 population placed at 5,816, the Drung constitute one of the smallest of the officially recognized minority nationalities in the People's Republic of China (PRC). They are also known locally as the Derung, Dulonh, Dulong, Dulongzu, Qiu, Tulung, and Tulong. Their language was formerly known as Qiuyu. The Drung homeland is an extremely remote one-hundred-mile stretch of territory in the river valleys branching off the Dulong River in northwestern Yunnan Province, near the frontier with neighboring Myanmar (Burma). Today it is politically organized as Drung-Nu Autonomous County, which is located at the juncture of farther northern Myanmar, northwestern Yunnan Province, and southeastern Tibet. The Dulong River drainage system is characterized by mountain ranges with peaks ranging from 13,000 to 16,000 feet, which surround Drung territory. At the lower elevations in the valleys, the climate is semitropical, while at higher altitudes the region is characterized by heavy snowfall in winter months.

The Drungs speak a language that ethnolinguists consider to be part of the

Tibeto-Burman* cluster within the Sino-Tibetan family. It is closely related to the language of the neighboring Nu* group. Over the centuries, the Drungs have been alternatively under the control of Han* dynasties, Lisu* slaveholders, and Tibetan* monks, and their vocabulary reflects that history. There is no written Drung language, and because of their tiny population, the PRC made no attempt after 1949 to develop a written Drung script, as it did for a number of the other minority nationalities.

The Drung economy has traditionally revolved around foraging and hunting in the thick forests of the Dulong River valleys. They also fished in the river and its tributaries and practiced a rudimentary slash-and-burn form of agriculture to produce maize, wheat, and beans. The lifestyle was essentially a subsistence one and relatively independent of surrounding commercial networks. Since the 1950s, government economic planners have tried, without a great deal of success, to wean the Drung away from their traditional economic activities and help them make the transition to paddy rice farming and the raising of cattle and pigs.

The government has also worked at altering the traditional Drung social structure in order to foster acculturation and assimilation. Drung society had long been organized around fifteen exogamous clans that were patrilineal. Each clan, called a *nile*, owned particular valleys, mountains, and forests. The fifteen clans were then subdivided into villages, known as *ke'engs*. Each village contained a number of households containing muligenerational families of anywhere from twenty to thirty-five people, and village leaders assigned communally owned land to particular households. Residence is patrilocal.

In 1956, when the central government formed the Drung-Nu Autonomous County, it began to implement an ambitious land reform scheme designed to reshape Drung society along more recognizably Marxist lines. Drungs were organized into agriculture collectives and communes that did not respect traditional clan affiliations. Drungs from different villages and different clans were forced to work together in labor units, and sometimes they had to work with other ethnic groups. The government also put them to work on vast, irrigated wet-rice projects. Many Drungs, however, resisted collectivization by relocating their villages to higher elevations more inaccessible to government agents.

In many ways, however, government acculturation policies have forever altered Drung society. Young women no longer receive the characteristic ritualized tattooing of their faces at puberty, and Drung families must now adopt a Han family name for government census purposes. Paddy rice farming is consuming more Drung energy now than hunting and foraging. Although most Drungs continue to wear their ethnically characteristic dress—striped flax cloth worn by day as a coat, skirt, or wrapping and used by night as a blanket—many are adopting Han clothing under pressure from the government.

Drung religion is an eclectic mix of traditional animism, shamanism, Buddhism, and Christianity. In the indigenous Drung religion, animals, plants, minerals, sun, moon, stars, and the earth are alive, are imbued with a measure of knowledge, individual consciousness, and awareness of the things around them. The Drungs give names to every tree, animal, river, stream, meadow, mountain, hill, and valley, as well as to days, weeks, months, and seasons. All of creation has a spiritual essence, and there is a balance and solidarity to nature. A strong element of shamanism also imbues Drung religion. Like other indigenous, animist peoples, the Drung believe that the natural world's balance depends upon respect for nature. Disobedience and disrespect toward the natural world can result in vengeance and retribution. Beyond the world of animals, objects, and natural phenomena, Drung religion functions in the world of spirits. Strong elements of Han religious traditions are also present in Drung spirituality. Ancestor worship, which derives from Confucianism and Daoism, is very important to daily Drung religious devotions, and a belief in reincarnation is not uncommon among them. Late in the 1930s, with the completion of the Burma Road, British missionaries made their way into Drung country and converted large numbers of them to Christianity. Today, approximately one-third of the Drungs remain faithful to a Christian sect.

SUGGESTED READINGS: Norma Diamond, ''Drung,'' in Paul V. Hockings, ed., *The Encyclopedia of World Cultures*, vol. 6, *East and Southeast Asia*, 1991; Ma Yin, ed., *China's Minority Nationalities*, 1989; Shen Che and Lu Xiaoya, *Life Among the Minority Nationalities of Northwest Yunnan*, 1989.

DULONG. See **DRUNG.**

DULONGZU. See **DRUNG.**

DUNGAN. See **HUI.**

DUNGANE. See **HUI.**

E

EAST GOVI. East Govi is a vernacular of the Korchin dialect of Mongolian. Most people who speak East Govi live in the East Govi subdivision of Mongolia and across the border in the corresponding regions of the Inner Mongolian Autonomous Region in the People's Republic of China. See **MONGOL**.

EASTERN KHAM. The Eastern Kham people are ethnic Tibetans* who speak the eastern vernacular of the Kham* dialect. Eastern Kham speakers today can be found living in the following areas of the Tibetan Autonomous Region: Dege, Garza, Peyu, Kangding, Yajiang, Konjo, Qamdo, Denggen, Riwoqe, Chaqyab, Litang, Batang, Mangkam, Zogang, Baxoi, Lhorong, Banbar, Baqen, Biru, Sogxian, Lhari, Bome, Zayu, Dabba, Luding, Danba, Xisangcheng, and Medog.

EASTERN MANDARIN. Chinese linguists classify the Mandarin language, which is spoken by the vast majority of citizens in the People's Republic of China, into several primary subgroups, and each subgroup contains many mutually intelligible dialects. All but a few of the Mandarian dialects and subdialects are mutually intelligible. Eastern Mandarin is one of the subgroups, which, too, is divided into dialects of its own. The Eastern Mandarin dialects, also identified as Lower Yangtze Mandarin, are found today in the Nanjing region of Anhui and Jiangsu provinces. See **MANDARIN**.

EASTERN MIAO. See **XIANG XI.**

EASTERN NAXI. See **NAXI.**

EDAW. See **AKHA.**

EKAW. See **HANI.**

EKHIRIT. The Ekhirits are a subgroup of the Buryat* people, who represent a Mongol* group of Siberian Russia and the Inner Mongolian Autonomous Region in the People's Republic of China.

EMU. The Emus are considered to be an ethnic subgroup of the Hani* people, an officially recognized minority nationality, who are located primarily in the far southwestern reaches of Yunnan Province in the People's Republic of China. Other Emus live in northern Laos, northern Thailand, and east central Myanmar (Burma). Their economy is largely a subsistence one. Farmers employ slash-and-burn techniques to raise maize, millet, tubers, and potatoes. For a cash crop they have produced tobacco for several decades, and more recently, farmers have turned to opium as a cash crop, which they sell to Han* traders in exchange for metal tools, cloth, and different types of food. Central government efforts to suppress the opium traffic, however, have in recent years reduced Emu income. Foraging and hunting are important economic and social activities. Indigenous Hani animism remains important to their religious beliefs.

EN. The En people are a tiny ethnic group living today in far northern Myanmar (Burma), with a small number probably across the border in the southern reaches of Yunnan Province of the People's Republic of China (PRC). The total En population numbers no more than 1,500 people, and the vast majority of them are on the Myanmar side of the Sino-Burmese frontier. They speak a Mon-Khmer* language in the Austroasiatic linguistic family. Some ethnolinguists have tried to classify the En people as a subgroup of the Wa,* but their languages, though related, are not mutually intelligible. Ens are closely related to the neighboring Son* people. They are primarily slash-and-burn agriculturalists who raise a variety of products, including maize, millet, rice, tubers, goats, pigs, and chickens. The En religion is a syncretic mix of Buddhism and their indigenous animistic faith.
SUGGESTED READINGS: Robert Parkin, *A Guide to Austroasiatic Speakers and Their Languages*, 1991; Wang Aihe, "Wa," in Paul V. Hockings, ed., *The Encyclopedia of World Cultures*, vol. 6, *East and Southeast Asia*, 1991; Wen Yiqun, "Women of the Highlands," *China Today* 44 (May 1995), 33–35.

ENGER. The Engers (Engees) are a subgroup of the Yugur* people of the People's Republic of China. They live in the western region of Sunan Yugur Autonomous County in Gansu Province. The question of whether they should be considered an independent ethnic group in their own right is a controversial one in China. Enger roots are the same as those of the other Yugur subgroup— the Yohurs*—but their languages are distinctly different. Yohur belongs to the Turkic branch of the Altaic* linguistic family, while Enger is classified with the Mongolian branch of the Altaic family. While Yohur is closely related to Uigur* and Salar,* Enger is more closely tied to Bonan,* Tu,* and Mongolian. Neither Yohur nor Enger has a written script.

The Yohurs and Engers, as the Yugur people, descend from a group of Uigurs who, in the ninth century, fled Mongolia after a series of genocidal attacks conducted by Kirgiz* armies. The Uigurs who settled in Dunhuang, Zhangye, and Wuwei slowly evolved their own distinct ethnic identity and became known as the Hexi Quigurs. That ethnonym later evolved into Yugur. Today they are a pastoral people. Yohurs living at higher elevations raise oxen, sheep, goats, and horses, while those at lower altitudes raise oxen, sheep, camels, and goats.

ENI. The Enis (Kados) are an ethnic subgroup of the Hani* people of the People's Republic of China (PRC). Scattered groups of Enis can also be found living in Thailand and Myanmar (Burma). The PRC Enis are located in the far southeastern corner of Yunnan Province, between the Mengle and the Ailao mountain ranges. Their society is patrilineal and patriarchal, with kinship relations organized around patrilineal clans. Each clan consists of from thirty to forty households, and each clan maintains elaborate ancestral histories. Their group identity is based more on a sense of being Eni than on being Hani. Most Enis remain tied to the agricultural economy, and a few still work in a traditional subsistence economy. They raise a variety of crops, including rice, maize, beans, buckwheat, millet, tea, peanuts, sugarcane, cotton, chili peppers, ginger, and indigo. Because of recent economic development programs in southwestern Yunnan, increasing numbers of Eni men can be found working in local factories and mines.

EONI. See **HANI.**

ERGONG. The Ergong people are a recently discovered minority nationality in the People's Republic of China (PRC). PRC social scientists are currently conducting ethnographic research into Ergong origins, trying to determine how to classify them, and until that research is completed, the process of extending them official recognition will be postponed. The Ergong language has not yet been classified. PRC demographers estimate the Ergong population at approximately 35,000 people, the vast majority of whom live in the Ganzhi Tibetan Autonomous Prefecture in Sichuan Province. Most Ergongs live in highland villages where they raise rice, maize, millet, pigs, poultry, and wheat.
SUGGESTED READING: S. A. Wurm, B. T'sou, D. Bradley, et al., eds., *Language Atlas of China*, 1987.

ERSU. The Ersu are one of the smaller subgroups, in terms of population, of the Qiang people of the People's Republic of China. Their language, one of the Qiang* dialects, is part of the Qiang branch of the Sino-Tibetan language family. No written script exists for Qiang, and a Chinese* dialect is gradually becoming the native language of more and more Ersus. They live in the mountain pass separating the Chinese lowlands in the east from the Tibetan highlands to the west. Most Ersus reside in rugged mountain villages, and their homes consist of multistoried, flat-roofed houses constructed of stone. Subsistence farmers, they raise barley, buckwheat, potatoes, and beans using both slash-and-burn hoe farming, and double-team cattle plowing techniques. In Ersu villages located below 7,000 feet in elevation, maize has become the staple product. As cash crops, Ersus produce apples, walnuts, peppers, and opium, and they collect bundles of firewood and medicinal herbs for commercial sale. Most Ersus remain loyal to their ancestral animistic religion.

Like other Qiang subgroups, many Ersu consider themselves a distinct ethnic entity, not simply an extension or a subgroup of the Qiang people. Following the lead of Pumi* nationalists, who in 1960 secured official recognition as a minority nationality, Ersu nationalists have made requests for similar recognition. With a population of as many as 30,000 people, they argue that their claim is as compelling as that of the Pumi. As of yet, the central government has not agreed with them.

ETALL. See ATAYAL.

EURASIAN. Hundreds of thousands of Eurasians can be found living today in the People's Republic of China (PRC) and on Taiwan in the Republic of China. On December 20, 1999, when Macao is transferred from Portuguese to Chinese sovereignty, tens of thousands of additional Eurasians will become part of the PRC. The bulk of the Eurasians in China today are the descendents of Han*-British* marriages in Hong Kong, during the years of British sovereignty there, and Han-Portuguese* marriages on Macao. See **HONG KONGESE** and **MACANESE**.

EVENK. The Evenk—also known as the Evenki, Tungus (Tongus), Lamut, Owenk, Birars, and Manegry—make up one of the smallest of the recognized ethnic minorities in the People's Republic of China (PRC). In China, their estimated 1997 population was 27,000 people, although Chinese ethnologists consider that a highly inflated number, since it most likely includes nomadic pastoralists from other ethnic groups. Chinese demographers have lumped Negidals* and Yakuts* in with the Evenks.

There are approximately 25,000 Evenk people in Russia. Arriving at an exact census figure is difficult because the Evenks move so often from place to place. In Russia, the Evenks are scattered over a huge expanse of territory, from the Yeneisei River to the Sea of Okhotsk, ranging over three million square kilometers of the Russian Far East. In the People's Republic of China, the Evenks can be found in the Ewenki Autonomous Banner, Chen Barag Banner, Butha Banner, Arun Banner, Ergun Left Banner, and the Morin Dawa Daur Autonomous Banner of the Hulun Buir League in the Inner Mongolian Autonomous

Region (IMAR), as well as in Nehe County of Heilongjiang Province. The majority of Chinese Evenks live in the taiga regions of the Northern Great Hinngan Mountains. Sixty percent of China's 27,000 Ewenki people live in Ewenki Autonomous Banner.

Ethnographers surmise that the Evenks descend from a mixture of Tungusic People* and Yukagir* cultures. Their language is part of the Tungusic group of the Tungus-Manuchu division of the Uralo-Altaic languages. The speakers of the ancient Tungus languages roamed over the vast Kolyma, Yana, and Indigirka river basins and in the process absorbed a great deal of Yukagir culture. By the eighteenth century, people identified as Lamut Yukagirs were migrating east toward the Sea of Okhotsk, and it was not until the 1840s that these people, who became the Evenks, reached the Kamchatka Peninsula. They were first identified as an ethnic group as early as the fourteenth century. Archaeologists suspect that the most dominant people who mixed with them to become the Evenks had their origins in the region of Lake Baikal and the Amur River.

Russian Cossacks constructed the Ket Fortress in 1602 and then began moving up the Yenesei River, where they confronted the Evenks for the first time in 1606 or 1607. By the mid-1620s, most of the Evenks living near the Yenesei River were paying the Russian fur tax on sable, fox, ermine, and squirrels. Russians* made sure that the taxes were paid by taking hostages from each Evenk clan and holding them for a tax ransom. The Evenks suffered a rapid population decline because of the diseases imported by the Russian settlers and because of the effects of alcohol on them. Missionaries from the Russian Orthodox Church moved into Evenk land in the late seventeenth century, and over the years they made thousands of converts, but the conversions were superficial at best, and even today the Evenks are only nominally Christians. The animistic tribal religion still exerts a strong pull on their spiritual and cultural loyalties. Christianity mixed with that shamanistic faith produced such religious fusions as Saint Nicholas, the Russian Orthodox saint who functions in the Evenk pantheon of gods as the deputy to the master-spirit of the upper world. The Evenk resented their Russian overlords and resisted, passively most of the time but also violently between 1825 and 1841, when Evenk rebellions were common.

The Evenk economy was regionally divided. The "Foot" or "Sitting" Evenks lived along the Sea of Okhotsk and Lake Baikal, where they hunted large sea mammals and fished. The "Horse" Evenks lived in the southern Baikal, the Transbaikal, and the Upper Amur River regions. The Evenks living near the Yakuts or Russians on the Lena, Lower Tunguska, Kirenga, and Amur rivers learned to raise cattle and also became settled farmers. Most of these Evenks supplemented their economic life by hunting elk and wild reindeer and by trapping for fur to sell for cash or to pay their taxes. Those Evenks living in the northern reaches of their territory turned to reindeer breeding as the basis of their economy. Today the Evenk economy remains divided. The northern Evenks are primarily still hunters, fishermen, and reindeer breeders, while the southern Evenk raise horses and cattle.

The Bolshevik Revolution brought dramatic changes to Evenk life. In 1927 the Soviet Union began establishing "cultural bases" in Evenk territory. The first one, which opened at the mouth of the Tura River in October 1927, included a boarding school for Evenk children, a health clinic, a bathhouse, and a community center. A library and theater were quickly added, and other cultural bases were established for the Evenks. In order to move the Evenks from clan-based government to a modern society, small-scale soviets were established among them beginning in the mid-1920s. By 1927 thirty-six soviets were functioning in the broader Yenesei River basin, and half of them were among the Evenks.

In 1929 the Soviet government began the forced collectivization of Evenk economic activities, but the plans encountered fierce resistance. The government declared all fur-bearing animals and all reindeer to be state property subject to state regulations. Many Evenks destroyed their reindeer herds rather than turn them over to the state, and others fled with their herds to the most inaccessible areas where they were out of reach. That brought several thousand Evenks into China, where they hoped to be left alone.

Substantial numbers of Evenks had lived in China for centuries. They were often referred to as the Sulun tribes. During the mid-seventeenth century, as Russian troops and settlers invaded much of the Heilongjiang Valley, Qing dynasty administrators relocated large numbers of Evenks to the Nen River Valley, where they were politically integrated into the banner system. Other Evenks were driven out of Russia and into China during the nineteenth century by Yakut pressures. The Manchus* extracted tribute from the Evenks and recruited them into the Chinese army. Evenks participated in the Boxer Rebellion, and during the 1930s and 1940s, they fought an extended guerrilla war against Japanese occupation forces in Manchuria. In the process, the Evenks sustained a dramatic decline in population. Today, because of disease and assimilation, there may be only a few hundred people left in China who identify themselves specifically as Evenks.

Historically, the Chinese Evenks did not fare much better under communism than their Russian counterparts had. The traditional Evenk economy was a seminomadic one revolving around animal husbandry. They were hunters, fishermen, and horse, cattle, and reindeer breeders and used horses and cattle for hides, meat, milk, and transportation. During the late eighteenth and early nineteenth centuries, many Evenk pastoralists had gone through a transition when cattle raising became more economically important than horse breeding. Evenks were also familiar with the range grasses of Siberia and Heilongjiang and harvested them with scythes in order to feed their animals during the long winter months. Because of their skills in working with horses, some Evenks also developed sophisticated blacksmithing skills, extracting iron ore and smelting it in primitive forges.

After Mao Zedong's 1949 revolution, Chinese Communist party officials decided to bring an end to Evenk nomadism. Early in the 1950s, government officials launched a forced collectivization program among the Evenks that was uniquely heavy-handed in its ideological fervor. Most of the Evenks living in China at the time fled China and resettled in Russian Siberia. Today, most of the surviving Evenks in the People's Republic of China are either settled farmers or settled livestock raisers. All Evenk reindeer breeders combined maintain fewer than one thousand animals today.

In recent years, the Evenk economy has undergone dramatic change. Government policies to end Evenk nomadism have reduced the number of truly nomadic families to a relatively few. Most of the others have turned to settled agriculture and livestock raising. Because the Ewenki Autonomous Banner possesses huge coal reserves, increasingly large numbers of Evenks are finding work in the region's mines.

Evenks in the PRC remain loyal to an extraordinarily eclectic religious theology. Evenk animism—with its worship of the wind god, mountain god, rain god, and fire god and reverence for the bear—still survives, but it is mixed today with elements of Russian Orthodox Christianity and Lamaist Buddhism. Evenk shamans still play an important role in the social and religious life of the Evenk community.

SUGGESTED READINGS: Alice Bartels and Dennis Bartels, "Soviet Policy toward Siberian Native People," *Canadian Dimension* 19 (1985), 36–44; Mike Edwards, "Siberia: In from the Cold," *National Geographic* 177 (March 1990), 2–49; F. George Heyne, "Reindeer Breeders in China," in Thomas Heberer, ed., *Ethnic Minorities in China: Tradition and Transformation*, 1984; Walter Kolarz, *Russia and Her Colonies*, 1952; Constantine Krypton, "Soviet Policy in the Northern National Regions after World War II," *Slavic Review* 13 (October 1954), 339–53; Liu Xingwu, "Ewenki," in Paul V. Hockings, ed., *The Encyclopedia of World Cultures*, vol. 6, *East and Southeast Asia*, 1991; Peng Jianqun, "Miners and Herders Hand in Hand," *China Today* 42 (February 1993), 55–57; William J. Pomeroy, "The Evenks: Affirmative Action in the USSR," in Marilyn Bechtel and Daniel Rosenberg, eds., *Nations and Peoples of the Soviet Union*, 1981, pp. 101–112; Piers Vitebsky, "Perestroika among the Reindeer Herders," *Geographical Magazine* 61 (June 1989), 23–34.

EVENKI. See **EVENK.**

EWEN. See **EVENK.**

EWENK. See **EVENK.**

F

FILIPINO. Thousands of Filipinos can be found living today in the People's Republic of China (PRC) and in the Republic of China on Taiwan, although the majority of them are located in Taiwan. Most of the Filipinos in Hong Kong and Taiwan are Tagalog-speaking people from Central Luzon in the Philippines. There are also, however, some Llocano-speaking immigrants from the Cagayan Valley on Luzon and Visayan-speaking people from the central region of the Philippine archipeligo. Most Filipinos living in Hong Kong and Taiwan today are Roman Catholics, descendents of forebears converted to Christianity by Spanish missionary priests in the seventeenth, eighteenth, and nineteenth centuries.

Beginning in the 1960s, Filipinos began to migrate to Taiwan and Hong Kong on temporary work permits. The maturing industrial and commercial economies there created a new demand for unskilled service workers, and Filipinos, who could make much more money abroad than they could at home, began making their way north to China. When Hong Kong became part of the PRC on July 1, 1997, those Filipinos suddenly found themselves under the political sovereignty of Communist China. Today, there are an estimated 200,000 ethnic Filipinos living and working in Hong Kong and Taiwan.

SUGGESTED READING: "Chinese Maids and Foreign Helpers in Hong Kong," *Modern China* 22 (October 1996), 448–79.

FISHKIN TATAR. See **HEZHEN.**

FORMOSAN. See **TAIWANESE.**

FUCHE. The Fuches are one of the most prominent clans of the Lisu* people of the People's Republic of China.

FUCHENG. The Fucheng people are a subgroup of the Qiongwen people, themselves a linguistic subgroup of the Min language of Chinese* in the People's Republic of China and the Republic of China on Taiwan. Fucheng speakers can be found today in the Haikou, Qiongshan, Chengmai, Ding'an, Tunchang, and Qiongzhong reigons of Hainan Province. See **HAN, MIN,** and **MINNAN.**

FUGUANG. The Fuguang people speak a dialect of Gan, one of the primary languages spoken by Han* Chinese* people in the People's Republic of China. Most Fuguang speakers live in the Fuguang region of southern Jiangxi Province and the Jianning and Taining regions of Fujian Province. See **GAN.**

FULARJI. The Fularjis are a Qiqihar*-speaking subgroup of the Daur* people.

FUNING. The Funing people are a subgroup of the Mindong people, themselves a linguistic subgroup of the Min language of Chinese* in the People's Republic of China and the Republic of China on Taiwan. Funing speakers can be found today in the Fu'an, Shouning, Zhouning, Zherong, Xiapu, and Funing regions of northeastern Fujian Province. See **MIN** and **MINNAN.**

FUSA. The Fusa people are one of the two primary subgroups of the Achang* people of western Yunnan Province in the People's Republic of China. Most Fusas are faithful to the Theravada branch of Buddhism.

G

GAN. The term Gan is used by linguists and anthropologists to refer to people of Han* descent who speak the Gan Chinese* language. Discussing the structure of the Chinese language is not as simple as it might appear, primarily because the government of the People's Republic of China (PRC) insists that there is only one Chinese dialect, and that it is divided into a series of subdialects. To argue otherwise would require government officials to recognize major ethnic divisions with the dominant Han people, something Chinese officials have been extremely reluctant to do.

Most linguists argue, however, that the definition of "dialect" means that it is mutually intelligible with other "dialects" of the same language. The Chinese* government claims that eight dialects of the language exist within the national boundaries: Mandarin,* Wu,* Jin,* Gan, Xiang,* Hakka,* Yue,* and Min.* The problem with that definition, of course, is that none of these so-called dialects is mutually intelligible with any other. The people who speak them may very well be united by their Han descent and their shared eclectic mix of Buddhist, Taoist, and Confucian religious beliefs, but they cannot understand one another's spoken languages, which should render them members of different ethnic groups. Complicating the issue even more is the fact that each of the Chinese languages possesses many dialects, and some of those dialects are not mutually intelligible to speakers of related dialects.

At the same time, however, they share an unusual linguistic similarity. The spoken Chinese languages cannot be mutually understood, but all employ the same written script, which is mutually readable. Some linguists have begun employing the term "regionalect" to describe the eight Chinese languages. Whether or not Mandarin, Wu, Gan, Xiang, Hakka, Jin, Yue, or Min are dialects, regionalects, or languages, they divide the more than 1.1 billion Han people into distinguishable, individual groups whose members share loyalty and a sense of identity with one another because of language.

Gan is one of the eight recognized Chinese languages. It is spoken by more than 30 million people—approximately 2.5 percent of all Chinese speakers. Jiangxi Province is home to most Gan speakers, who can also be found today living in eastern Hunan Province and far southeastern Hubei Province. The language is named after the Gann River, which is the major geographical feature of Jiangxi Province. Different Gan dialects exist all along the Gan River drainage system in Jiangxi, although most of them are mutually intelligible, at least on a fundamental level. Included in the major Gan dialects are Changjing, Yiliu, Jicha, Fuguang, Yingyi, Datong, Leizi, Dongsui, and Huaiyue. Many linguists consider Gan to be a transitional tongue, between the northern and southern Chinese languages. This is largely a geographical phenomenon, because the Gan River serves as a conduit from northern Chinese provinces into the deep south. SUGGESTED READINGS: S. Robert Ramsey, *The Languages of China*, 1987; S. A. Wurm, B. T'sou, D. Bradley, et al., eds., *Language Atlas of China*, 1987.

GANKUI. The Gankuis are the principal subgroup of the Oroqen* people of the People's Republic of China. Gankuis can be found primarily in Heilongjiang Province and in the eastern reaches of the Inner Mongolian Autonomous Region.

GANSU BONAN. The Gansu Bonans are the primary subgroup of the Bonan* people of the People's Republic of China. The Gansu Bonans live in Gansu Province. They are overwhelmingly Muslim in their religious loyalties. A smaller group of Bonans, who are primarily Lamaist Buddhists, dwell in Qinghai Province. The religious difference between the Bonans is significant enough to divide them into distinct ethnic groups.

GAO'AN. The Gao'an people speak a dialect of Gan, one of the primary languages spoken by Han* Chinese* people in the People's Republic of China. Most Gao'an speakers live in southern Jiangxi Province. See **GAN**.

GAOLAN NONGAN. See **ZHUANG**.

GAORI. The Gaori people, also known as Gauris, are a dialect subgroup of the Jingpo* branch of the Jingpo people of the People's Republic of China. They all live in Yunnan Province.

GAOSHAN. The term Gaoshan is a generic reference used today in the People's Republic of China to refer to the aboriginal people of Taiwan and Fujian Province. In mainland China, particularly in Fujian, the Gaoshan people have all but completely acculturated to Han* institutions. There they work primarily as farmers and speak the Min* Chinese* language, which was the common language of an earlier generation of Han settlers on Taiwan. On Taiwan, the Gaoshans include the Ami,* the Atayal,* the Bunun,* the Tsou,* the Puyuma,* the Paiwan,* the Rukai,* the Saisiyat,* and the Yami.* Most of the Taiwanese Gaoshans have been assimilated as well. Gaoshans speak Malayo-Polynesian languages, and some Chinese anthropologists speculate that they migrated to their present locations from the Malay Archipeligo. See **TAIWANESE.**

GAOYANG. The Gaoyang people are a dialect subgroup of Yue*-speaking Han* Chinese* in the People's Republic of China. Approximately 5.4 million people speak Gaoyang, and most of them live in the Yangjiang, Yangchun, Gaozhou, Maoming, Xinyi, Lianjiang, Zhanjiang, Huazhou, and Wuchuan regions of Guangdong Province.

GARIA. The term Garia is used to refer to people of Assamese* ethnic heritage who have converted to Islam. The vast majority of them live today in Assam State in northeast India, although scattered numbers of them can also be found in far southeastern Tibet.

GAURI. See **GAORI.**

GE. The Ge people constitute an ethnic group in the People's Republic of China (PRC), although the central government has never extended to them formal recognition as a minority nationality. Official PRC publications classify the Ge people as a subgroup of the Miao,* and, indeed, they speak a Miao language. But the language is not mutually intelligible with the vast majority of other Miao languages, and the Ge give themselves a distinct, separate identity. They will acknowledge a certain cultural affinity with other Miao peoples, but they insist that they are separate. The total Ge population today exceeds 70,000 people, most of whom live in the Qiandonngnan Miao-Dong Autonomous Prefecture in southeastern Guizhou Province.

Ge settlements vary in size depending upon their elevation. At the higher altitudes, such as the plateau connecting Guizhou and Yunnan provinces, villages are rarely larger than twenty households. At lower elevations, Ge settlements can be as large as one thousand households. The Ge economy also varies from region to region. Unlike many of the mountain peoples of southwestern China, the Ge do not build their houses on elevated pilings. Most high-altitude villages support themselves through swidden farming techniques by raising buckwheat, oats, potatoes, corn, and hemp. When they are surrounded by Han* farmers, the Ge use more sophisticated farming techniques, employing plows, fertilizers, and irrigation systems. Some Ge people are settled agriculturalists who raise tobacco, millet, wheat, beans, vegetables, and wet-rice.

Over the centuries, the Ge people have adopted elements of folk Daoism and Buddhism, which they have have added to their traditional animism. Many converted to Christianity during the early decades of the twentieth century. As a result, Ge religion is quite eclectic. Traditional Ge animism sees the world as inhabited by a vast number of unseen ghosts, dragons, demons, angels, and spirits, which represent the afterlife of one's ancestors or the unseen spirits of trees, animals, bridges, rivers, mountains, heavenly bodies, wells, stones, and valleys. Guardian spirits watch over households and villages, but evil spirits can also interfere in human affairs, and people need the intervention of shamans to protect them.

SUGGESTED READINGS: Bai Ziren, ed., *A Happy People*, 1988; Robert G. Cooper, *Resource Scarcity and the Hmong Response: Patterns of Settlement and Economy in Transition*, 1984; Qiu Huanxing, "Unusual Customs of the Ge Minority," *China Today* 39 (September 1990), 66–70.

GEI. See **QI.**

GEJIA. The Gejia are one of hundreds of ethnic groups in the People's Republic of China. They have a contemporary population approaching 35,000 people, most of whom live in highland villages in and around Chong'an in southern Guizhou Province. Most Gejias are slash-and-burn farmers who raise rice, corn, maize, millet, vegetables, and, at higher altitudes, barley and buckwheat. Their animistic and shamanistic religion revolves around the need to appease unseen spirits in the environment in order to prevent disease, tragedy, and death and to guarantee good harvests. They speak a Miao* language.

Over the years, Gejias have applied repeatedly to the central government for official recognition as a minority nationality. They insist that their language is mutually unintelligible to speakers of any other Miao language or dialect, that they live in differently arranged villages from most Miao, that their clothing bears no resemblance to the brightly colored patterns on the dresses of Miao women, and that their religion is quite different. Nevertheless, Miaos greatly outnumber Gejias in southern Guizhou, and the Chinese government has consistently classified them as a Miao subgroup even though neither the Gejias nor the Miaos consider them to be part of the Miao culture.

SUGGESTED READING: Colin Mackerras, *China's Minorities: Integration and Modernization in the Twentieth Century*, 1994.

GELAO. The Gelaos are one of the officially recognized minority nationalities of the People's Republic of China (PRC). They refer to themselves as the Klo or Klau people. Most Gelaos—who are also known as Ch'i-lao, Gelo, Kopu, Shagai, Thi, Thu, Ilao, Keilao, Kelao, Kha Lao, Khi Lao, Xan Lao, and Bendiren—live today in the western and northwestern reaches of Guizhou Province, scattered widely throughout twenty counties there. Gelaos prefer their settlements to be in the highlands. They are especially concentrated demographically near Zunyi and Anshun. Some Gelaos can also be found in the Zhuang* regions of Yunnan and Guangxi provinces. Smaller numbers of Gelaos live in Hunan Province and across the Yunnanese border in Vietnam. Exact descriptions of the Gelao population are impossible to obtain, primarily because of the widely varying results of different Chinese censuses. The 1982 census, for example, stated that there were 54,000 Gelao people, but the 1990 census placed their number at around 438,000. The 1990 numbers are more accurate than the 1982 estimates.

Much of the discrepancy is political. Over the centuries, the Gelaos walked far down the road toward Han* acculturation. By the mid-twentieth century, few of them still spoke their own language, which ethnolinguists place in the Sino-Tibetan family. Most Gelaos spoke Chinese,* Yi,* Miao, and Bouyei* as their native languages. They had also largely abandoned their traditional dress, with its characteristic long scarves and black-and-white striped linens, in favor of the Han clothing styles worn by most people in Guizhou Province. Because of their advanced state of acculturation, it was easy for ethnic Gelaos to deny their ethnicity. During the Cultural Revolution from 1966 to 1976, when ideological Red Guard crusaders tried to purify China of its bourgeois remnants and to stamp out ethnic diversity, many Gelaos had to deny their heritage. By claiming to be ethnic Hans, they escaped persecution. Data for the 1982 census was collected not long after the end of the Cultural Revolution's excesses, when many Gelaos still worried about the political repercussions of their heritage. A decade later, when new census takers appeared and the Cultural Revolution had become part of the more distant past, they felt freer to acknowledge their Gelao ethnicity. Nevertheless, most Gelaos are in an advanced state of assimilation with neighboring Han or Tai*-speaking people.

Considerable debate continues today about the exact linguistic classification of the Gelao language. Many Chinese linguists insist on putting it in an unclassified category, since so few studies about the language have been conducted in the PRC. Some western linguists, based on studies completed before the triumph of Mao Zedong in 1949, believe that Gelao is a member of the Tai language family, although its links to existing Tai languages must be extremely ancient. They argue that Gelao's closest relative is Li.*

In any event, the Gelao language is losing ground in Western Guizhou, Yunnan, and Guangxi provinces. Linguistic scholars today believe that the number of people who speak Gelao as a native tongue is less than 5,000. Gelao is divided into four mutually intelligible dialects: Qua, Ysu, Hakei, and No.

Most Chinese archaeologists and historians believe that the Gelao people are descendents of the ancient Liao people of southwestern China. They came under the control of the Yelang Kingdom, which was conquered by Han armies nearly two thousand years ago. Documents from the Ming and Qing dynasties mention the Gelaos many times.

To most outside observers, Gelao society does not seem to be much different today from that of the surrounding Han people. They live in concentrated villages with houses patterned after those of their Han neighbors. Gelao staples are sweet potatoes and maize, although they also raise wheat, millet, and rice where soil conditions and climate permit. Since the late 1950s, state incentives have also encouraged commercial-level production of tobacco, tung oil, and palm trees.

But the Gelaos still engage in a variety of religious and cultural practices that evoke earlier, animistic traditions. At funerals, they still practice animal sacrifices, and to encourage good rice crops annually, they sacrifice chickens and make offerings of wine. Worship of village ancestors, which most likely came from Han traditions, is still accompanied by ancient Gelao sacrifices of oxen, pigs, and sheep. Once a year, the Gelaos enjoy a festival to honor the god of oxen. During the years of the Cultural Revolution, Red Guard cadres suppressed most of these ancient practices, but as soon as the pressure was lifted in 1980, when the central government announced its willingness to allow such religious observances to continue, Gelao religious traditions reappeared.

SUGGESTED READINGS: Norma Diamond, "Gelao," in Paul V. Hockings, ed., *The Encyclopedia of World Cultures*, vol. 6, *East and Southeast Asia*, 1991; Ma Yin, *China's Minority Nationalities*, 1989; Peng Jianqun, "In the Mountains of the Gelao," *China Reconstructs* 36 (1987), 66–69.

GELO. See **GELAO.**

GEMAN. See **KAMAN.**

GETSUO. The Getsuos (Getsos) are an ethnic subgroup of the Hani* people of the People's Republic of China (PRC). Scattered groups of Getsuos can also be found living in Thailand and Myanmar (Burma). The PRC Getsuos are located in the far southeastern corner of Yunnan Province, between the Mengle and the Ailao mountain ranges. Their society is patrilineal and patriarchal, with kinship relations organized around patrilineal clans. Each clan consists of from thirty to forty households, and each clan maintains elaborate ancestral histories. Their group identity is based more on a sense of being Getsuo than on being Hani. Most Getsuos remain tied to the agricultural economy, and a few still work in a traditional subsistence economy. They raise a variety of crops, including rice, maize, beans, buckwheat, millet, tea, peanuts, sugarcane, cotton, chili peppers, ginger, and indigo. Because of recent economic development programs in southwestern Yunnan, increasing numbers of Getsuo men can be found working in local factories and mines.

GIN. See **JING.**

GOLD. See **HEZHEN.**

GOLDI. See **HEZHEN.**

GONGSHAN. The Gongshan people are not an officially recognized minority nationality in the People's Republic of China because government officials classify them as a subgroup of the Nu.* But such a classification is problematic because the Gongshan language which, though closely related to Nu, is not mutually intelligible with the other Nu dialects. In fact, it is mutually intelligible with Drung.* Gongshan is part of the Tibeto-Burman* cluster of languages in the Sino-Tibetan linguistic family. The Gongshans, or Gongshan Nus or Gong-shan Drungs, live in Gongshan County in the Nujiang Lisu Autonomous Pre-fecture in northwestern Yunnan Province. Their population is approximately 12,000 people.

The Gongshan people have a profound sense of ethnic identity and consider themselves to be culturally and even racially separate from surrounding peoples, although modern ethnologists would certainly disagree with that point of view. Not surprisingly, Gongshans are convinced that they have been the original inhabitants of what is today Gongshan County since the creation of the world, and that every other group is a later arrival and, by definition, an interloper.

Like the other long-time residents of northwestern Yunnan, the Gongshans fell under the authority of the Nanzhao Kingdom in the eighth and ninth cen-turies and the Dali Kingdom in the tenth, eleventh, and twelfth centuries. Early in the thirteenth century, Naxi* armies seized control of the region, and Gong-shans were frequent victims of Lisu* slave raiding parties. Han* military au-thority and later hundreds of thousands of Han settlers came to Nu country, but the Gongshans did not possess the technology or the organization to resist Han imperialism. Periodically, they rebelled and fought guerrilla wars against Han officials, but the rebellions were always suppressed. The most recent rebellion occurred in 1935, when the Gongshan participated in a panethnic rebellion against Han administration in what was then known as the Guomindang Frontier Administration. Such a history has bequeathed to Gongshans a healthy suspicion toward ethnic outsiders. The People's Republic of China established the Nujiang Autonomous Prefecture in 1954, and Gongshan Autonomous County was cre-ated in 1956.

Most Gongshans live in relatively compact villages built at some distance from neighboring villages. Each village consists of perhaps 150 people who descend from the same patriline. Single-story wood-plank houses are the norm. Gongshan villages are among the poorest in China, in spite of government ef-forts to encourage economic development. While some Gongshan farmers em-ploy plow technologies, most still use slash-and-burn techniques to raise buckwheat, rye, barley, oats, and maize. They grow hemp to supply their cloth-ing. Gongshans also pasture cattle, sheep, pigs, and horses in commonly held, unused fields. A few cottage industries supply most manufacturing needs.

Before the Communist Revolution, pastures, forests, and uncultivated high-land land was communal property owned by patrilines or villages. Farm land was owned by individual households and could be bought and sold. Collectiv-ization in the 1950s turned all land over to the state, and government officials encouraged multilineage and, where possible, multiethnic labor teams to work the land. It was not until the early 1980s that economic reforms restored a measure of economic power to individual households.

Their religion reflects contact in the past with many other groups. Gongshan animism was so complex that quite different religious ceremonies characterized the dozen or so patriclans around which society was organized. Shamans maintained environmental balance and community well-being. Because Gongshan communities are in far northwestern Yunnan, near the Tibetan border, Lamaist Buddhism also made its way into their religion. Many Gongshan young men have become Lamaist priests. Beginning in the 1930s, Protestant and Catholic missionaries came to Gongshan country and experienced great success in converting thousands of people to Christianity. Many Gongshan villages today are primarily Christian.

SUGGESTED READINGS: Norma Diamond, ''Nu,'' in Paul V. Hockings, ed., *The Encyclopedia of World Cultures*, vol. 6, *East and Southeast Asia*, 1991; Ma Yin, ed., *China's Minority Nationalities*, 1989; Shen Che and Lu Xiaoya, *Life among the Minority Nationalities of Northwest Yunnan*, 1989.

GOULOU. The Goulou people are a dialect subgroup of Yue*-speaking Han* Chinese.* Approximately 6.9 million people speak Goulou, and most of them live in the Sihui, Guangning, Deqing, Luoding, Yunan, Fengkai, Huaiji, Xinyi, Yangshan, Lianxian, and Lianshan regions of Guangdong Province and in the Yulin and Wuzhou regions of the Guangxi Zhuang Autonomous Region in the People's Republic of China.

GOVI-ALTAY. Govi-Altay is a vernacular of the Ordo* dialect of the Mongolian language. It is spoken primarily in the Govi-Altay Banner of southwestern Mongolia and across the immediate frontier in the Inner Mongolian Autonomous Region of the People's Republic of China. See **MONGOL**.

GREEN MIAO. See **MIAO**.

GTSANG. The Gtsang people are ethnic Tibetans* who speak the Gtsang vernacular of the Dbusgtsang* dialect. Most Gtsang speakers live in the Xigaze Prefecture of Tibet.

GUANGFU. The Guangfu people are a dialect subgroup of Yue*-speaking Han* Chinese.* Approximately 13 million people speak Guangfu, and most of them live in the Guangzhou, Panyu, Shunde, Nanhai, Foshan, Sanshui, Qingyuan, Longmen, Huaxian, Conghua, Fogang, Dongguan, Bao'an, Shenzhen, Zengcheng, Zhongshan, Zhuhai, Yingde, Zhaoqing, Gaoyao, Gaoming Xinxing, Yunfu, and Dianbai regions of Guangdong Province, as well as in Pingnan County in the Guangxi Zhuang Autonomous Region of the People's Republic of China. Guangfu is also commonly spoken in Hong Kong and in the overseas Han Chinese communities.

GUANGPYAT. See **TAME WA** and **WA.**

GUANGZHOUESE. The term Guangzhouese here refers to the residents of the city of Guangzhou (Canton) and its surrounding culture area in the southeastern reaches of the People's Republic of China (PRC). Guangzhou sits at the mouth of the Pearl River in Guangdong Province. Demographers place the city's current population at nearly 3,600,000 people. Ever since the years of the Ming dynasty, Guangzhou has been the economic and cultural center of southern China. Its residents are overwhelmingly of Han* descent and speak the Guangzhou dialect of the Yue* Chinese* language. Guizhou is considered to be the most sophisticated Yue dialect, the standard by which all of the other Yue dialects are measured. Like Mandarin—but unlike Gan,* Jin,* Xiang,* Hakka,* Min,* and Wu*—Yue developed its own vernacular literature with a series of nontraditional characters for colloquial words and expressions. Government officials in the PRC discourage publications using the Yue vernacular characters, but they still appear everyday, especially in Hong Kong.

The Guangzhouese constitute a distinct ethnic community in the PRC largely because of the way in which they view themselves. Their Han background is certainly similar to that of the rest of the country, and their religious beliefs revolve around an eclectic mix of Daoism, Buddhism, Confucianism, and Chinese folk tradition. What sets them apart is their Yue dialect, which they and many other non-Guangzhouese consider to be a superior language, and their history of commercial acumen earned over the millenia as the heart of the Pearl River economy. When asked to identify themselves, they usually prefer "Guangzhouese" to "Chinese."
SUGGESTED READING: S. Robert Ramsey, *The Languages of China*, 1987.

GUANTING. See **TU.**

GUARI. The Guari people, who are also known as the Hkauris, are a subgroup of the Jingpo* people of Myanmar (Burma) and the People's Republic of China. The Jingpo themselves are one of the Kachin*-speaking people, a transnational ethnic group living today in Myanmar, China, and India.

GUBEI. The Gubei people are a subgroup of the Zhuang* people of the People's Republic of China. The Gubei language is classified as one of the Northern Zhuang* dialects, and most of its speakers live today in Hechi, Nandan, Tian'e, Donglan, Bama, Rongshui, Luocheng, Huanjiang, Yongfu, Rong'an, Sanjiang, and Longsheng counties in the Guangxi Zhuang Autonomous Region.

GUIBIAN. The Guibian people are a subgroup of the Zhuang* people of the People's Republic of China. The Guibian language is classified as one of the

Northern Zhuang* dialects, and most of its speakers live today in Tianlin, Longlin, Xilin, Lingyun, Leye, and Fengshan counties in the Guangxi Zhuang Autonomous Region, as well as in Funing and Guangnan counties in Yunnan Province.

GUICHONG. The Guichong people are a recently discovered minority nationality in the People's Republic of China (PRC). PRC social scientists are currently conducting ethnographic research into Guichong origins, trying to determine how to classify them, and until that research is completed, the process of extending them official recognition will be postponed. The Guichong language has not yet been classified. PRC demographers estimate the Guichong population at approximately 35,000 people, the vast majority of whom live in the Ganzhi Tibetan Autonomous Prefecture in Sichuan Province. Most Guichongs live in highland villages where they raise rice, maize, millet, pigs, poultry, and wheat.
SUGGESTED READING: S. A. Wurm, B. T'sou, D. Bradley, et al., eds., *Language Atlas of China*, 1987.

GUMA. Guma is one of the vernacular subgroups of the Uigur* language spoken in Xinjiang Uigur Autonomous Region of the People's Republic of China. Most Guma speakers live in or around the oasis community of Guma.

GUOZHOU. The Guozhou, also known as the Black Kucong and the Lahu Ni, are one of the subdivisions of the Lahu* peoples of Yunnan Province in southwestern China.

GURUNG. The Gurungs, an ethnic group of approximately 190,000 people, live today in Nepal, primarily in the foothills of the Annapurna and Lamjung Himalayas. Lamjung, Syangja, Kaski, Gorkha, Tanahu, and Parbat districts have the largest concentrations of Gurungs. Most Nepalese Gurungs live between 3,500 and 6,500 feet in altitude. Several thousand Gurungs also live in Bhutan, and some of them make their way into Tibet along commercial trade routes. Gurung is a Tibeto-Burman* language and part of the larger Sino-Tibetan linguistic family, and it is closely related to Thakali* and Tamang. Gurungs trace their ethnic roots back to the Mongols,* and most of them are Lamaist Buddhists. During the nineteenth and twentieth centuries, at least until the Chinese conquest of Tibet, Gurung merchants dominated the salt trade between Nepal and Tibet, moving back and forth across the international boundary as economic demand dictated. Since the early 1950s, that trade has largely disintegrated, although there remain in Tibet a handful of people who are aware of their Gurung heritage.
SUGGESTED READINGS: Alan Macfarlane, *Resources and Population: A Study of the Gurungs of Nepal*, 1976; Donald A. Messerschmidt, *The Gurungs of Nepal*, 1976.

GUYIANG MIAO. The Guiyang Miao comprise an ethnic group of approximately 135,000 people who live in Guizhou Province, particularly in and around the towns of Guiyang and Anshun and in Pingba, Qianxi, Jinsha, Qingzhen, Kaiyang, Changshun, and Zhenning counties in the People's Republic of China (PRC). The Guiyang language is further divided into four mutually intelligible dialects. Although PRC demographers and ethnologists classify them as a Miao* subgroup, the Guiyangs have a distinct sense of identity.

GYARUNG. The Gyarungs (Gyrongs) are not officially recognized by the People's Republic of China (PRC) as one of the minority nationalities, but they nevertheless constitute a distinct ethnic entity whose members live in southeastern Tibet and northern Suchuan Province. Their population is approximately 100,000 people, and they are closely related to Moinbas* and Tibetans.* They are surrounded by ethnic Tibetans, with whom they have intermarried for decades. Gyarungs speak a Tibeto-Burman* language, part of the Sino-Tibetan family. It is subdivided into a number of mutually intelligible dialects. Most Gyarungs refer to themselves as the Keru people. They are most likely to be found today living in the Lixian, Barkam, Jinchuan, Xiaojin, Wenchuan, and Heishui regions in Aba Tibetan Autonomous County and in the Danba, Dawu, and Ya'an region in the Garze Tibetan Autonomous Region.

Most Gyarung families are farmers and pastoralists. Because of persecution from ethnic Tibetans over the years, Gyarungs live in isolated, forested, mountainous, or deep gorge areas of southern Tibet. Their local climate is subtropical and the soil fertile. Gyarung farmers produce rice, maize, millet, buckwheat, soybeans, and sesame seeds, and pastoralists herd cattle and sheep. Hunting remains important as a source of protein and male bonding. They are also well known regionally for their skills in manufacturing saddle bags, carpets, and mats. Although some elements of traditional Gyarung animism survive in contemporary culture, most Gyarungs are Lamaist Buddhists, just like their Tibetan neighbors. They are devoutly religious, committed to pursuing individual enlightenment; accept the idea of reincarnation; and believe that after many cycles of the recurrent process of life, death, and rebirth, the individual soul finds enlightenment and enters nirvana.

SUGGESTED READINGS: Tiley Chodag, *Tibet: The Land and Its Peoples*, 1988; Paul V. Hockings, "Moinba," in Paul V. Hockings, ed., *The Encyclopedia of World Cultures*, vol. 6, *East and Southeast Asia*, 1991; Ma Yin, ed., *China's Minority Nationalities*, 1989; S. Robert Ramsey, *The Languages of China*, 1987; S. A. Wurm, B. T'sou, D. Bradley, et al., eds., *Language Atlas of China*, 1987.

H _____

HA. The Ha make up one of the many subgroups of the Li* people of Hainan Province in the People's Republic of China. They are concentrated in the western region of the Li-Miao Autonomous Prefecture, primarily in Ledong, Yaxian, and Dongfang counties. Ha people can also be found in Baisha, Changjiang, Baoting, and Lingshui counties. Like other Li groups, the Ha have earned a reputation over the years for ferocious anti-Han* xenophobia, which often took the form of guerrilla warfare against Han immigrants to Hainan. Their hatred of the Nationalist government in the 1930s and 1940s also made them willing allies of Mao Zedong and the Communists, and when Mao triumphed, the Li were afforded recognition as heroes. Most Ha people today are farmers who raise coconuts, coffee, cocoa, sisal, rubber, cashews, pineapples, mangoes, and bananas. Rice is their staple, and because of the tropical climate of Hainan and its fertile soil, the Ha are able to produce three rice crops a year. The Ha are themselves divided into three subgroups based on language. The Luoluo* dialect is spoken mainly in Ledong County and along the Changhua River in Dongfang County. Approximately 38 percent of Has speak the Luoluo dialect. The Hayan* dialect, which is spoken by 44 percent of Ha people, is relatively scattered but is found in the southern and western fringe regions of Ha territory. Finally, the Baoxian* dialect is spoken by Ha people living along the Ningyuan River from Yaxian County to Ledong County. Accounting for only 16 percent of all Ha speakers, Baoxian is the smallest of the Ha dialects.

HA-AI. The Hani* people of Yunnan Province in the southwestern reaches of the People's Republic of China, northern Myanmar (Burma), northern Laos, northern Vietnam, and northern Thailand are subdivided into three general linguistic clusters. Because the dialects are barely mutually intelligible to members of the other dialect groups, some ethnolinguists prefer to use the term "regionalect" to describe them. One of the three Hani regionalects is Ha-Ai.

HAI. See **WA.**

HAILAR. The Hailars are an ethnic subgroup of the Daur* people, who live in the Molidawa Daur Autonomous Banner District of far northeastern China in the Inner Mongolian Autonomous Region and across the border in Heilongjiang Province. The remainder of the Daurs can be found on the other side of the country, living near the city of Qiqihar in the Xinjiang Uigur Autonomous Region. Spoken by 15,500 speakers, Hailar is different enough from Qiqihar and Butha to be understood by those groups only with great difficulty. It has two vernaculars of its own: Nantun, which is spoken in Hailar City and in Nantun, the seat of the Evenk Autonomous Banner; and Mokertu, which is spoken in and around the towns of Bayintala and Mokertu in the Evenk Autonomous Banner. Because of the distinctiveness of their dialect, many Hailars consider themselves ethnically different from other Daurs, especially the Qiqihar Daurs and the Butha Daurs. They have frequently requested, and been denied, official recognition as a minority nationality from the central government.

HAINAN YAO. Thousands of Yao* people live today on the island of Hainan in the South China Sea. Although they are locally referred to as Miaos,* their ethnic ancestry is Yao. Chinese historians and archaeologists believe that the Yao people emerged from a process of ethnogenesis that included centuries of widespread intermarriage between Han,* Zhuang,* Dong,* and various Miao peoples. During the Tang dynasty, Han imperial administrators first identified them as "Mo Yao" people because they had adopted the ethnonym of "Yao" to refer to themselves.

For more than a thousand years, Yaos have worked as settled agriculturalists. A minority of Yao farmers remain loyal to swidden, slash-and-burn techniques, but most of them employ more modern plowing techniques to produce rice. Where heavily forested regions border Yao farmlands, the people continue to hunt actively, often in carefully organized communal groups. Their social system is based on patrilineal descent, with inheritance going from father to son. Patrilineal clans are the most important governing institutions in Yao society, and residence is patrilocal. Yaos prefer that all marriages be cross-cousin arrangements, in which young men marry their mother's brother's daughters.

HAKEI GELAO. The Hakei Gelaos are one of the four linguistic subdivisions of the Gelao* people of the People's Republic of China.

HAKKA. In Cantonese, the word "Hakka" translates as "guests," "newcomers," "strange visitors," or even "settlers." The Hakka (Kechia) population in the People' Republic of China (PRC) today exceeds forty million people, and another forty million live abroad in Chinese settlements around the world. The center of Hakka settlement in China today is Meixian Prefecture, which is located in the mountains east of the North River in northeastern Guangdong Province. Other large settlements of Hakkas can be found today in southwestern Fujian Province, southern Jiangxi Province, eastern Guangxi Province, Hainan Island, Hong Kong, and Taiwan. Today, Hakkas constitute more than 60 percent of the population of Fujian, Guangxi, and Jiangxi provinces. Smaller clusters of Hakkas live in Suchuan and Hunan provinces.

Over the last century, ethnolinguists, archaeologists, and historians in China have argued over the issue of Hakka origins and identity. Because their own ethnonym designates them as "outsiders" or "strangers," Hakkas have traditionally been considered to be a non-Han* people. Part of that conclusion also owes to the fact that Hakka is not mutually intelligible with any other Chinese languages, so much so that even labeling it a dialect is impossible. In recent decades, however, a consensus has begun to emerge that Hakkas are indeed Han people who are differentiated ethnically by their language.

Hakkas themselves claim that their language is closely related to Mandarin,* not to Cantonese, but ethnolinguists today classify Hakka as a southern Chinese language, related to Yue* (Cantonese) and Min* (Hokkien), not really to the Mandarin Chinese of northern China. Hakka emerged out of the Chinese* spoken in southern China more than two thousand years ago. Millions of Hakkas, however, no longer speak Hakka as their native language. Instead, they have adopted the Chinese language spoken by the other Han people among whom they live. Hakka is divided into a great variety of dialects; the dialect spoken in the Meixian region of Meizhou Prefecture in Guizhou Province is considered the "purest" form of Hakka. The other major Hakka dialects, which are not necessarily mutually intelligible, are Yuetai, Yuezhong, Huizhou, Yuebai, Tingzhou, Ninglong, Yugui, and Tonggu. The Yuetai dialect is further subdivided into Jiaying, Xinghua, Xinhui, and Shaonan.

In terms of origins, however, the Hakkas can trace their beginnings back to north-central China, particularly the regions of what is today southern Shanxi, Henan, and Anhui. Hakkas began migrating out of north-central China in the fourth century at the time of the fall of the Western Jin dynasty. They first reached central Jiangxi, Hubei, and south Henan. During the tenth century, the ancestors of today's Hakka people were on the move again, this time relocating in southern Jiangxi, Fujian, and Guangdong. A third Hakka migration took place between the twelfth and seventeenth centuries, when Mongol* depradations destabilized Chinese society and forced the exile of the Southern Song dynasty. This migration brought Hakka people into what is today northern and eastern Guangdong Province. By 1400, the northern and eastern regions of Guangdong were inhabited almost exclusively by Hakka people. Another Hakka migration developed in the middle of the seventeenth century, when the Manchu* conquest of northern China began. Throughout the conquest period and during the Hing dynasty into the mid-1800s, this Hakka migration continued, bringing them to the coast of Guangdong Province and into Suchan, Guangxi, Hunan, and southern Guizhou provinces. It was during this period that some Hakkas also settled in Taiwan for the first time.

Their migrations, of course, often put the Hakkas at odds with the local Chinese speakers into whose homelands they were settling. When they began arriving in what is today Fujian Province and Taiwan, they frequently found themselves engaged in power struggles with local Min-speaking Han people. In Guangdong Province, Hakkas battled with local Yue-speaking Hans. Those Hakka-Yue confrontations were particularly violent during the Taipeng Rebellion of the 1850s, when Hakkas played a key role in the uprising against the Han government, and during what is known today as the Hakka-Bendi War, a violent power struggle between Hakkas and Yue-speaking Han people. The Hakka-Bendi War lasted from 1854 to 1867. It was during the mid-nineteenth century that Yue- and Min-speaking Chinese, who found Hakka so linguistically distinct, began referring to the Hakkas as ''barbarians'' or ''savages'' and comparing them to the mountain, tribal peoples of Yunnan Province. Hakkas greatly resented such ethnocentrism. In the wake of the Taipeng Rebellion and the Hakka-Bendi War, large numbers of Hakkas became migrants again, this time moving into southern Guangdong, out to Hainan Island, and overseas to Chinese settlements in Malaysia, Borneo, and California.

The final major movement of the Hakka people has occurred in recent years. Early in the 1990s, with the reality of Hong Kong's eventual transfer to the sovereignty of the PRC, large numbers of Han and Hakka people on the island began making plans to leave. They sold their businesses and property in Hong Kong and transferred their assets to overseas accounts; when their plans were completed, Hakkas began relocating to overseas Chinese communities.

Because of their immigration history, the Hakkas have often found themselves confined to marginal lands, usually in hilly regions where soil fertility left much to be desired. In Guangdong and Guangxi provinces, Yue-speaking Han people had already assumed ownership of the river valleys. In Hong Kong, Hakkas ended up in the New Territories. On Taiwan, Hakkas settled on land that Min-speaking Han did not want. Throughout southeastern China, Taiwan, and Hong Kong, Hakkas often had to rent land from Han landlords. Communist land reform schemes often worked to the advantage of the Hakkas during the 1950s.

Compared to Yue- and Min-speaking Han people, Hakkas have lived in very different settlements. Min and Yue speakers have preferred large, single-surname settlements, while Hakkas villages were frequently multisurnamed. Hakka settlements were also smaller and more dispersed. Their homes, often built for defensive purposes, were circular, constructed of adobe or tamped earth mixed with lime. Although Hakkas have traditionally been a rural, agricultural people, more and more of them have made their way into cities in recent years.

Hakka society and culture today are closely related to those of Yue- and Min-speaking peoples. Hakkas insist, as do other Chinese, that marriages be surname exogamous. Communities are organized along kinship lines. Family units consist of extended patrilineal relationships. Hakka religion is an eclectic mix of Buddhism, Daoism, Confucianism, and local folk traditions. More so than other Chinese, Hakkas have been willing to convert to Christianity.

The Hakka sense of ethnicity remains healthy and distinct into the 1990s. Part of that identity derives from the political success of prominent Hakkas, like Deng Xiaoping in the PRC, President Lee Teng-hui of the Republic of China, and President Lee Kwan Yew of Singapore. Millions of Hakkas maintain membership in such international societies as the United Hakka Association. The associations promote Hakka identity and protest anti-Hakka sentiments, especially any hint that Hakkas are not ethnic Chinese.

SUGGESTED READINGS: Char Tin Yuk, *The Hakka Chinese—Their Origin and Folk Songs*, 1929; Myron L. Cohen, "The Hakka or 'Guest People': Dialect as a Sociocultural Variable in Southeastern China," *Ethnohistory* 15 (1968), 237–52; Nicole Constable, *Christian Souls and Chinese Spirits: A Hakka Community in Hong Kong*, 1994; H. C. Feng, *The Chinese Kinship System*, 1948; Paul V. Hockings, "Hakka," in Paul V. Hockings, ed., *The Encyclopedia of World Cultures*, vol. 6, *East and Southeast Asia*, 1991, and *Guest People: Studies of Hakka Chinese Identity*, 1994; Mantaro J. Hashimoto, *The Hakka Dialect: A Linguistic Study of Its Phonology, Syntax, and Lexicon*, 1973; Clyde Kiang, *The Hakka Odyssey and Their Taiwan Homeland*, 1994, and *The Hakka Search for a Homeland*, 1991; S. T. Leong, "The Hakka Chinese of Lingnan: Ethnicity and Social Change in Modern Times," in David Pong and Edmund S. K. Fung, eds., *Ideal and Reality: Social and Political Change in Modern China, 1860–1949*, 1985; Leo J. Moser, "The Controversial Hakka: 'Guests' from the North," in Leo J. Moser, ed., *The Chinese Mosaic: The Peoples and Provinces of China*, 1985; S. A. Wurm, B. T'sou, D. Bradley, et al., eds., *Language Atlas of China*, 1987.

HAN. The largest Chinese ethnic group refers to themselves as "people of the Han dynasty" or *Han ren*, claiming kinship to a common ancestor, the Yellow Emperor, Huangdi. Huangdi, a mythical figure thought to have reigned from 2697 to 2597 B.C., is hailed as the first ancestor (*shizu*) of the Han race that grew up around the Huanghe or the Yellow River. The Han comprise 91.9 percent of China's population, estimated to be 1,203,097,268 in 1995, and stretch over 3.7 million square miles—from the Amur River in the north to Southeast Asia and the South China Sea, and from the Pamir Mountains in the west to the Pacific Ocean in the east. The Han practice Confucianism, Daoism, and Buddhism, but it was Confucianism that provided the foundation for Han-dominated imperial government until 1912. Like most of East Asia, the Han are part of the Sinitic or Sino-Tibetan family of languages and are Mongoloid, with distinctive features that include fleshy, narrow eyelids, straight black hair, relatively flat faces, and dark eyes. The term Han is commonly used interchangeably with the term Chinese. This conveys the false impression that China is homogeneous and unified, belying the presence of scores of minority groups within its borders who would not call themselves Han. It reflects, however, the hegemony of Han Chinese "culturalism."

HAN CHINESE CULTURALISM

China's topography has historically encouraged regional separatism, but Han culturalism provided unity for the Chinese. Han Chinese culturalism arose to distinguish between the culture of the Han, or inner people (*nei ren*), and the "barbarians," the outer people (*wai ren*). Chinese social institutions and feelings of cultural and aesthetic superiority have provided reassurance for the Han Chinese in the face of barbarian penetration and conquest.

The concept of Han culture began with the Shang dynasty, 1750–1040 B.C., whose political center was located north of the Yellow River. The Shang provided China's first written history as well as the assertion of central cultural superiority over the surrounding peoples by designating as barbarians everyone who did not yet acknowledge the central government's supremacy. The Chinese distinguished between "raw barbarians" (*shengfan*), or the unassimilated peoples, and "cooked barbarians" (*shufan*), or assimilated taxpayers who enjoyed the fruits of Chinese culture. For example, Han Chinese officials separated the "cooked" Li* of the coast of Hainan, who enjoyed the benefits of Chinese civilization, from the wild, "uncooked" Li of the central forests, far from the influences of the Han culture.

Barbarians were given generic names in the Chinese classics and histories: the Yi barbarians to the east, the Man to the south, the Rong to the west, and the Di to the north. (When Westerners arrived by sea, they were officially designated until the late nineteenth century as Yi.) Until the 1930s, the names of outgroups (*wai ren*) were commonly written in characters with an animal radical: the Di, a northern tribe, were linked to the dog; the Man and the Min* of the south were characterized with reptiles; and Qiang* was written with a sheep radical. This reflected the Han Chinese conviction that civilization and culture were linked with humanity; alien groups living outside the pale of Chinese society were regarded as inhuman savages. To be labeled a barbarian was a cultural rather than a racial distinction.

The custom of sharply distinguishing between inside and outside went along with calling China the Middle Kingdom (*zhong guo*), which began by ruling the Central Plain (*zhongyang*) in North China. Rather than using outright military conquest of outsiders, the theory of "using the Chinese ways to transform the barbarians" (*yongxiabianyi*) was promulgated. By Chinese cultural absorption or racial integration through intermarriage, a barbarian could become Han Chinese (*hanhua*). To be counted within China, groups accepted the rituals and cosmology that gave the Han dynastic state the Mandate of Heaven to rule over mankind. Nonacceptance of this politicized culture left one outside of *Zhongguo* or China.

State building during the Three Dynasties of the Bronze Age entailed the widening of submission to or acceptance of the central dynastic ruling house. The dynastic ruler served social, religious, and judicial functions and directed public works and war, processes that culminated in the development of cultural and political unity. Thus, by the time of the era of written history, the Chinese people had a high degree of cultural homogeneity with an inbred assumption of Han power and superiority.

EARLY HISTORY AND TERRITORIAL EXPANSION

In China, the study of prehistory through archaeological excavation is a comparatively new development. This is perhaps a reaction to earlier thinking by Western scholars that China had no prehistory of its own but rather benefited from the diffusion of such West Asian cultural traits as wheat, pottery, autocratic government, and writing to create a "civilization by osmosis." Archaeological advances since 1920, however, indicate a cultural continuity between contemporary Chinese life and prehistory.

The discovery of the skull of Peking man (*Homo erectus*) in 1929 near Beijing proved to be a major archaeological finding. Peking man and woman inhabited caves in limestone hills located twenty-seven miles southwest of Beijing beginning around 400,000 B.C. and ending around 200,000 B.C. They were hunter-fisher-gatherers who used fire to illuminate their caves and to cook meat. Their primary source of meat was deer, but leopard, bear, saber-toothed tiger, hyena, elephant, rhinoceros, camel, water buffalo, boar, and horse bones have also been found. Although no complete skeletons or burial sights have been discovered, some skulls were bashed, which suggests that Peking man might have been a cannibal or headhunter. Post-1949 construction projects have unearthed skulls of *Homo erectus* at a dozen different sites, which seems to indicate that the species was widely dispersed throughout China, particularly in the western mountains.

Excavations since the 1970s have produced remains of *Homo sapiens* dated between 200,000 and 50,000 years ago and *Homo sapiens* from 50,000 to 12,000 years ago. The remains of the latter were also widely dispersed throughout China but were usually situated at points where mountains meet plains and hunting could be combined with fishing and gathering, including areas such as the middle Yellow River Valley, the Ordos region, the loess plateau of Shaanxi Province and the western edge of the North China Plain. Archaeologists suggest that basic ideas of kinship, authority, religion, and art that can still be found in China today were already developing in these early cultures.

NEOLITHIC CHINA

The Neolithic Age, which began in China around 12,000 years ago, was marked by the spread of settled agricultural communities. Discoveries of Neolithic sites reveal that the great bend of the Yellow River in North China was the center of early Chinese civilization. In this area, between wooded highlands on the west and swampy lowlands on the east, hunting and fishing people domesticated animals and began to cultivate plants for food. With time, this culture spread along the middle and lower course of the 2,700 miles of the Yellow River into the North China Plain, which was well suited to agriculture. Irregular rainfall in this semiarid region, often called "brown China," meant that precipitation did not produce forests that had to be removed before tilling could begin. One crop a year of wheat, millet, or soy beans could be harvested. Frequent flooding by the Yellow River enriched the soil but often caused great destruction, earning for the river the epithet "China's Sorrow."

The culture that arose around the bend of the Yellow River in northwest China was probably based on East Asian culture enriched from Western Eurasia. The North China Plain is the part of East Asia most accessible by land from India and West Asia. Therefore, scholars believe that the cultivation of grains like wheat, the domestication of animals such as sheep, cattle, and horses, and the wheel, chariot, bronze, and iron may have slowly spread to the North China Plain via the steppes and mountains of Central Asia. There also is evidence that East Asian agriculture and early civilization developed independently of Western Eurasia, a conclusion borne out by discoveries of pottery dating from 10,000 years ago and evidence that bronze may have been produced in Thailand even earlier than in the Middle East.

Rice, the chief cereal of East Asia today, is of Southeast Asian origin, and its cultivation in the Yangzi River Valley had been established by prehistoric times. The Yangzi, China's longest river, is 3,100 miles long and is nicknamed "green China." This region records forty inches of rainfall a year and produces tea, rice, and silk. The lower Yangzi valley became in time the population center and heart of the country. China's largest city, Shanghai, lies near the river's mouth. The prehistoric Chinese also produced silk; raised pigs, chickens, and dogs for food; and used water buffalo to cultivate rice. Their basic agricultural tool was the hoe. Thus, the Neolithic peoples of North China appear to have been the direct ancestors of the modern Han Chinese.

PAINTED AND BLACK POTTERY CULTURES

Two distinct cultures, named for their characteristic pottery, occupied North China in late Neolithic times. The Painted Pottery culture is believed to have predated Black Pottery but occupied approximately the same region.

The Painted Pottery culture, also known as Yangshao from a type site in northwest Henan, is found throughout northwest China. Its most famous site is the partially excavated village at Banpo located near the modern city of Xian, the ancient capital city of Chang An, which dates from the fifth millennium B.C. The culture is typified by large bulbous pots, painted in red and black, usually with bold geometric designs. People of the Yangshao culture lived on millet supplemented by hunting and fishing, used hemp for fabrics, lived in clustered dwellings that suggest kinship units, raised pigs and dogs as their principal domesticated animals, and stored their grain in pottery jars decorated with fish, animal, and plant designs as well as symbols that were evidently clan or lineage markers. There are also arrowheads which indicate hunting with bows. Despite a resemblance to West Asian pottery, there is no archeological link to indicate cultural borrowing.

By about 2000 B.C. the Black Pottery culture, also known as Longshan from type sites in Shandong, emerged. It overlaid virtually the same area as the Yangshao, with extensions that included Shandong, the middle and lower Yangzi valleys, and even the southeast coast. Thin, shiny, black pottery was the most characteristic artifact of the culture. There is a discernible West Asian influence, indicated by the domestication of sheep and horses and the use of the potter's wheel. There was also a cultural continuity between the Yangshao and the following bronze age of the Shang Dynasty. They shared the same hollow-legged tripods used for divination, and both had begun to build walls of pounded earth around settlements that were larger than villages.

Scattered deposits of Yangshao and Longshan pottery existing today on the North China Plain and along the Yellow and Yangzi rivers show the differentiation of local cultures. As contact grew among these Neolithic farming villages, networks of kinship and allied relationships created an opportunity for broader government from a central capital. It appears that family lineages, derived from large tribal clans, each established their own separate walled towns. One lineage headed by a patriarch would establish relations by marriage with other lineages in other walled towns. Branch lineages could also be set up by migration to new town sites. As relationships were defined delineating superior to subordinate, so grew the concept of central authority which was expanded during the Three Dynasties.

THE THREE DYNASTIES OF XIA, SHANG, AND ZHOU

As of 1920 only the Zhou of the legendary Three Dynasties of ancient China—Xia, Shang, and Zhou—was known directly from its own written records. Details of Shang rule were known through chronicles compiled during the Zhou dynasty, but it was not until 1899 that scholars noted that Chinese pharmacists were selling "dragon bones" inscribed with archaic characters. These "oracle bones" were traced back to a site near Anyang north of the Yellow River in Henan province in the late 1920s, but the war with Japan curtailed further excavations. It was not until 1950 that one of the seven Shang capitals was found near the present-day city of Zhengzhou, complete with inscriptions which listed the dynasty's thirty kings, exactly as the traditional texts had listed them. Just as modern historians discounted the existence of the Shang, despite its mention in traditional texts, until the bona fide archaeological discoveries of the 1920s, they also discounted the Xia dynasty, which was said to be founded by Yu, the last culture hero to rule China.

Before the advent of archaeological science, the Chinese, like other cultures, developed a mythical explanation for the origins of their first societies. According to Chinese legend, there were three early rulers (*huang*), or possibly fraternal groups of rulers, followed by five emperors (*di*), who were in turn followed by three dynasties, which explains Chinese evolution to historical times. The three rulers and five emperors are often called culture heroes who, according to the myth, taught civilized life to the Chinese. Early achievements of civilization are attributed to them, including the discovery of fire, the origination of fishing, hunting, and agriculture, the devising of the calendar, the development of medicine, the invention of writing, and the introduction of the bow and arrow. In addition, the culture heroes instituted family life and created a rudimentary central government. The wife of the first of the five emperors is credited with the development of sericulture, since silk production is typically the work of women. The last two of the five emperors, Yao and Xun (Shun), passed on their rule to worthy ministers rather than to their sons. Yao selected Xun who in turn selected Yu. Together they are known as the three model emperors. Yu is credited with the building of dams for flood control and the establishment of China's first recorded dynasty, the Xia, around 2205 B.C. It was from the titles of these culture heroes that the Chinese derived the name for their imperial leaders: emperor or *huangdi*.

The Xia dynasty dated from 2205 to 1766 B.C., and according to ancient texts, the Xia are the result of the blending of Neolithic cultures, such as the Longshan and the Yangshao. Excavations at Erlitou, in the city of Yanshi not far from Luoyang and just north of the Yellow River, appear to confirm the ancient writing. In 1959 large palaces were uncovered that may have been a capital of the Xia dynasty. The Erlitou culture was widespread in the region of northwest Henan and southern Shanxi provinces and appears to be a direct successor of the Longshan Black Pottery culture. Radiocarbon dating analysis dates the Erlitou from 2100 to 1800 B.C., making them predecessors of the Shang.

The Three Dynasties can now be viewed as successive phases of a single cultural development which ultimately became the Han. There seems to have been a smooth transition from the innumerable Neolithic villages of the Longshan culture to the Bronze Age capital cities of the Three Dynasties. There is a high degree of cultural homogeneity and continuity, evidenced by the tools, weapons, pots, bronze vessels, the domestication of crops and animals, the architectural layout of settlements and burials, and the practices of religion and government. Each dynasty succeeded the other through warfare, but there is no evidence of violent intrusion by an outside culture. The Xia, Shang, and Zhou centered in three distinct but overlapping areas and seem to have coexisted. From the melting of the Shang with the Zhou emerged the dominant center of ancient North China, located along the Yellow River. The ancient capitals confirm the power of a kingship based on sedentary, landlocked agriculture, rather than mobile, waterborne trade with other areas.

The making of bronze from copper and tin during the Xia and Shang dynasties coincided with the expansion of central government authority over a broad area. Although bronze metallurgy may have been the natural next step in

China's technological development, it could not have been accomplished without a central authority to oversee the backbreaking, labor-intensive process. First the ore had to be mined under hazardous conditions and then cast by the piece-mold process, which required hundreds of skilled artisans. The end product was usually a ritual vessel used by the Xia and Shang ruling families to confirm their power to govern.

The Shang king was served by diviners who practiced scapulimancy. The diviners applied a hot point to create cracks in animal shoulder blades or tortoise shells, interpreted these cracks as the advice of the ancestors, and inscribed the results on the bones, thereby producing the oracle bones. Questions asked of the ancestors ranged from "Will the queen's toothache be cured?" to "Will the campaign against a rival or barbarian group succeed?" Certain animals were considered to have a totemic relation to the ancestors, and Shang bronze ritual vessels representing animal designs were used to assist the king or shaman in asking the spirits of the ancestors for help and guidance.

The existence of the bronze ritual vessels, together with the inscriptions on the oracle bones, reveals a highly stratified society in which animals and sometimes humans were used in ritual sacrifices for the state religion. By practicing a religious cult of the ancestors, local rulers legitimized their authority. Some became lords over groups of towns, and group vied with group as well as region with region until a single ruling dynasty could emerge in a distinct area. Central authority was expanded through warfare. The Shang walled in their chief settlements and took advantage of a superiority in military hardware, provided by horse-drawn chariots, to subdue their neighbors.

There was also peaceful expansion. Under the Xia and Shang, new towns were planned and created by local rulers who carefully monitored the opening of new farmland. Undoubtedly, the most important legacy of the Shang are the oracle bones, which provide the oldest known form of Chinese writing. The bones reflect an early stage in the development of the Chinese ancestor veneration or ancestor worship that came to be closely identified with the practice of Confucianism. Although Shang prisoners of war were often enslaved and killed, this did not conflict with ancestor worship, since it was believed that slaves lacked souls or spirits. The script of the oracle bones reflects the basic features and principles that characterize the present-day Chinese writing system, which was in place by the end of the Shang.

THE ZHOU DYNASTY

Relations between the Shang and their vassals were never easy. The last Shang emperor is said to have been a physical giant and a depraved monster who made drinking cups from the skulls of his vanquished enemies. The dynasty ended in a great slave revolt around 1050 B.C., when the Zhou joined with the slaves in ransacking the Shang capital, Anyang, where the last king burned to death in his palace. Consequently the Zhou declared a new dynasty, which lasted from 1050 B.C. until the end of the ninth century B.C.

Before coming to power, the Zhou tribe interacted with nomads on the north and with proto-Tibetan* Qiang people on the west. Early on they learned how to tolerate and work with people of different cultures. After settling in the Wei River Valley, the Zhou became vassals of the Shang and were charged with the protection of the western frontier. After mobilizing from seven to eight hundred villages, the Zhou successfully overthrew the Shang. The Zhou conquest of the Shang and the establishment of a new dynasty did not represent a sharp break in any respect.

The Zhou dynasty continued the cultural and technical evolution already begun by the Shang. The Zhou transplanted Shang elite families to manage the work of building their new capital and made use of Shang skills in ritual and government. The Chinese writing system continued to evolve, until, by mid-Zhou, it was close to modern or classical Chinese script. Both oracle bone divination and ancestor veneration continued to be practiced. The victorious Zhou institutionalized a feature borrowed from the Shang to justify the dynastic transition, the "Mandate of Heaven." They legitimized their power by claiming that they had come to the throne by means of the rebellious actions of the people and with the Mandate of Heaven (tian-ming). Certainly, the Zhou rulers provided better leadership than the late Shang, and they proclaimed, "Heaven sees and hears through the eyes and ears of the people." Therefore, the new leaders assumed the title "Son of Heaven," by which the ruler's right to rule included a moral criterion for holding office. This political theory subsequently justified every dynastic change in China until the abolition of the imperial system in 1912.

As the Zhou expanded their power, they established a feudal network to maintain control from the center. The Zhou defeated nomads on the northwest and launched successful campaigns southward into the Han and Yangzi River areas and southeast along the Huai River. Expansion of Zhou central power and authority also involved a degree of acculturation, as barbarians submitted to the superiority to the culture of the Central Plain. To control these newly conquered peoples, sons of the Zhou rulers were asked to preside over fifty or more vassal states. The investiture ceremony was an elaborate delegation of authority of a contractual nature, in which vassals exchanged oaths of loyalty to the Zhou king for grants of land and titles translatable as duke, earl, baron, marquis, or count and were supplied troops on request from the Zhou king for mutual defense.

The Zhou feudal system, which was based on kinship or family ties to ensure loyalty and cooperation, worked relatively well for approximately two hundred years. Over time, however, the power of the Zhou royal family declined and was eclipsed by the rise of its former vassals. The weakness of the Zhou was highlighted by their inability to prevent former vassals from developing kingdoms ruled by self-proclaimed kings, a title previously reserved for the Zhou rulers. By the end of the eighth century B.C., there were as many as two hundred kingdoms. In 771 B.C. the royal capital was sacked by northern invaders in league with dissident vassals, and the Zhou king was killed, ending what is called the Western Zhou period. Despite the inauguration of the Eastern Zhou period with the rebuilding of the Zhou capital at Luoyang, surrounded by long-settled Chinese territory, the Zhou were unable to maintain effective control over their conquered territories. Royal authority disintegrated, and dependent vassals became rival states. The Zhou dynasty continued to exist in name only until 256 B.C.

Despite its prolonged deterioration, the Zhou made major contributions to the development of Han Chinese culture. This includes the writing of several Chinese classics, including the *I-ching* or Book of Changes, which was a handbook for diviners and provided a basis for Daoism; the Book of Songs; the Book of Rituals, also known as *I-chi* or Book of Rites; and the collection of historical documents or *Shu Ching*, which gives the story of the five culture hero emperors and the Xia, Shang, and Zhou dynasties. In addition, large-scale irrigation and water control projects were undertaken and internal transport canals were constructed, indicating the growth of the economic unit and the rising need to move large quantities of tax grains and other commodities great distances. The use of copper cash appeared near the end of the Zhou. Other characteristic features of Chinese civilization, such as the use of chopsticks and lacquer, also appeared in the late Zhou.

CONFUCIANISM

Amidst the social and political chaos of the later Zhou period, a small group, mostly from aristocratic families, began to devote themselves to study and contemplation. This period has come to be known for its philosophical flowering as the Hundred Schools of Thought. Of lasting significance for Chinese culture was the school of thought known as Confucianism.

Confucianism was the intellectual product of Confucius, a man known as Kongzi to the Chinese. He was born in 551 B.C. to a lower-ranking, possibly impoverished aristocratic family. Despite attempts to serve as a court adviser in North China, Confucius devoted his later years to education. In his day, he was called by the exalted title teacher and is hailed yet today by Chinese governments as China's first teacher.

Confucius viewed politics as an ethical problem and social improvement as a matter of individual morality. Order and good government would return to society only when the ruler and administrators reformed themselves and set moral standards for the rest of the population. As "grass bends to the wind," so society is influenced by the ruler, Confucius argued. He believed that knowledge led to virtue, and he emphasized the major role that education should play in ensuring proper leadership.

Confucius also upheld what the Chinese call *ren*, a virtue that encompasses benevolence, love, compassion, and sympathy toward fellow human beings. The stress on *ren* reveals the central humanism of this philosophy. Cultivation of *ren* produces a gentleman, or *jun-zi*, who is more concerned about what is right than about what is profitable. Confucianism is considered by some to have been revolutionary because it challenged the Zhou aristocracy by asserting that any man, regardless of birth or wealth, could aspire to become an honored *jun-zi*.

In its practice, however, Confucianism is explicitly conservative. Confucius proclaimed the writings of the ancients to be the most important guides to virtuous behavior, and he extolled the Duke of Zhou, of the twelfth–eleventh century B.C., as the ideal ruler. He taught respect for authority and deference to superiors as expressed in the term *li*, defined as social and moral propriety and the proper maintenance of the five basic human relationships: ruler to subject, father to son, elder brother to younger brother, husband to wife, and friend to friend. These relationships stressed the preeminence of the family, which was the fundamental social unit for Confucius.

One of Confucius' most important disciples was Menzi or Mencius, 372–289 B.C., known as the Second Sage. Menzi emphasized the equation between knowledge and virtue, especially for the ruler who should cultivate ''sageliness within and kingliness without.'' More significantly, Mencius stressed that the virtue of a ruler must be measured by benevolence to the people. Thus the first duty of a government was to ensure the material well-being of the populace; failure to do so provided grounds for popular rebellion. If successful, the revolt would clearly signify the withdrawal of the Mandate of Heaven.

Confucianism became the underlying basis for Chinese government and the cornerstone of the Chinese exam system until 1905. Despite reinterpretations of the basic doctrines of Confucianism over the centuries, it survived. Its survival is due to its humanity; its simplicity; its appeal to the nobler instincts through reverence for virtue, respect for learning, and devotion to family; and its lack of mysticism.

SPRING-AND-AUTUMN AND WARRING STATES PERIODS

The so-called Spring-and-Autumn period, from 722 to 481 B.C., saw the emergence of 170 aristocratic family states that were beyond Zhou central control. Each of these states, centered around a walled capital, engaged in diplomatic alliances and leagues, which resulted in a diplomatic-military free-for-all that gave rise to seven major states on the North China Plain. The competition for supremacy among the seven states is known today as the Warring States period of from 403 to 221 B.C.

The principal rival kingdoms included the Qin, who controlled the old Zhou base in the Wei valley; the Jin, who were situated north of the Yellow River; the Yan, located northeast of the modern city of Beijing; the Qi, east of Shandong; the Qu of the central Yangzi valley; the Shu in Sichuan; the Wu* in the lower Yangzi; the Yue* in the southeast, and a number of smaller states, including the Lu, in Shandong.

It would be incorrect at this point to refer to any one of these rivals, even the Zhou, as "China." Each state was culturally, linguistically, and politically distinct, and there were also minor physical differences. By this period, however, two major components of the eventual Chinese imperial government had already emerged—military rulers and scholar-teachers. Both were concerned with the performance of ritual and ceremonies to keep human society in proper accord with the cosmic order.

Paradoxically, the Warring States period fostered a philosophical movement known as Daoism. In opposition to the humanism of Confucianism, Daoism emphasized nature and the achievement of harmony. The Daoist answer to the chaos of the Warring States was in effect to withdraw from all worldly matters and to seek solace, and answers, in nature. Daoism expressed the common people's naturalistic cosmology and belief in the unseen spirits of nature and was an enormous reservoir of popular lore. The Daoist aim was to achieve "tranquility in the midst of strife" and to assert the independence of the individual, free of the rigid social and political controls implicit in Confucianism. Daoism stresses "doing what comes naturally," noninterference, and personal spontaneity.

The ideal society for the Daoists had existed in primitive times before people needed conventions; by the same token, the unborn child represented the perfect person. As the way to happiness, the *dao* defies precise definition; it is "nameless," "formless," and "fathomless." The individual must become accommodated to the impersonal natural order, actually realizing and attaining everything by doing nothing. While Confucians had urged the ruler to direct society by moral example, the Daoists preferred that authority be discreet, governing without appearing to govern.

In most ways contradictory, Confucianism and Daoism complemented each other in molding the Chinese mind. Although the Daoists had mass support and many sects, its monasteries and temples were disconnected units that catered to popular beliefs and were not organized enough to become embroiled to any great degree in Chinese politics. Rather than threatening the exalted position of Buddhism, they both flowed through Chinese philosophy, art, and literature, appealing simultaneously to opposite sides of the Chinese character. While Confucianism taught the Chinese to be sober, moralistic, and hardworking, Daoism urged them to relax, enjoy life a little more, and cultivate their individuality. In both philosophies, the Chinese found principles of enormous value that served some part of their social and personal needs.

QIN UNIFICATION

China as we know it emerged in the third century B.C., with the forced unification of north and most of south China by the Qin, from 221 to 206 B.C. The ingredients for Qin success included the use of infantry armies in hilly terrain on the northern and southern frontiers, which were not conducive to chariot battle; the use of iron for tools as well as weapons, which led to greater agricultural production, more trade, and larger armies; the adaptation of the horse to cavalry warfare; and the strategic location of the Qin in the Wei Valley. The Qin put their stamp on what was to become the dominant Han Chinese style in language, culture, statecraft, and social organization for the next two millennia. Indeed, the name China is derived from the Qin, whose king created the title First Emperor, or Shi huangdi.

The victory of the Qin in 221 B.C. marks a turning point in Chinese history, dividing China's ancient feudal past from the imperial centuries which followed. Qin rule was marked by the authoritarianism of its rulers, who were dominated by the Legalist school of thought. Shi huangdi initially benefited from the reforms instituted by his Legalist adviser, Shang Yang (Lord Shang, d. 338 B.C.). The Legalist school, so called for its reliance on hard and fast rules, advocated rewards and punishments as the "two handles" to keep people in order. Today it might be called the "carrot and stick." The aim of the ruler was to preserve power at all costs. Harmony of interests did not exist between the ruler and the ruled. Legalists insisted that "right" was what the ruler wanted, and "wrong" what the ruler did not want. Everyone was held responsible and punished collectively.

In the short term, Qin power was strengthened by Lord Shang's reforms. The First Emperor divided his new empire into thirty-six commanderies (*jun*), each subdivided into a number of counties (*xian*). Junxian has been the shorthand for centralized bureaucratic rule ever since. Each commandery was headed by a civil governor and a military commander, with an imperial inspector to watch the governor. County magistrates were centrally appointed, salaried, required to report to the capital in writing, and subject to recall. Local aristocratic families were moved to the capital, nongovernmental arms were melted down, and some city walls were destroyed. Writing, weights, and measures were all standardized and imperial highways totalling over 4,000 miles were built along with a 1,200 mile canal that extended from the Yangzi to Guangzhou. Even axle lengths for carts were standardized, so that all carts would fit the same ruts. The ultimate glory of the Qin was the building of the First Emperor's tomb near Xian, which was rediscovered in 1974 and which is still being excavated today. Discovery of the existence of some 7,500 life-sized ceramic soldiers has amazed scholars who believed that this type of art was not introduced to China until after the advent of Buddhism. It should be noted that the Qin have long been credited erroneously with the building of the Great Wall, but it was constructed primarily during the Ming dynasty in the sixteenth century.

The glory of the Qin is often obscured by its repressive authoritarianism. Scholars long believed that the First Emperor's dislike of people's complaints had resulted in some 460 being buried alive. Apparently this was a mistranslation; the scholars involved were merely murdered. Book learning was condemned. Unlike the Confucianists, the Qin preferred to keep people "dull and stupid." The Qin also sought to control history by burning books. Although the book burning was incomplete, the archives of conquered states were largely destroyed, and the records of the Qin alone were saved. The oppressive Qin government abused the resources of the state and its people. Thus, when the First Emperor suddenly died at the age of forty-nine in 210 B.C. after thirty-seven years of rule, the Qin empire quickly disintegrated.

In retrospect, the swift demise of the Qin within two decades of its establishment suggests that the regime's ideology was inadequate to rule a country. The Qin, however, believed firmly that their new order represented progress; they had a visionary conviction that they were creating a better society. The break from China's feudal past to a system based on merit rather than on birth was certainly welcomed by most of the people. The parallels with Communist China are striking, and the First Emperor was praised during the Cultural Revolution in the late 1960s. The Chinese Communists used the Qin adage, ''A thousand die so a million may live.''

THE HAN DYNASTY

Emerging from the chaos that followed the collapse of the Qin, a new dynasty assumed power in 206 B.C., which lasted until A.D. 200. The founder of the Han dynasty, Liu Bang, who personally had risen from peasant origins by his own ability, underlined the point that leadership was no longer the exclusive preserve of the aristocracy. Under the Han, China took both the territorial and social shape it was to retain until the present century. The Chinese still call themselves ''people of the Han,'' in distinction from Mongols,* Tibetans, other domestic minorities, and more distant foreigners. It is a label they carry with much pride.

The China of Han times was roughly the size of all Europe, with a population of over sixty million that required continuation of the Qin bureaucracy. The Han sought to avoid the excesses of Qin legalism and added to it a comprehensive moral cosmology centering around the emperor. The first Han emperor, who took the title of High Progenitor, emphasized the Confucian precept that government exists to serve the people and that unjust rulers should forfeit both the Mandate of Heaven and the support of the ruled. Although army conscription and forced labor for public works continued, the first Han emperor abolished the controls on travel, education, and thought; lowered taxes; and, most important for the future of China's bureaucracy, encouraged learning. The renewed emphasis on education created a pool of talented men whose abilities, in the Confucianist mode, could be called upon to serve the state. After the Han government invited Confucian scholars into official service, Confucianism rose to such prominence that it was finally declared the state ideology in 124 B.C. With the introduction of a Confucian curriculum into the national university founded in that same year and the establishment of a competitive civil service examination system based on Confucian writings, the Confucianization of Chinese culture and politics was well under way.

The early Han was a period of great prosperity and enthusiasm, but the bitter memories of the Qin had faded by the time of the rule of emperor Wu Di from

141 to 87 B.C. Wu Di imposed state regulations on trade and merchants and set new taxes and new state controls on salt, iron, and the supply of grain. The last measure, which became known as the "ever normal granary system," was intended to prevent famine by state collection of grain in good years or surplus areas for sale at low, controlled prices during lean years. Although this popular idea was also practiced by subsequent dynasties, it was not always popular with local producers or with merchants.

After putting the imperial household in order and increasing state revenues and state power, Wu Di began in 111 B.C. an ambitious program of new conquests. He incorporated the Yue of the Fujian and Guangzhou areas, which had broken away after the fall of the Qin dynasty. The Yue kingdom included the related people and culture of coastal Annam and Tonkin in what is now northern Vietnam, beginning the long struggle of the Vietnamese* to reassert and maintain their separate identity. Wu Di's armies also conquered southern Manchuria and northern Korea; other campaigns established a looser control over the still non-Chinese populations of Yunnan and Guizhou in the southwest. Like the Vietnamese, the Koreans* remained anxious to reclaim their nationality, identity, and independence and to maintain their own civilization and cultural style.

After the Han collapse in A.D. 220, both Vietnam and Korea broke away from Chinese control. Korea remained nominally a tributary state of China (until 1895), whereas Vietnam endured later Chinese reconquest under the Tang and then successive wars of independence until modern times. Wu Di also pacified the Xiong-nu and for a time drove them out of most of Inner Mongolia, Gansu, and Sinkiang, which allowed the Chinese to plant Chinese military colonies and garrisons in those areas and along the Silk Road (still marked by Han watchtowers) and allowed the expansion of trade links between China and ancient Rome. Although Sinkiang and Inner Mongolia were to fall away from Chinese control in later periods when the central state was weak, they were reclaimed by most subsequent dynasties as part of the empire and are incorporated into the boundaries of China today.

In order to maintain nominal suzerainty over these outlying territories, the Han originated the tribute system, which would later be institutionalized by the Tang and maintained until the beginning of the twentieth century. This system enabled foreign people to retain their native leaders (although they were prohibited from using the title emperor but could use, instead, the title of king) yet secure Chinese protection in return for periodic tribute in the form of native products which were largely symbolic and homage rendered to the emperor at the imperial capital. The hundreds of tribute missions recorded for one year suggests that many people used the tribute system to cloak trade in prized Chinese goods, such as the silks which the emperor might present to a tribute mission. Others, such as the Koreans, accepted their subservient status vis-à-vis the Chinese. Yet even in the case of the Koreans, Han culture was not imposed on their society, and they retained their own ethnic identity separate from the Han Chinese.

The Han Dynasty ruled continuously for over four hundred years except for a brief hiatus between A.D. 9 and 23 when Wang Mang, a highly popular chief minister, usurped the throne. The four centuries of Han rule are noteworthy for major developments in several fields. The civil service examination system is one of the greatest legacies of the Han. It created a meritocracy by promoting men of talent from all backgrounds to government service, based on the successful completion of three exams—metropolitan, provincial, and national—the content of which continued to be based on Five Classics until 1905. Office-holding by the scholar-gentry class, who were enriched each generation by new blood rising from peasant or commoner ranks through the imperial examinations, became the most prestigious of all occupations. Whereas the sons of rich or gentry families enjoyed an obvious advantage because their parents could afford to spare them from work and provide them with a classical education, often with a private tutor, gentry status could not be inherited. The failure of one generation to pass the imperial examinations could result in a powerful scholar-gentry family's relegation to obscurity. Few rich families kept their position more than two or three generations.

The empire of the Han disintegrated in the early third century A.D. in ways similar to the decline of Rome. In both instances, causal factors included an imbalance of wealth, a decline of loyalty to the empire, and a shortage of arable land. The final collapse of the imperial structure resulted in the abdication of the last Han emperor in A.D. 220. Great landed families and rival generals carved up the empire into their own satrapies. Three regional states reasserted their independence as separate kingdoms: the Shu in Sichuan, the Wu in the lower Yangzi Valley and the southeast, and the Wei in the north. This was the time of Zhu Geliang (181–234), the famous Shu statesman, general, and strategist who tried unsuccessfully to reestablish the Han tradition of unity.

BUDDHISM

Buddhism, which flourished in this period, began to appeal to increasingly wider audiences as the political order disintegrated. Buddhism first arrived in China in the first and second centuries A.D. It expanded from its Indian origins to central Asia and gradually spread into China during the Han empire. When China's unity under the Han disintegrated after A.D. 220 and state Confucianism went into decline, Buddhism gained adherents.

Buddhism is an offshoot of Hinduism, founded by Gautama Siddartha, the son of a minor king in the Himalayan foothill region of Nepal, who was born in about 563 B.C. According to Buddhist lore, up until the age of twenty-nine, Gautama enjoyed the conventional life of a prince. One day he walked away from the confines of the walled palace and, overwhelmed by the sufferings of mortal life, the emptiness of worldly pleasure, and the promise of ascetic devotion, abandoned palace security forever, as well as his wife and son. After many years of wandering and begging, Gautama determined to solve the riddle of suffering through intense meditation. During forty-nine days of contemplation while sitting under a tree, he was tempted by the prince of demons with promises of riches, power, and, sensual pleasures. Instead, Gautama achieved an illumination in which he realized the great principle of the wheel of the law, or the wheel of the Buddha. From this moment, he was known as the Buddha or the Enlightened One. He soon acquired a band of disciples and spent the remainder of his life as an itinerant preacher of the faith.

The basic tenets of Buddhism are contained in the Four Noble Truths. First, all life is suffering, filled with pain, sorrow, frustration, impermanence, and dissatisfaction. Second, the root of all suffering is desire, attachment, and the urge for existence. Third, to end suffering and sorrow, one must end desire and become desireless—to change one's self rather than trying to change the world. And fourth, desirelessness can be gained only by following the Noble Eight-Fold Path of "right conduct"—kindness to all living things, purity of heart, truthfulness, charity, and avoidance of fault finding, envy, hatred, and violence. Success in conquering desire led to the attainment of nirvana, a state of perfect peace and bliss, by which one can escape the cycle of rebirth and achieve reabsorption with spiritual infinity.

Soon after the third century B.C., Buddhism was split into two major schools known as Theravada or "the lesser vehicle" and Mahayana, "the greater vehicle." It was the latter that was ultimately transplanted in China. The Mahayana sect popularized and humanized Buddhism. The Buddha was transformed into a supernatural god. Bodhisattvas, Buddhas who out of compassion delayed their entrance into nirvana in order to help those still on earth to attain salvation, were a welcome addition. Bodhisattvas became the chief gods of Mahayana Buddhism. Mahayana Buddhism stressed the redemptive power of charity and good works, both to help others and to contribute to one's own salvation. Indeed, the further Mahayana Buddhism wandered from the original teachings of Gautama, the more converts it attracted.

SUI AND TANG REUNIFICATION OF CHINA

The non-Chinese founders of the Sui and Tang empires (A.D. 589–907) are good examples of the success of Han culturalism. Although the concept of a united empire had survived despite the chaos characterizing the end of the Han dynasty, it was non-Chinese who resuscitated it under the Sui and, later, Tang rulers. The founders of the Sui and Tang came from a part-nomad Yang family and from a part Li family of Turkic military origins, respectively, whose ancestors had intermarried with the Chinese. The roots of the Sui and Tang were both in northwest China in the region of modern day Shanxi province, the Wei Valley, the Yellow River Valley, and the North China Plain. This intermingling benefited the Chinese, who acquired trousers for riding astride, saddles, stirrups, the breast harness, and the horse collar in exchange for Han culture. The nomads adopted Chinese ways, including language, dress, and methods of government, and were fully sinicized.

With the exception of state Confucianism, the sinicized Sui continued several institutions dating from earlier kingdoms, including the equal-field system that annually alloted several acres of cultivable land to each adult male, the system of collective responsibility, the system of price-regulating granaries, and a unified bureaucracy to facilitate the collection of tax revenues. The most significant break with the past was the growth of Buddhist monasteries, which were allowed to become great landowners. The emperor's devout patronage not only created what has been called "imperial Buddhism" but also gave the Buddhists great influence at court. By 618, however, the Sui ruler, Sui Yangdi, had lost the Mandate of Heaven. He had overreached himself; his failed attempt to conquer Korea had exhausted his resources, resulted in widespread rebellion, and ended the Sui dynasty within one generation of its founding.

Despite its short life, the Sui prepared the way for the establishment of an equally sinicized but much more powerful and longlived dynasty, the Tang (A.D. 618–806). The Tang retained the Sui capital at Chang An and established a secondary capital at Luoyang. They expanded the Sui system of six ministries, which had in itself been an improvement on the Han system. The six ministries comprised administration, finance, rites, army, justice, and public works along with the censorate that had oversight over official and imperial conduct and the examination system, all of which would form the main echelons of China's government until the twentieth century. Virtually all government job seekers were subject to the imperial exams, the last of which was administered at the imperial palace itself, and the title *jin shi*, or "advanced scholar worthy of government appointment," was awarded to the successful applicant. Tang military prowess extended the empire's frontiers to their greatest limits, institutionalizing tribute relations with Korea, parts of Manchuria, Tonkin, and the areas of present-day Xinjiang and Tibet. The expansion of international trade, stimulated by foreign demand for Chinese silk and porcelain, ultimately led to the introduction by traders of new religions such as Islam. The Tang capital became a great international metropolis, with a population of over two million, and the focal point of the Eurasian world.

The reunification of China under the Tang heralded the reinvigoration of Confucianism. The appeal of Confucianism to Tang rulers was its inherent support of strong government. The peaceful coexistence of these two state-backed religions was made possible by the successful adaption of Buddhism to Chinese ways. For one, the Buddhist Way, like Confucianism, emphasized moral behavior, good works, and charity. Second, Buddhism did not diminish the power of the state as the sole source of political and social order and allowed high culture to be dominated by Confucianist literati. Third, clerical examinations for Buddhists, as for Confucian classical scholars, came under the Ministry of Rites, and Buddhist monasteries included Confucianism in their field of studies. Thus, the suppression of Buddhism in the ninth century was due less to Buddhism's threat to China's political tradition and rather more to economics. Buddhism reached its zenith under the Tang, but when Buddhists claimed autonomy from the state, free from government control and taxation, persecution ensued and the Buddhist lands were confiscated.

Despite cultural achievements such as block printing and the publication of the first book in the seventh century, long before a similar development in Western Europe, decline was inevitable. The final half century of the Tang dynasty is best characterized as anarchic. Corruption at all levels weakened political loyalties, resulting in widespread banditry, which the crumbling and morally bankrupt central government was unable to curtail. By 907, Turkic and other non-Chinese peoples occupied much of North China and, as in the case of other periods of Chinese history when there was no effective central government, warlordism flourished. The regional states, known in North China as the Five Dynasties and in Central and South China as the Ten Kingdoms, were not subdued until the imperial army of the Song began the process of reunification in A.D. 960.

SONG DYNASTY

Ironically, in the fields of population, cultural attainment, productivity, and wealth, the south outpaced the north during the interim between Tang decay and Song unification. But stability was once again restored by a northern regime—the Song—who ruled from 960 to 1270. The dynasty began when, in 960, the commander of the palace guard under the last of the Five Dynasties in North China was acclaimed by his troops as a new emperor. Zhao Kuangyin, the founder of the Song, and his successor replaced the military governors (warlords) with civil officials, built up their bureaucracy from examination graduates, and centralized the revenues. The Song gradually incorporated the former independent states of northern and southern China into their empire, inaugurating one of China's most creative periods.

Many Song accomplishments are by-products of the population explosion that occurred during the early years of Northern Song rule. At the height of the Tang dynasty, China's population was approximately sixty million, but it grew to about one hundred million during the early tenth century and was one hundred and twenty million by the end of the twelfth century.

Population growth resulted in a rise of city life, which was most spectacular in the Song capital of Kaifeng. Situated near the junction of the early Grand Canal and the Yellow River, it had a population—including officials, service personnel, and troops—of approximately 1.4 million. A water system of over 30,000 miles, created by the Grand Canal, the Yangzi, and other river and canal systems, generated the world's most populous trading area and industrial complex. The exhaustion of the forests around A.D. 1000 made the use of coal instead of charcoal in coke-burning blast furnaces a necessity. The water system made the shipment of coal and iron cheap and easily accessible to the capital, creating a national market that allowed Song ironworkers to develop a decarbonization method for steelmaking. By 1078, North China produced more than 114,000 tons of pig iron per year, in contrast to England which, seven centuries later, would produce half that amount.

The marriage of iron and weaponry revolutionized warfare. Coats of mail, steel weapons, the catapult, and the use of gunpowder in fire lances, grenades, and bombards turned the tide in favor of the attacker in siege warfare. Before these developments, sieges had been risky if the besieged city had stored supplies, permitting it to outlast its poorly supplied attackers. Unfortunately for the Northern Song, Ruzhen invaders used the new Song war technology to capture Kaifeng in 1126 where they declared their new Jin dynasty.

Not yet prepared to yield the Mandate of Heaven, the Song moved the capital of their truncated empire south to Hangzhou, where they prospered until 1279, when the Southern Song capital was captured by the Mongols. Marco Polo is said to have visited the Southern Song capital and was greatly impressed by the degree of urbanization and its 2.5 million inhabitants. The demand for luxuries at Hangzhou—especially spices, silk, and porcelain—contributed to a rapid growth in Song foreign trade at seaports such as Guangzhou, Xiamen, Fuzhou, and Hangzhou. Chinese shipping went down to Africa, but its foreign trade was largely in Muslim Arab hands. The extent of foreign trade outstripped the supply of Chinese copper cash and led to the revived use of paper money, which had first been developed by the Tang, and promissory notes.

In spite of the prosperity that an expanding economy brought to the Song, social problems and foreign affairs continued to pose challenges to the dynasty. In the northeast, the Khitan tribes of Manchuria had united to form the state of Liao in 907 and had carved out a kingdom for themselves that included some territory inside of the Great Wall. The Song, unable to conquer the Liao, negotiated a treaty in 1004 whereby both sides agreed to exchange envoys, develop trade, and respect each other's territorial integrity. In a dramatic reversal of traditional Chinese practice, the Song agreed to pay annual tribute to appease the Liao. In 1044 the Song struck the same deal with the Tanguts of the northwest, which left the Song with crippling tribute payments and high defense costs.

The Southern Song, facing a constant threat from northern tribes, became increasingly self-centered and less receptive to alien institutions. One example was the rejection of Buddhism as a foreign religion by Chinese intellectuals, who looked to their native Confucianism for inspiration. Western missionaries eventually called the eclectic combination Neo-Confucianism. One of Neo-Confucianism's greatest thinkers, Zhu Xi, incorporated elements of Daoism and Buddhism into his philosophy to broaden and enrich Confucian concepts. While still continuing to emphasize virtuous behavior and loyalty to the ruler, Neo-Confucianists sought to "repossess the Way." Zhu Xi believed that *dao*, the Way, is a vast energizing force that pervades the universe and all things in it; only through disciplined self-cultivation could a man understand the Way. This new philosophy was both rational and human and challenged the Song court and Song scholars to be less selfish and to live up to their Confucian ideals. Neo-Confucianism became the living faith of China's elite.

YUAN DYNASTY

The period of Southern Song rule proved to be an exceptionally peaceful and prosperous time, which might have continued had its leaders not responded to the Ruzhen's appeals in 1215 for assistance against the Mongols. Later, after the Mongols defeated the Ruzhens in 1234, the Song sealed their fate when they attempted to reconquer North China from Kublai Khan, who promptly launched an invasion against the Southern Song. After decades of war, the Mongols finally subdued the region in 1279 and founded the Yuan dynasty. This marks the first time that the whole of China had been ruled by non-Chinese nomads who had not previously been sinicized. Although they would adopt Chinese institutions and techniques, the Mongols remained totally alien to the Chinese, whom they ruled until 1368.

Direct rule of China by non-Hanized tribal invaders from the north was always a credible possibility, but rule by cultural aliens was more problematic. The earliest tenet of Chinese culturalism was that the cultural superiority of the Middle Kingdom would inevitably dominate the military violence of barbarians. Non-Chinese tribal chieftains acknowledged China's superiority by bowing down before the Chinese emperor. After the disintegration of state power under the Tang, however, non-Chinese rulers on the periphery for the first time began to govern a Chinese populace in North China. This alien rule began with the Qidan, a Mongolian people from whom North China received the medieval European name Cathay. The Qidan, who were originally seminomadic, rose to power in North China, Manchuria, and Mongolia.

The federation of tribes that founded the empire was led by the imperial Yelu clan, who prolonged their rule by adopting Chinese institutions, such as a hereditary monarchy and Confucianist government. This became known as the Liao dynasty, which ruled a population of about 4 million from 916 to 1125 and peacefully coexisted with the Song with whom they concluded a treaty in 1005. The Tungusic Ruzhen tribes from northern Manchuria, who took the dynastic name of Jin, or "Golden," conquered the Liao state in 1125. The Jin also combined their cavalry and grain to mount successful military campaigns that forced the Song to retreat southward. The Southern Song were hamstrung by a debate on whether to fight or appease, which ended only after the murder of the leading general, Yue Fei, who was thereby immortalized as a model for later Chinese patriots. In 1142 the Song concluded what could rightly be called an unequal treaty, when they formally ceded North China down to the Huai River to the barbarians and agreed to pay annual tribute to the Jin. Although the Jin used the framework of Confucian government, they resisted sinicization. Instead of becoming Chinese, Ruzhen rulers developed their role as supporters of civil order by sponsoring Confucian schools and holding exams, but they promoted Chinese culturalism to facilitate the rule of Chinese subjects, always maintaining their own ethnic, tribal, identity. Their theory of multiethnic empire would later be adopted by the Manchus* of the Qing dynasty.

The Mongol conquest of China can be compared to Western imperialism in the nineteenth century when Chinese society was laid open to foreign influences. The ferocity and destructiveness of the Mongols, who had been united by Genghis Khan in 1206, had given them a bad reputation among the moral-minded Confucians who were particularly concerned with reports that ninety Jin towns in North China had been destroyed by the Mongol hordes. The gap of forty-five years between the conquest of the Jin in 1234 and the subjugation of the Southern Song in 1279 had taught the conquerors that, although the Chinese empire could be conquered on horseback, it could not be ruled on horseback. The Mongols were too different in speech, dress, customs, and background to narrow the cultural gap between themselves and the Chinese, who despised them and said they stank so badly that their foul scent could be picked up downwind. The cultural gap made for light government. Yuan punishments were less severe, and fewer irregular taxes were levied than during the Song. During the last twenty-two years of the dynasty, there were seven different emperors, mismanagement of the imperial finances, a series of military defeats, and widespread famine in the north caused by the flooding of the Yellow River, which historically has been a sign from heaven that the ruling family has lost the mandate to rule. The famine was followed with popular revolts in the 1360s and the retreat of the Mongols to the steppes in 1368. Zhu Yuanzhang, the leader of the successful anti-Mongol revolt, declared his new dynasty, the Ming, that same year.

MING DYNASTY

The character of the Ming, or "bright," dynasty, which ruled China from 1368 to 1644, began with the mentality of its dynastic founder, Zhu Yuanzhang. He was the first peasant to establish a dynasty in a millennium and a half. His childhood was marked by starvation and beggary. He received an informal education from Buddhist priests and rose to prominence after joining an anti-Mongol religious sect as a rebel warlord. After beating his competitors in the lower Yangzi region, Hongwu got the help of Confucian scholars in issuing proclamations and performing rituals to claim the mandate, drove out the Mongols, and built a great capital at Nanjing, where he used repression to restore the empire to the glory of Tang times, creating a stable, prosperous, and militarily strong China that once again dominated East Asia.

Many of the peculiarities of Ming rule are said to stem from the personal characteristics of Hongwu, who enjoyed enormous organization skills but had violent fits of temper and was suspicious of conspiracies against him. Hongwu's admonitions and regulations were aimed at maintaining his centralized control over the world's largest and most diversified state, which grew to over 160 million during the domestic peace of Ming rule. Even Ming domestic success sowed the seeds of its ultimate demise. Hongwu's economic vision was limited to the conventional Confucian view of agriculture as the source of the country's wealth, trade as ignoble and parasitic, and frugality as the prime imperial virtue. Farmers, however, benefited from Ming policies. Farm taxes were held to a minimum, trees were planted to prevent further soil erosion, dikes were maintained on the Yellow and Yangzi rivers, granaries were kept stocked to ensure against famine, and a mutual-responsibility system was supported to suppress banditry, complete and maintain public works projects through corvée labor, and encourage the gentry to care for the needy thus creating self-sustaining communities.

The overemphasis on state frugality, however, led to low government salaries and official corruption and a weak military. Soldiers did not receive regular pay and often reverted to farming. Army ranks shrank to 10 percent of their original size. In 1597 the Ming sent troops to protect its tributary, Korea, from invading Japanese forces in a campaign that was ultimately successful but placed a heavy burden on the imperial treasury. The burdensome costs of such military campaigns influenced the decision of the court not to send troops to contain the rise of a minor Manchurian chieftain.

Despite these endemic weaknesses, China basked in the reflection of Ming success and glory. The Chinese are heirs to the Ming's greatest accomplishments. These include the Great Wall, which was largely constructed during this period, and Beijing's Forbidden City. In 1421 the Yonglo emperor moved the capital from Nanjing to Beijing, concentrating the empire's defense where it was most needed, in the north. The Ming also launched a great naval exploration, which took Chinese ships all the way to India, Africa, and the Middle East.

QING DYNASTY

The Qing dynasty was founded by the Manchus in 1644. During the last generations of the late sixteenth and seventeenth centuries, a tribe of Manchus, under the personal rule of Nurhaci (1559–1626), quietly consolidated its military power through diplomacy and conquest over the clans in the southern part of Manchuria. They established their capital at Mukden. The Manchus took advantage of their strategic position just beyond the Great Wall to learn Chinese ways and yet not be entirely subjected to Chinese rule. By the time the Manchus were ready to challenge Ming rule, they had already developed a writing system for the Manchu language and had translated some of the Chinese classics into it, had adopted the veneration of ancestors, had established the state cult of Confucius, had adopted an administrative system based on the six Ming ministries, and had come to enjoy the support of large numbers of Chinese farmers who had settled beyond the Great Wall. They finally proclaimed the Qing, or "pure," dynasty in 1636.

In 1644 the Manchus took advantage of massive internal rebellions. A disgruntled Ming general who protected the strategically significant Shanhaiguan—

the mile-long pass where the Great Wall meets the sea—welcomed the Manchus. The Manchus entered the Ming capital ostensibly to restore the rightful emperor to the Dragon Throne but, finding the emperor dead, proceeded to take the throne for themselves. Consolidation of the Qing required another generation to complete. The switch of loyalties of many Ming officials facilitated a relatively smooth transition from Ming to Qing rule.

The Qing instituted devices to prevent sinicization and to preserve their dynastic vitality and separate identity. Summers were spent in Inner Mongolia to promote physical fitness for riding, hunting, and shooting. Manchuria was cut off from Chinese settlement, and an artificial border extending several hundred miles was created by digging a ditch and planting willows to mark the boundary. Racial purity was maintained by banning intermarriage between Chinese and Manchus. Cultural differences were fostered. For instance, Manchurian women did not bind their feet like Chinese women. Manchus were not supposed to engage in trade or labor. Manchu clan organization was preserved by a shamanistic religious system. The Manchu language was promoted, and all official documents were translated into both Chinese and Manchu, although many documents were generally unavailable to the Chinese officials. The key to Manchu military control was the establishment of Manchu banner garrisons at strategic points. Chinese troops were used only at the provincial level for policing postal routes and guarding against banditry. To limit the Chinese military threat to Qing rule, Chinese were trained only in defensive military tactics.

To ensure the success of their dynasty, the Manchus promoted themselves as the protectors of Chinese culture. They made few changes in the Ming administrative system, except to balance Chinese officials with Manchus in a system referred to as a dyarchy or synarchy. Joint Chinese and Manchu presidents were appointed to the Six Ministries at the capital, and Manchu and Chinese governors-general and governors were paired in the provinces. These high officials reported jointly to the emperor. The examination system, with its Neo-Confucian basis, remained an integral part of the political and social setting, although different exams were administered to the Manchus and the Chinese. The emperors, particularly Kangxi and Qianlong, patronized scholarly endeavors, which included some of the most monumental projects ever undertaken, such as the Complete Library in Four Branches of Literature in thirty-six thousand manuscript volumes. They also attempted to become ideal Confucian rulers by assiduously practicing the proper rites and by writing and painting in the manner of the scholar-bureaucratic elite. The Qing adoption of state Confucianism provided moral legitimacy for Qing rule, even if it was non-Chinese. The outward sign of Chinese acceptance of the Manchu Mandate of Heaven was the wearing of the queue—keeping the forehead shaved and the hair braided in a queue—by Chinese males. Nonacceptance resulted in death.

Paradoxically, imperial China reached the zenith and the nadir of its development under Manchu rule. Under the first three emperors—Kangxi, Yongzheng, and Qianlong (1661–1796)—the empire enjoyed an extraordinarily long and dynamic leadership. On the domestic scene, peace and stability provided the background for such prosperity that under the Qianlong emperor taxes were cancelled on more than one occasion. Trade expanded throughout the period and handicraft industries flourished. Brilliant military campaigns extended the borders of the empire to Mongolia, much of Central Asia, and Tibet. In the south, Burma, Annam, and Nepal fell under Chinese domination.

As great as these accomplishments might appear, China was already being eclipsed by the West. By the 1750s, when the Qing had consolidated their control of Mongolia, Central Asia, and Tibet, a contemporary struggle between the British and French empires, during the Seven Years' War, had secured Canada and India and had established England's domination of the world's sealanes. Qing domination of marginal caravan routes would pale in comparison to Britain's conquest of the oceans.

Although some have claimed that the West caused the decline of the Qing empire, history is more complex than that. Between 1790 and 1840, the Chinese population had doubled to 432 million because of early ripening varieties of rice that made double-cropping possible; the introduction of such new crops as corn, sweet potatoes, and peanuts; and the expansion of irrigation. What did not occur in China was systematic industrialization, and, as a result, in the nineteenth century, the Qing experienced a long, drawn out process of dynastic decline characterized by domestic rebellion, foreign invasion, and futile efforts at reform to preserve the rule of the elite.

Even without the intrusion of British gunboats, the Qing dynasty faced a serious challenge to its continued rule from civil unrest, such as the White Lotus and the Taiping rebellions. The White Lotus Society, an antiforeign cult dating back to the Mongol period, believed that the Maitreya Buddha would descend into the world, restore the Ming dynasty, and end disaster, disease, and personal suffering. The White Lotus sect appealed especially to peasants. Cult leaders added to their popular appeal with an anti-Manchu racial doctrine. The rebellion began in 1796 as a protest against the exactions of minor tax collectors and was quelled in 1804, but at tremendous cost to the dynasty. The Qing lost a national fortune in uncollected taxes, as well as its reputation for invincibility.

The Taiping Rebellion, from 1851 to 1864, reduced China to civil war. In 1843 Hong Xiuquang founded the Taiping sect after failing the imperial examination for the fourth time. He became fanatically anti-Manchu and, after reading a series of Christian missionary tracts, came to believe that he was the younger brother of Christ who had been sent by God to save mankind. Hong, who spoke Hakka,* enjoyed great success proselytizing among other Hakkas. The Taiping, or "Heavenly Kingdom," with some 20,000 militant believers, waged war against the Qing government and, at the height of their success, established their headquarters at Nanjing, a former Ming capital. During the civil war, more than twenty million people died. Internal squabbling weakened the Taiping who fell to Qing forces in 1864. Although Christianity gained a bad reputation, the Qing enjoyed a brief respite known as the Qing Restoration.

Foreign invasion is the second prong of Qing collapse. In the seventeenth century, the British developed a brisk trade with China, importing tea, silk, and porcelain in exchange for silver, woolen textiles, and eventually opium. After 1759 Guangzhou (Canton) was made the sole port open to Europeans. The government commissioned a group of Chinese merchant families to act as brokers and superintend the foreign traders. The British chafed under such a monopolistic system. In 1839 war broke out when the Manchu government tried to suppress the opium trade, which the British imported to pay for Chinese exports. Ultimately, the British won the Opium War of 1839–1842 and secured Qing agreement to the Treaty of Nanjing in 1842. The treaty provisions included extraterritoriality, an indemnity of 21 million pounds sterling, a tariff later set at 5 percent, the opening to commerce of Guangzhou, Xiamen, Fuzhou, Ningbo, and Shanghai as treaty ports, and the cession of Hong Kong to Great Britain. The failure of the Chinese to live up to its agreements with the British and other Western powers led to the joint Anglo-French occupation of Beijing from 1858 to 1860.

Although the Manchus tried to deal with domestic rebellion and international agression with what later became known as the Qing Restoration, the dynasty was doomed. After 1870 rebellions by the Taiping, Nian, Muslims, and other peasant groups took a heavy toll in terms of human life—it is estimated that nearly sixty million lives were lost collectively—and sapped the energy of the Qing rulers, who were increasingly identified as ''foreign,'' non-Chinese.

Cultural institutions accelerated the decline. Antiforeign sentiments and the Han and Manchu sense of superiority inhibited technological developments, especially if they originated in the West. Chinese scholars often objected to the teaching of science and foreign languages in the country's schools out of fear of Westernization. Traditionalists also prevented the reform of school curricula, insisting that the imperial examinations remain based on the classics. Industrialization was hampered by fears that mines, railroads, and telegraph lines would upset the harmony between man and nature and disturb dead imperial ancestors. Ultimately, railroad building was taken over by the imperialist powers in their spheres of influence after 1898.

But while China remained tied to its traditional premodern institutions, Japan was readily adopting Western technologies. The stage was set for the Sino-Japanese War of 1895–1896, which the Chinese fully expected to win. But the Japanese military made short work of the Chinese, destroying their navy and humiliating their army. The war ended with the signing of the Treaty of Shimonoseki in 1895, in which China agreed to surrender Taiwan and the Pescadores and pay an indemnity to the Japanese. In a major break from China's past, China was forced to acknowledge Korea's independence; the Japanese formally annexed Korea in 1907.

Japan's victory revealed China's military impotence, and the Western powers were quick to exploit it. In 1897 the Germans seized the Shangdong port of Qingdao. Russia took over Port Arthur in Manchuria. The French negotiated a lease for the southern port of Guangzhou. The British moved into Weihaiwei and the following year claimed the entire Yangzi River Valley. In 1899 the United States issued what is known as the Open Door Notes—a foreign policy demand that all nations respect China's territorial integrity and allow equal commercial access everywhere.

China's humiliating defeat by Japan, a former tributary, and the impending dismemberment by Western powers gave rise to a new era of reform. Intellectuals outside the imperial court began to call for radical reforms, such as abolishing the civil service exams and the introduction of representative government. During the 1890s secret societies opposed to Manchu rule arose in many areas of China. One of these groups, known as the Righteous and Harmonious Fists, or the Boxers to Europeans, shifted the focus of their enmity to the foreigners who had humiliated China. In the summer of 1898, the empress dowager, fearing an attempt by the Western powers to restore the Guangxu emperor to the throne, ordered provincial authorities to organize the Boxers to fight an expected foreign invasion. In the countryside, fanatical bands of Boxers, who believed themselves to be immune to Western bullets, attacked Westerners. Boxers laid siege for fifty-five days to the foreign enclave in Beijing, where the Western embassies were located. A combined British-French-German-American military force finally broke the siege and imposed a humiliating settlement on China—an indemnity of $334 million to be paid over forty years at a high interest rate, a fixed tariff of 5 percent, the immediate execution of ten specified Chinese officials, the permanent stationing of foreign troops in the Chinese capital, and the destruction of some twenty-five Qing forts. The Manchus were hopelessly discredited and demoralized; the only reason the Qing dynasty survived until 1912 was because there was no regime in sight to replace it and because both Chinese and foreigners in China preferred order to disruption.

THE REPUBLICAN ERA

The Chinese revolution was touched off by the building of a railroad in Sichuan Province. The local Chinese elite had invested in a railroad which was to be financed largely by foreign loans. The Chinese investors did not want to share their profits with the Qing central government. Qing attempts at suppression failed. An open revolt began in Wuchang on October 11, 1911, when the explosion of a munitions storehouse led to an open revolt. The explosion triggered a series of defections in which most provinces declared their independence from the Qing. Sun Yatsen, leader of the Revolutionary League, proclaimed the Chinese Republic on January 1, 1912, and named himself as its provisional president.

Sun was born in 1866 to a poor peasant family in a village near Canton. At the age of thirteen, Sun went to live with his brother in Hawaii, where he attended a local missionary school and later graduated from Oahu College in 1883. While studying for a medical degree in Canton and Hong Kong, Sun planned for the day when he would help topple the Manchu dynasty. In 1895 he began to travel to raise funds among the overseas Chinese. Sun's revolutionary thought was based on what he called *San Min Zhu Yi*, or the Three Principles of the People: the people's nationalism, the people's democracy, and the people's livelihood. Sun never put these vague principles to practical use, but both the Nationalists and Communists claim to be his political and intellectual heirs. In terms of the revolution itself, Sun envisioned progressive development of government through three stages: military government, political tutelage, and constitutional democracy. Sun was not a democrat in the Western sense, but he was certainly committed to the idea of a constitutional government.

Following the revolution, there was a general agreement that China should have a representative parliament, that unity must be achieved to forestall foreign intervention, and that the reform-minded Yuan Shikai, who had trained the new army that had defended Beijing, had the capacity to head a new Chinese government. China avoided a potential civil war and peasant uprisings, as well as foreign intervention, through a series of compromises. The Qing emperor abdicated, and Sun Yatsen, acknowledging his lack of a military power base, resigned, and in March 1912 Yuan became president.

Yuan Shikai was born in Hunan Province in 1859 to a peasant family. After failing to pass the civil service examinations, he entered the military and eventually gained favor with the empress dowager. He soon came to be one of the most powerful men in China. The success of the Chinese revolution revolved around his changing allegiances because the Manchus abdicated when they learned of Yuan's decision. Upon becoming president of the Republic of China, Yuan obtained loans from the Western powers in return for a guarantee of their treaty rights.

The new Chinese republic had the trappings of liberalism but no liberal tradition. They had elected assemblies representing the local elite in many counties, prefectures, and provinces and a national parliament organized by the newly created Nationalist party or Guomindang. As president, however, Yuan, a former Qing official and military man who later came to be called the "father of the warlords," was distressed by discordant proposals and political factionalism. He concluded that his only hope of governing China lay in the reassertion of autocracy. The Revolutionary League had joined with smaller parties to form the Nationalist party under the leadership of Song Jiaoren. After winning the 1913 elections, Song was slated to become the leader of the national parliament in Nanjing, but instead he was assassinated on the orders of Yuan, who abolished the parliament along with the county assemblies. Sun Yatsen exiled himself to Japan.

In 1915 Yuan scrapped the constitution and proclaimed himself president for life. One year later, he tried to declare himself emperor and assume the duty of imperial ancestor worship, but a storm of public protest drove him to renounce the throne and withdraw from politics. Yuan died a few months later. China's first liberal experiment was at an end.

THE SEARCH FOR NATIONAL UNITY

In the decade after Yuan Shikai, Republican China consisted of two areas and two regimes—warlord China and treaty-port China. The warlords were military men who controlled certain regions. Although the fiction of republicanism was preserved, there was in fact no strong central government. As during previous dynasties, the lack of central authority was marked by a rise in such regional powers. The treaty-port cities, however, included most cities, where Chinese banks, industries, universities, and professional classes were concentrated. The treaty-port part of the Chinese state's power structure provided a degree of stability during the years of warlord disruption. Chinese patriots had to confront the paradox that the unequal treaties, while humiliating in principle, provided them with protection from pillaging by the warlords. For his part, Sun Yatsen returned to China from Japan and based himself in the treaty-port city of Guangzhou (Canton), from which he hoped to lead the struggle for national unification.

THE NEW CULTURE MOVEMENT

While the West focused on World War I, Japan in 1915 issued the Twenty-One Demands which, if implemented, would have rendered China a protectorate of Japan. Although not implemented, the Twenty-One Demands stimulated China's modern nationalism. The controversy coincided with the New Learning movement, in which scholars rejected government service in order to step back and analyze old Confucian values and determine what had retarded Chinese development.

The first point of attack for the New Culture Movement was the Chinese writing system. Chinese characters had many layers of meaning, which had been accumulated since their inception around 200 B.C. To write Chinese, one first had to be familiar with the Chinese classics, which served as the point of reference for the meaning of the characters. Classical writing was no longer convenient, however, for modern Chinese living in the postimperial examination era. The first stage of the literary revolution was the use of everyday speech in written form. Leadership was taken by Hu Shi, who advocated the use of spoken Chinese as a medium for scholarship, education, and written communication. The use of *baihua* spread rapidly. Literary criticism was thus extended to the myths and legends of early Chinese history; the tyranny of the classics was ended.

THE MAY FOURTH MOVEMENT

The May Fourth Movement fostered anti-imperialism, nationalism, and the spread of communism in China. On May 4, 1919, as part of their deliberations to work out the Treaty of Versailles, the Western powers agreed to cede to Japan the former German concessions in Shandong Province. In reaction to the decision, more than three thousand Beijing University students demonstrated in Tiananmen Square. They also burned the house of a pro-Japanese cabinet minister and beat the Chinese minister to Japan. When the police attacked, the students responded by calling a national strike throughout China. Demonstrations grew in strength when sympathetic merchants closed their shops and labor unions staged strikes. A national boycott of Japanese goods, which continued for well over a year, constituted the deepest, most widespread demonstration of national feeling that China had ever experienced.

THE UNITED FRONT

By 1922 Sun Yatsen had reached a low point in his fortunes. After stepping aside as president of the Chinese Republic in 1912 only to see his country disintegrate in warlordism, he was unsuccessful in his attempt to reunify China from Canton, and in 1922 he fled to Shanghai. Although Sun was the undisputed Chinese Nationalist leader, he was hindered by his failure to complete the revolution. In desperation, he turned to the Comintern and began to reorganize the Guomindang (GMD), his political organization, along Soviet lines in September 1922.

Although Sun did not subscribe to the Communist idea of class struggle, he recognized the usefulness of Communist methods and, therefore, accepted Communist collaboration in his Nationalist cause. The Russian Bolsheviks organized the Comintern in 1919 to encourage revolution throughout the world. Establishment of the Chinese Communist party (CCP) in Shanghai during the fall of 1920 was the work of a Comintern agent. Through propaganda journals, bookstores, translations, study groups, and labor organization, Chinese communism quickly established itself as an ideology of action. Furthermore, the Soviet appeal to the Chinese was strengthened by Russian renunciation of the czar's unequal treaties and the fact that the Russians had not been a party to the Treaty of Versailles of 1919.

Employing a Communist model was not Sun Yatsen's first choice. As he wrote to Jiang Jieshi (Chiang Kai-shek), he had to seek aid where he could, and the Western democracies offered none. The Soviet Union helped set up a political institute for the training of propagandists and taught GMD politicians how to secure mass support. By using the Soviet model to develop local cells, which in turn elected representatives to a party congress, the first national congress was convened in January 1924. By 1925, however, the CCP had only 1,500 members, in comparison to the GMD's 50,000 members. Sun Yatsen agreed, however, for all CCP members to join the GMD as individuals, which he believed would strengthen his ability to hold off Western imperialists. The arrangement created the United Front. Actually, however, the agreement only gave Communists a foothold in the GMD, which they would use to take over the entire country. Sun Yatsen died in March 1925.

Between 1926 and 1927, Jiang Jieshi, with Russian weapons and Russian military advisors, defeated thirty-four warlord forces in South China and was well on the way to unifying China. The focus of Chinese nationalism during that period was Great Britain, the chief imperialist power in China. In response to Jiang Jieshi's military successes, the British restored to China the concessions at Hankou and Jiujiang along the Yangzi River.

Jiang Jieshi was born in 1887 to a poor merchant family in Zhejiang Province. Educated in Japan, he became the director of the Whampoa Military Academy near Guangzhou, married the sister of Sun Yatsen's wife, and became a Christian to consolidate the relationship. After 1923 Jiang rose to prominence in the GMD and succeeded Sun Yatsen as leader. He was deeply suspicious of Communist intentions. In April 1927, Jiang betrayed the Communists. At Shanghai, foreign troops and warships confronted the Communist-led unions, which had seized local control. Expecting the support of Jiang's forces, the Communists were instead attacked and decimated in a bloody assault. After establishing his capital at Nanjing, Jiang continued to purge Communist elements. The Communist survivors, led by Mao Zedong and Zhu De, retreated to the frontiers of Jiangxi, a southeastern province surrounded by mountains and forests. There they kept the Communist movement alive, regrouped, and turned to guerrilla action against the GMD.

Jiang's timely break from the Communists allowed him to consolidate the gains of the national revolution while stopping short of class struggle and social revolution, achieve at least a facade of national unity, secure recognition by the Western powers, and begin the process of administrative development necessary to abolish the unequal treaties. In the spring of 1928, he led a northern expedition from the Yangzi to Beijing, which he renamed Beiping, or "Northern Peace," since it was not the capital of the Republic of China. In November 1928, Chinese unification was ostensibly completed when the warlord of Manchuria recognized the jurisdiction of the Nanjing government.

Soon, however, the Nationalists found themselves on the defensive against both the CCP and Japan. On September 18, 1931, a minor explosion occurred along the South Manchurian Railway near Shenyang, marking the renewal of Japanese interest in China. Although the bomb was set off by Japanese, Japan blamed the Chinese, which gave Tokyo a pretext for invading Manchuria. Jiang chose not to fight. Meeting little resistance, the Japanese overran the entire territory within five months.

In the southeast, Jiang's armies were still clashing with the Communists, whom Jiang regarded as the more dangerous army. As he was once said to have remarked, "The Japanese are a disease of the skin, whereas the Communists are a disease of the heart." The League of Nations found Japan guilty of aggression, which prompted Japan's secession from the international organization. Jiang's decision to sign a truce with Japan put a temporary halt on Japanese expansion but proved costly in the long run. Jiang's refusal to resist Japan angered many Chinese nationalists and cost him a major opportunity to mobilize the Chinese people.

The remnants of the Communist movement, which had fled to Jiangxi in 1927, took advantage of popular discontent to broaden its base of support. The Communists also created a professional military, the Red Army, which refined the techniques of guerrilla warfare into an effective strategy allowing the Communists to resist Jiang's armies. It was during this period that Mao Zedong began to emerge as the intellectual, military, and political leader of the Chinese Communists.

Mao was born in 1893 to a relatively well-to-do peasant family. One of the original founders of Chinese communism in 1921, he had been responsible for organizing the peasants during the first United Front. From his experiences in the countryside, Mao became convinced that the success of the Communist cause in China depended upon the mobilization of the peasantry, who made up more than 90 percent of China's population. Mao's theory contradicted the Marxist-Leninist interpretation of Soviet Communists, who instead wanted to focus CCP organization attempts on China's small urban proletariat. Mao's position would eventually triumph.

In the meantime, Mao and the Communist leaders decided to flee their base in Jiangxi during Jiang's fourth campaign against the Communists. The success of the Nationalist blockade led to the epic "Long March." In October 1934, over 100,000 men, women, and children slipped through Jiang's blockade, headed westward toward Tibet, and ultimately turned north to settle Yenan. The Long Marchers crossed twenty-four rivers, eighteen mountain ranges, twelve separate provinces, and ten hostile warlord-held areas in a period of 368 days, covering more than 5,000 miles. Only 20,000 exhausted survivors reached Yenan. Jiang dispatched Zhang Xueliang, the warlord of Manchuria, to finish off any survivors. When Zhang failed to move against the Communists, Jiang flew to Xian in December 1936, where he confronted rebellious officers who wanted an end to the fighting and the formation of a united front against Japan. After being held hostage for two weeks, Jiang agreed to a Second United Front. He never forgave Zhang, who remains under house arrest on Taiwan to this very day.

WORLD WAR II

When Chinese and Japanese troops clashed at the Marco Polo Bridge near Beijing on July 7, 1937, Japan did not expect the incident to lead to all-out war. Japanese goals were limited to consolidating control over northern China to prevent Soviet interference. The Japanese probably expected Jiang to follow his usual policy of negotiating to avoid war, but the Xian incident and public objection to further concessions limited his options. Japanese military action against Shanghai, however, led to the outbreak of major hostilities on August 13, 1941.

The Japanese overran most of eastern China, forcing the Nationalists to transfer the capital far inland to Chongqing. The declaration of war on Japan by the

United States following the bombing of Pearl Harbor on December 7, 1941, changed the war for Jiang, who could now wait for the Americans to defeat this Asian imperialist power. Jiang also benefited from the abrogation of the unequal treaties by the United States and Britain in 1943. He avoided costly operations against Japan and preserved his resources for the day when the war ended and action against the Communists resumed. The evacuation from the east coast, however, left millions of Chinese to suffer the brutality of Japanese occupation. Many peasants in response rejected the Nationalists in favor of the Communists, whose guerrilla units were trying to protect them from the Japanese. The apparent honesty of the Communists in the face of widespread Nationalist corruption also drew many Chinese to the Communist party. Communist programs, such as the education movement of 1944 which sought to end adult illiteracy, won further converts. By the time of the surrender of the Japanese forces in August 1945, the CCP had preempted Chinese nationalism.

After the war, both Nationalist and Communist forces scrambled to fill the void left by the Japanese. The Nationalists started out with a clear advantage: the Japanese were ordered to surrender only to Jiang's forces, and American ships and planes facilitated the movement of Nationalist troops from their inland positions to the coastal areas and northern China. Jiang, however, made two tactical blunders, which significantly affected the outcome of the civil war. The first was his decision to concentrate on occupying China's principal cities, which allowed the Communists to consolidate and spread their control over the countryside. The second resulted from Jiang's decision to commit his best forces to Manchuria. He wanted to prevent the division of China between north and south and wished to keep this important industrial region out of CCP hands. The decision, however, dangerously stretched Jiang's supply and communication lines. He also squandered much of the goodwill accrued to him as the national leader nominally responsible for the defeat of a brutal, imperialist power. For example, he retained Japanese officials in areas where the Nationalists were understaffed. Mao Zedong and the Communists steadily gained power, and in 1949 Jiang Jieshi and the GMD fled the mainland for Taiwan.

THE NATIONALISTS ON TAIWAN

The GMD soon controlled the central government, while native Taiwanese, who were mostly descendants of seventeenth-century Chinese immigrants, continued to run the local administration. For the next forty years, the leaders of the Republic of China on Taiwan maintained the legal fiction that it was the government of all China. From 1949 to 1987, Taiwan remained under martial law and was dominated by the Nationalist party. By the mid-1980s, however, modernization and the growing strength and maturity of the political opposition created conditions favorable to liberalization. Jiang's son Jiang Jingkuo (presidency, 1978–1988) ended martial law and removed the ban on organizing new political parties. Lee Denghui, a native Taiwanese who has served as president since 1988, has continued Taiwan's political liberalization, culminating in 1996 with the holding of Taiwan's first direct elections for president. Taiwan's stunning economic success has paved the way for political liberalization. Although small and resource poor, Taiwan has benefited from a sound economic strategy that, until the 1970s, gave priority to agriculture and light industry and then moved to more sophisticated and heavier industry. By 1994 Taiwan was second only to Japan among East Asian nations in terms of industrialization, foreign currency reserves, and quality of life.

THE PEOPLE'S REPUBLIC OF CHINA

The establishment of the People's Republic of China (PRC) on October 1, 1949, brought forth a Chinese government that broke from the traditions of the imperial past and launched a new era of Han culturalism grounded in the CCP's inherent right to rule.

After decades of disunity and civil war, the CCP's first priority was to unify China and reconstruct its shattered economy. Land reform between 1950 and 1952 broke up large landholdings, equalizing the distribution of land among farm owners and laborers and undercutting the traditional power of the landlord class. Marriage laws elevated the status of women and introduced them into public life. Thought reform campaigns employed self-evaluation, mutual criticism, and indoctrination to attack traditional and bourgeois ideas. In foreign affairs, the Chinese fulfilled their anti-imperialist promise between 1950 and 1953 by assisting North Korean forces in their war against the United States.

In the mid-1950s, Mao moved ahead with his radical Great Leap Forward, an accelerated economic development crusade characterized by mass mobilization, socialist education, economic decentralization, competition and quotas rising to extraordinary heights, agricultural collectivization, and the reorganization of rural life into communes. By 1958, however, it was apparent that the Great Leap Forward was in trouble. Crop yields had dropped dramatically, resulting in a man-made famine that claimed millions of lives. Indeed, the Chinese government continued to export rice to Asian countries rather than admit that a shortage existed. Rather than advance the economy, the Great Leap Forward nearly wrecked it; and rather than leading China to some golden age, it only engendered crisis.

The failure of the Great Leap Forward led in 1959 to the replacement of Mao as head of state with Liu Shaoqi, a pragmatist. Mao defended the ill-fated policy and branded his critics as rightists. By 1965 he sensed a further erosion of his political position due to the success of Liu Shaoqi's policies. Liu had centralized economic planning; increased production of consumer goods; established incentives for the peasants, such as permitting the use of private plots and the organization of free markets; emphasized expertise rather than "redness"; and deradicalized the communes.

As the struggle for power between Mao and the pragmatists became increasingly public, Mao appealed to China's youth to rally to his cause and organized students into Red Guard units. In 1966 he launched a nationwide campaign known as the Great Proletarian Cultural Revolution. The chairman succeeded in toppling Liu, as well as Deng Xiaoping, another pragmatist. The Cultural Revolution was characterized by the destruction of antiques, the burning of libraries, the desecration of shrines and monuments, the closing of schools, an extraordinary cult of personality built around Mao Zedong, and the withdrawal of China from world affairs. Although Mao, probably under the calming influence of Premier Zhou Enlai, began the process of restoring order and phasing out the Red Guards in 1968, the Cultural Revolution continued until approximately 1978. It had been a political victory for Mao, who was once again the undisputed leader of the country, but it had been tremendously expensive for the country and its people.

HAN CULTURALISM, THE CCP, AND THE MINORITY NATIONALITIES

Like every other nation in the world with an ethnically diverse population, the People's Republic of China has faced complicated political, social, and cultural issues in dealing with its minority peoples. Part of the problem, of course, is defining the exact nature of ethnic identity which, as most anthropologists will agree, is an impossible task. Group identity is a complex phenomenon revolving around individual loyalties to a group because of physical, linguistic, social, religious, and economic similarities. Ethnicity can be based on just one of these or on combinations of several or all of them. Nor is ethnic loyalty static. Over time, as social, linguistic, and economic factors change, so does ethnicity.

Chinese officials preferred a more stringent definition of ethnicity. In 1913 Josef Stalin had described a *minzu*, or nationality, as a "nation that is a historically constituted, stable community of people, formed on the basis of common language, territory, economic life, and psychological make-up manifested in a common culture. None of the characteristics taken separate [*sic*]," Stalin went on, "is sufficient to define a nation." And if one of these elements is missing, he claimed, "the nation ceases to be a nation."

Such a definition of ethnicity, of course, is too static and limiting because it ignores the historical reality of cultural evolution, intermarriage, demographic change, and economic development. The Manchu people, for example, today speak Han Chinese as their native language, but few can deny that they are a distinct ethnic minority. Nor do the Hui* people fill Stalin's requirement of territorial integrity. They are scattered throughout the entire country and usually speak the language of their closest neighbors. But most people in China acknowledge them as a distinct minority people.

The realization of just how complex ethnicity can be first dawned on Chinese officials soon after the revolution. In 1949 the government invited the country's ethnic groups to apply for recognition as official minority nationalities. To their astonishment, more than four hundred groups applied. In 1956 the government set up sixteen teams of historians, linguists, anthropologists, and archaeologists to settle in minority regions and conduct scholarly investigations, all with the intent of identifying just how many minority nationalities existed in the PRC. They lived, ate, worked, and relaxed with the people they were studying.

But when the time came to extend official recognition, the recommendations of the scholars had to fit Stalin's 1913 definition. To recognize the presence of more than four hundred minority groups would make even more daunting the Marxist goal of creating a classless, homogenous society. To acknowledge such complexity was politically impossible, so the government approached the task more arbitrarily.

Ethnicity can become highly politicized. In the People's Republic of China, for example, government officials insist that the more than one billion Han people speak the same language and that the differences between Mandarin or Yue or Hakka are differences in dialect, not in language. But most linguists argue that dialects, by definition, must be mutually intelligible. The so-called Chinese dialects are not mutually intelligible. The Chinese government, however, will not divide the Han people into subgroups based on their mutually unintelligible languages. Miaos* provide another illustration. The Chinese Miao speak three mutually unintelligible languages, which are themselves divided again into many mutually unintelligible subdialects. Vast cultural differences also exist from Miao subgroup to Miao subgroup. Because of these existing linguistic, cultural, and geographical differences, some scholars argue that there may be as many as eighty to more than one hundred Miao ethnic groups. Government demographers, however, recognize the Miaos as a single group. When the government finished evaluating all of the applications, it began the process of extending official recognition. By 1979 the government had identified fifty-five official minority nationalities. Including the Han, there are fifty-six official nationalities in the People's Republic of China.

During the first decade of the People's Republic of China, government officials labored to do a better job of dealing with the minority nationalities than the Nationalist government had done. They declared that the country was a "unitary multinational state. All the nationalities are equal. Discrimination against or oppression of any nationality, and acts which undermine the unity of the nationalities, are prohibited." The government went on to protect the right of nationalities "to use and develop their own spoken and written languages." Finally, the government stated that "regional autonomy" applies in areas where a minority nationality lives in a compact community. All the national autonomous areas are inseparable parts of the People's Republic of China.

To put it mildly, the government was walking a tightrope. They initially wanted to reassure minority nationalities about their equality and their right to express themselves, but, at the same time, the PRC would not tolerate ethnic separatism or secessionism. National minorities should enjoy equality and autonomy, but they could do nothing that might threaten the territorial integrity or sovereignty of the PRC. They did not want ethnic pride to turn into ethnic nationalism, nor, theoretically at least, did they want the huge Han majority to suppress other groups. Actually, government policy over the years has been the proverbial pendulum, swinging back and forth between ethnic autonomy and assimilation.

An early item on the nationalities agenda of Mao Zedong and the leaders of the CCP was the assertion of authority over regions considered to be part of "greater China." When the Korean War broke out in 1950, China used the crisis as an excuse for annexing the Yanbian region, whose population was overwhelmingly made up of ethnic Koreans. On September 3, 1952, China established its first autonomous prefecture—the Yanbian Korean Autonomous Prefecture. They then encouraged Han migration into the region, and by 1962 only half of the population was Korean.

Throughout the 1950s, the new Communist government found itself fighting an ongoing guerrilla war against a number of minorities in Yunnan Province, where people resisted the imposition of CCP authority, often equating the CCP with Han oppresssion. It was also apparent to many minority leaders that the new CCP cadres could quickly become an omnipresent force in Yunnan Province. Yunnan was important to the Chinese government; the last thing CCP officials wanted was to have Yunnan Province disintegrate into dozens of minority principalities and expose southern China to political instability and possible foreign intervention.

Tibet, however, was a far greater problem than Yunnan. Ever since the nineteenth century, Chinese government officials had viewed Tibet as the fulcrum of Central Asia. Great Britain had established an imperial foothold in Hong Kong and Guangdong Province in the east, and their hold on the subcontinent to the south was another threat. The French had not succeeded in making their way up the Mekong River through French Indochina into southern China, but Chinese leaders harbored no illusions that the British were as weak as the French. British designs on Nepal and Tibet had been obvious throughout the late nineteenth and early twentieth centuries. Having the British in Nepal, India, and Pakistan was bad enough, but at least the Himalayan mountains served as a great natural barrier protecting Tibet and China. But if Great Britain crossed the mountains and seized control of Tibet, China would be wide open to British invasion. To prevent that possibility, China claimed Tibet as its own, although Tibetans certainly disagreed with that position.

Late in 1950, Chinese troops marched into Tibet, fighting their way to Qabdo, which they then claimed was part of Xinjiang Province. In 1951 People's Liberation Army troops entered the Tibetan capital at Lhasa. A group of Tibetan representatives signed an agreement making Tibet an autonomous region in the PRC, but the Dalai Lama did not accept the agreement, and fighting continued for years between Tibetan guerrillas and the Chinese People's Liberation Army.

More than one million Tibetans died in the fighting. In 1959 the Dalai Lama fled Tibet for India, where he established a government in exile.

While the war in Tibet was taking place, Chinese officials consolidated their authority and implemented their policy of nationality autonomy. They created three autonomous regions: the Xinjiang Uigur Autonomous Region in October 1955, the Guangxi Zhuang Autonomous Region in March 1958, and the Ningxia Hui Autonomous Region in October 1958. The government also established twenty-nine autonomous prefectures during the decade and fifty-four autonomous counties (banners in Inner Mongolia).

Late in the 1950s, relations between the central government and many of the minorities began to deteriorate. What the Great Leap Forward meant for minorities was new, heavy-handed Han assimilationist pressures. In Xinjiang, Yunnan, and Tibet, armed rebellion broke out. The People's Liberation Army ruthlessly crushed the rebellions, and in the process the central government tightened its economic, political, and social grip on the minorities. During the next several years, after the exile of the Dalai Lama, China worked to abolish serfdom in Tibet, a land reform that incited intense opposition from Tibetan landlords. In September 1959, China established the Tibet Autonomous Region.

During the years of the Cultural Revolution, the government pursued assimilation with an ideological vengeance. All forms of minority nationalism and cultural expression were condemned as reactionary because they would retard efforts to create a classless society which, in the view of CCP ideologues, was a far more important political objective than ethnic nationalism. A new constitution called for the "unity of all nationalities" on the basis of the thought of Chairman Mao Zedong. Pure socialism should take precedence over nationalism. Han cadres, in the name of socialist purity, engaged in a ruthless assault on minority nationalism, particularly among the Muslim nationalities. Savage, brutal, and uncompromising, the Cultural Revolution brought about a temporary suppresion of ethnic expression in the People's Republic of China, but it also intensified minority resentment of Han ethnocentrism.

ERA OF REFORM

The year 1976 proved to be a major turning point in China's post-1949 history. Within three months of each other, Zhou Enlai, Marshall Chu De, and Mao Zedong died. It was an intense year for jockeying for power. After giving a stirring eulogy of Zhou, Deng Xiaoping suddenly disappeared. In the interim, the dying Mao named Hua Guofeng as his handpicked successor. Hua did not get along with Mao's widow, Jiang Qing, who was preparing with three other leaders, the notorious Gang of Four, to seize power. Hua had the Gang of Four arrested and placed in solitary confinement. Meanwhile, public sympathies for Deng were revealed on April 5, 1976, when a spontaneous demonstration of 100,000 in Tiananmen Square began chanting anti-Mao slogans and hoisting pro-Zhou and pro-Deng banners. In 1977 Deng was fully rehabilitated and reappointed to a vice premiership, to the Politburo, and to the Military Affairs Commission. Deng Xiaoping soon became "the chief engineer of reform."

For Deng, the Cultural Revolution had nearly ruined the country, setting it back economically in incalculable ways and undermining the legitimacy of the CCP. Deng was committed to achieving economic development, which would move China forward into the ranks of the most highly productive societies in the world while, at the same time, preserving popular loyalty for the CCP. While insisting on political loyalty, Deng allowed China's latent entrepreneurial instincts to flourish, permitting market forces and profit motives to stimulate economic growth. The economy boomed.

Reform also meant changes in minorities policy. Hua Guofeng was convinced that the excesses of the Cultural Revolution had devastated the Chinese economy and made even more likely the possibility of ethnic separatism. He insisted that minority peoples deserved to be treated with equality, that political autonomy should become a reality, and that the Han cadres laboring in nationality regions must "learn the area's language and respect its customs and ways." Deng agreed and continued Hua's policies.

The real shift, however, occurred in 1980, when CCP officials published the contents of a speech delivered by Zhou Enlai in 1957. Not surprisingly, Zhou condemned ethnic chauvinism as dangerous to the motherland, but he also called for the protection of minority rights and the implementation of real regional autonomy whenever possible. Early in the 1980s, the CCP decided to lift political restrictions in Tibet, allowing the full expression of Tibetan culture, and also promised to replace Han government officials with ethnic Tibetans as soon as possible. Official ideologists acknowledged that ethnic differences were likely to long outlast class differences. Such a statement seemed commonsensical, but it actually turned traditional Marxist-Leninst theory upside down, which argued that ethnic differences are simply manifestations of an oppressive class structure.

The new frame of mind also found its way into formal policy. A new state constitution, adopted in December 1982, proclaimed minority equality and praised the virtues of regional autonomy, but it also allowed autonomous political units to organize their own police forces and required that the administrative head of an autonomous unit be a native of the local majority nationality. The constitution also required that legal hearings in minority political units had to be conducted in the local minority language, not in Chinese, and that all legal documents had to be written in the local language. In May 1984, the government implemented the Law on Regional Autonomy for Minority Nationalities. More minority members had to be included on governing committees, and autonomous political units were given the authority to reject, or at least not to implement, central government decisions they found obnoxious or not in their best interests. The 1984 nationality legislation also guaranteed the right of minorities to conduct litigation in their own language.

AFTER TIANANMEN

Deng Xiaoping's economic and social reforms, however, inevitably led to demands for political reform and to the mass student demonstrations held at Tiananmen Square in Beijing in 1989. Deng ruthlessly quashed the movement. The campaign against domestic counterrevolutionaries soon involved foreign nations critical of the bloody suppression of the pro-democracy protests, particularly the United States. The threat of economic sanctions, China's exclusion from membership in the World Trade Organization, and the 1993 decision of the International Olympic Committee not to award the 2000 Olympics to Beijing raised the hackles of Chinese nationalists, who viewed the exclusions as a hybridization of gunboat diplomacy.

There is a common feeling among Chinese that the United States is a superpower in decline and, therefore, determined to contain China, a superpower on the rise. The Chinese feel that they deserve recognition and respect befitting a future superpower, and they put great stock in forecasts that they will soon have the world's largest economy. The Beijing government has responded to foreign criticism by fanning the flames of nationalism. By harping on China's past humiliations and present glory, the CCP is pursuing a campaign of "patriotic education." The message is that calls for democracy and human rights can bring disunity and disorder and open the door to foreign aggression and new humiliation.

Today, the minority nationalities are still vastly underrepresented in positions of political power in the People's Republic of China. On the surface, it has appeared that minorities enjoy considerable power. In 1954, for example, 14.5 percent of the National People's Congress were minority nationalities. Nearly four decades later, that number has remained steady at just over 15 percent. That was almost double the proportion of minority nationalities in the total population. But representation in the National People's Congress is not the best indication of power, since it rubber stamps CCP decisions. Party membership is a better measure. In 1957, 5.5 percent of CCP membership were minorities, and in 1990 that number had increased to only 6.6 percent, even when the minority proportion of the Chinese population had gone past 8 percent.

The number of minority cadres increased from 1,020,000 people in 1981 to 2,060,000 million in 1990, but that percentage was only up from 5.4 to 6.6 percent. Minorities had actually lost a little ground proportionally, even though their number of cadres had doubled. Also, minority cadres were far more likely to hold positions of relatively little authority in the political structure, while Han cadres rose quickly to the top.

Government minority policies have worked successfully in some areas and not so successfully in others. Over the years, some groups—including the Zhuang,* the Manchus, and the Tujias*—have become highly sinicized in a process that has greatly reduced friction with their Han neighbors. The number of Zhuang minority cadres today exactly reflects the Zhuang percentage of the total Chinese population. Other groups, like the Koreans, are less sinicized but still comfortable with central government policies. In the Yanbian Korean Autonomous Prefecture, Koreans constitute only 41 percent of the population but account for more than 50 percent of all judges and police. Koreans have served as leaders of political units at every level, and the Korean language is given precedence over Chinese in legal and political proceedings.

But in other regions, ethnic separatism still challenges central government and CCP authority. In September 1987, lamaist monks in Llasa, Tibet, took to the streets demanding the restoration of the Dalai Lama and of Tibetan independence. Chinese troops moved in to crush the rebellion, and an ensuing firefight resulted in the deaths of several people. In 1988 and 1989, more demonstrations erupted; Tibetans rioted in several areas and ransacked the homes of Han settlers. The central government imposed martial law in Tibet, and foreign observers were expelled from Tibet. Pro-independence Tibetans were imprisoned. Martial law was lifted in 1990, but more demonstrations occurred in 1991, 1993, and 1994.

Xinjiang Province has also posed secessionist problems. Chinese authorities had long claimed that "Eastern Turkestan is an inalienable part of China," and events in Central Asia in the late 1980s and early 1990s created new political tensions there. The rise of Islamic fundamentalism among Arabs, Iranians, and Afghans threatened to create a new pan-Islam spirit in Central Asia. Chinese Muslims—particularly Uzbeks,* Uigurs,* Kazaks,* and Kirgiz*— feel a kinship with their ethnic compatriots in the Soviet Union, and when the Soviet Union collapsed and independence came to Uzbekistan, Kazakstan, and Kirghizia, secessionist movements emerged in the PRC. A number of terrorist bombings against CCP buildings and buses in Xinjiang in 1991 and 1992 were blamed on Muslim secessionists, and the government deployed more than 100,000 People's Liberation Army troops to maintain order and suppress any further eruptions of secessionist sentiment. Laws were also passed prohibiting Xinjiang residents from even talking to foreigners.

The collapse of the Soviet Union also inspired secessionist sentiments among some Mongol leaders. The Soviet Union had long kept a very tight rein on the Mongolian People's Republic, but when Mikhail Gorbachev's empire disintegrated in 1991 and independence came to Mongolia, Mongolian nationalists in China's Inner Mongolia began pushing for secession and reunification. The nationalists were neither as violent nor as well organized as those in Xinjiang and Tibet, but Chinese officials nevertheless arrested and imprisoned them. People's Liberation Army troops were also depoloyed to Inner Mongolia to act as a deterrent to secessionists.

In the disintegration of the Soviet Union, CCP leaders had witnessed the playing out in another country of their worst nightmare. The Soviet economy, in spite of Gorbachev's perestroika reform policies, collapsed late in the 1980s, and the central government lost the ability to enforce its edicts in the various republics. At the same time, Gorbachev's glasnost policies, which lifted most restricitons on freedom of speech and the press, brought on an unprecedented expression of nationalism in the ethnic republics. Gorbachev had essentially set in motion a process of political disintegration that he could not stop. The results were extraordinary. Within just two years, the Soviet Union had collapsed and the following Soviet republics became independent nations: Latvia, Lithuania, Estonia, Russia, Belarus, Ukraine, Moldova, Armenia, Azerbaijan, Uzbekistan, Kazakstan, Turkmenistan, and Kirghizia.

China's response was to make sure that they did not make the same mistakes. They accelerated the economic reform movement that had been launched early in the 1980s; government officials felt certain that economic prosperity rather than economic degeneration was the best way to keep the multicultural state together. They also decided to maintain, indeed even to tighten, political controls on freedom of expression. The student rebellion in Beijing in 1989 gave them a taste of how quickly the desire for democracy could get out of control. Throughout the 1990s, the People's Republic of China kept the country intact by continuing to extend a level of autonomy to the minority nationalities, promoting economic reform, suppressing political freedom, and not countenancing any expressions of nationality separatism. In the People's Republic of China today, two political doctrines remain sacrosanct. First, the power and authority of the Chinese Communist party must not be challenged in any way, and, second, the minority nationalities and the geographical regions they inhabit must remain part of the nation state.

SUGGESTED READINGS: Cyril E. Black, Louis Dupree, et al., *The Modernization of Inner Asia*, 1991; Frank Dikotter, *The Discourse of Race in Modern China*, 1995; June Teufel Dreyer, *China's Forty Millions: Minority Nationalities and National Integration in the People's Republic of China*, 1976; John K. Fairbank, *China: A New History*, 1992; Fei Hsiao Tung, *Toward a People's Anthropology*, 1981; Dru C. Gladney, *Muslim Chinese, Ethnic Nationalism in the People's Republic*, 1991; Steven Harrel, ed., *Cultural Encounters on China's Ethnic Frontiers*, 1995; Thomas Heberer, *China and Its National Minorities, Autonomy or Assimilation?*, 1989; Akira Iriye, Edward Lazzerini, David Kopf, William Miller, and J. Norman Parmer, *The World of Asia*, 1995; Colin Mackerras, *China's Minorities: Integration and Modernization in the Twentieth Century*, 1994; Donald H. McMillen, *Chinese Communist Power and Policy in Xinjiang, 1949–1977*, 1979; George V. H. Moseley III, *The Consolidation of the South China Frontier*, 1973; Rhoads Murphy, *A History of Asia*, 1992; Michael Oksenberg, ed., *China's Developmental Experience*, 1973; Laurence Thompson, *Chinese Religion: An Introduction*, 1996; David Y. H. Wu, ed., *National Policy and Minority Cultures in Asia*, 1988; Graham Young, ed., *China: Dilemmas of Modernisation*, 1985.

TRACY STEELE

HAN BAIYI. See DAI.

HAN DAI. See DAI.

HANGZHOU. The Hangzhou people are a dialect subgroup of the Taihu* people, themselves a linguistic subgroup of the Wu*-speaking Han* people of the

People's Republic of China. More than 1.3 million people speak the Hangzhou language, and the vast majority of them live in and around Hangzhou City.

HANI. The Hani people—also known as Hounis and Wonis—are a prominent ethnic group in the northern reaches of Southeast Asia. Over the years, and today as well, they have been identified by a variety of ethnonyms. Demographers in the People's Republic of China (PRC) call them Hani, but they also appear in Chinese historical documents as Heyis, Hemans, Henis, Hinis, Wonis, Wunis, Wumans, and Ahnis. Their self-designations include Kaduo, Aini, Haoni, Biyue, and Byues. The Hani people living in Thailand identify themselves as the Akha. To the Dai*-speaking peoples in Myanmar (Burma), Thailand, Vietnam, and southwestern China, the Hanis are known as Kaw, Ekaw, and Kha Ko. The term "Kutsung" has also been used when referring to the Hani people.

The Hani language is part of the general Sino-Tibetan linguistic family, and scholars place it within the Yi* branch of the Tibeto-Burman* cluster. There is no written script for the Hani language, except for a pinyin-based romanized version that is rarely used. Hani is divided into three regional dialects that are only barely mutually intelligible. Since many linguists require dialects of one language to be mutually intelligible, classifying the subgroups of Hani is somewhat difficult. The term "regionalect" has been used by some linguists. In any event, there are three Hani dialects: Ha-Ai,* Bi-Kaw,* and Hao-Bai. When dialect, region, and material culture are combined, it becomes possible to identify a variety of Hani subgroups, including the Baihong, Biyue,* Getsuo,* Asiluma,* Doni,* Emu,* Lau,* Lomai,* Soni,* Haoni,* Puli,* Tyitso,* Akho,* Nuquay,* Eni* (Kaduo, Kado), Jen G'we,* and Hteu La.* Their differences from one another are significant enough to cause many anthropologists to classify the Hani subgroups as distinct ethnic groups in their own right.

Between the 1982 Chinese census and its 1990 follow-up, the Hani population increased from 1,058,836 people to 1,253,952. Most Chinese demographers place the total today at more than 1.4 million people. These numbers do not include the Hani in Myanmar, Laos, Thailand, and Vietnam. The vast majority of them can be found in far southeastern Yunnan Province, between the Mengle and the Ailao mountain ranges. They are the southernmost of China's officially recognized minority nationalities. This region is drained by the Red River and the Lancang River. Approximately 800,000 Hanis are concentrated in the region surrounding Mount Aiqian. More particularly, Hanis can be found in Honghe, Yuanyang, Luchun, and Jinping counties in Honghe Hani-Yi Autonomous Prefecture; Mojiang Hani Autonomous County; Jiangcheng Hani-Yi Autonomous County; Lancang Lahu Autonomous County; Puer and Zhenyuan counties in Simao Prefecture; Menghai, Jinghong, and Mengla counties in Xishuangbanna Autonomous Prefecture; and in Yuanjiang Hani-Hi-Dai and Xinping Yi-Dai Autonomous counties in the Yuxi Prefecture.

Chinese archaeologists speculate that the Hani people originated in the region of the central frontier between Yunnan and Sichuan provinces, probably as part of the Yi* people, and Hani oral traditions recall a long-ago migration from "northern regions" to their present homeland. The historians of the eighth-century Nanzhao Kingdom described Hanis as the Henis, and in the twelfth century they were known to the Mongol* conquerors as Hezis. By the fourteenth century, with the Han* Chinese in firm control of Hani country, the hereditary *tusi* system of government was imposed on the region, in which the imperial government appointed Hani leaders as its political agents. That system continued for centuries, although the central government gradually replaced Hani *tusis* with rotating Han administrators.

To deal with its minority nationalities, the People's Republic of China adopted the policies of the former Soviet Union. Worried about ethnic unrest in its border territories, China wanted to pacify the minorities while assimilating them. It was a difficult task. Han settlers were relocated by the tens of millions to minority areas, where they tended to dominate political, cultural, educational, and economic life. But at the same time, China implemented the practice of establishing autonomous political units for minority nationalities. For the Hani, that meant the creation of the Xishuangbanna Gelang He Hani Autonomous Prefecture in 1952. Its name was changed to the Honghe Hani, Yi, and Dai Autonomous Prefecture in 1957.

The Hani have often chafed under Han control or, for that matter, under the control of any outsiders. During the mid-nineteenth century, many Hanis actively supported the Taipeng Rebellion against the imperial government. When France tried to make Yunnan Province part of its Indochinese Union in the late 1800s and early 1900s, the Hani participated in guerrilla warfare against them. Lu Meibei, a Hani woman, led a rebellion in 1917 against Han officials and their Hani *tusi* subordinates. During World War II, the Hani fought against Japanese occupation forces, and in the immediate postwar years, the Hani assisted Mao Zedong's forces in fighting against the nationalist Han government.

The triumph of the Chinese Communists in 1949, however, brought about major changes in Hani life. Land tenure changed, as it did throughout China. Before 1949, most Hani villages, which consisted of anywhere from ten to several hundred households, owned all the land. Land was essentially unregulated, however, and individual Hani farmers were free to work it. Land could not be sold, bartered, or leased. Early in the 1950s, the central government collectivized Hani agriculture, assumed ownership of the land in the name of "the people," and organized Hani local farmers into communal labor systems that were often multicultural. Incentives were few, and productivity declined. The government maintained the system for nearly thirty years, but early in the 1980s collective farming was replaced by the "responsibility system." Land remained the property of the state, but individual families could work private plots and keep the profits of their labor. Productivity increased dramatically.

Hani society is patrilineal and patriarchal. Kinship relations are organized around patrilineal clans. Each of these clans consists of from thirty to forty households, and each clan maintains elaborate ancestral histories, which trace their origins back more than forty generations. After twenty or so generations, those ancestors cease to be real individuals and become spirits and mythological beings. At that point, genealogy merges with religion.

Although Buddhist missionaries worked for centuries among the Hani, they had little success. Nor did Christian missionaries in the late nineteenth and early twentieth centuries. The Hani remain animistic, polytheistic, and shamanistic. They believe that untold numbers of spirits inhabit the world, manifesting themselves in the weather, natural geography, and in capricious events. Each village has a *zuima*, or shaman, who presides over planting and harvesting ceremonies, predicts natural and human events, and practices herbal medicine. Not all of the Hani worship the same spirits. In the Honghe region, they revere a heavenly deity named Ao Ma, who is considered to be the creator of the world. Most Hani believe that trees are guardian spirits that protect them, and they perform annual ceremonial sacrifices for them. Individual homes have guardian spirits, as do villages. There are spirits of the heavens and the earth, and the Hanis worry about an underworld of dangerous, hostile spirits who can upset their lives and bring harm to them. Disease and misfortune are the work of these spirits, and only *zuimas* can nullify their powers.

The Hani economy today is in a rapid state of industrial and commercial development. After 1949 and the Chinese Communist revolution, major changes have been brought about in the Yunnan Province infrastructure—roads, highways, railroads, and telephones—and PRC officials are integrating the Hani into the larger Chinese society and economy. The region's rich reserves of bronze, gold, nickel, silver, and lead can now be exploited, as can valuable timber resources in the thick mountain forests. A variety of factories have also been constructed in Hani country, especially mines, smelters, chemical, and plastics manufacturing facilities.

Most Hanis, of course, remain tied to the agricultural economy. Some Hani farmers still work in a traditional subsistence economy. Farmers in Xishuangbanna and Lancang still practice slash-and-burn techniques, but in the Honghe area, more sophisticated techniques are used. Hani staples are rice and maize, with beans, buckwheat, and millet produced as secondary crops. Honghe Hani raise tea, peanuts, sugarcane, cotton, chili peppers, ginger, and indigo as cash crops.

SUGGESTED READINGS: Amiram Gonen, *The Encyclopedia of the People's of the World*, 1993; Syed Jamal Jaafar and Anthony R. Walker, "The Akha People: An Introduction," in Anthony R. Walker, ed., *Farmers in the Hills*, 1986; Peter Kunstadter, ed., *Southeast Asian Tribes, Minorities, and Nations*, 1967; Bruno Lasker, *Peoples of Southeast Asia*, 1944; Paul W. Lewis and Elaine Lewis, *Peoples of the Golden Triangle*, 1984; Beth E. Notar, "Hani," in Paul V. Hockings, ed., *The Encyclopedia of World Cultures*, vol. 6, *East and Southeast Asia*, 1991; S. Robert Ramsey, *The Languages of China*, 1987; Joseph Spencer, *Shifting Cultivation in Southeastern Asia*, 1966.

HANSA. See **ACHANG.**

HANXIN. The Hanxin people are a subgroup of the Jin*-speaking Han* Chinese.* Hanxins are divided into two dialect subgroups of their own: Cizhang and Huoji. Most Hanxins live today in thirty-seven cities and counties in southern Hebei Province, northern Henan Province, and southeastern Shanxi Province in the People's Republic of China.

HAO-BAI. The Hani* people of Yunnan Province located in the southwestern reaches of the People's Republic of China (PRC), northern Myanmar (Burma), northern Laos, northern Vietnam, and northern Thailand are subdivided into three general linguistic clusters. Because the dialects are barely mutually intelligible to members of the other dialect groups, some ethhnolinguists prefer to use the term "regionalect" to describe them. One of the three Hani regionalects is Hao-Bai.

HAONI. The Haonis are an ethnic subgroup of the Hani* people of the People's Republic of China (PRC). Scattered groups of Haonis can also be found living in Thailand and Myanmar (Burma). The PRC Haonis are located in the far southeastern corner of Yunnan Province, between the Mengle and the Ailao mountain ranges. Their society is patrilineal and patriarchal, with kinship relations organized around patrilineal clans. Each clan consists of from thirty to forty households, and each clan maintains elaborate ancestral histories. Their sense of group identity is based more on a sense of being Haoni than on being Hani. Most Haonis remain tied to the agricultural economy, and a few still work in a traditional subsistence economy. They raise a variety of crops, including rice, maize, beans, buckwheat, millet, tea, peanuts, sugarcane, cotton, chili peppers, ginger, and indigo. Because of recent economic development programs in southwestern Yunnan, increasing numbers of Haoni men can be found working in local factories and mines.

HASAK'O. See **KAZAK.**

HAYAN. The Hayan people speak one of the three dialects of Ha,* itself a dialect of the Li* language of Hainan Island in the People's Republic of China. Hayan, spoken by 44 percent of Ha people, is relatively scattered, and Hayan speakers can be found today occupying the southern and western fringe regions of Ha territory.

HBROGPA. The Hbrogpa people are ethnic Tibetans* who speak the Hbrogpa vernacular of the Amdo* dialect. Most Hbrogpa speakers live today in a variety of Tibetan autonomous prefectures in Qinghai and Sichuan provinces. See **KHAM.**

HBRUGCHU. The Hbrugchu people are ethnic Tibetans* who speak the Jone* vernacular of the Kham* dialect. Most Hbrugchu speakers live today in Zhugqu County in the Gannan Tibetan Autonomous Prefecture in Gansu Province.

HEI-I. The Hei-is constitute an ethnic group in the People's Republic of China (PRC), although the central government has never extended to them formal recognition as a minority nationality. Official PRC publications classify them as a Yi* subgroup, and, indeed, they speak a Yi language. But the Hei-i language is not mutually intelligible with the vast majority of other Yi languages, and the Hei-is give themselves a distinct, separate identity. They will acknowledge a certain cultural affinity with the Yi, but they still insist that they are a separate people. Most Hei-is live today in Yunnan Province.

The traditional Hei-i economy is primarily agricultural. Farmers at lower altitudes cultivate maize, potatoes, buckwheat, and oats; cattle, sheep, goats, and horses are raised in the highlands. Poorer Hei-i families still engage in foraging activities to supplement their diet. Villages are quite small, more like hamlets, and their homes are constructed of wood and dirt. Their religious beliefs today remain an eclectic mix of Daoism, Buddhism, animism, and shamanism; a few thousand Hei-is practice Christianity.

HEI-KU. The Hei-kus are considered to be one of the subgroups of the Yi* people of the People's Republic of China (PRC). Although the Yi are an officially recognized minority nationality of more than seven million people, they are divided into a variety of subgroups whose sense of ethnic identity is quite parochial, based on region and dialects that are usually not mutually intelligible. Hei-kus can be found living today in Guizhou Province, usually in autonomous political subdivisions established by the PRC government for the Yi. They descend from the ancient Tusan people native to the Kunming region of Yunnan and the Chengdu in Sichuan. Their economy is overwhelmingly agricultural. At lower elevations, farmers produce maize, potatoes, buckwheat, and oats as staples. In the highlands, they raise cattle, sheep, goats, and horses. Chickens and pigs are ubiquitous in Hei-ku villages. Poorer families supplement their diets by collecting acorns, roots, wild vegetables, and herbs, and by fishing and hunting. Most Hei-kus live in mountain hamlets of less than twenty households. They continue to be devoted to an eclectic religion that fuses elements of Buddhism, Daoism, and their indigenous animism, although a minority was converted to Christianity in the 1920s and 1930s.

HEISUHUI QIANG. The Heisuhuis are a subgroup of the Qiang* people, who are themselves a subgroup of a larger cluster of Qiang-speaking people near the Tibetan frontier in northern Yunnan Province and northwestern Sichuan Province in the People's Republic of China.

HEIZIWEI. The Heiziweis are a subgroup of the Kirgiz* people. They speak a Northern Kirgiz* dialect and can be found living today in Uqia County in the Xingiang Uigur Autonomous Region of the People's Republic of China.

HEMAN. See **HANI.**

HENGCHUN. The Hengchun Amis are one of the five primary subgroups of the Ami* people of Taiwan in the Republic of China. They are closely related to the Coastal Amis.* The Hengchun are concentrated in north central Taidong County.

HENI. See **HANI.**

HEYI. See **HANI.**

HEYZA. The Heyzas are one of the most prominent clans of the Lisu* people of the People's Republic of China.

HEZHEN. The Hezhen people—also known as the Achas, Fishkin Tatars, Golds, Goldis, Heshes, Nabeis, Nanais, Naniaos, Nanaitsis, Hoches, Hochihs, Khechkis, Natkis, Sushens, Wild Nuchens, and Yupibos—account for one of the smallest officially recognized minority nationalities in the People's Republic of China (PRC). They live in the far northeastern reaches of Heilongjiang Province, along the Sungari River watershed, particularly in Jiejinkou and Bacha, as well as in Sipai in Raohe County in the Wusuli River Valley. Across the border in Siberian Russia, they are known as the Nanais. In 1980 the official census of China placed their total number at 2,745 people, but in 1990 the number had increased to 4,245. Demographers know that their population is growing, and today it could be in the neighborhood of 5,000 people. Most Hezhens live near the point where the Songhua and Heilong rivers merge. Hezhens are closely related to the Ulchis, Oroks, and Orochis, who live in Russian Siberia. The Hezhen language is part of the Manchu*-Tungus branch (see Tungusic People) of the Altaic* linguistic family. Only one dialect is spoken by the Hezhens living in Heilongjiang, and it differs substantially from the dialect spoken by the Russian Nanais.

Hezhen history is intimately linked with that of the Manchus, an ethnic group of more than five million people who live in northeastern China, particularly in southern Manchuria. They are descendants of the ancient Tungus people who were present in Manchuria as early as the third century B.C. The Tungus represented a consolidation of such local tribes as the Sushen, Ilu, Wochu, Wuchi, and Moho, as well as a variety of neighboring Turkic people* and Mongol* tribes. By the early seventeenth century, the Manchus, who had become a self-conscious ethnic entity, were led by Emperor Nurhatsi, who established an imperial capital at Mukden. The name "Manchu" by that time referred to the people of the region. Later in the seventeenth century, the Manchus established the Ch'ing Empire by conquering Korea, Mongolia, and China. It was during this era that the Hezhens came under Manchu control.

Russia's first annexations of Manchu land occurred in 1850, when Saint Petersburg seized the Amur Delta. The first Russian* settlement among Hezhen people was established in the same year at Nikolayevsk-na-Amure, at the mouth of the Amur River. Russia's eastward thrust occurred at the same time that Japan was extending its own influence northward. Both powers wanted control of Sakhalin Island and, in 1855, a Russo-Japanese condominium was reached, which established dual control of the 29,000-square-mile island. This agreement was dissolved in 1875 when Russia ceded the Kurile Islands to Japan. Sakhalin Island then became part of the Russian empire and was used primarily as a penal colony until 1905. After ceding southern Sakhalin to Japan following the Russo-Japanese War, the Romanovs tried to develop northern Sakhalin by encouraging Russian settlements.

A power vacuum caused by the collapse of the czarist government and the Russian civil war prompted local people in August 1918 to invite Japanese forces to occupy the region, bolstering the influence of the local Japanese minority who were opposed to the Bolsheviks. Unrest between the Bolsheviks and the Japanese culminated in the infamous Nikolayevsk Massacre of March 11-15, 1920, when Red forces murdered countless ''reactionaries,'' primarily the Japanese minority. Gradually, the Japanese presence was replaced by the Far Eastern Republic, a Leninist creation based in Chita. By 1922 this republic had annexed all the Manchu territories, and, in the same year, the republic was merged into the Soviet Union.

The Japanese took out their revenge on the people of Manchuria. In 1931 Japan invaded Manchuria and established the puppet Manchuko state. Japanese military officials then began a forced relocation of the Hezhens, taking them out of their clan-based villages and moving them to useless marshlands or heavily forested areas, or forcing them into slave labor conditions working in mines and on railroad lines. To cope with their changing circumstances, large numbers of Hezhens began to use opium. The combination of heavy opium use and Japanese brutality resulted in the deaths of between 80 and 90 percent of the Hezhen population by 1945.

The traditional Hezhen economy revolved around hunting, fishing, and foraging, and early in the 1900s, because of the plentifulness of fish in the region, Hezhens made the transition from subsistence fishing to commercial fishing. With a commercial economy came the demise of traditional communal property systems. Private property in the form of individually owned boats and nets, as well as hired labor, soon came to characterize the Hezhen economy.

Hezhen society has also undergone significant changes in recent years. Throughout the twentieth century, large numbers of Han* people settled in Heilongjiang Province, and the rate of intermarriage between Hezhen men and Han women increased. Relatively few Hezhen women marry Han men. During the

1950s, that process accelerated when the new Communist government established multiethnic fishing cooperatives, forcing Hezhens to live and work with Hans, Manchus, and Koreans.

In terms of religion, Hezhens retain many beliefs of their traditional animist, indigenous religions, although they have also incorporated elements of Russian Orthodoxy, Buddhism, and Confucianism into their faith. They believe in the god Sangi, ruler of the skies, who intervenes in human affairs to prevent sadness or to punish people for damaging the environment.

The environmental issue has assumed enormous importance to the Nanais in Russia and the Hezhens in China in recent years. Soviet economic policies abruptly changed Hezhen life. During the 1960s, 1970s, and 1980s, local oil refineries and pulp and paper mills badly polluted the Amur River watershed, destroying much of the fish population and depriving many Hezhens living downriver of their livelihoods. Construction plans to build a nuclear power plant near Lake Evoron in Russia, where Hezhens believe Mudur, the heaven dragon, lives, have precipitated a bitter protest movement. Hezhen activists, such as Yevdokia Gayer and Pongsa Kile, are urging the Russian and Chinese governments to slow down the process of economic development so that the Hezhens can preserve their traditional way of life.

Ironically, the collapse of the Communist party and the disintegration of the Soviet Union in 1991, as well as economic reforms implemented in the People's Republic of China during the 1980s and early 1990s, made the retention of Hezhen identity less likely to occur. Government-imposed restraints on economic development are highly unlikely, either in Russia or China. Since huge volumes of natural resources exist in Siberia, exploitation and exportation of those resources—especially coal, iron ore, natural gas, timber, and petroleum—is a relatively quick way of earning hard currency to develop the rest of the economy. Russians began importing Western technology to develop Siberia, and if the Chinese do the same in Heilongjiang, the traditional Hezhen economy will not be able to survive.

SUGGESTED READINGS: Alice Bartels and Dennis Bartels, "Soviet Policy toward Siberian Native People," *Canadian Dimension* 19 (1985), 36–44; Alina Chadayeva, "Land of the Ancient Mangbo," *Soviet Life* (December 1990), 25–28; Norma Diamond, "Hezhen," in Paul V. Hockings, ed., *The Encyclopedia of World Cultures*, vol. 6, *East and Southeast Asia*, 1991; Mike Edwards, "Siberia: In from the Cold," *National Geographic* 177 (March 1990), 2–49; Constantine Krypton, "Soviet Policy in the Northern National Regions after World War II," *Slavic Review* 13 (October 1954), 339–53; Owen Lattimore, *The Gold Tribe: Fishkin Tatars of the Lower Sungari*, 1933; Li Fugen, "Hezhe Nationality Fishermen," *China Today* 43 (February 1994), 14–15; Liu Zhongpo, "China's Smallest Minority," *China Reconstructs* 29 (1980), 22–23; Ma Yin, ed., *China's Minority Nationalities*, 1989; Henry G. Schwarz, *The Minorities of Northern China: A Survey*, 1984; Piers Vitebsky, "Perestroika among the Reindeer Herders," *Geographical Magazine* 61 (June 1989), 23–34.

HEZI. See HANI.

HIAI. See **LI.**

HKAKU. The Hkaku people are a subgroup of the Jingpo* people of Myanmar (Burma) and the People's Republic of China. The Jingpos themselves are one of the Kachin*-speaking people, a transnational ethnic group living today in Myanmar, China, and India.

HKAURI. See **GUARI.**

HKAWA. The Hkawas are considered by many ethnologists in the People's Republic of China to be a subgroup of the Wa,* an officially recognized minority nationality. Most Hkawa live in the southwestern reaches of Yunnan Province, primarily in Ximeng County, with other clusters in Canghyuan, Menglian, Gengma, Lancang, Shuangjiang, Yongde, and Zhenkang counties. Most Hkawas are slash-and-burn farmers who raise maize, millet, wet and dry rice, tubers, chickens, and pigs. Classifying them as a subgroup of the Wa, however, poses problems to ethnologists and ethnolinguists. Their "dialect" is not mutually intelligible with most of the other Wa dialects, and most Hkawas view themselves more as Hkawa than as Wa.

HKUN. The Hkuns, also known as Hkun Lois, are considered by many ethnologists in the People's Republic of China to be a subgroup of the Wa,* an officially recognized minority nationality. Most Hkuns live in the southwestern reaches of Yunnan Province, primarily in Ximeng, Cangyuan, Menglian, Gengma, Lancang, Shuangjiang, Yongde, and Zhenkang counties. They are concentrated demographically in Ximeng and Cangyuan counties. Most Hkuns are farmers, but their techniques vary from village to village; some use traditional slash-and-burn methods, and others employ more modern sophisticated techniques. They raise wet rice, dry rice, maize, millet, tubers, and wheat.

HKUN LOI. See **HKUN** and **WA.**

HLIKHIN. See **NAXI.**

HMONG. See **MIAO.**

HMU. See **MIAO.**

HMUNG. See **MIAO.**

HO. See **HUI.**

HOCHE. See **HEZHEN.**

HOCHIH. See **HEZHEN.**

HOKKIEN. See **MIN.**

HONG KONGESE. Ethnicity is a sense of group identity based on race, religion, national origins, language, and economic class, or any combination of these factors. Given that broad definition, it is possible today to speak of a Hong Kongese minority in the People's Republic of China (PRC), even though official government ethnologists do not recognize them as a minority nationality.

Hong Kong, which was a British colony from June 26, 1843, to July 1, 1997, is located on the coast of Guangdong Province on the southern Chinese coast, approximately forty miles down the Pearl River from the city of Guangzhou (Canton). In 1842 the Chinese government signed the Treaty of Nanjing with Great Britain, which ceded the 29-square-mile island of Hong Kong to the British. One year later, Hong Kong was named a crown colony in the British empire. In 1860 the colony was expanded when the British acquired from China the 3.5-square-mile peninsula of Kowloon, situated on the mainland across the bay from Hong Kong. That same year, Great Britain also acquired Stonecutters Island. In 1898 the crown colony of Hong Kong expanded again when Great Britain acquired the New Territories, a region of 365.5 square miles on the mainland north of the island of Hong Kong, along with 235 small islands offshore.

Originally, the island of Hong Kong was inhabited by a mixture of Yue*- and Hakka*-speaking Han* settlers. With the establishment of the British crown colony, Anglo businessmen and their families settled in Hong Kong as well. During the nineteenth century, Hong Kong evolved into Asia's busiest, most prosperous commercial entrepôt—the trading nexus among East Asia, South Asia, Europe, and North America. Because the Anglo settlers remained only a tiny minority of the Hong Kong population, Great Britain did not push the colony toward democracy. To have devolved political power upon the Anglos would have meant the long-term denial of fundamental privileges to the Chinese majority. But true democracy would have put the Han in charge of the colony. Great Britain thus developed a policy of laissez-faire toward the economy and enough political power to maintain order.

On December 7, 1941, Japan bombed Pearl Harbor and invaded Hong Kong simultaneously. Hong Kong surrendered little more than three weeks later on Christmas Day. Japan imposed a harsh military regime, which survived until the end of the war. The British restored colonial civil government on May 1, 1946. After World War II, as the Japanese economy at first revived and then boomed, several thousand ethnic Japanese settled in Hong Kong to represent their country's corporate interests there.

In 1949 the history of Hong Kong took a dramatically different course when Mao Zedong and the Chinese Communists drove Jiang Jieshi (Chiang Kai-shek) and the Nationalists from the mainland and declared the existence of the People's Republic of China. Mao Zedong's triumph triggered an exodus of Han people from Guangdong Province into Hong Kong. Over the next four decades, millions of Han Chinese and Hakkas crossed the border into Hong Kong, and this refugee migration frequently caused diplomatic tensions between the PRC and Great Britain. The crown colonial government in Hong Kong worked to repatriate the refugees, but they could never really stem the tide. By the mid-1980s, the population of Hong Kong had reached more than 5.5 million people; all but 70,000 of them were Chinese.

Time was also catching up with Hong Kong. When Great Britain had acquired the New Territories from China in 1898, the agreement stipulated a ninety-nine-year period of British sovereignty, after which the region would revert to Chinese control. In 1997 the agreement would be fulfilled. The PRC was also demanding the repatriation of the rest of the crown colony, including the island of Hong Kong. Early in the 1980s, negotiations over the issue commenced, and in 1984 the joint declaration concerning Hong Kong was signed by British Prime Minister Margaret Thatcher and Chinese Prime Minister Zhao Ziyang. The agreement dictated that on July 1, 1997, Hong Kong would revert to the PRC. The central government in Beijing would assume sovereign authority over Hong Kong, but the former British colony would be afforded a great deal of autonomy. Although China would assume responsibility for Hong Kong's defense and foreign affairs, Hong Kong would maintain control of its revenues and taxes, and the Hong Kong dollar would remain convertible on world monetary exchanges. The free flow of capital in and out of Hong Kong would not be interrupted. China also guaranteed freedom of speech, press, assembly, religion, travel, and correspondence, and the people of Hong Kong would enjoy the right to choose their occupations and to strike against their employers. All foreign exchange, securities, and futures markets would be allowed to operate freely.

Doubts about just how far China would go to implement these promises, and just how far Great Britain would go to protect them after the transfer of sovereignty, increased exponentially in the spring of 1989 after the violent suppression of the Chinese student protests at Tiananmen Square in Beijing. British Foreign Secretary Sir Geoffrey Howe visited Hong Kong in July 1989 to reassure nervous residents, but he said nothing specific about just what Great Britain would do in the event that the PRC did not live up to the agreement after July 1, 1997. The transfer of authority took place as planned on July 1, 1997, and Hong Kong officially became part of the People's Republic of China.

Between 1843 and 1997, however, British control of Hong Kong had created a new ethnic group there. The population of Hong Kong was just approaching six million people in 1997, and less than 2 percent of them were non-Chinese. But the 5.9 Chinese people of Hong Kong did not necessarily identify ethnically with the Chinese of the mainland. The vast majority of them, of course, were of Han Chinese ancestry, but while Mandarin* was the official language of the PRC, Yue (Cantonese) was the primary language of Hong Kong. And over the years, the British public school system in Hong Kong had pushed English, not

Mandarin, as the most important second language. Even before the transfer of power, the Beijing government did not hide its intention of increasing the teaching of Mandarin in Hong Kong. The ultimate cultural integration of Hong Kong into mainland society, PRC officials argue, will not take place until Mandarin has made the necessary inroads into Hong Kong.

But it was not just language that separated the people of Hong Kong from the mainland. The vast majority of the Chinese citizens living in Guangdong Province, just across the border from Hong Kong, were also Yue-speaking, but the Hong Kongese did not identify ethnically with them either because of the economic and cultural chasm existing between the two societies. Ethnic identity is not just a function of race, religion, or language. It also possesses an economic dimension.

At the time of the transfer, more than half of the people of Chinese descent living in Hong Kong were native to the region. They had never lived under the authority of the Communist regime in Beijing, with its ideological purity and attempts to direct the course of history bureaucratically. The crown colony had adopted a strictly laissez-faire approach to economic development, and many economists argue that Hong Kong enjoyed the purest form of capitalism in the world. Making money was the primary reason for being. Values were materialistic, the economy consumer oriented, and personal goals highly commercialized. In Hong Kong, the dollar was almighty. The people of Hong Kong were also accustomed to freedom of religion, association, and expression. The government had long stayed out of their businesses and out of their bedrooms. They were used to governments playing only a minimal role in their lives. In fact, among all the people of the developed world, the Hong Kongese lived with the least amount of government interference. Thousands of Eurasians*—people of mixed British, Portuguese, and Chinese ancestry—also lived in Hong Kong, and they considered themselves neither British nor Chinese.

As a result of these social, economic, and historical processes, the People's Republic of China acquired a new ethnic group on July 1, 1997. In the former British territory of Hong Kong lived several million ethnic Hong Kongese-Yue-speaking capitalists who viewed their way of life as decidedly superior to that of the mainland Chinese, where a heavy-handed government left little to the social and economic imagination.

SUGGESTED READINGS: Nigel Cameron, *Hong Kong, The Cultured Pearl*, 1978; Mike Edwards, "Hong Kong: Countdown to China," *National Geographic* 191 (March 1997), 32–39; G. B. Endacott, *Government and People in Hong Kong, 1841–1962*, 1964; *New York Times*, June 30–July 5, 1997; Roy E. Thoman, "Hong Kong," in James S. Olson and Robert Shadle, eds., *Historical Dictionary of the British Empire*, 2 vols., 1996.

HONGHE HANI. See HANI.

HONGSHUIHE. The Hongshuihe people are a subgroup of the Zhuang* people of the People's Republic of China. Hongshuihe is classified as one of the

Northern Zhuang* dialects, and most of its speakers live today in Du'an, Mashan, Shanglin, Xinxheng, Laibin, Wuxuan, Xiangzhou, Luzhai, Lipu, Yangsuo, Guixian, and Hexian counties in the Guangxi Zhuang Autonomous Region.

HOTAN. Hotan is the dialect of Uigur* spoken in the southern region of Xinjiang Uigur Autonomous Region in the People's Republic of China.

HOUGUAN. The Houguan people are a subgroup of the Mindong* people, who are themselves a linguistic subgroup of the Min language of Chinese* in the People's Republic of China. Houguan speakers can be found today in the Fuzhou, Minqing, Minhou, Yongtai, Changle, Fuqing, Pingtan, Luoyuan, Gutian, Ningde, Pingnan, Lianjiang, and Youxi regions of northeastern Fujian Province. See **HAN, MIN,** and **MINNAN**.

HOUNI. See **AKHA**.

HOUNI. See **HANI**.

HOVD. Hovd is a vernacular of the Ordos dialect of the Mongolian language. It is spoken primarily in the Hovd banner of southwestern Mongolia and across the immediate frontier in the Inner Mongolian Autonomous Region of the People's Republic of China. See **MONGOL** and **ORDO**.

HRUSSO. See **AKHA**.

HSAP TAI. See **TAME WA** and **WA**.

HSEN. The Hsens, or Hsensums, are considered by many ethnologists in the People's Republic of China to be a subgroup of the Wa,* an officially recognized minority nationality. Most Hsens live in the southwestern reaches of Yunnan Province, primarily in Ximeng, Canghyuan, Menglian, Gengma, Lancang, Shuangjiang, Yongde, and Zhenkang counties. Hsens are farmers, but their techniques vary from village to village; some use traditional slash-and-burn methods, and others employ more modern sophisticated techniques. They raise wet rice, dry rice, maize, millet, tubers, and wheat. Classifying them as a subgroup of the Wa is difficult because the Hsen ''dialect'' is not mutually intelligible with most of the other Wa dialects, and, because of that reality, most Hsens tend to view themselves more Hsen than Wa.

HSENSUM. See **HSEN**.

HSIPO. See **XIBE**.

HSI-SHUANG PANNA TAI. See **DAI**.

HSIUKULUAN. The Hsiukuluan Amis are one of the five primary subgroups of the Ami* people of Taiwan in the Republic of China. They are closely related to the Coastal Ami.*

HTEU LA. The Hteu Las are a subgroup of the Hani* people of Yunnan Province in the People's Republic of China. Other Hteu La communities exist in northern Laos, northern Thailand, and east central Myanmar (Burma). Their economy is largely a subsistence one, in which Hteu La farmers employ slash-and-burn techniques to raise maize, millet, tubers, and potatoes. For a cash crop they have produced tobacco for several decades, and more recently, Hteu La farmers have turned to opium, which they sell to Han* traders in exchange for metal tools, cloth, and different types of food. Foraging and hunting remain significant economic and social activities. Indigenous Hani animism remains important to their religious beliefs.

HUAIYUE. The Huaiyue people are a subgroup of the Gan-speaking Han* Chinese* of the People's Republic of China. Most Huaiyues today live in Huaining, Yuexi, Qianshan, Taihu, Wangjiang, Susong, Dongzhi, Shidai, and Guichi counties in Anhui Province. See **GAN** and **HAN**.

HUI. The Hui are the second largest and most widely distributed of China's minority groups. They are also known as the Huihui, Huizo, Panthay, Dungan (Dungane), Donggan Ren, Tung-an, Mumin, Jiaomen, Zhongyuan-ren, Lao Hui Hui, Lao Khuei Khuei, Yuan' Zhyn, and Huijiaoren, which is their self-designation. The Hui, the most ancient of the ten Muslim groups in the People's Republic of China (PRC), can be found in every province, as well as in Hong Kong, Taiwan, Macao, and the overseas Chinese communities. They are especially concentrated in two areas of northwestern China: the Linxia Hui Autonomous Prefecture west of the city of Lanzhou in Gansu Province, and the Ningxia Hui Autonomus Region which, until 1958, was part of Gansu Province. The 1982 Chinese census put the Hui population at 8.2 million people, but population growth over the past fifteen years, as well as the non-mainland Huis, must put their population closer to 10 million. They have the most rapidly growing population of any Chinese ethnic group.

Russian ethnographers argue that they are ethnic Han* people who converted to Islam because of their sustained contact with Arab, Persian, and Turkic (see Turkic people) traders over the centuries. In the former Soviet Union, there are approximately 65,000 Hui people, who are called Dungan, Dunganne, or Tung-an there. They can be found today living in Kazakstan, Kirgizia, and far southeastern Russia.

During the Tang dynasty, between A.D. 618 and 906, Islam made its way into China. Arab merchants and sailors, along with Persian traders, brought the Sunni Muslim faith to China soon after its founding by Mohammed. Thousands of those Muslim merchants settled in China and married Han women. For centuries, the Chinese forced them to live in separate enclaves—"barbarian settlements"—where they were allowed to run their society according to Muslim law. Their children were raised as Han-speaking Muslims. Because of more Muslim immigration and natural population increase, the size of the Hui community in China grew rapidly.

A second influx of thousands of Muslims occurred in the thirteenth century when the Mongols* conquered much of China. A nomadic people accustomed to frequent movement, the Mongols were not well-suited to administering a large, far-flung empire. To assist them in ruling China, the Mongols imported thousands of teachers, accountants, scholars, artisans, and administrators from Central and West Asia. Most of these new immigrants were Muslims who augmented the Hui population. Some Chinese ethnographers claim that the Hui are Arab, Persian, and Turkish Muslims who first came to China as prisoners of the Mongol rulers and who then assimilated, except for their religious loyalties, into the surrounding Han population. During the century of Mongol domination, Muslims permeated the Chinese civil service, educational system, and financial administration. Muslim migration to China slowed dramatically in the sixteenth century when Europeans seized control of the Indian Ocean's sea-lanes from Arab mariners.

By that time, the Sinicization of Hui culture was well under way. Intermarriage with Han women continued over the course of the centuries, and in the process, the Hui became culturally and even physically similar to the Hans. They adopted Han surnames, the Han language, and Han food and customs. But they still retained their identity as Hui people, and their population steadily grew through conversion to Islam and natural increase.

Cultural and physical similarities, however, did not necessarily imply peaceful coexistence. From the sixteenth to the twentieth centuries, violent ethnic conflict has frequently characterized the relationship between Han and Hui. Over the centuries, more than ten million people have died in China as a result of ethnic confrontations over religion. Dongxiang,* Salar,* Bonan,* and Hui rebellions in north central China and Yunnan occurred whenever Han authorities tried to suppress the Muslim faith officially.

Much of that violence ended in 1912 with the founding of the Republic of China. Han authorities, interested now in attempting to win the loyalty of the minority nationalities, officially recognized the Hui as one of China's "five great peoples." The Hui readily joined in reform movements of the 1920s and 1930s, although they were not usually inspired by the Communist party because of its antireligious overtones. When Mao Zedong triumphed in 1949, thousands of Hui fled the mainland for Taiwan, where they constitute today one of the island's identifiable ethnic minorities. Hui refugees also made their way to Hong Kong, Macao, and the overseas Chinese communities.

In more recent decades, except for the ideological crusades of the Cultural Revolution in the mid-1960s, in which Chinese zealots often attacked any manifestation of religious devotion, the central government has been somewhat accommodating toward the Hui. The country's policy toward ethnic minorities was patterned after that of the former Soviet Union, which had offered minority nationalities substantial autonomy in return for political support. Just as the Soviet Union had done, China created autonomous political subdivisions in regions where minority populations were concentrated. By 1980 there were 107 autonomous political entities, including five provinces, thirty prefectures, and seventy-two counties. Twelve of those self-governing regions were designated for Hui peoples. Approximately half of the Hui live in Gansu, Ningxia, Shaanxi, Qinghai, and Xinjiang provinces or autonomous regions. They form a majority in none of those provinces, but they are highly influential in political, economic, and social circles.

To outside observers, few factors distinguish the Hui from the Han in China. They often look the same, dress the same, and live among one another. But the Hui are aware of profound differences. Some Hui claim that there are still, even after considerable intermarriage over the centuries, recognizeable physical differences. Included in these differences, allegedly, are larger noses, more body hair, and more deeply set eyes. Most Hui acknowledge that they are Chinese by language and citizenship but not by blood. Nor are Hui simply Han who have converted to Islam. The Hui claim to have the blood of foreigners, particularly Arabs, running through their veins. As a result, even Hui who no longer observe Muslim rituals or maintain Muslim beliefs still identify themselves as Hui.

What clearly does distinguish the Hui from the Han is their refusal to eat pork, which the Han describe as an extremely "peculiar" cultural trait. The Hui also consider the Han religious amalgamation of Buddhism, Confucianism, Taoism, and ancestor worship to be hopelessly superstitious and to be avoided at all costs. The Hui also have long memories. The centuries of conflict between Hui and Han characterizing recent Chinese history have sharpened the Hui sense of identity. It has been only thirty years since Han ideologues launched their anti-Muslim crusade during the infamous Cultural Revolution. Red Guards, who were overwhelmingy Han, forced Muslims, under threat of death, to eat pork and cremate their dead, both of which are forbidden in Islam. Sometimes they forced Muslim religious leaders to tend pigs or to parade through town carrying part of a pig's body. Mosques were invaded and desecrated. Although the excesses of the Cultural Revolution disappeared after a few years, most Hui feel that Han hostility remains bubbling just below the political surface.

The Communist regime has brought significant changes to Hui life since 1949. To control population growth, national legislation has outlawed the arranged marriages and polygamy common to pre-1949 Hui society, has extended equal inheritance and divorce rights to women and men, and has forbidden early marriages and rewarded one-child families. At the same time, the government extends tax exemptions to mosques, respects Muslim dietary requirements in the military, and provides paid vacation days for Muslim workers to observe Islamic holidays. The government also sponsors the Chinese Islamic Association to co-ordinate church-state relations.

Although the Hui sense of identity remains quite strong today, there are religious divisions among them. The Old Teaching and New Teaching division, which affects the Salars, Bonans, and Dongxiang, also divides the Huis. Old Teaching Hui were comfortable with the ancient Chinese rituals that had survived the conversion to Islam. New Teaching adherents wanted to purify Islam of its Chinese remnants. From the sixteenth to the early twentieth centuries, this factional division often erupted into violence in Hui communities. More recently, the split no longer consumes so much energy. Religious Huis are also divided from their atheistic counterparts. Religious Hui are Sunni Muslims of the Hanafi school, but there are large numbers of Hui who are not religious at all. In fact, many of them are atheists without any religious dimension to their lives; they consider themselves to be atheistic Muslim Huis. Islam dominates the daily life of most Hui in Gansu and Ningxia; however, in the cities of Quanzhou and Changzhou in Fujian Province, Islam is much less visible.

During the 1990s, the Chinese Communist party has become somewhat more tolerant of Hui religious devotions. The disintegration of the Soviet Union under the centrifugal forces of ethnic nationalism has greatly concerned Chinese leaders, as has the rise of Islamic fundamentalism in the Middle East. In an attempt to appease their Muslim minorities, particularly the Hui, the central government has allowed the construction of more mosques, approved the opening of Koranic schools, and allowed Hui religious leaders to make their pilgrimage to Mecca. The central government has also exempted the Hui from population control measures, allowing them to marry earlier than Han Chinese and permitting them to have more than one child.

SUGGESTED READINGS: Cheng Degan, "Muslims in Inner Mongolia," *China Reconstructs* 33 (February 1984), 59–60; Michael Dillon, *China's Muslims*, 1996; Svetlana Rimsky-Korsakoff Dyer, "Muslim Life in Soviet Russia: The Case of the Dungans," *Journal of the Institute of Muslim Minority Affairs* 3 (1981), 42–53, and *Soviet Dungan Kolkhozes in the Kirghiz SSR and the Kazakh SSR*, 1979; Wolfram Eberhard, *China's Minorities: Yesterday and Today*, 1982; Andrew Forbes, "The Muslim National Minorities of China," *Religion* 6 (1976), 67–87; Raphael Israeli, *Muslims in China: A Study in Cultural Confrontation*, 1980; Jonathan Lipman, "The Border Worlds of Gansu, 1895–1935," Ph.D. diss., Stanford University, 1981, and "Ethnicity and Politics in Republican China: The Ma Family Warlords of Gansu," *Modern China* 10 (July 1984), 285–316; Ma Yu-huai, "Twenty Years of the Ningsi Hui Autonomous Region," *China Reconstructs* 28 (February 1979), 23–26, 40; *New York Times*, July 3, 1990; Barbara L. K. Pilsbury, "Hui," in Richard V. Weekes, ed., *Muslim Peoples*, 1984, and "Cohesion and Cleavage in a Chinese Muslim Minority," Ph.D. diss., Columbia University, 1973; "Vignettes of Hui Life," *China Reconstructs* 28 (1979), 44–46, 75–77.

HUIHU. See UIGUR.

HUIHUI. See HUI.

HUIJIAOREN. See **HUI.**

HUISHUI. The Huishui Miao are an ethnic group of approximately 145,000 people who live in Guizhou Province, particularly in Huishui and Changshun counties. The Huishui language is divided into four mutually intelligible dialects. Although demographers and ethnologists in the People's Republic of China classify them as a Miao* subgroup, the Huishui have a distinct sense of identity.

HUITZE. See **HUI.**

HUIZHOU. The Huizhou people are a linguistic subgroup of the Hakka*-speaking Han* people of the People's Republic of China (PRC). Huizhou speakers can be found today living in the city of Huizhou in Guangdong Province of the PRC.

HUIZI. See **HUI.**

HUMAI. See **DE'ANG.**

HUNZU. See **BURUSHO.**

HUNZUKUT. See **BURUSHO.**

HUZHU. The Huzhus are one of the two primary subgroups of the Tu* people who live in the Huzhu Tu Autonomous County of Qinghai Province in the People's Republic of China. Most Huzhus live in the northern region of the county.

HWEI. See **HUI.**

HYIN. The Hyins are one of the many subgroups of the Li* people of Hainan Province in the People's Republic of China. Like other Li groups, they have earned a reputation over the years for ferocious anti-Han* xenophobia, which has often taken the form of guerrilla warfare against Han immigrants to Hainan. Their hatred of the Nationalist government in the 1930s and 1940s also made them willing allies of the Communists. Most Hyins today are farmers who raise coconuts, coffee, cocoa, sisal, rubber, cashews, pineapples, mangoes, and bananas. Rice is their staple, and because of the tropical climate of Hainan and its fertile soil, they are able to produce three rice crops a year.

I

I. See **YI.**

IAKUT. See **YAKUT.**

I-CHIA. See **YI.**

ICHIA. See **BOUYEI.**

ICHIA. The Ichias are an ethnic group in the People's Republic of China (PRC), although the central government has never extended to them formal recognition as a minority nationality. Official PRC publications classify them as a Yi* subgroup, and, indeed, they speak a Yi language. But Ichia is not mutually intelligible with the vast majority of other Yi languages, and the Ichias give themselves a distinct, separate identity. They will acknowledge a certain cultural affinity with the Yi, but they still insist that they are a separate people. Most Ichias live today in Yunnan Province.

The traditional Ichia economy is primarily agricultural. Ichia farmers at lower altitudes cultivate maize, potatoes, buckwheat, and oats; in the highlands, they raise cattle, sheep, goats, and horses. Poorer Ichia families still engage in foraging activities to supplement their diet. Ichia villages are quite small, more like hamlets, and their homes are constructed of wood and dirt. Their religious beliefs today remain an eclectic mix of Daoism, Buddhism, animism, and shamanism; a few thousand Ichias practice Christianity.

IJEN. See **BOUYEI.**

IKAW. See **AKHA.**

IKHO. See **AKHA.**

I-LAO. See **GELAO.**

ILI. The so-called Ili people speak one of the vernaculars of the Uigur* language in Xinjiang Uigur Autonomous Region of the People's Republic of China.

ILI. The Ilis are a subgroup of the Daur* people. Approximately 5,000 Daurs speak the Ili dialect, which can be heard today in the Xinjiang Uigur Autonomous Region of the People's Republic of China. Ili reflects the long interaction between the Daur and the Kazak* people in Xinjiang.

INDEPENDENT YI. The term ''Independent Yi'' has been used during the last century to describe the Yi* residents of southern Sichuan Province in the People's Republic of China.

IS. The Is make up one of the subgroups of the Yi* people of the People's Republic of China (PRC). Although the Yi are an officially recognized minority nationality of more than seven million people, they are divided into a variety of subgroups whose sense of ethnic identity is quite parochial, based on region and dialects that are usually not mutually intelligible. The Is can be found living today in Guizhou Province, usually in autonomous political subdivisions established by the PRC government for the Yi. They descend from the ancient Tusan people native to the Kunming region of Yunnan and the Chengdu in Sichuan. The Is economy is overwhelmingly agricultural. At lower elevations, the farmers produce maize, potatoes, buckwheat, and oats as staples. In the highlands, they raise cattle, sheep, goats, and horses. Chickens and pigs are ubiquitous in Yi villages. Poorer families supplement their diets by collecting acorns, roots, wild vegetables, and herbs, and by fishing and hunting. Most Is live in mountain hamlets of fewer than twenty households. They continue to be devoted to an eclectic religion comprising elements of Buddhism, Daoism, and their indigenous animism; a minority converted to Christianity in the 1920s and 1930s.

ISIBUKUN. The Isibukun people are one of the primary subgroups of the Bunun* people of Taiwan in the Republic of China. In terms of population, the Isibukuns are the largest of the Bunun subgroups.

ISMAILI KHO. See **KHO.**

IU MIEN. See **YAO.**

J

JAIZI. The Jaizi are one of the most prominent clans of the Lisu* people of the People's Republic of China.

JALI. The Jali are one of the most prominent clans of the Lisu* people of the People's Republic of China.

JAOCHIA. See **BOUYEI.**

JEKO. See **YAKUT.**

JEN G'WE. The Jen G'wes are an ethnic subgroup of the Hani* people, who are located primarily in the far southwestern reaches of Yunnan Province in the People's Republic of China. Other Jen G'we communities exist in northern Laos, northern Thailand, and east central Myanmar (Burma). Their economy is largely a subsistence one; farmers employ slash-and-burn techniques to raise maize, millet, tubers, and potatoes. Tobacco has long been their cash crop, but more recently, Jen G'we farmers have turned to opium, which they sell to Han* traders in exchange for metal tools, cloth, and different types of food. Foraging and hunting remain significant economic and social activities. Indigenous Hani animism remains important to their religious beliefs.

JIAMANSU. The Jiamansus are a subgroup of the Kirgiz* people. They speak a Northern Kirgiz dialect and live primarily in Uqturpan County in the Xinjiang Uigur Autonomous Region of the People's Republic of China.

JIAMAO. The Jiamaos are one of the many subgroups of the Li* people of Hainan Province in the People's Republic of China. They are concentrated in the eastern and southern reaches of Baoting County. Like other Li groups, they have earned a reputation over the years for ferocious anti-Han* xenophobia, which has often taken the form of guerrilla warfare against Han immigrants to Hainan. Their hatred of the Nationalist government in the 1930s and 1940s also made them willing allies of Mao Zedong and the Communists, and when Mao triumphed, the Lis were afforded recognition as heroes. Most Jiamaos today are farmers who raise coconuts, coffee, cocoa, sisal, rubber, cashews, pineapples, mangoes, and bananas. Rice is their staple, and because of the tropical climate of Hainan and its fertile soil, they are able to produce three rice crops a year. There are approximately 55,000 Jiamaos.

JIANGDONG. The Jiangdong are a Qiqihar*-speaking subgroup of the Daur* people.

JIANGXI. The Jiangxi are a Qiqihar*-speaking subgroup of the Daur* people.

JIANNING. The Jianning people are a linguistic subgroup of Gan*-speaking Han* Chinese.* Most Jiannings live in Jianning County in northwestern Fujian Province of the People's Republic of China.

JIAOMEN. See **HUI.**

JIARONG. The Jiarongs are the second largest of the subgroups of the Qiang* peoples of the People's Republic of China. Their language, one of the Qiang dialects, is part of the Qiang branch of the Sino-Tibetan language family. No written script exists for Qiang, and a Chinese dialect is gradually becoming the native language of more and more Jiarongs. They live in the mountain pass separating the Chinese lowlands in the east from the Tibetan highlands to the west. Most Jiarongs are concentrated in the western reaches of that mountain corridor. Han, Yi,* and Tibetan* peoples also live among them.

Most Jiarongs reside in rugged mountain villages, in multistoried, flat-roofed houses constructed of stone. Subsistence farmers, they raise barley, buckwheat, potatoes, and beans, using both slash-and-burn hoe farming as well as double-team cattle plowing. In Jiarong villages located below 7,000 feet in elevation, maize has become the staple product. As cash crops, Jiarongs produce apples, walnuts, peppers, and opium, and they collect bundles of firewood and medicinal herbs for commercial sale. Most Jiarongs remain loyal to their ancestral animistic religion.

Like other Qiang subgroups, many Jiarongs consider themselves a distinct ethnic entity, not simply an extension or a subgroup of the Qiang people. Following the lead of Pumi* nationalists, who in 1960 secured official recognition as a minority nationality, Jiarong nationalists have made requests for a similar classification from the central government. With a population of as many as 190,000 people, they argue that their claim is at least as compelling as that of the Pumis. As of yet, the central government has not agreed with them.

JIAYING. The Jiaying people are a subgroup of the Hakka*-speaking Han* Chinese living in Taoyuan, Xinzhu, and Miaoli counties on Taiwan in the Republic of China, as well as in the Meixian, Jiaoling, and Pingyuan counties in Guangdong Province of the People's Republic of China. Approximately 1.3 million people speak Jiaying.

JICHA. The Jicha people are a subgroup of the Gan*-speaking Han* Chinese* of the People's Republic of China. Most Jichu speakers can be found today in the Youxian, Chaling, and Lingxian regions of Hunan Province and in the Ji'an, Jishui, Xiajiang, Taihe, Yongfeng, Anfu, Lianhua, Yongxin, Ninggang, Jinggangshan, Wan'an, and Suichuan regions of Jiangxi Province.

JIEZI. The Jiezis are a subgroup of the Salar,* one of the Muslim minorities in the People's Republic of China. The Jiezi dialect is spoken in Jiezi, Qingshui, and Baizhuang in Xunhua County, in Gandu in Hualong County, in Dahejia in Gansu County, and in Yining County. All of these are located in the Xinjiang Uigur Autonomous Region.

JILIAN. The Jilian people speak a dialect of Gan,* one of the primary languages spoken by Han* Chinese* people in the People's Republic of China. Most Jilian speakers live in the Jilian region of southern Jiangxi Province.

JIN. See **MULAM.**

JIN. The term Jin is used here to describe the speakers of the Jin Chinese language. Linguists disagree about whether to separate Jin out from Mandarin* or whether to include it as a dialect. Chinese linguists are increasingly prone to make the separation. Jin is spoken by more than 48 million people in 175 cities and counties of Shaanxi, Hebei, and Henan provinces and in the Inner Mongolian Autonomous Prefecture. Whether Jin is a language or a dialect is actually as much of a political question as it is an intellectual one. Government officials in the People's Republic of China (PRC) insist that there is only one Chinese language which possesses eight "dialects": Mandarin, Wu,* Gan,* Xiang,* Hakka,* Jin, Yue,* and Min.* Calling them dialects poses a problem, however, because they are not mutually intelligible, which many linguists insist is the real definition of a dialect. If one dialect is not mutually intelligible with another dialect, they must constitute different languages. Complicating the issue even more is the fact that each of the eight Chinese languages possesses many dialects, and some of those dialects are not mutually intelligible to speakers of related dialects.

At the same time, however, they share an unusual linguistic similarity. The spoken Chinese languages cannot be mutually understood by different speakers, but all speakers employ the same written script. Also, when asked what language they speak, speakers of Mandarin, Wu, Gan, Xiang, Hakka, Yue, Jin, and Min all reply, ''Chinese.'' Some linguists have begun employing the term ''regionalect'' to describe the eight Chinese languages. Whether or not Mandarin, Wu, Gan, Xiang, Hakka, Yue, are Min are dialects, regionalects, or languages, they all divide the more than 1.1 billion Han people into distinguishable, individual groups whose members share loyalty and a sense of identity with one another because of their language. The Jin dialects include Bingzhou,* Luliang,* Fenzhou, Xiang Xi,* Wutai,* Dabao,* Zhanghu,* Hanxin,* and Zhiyan.

SUGGESTED READINGS: S. Robert Ramsey, *The Languages of China*, 1987; S. A. Wurm, B. T'sou, D. Bradley, et al., eds., *Language Atlas of China*, 1987.

JING. The Jing people—also known as the Chins, Chings, Gins, and Yuezus—constitute one of the smaller recognized minority nationalities in the People's Republic of China (PRC). Their current population is approximately 20,000 people, most of whom live very near to the border of China and Vietnam and on three islands in the Gulf of Tonkin: Jiangwei, Wutou, and Shanxin. They are part of the Fangcheng Multi-National Autonomous County in the Guangxi-Zhuang Autonomous Region.

Jings possess a unique identity, one that scholars and ethnolinguists have had difficulty tracing accurately. According to oral tradition and old Vietnamese texts, the Jings originated in Vietnam and moved north to their present locations in the sixteenth century. But their linguistic origins are not Vietnamese because they speak a Yue* dialect, one related to those in Guangdong Province. Literate Jings read and write using Mandarin* Chinese characters; a few use Zinan, an ancient written script.

The traditional Jing economy revolved around fishing, both freshwater fishing on inland rivers and streams and saltwater fishing on the coast— farming was quite secondary to their economy—and Jing culture reflected that fishing economy. None of their pots or pans, for example, are ever placed upside down because it signifies a capsized boat. They never use the word ''oil'' because it resembles ''swim'' in Chinese, and the only Jing who ever swim are those whose boats have capsized.

The Communist revolution of 1949 brought important changes to Jing economic life. Fishing is still an important dimension of their economy, but it is no longer a subsistence activity. Jing now are active in commercial deep-sea fishing in the Gulf of Tonkin. In 1958, with encouragement from the central government, the Jing established oyster farming and pearl production. The government also launched highly ambitious reclamation schemes to reclaim land from the Gulf of Tonkin. By the 1980s, those plans had reached fruition, and the Jing islands were actually connected to the mainland. Because of the availability of new land, agriculture has assumed a previously unknown importance in Jing life. Rice, sweet potatoes, taro, bananas, papayas, coconuts, and a variety of other tropical fruits are now raised successfully.

More than a third of all Jings today live in urban settings. The others, however, still reside in traditional villages, which often consist of several hundred households. Each village usually contains several temples, reflecting eclectic religious commitments to Buddhism, Daoism, and animism. Male shamans exist in each Jing village to counter the magic of evil spirits and help communities maintain balance and tranquility. Perhaps 10 percent of the Jings are Roman Catholics, who were converted by French missionary priests working out of Indochina in the late nineteenth century.

SUGGESTED READINGS: Paul V. Hockings, "Jing," in Paul V. Hockings, ed., *The Encyclopedia of World Cultures*, vol. 6, *East and Southeast Asia*, 1991; Ma Yin, ed., *China's Minority Nationalities*, 1989; Peng Jianqun, "Adding Tourism and Trade to an Old Tradition," *China Today* 42 (June 1993), 60–62.

JINGPO. The Jingpo people are considered one of the officially recognized minority nationalities of the People's Republic of China (PRC). They are part of the much larger Kachin* people, a transnational ethnic group numbering as many as 700,000 people. Other ethnonyms by which they have been known are Jingpaw, Chingpo, Chingpaw, Kachin, Kakhieng, Singhpo, and Thienbaw. Virtually all of the Chinese Jingpo live in Yunnan Province, most of them in the Dehong Dai and Jingpo Autonomous Prefecture in far western Yunnan. There are perhaps 550,000 Kachins living in Myanmar (Burma), and a few thousand more live in the Assam region of India, where they are known as the Singhpos. The Chinese Jingpo population in the 1990 national census was placed at 119,209, but that number included the Zaiwa* and closely related Lashi* and Langwo,* whose languages are not mutually intelligible with Jingpo. The number of Jingpos proper, who are called the Jingpaws in Myanmar, is approximately 30,000 people.

The Jingpo name was not applied to them by the central government of China until 1953. Before then they were known to Han* people as the Shantou Rens, which translated as "people of the mountaintops" or as Ye Ren, which means "savages." Obviously, Jingpos consider the reference Ye Ren to be a pejorative ethnic slur. Over the centuries, the Jingpos have been identified as Achas, Ajis, Cashans, Dashans, Jingpaws, Khangs, Kangs, Lalangs, Langshus, Lashis, Marus, Shidongs, Singhpos, and Xiaoshans. Because of the presence of so many other minority nationalities in Yunnan, there are dozens of other terms for the Jingpos.

The Jingpo language is a complex one that has created problems for ethnolinguists studying it. Most agree that it is part of the large Tibeto-Burman* branch of the Sino-Tibetan language family. In the People's Republic of China, there are three major Jingpo subgroups, each of them based on dialect differences. The largest of the subgroups, with a population of as many as 25,000 people, are the Jingpos. Jingpo is further subdivided into its own dialects, which include Gaori (Gauri), Monzhi, and N'kung. A major scholarly controversy exists in China over whether the Zaiwa people of Yunnan Province are a distinct ethnic group in their own right or a subgroup of the Jingpos. They are officially classified for political purposes as a Jingpo subgroup, but Zaiwa is not mutually intelligible with Jingpo. In fact, some ethnolinguists classify them into different branches of the Tibeto-Burman language family. Because language is a defining characteristic of ethnic identity, Zaiwas are treated as a separate group in this dictionary.

Given the linguistic debate over the Jingpo, it is hardly a surprise to find archaeologists and historians disagreeing over Jingpo origins. Most scholars, however, contend that the ancestors of the Jingpo originated near the headwaters of the Irrawaddy River in Tibet and began moving south some 1,500 years ago. The Jingpo entered the Dehong area in the fifteenth century. The region was already occupied by Dai,* De'ang,* and Han peoples, and the Chinese *tusi* system, an administrative structure in which the Chinese imperial government ruled the region through local, hereditary ethnic leaders, was already in place when the Jingpo arrived. At first, the Jingpo found themselves under Dai control, but Jingpo militarism soon made them a valuable, and eventually independent, political force.

Most Jingpo villages, which are relatively small with only twenty to thirty households, are located on the slopes of the Gaoligong mountains. They prefer the higher elevations; most Jingpo villages can be found between 4,500 and 7,000 feet in altitude. Jingpo country catches the Indian Ocean monsoons, which guarantee abundant summer rainfall. The climate is semitropical.

Until a century ago, most Jingpos were slash-and-burn cultivators who were forced to relocate their villages every few years. Many Jingpo farmers still raise rice through these swidden techniques, but other Jingpos have made the transition to sedentary, terraced cultivation of rice, and they live in permanent villages. Other crops include dry rice, maize, millet, soybeans, kidney beans, potatoes, chili peppers, ginger, garlic, cucumbers, pumpkins, and sugarcane. Livestock are also important in the Jingpo economy, with water buffalo, cattle, and pigs the most popular animals. Jingpos also earn cash by collecting and selling mushrooms, wild vegetables, timber, firewood, and herbal medicines. They have, as well, a long history of producing opium.

At the time of the Communist revolution in 1949, the Jingpo enjoyed limited private ownership of property. Rice paddy fields could be bought, sold, and leased, although only to members of the village. Forests lands were considered to be communal property. In 1957 the central government tried to take a step toward realizing the goal of a completely socialist economy and collectivized Jingpo agriculture. All land was owned either by the state or by agricultural cooperatives. Production plummeted, and no amount of government tinkering could fix the problem until 1981, when central economic planners established the household contract-responsibility system. Under this arrangement, individual Jingpo families could contract for a certain portion of paddy land and make their own decisions about resource allocation. They had to pay a tax in rice to the state and sell a set quota of their harvest at state prices, which happened to be 40 percent below market prices. But those families with surpluses after the rice tax and the quota sale could keep the proceeds of their extra production.

Jingpo society is patrilineal and clan based. Families are organized around the principles of lineage exogamy, asymmetrical matrilateral cross-cousin marriages, strict class endogamy between aristocrats and commoners, and occasional polygyny. With the advent of the Communist victory in 1949, prohibitions against class exogamy were eliminated. The necessity of matrilateral cross-cousin marriage is also easing, although most Jingpo men still marry their mother's brother's daughter. Lineage exogamy, however, remains strictly enforced in Jingpo society.

Although some elements of Han Confucianism and Dai Buddhism have made their way into Jingpo religion, most Jingpos remain loyal to their indigenous, animist faith. It is a dualist theology in which reality is occupied by an ongoing struggle between good and evil spirits. Jingpos believe that all unseen spirits were once human beings. Upon death, every individual becomes a supernatural, invisible spirit, some capable of evil and others of good. Those spirits do not leave the world but occupy it, interjecting themselves constantly into the lives of the living. Jingpos call these spirits *nats*. Because all human beings eventually become *nats*, Jingpo theology finds *nats* everywhere throughout the natural world. There are an infinite number of *nats*, all of whom are responsible for sickness and healh, good fortune and bad luck, drought and abundant harvests, fertility, and human destiny. *Nats* also have an edge to them and are easily offended. Human beings must appease them through prayer, worship, reverence, animal sacrifices, and the intervention of shamans known as *dumsas*.

SUGGESTED READINGS: Edmund R. Leach, *Political Systems of Highland Burma*, 1954; F. K. Lehman, "Kachin Social Categories and Methodological Sins," in W. Mc-Cormack and S. Wurm, eds., *Language and Thought: Anthropological Issues*, 1977; Lei Honghua, "A Jingpo Nationaliy Law Student," *China Reconstructs* 38 (January 1989): 20–21; LaRaw Maran, "Towards a Basis for Understanding the Minorities of Burma: The Kachin Example," in Peter Kunstadter, ed., *Southeast Asian Tribes, Minorities, and Nations*, vol. 1, 1967, 125–46; David Nugent, "Closed Systems and Contradictions: The Kachin in and out of History," *Man* 17 (1982), 508–27; Wang Zhusheng, "Jingpo," in Paul V. Hockings, ed., *The Encyclopedia of World Cultures*, vol. 6, *East and Southeast Asia*, 1991; Xie Jun, "Jingpo Song and Dance Festival," *China Reconstructs* 37 (August 1987), 18–20.

JINGPO. In addition to describing one of the officially-recognized minority nationalities of the People's Republic of China, Jingpo is also used by ethnolinguists to describe a branch of the Tibeto-Burman* language family. In fact, Jingpo is considered to be an extremely important language because it is transitional between Tibetan to the north and Burmese to the south, and it also connects both of those language groups with the Yi* family to the east in the

PRC. Included in the Jingpo branch of the Tibeto-Burman family are Jingpo, Drung,* and Singhpo.

SUGGESTED READING: S. Robert Ramsey, *The Languages of China*, 1987.

JINO. The Jinos (Junos) constitute one of the smallest of China's officially recognized minority nationalities. They are sometimes called the Youle people because of their homeland in the Youle mountains. Since the official recognition came in 1979, they are also the most recent ethnic group in the People's Republic of China (PRC) to achieve such recognition. As such, they are considered the PRC's fifty-sixth nationality. Their current population is just under 19,000 people, the vast majority of whom live in Jinghong County of Xishuangbanna Autonomous Prefecture of Yunnan Province in the PRC, just north of the Laotian frontier. They live in forty-six villages stretched across the Youle mountains. Their language, which is closely related to Yi* and Burmese, is part of the Tibeto-Burman* branch of the Sino-Tibetan family. The Jinos never developed a written language, and because their population is so small, the Chinese government has made no effort to generate one for them.

The Jinos first appear in Chinese historical documents in the eighteenth century. Oral traditions among the Jinos and their Dai* neighbors claim that the Jinos originated to the north and migrated into Yunnan centuries ago. When they arrived, they came under the political domination of the more powerful Dai people, whom they served as vassals. Han* settlers sent by the Chinese imperial government arrived in Dai country beginning in the fourteenth century, and ever since then, Han officials have considered the Jinos to be a Dai subgroup. It was not until 1979 that the central government afforded the Jinos the status of an officially recognized national minority.

Most Jino villages are located on mountain slopes, where they build their homes out of bamboo and place them on stilts. As the economy has improved recently, many Jino villages now see the addition of a few brick homes. Several Jino villages have recently received electricity. Villages contain anywhere from thirty to more than one hundred households. The subtropical climate is characterized by heavy summer rainfall. In 1950 Chinese government economic planners began weaning Jino farmers away from traditional swidden techniques. The introduction of irrigation systems did more than anything else to help Jinos make the transition to more large-scale, efficient production systems. Today, Jinos raise wet and dry rice, maize, bananas, papayas, and cotton. Their tea, known as Puer tea, is popular throughout China. Jino men retain, however, a fascination with hunting. Armed with crossbows, shotguns, poisoned arrows, and traps, they hunt game for meat and furs. Jino women also continue to forage, collecting herbs, nuts, and wild fruits. They sell tea, cotton, and handmade rattan furniture, and with the cash they make they purchase iron, cloth, and some foodstuffs.

Although the Jinos continue to practice a traditional polytheistic, animistic religion, their society is undergoing rapid change. In 1900 most Jinos lived in large extended families that consisted of up to twenty patrilineally related men and their wives and children. They shared a single budget, worked communally held land, and cooperated in their labor requirements. Today, most Jinos live in nuclear family settings. Families are monogamous.

SUGGESTED READINGS: Paul V. Hockings, "Jino," in Paul V. Hockings, ed., *The Encyclopedia of World Cultures*, vol. 6, *East and Southeast Asia*, 1991; *New York Times*, April 21, 1991; Rong Ye, "Among the Jino of the Youle Mountains," *China Today* 43 (December 1994), 14–17; Zhi Exiang, "The Jinuos: China's Newest Nationality," *China Reconstructs* 29 (February 1980), 55–56.

JINPING DAI. Jinping Dai is one of the six written versions of the Dai* language of southwestern China and the northern reaches of southeast Asia. People who read and write the language are sometimes referred to as Jinping Dai.

JIONGNAI. Jiongnai is a subdialect of the Bunu* language, which is part of the larger Yao* cluster of people in the People's Republic of China.

JIREM. See **KHORCHIN.**

JIXU. The Jixu people are a subgroup of the Xiang*-speaking Han* Chinese* of the People's Republic of China. Most Jixus live today in the Jishou, Baojing, Huahuan, Guzhang, Luxi, Chenxi, Xupu, and Yuanling regions of Hunan Province. See **GAN.**

JONE. The Jone people are ethnic Tibetans* who speak the Jone vernacular of the Kham* dialect. Most Jone speakers live today in Jone and Tewo counties in the Gannan Tibetan Autonomous Prefecture of Gansu County.

JTU. See **TU.**

JUI. See **BOUYEI.**

JUMA. See **QIANG.**

JUMEI. See **QIANG.**

JUNNONG. The Junnong are one of the three subgroups of the De'ang* people of Yunnan Province in the People's Republic of China. The Junnongs live in the Junnong region of Zhenkang County.

JUNO. See **JINO.**

JURCHEN. See **MANCHU.**

JUU UD. The Juu Uds are one of the subgroups of the Mongol* peoples of the Inner Mongolian Autonomous Region in the People's Republic of China.

K

KA VA. The Ka Vas are considered by many ethnologists in the People's Republic of China to be a subgroup of the Wa,* an officially recognized minority nationality. Most Wa live in the southwestern reaches of Yunnan Province, primarily in Ximeng, Canghyuan, Menglian, Gengma, Lancang, Shuangjiang, Yongde, and Zhenkang counties. The Ka Va are farmers who raise wet rice, dry rice, maize, millet, tubers, and wheat. Since their language is not mutually intelligible with that of other Wa peoples, the Ka Va consider themselves to be a distinct entity.

KACHIN. The Kachins are a transnational ethnic group who live today in Myanmar (Burma), the People's Republic of China (PRC), and India. Most Kachins can be found in the Kachin State and northern Shan State in Myanmar, southwestern Yunnan Province in China, and Assam State and Arunachal Pradesh State in India. Although it is difficult, because of political turmoil in Myanmar and the PRC in recent decades, to come up with reliable census figures, most southeast Asian demographers estimate the Kachin population at approximately 1.1 million people. Of that number, nearly a million are citizens of Myanmar and another 100,000 are Chinese citizens in Yunnan. Less than 10,000 Kachins can be found in northeastern India.

Linguists classify the Kachin languages in the Tibeto-Burman* language family, although the various Kachin subgroups are not necessarily members of the same branch of that linguistic cluster. In the PRC, one Kachin subgroup is the Jingpo,* which is a branch of its own in the Tibetan-Burman language family. Jingpo is divided into four dialects. The Sinli dialect of Jingpo is concentrated in the southern reaches of Jingpo country, especially in and around the towns of Bhamo and Myitkyina. The Mungun dialect of Jingpo is spoken primarily in the Assam State of India. Guari, also known as Hkauri, is spoken in the eastern reaches of Jingpo country. The fourth Jingpo dialect—Hkaku—is spoken in what is known as "Red Earth country" in the northern and western sections of Jingpo country. In addition to Jingpo, the other Kachin subgroups that speak a Kachin language include the Achang,* the Zaiwa,* and the Lashi.* The Rawang* are considered a Kachin subgroup, but their language is more closely associated with that of the Nung* people in a different Tibeto-Burman language branch. Maru (see Maru Dangbau) is in the Burmese-Lolo branch of Tibeto-Burman, while Yawyin* is a Loloish tongue in the Lolo-Burmese branch. Because these languages are not mutually intelligible, many ethnologists believe that the general classification of "Kachins" is not useful for ethnographic analysis.

Kachins first appear in Chinese historical documents in the fourteenth century, when Jingpos are identified in Yunnan Province and Singhpos in Assam State in India. Both groups are classified as Kachin peoples. By the eighteenth century, the Kachins are noted for being closely involved with the Dai,* known as the Shan people in Myanmar. In the fourteenth century, the power of the Chinese imperial government reached Kachin country in southwestern Yunnan Province. The imperial court implemented the *tusi* administrative system, in which local ethnic leaders were used to enforce Han* policies. The imperial court relied heavily on Jingpo ethnic leaders to serve as *tusis*, which gave them control of the political apparatus and the economic system. As the Chinese caravan system expanded south and east in the nineteenth century, Kachin expansion occurred as well, which brought them into conflict with resident Dai communities.

While the Kachins were expanding southward in the nineteenth century, the British empire was expanding north out of India into Burma. The collision of the two empires resulted in considerable frontier violence during the late 1800s and early 1900s. The British triumphed and pacified the Kachins. The Japanese invasion of Burma in 1942 led to more warfare. In the years after World War II, Kachins became deeply involved in the multiethnic insurgency movement against the Burmese government. Rebels occupied the mountainous areas of the border region of Myanmar-China-Thailand. In 1952 China established the Jingpo Autonomous Region in southwestern Yunnan Province, and Burmese Kachins have frequently sought refuge among their ethnic compatriots there.

Kachin people are primarily farmers who use swidden techniques, except in regions bordering Dai communities, where more sophisticated agricultural techniques are employed. Rice is the staple crop, but Kachins also produce maize, sesame, buckwheat, tobacco, millet, pumpkin, cotton, and opium. Fishing with traps and poison used to be an important source of protein for Kachin families, but in recent years it has become relatively insignificant. Although they hunt during the cold season in December, January, and February, hunting is no longer as economically significant as in earlier times. Kachins raise cattle, pigs, dogs, buffalo, and fowl, but these animals are used for sacrificial purposes more often than for food.

The Kachin social system is quite unique, at least among Southeast Asian ethnic groups. Their society is organized around a series of eponymous clans, in which Kachins trace their patrilineages back to mythological ancestral figures. Clan lineage loyalties, however, are not confined to the individual Kachin subgroups. They cross the linguistic subgroups. Fixed correspondences exist for clan names in the different languages. There are, for example, five aristocratic clans among Kachin people—the Marips, the Lahtaws, the Lahpais, the N'Hkums, and the Marans. An individual from the Maran clan of the Jingpo group, for example, possesses a strong ethnic identification with a Maran from the Singhpo group, even though Jingpos and Singhpos find it difficult to understand one another's languages and possess different material cultures. For this reason, some ethnologists have argued that the most compelling way to divide Kachins into subgroups is based on clan affiliation, not language.

Late in the nineteenth century, large numbers of Protestant and Roman Catholic missionaries made their way into northern Burma and southwestern China. During their labors in Yunnan Province, they converted large numbers of Kachin people to Christianity. More than the other indigenous peoples of northern Southeast Asia, the Kachins have a strong cohort of Christians among them, although that is more true of Kachins in Burma than those in China. Even Christian Kachins, however, still believe in local gods, whom they call *nats*. *Nats* preside over the earth and sky and govern other invisible spirits who influence human affairs.

SUGGESTED READINGS: W. J. S. Carrapiet, *The Kachin Tribes of Burma*, 1929; Jonathan Friedman, *System, Structure, and Contradiction*, 1979; Charles Gilhodes, *The Kachins: Religion and Customs*, 1923; Olaf Hanson, *The Kachins: Their Customs and Traditions*, 1913; Edmund R. Leach, *Political Systems of Highland Burma*, 1954, and *Rethinking Anthropology*, 1961; F. K. Lehman, "Kachin," in Paul V. Hockings, ed., *The Encyclopedia of World Cultures*, vol. 3, *Southeast Asia*, 1991, "Kachin Social Categories and Methodological Sinns," in William McCormack and Stefan Wurm, eds., *Language and Thought: Anthropological Issues*, 1977, and "Internal Inflationary Pressures in the Prestige Economies of the Feast-of-Merit Complex," in Susan D. Russell, ed., *Ritual, Power, and Economy: Upland-Lowland Contrasts in Mainland Southeast Asia*, 1989; Bertil Lintner, *Land of Jade: A Journey through Insurgent Burma*, 1990; LaRaw Maran, "Towards a Basis for Understanding the Minorities of Burma: The Kachin Example," in Peter Kunstadter, ed., *Southeast Asian Tribes, Minorities, and Nations*, vol. 1, 1967.

KADO. See **ENI.**

KADUO. The Kaduos are considered to be an ethnic subgroup of the Hani* people, an officially recognized minority nationality, who are located primarily in the far southwestern reaches of Yunnan Province in the People's Republic of China. Other Kaduos live in northern Laos, northern Thailand, and east central Myanmar (Burma). Their economy is largely a subsistence one; farmers employ slash-and-burn techniques to raise maize, millet, tubers, and potatoes. For a cash crop they have produced tobacco for several decades, and more recently, farmers have turned to opium, which they sell to Han* traders in exchange for metal tools, cloth, and different types of food. Central government efforts to suppress the opium traffic, however, have in recent years reduced Kaduo income. Foraging and hunting remain important economic and social activities.

KAHABU. Kahabu is one of the dialects of the Pazeh* language, which is spoken by a handful of people living on the far northwestern coast of Taiwan in the Republic of China.

KAISHIN. Kaishin is one of the subdialects of Nu,* a dialect of the Black Lahu* language of the People's Republic of China.

KAKHIENG. See **JINGPO.**

K'ALA. The K'ala people, whom some ethnolinguists consider to be a subgroup of the Wa,* are an officially unrecognized minority in the People's Republic of China (PRC). They have sometimes been identified as the Angku. The major dilemma with naming K'alas as a Wa subgroup is that their languages, although both Mon-Khmer* in linguistic classification, are mutually unintelligible. Most K'alas live today in the Kengtung State of Myanmar (Burma), but several thousand can also be found across the border in Yunnan Province of the PRC.

The K'ala language is closely related to De'ang* and to Bulang, which are spoken in Yunnan and Myanmar. K'alas have a common, long history with De'angs and Bulangs. More than two thousand years ago, Han* expansion reached K'ala country. By the Tang dynasty of the seventh and eighth centuries, K'alas had begun to distinguish themselves ethnically from surrounding peoples, acquiring a sense of group identity based on language and religion. During the centuries of the Tang dynasty, they found themselves under the political domination of the Nanzhao Kingdom. The Dali Kingdom controlled them during the Song dynasty from the tenth to the thirteenth centuries.

Until then, the K'alas had consistently pursued a hunting and foraging lifestyle, and their social system was based on matrilineal descent values. Changes came to their society during the Yuan and early Qing dynasties from the thirteenth through the eighteenth centuries. Massive in-migration of Han and Dai* people during these years stimulated a dramatic change in the K'ala economy, from hunting and foraging to agriculture, and the social system gradually changed from matrilineal to patrilineal descent. Farming became central to their economy and hunting became secondary, although it retained its ritualistic, ceremonial, and social importance.

Today, K'alas live in mountain villages that contain anywhere from one hundred to four hundred families. Houses, constructed of bamboo, are elevated above the ground, and the area underneath is used for livestock. They are mountain farmers who use agricultural techniques consistent with different ecological settings. Some K'ala farmers still use thirteenth-century techniques of slash-and-burn, fertilizing land with ashes and using a stick to plant seeds. Others combine slash-and-burn methods with plowing and hand seeding. Crop rotation, mixed-crop planting, and leaving land periodically fallow preserve fertility. Wheat, dry rice, maize, millet, and tubers are the most common crops. Other K'ala farmers cultivate rice paddies, but only where the land is level and access to water is relatively easy.

SUGGESTED READINGS: Fang Dong, ''A Long Road Upward for the Wa Nationality,'' *China Reconstructs* 31 (March 1982), 10–17; Robert Parkin, *A Guide to Austroasiatic Speakers and Their Languages*, 1991; Peng Jianqun, ''Bao Hongzhong, A Wa Headman,'' *China Today* 44 (July 1995), 56–58; Wang Aihe, ''Wa,'' in Paul V. Hockings, ed., *The Encyclopedia of World Cultures*, vol. 6, *East and Southeast Asia*, 1991; Wen Yiqun, ''Women of the Highlands,'' *China Today* 44 (May 1995): 33–35.

KALAJUN. The Kalajuns are a subgroup of the Kirgiz* people. They speak a northern Kirgiz dialect and live primarily in Akqi County in the Xinjiang Uigur Autonomous Region of the People's Republic of China.

KALAKQIK. The Kalakqiks are a subgroup of the Kirgiz* peoples. They speak a southern Kirgiz dialect and live primarily in Akto, Yengishar, and Guma counties in the Xinjiang Uigur Autonomous Region of the People's Republic of China.

KALMUCK. See **MONGOL** and **OIRAT**.

KALMUK. See **MONGOL** and **OIRAT**.

KALMYK. See **MONGOL** and **OIRAT**.

KAM. See **DONG**.

KAMAN. Kaman is one of the two primarily linguistic divisions of the Deng* people of the Tibetan Autonomous Region in the People's Republic of China. Approximately 8,000 people speak the Kaman language.

KAMBA. See **KHAM**.

KAMBE. See **KHAM**.

KAMMU. See **KMHMU**.

KANAKANABU. The Kanakanabu are one of the primary linguistic subdivisions of the Tsouic*-speaking peoples of Taiwan in the Republic of China. The Kanakanabu language is today spoken by only about three hundred people who live along the upper extension of the Nanzixianxi River. Most Kanakanabus are slash-and-burn agriculturalists. Demographers and ethnolinguists have little hope that the Kanakanabu language will survive for more than one or two more generations.

SUGGESTED READING: S. A. Wurm, B. T'sou, D. Bradley, et al., eds., *Language Atlas of China*, 1987.

KANG. See **JINGPO.**

KAOCH'E. See **UIGUR.**

KARGALIK. Kargalik is one of the vernacular subgroups of the Uigur* language which is spoken in Xinjiang Province of the People's Republic of China. Most speakers of Kargalik live in or around the oasis town of Kargalik.

KASHGAR. Kashgar, one of the vernaculars of the Uigur* language, is spoken in the Xinjiang Uigur Autonomous Region of the People's Republic of China.

KASHGARLIK. See **UIGUR.**

KASHMIRI. The Kashmiris, who number more than 4.5 million people, are the dominant ethnic group in the region of Jammu and Kashmir, which is today divided primarily between Pakistan and India. Most Kashmiri speakers are Muslims, and perhaps as many as 5 percent are Hindu in their religious loyalties. Kashmiris originate in the Vale of Kashmir, the Himalayan kingdom in North India that was once a princely state.

Kashmiri society is fractured by profound divisions which in themselves constitute different ethnic groups. Although all Kashmiris speak the language, which is classified as part of the Indo-Iranian family, they are badly divided by religion. Kashmiri Muslims constitute a different ethnic group from Kashmiri Hindus, even though they speak the same language. Kashmiri Muslims are further divided into a variety of sects. Nearly 95 percent of Kashmiri Muslims are Sunnis; the rest are Shiites. Kashmiri Sunnis, in turn, are divided by those faithful to the ancient Sufi worship of saints and the contemporary revivalists who want to purge Islam of such superstitions.

Caste lines also divide the Kashmiris, although they are not as rigid as those of the Hindus. At the very top of the Kashmiri social structure are the Sayyids, who claim direct descent from the Prophet Muhammad and marry endogamously. Just below the Sayyids are the Shaikhs, who claim descent from the prophet's earliest disciples. Shaikhs also marry endogamously. Sayyids control the Muslim religious establishment, whereas Shaikhs are merchants and traders. At the very bottom of the social structure are the so-called occupational subcastes. The Teli are oil pressers, the Lohars are blacksmiths, the Kumiar are potters, the Hanji are fishermen, the Hajjam are barbers, and the Machis are leather workers.

When China seized control of portions of Jammu and Kashmir in 1959, it acquired sovereignty over a handful of Kashmiris who were living in the region at the time. Most of them were Shaikh businessmen, but there were no doubt representatives of the other groups as well. India still claims them, but China controls them.

SUGGESTED READINGS: Sisir Gupta, *Kashmir: A Study in India-Pakistan Relations*, 1966; Trioki Madan, "Religious Ideology in a Plural Society: The Muslims and Hindus of Kashmir," *Contributions to Indian Sociology* 6 (1972), 106–41.

KATHMANDU. The Kathmandus, who live in the Kathmandu Valley, are one of the primary linguistic subgroups of the Newar* people of Nepal. Their dialect is considered by most people in the region to be the standard for the Newar language.

KAVALAN. Kavalan is an all but extinct language of Taiwan in the Republic of China. At one time, thousands of Kavalan speakers lived on the Yilan Plains of northeastern Taiwan, especially in Yilan and Hualien counties. Today, there are no Kavalan speakers left in Yilan County, although there are several hundred people who realize that they are of Kavalan descent. In nearby Hualien County, however, there are several dozen slash-and-burn farmers who still speak Kavalan.

SUGGESTED READING: S. A. Wurm, B. T'sou, D. Bradley, et al., eds., *Language Atlas of China*, 1987.

KAW. See **AKHA** and **HANI.**

KAWA. See **TAME WA** and **WA.**

KAZAK. There are approximately 1.2 million ethnic Kazaks (Kazakhs, Khazaks) living today in the People's Republic of China (PRC). The vast Kazak homeland—Kazakistan—is located between the Caspian Sea and the Urals and the Tien Shan mountains in northwestern China. Their population approaches ten million people. Another million Kazaks live in Turkmenistan, Mongolia, and Afghanistan. Kazaks constitute one of the PRC's fifty-five officially recognized minority nationalities. Most Chinese Kazaks live in the Xinjiang Uigur Autonomous Region, as well as in the western reaches of Gansu and Qinghai provinces. They speak a language that is part of the Kipchak branch of the Turkic cluster of languages in the Altaic* family of languages. Because of the complicated history of the Kazak people, their language possesses an abundance of loan words from Russian,* Mongol,* Persian, Arabic, and Chinese.*

Kazaks claim to be the direct descendents of Genghis Khan, but Central Asian ethnologists believe that they first emerged as a conscious ethnic identity in the thirteenth century. For centuries, a variety of Turkish tribes in the region had mingled and intermarried, but the Mongol invasions in the early thirteenth century gave them a unity and a political consciousness. Not until the early sixteenth century, however, after the breakup of the Mongol empire and several of its succeeding khanates, did the Kazaks unite under the leadership of Kasim Khan, at which point they rapidly began to construct an identity based on shared political, linguistic, and social institutions. They also converted to Islam.

During the seventeenth, eighteenth, nineteenth, and twentieth centuries, Kazak history has been largely defined by their political relationships with Russians and Han* Chinese, who have repeatedly attempted to impose their own political controls on the Kazak people. Kazak rebellions against Russian authority occurred in 1772–1776, 1782–1783, 1827–1829, 1837–1846, and 1916–1917. Kazak ethnicity was cut on the edge of anti-Russian sentiment for hundreds of years. The Bolshevik Revolution encouraged some Kazak leaders to believe that Kazak-Russian relations were about to improve, and in 1920 the Soviets established the Kirgiz (Kazak) Autonomous Soviet Socialist Republic.

The honeymoon was short-lived. The traditional Kazak economy revolved around a nomadic pastoral lifestyle, in which Kazak extended families herded cattle, sheep, and horses. They lived in portable tents, known as *yurts*, during the late spring, summer, and early fall and then wintered in permanent adobe houses. When Joseph Stalin began the forced collectivization of their herds in the 1920s and 1930s, it touched off a fierce sense of Kazak nationalism. Large numbers of Kazak people fled into the Xinjiang region of China and into what is today Uzbekistan. Those Kazaks left behind in the Soviet Union had to endure decades of political oppression and carefully orchestrated attacks against their culture. The Soviet government even prohibited use of the Arabic script in printed Kazak and imposed use of the Cyrillic alphabet.

The Chinese Kazaks soon found themselves facing similar problems. After Mao Zedong's triumph in 1949, they were subjected to similar pressures from collectivization and political oppression. The independent-minded Kazaks of China were no more likely than their Russian counterparts to accept socialist schemes. In 1961, as part of the PRC's Great Leap Forward, mandatory collectivization of Kazak livestock and breeding programs was imposed. Kazaks violently resisted collectivization, and troops from the People's Liberation Army deployed to far western Xinjiang to maintain order. Tens of thousands of Kazaks fled with their herds across the Soviet border into the Kazak Soviet Socialist Republic. In 1963, when the Sino-Soviet border dispute erupted, both countries placed armies along the border, cutting the two Kazak groups off from one another. Those borders remained closed for nearly thirty years.

When the Soviet Union began to disintegrate late in the 1980s, Kazak nationalism surfaced again. In 1991, when the Soviet Union collapsed, Kazakstan became an independent nation allied with the new Commonwealth of Independent States. Chinese Communist party (CCP) officials viewed the breakup of the Soviet Union with alarm. The rise of Islamic fundamentalism among

Arabs, Iranians, and Afghans had already created a new pan-Islamic spirit in Central Asia. Chinese Muslims—particularly Uzbeks,* Uigurs,* Kazaks, and Kirgiz*—felt a kinship with their ethnic compatriots in the Soviet Union, and when the Soviet Union collapsed and independence came to Uzbekistan, Kazakstan, and Kirgizia, secessionist movements emerged in the PRC. A number of terrorist bombings against CCP buildings and buses in Xinjiang in 1991 and 1992 were blamed on Muslim secessionists, and the government deployed more than 100,000 People's Liberation Army troops to maintain order and suppress any further eruptions of secessionist sentiment. Laws were also passed prohibiting Xinjiang residents from even talking with foreigners. At the same time, however, border tensions relaxed somewhat, and Kazaks in Kazakstan and Xinjiang enjoyed more contact with one another. In recent years, use of the Arabic script for written Kazak has been revived, and Cyrillic is falling into disuse.

Late in 1997, Muslim insurgency appeared for the first time in several years in Xinjiang. Tensions between Han Chinese and the Turkic Uigurs had been mounting for years. The Muslim revival throughout Central Asia, South Asia, and the Middle East had fanned the flames of Muslim nationalism and pan-Islamic ideas. Many Muslims still resented the persecution of the Cultural Revolution years and believed that the central government in Beijing still retained its discriminatory attitudes toward Islam. Muslims—Kazaks, Tatars,* Uzbeks, and Uigurs—also resented government development policies, which invested huge amounts of capital in order to relocate millions of Han Chinese to Xinjiang. As far as the Muslims were concerned, the arrival of so many Han settlers was just another government attempt to assimilate them.

Violence erupted. A series of bombings, kidnappings, and assassinations occurred, usually targeted at pro-Beijing Muslims and at Han Chinese in Xinjiang. In February 1997, more than one thousand Muslim separatists rioted in the town of Yining, which is located in far western Xinjiang, just thirty miles from the border of Kazakstan. A few weeks later, more rioting and bombings occurred in the cities of Urumqi and Kashgar. Chinese government security forces crushed the rebellion, but not before ten people had been killed, more than one hundred injured, and five hundred arrested. What triggered the rioting was the attempt by a Han Chinese policeman to arrest a Uigur criminal suspect. When the Uigur resisted arrest, he was beaten. A crowd, which formed to observe the confrontation, soon turned into a mob and attacked several government buildings.

Chinese political officials have been quick to respond militarily to the smallest signs of political insurgency among Kazaks. They have also recently negotiated diplomatic agreements with Kazakstan to protect the PRC-Uzbekistan border. To prevent Kazak nationalists from moving back and forth across the frontier, the agreement provides for PRC-Kazak police cooperation in searching travelers for guns, explosives, currency, and propaganda literature. Nevertheless, a number of Xinjiang Kazaks now live in Almaty, the Kazakstan capital city, from which they continue their efforts to expand Kazakstan east into the People's Republic of China.

SUGGESTED READINGS: Shirin Akiner, *Islamic Peoples of the Soviet Union*, 1983; Milton J. Clark, "How the Kazaks Fled to Freedom," *National Geographic* 106 (1954), 621–44; Michael Dillon, *China's Muslims*, 1996; Ned Gillette, "Adventure in Western China," *National Geographic* 159 (February 1981), 174–99; Rick Gore, "Journey to China's Far West," *National Geographic* 157 (March 1980), 292–332; René Grousset, *The Empire of the Steppes: A History of Central Asia*, 1970; A. E. Hudson, *Kazakh Social Structure*, 1938; Ma Yin, ed., *China's Minority Nationalities*, 1989; George Miseley, *A Sino-Soviet Cultural Frontier: The Ili Kazakh Autonomous Chou*, 1966; *New York Times*, February 28, 1997; Martha Brill Olcott, *The Kazakhs*, 1987; Lee Pappas, "Kazaks," in James S. Olson, ed., *Historical Dictionary of the Russian and Soviet Empires*, 1993; Peng Jianqun, "In a Kazak Herdsman's Home," *China Reconstructs* 35 (July 1986), 58–60; Richard Pipes, *The Formation of the Soviet Union: Communism and Nationalism, 1917–1923*, 1980; Michael Rywkin, ed., *Russian Colonial Expansion to 1917*, 1988; Henry G. Schwarz, *The Minorities of Northern China: A Survey*, 1984; M. Wesley Shoemaker, ed., *Russia, Eurasian States, and Eastern Europe*, 1972; Wayne S. Vucinich, ed., *Russia and Asia: Essays on the Influence of Russia on the Asian Peoples*, 1972; *Washington Post*, February 11, 1997; Joseph L. Wieczynski, *The Modern Encyclopedia of Russian and Soviet History*, vol. 38, 1984; Wong How-Man, "Peoples of China's Far Provinces," *National Geographic* 165 (March 1984), 283–377.

KAZAKH. See **KAZAK.**

KECHIA. See **HAKKA.**

KEILAO. See **GELAO.**

KELAO. See **GELAO.**

KELAOZU. See **GELAO.**

KEREI. The Kereis are a subgroup of the Kazak* people of the Xinjiang Uigur Autonomous Region, Gansu Province, and Qinghai Province in the People's Republic of China.

KERGEZ. See **KIRGIZ.**

KERU. See **GYARUNG.**

KEZEI. The Kezeis are a subgroup of the Kazak* people of the Xinjiang Uigur Autonomous Region, Gansu Province, and Qinghai Province in the People's Republic of China.

KHA. See **KMHMU.**

KHA CHE. See **KMHMU.**

KHA DOY. See **KMHMU.**

KHA KHO. See **AKHA** and **HANI.**

KHA KO. See **AKHA.**

KHA LAMET. See **LAMET.**

KHA LO. See **GELAO.**

KHA QUY. See **AHU.**

KHAE LISAW. The Khae Lisaws are a subgroup of the Lisu* people of Yunnan Province in the People's Republic of China. Along with other Lisu peoples, most of the Khae Lisaws are concentrated between the Sawleen River and the Mekong River in western Yunnan Province. The Khae Lisaw language is not mutually intelligible with most of the other Lisu tongues, but it is closely related to Akha,* Lahu,* and Yi.* They are more likely to identify themselves as ethnic Khae Lisaws than as Lisus. They employ a social system that revolves around a variety of patrilineal, exogamous clans which exercise great political power. Most Khae Lisaws live at higher elevations, usually in ridgeline villages between 3,500 and 10,000 feet in altitude. Swidden farmers, they raise maize, mountain rice, millet, and barley.

KHAL'MG. See **MONGOL** and **OIRAT.**

KHAM. Kham is one of the three primary dialects of Tibetan.* Calling it a dialect, however, is complicated by the fact that it is only marginally intelligible to speakers of Amdo* and Dbusgtsang,* the other Tibetan dialects. Kham is spoken in the Changdu region of the Tibetan Autonomous Region; the Ganzi Tibetan Autonomous Prefecture in Sichuan Province, the Diqing Tibetan Autonomous Prefecture in Yunnan Province; the Yushu Tibetan Autonomous Prefecture in Qinghai Province, and in the Gannan Tibetan Autonomous Prefecture in Gansu Province. It is divided into six vernaculars: Eastern Kham, Southern Kham, Western Kham, Northern Kham, Jone, and Hbrugchu. All of these regions are located within the national boundaries of the People's Republic of China.

KHAMBU. The Khambus are a subgroup of the Rai* people, who themselves are one of the two subgroups of Kiranti* people of Nepal. See **NEPALESE.**

KHAMPA. The Khampas, who are ethnic Tibetans,* reside in the Kham* region of southeastern Tibet. Khampas have been the most militantly anti-Chinese Tibetans in the country since the Chinese takeover occurred in the 1950s. They fought a guerrilla war against People's Liberation Army troops during the invasion of the early 1950s, and they violently resisted Han*-implemented schemes to collectivize Tibetan agriculture. For a time in the late 1950s, Khampa guerrilla forces controlled a good portion of the Kham countryside. In October 1958, Khampas attacked and killed several thousand Chinese living south of the Brahmaputra River in southeastern Tibet. Ever since then, Khampas have been among the most vociferous advocates of Tibetan independence.

KHAMU. See **KMHMU.**

KHARACHIN. The Kharachin people are a subgroup of the Mongol* people of the People's Republic of China. Their dialect is spoken primarily in the southern section of the Inner Mongolian Autonomous Region (IMAR). Most Kharachins are farmers and herders, who raise barley, wheat, oats, corn, millet, potatoes, buckwheat, sorghum, apples, and a variety of vegetables. Mongols also raise horses, cattle, camels, and goats, although their preferred livestock today is sheep. Approximately 600,000 people in the IMAR speak the Kharachin vernacular.

KHECHKE. See **HEZHEN.**

KHELAO. See **GELAO.**

KHIANGAN. The Khiangans are one of the subgroups of the Mongol* people of the Inner Mongolian Autonomous Region in the People's Republic of China.

KHIK. See **WAKHAN.**

KHI'LAO. See **GELAO.**

KHIRGIZ. See **KIRGIZ.**

KHMER. The Khmer, who are ethnic Cambodians, are primarily Hinayana Buddhists. Khmers living today in the People's Republic of China (PRC) are recent arrivals, refugees from revolutions and wars that have swept through Indochina. In the mid-nineteenth century, France established imperial control over Cambodia, and, along with Laos, Annam, Cochin China, and Tonkin, Cambodia became part of the French union. After the Vietminh defeated France in 1954 at the Battle of Dienbienphu, an international conference convened in Geneva to consider the future of Indochina. Cambodia received its independence.

But during the next forty years, Cambodia became involved in the Indochinese conflict and underwent a tumultuous revolution of its own. Prince Norodom Sihanouk tried to maintain a neutral position between the United States, South Vietnam, North Vietnam, and the Vietcong, but it proved to be an impossible task. In 1970, before the United States invaded Cambodia, the Central Intelligence Agency engineered a coup d'état that deposed Sihanouk in favor of the pro-American military leader Lon Nol. During the next five years, while the United States and South Vietnam battled North Vietnam and the Vietcong, the Lon Nol government fought against the Khmer Rouge, its own Communist insurgency. During the early 1970s, while the United States was reducing its presence in Indochina, the Communists gained power everywhere. In the spring of 1975, South Vietnam, Laos, and Cambodia all fell to Communist insurgents.

The Cambodian elite, particularly those who had supported the Lon Nol government, were in trouble. Their pro-American pro-capitalist history made them vulnerable to ideological reprisals from the Khmer Rouge. Little did they know just how vulnerable they were. Pol Pot, the leader of the Khmer Rouge, had ideological purification in mind, and he implemented what he called Year Zero—the destruction of the Cambodian intelligentsia, the depopulation of the cities, and the ideological retraining of an entire people. During the next decade, Cambodia was transformed into a "killing field" as Pol Pot's ideological crusade turned into genocide. More than two million ethnic Khmers died at the hands of the Khmer Rouge.

Refugee Khmers fled Cambodia, just as hundreds of thousands of Vietnamese fled Indochina. Thousands of them ended up in Hong Kong during the late 1970s and early 1980s. The Hong Kong government worked diligently to resettle them. Even during the 1980s, when it had become obvious that most Vietnamese refugees reaching Hong Kong were fleeing economic privation, not political persecution, the Khmer remained political refugees. Most Khmer refugees were resettled in the United States, Canada, France, and Great Britain, but several thousand remained in Hong Kong. When Hong Kong reverted to the People's Republic of China on July 1, 1997, several hundred Khmers still lived there.

SUGGESTED READINGS: Nigel Cameron, *Hong Kong, The Cultured Pearl*, 1978; François Ponchaud, *Cambodia: Year Zero*, 1978; William Shawcross, *The Quality of Mercy: Cambodia, Holocaust, and the Modern Conscience*, 1984, and *Sideshow: Kissinger, Nixon, and the Destruction of Cambodia*, 1979.

KHMU. See KMHMU.

KHO. The Kho people are the most important ethnic group in the Chitral region of northern Pakistan. Their current population is approximately 300,000 people, most of whom live in the mountain valleys between the Hindu Kush and the Hindu Raj ranges in the North-West Frontier Province. Historically, the surrounding mountain ranges and the border with Afghanistan have kept the Chitral region quite isolated geographically. They are an Indo-Aryan people who are Muslims, primarily Sunnis of the Hanafi tradition. In the Upper Chitral region, most Kho are Ismaili Muslims, whom the Hanafi Sunnis consider to be an inferior people.

There have not been any Kho living in China until quite recently. Infrastructural improvements in northern Pakistan in the 1970s, 1980s, and 1990s enhanced transportation and communications networks with neighboring regions of Pakistan, China, India, and Afghanistan. The recent completion of the Karakoram Highway through the Karakoram mountains, which linked the Chinese and Pakistani economies, has increased the traffic between them. A few Kho merchants and truck drivers make their way regularly into China.

SUGGESTED READINGS: Fredrik Barth, *Indus and Swat Kohistan: An Ethnographic Survey*, 1956; Richard F. Strand, ''Kho,'' in Richard V. Weekes, ed., *Muslim Peoples*, 1984.

KHO KO. See **AKHA.**

KHO' MU. See **KMHMU.**

KHONGODOR. The Khongodors are a subgroup of the Buryats,* a Mongol* people of Siberian Russia and the Inner Mongolian Autonomous Region in the People's Republic of China.

KHORA. The Khoras are a subgroup of the Buryats,* a Mongol* people of Siberian Russia and the Inner Mongolian Autonomous Region in the People's Republic of China.

KHORCHIN. The Khorchin people, who are also known as the Jirems, are a subgroup of the Mongol* people of the People's Republic of China. Their dialect is spoken primarily in the southeastern section of the Inner Mongolian Autonomous Region. Most Khorchins are farmers and herders, who raise barley, wheat, oats, corn, millet, potatoes, buckwheat, sorghum, apples, and a variety of vegetables. They also raise horses, cattle, camels, and goats, although their preferred livestock today is sheep.

KHOTON. There may be several hundred Khotan people still living in the People's Republic of China (PRC), and there certainly is a remnant of people there who are at least aware of their Khotan ancestry. The Khotons are a Muslim people whose original homeland was in Mongolia, north and east of the Gobi Desert. They are of Turkic ethnic heritage with close connections to the Kazaks* and the Kirgiz.* They were a nomadic people whose economy revolved around their sheep herds. The Khotons were divided into two nomadic camps which, for all intents and purposes, constituted subgroups of their own. They were known as the Bayan Mandal people and the Altan Degeli camp. Since the Bayan Mandal people usually worked the grasslands to the north and west, any surviving Khotons in the PRC are probably descendents of the the Altan Degeli group. They most likely reside in Inner Mongola, across the border from the Sak Batar region of Mongolia.

SUGGESTED READINGS: Larry W. Moses, "Khoton," in Richard V. Weekes, ed., *Muslim Peoples*, 1984, and "The Khotons: Muslims of Mongolia," *Mongolia Society Bulletin* 6 (Spring 1967), 11–14.

KHU XUNG. See **LAHU.**

KHUCONG. See **LAHU.**

KHURUKUT. The Khurukuts are one of the four primary clans of the Burusho* people of the Hunzu Valley in Pakistan.

K'IANG. See **QIANG.**

KIM MIEN. See **YAO.**

KIM MUN YAO. The Kim Mun Yaos are currently considered by the People's Republic of China to be a subgroup of the Yao* people, who live in Guangxi, Hunan, Guangdong, Jiangxi, Guizhou, and Yunnan provinces. The problem with classifying Kim Mun Yaos with the other so-called Yao peoples is language. The government argues that there are four subgroups of the Yao people—Byau Min Yao,* Kim Mun Yao,* Mien Yao,* and Yao Min*—but these subgroups are not really dialects. Although all four are classified in the Miao-Yao linguistic family, they are not mutually intelligible. If the language spoken by Kim Mun Yao is not comprehensible to the other Yao subgroups, then the argument for separate and official ethnic status is a compelling one.

Demographers estimate that there are more than 450,000 Kim Mun Yao people. Their economies vary according to ecological setting, with agriculture, hunting, and foraging occupying the Kim Mun Yao. Their social system is based on patrilineal descent, and young people are expected to marry endogamously. Elders frown on an individual who marries somebody from another Yao group. That stigma against exogamous marriage to any other people, including other Yaos, is more evidence that Kim Mun Yaos constitute a distinct ethnic entity.

KIMMUN. See **KIM MUN YAO.**

KIORR. See **TIOL.**

KIRANTI. The Kirantis are one of the ethnic groups living today in Nepal and Bhutan. They are broken down into two primary subgroups: the Khambus and the Yakhus. At any given moment, several hundred Kirantis can be found living today in Tibet, where they work the commercial trade routes with Bhutan, Sikkim, and Nepal. See **BHUTANESE.**

KIRGIZ. The Kirgiz—also variously spelled Kyrgyz, Khirghiz, Qyrqyz, and Khirgiz—are a Central Asian, Turkic-speaking people whose homeland is the Republic of Kirgizstan. The country is bordered by Kazakstan to the north and Tajikistan and Uzbekistan to the south. The population of the Kirgiz Republic today exceeds 2.7 million people. Another 130,000 ethnic Kirgiz can be found in the Namangan, Andidzhan, and Fergana districts of Uzbekistan; in the Gorno-Badakhshan, Garm, and Pamir regions of Tajikistan; and in the neighboring regions of Kazakhstan.

The Kirgiz are also one of the officially recognized minority nationalities of the People's Republic of China (PRC). The 1990 national census counted 141,549 Kirgiz people in China, so it is reasonable to estimate a contemporary Kirgiz population of more than 150,000. Chinese Kirgiz represent only 7 percent of the total Kirgiz population in the world. The PRC Kirgiz are concentrated in the Xinjiang Uigur Autonomous Region, particularly in the southwest on the southern slopes of the Tian Shan mountains, especially in the Kizilsu Kirgiz Autonomous Prefecture. Some live in and around the cities of Khotan, Kashgar, and Aksu. They are a nomadic people who work herds of sheep and cattle about the Pamir highlands and the Tian Shan and Kunlun mountains. A small contingent of Kirgiz people also live in Heilongjiang Province.

Kirgiz people speak a language, Turkish in origin, that is part of the larger Altaic* family. Kirgiz possesses two major dialects, Northern Kirgiz and Southern Kirgiz, which correspond to the historical and cultural differences between the northern and southern Kirgiz. For example, the southern dialect contains a major fund of loan words from Persian, due to Iran's and Tajikistan's geographical proximity to Kirgizstan. Among the PRC Kirgiz, the two dialects are further subdivided into a number of distinct vernaculars that correspond to different regions of Kirgizia. The northern dialect, spoken in the region north of the Kizilsu River, is divided into Heiziwei, Ulukqiat, and Toyun, which are spoken in Uqia County; Kalajun and Tugaimait, which are spoken in Akqi County; Jiamansu, which is spoken in Uqturpan County; Baozitong, which is spoken in Wensu County; Kuoketielik, which is spoken in Tekes County; and Shato, which is spoken in Monggolkure County. Southern Kirgiz is divided into the following vernaculars: Posdantielik, in Uqia County; and Kalakqik, Zhulukbash, Subash, Bulongkol, Kiziltao, and Qiarleng in Atko, Yengishar, and Guma counties.

The Kirgiz people are Muslims who began to convert to Islam during the late seventeenth century when they found themselves in a bloody conflict with the Oirats.* The Hanafi school of Sunni Islam now absorbs their religious energies, and they are also devoted followers of several Sufi orders. Large numbers of Kirgiz fled into what is today the Xinjiang Uigur Autonomous Region of China. After the Manchus* defeated the Oirats in 1758, many Kirgiz became Chinese subjects, although their nomadic pastoral economy gave them almost complete independence.

During the eighteenth and nineteenth centuries, the Kirgiz people of Central

Asia had to deal with the expanding Russian empire, and battles with ethnic Russians* sharpened Kirgiz ethnic identity. In fact, their resistance to Russian authority often took the form of a Muslim holy war. It was not until the 1860s that Russia pacified the region. In 1867 Russia established the government of Turkestan and followed that up in 1882 with the Government of the Steppes. Both political entities were committed to the destruction of Kirgiz identity. Incoming Russian, Ukrainian, and German immigrants seized large portions of Kirgiz land.

Kirgiz frustration erupted into open rebellion during World War I. The Russian government began forcibly conscripting Kirgiz men into the army, and a virtual civil war developed in Kirgizia. Thousands of Russian colonists and Kirgiz were killed, and more than 150,000 nomads abandoned their possessions and fled into neighboring China. After the Bolshevik Revolution, the immigration of non-Kirgiz into the region increased. In 1919 the Kirgiz became part of the newly created Turkestan Autonomous Soviet Socialist Republic, and Soviet officials ruthlessly suppressed any manifestation of Kirgiz nationalism.

Early in the 1920s, Soviet officials decided to implement a more conciliatory stance toward Kirgizia. Some lands taken by ethnic Russians and Ukrainians were returned to Kirgiz pastoralists, and in 1926 the government established an autonomous Kirgiz *oblast*, or province, in Turkestan. A decade later, the Soviet Union declared the establishment of the Kirgiz Autonomous Soviet Socialist Republic, and leading Kirgiz politicians were given important positions in the new government.

By that time, however, the Kirgiz had become deeply alienated again. Joseph Stalin's brutal attempt to collectivize Kirgiz economic activities, which revolved around the herding of cattle, sheep, and horses, and to terminate their nomadic wanderings precipitated widespread resistance. The Kirgiz slaughtered their livestock and fled toward the Chinese border rather than submit. Then, during Stalin's political purges of the late 1920s and 1930s, leading Kirgiz political and intellectual leaders were murdered. The purges drove tens of thousands more of frightened Kirgiz across the border into Xinjiang.

The triumph of Mao Zedong and the Chinese Communist party in 1949 brought a similar series of pressures to bear on Kirgiz society in the People's Republic of China. In 1961, as part of the PRC's Great Leap Forward, mandatory collectivization of Kirgiz livestock and breeding programs was imposed. The Kirgiz violently resisted collectivization, and troops from the People's Liberation Army deployed to far western Xinjiang to maintain order. Tens of thousands of Kirgiz fled with their herds across the Soviet border into the Kirgiz Soviet Socialist Republic, where they hoped to preserve their traditional pastoral lifestyle, since Soviet ideologues had recently relaxed some of the more heavy-handed of Stalin's collectivization schemes.

Events in the Soviet Union early in the 1990s stimulated Kirgiz nationalism. When the Soviet Union began to disintegrate late in the 1980s, Kirgiz nationalism surfaced again. In 1991, when the Soviet Union collapsed, Kirgizstan became an independent nation. Chinese Communist party officials viewed the breakup of the Soviet Union with alarm. The rise of Islamic fundamentalism among Arabs, Iranians, and Afghans had already created a new pan-Islamic spirit in Central Asia. Chinese Muslims—particularly Uzbeks,* Uigurs,* Kazaks,* and Kirgiz—felt a kinship with their ethnic compatriots in the Soviet Union, and when the Soviet Union collapsed and independence came to Uzbekistan, Kazakstan, and Kirgizstan, secessionist movements emerged in the People's Republic of China. Many Muslims still resented the persecution of the Cultural Revolution years and believed that the central government in Beijing still retained its discriminatory attitudes toward Islam. Muslims—Kazaks, Tatars,* Uzbeks, and Uigurs—also resented government development policies, which invested huge amounts of capital in order to relocate millions of Han* Chinese to Xinjiang. As far as the Muslims were concerned, the arrival of so many Han settlers was just another government attempt to assimilate them. Some Kirgiz leaders looked to Askar Akayev, the anticommunist president of Kirgizstan, for leadership and talked of Kirgiz reunification, a policy Chinese Communist party leaders found absolutely unacceptable.

A number of terrorist bombings against CCP buildings and buses in Xinjiang, as well as against people of Han descent, in the 1990s were blamed on Muslim secessionists, and the government sent in tens of thousands of troops to maintain order and suppress expressions of ethnic nationalism and secessionism. Laws were also passed prohibiting Xinjiang residents from talking with foreigners. Foreign journalists were expelled. At the same time, however, border tensions relaxed somewhat, and Kirgiz in Kirgizstan and Xinjiang were able to enjoy more contact with one another. Also in recent years, the use of the Arabic script for written Kirgiz has been revived, and Cyrillic is falling into disuse.

Chinese authorities are playing their political hand carefully, because they do not want to antagonize their Muslim minorities and generate Muslim rebellions on their western frontiers. PRC political officials have been quick to respond militarily to any sign of political insurgency among the Kirgiz. They have also recently negotiated diplomatic agreements with Kirgizstan to protect the PRC-Kirgiz border and to make the movement of Kirgiz nationalists back and forth across the border more difficult.

SUGGESTED READINGS: Shirin Akiner, *Islamic Peoples of the Soviet Union*, 1983; Edward Allworth, *Central Asia: A Century of Russian Rule*, 1967; Azamat Altay, "Kirghiziya during the Great Purge," *Central Asian Review* 12 (1964), 97–107; Elizabeth E. Bacon, *Central Asia under Russian Rule*, 1966; Alexander Bennigsen and Chantal Lemercier-Quelquejay, *Islam in the Soviet Union*, 1967; Michael Dillon, *China's Muslims*, 1996; Ned Gillette, "Adventure in Western China," *National Geographic* 159 (February 1981), 174–99; Rick Gore, "Journey to China's Far West," *National Geographic* 157 (March 1980), 292–332; René Grousset, *The Empire of the Steppes: A History of Central Asia*, 1970; Charles W. Hostler, *Turkism and the Soviets*, 1957; "The Kirgiz of the Far West Border," *China Reconstructs* 34 (May 1985), 62; Lawrence Krader, *Peoples of Central Asia*, 1963; Ma Yin, ed., *China's Minority Nationalities*, 1989; *New York Times*, February 28, 1997; Alec Nove and J. A. Newth, *The Soviet*

Middle East: A Communist Model for Development, 1966; Lee Pappas, "Kirgyz," in James S. Olson, ed., *Historical Dictionary of the Russian and Soviet Empires,* 1993; Alexander G. Park, *Bolshevism in Turkestan, 1917–1927,* 1957; Richard Pipes, *The Formation of the Soviet Union: Communism and Nationalism, 1917–1923,* 1980; Michael Rywkin, ed., *Russian Colonial Expansion to 1917,* 1988; Michael Rywkin, *Russia in Central Asia,* 1963; Henry G. Schwarz, *The Minorities of Northern China: A Survey,* 1984; M. Wesley Shoemaker, ed., *Russia, Eurasian States, and Eastern Europe,* 1992; Wayne S. Vucinich, ed., *Russia and Asia: Essays on the Influence of Russia on the Asian Peoples,* 1972; *Washington Post,* February 11, 1997; Geoffrey Wheeler, *The Peoples Soviet Central Asia,* 1966; Wong How-Man, "Peoples of China's Far Provinces," *National Geographic* 165 (March 1984), 283–377; Serge A. Zenkovsky, *Pan-Turkism and Islam in Russia,* 1960.

KIZILTAO. The Kiziltaos are a subgroup of the Kirgiz* people. They speak a Southern Kirgiz dialect and live primarily in Akto, Yengishar, and Guma counties in the Xinjiang Uigur Autonomous Region of the People's Republic of China.

K'LAI. See **LI.**

KLAU. See **GELAO.**

KLO. See **GELAO.**

KMHMU. The Kmhmu are one of the indigenous tribal peoples of southeastern Asia. They can be found today in Laos, Thailand, the People's Republic of China (PRC), the United States, Canada, and France. To their neighbors in Indochina, as well as to many anthropologists, the Kmhmus are also known by other ethnonyms, including Kammu, Khamu, Khmu, Kho' Mu, Kmhmu', Kumhmhu, and Lao Theung. There is also another group of ethnonyms which the Kmhmu people consider to be pejorative slurs: Kha, Kha Che, Kha Doy, and Xa Cau.

Ethnologists consider the Kmhmu to be the indigenous inhabitants of northern Laos. Today, there are more than 400,000 Kmhmus in Laos, most of them concentrated in the north, where they are the largest of the country's minority groups. Originally, the Kmhmus dwelled in the Nam Ou, Nam Tha, and Nam Beng river valleys, particularly where those rivers merged with the Mekong River. Until the thirteenth century, they were the dominant ethnic group in the region of Laos that today includes the city of Luang Prabang. The Lao* people conquered the Kmhmus in the thirteenth century and subjected many of them to feudal serfdom or drove them into remote mountain settlements. Beginning in the eighteenth century, the expansion of Tai*-speaking people into northern Laos displaced the Kmhmus again, and many of them moved into far northern Laos, across the border into China, and into Thailand. Today approximately 30,000 Kmhmus live in Thailand and 2,500 in southern China. The Chinese

Kmhmus are found now in the jungled highlands between the towns of Muong Sing, Laos, and Mengla in far southern Yunnan Province.

During the Indochinese wars of the 1950s, 1960s, and 1970s, most Kmhmus could be counted on to be anti-French and anti-American. Kmhmu people were the leaders of the Pathet Lao, the Laotian nationalist movement which also happened to be communist in its ideology. Military historians and ethnologists now realize that the Kmhmus constituted the bulk of the Pathet Lao military forces between 1945 and 1975. A tiny segment of the Kmhmu people supported the Royal Laotian government, which was pro-American, during the Indochinese war. In 1975, when the Pathet Lao seized control of Laos and U.S. forces were finally driven out of Laos, Cambodia, and Vietnam, a contingent of pro-American Kmhmus fled the country rather than face retaliation and ''reeducation'' by the Communists. Their emigration explains the presence today of about 3,000 Kmhmus in Canada and the United States and approximately 1,000 in France.

Ethnolinguists classify the Kmhmu language as part of the Khmuic group of the northern Mon-Khmer branch of the Austroasiatic language family. The language can be divided into two primary dialect groups: Northern Kmhmu and Southern Kmhmu. Northern Kmhmu is characterized by a distinct difference between voiced and voiceless initials; Southern Kmhmu distinguishes between a low tone and a high tone. Those two groups are further divided into several dozen dialects, all of which are mutually intelligible. The Chinese Kmhmus speak one of the northern dialects.

The traditional Kmhmu village is located in tropical rain forests at lower elevations on mountain ridges. Their villages typically have contained from fifteen to one hundred households, with anywhere from 150 to 1,200 people. They dwell in bamboo and wooden houses built on stilts, which permit the people to remain dry during the monsoon rainy season. Most Kmhmu farmers raise dry rice on mountain slopes using slash-and-burn agricultural techniques. Fields are usually planted for one or two years and then left fallow for as long as ten years. They plant seeds using planting sticks, not plows, and their major crops in addition to dry rice are maize, legumes, chilies, taro, and yams. To boost their sources of protein, most Kmhmu villages raise pigs, chickens, ducks, goats, and water buffalo. During lean periods when food supplies are diminished and the harvest is still weeks or months away, Kmhmu people revert to ancient hunting and foraging activities, collecting wild plants, berries, and small game animals.

In terms of their political organization, the Kmhmu people tend to be subservient today to their Tai, Lao, and Han* Chinese neighbors. Only in completely Kmhmu communities, which are rare because the Kmhmu tend to live in close proximity with other ethnic groups, can they enjoy the benefits of an ethnic Kmhmu village head. Because of their loyalty to the Pathet Lao during the Indochinese wars, however, more acculturated Kmhmus can be found occupying every level of the contemporary Laotian military and civil service.

Religious beliefs today reflect the complex history of the Kmhmu people. In more isolated settlements, the indigenous, animistic faith of the Kmhmu people remains alive and well. It is a religion based on beliefs in a great variety of ghost spirits, known in Kmhmu as *hrooy*. Those spirits include the souls of dead ancestors, house spirits, village spirits, rice spirits, and spirits associated with animals, plants, and environmental forces. Each living person possesses a soul of his or her own, known as *hrmaal*. In areas where the Kmhmus have had more contact with European imperial forces, an eclectic variety of Christian doctrines have been superimposed on the indigenous faith. Protestant missionaries made their way into Kmhmu communities in Thailand, Laos, and China beginning in the late nineteenth century, and Roman Catholic missionaries worked among the Kmhmu during the late 1940s and 1950s. In addition, a veneer of Buddhism has been accepted by most Kmhmu people for the past century.

SUGGESTED READINGS: Kristina Lindell, Hakan Lundstrom, Jan-Olof Svantesson, and Damrong Tayanin, *The Kammu Year: Its Lore and Music*, 1982; Kristina Lindell, Jan-Ojvind Swahn, and Damrong Tayanin, *Folk Tales from Kammu*, 4 vols., 1977–1989; Frank Proschan, "Kmhmu," in Paul V. Hockings, ed., *Encyclopedia of World Cultures*, vol. 6, *East and Southeast Asia*, 1991, and "Kmhmu Verbal Art in America: The Poetics of Kmhmu Verse," Ph.D. diss., University of Texas at Austin, 1989; Dang Nghiem Van, "The Khmu in Vietnam," *Vietnamese Studies* 36 (1973), 57–64.

KMHMU'. See **KMHMU.**

KOERH-K'OSSU. See **KIRGIZ.**

KOK NUR. Kok Nur is one of the vernaculars of the Oirat* language of the People's Republic of China.

KONDOMA. See **SHOR.**

KONKEU. The Konkeus are a small ethnic group living today in the People's Republic of China (PRC), especially in far southern Yunnan Province, and across the border in Myanmar (Burma). They are closely related linguistically and culturally to the K'alas,* and many Chinese anthropologists classify them as a Wa* subgroup. The PRC has not extended them recognition as an official minority nationality, although some Konkeu leaders have tried to make a case for separate status. Difficulties arise with any attempt to classify Konkeus as a Wa subgroup because their languages, although Mon-Khmer* in their linguistic classification, are mutually unintelligible. Most Konkeus live today in the Kengtung State of Myanmar, but several thousand can also be found across the border in Yunnan Province of the PRC. Most Konkeus live in mountain villages that contain anywhere from one hundred to four hundred families. They are a farming people who raise rice, millet, maize, and tubers.

SUGGESTED READINGS: Fang Dong, "A Long Road upward for the Wa Nationality,"

China Reconstructs 31 (March 1982), 10–17; Robert Parkin, *A Guide to Austroasiatic Speakers and Their Languages*, 1991; Peng Jianqun, "Bao Hongzhong, A Wa Headman," *China Today* 44 (July 1995), 56–58; Wang Aihe, "Wa," in Paul V. Hockings, ed., *The Encyclopedia of World Cultures*, vol. 6, *East and Southeast Asia*, 1991; Wen Yiqun, "Women of the Highlands," *China Today* 44 (May 1995), 33–35.

KOPU. See **GELAO.**

KORCHIN. The Korchin people, who are ethnic Mongols,* live in southeastern Mongolia and in the northeastern reaches of the Inner Mongolian Autonomous Region in the People's Republic of China. Korchin, a dialect of Mongolian, is divided into a number of vernaculars, including Subhaatar, East Govi, and South Govi.

KOREAN. In the 1990 national census of the People's Republic of China (PRC), demographers placed the Korean ethnic population at 1,920,597. No doubt today the Korean population in China exceeds two million people. They are divided into two groups. By far the smaller group of Koreans can be found in the Xinjiang Uigur Autonomous Region of Central Asia. At least half a million Koreans live in the former Soviet Union, especially in the new republics of Uzbekistan, Kazakstan, and Kirgizstan. Some Koreans can also be found across the border in Chinese Central Asia, where they are often in a state of advanced assimilation with Uzbeks,* Kazaks,* and Kirgiz.* The bulk of the Chinese Koreans, however, are concentrated in northeastern China; 63 percent of them live in five counties of Jilin Province, 27 percent in Heilongjiang Province, and 10 percent in Liaoning Province. The five counties constitute the Yanbian Korean Autonomous Prefecture, which was established in 1952. The largest group of Central Asian Koreans are located in Uzbekistan.

The Korean presence in the People's Republic of China today is also a consequence of their traditional skills as cold weather wet-rice farmers. Although several thousand Koreans arrived in northeastern China in the seventeenth century, the great migration did not take place until two centuries later. For centuries, the Chinese emperors had prohibited private citizens from settling in what is today Jilin Province. They had declared the region a hunting preserve for the imperial elite. But in 1860, Han* immigrants were allowed to settle there, and in 1869, when a major famine hit Korea in 1869, substantial numbers of Koreans entered China. During the late nineteenth and early twentieth centuries, when Japan tightened its grip on Korea, virtually transforming the country into a Japanese colony, tens of thousands of Koreans migrated into northeastern China. The first Korean public schools were already operating in China by 1901.

The number of frost-free days each year in Jilin Province varies from 110 to 150, and the Korean immigrants settled in the swampy stretches of the Yalu and Tumen river watersheds and began wet-rice cultivation, an art they had developed long ago in Korea. The Koreans constructed elaborate irrigation canals and introduced paddy-rice farming in Jilin, Heilongjiang, and Liaoning provinces. In doing so, they became some of the most productive farmers in the entire country.

The number of Koreans in the PRC also increased in 1950. At the end of World War II, Soviet troops had occupied North Korea, and a Communist government took control there, dividing Korea at the 38th parallel into two countries. In 1950, when the Korean war erupted, tens of thousands of northern Koreans migrated across the Yalu and Tumen rivers into the PRC. The war had, for the most part, been of Soviet–North Korean design, with China hardly involved at all in its planning. But as United Nations forces crossed the 38th parallel into North Korea in the summer of 1950, the People's Republic of China found itself badly threatened. North of the Yalu and Tumen rivers, in the region known as Manchuria, sat the vast majority of China's industrial resources. Worried that United Nations forces in general and United States troops in particular might decide to invade Manchuria themselves and seize China's industrial heartland, Chinese Communist officials decided to enter the war. More than 300,000 Chinese troops invaded North Korea and then took the war to South Korea. An agreement ending the war did not materialize until 1953. By that time, the Chinese–North Korean border was heavily fortified, and ethnic Koreans settled in Jilin, Heilongjiang, and Laoning provinces had become permanent Chinese residents.

SUGGESTED READINGS: R. Sh. Dzharyglasinova, "The Koreans in Central Asia," *Central Asian Review* 15 (1967), 212–18; William S. Ellis, "The Aral: A Soviet Sea Lies Dying," *National Geographic* 177 (1990), 73–92; Huang Yubox, "Home of Koreans in China," *China Reconstructs* 32 (May 1983), 66–69; Walter Kolarz, *The People of the Soviet Far East*, 1965; Ross Marlay, "Korean," in James S. Olson, ed., *Historical Dictionary of the Russian and Soviet Empires*, 1993; Bohdan Nahaylo and Victor Swoboda, *Soviet Disunion: A History of the Nationalities Problem in the U.S.S.R.*, 1989; Alexsandr M. Nekrich, *The Punished Peoples: The Deportation and Fate of Soviet Minorities at the End of the Second World War*, 1978; *New York Times*, February 2, 1992; Harry G. Schwarz, *The Minorities of Northern China: A Survey*, 1984; Dae-Sook Suh, ed., *Koreans in the Soviet Union*, 1987.

KORLA. Korla is one of the vernacular subgroups of the Uigur* language, spoken in Xinjiang Uigur Autonomous Region of the People's Republic of China. Most speakers of Korla live in or around the oasis town of Kuqa.

KOSUNG. See LAHU.

KU T'OU. See YI.

KU TOUS. The Ku Tous are an ethnic group in the People's Republic of China (PRC), although the central government has not yet extended to them formal recognition as a minority nationality. Official PRC publications classify them as a Yi* subgroup, and, indeed, they speak a Yi language. But Ku Tous is not mutually intelligible with the vast majority of other Yi languages, and the Ku Tous give themselves a distinct, separate identity. They will acknowledge a certain cultural affinity with the Yi, but they nevertheless insist that they are a separate people. Most Ku Tous live today in Yunnan Province.

The traditional Ku Tous economy is primarily agricultural. Ku Tous farmers at lower altitudes cultivate maize, potatoes, buckwheat, and oats, and raise cattle, sheep, goats, and horses in the highlands. Poorer Ku Tous families still engage in foraging activities to supplement their diet. The villages are quite small, more like hamlets, and their homes are constructed of wood and dirt. Their religious beliefs remain an eclectic mix of Daoism, Buddhism, animism, and shamanism; a few thousand Ku Tous today practice Christianity.

KUCONG. See **LAHU.**

KUMANDIN. The Kumandins are one of the primary subgroups of the Altai,* a minority ethnic group living today in far northern Xinjiang Uigur Autonomous Region in the People's Republic of China.

KUMHMHU. See **KMHMU.**

KUNGNUNG. See **MAONAN.**

KUNLOI. See **DE'ANG.**

KUOKETIELIK. The Kuoketieliks, a subgroup of the Kirgiz* people, speak a Northern Kirgiz dialect and live primarily in Tekes County in the Xinjiang Uigur Autonomous Region of the People's Republic of China.

KUQA. Kuqa, one of the vernacular subgroups of the Uigur* language, is spoken in the Xinjiang Uigur Autonomous Region of the People's Republic of China. Most speakers of Kuqa live in or around the oasis town of Kuqa.

KUT WA. See **TAME WA** and **WA.**

KUTSUNG. See **HANI.**

KUZNET TATAR. See **SHOR.**

KWI. See **LAHU.**

KYRGHYZ. See **KIRGIZ.**

KYRGYZ. See **KIRGIZ.**

L

LA. The La people are a tiny ethnic group living today in far northern Myanmar (Burma); a handful of La people probably live across the border in the southern reaches of Yunnan Province of the People's Republic of China. The total La population numbers no more than 3,000 people, and the vast majority of them are on the Myanmar side of the Sino-Burmese frontier. They speak a Mon-Khmer* language in the Austroasiatic linguistic family. Some ethnolinguists have tried to classify the La people as a subgroup of the Wa,* but their languages, though related, are not mutually intelligible. They are primarily slash-and-burn agriculturalists who raise a variety of crops, including maize, millet, rice, tubers, goats, pigs, and chickens. Their religion is a syncretic mix of Buddhism and their indigenous animistic faith.

SUGGESTED READINGS: Robert Parkin, *A Guide to Austroasiatic Speakers and Their Languages*, 1991; Wang Aihe, "Wa," in Paul V. Hockings, ed., *The Encyclopedia of World Cultures*, vol. 6, *East and Southeast Asia*, 1991; Wen Yiqun, "Women of the Highlands," *China Today* 44 (May 1995), 33–35.

LA SAM. See **DAI.**

LACHI. See **LASHI.**

LA-ENG. See **DE'ANG.**

LAFUFA. The Lafufas are one of the most prominent clans of the Lisu* people of the People's Republic of China.

LAHO. See **LAHU.**

LAHO ALEH. Laho Aleh is a subdialect of Shehleh, a dialect of the Black Lahu* language of the People's Republic of China.

LAHOSHI. Lahoshi is one of the dialects of the Yellow Lahu* language of the People's Republic of China.

LAHU. The Lahu, sometimes known as Kucongs, are an Asian ethnic group who can today be found in the southwest corner of Yunnan Province in the People's Republic of China (PRC), the Shan State in Myanmar (Burma), northwestern Laos, northern Thailand, and northwestern Vietnam. Demographers estimate their contemporary population at approximately 650,000 people, with the largest contingent in China, where perhaps as many as 420,000 of them reside. There are about 150,000 Lahu in Myanmar, 10,000 in Laos, 65,000 in Thailand, and 5,000 in Vietnam. Their language is closely related to that of the Lisu* people, and together they constitute part of the central Loloish branch of the Lolo-Burmese subgroup of the Tibeto-Burman* language family. There is no written language in use by the Lahu people, although Protestant and Roman Catholic missionaries, as well as the Chinese government, have developed scripts.

In the People's Republic of China, the Lahu language is divided into two major languages and a variety of dialects and subdialects. Those dialects and subdialects often cross national boundaries into Thailand, Myanmar, Vietnam, and Laos. Approximately two-thirds of all Lahus speak the Black Lahu dialect, which is sometimes referred to as Muhsur. Black Lahu possesses three major dialects. The Lahuna dialect includes, in China, the Meuneu and Panai subdialects. Divergent Lahu,* or the Nu dialect, has the Kaishin and Namhpehn subdialects. The Shehleh dialect in China has one subdialect: Laho Aleh. The other Lahu language is known as Yellow Lahu. One of its major dialects is Lahu, and Lahu has one subdialect of its own that is spoken in China: Bankeo. Lahoshi is another Yellow Lahu dialect, and its two dialects are Banlan and Nankeo.

Because they range so widely over the region and reside in five different nations, a number of names have been used to identify the Lahus. The most common ethnonyms are Co Sung, Co Xung, Guozhou, Kha Quy, Khu Xung, Kucong (Kosung), Kwi, Laho, Lahuna, Lahupu, Lahuxi, Lohei (considered a pejorative slur by the Lahus), and Mussur. The Lahus can be divided into a variety of subgroups based upon environmental and economic adaptation, dialect, and culture. The two most fundamental divisions are the Lahu Na (Black Lahu) and the Lahu Shi (Yellow Lahu), which divide the Lahu people in Yunnan. The Lahu Hpus (White Lahus) are a smaller subgroup in Yunnan, as are the Lahu Sheh Leh. Two other Yunnanese subdivisions of the Lahus are the Guozhou (Black Kucong and Lahu Ni) and the Lahu Shi (Yellow Kucong). The Lahu people in Myanmar, as well as small numbers of Chinese Lahu, are known as the Mussur, Mussur Kwi, or simply Kwi. Other Myanmar Lahus are known as Lahu Nyi, or Red Lahus.

Anthropologists and historians consider the Lahus to be descendents of the ancient Qiang* people of the Qinghai-Tibetan plateau. Between the third and fifth centuries, they began a southern migration into the Dali region of Yunnan, where they became known as the Kun or Kunming people. During the tenth century, the Lahu migration began anew, once again in a southern direction, and they then split into two groups. The Lahu Na went to the west, while the Lahu Shi and Lahu Nha traveled east. For centuries they found themselves under the control of Tai* overlords, who were gradually replaced by Han* administrators during the Ming and Qing dynasties. From the eighteenth through the early twentieth centuries, the Lahus chafed under Han control, but Chinese military officials always managed to suppress any Lahu rebellions.

Most Lahus acquiesced in Chinese domination, but others fled south, where they became the nucleus of the Lahu communities in Thailand, Laos, and Vietnam. Today, the farther northeast one travels through Lahu country, the more sinicized the people have become. Naturally, to the southwest, it is more common to find Lahu people adhering to their own indigenous traditions.

Today, the Lahus of Yunnan reside in villages containing between 200 and 1,000 people. To the southwest and into Myanmar, northern Thailand, and northwest Laos, Lahu villages are much smaller. Most Lahu villages are situated in mountainous areas, above the Tai, Wa,* and Akha* peoples who occupy the valleys and foothills. Lahu culture is a mountain culture. They dwell in earthen homes topped by thatch or wood plank roofs.

In the sinicized areas of Lahu country, particularly in Yunnan Province, most Lahus are wet-rice farmers who employ irrigation systems. Rice provides the staple of their diet. They also engage in fruit tree siviculture and raise tea and vegetables. But as one moves southwest across the region of the Yunnanese Lahus, the economy changes, reverting to more primitive swidden agricultural techniques. There they raise dry rice for themselves, corn for their pigs, and chilies, which they use as a cash crop and to spice up all of their meals. Pigs, cattle, and water buffalo are also common in the Lahu economy. Even the Lahu still practicing swidden agriculture are familiar with the use of money, trade, and the need to exploit lowland markets.

Among the mountain peoples of the region, the Lahu are known for their fierce sense of egalitarianism. Status in the community tends to be based on age rather than on gender, wealth, or fertility. Individual households are highly autonomous; only the weakest patrilineages unite various households. Village headmen must work to achieve consensus to govern effectively. Those headmen often form alliances with lowland Tai leaders, seeking formal recognition from them, in return for which they supply cash, labor, and allegiance in what is almost a feudal relationship.

Lahu religion, which is extraordinarily complex owing to the forces of acculturation and assimilation, is a syncretic mix of their original animist faith, Protestant doctrine and Catholic rituals received from late nineteenth- and early twentieth-century missionaries, Mahayana Buddhist ideas from the Han Chinese,

Theravada Buddhism from their Tai neighbors, and even traces of Marxist ideology from the post-1949 Chinese Communists. Most Lahus, however, remain faithful to the animistic notions of the past. They believe in a world of capricious spirits known as *ne*, who must be appeased through the actions of shamans known as the *maw-pa*. They also believe in a powerful deity known as G'ui-sha, or "Sky Ghost," which Christian Lahus accept as the supreme deity. In Protestant Lahu communities, pastors have replaced the *maw-pas*, as have priests in Roman Catholic Lahu villages.

SUGGESTED READINGS: David Bradley, *Lahu Dialects*, 1979; Lin Zhenyu, "Dramatic Changes for the Kucongs," *China Reconstructs* 30 (July 1981), 68–69, 72, and "Transformations of Buddhism in the Religious Ideas and Practices of a Non-Buddhist Hill People: The Lahu Nyi of the Northern Thai Uplands," *Contributions to Southeast Asian Ethnography* 5 (1986); Anthony Walker, "Lahu," in Paul V. Hockings, ed., *Encyclopedia of World Cultures*, vol. 6, *East and Southeast Asia*, 1991, and "The Divisions of the Lahu Peoples," *Journal of the Siam Society* 62 (1974), 72–82; Xu Yongan and Li Chuang, "The Lahu People of Yunnan," *China Reconstructs* 30 (May 1981), 33–39.

LAHU HPU. The Lahu Hpus, who are also known as the White Lahu, are one of the primary subdivisions of the Lahu* people of Yunnan Province in southwestern China.

LAHU NA. The Lahu Na, who are also known as the Black Lahu, are one of the primary subdivisions of the Lahu* people of Yunnan Province in southwestern China.

LAHU NI. See **LAHU.**

LAHU NYI. See **LAHU.**

LAHU SHE LEH. The Lahu She Neh are one of the primary subdivisions of the Lahu* people of Yunnan Province in southwestern China.

LAHU SHEH. See **LAHU.**

LAHU SHEH LEH. See **LAHU.**

LAHU SHI. The Lahu Shi, who are also known as the Yellow Lahu and Yellow Kucong, are one of the primary subdivisions of the Lahu* people of Yunnan Province in southwestern China.

LAHUL. The Lahul (Lahoul) people speak a dialect of Kham,* one of the two major languages of Tibet. Lahul speakers can be found in the Nga-Ri region of far western Tibet and across the border in Jammu and Kashmir. See **TIBETAN** and **WESTERN KHAM.**

LAHUNA. Lahuna is one of the major dialects of the Black Lahu* language in the People's Republic of China. Lahuna includes the Meuneu and Panai subdialects.

LAHUNA. See **LAHU.**

LAHUPU. See **LAHU.**

LAHUXI. See **LAHU.**

LAI. The Lai people are a recently discovered minority nationality in the People's Republic of China (PRC). PRC social scientists are currently conducting ethnographic research into Lai origins, trying to determine how to classify them, and until that research is completed, the process of extending them official recognition will be postponed. The Lai language has not yet been classified. PRC demographers estimate the Lai population at less than 1,000 people, the vast majority of whom live in the Longlin Nationalities Autonomous County in Guangxi. Most Lai people live in highland villages where they raise rice, maize, millet, pigs, poultry, and wheat.
SUGGESTED READING: S. A. Wurm, B. T'sou, D. Bradley, et al., eds., *Language Atlas of China*, 1987.

LAI. See **LI.**

LAKKYA. The Lakkyas (Lakkias) are a subgroup of the Yao* people of the People's Republic of China. The 1990 national census counted 2,134,000 Yao people in China, and given their birthrate, which is above the national average, it is safe to say that the Yao population is approaching 2.4 million people today. More than 1.5 million Yaos live today in Guangxi Province, usually in mountain villages, but another 900,000 Yaos can be found scattered throughout the border regions of surrounding Hunan Province, Guangdong Province, Jiangxi Province, Guizhou Province, and Yunnan Province. They are particularly concentrated demographically in the Guangxi Zhuang Autonomous Region. Lakkyas constitute roughly 1 percent of the total Yao population, which gives them a population of from 20,000 to 25,000 people. Most of them live in the Jinxiu Yao Autonomous County of the Guangxi Zhuang Autonomous Region and across the border in Pingnan County.

For linguistic reasons, it is probably a mistake to classify the Lakkyas as a subgroup of the Yao people. It is mutually unintelligible with other Miao* and Yao languages in the region, and they view themselves as an ethnically distinct people. Most contemporary linguists are classifying Lakkya as an independent language within the Kam-Sui family.

For more than a thousand years, Lakkyas have worked as settled agriculturalists. Today, a small minority remain loyal to swidden, slash-and-burn techniques, but most of them employ modern plowing techniques to produce rice. Where heavily forested regions border Lakkya farmlands, the people continue to hunt actively, often in carefully organized communal groups. Foraging as a significant economic activity no longer exists. The Lakkya social system is based on patrilineal descent, with inheritance passing from father to son. Patrilineal clans are the most important governing institutions in Lakkya society, and residence is patrilocal. Yaos prefer that all marriages be cross-cousin arrangements, with young men marrying their mother's brother's daughter.

SUGGESTED READINGS: Jacques Lemoine and Chiao Chien, eds., *The Yao of South China: Recent International Studies*, 1991; Ma Yin, ed., *China's Minority Nationalities*, 1989; S. Robert Ramsey, *The Languages of China*, 1987; S. A. Wurm, B. T'sou, D. Bradley, et al., eds., *Language Atlas of China*, 1987; Paul V. Hockings, "Yao," in Paul V. Hockings, ed., *The Encyclopedia of World Cultures*, vol. 6, *East and Southeast Asia*, 1991.

LAKU. See **LAHU.**

LALANG. See **JINGPO.**

LAMET. The Lamet are one of the indigenous tribal peoples of southeastern Asia. They can be found today in far northwestern Laos as well as across the border in far southern Yunnan Province of the People's Republic of China. Closely related to the Kmhmu* people, the Lamets are also known as the Kha Lamet and the Le-Met. Their total population today is less than 8,000 people, most of whom reside in Laos. They claim to be the original inhabitants of the region, and most ethnologists agree that they have occupied the area since prehistoric times. Ethnolinguists classify their language with the Mon-Khmer* group, and it has close links to Wa.*

The traditional Lamet village is located in tropical rain forests at lower elevations on mountain ridges. Most Lamet farmers raise dry rice on mountain slopes using slash-and-burn agricultural techniques. Fields are usually planted for one or two years and then left fallow for as long as ten years. When more frequent planting is necessary, soil depletion occurs and the Lamets must relocate their villages. Instead of using plows, they employ planting sticks, and their major crops in addition to dry rice are maize, legumes, chilies, taro, and yams. To boost their sources of protein, most Lamets also raise pigs, chickens, ducks, goats, and water buffalo. During lean periods, when food supplies are diminished and the harvest is still weeks or months away, Lamets revert to ancient hunting and foraging activities, collecting wild plants, berries, and small game animals.

Lamet religious beliefs today reflect their complex history. In more isolated settlements, their original animistic faith still thrives. It revolves around beliefs in a myriad of ghosts and spirits that inhabit the natural world, as well as the spirits of dead ancestors, who can exert influence on the mortal world. In areas where Lamets have had more contact with European imperial forces, an eclectic variety of Christian doctrines have been superimposed on the indigenous faith. Protestant missionaries made their way into Lamet communities late in the late nineteenth century, and Roman Catholic missionaries worked among them during the late 1940s and 1950s. In addition to that, a veneer of Buddhism has been accepted by most Lamet peoples for the past century.

SUGGESTED READINGS: Gerald C. Hickey, "Lamet," in Frank M. LeBar, Gerald C. Hickey, and John Musgrave, eds., *Ethnic Groups of Mainland Southeast Asia*, 1964; Paul V. Hockings, "Lamet," in Paul V. Hockings, ed., *Encyclopedia of World Cultures*, vol. 6, *East and Southeast Asia*, 1991; Karl Gustav Izikowitz, *Lamet: Hill Peasants in French Indochina*, 1951.

LAMUT. See **EVENK.**

LAN. The Lans are one of the lineage subgroups of the She* people, who can be found scattered throughout sixty counties in Zhejiang, Fujian, Guangdong, Jiangxi, and Anhui provinces in the People's Republic of China.

LANGSHU. See **JINGPO.**

LANGWO. The Langwos are a subgroup of the Zaiwa* people of Yunnan Province in the People's Republic of China.

LAO. Today several thousand ethnic Lao people live in the People's Republic of China (PRC). The Lao—also known as Lao Loum, Lao Meui, Lao Neua, Lao Phuan, and Lao Yuon—are lowlanders who live in Laos and northeastern Thailand. Two million Laos constitute the largest ethnic group in Laos. They speak a Tai* language and descend from the original Tai-speaking immigrants who migrated to Laos from southern China.

Three groups of Laotians constitute the ethnic Lao population of the PRC. First, there are ethnic Lao merchants and businessmen who work the trade routes between the far northern reaches of Laos and Yunnan Province in southwestern China, exchanging cloth, metal tools, and other manufactured goods for the handicrafts of some of the mountain people in the region.

Second, since the fall of Laos to the Communists in the spring of 1975, China has invited Laotian students to study at Chinese universities, and Laotian military officers are being trained at Chinese military academies. These ethnic Lao do not live permanently in China, but the coming and going of hundreds of soldiers and students each year nevertheless give Laotians a permanent, if tiny, presence in China.

Third, the transfer on July 1, 1997, of Hong Kong from British authority to the sovereignty of the PRC brought several hundred ethnic Laos into the country. During the 1950s, 1960s, and early 1970s, Laos found itself in a bitter civil war. Communist-inspired Pathet Lao guerrillas fought for control against the Laotian government, which moved back and forth from neutralist to pro-Western positions. As the Vietnam War spread throughout Indochina in the early 1970s, North Vietnamese troops came to the assistance of the Pathet Lao. The United States began a gradual withdrawal from Vietnam beginning in 1969, and by 1973 the Americans were all but gone from Indochina. The Pathet Lao then launched a concerted military campaign against their government, and in 1975 they triumphed.

Pro-Western ethnic Laos soon found themselves in difficult political circumstances. Their reputations were tainted by past loyalties to the United States, and they were vulnerable to the ideological fervor of the new Communist government. Tens of thousands of them fled across the border into northeastern Thailand, where large numbers of ethnic Laos lived. Thousands of Laotian refugees found themselves in refugee camps, and from there in the late 1970s and 1980s they found their way to Hong Kong, from which they hoped to be resettled in the West. Some of the Laotian refugees took up permanent residence in Hong Kong, and when the transfer of authority came on July 1, 1997, they once again found themselves under Communist authority.

SUGGESTED READINGS: W. Randall Ireson and Carol J. Ireson, "Laos: Marxism in a Subsistence Rural Economy," *Bulletin of Concerned Asian Scholars* 21 (1989), 59–75; Martin Stuart-Fox, *Laos: Politics, Economy, and Society,* 1987.

LAO HUI HUI. See **HUI.**

LAO KHUEI KHUEI. See **HUI.**

LAO LOUM. See **LAO.**

LAO MEUI. See **LAO.**

LAO NEUA. See **LAO.**

LAO PHUAN. See **LAO.**

LAO THEUNG. See **KMHMU.**

LAO YUAN. See **LAO.**

LASAW. See **LISAW** and **LISU.**

LASHI. The Lashi people are an officially unrecognized minority nationality in the People's Republic of China. They can be found today in western Yunnan Province and across the border in northern Myanmar (Burma). The Lashis are one of the subgroups of the larger Kachin* people of Myanmar, northwest Thailand, and Yunnan Province. They prefer to live in valleys and small plains that are surrounded by mountains. Lashis select their village sites at the foot of a mountain or the edge of a plain, and a typical village consists of several patri-lineally related groups.

Chinese historians first make note of the Lashi during the Tang dynasty more than a thousand years ago. They had originated to the north and to the east in what is today northern Myanmar and had settled in western Yunnan. Because of geographical isolation and indigenous economies, the region of far western Yunnan Province has never had a monoculture. Different ethnic groups live in close proximity to one another, even among one another in many pluralistic villages. Lashis are surrounded by a variety of other ethnic groups in the region, including the Dai,* the Jingpo,* the Han,* the De'ang,* and the Wa.* Because they have adopted so much of the material culture of the surrounding groups, the Lashis are hardly distinguishable any more to outsiders as a distinct ethnic group.

The Lashi language is classified by ethnolinguists as one of the Kachin lan-guages and part of the Tibeto-Burman* cluster in the Sino-Tibetan language family. It remains their primary language, although many Lashis are also bilin-gual in Dai, Chinese,* Jingpo, Wa, and/or De'ang.

Historically, the Lashi economy revolved around subsistence levels of wet-rice agriculture. The Lashi have adapted their planting and harvesting to the prevailing weather patterns, particularly the arrival of the monsoon season. To-bacco, sugarcane, and oil-producing plants generate cash for the Lashi economy. Textile production and silversmithing are also part of the local economy.

Since the Communist victory in 1949, the central government has become increasingly involved in Lashi economic life. State programs to resettle Han people throughout the country to encourage assimilation have brought tens of thousands of immigrants to western Yunnan Province. The newcomers have succeeded in taking control—through outright seizure, legal purchase, or gov-ernment condemnation—of large portions of Lashi land. Instead of working as subsistence farmers on communal land, the Lashis are rapidly becoming skilled workers, employed primarily by Shan businessmen. Since 1956 the Lashis still engaged in agriculture have been forced by law to sell their produce to the central government at a fixed price.

Land tenure has also evolved over the years. Land was once controlled by Dai feudal lords or Achang* chiefs. After the revolution, the landlords lost their land, although the peasant families still had to pay rent to them. A brisk com-merce in land sales took place among peasant households until 1956, when the central government mandated communal/state ownership of the land. They then experienced a steady, long-term decline in production, since peasants could no longer keep the fruits of their labor. In 1982 Chinese officials reversed their policy and redivided the communal land among peasants, a decision that has led to substantial increases in agricultural productivity.

The Lashi social structure is based on a system of patrilineal descent, in which members of a village or several villages trace their ancestry back to a common male. Individuals must marry outside their patrilineal group, and marriages are generally arranged by parents for economic advantage. The fundamental family unit of Lashi society is a patriarchal family that includes two or three generations.

Like other Kachin-speaking groups, the Lashis maintain very eclectic religious beliefs. For many centuries now, they have been Buddhists, a religion given to them by surrounding Dai-speaking people. At the same time, traditional Lashi animism survives. In the indigenous Lashi religion, animals, plants, minerals, sun, moon, stars, and the earth are alive, imbued with a measure of knowledge, individual consciousness, and awareness of the things around them. They give names to every tree, animal, river, stream, meadow, mountain, hill, and valley, as well as to days, weeks, months, and seasons. All of creation has a spiritual essence, and there is a balance and solidarity to nature. Shamanism is also present. Special religious practitioners function to bring good fortune to the Lashis and prevent natural disasters.

LASI. See **LISU.**

LAU. The Laus are an ethnic subgroup of the Hani* people of the People's Republic of China (PRC). Scattered groups of Lau can can also be found living in Thailand and Myanmar (Burma). The PRC Lau are located in the far southeastern corner of Yunnan Province, between the Mengle and the Ailao mountain ranges. Their society is patrilineal and patriarchal, with kinship relations organized around patrilineal clans. Each clan consists of from thirty to forty households, and each clan maintains elaborate ancestral histories. Their sense of group identity is based more on a sense of being Lau than on being Hani. Most Laus remain tied to the agricultural economy, and a few still work in a traditional subsistence economy. They raise a variety of crops, including rice, maize, beans, buckwheat, millet, tea, peanuts, sugarcane, cotton, chili peppers, ginger, and indigo. Because of recent economic development programs in southwestern Yunnan, increasing numbers of Lau men can be found working in local factories and mines.

LAWA. See **LE VA** and **WA.**

LAWNGWAW. See **MARU DANGBAU.**

LAVE. See **LE VA** and **WA.**

LE. See **LI.**

LE MET. See **LAMET.**

LE SHU O-OP'A. The Le Shu O-op'as (Lesuos) are a subgroup of the Lisu* people of Yunnan Province in the People's Republic of China. Along with other Lisu people, most Le Shu O-op'as are concentrated between the Sawleen River and the Mekong River in western Yunnan Province. Their language is not mutually intelligible with most of the other Lisu tongues, but it is closely related to Akha,* Lahu,* and Yi.* They are more likely to identify themselves as ethnic Le Shu O-op'as than as Lisu. They employ a social system that revolves around a variety of patrilineal, exogamous clans which exercise great political power. Most Le Shu O-op'a people live at higher elevations, usually in ridgeline villages between 3,500 and 10,000 feet in altitude. They are swidden farmers who cultivate maize, mountain rice, millet, and barley.

LE VA. The Le Va (Lave and Lawa) people are considered by many ethnologists in the People's Republic of China to be a subgroup of the Wa,* an officially recognized minority nationality. Most Wa live in the southwestern reaches of Yunnan Province, primarily in Ximeng, Cangyuan, Menglian, Gengma, Lancang, Shuangjiang, Yongde, and Zhenkang counties. They are concentrated demographically in Ximeng and Cangyuan counties. Most Le Vas are farmers, but their techniques vary from village to village; some people use traditional slash-and-burn methods, and others employ more modern, sophisticated techniques. They raise wet rice, dry rice, maize, millet, tubers, and wheat.

Classifying them as a subgroup of the Wa poses problems to ethnologists and ethnolinguists. The Le Va "dialect" is not mutually intelligible with most of the other Wa dialects, and because of that reality, most Le Vas tend to view themselves more as Le Va than as Wa. The process of ethnogenesis, by which they would see themselves primarily as Wa people, is not yet complete.

LEI. The Leis are one of the lineage subgroups of the She* people, who can be found scattered throughout sixty counties in Zhejiang, Fujian, Guangdong, Jiangxi, and Anhui provinces in the People's Republic of China.

LEISU. The Leisus are one of the subgroups of the Yi* people of the People's Republic of China. Although the Yi are an officially recognized minority nationality of more than seven million people, they are divided into a variety of subgroups whose sense of ethnic identity is quite parochial, based on region and dialects that are usually not mutually intelligible. Ethnolinguists believe that Leisu is more closely related to Hani* and Lisu* than to Yi.

Leisus can be found living today in Yunnan Province. They descend from the ancient Tusan people native to the Kunming region of Yunnan and the Chengdu in Sichuan. The Leisu economy is overwhelmingly agricultural. At lower elevations, Leisu farmers produce maize, potatoes, buckwheat, and oats as staples. In the highlands, they raise cattle, sheep, goats, and horses. Poorer families supplement their diets by collecting acorns, roots, wild vegetables, and herbs, and by fishing and hunting. Most Leisus live in mountain hamlets of less than twenty households. They continue to be devoted to an eclectic religion fusing elements of Buddhism, Daoism, and their indigenous animism, although a minority converted to Christianity in the 1920s and 1930s.

LEIZI. The Leizi people are a subgroup of the Gan*-speaking Han* Chinese of the People's Republic of China. Most Leizis live today in Leiyang, Changning, Anren, Yongxing, and Zixing counties in Hunan Province.

LEM. The Lems are considered by many ethnologists in the People's Republic of China to be a subgroup of the Wa,* an officially recognized minority nationality. Classifying them as a subgroup of the Wa, however, poses problems to ethnologists because their "dialect" is not mutually intelligible with most of the other Wa dialects, and most Lems view themselves more as Lems than as Wa.

Most Lems live in the southwestern reaches of Yunnan Province, primarily in Menglian County. They are farmers who use slash-and-burn techniques to cultivate maize, millet, wet and dry rice, and tubers, and they raise chickens and pigs.

LEPCHA. The Lepcha people are an ethnic group who live today in Nepal, primarily on the southern and eastern slopes of Mount Kanchenjunga, which borders Sikkim. Several thousand Lepchas can also be found today in Bhutan. The total Lepcha population in Nepal and Bhutan exceeds 75,000 people. Of Mongol* descent, they speak a language that is part of the Tibeto-Burman* branch of Sino-Tibetan; however, most Lepchas no longer speak their native tongue. They are far more likely to speak the language of a dominant, neighboring ethnic group. Most Lepchas practice a uniquely dual religion, maintaining a loyalty to the Lamaist Buddhism of their Tibetan* neighbors, as well as a faithfulness to their own animistic Mon religious tradition.

The Lepcha economy is primarily agricultural, although it is also quite diverse. They raise wet rice, dry rice, maize, millet, and buckwheat as staples, and cardamom is an important cash crop. In subtropical regions, Lepcha farmers also produce sugarcane and manioc. They raise vegetables in family gardens. Although hunting is no longer economically significant, Lepchas do continue to forage for wild vegetables and fruits. They also raise cattle, pigs, and goats.

Historically, there has been a great deal of contact between Tibetans and Lepchas because of the Himalayan passes from Sikkim into Tibet's Chumbi Valley. Sikkim also dominated the historic Kalimpong-Llasa trade route, which regularly brought Tibetans, Indians, Nepalese,* and Sikkimese* into contact. During the years of the British control of the subcontinent, Sikkim was considered the avenue of access to Central Asia. Today, because of that historical commercial relationship and their current proximity to the Tibetan border and Himalayan trade routes, it is likely that at any given time there are hundreds of Lepchas living in the Tibetan region of the People's Republic of China.

SUGGESTED READINGS: Jay DiMaggio, "Lepchas," in Paul V. Hockings, ed., *The Encyclopedia of World Cultures*, vol. 3, *South Asia*, 1991; John Morris, *Living with Lepchas: A Book about the Sikkim Himalayas*, 1938; Michael Tobias, *Mountain People*, 1967.

LESUO. See **LE SHU O-OP'A** and **LISU.**

LEUR SEUR. The Leur Seur, a subgroup of the Lisu* people of Yunnan Province in the People's Republic of China, are concentrated, along with other Lisu people, between the Sawleen and Mekong rivers in western Yunnan Province. Their language, which is not mutually intelligible with most of the other Lisu tongues, is closely related to Akha,* Lahu,* and Yi.* Leur Seurs are more likely to identify themselves as ethnic Leur Seurs than as Lisu. Their social system revolves around a variety of patrilineal, exogamous clans which exercise great political power. Most Leur Seurs live at higher elevations, usually in ridgeline villages between 3,500 and 9,000 feet in altitude. Swidden farmers, they produce maize, mountain rice, millet, and barley.

LHAI. The Lhais are one of the many subgroups of the Li* people of Hainan Province in the People's Republic of China. Like other Li groups, they have earned a reputation over the years for their ferocious anti-Han* xenophobia, which has often taken the form of guerrilla warfare against Han immigrants to Hainan. Their hatred of the Nationalist government in the 1930s and 1940s also made them willing allies of Mao Zedong and the Communists, and when Mao triumphed, the Lhai were afforded recognition as heroes. Most Lhais today are farmers who raise coconuts, coffee, cocoa, sisal, rubber, cashews, pineapples, mangoes, and bananas. Rice is their staple, and because of the tropical climate of Hainan and its fertile soil, they are able to produce three rice crops a year.

LI. The Li people are one of the officially recognized minority nationalities of the People's Republic of China (PRC). They have also been known over the years by a variety of ethnonyms, including B'lai, B'li, Dai Dli, Hiai, K'lai, Lai, Le, Loi, and S'lai. The 1990 national census put their population at 1,110,900 people, and today it surely exceeds 1.2 million people. The vast majority of them live in Hainan Li and Miao Autonomous Prefecture in Hainan Province. They are scattered throughout Ledong, Baoting, Baisha, Dongfang, Changjiang, Yaxian, Lingshui, and Qiongzhong counties. Outside the autonomous prefecture, Lis can be found in neighboring Wanning, Tunchang, and Chengmai counties. Anthropologists believe that the Li people migrated to Hainan in the eleventh century and settled in the central region of the island. The foothills of the Wuzhi mountains are considered to be the Li heartland. The island of Hainan is located in the South China Sea, off the coast of southern Guangdong Province.

The Li speak a language that is closely related to Zhuang,* Shui,* Dong,* Bouyei,* and Dai* and part of the Zhuang-Dong group of the Sino-Tibetan linguistic family. It is really quite impossible to speak of the Li as a single, identifiable ethnic community. Ethnolinguists speculate that there are five distinct Li languages, and that each of those languages has several dialects. The Ha dialect, which itself is divided into the Luohuo, Hayan, and Baoxian subdialects, is spoken by approximately 500,000 people. PRC ethnolinguists consider the Luohuo dialect to be the standard for the Li language. The Qi dialect, also known as Gei, is spoken by 190,000 people and is divided into three subdialects of its own: Tongahi, Qiandui, and Baocheng. The Bendi dialect has two subdialects—Baisha and Yuanmen—and is spoken by nearly 50,000 people. There is also the Meifu (Moifau) dialect, with 30,000 speakers, and the Jiamao dialect, with 55,000 speakers. Each of these linguistic groups is a subgroup of the Li that enjoys distinct ethnic identities. Li in general do not identify themselves as a single people. Most tend to identify more with their own ethnic subgroup than with the larger cluster of Li people. There is also a variety of regional subgroups based on geography, including the Lhais, Tlhais, Dais, Tsais, T'ais, Sais, Stais, Has, Geis, Nofus, Hyins, Xins, and Zins. Each of them is a distinguishable ethnic entity on Hainan Island.

Historians and archaeologists believe that the Li people have lived on Hainan Island for more than three thousand years. Han* settlers reached the island approximately two thousand years ago, and by the sixth century they had come into complete political control of Hainan. Sovereignty did not come without a fight. The Li, often known as the "wild Li of Hainan," put up a bloody resistance to the extension of Han authority. Chinese documents from as early as the Tang period identify the Li as hostile and rebellious. During the Ming and Yuan dynasties, dozens of Li insurrections had to be put down, each of which contributed to the stereotypical image of the Li among Han. Han authority for the most part controlled the Hainan coastal regions, but the Li were in charge of the central highlands. For the most part, the Chinese government adopted a hands-off policy toward the center of the island.

The negative Han opinion of the Li changed, however, during World War II. Japanese forces invaded Hainan Island in 1939, and the Chinese community, fleeing the coastal area in mass, headed into the interior. The migration precipitated a virtual civil war between Nationalist government troops, who were trying to protect the Han migrants, and the Li. In 1943 the Li rose up in a mass rebellion during which thousands of Kuomintang soldiers were killed. Li guerrillas eventually had to retreat deep into the interior highlands to avoid extermination.

There, however, the Li guerrilla leader, a man named Wang Guoxing, threw in his lot with Communist guerrillas in the area, and they put together a 15,000-man army, known as the "Li column," which dedicated itself to ridding Hainan of the Japanese and the Nationalist government. The Li military contingent was the largest minority army to fight in support of Mao Zedong, and in 1949, when the Communists rode to victory, the Li were accorded the status of national heroes. Since then, highly romanticized versions of Li dedication to the Communist cause have become standard in official histories of the PRC.

Most Lis are farmers who raise coconuts, coffee, cocoa, sisal, rubber, cashews, pineapples, mangoes, and bananas. Rice is their staple, and because of the tropical climate of Hainan and its fertile soil, they are able to produce three rice crops a year. Unlike many of their neighbors, the Li are communal farmers who own land collectively and share their harvests with one another.

SUGGESTED READINGS: Chen Jian, "The Double Three Festival Is a Big Day for the Li of Hainan," *China Today* 41 (October 1992), 22–25; Gao Daxian, "The Li People of Hainan Island," *China Reconstructs* 30 (October 1981), 59–65; Li Chunyou, "I Can Do It Too," *China Reconstructs* 32 (February 1983), 52; Paul V. Hockings, "Li," in Paul V. Hockings, ed., *The Encyclopedia of World Cultures*, vol. 6, *East and Southeast Asia*, 1991; Ma Yin, ed., *China's National Minorities*, 1989; Peng Jianqun, "The Li Nationality of Hainan Island," *China Reconstructs* 34 (October 1985), 40–42; S. Robert Ramsey, *The Languages of China*, 1987; Yai Wen, "Ancient Yi Totems Reborn in Li Yue's Wood Carvings," *China Today* 41 (November 1992), 52–55.

LI. Not to be confused with the Li* people of Hainan Island, these Li are a subgroup of the Lisu* people of Yunnan Province in the People's Republic of China. Along with other Lisu people, most Li are concentrated between the Sawleen and Mekong rivers in western Yunnan Province. Their language is not mutually intelligible with most of the other Lisu tongues, but it is closely related to Akha,* Lahu,* and Yi.* They are also more likely to identify themselves as ethnic Li than as Lisu. Their social system revolves around a variety of patrilineal, exogamous clans which exercise great political power. Most Lis live at higher elevations, usually in ridgeline villages between 3,500 and 10,000 feet in altitude. Swidden farmers, they produce maize, mountain rice, millet, and barley.

LI. In addition to describing an ethnic cluster of people living on the island of Hainan in the South China Sea, the term "Li" is employed by ethnolinguists to describe a branch of the Zhuang-Dong linguistic family, which is itself part of the Tai* language family. Although Chinese linguists argue that Li is divided into a variety of dialects, most of these so-called dialects are not mutually intelligible, or at least are understandable only with great difficulty. Western linguists, therefore, would prefer to describe these dialects as distinct languages within the Li branch of Zhuang-Dong.

SUGGESTED READING: S. Robert Ramsey, *The Languages of China*, 1987.

LIANG. See **DE'ANG.**

LIANGHE. The Lianghe people are one of the two primary subgroups of the Achang* people of western Yunnan Province in the People's Republic of China.

LIANHUA. The Lianhua people live today primarily in Huidong and Haifeng counties in Guangdong Province of the People's Republic of China. The Lianhuas are one of the two subgroups of the She* people.

LIANSHAN. The Lianshans are a subgroup of the Zhuang* people of the People's Republic of China. The Lianshan language is classified as one of the Northern Zhuang* dialects, and most of its speakers live today in Lianshan Zhuang-Yao Autonomous County and in Huaiji County in Guangdong Province.

LIAONING XIBE. The Liaoning Xibes, also known as the Northeastern Xibes,* are one of the two subgroups of the Xibe* people of Xinjiang and Liaoning provinces in the People's Republic of China. They are known as the more liberal of the Xibes, at least in terms of their willingness to acculturate to many Han* institutions.

LIHSAW. See **LISAW** and **LISU.**

LIJIANG NAXI. The Lijiang Naxis are one of the primary subgroups of the Naxi* people of Yunnan Province in the People's Republic of China.

LIMBU. The Limbu people are an ethnic group who live today primarily in Nepal, especially in far eastern Nepal between the Arun River and the Sikkimese border. Several thousand Limbus can also be found today in Bhutan. The total Limbu population in Nepal and Bhutan exceeds 500,000 people. Of Mongol* descent, they speak a language that is part of the Tibeto-Burman* branch of Sino-Tibetan. Most Limbus maintain a loyalty to ancient animist traditions although they willingly participate in various Hindu festivals. They tend to be farmers raising wheat, rice, and maize.

Historically, there has been a great deal of contact between Tibetans* and Limbus because of the Himalayan passes from Sikkim into Tibet's Chumbi Valley. Sikkim also dominated the historic Kalimpong-Llasa trade route, which regularly brought Tibetans, Indians, Nepalese,* and Sikkimese* into contact. During the years of the British control of the subcontinent, Sikkim was considered the avenue of access to Central Asia. Today, because of that historical commercial relationship and their current proximity to the Tibetan border and the Himalayan trade routes, it is likely that at any given time hundreds of Limbus are living in the Tibetan region of the People's Republic of China.
SUGGESTED READINGS: Rex L. Jones and Shirley K. Jones, *The Himalayan Woman: A Study of Limbu Women in Marriage and Divorce*, 1976; Pradyumna Karan and William M. Jenkins, *The Himalayan Kingdoms: Bhutan, Sikkim, and Nepal*, 1963.

LIMKOU. The Limkous (Lingao, Vo Limkou), also known historically as the Be people or the Ongbe people, are an ethnic group who live today on Hainan Island in the People's Republic of China. Their total population exceeds 550,000 people, most of whom can be found in Lingao, Chengmai, Danxian, and Qiong-shan counties. They are not an officially recognized minority nationality in the PRC because government officials classify them as a subgroup of the Han* majority. Although most Limkous also see themselves as Han, they speak Chinese* only as a second language. Their native tongue is an extremely complex language whose roots constitute a linguistic mystery. Various ethnolinguists classify Limkou as Zhuang,* Li,* or Tai,* although it does contain large numbers of Li and Chinese words. There are two Limkou subgroups based on dialect. The Linchengs live in Lingao and Danxian counties and in the Fushan and Bailian regions of Chengmai County. The Qiongshans live in Qiongshan County, near the city of Haikou. Most Limkous are farmers who raise coconuts, coffee, cocoa, sisal, rubber, cashews, pineapples, mangoes, and bananas. Rice is their staple, and because of the tropical climate of Hainan and its fertile soil, they are able to produce three rice crops a year.

SUGGESTED READING: S. A. Wurm, B. T'sou, D. Bradley, et al., eds., *Language Atlas of China*, 1987.

LINCANG. The Lincangs are one of the three subgroups of the De'ang* people of Yunnan Province in the People's Republic of China. Lincangs can be found scattered throughout the Lincang Administration Area.

LINCHENG. The Linchengs are a subgroup of the Limkou* people of Hainan Island in the People's Republic of China. Most Linchengs live in Lingao County and Danxian County, as well as in the Fushan and Bailian regions of Chengmai County. More than 360,000 people speak the Lincheng dialect of Limkou.

LING. See **MULAM.**

LINGAO. See **LIMKOU.**

LINGNAN YAO. See **YAO.**

LINSHAO. The Linshao people are a dialect subgroup of the Taihu* people, who themselves are a linguistic subgroup of the Wu*-speaking Han* people of the People's Republic of China. The vast majority of the more than eight million people who speak the Linshao language live in the Fuyang, Xiaoshan, Tonglu, Shaoxing, Zhuji, Shengxian, Xinchang, Shangyu, Yuyao, Cixi, Lin'an, and Jiande regions of Zhejiang Province.

LIP'A. The Lip'as (Lipos, Lip'os) are a subgroup of the Lisu* people of Yunnan Province in the People's Republic of China. Along with other Lisu people, most Lip'as are concentrated between the Sawleen and Mekong rivers in western Yunnan Province. Their language is not mutually intelligible with most of the other Lisu tongues, but it is closely related to Akha,* Lahu,* and Yi.* Lip'as are more likely to identify themselves as ethnic Lip'as than as Lisus.

LIPO. See **LIP'A** and **LISU.**

LIP'O. See **LIP'A** and **LISU.**

LISAW. The Lisaws (Lasaws, Lihsaws, Li-shaws) are a subgroup of the Lisu* people of Yunnan Province in the People's Republic of China. Along with other Lisu people, most of the Lisaws live between the Sawleen River and the Mekong River in western Yunnan Province. Although the Lisaw language is not mutually intelligible with most of the other Lisu tongues, it is closely related to Akha,* Lahu,* and Yi.* They are more likely to identify themselves as ethnic Lisaws than as Lisus. Most Lisaw people are slash-and-burn farmers.

LI-SHAW. See **LISAW** and **LISU.**

LISHU. The Lishus are a subgroup of the Lisu* people of Yunnan Province in the People's Republic of China. Along with other Lisu peoples, they live primarily between the Sawleen and Mekong rivers in western Yunnan Province. Their language, which is not mutually intelligible with most of the other Lisu tongues, is closely related to Akha,* Lahu,* and Yi.* Instead of regarding themselves as ethnic Lisu, the Lishu people have a more parochial sense of their ethnic identity which is based on their language.

LISU. The Lisu people are a demographically large ethnic group who live today in southwest China, northeast India, Thailand, and Myanmar, formerly known as Burma. Their current total population probably exceeds 800,000 people, of whom the Chinese contingent, with more than 500,000 people, is the largest. The Lisu in China are concentrated between the Sawleen and Mekong rivers in western Yunnan Province in the People's Republic of China (PRC), particularly in the Nujiang Lisu Autonomous Prefecture and in Wiexi County of the Diqing Tibetan Autonomous Prefecture. Approximately 260,000 Lisus live in India and perhaps 20,000 in Myanmar. There are even a few Lisus living as far south as Kamphaeng Phet and Phitsunulok in Thailand and as far to the northeast as eastern Tirap in northeastern India.

Like many of the other peoples indigenous to the Yunnan region of southwestern China, the Lisus are divided into a number of subgroups whose differences from one another in terms of language, material culture, and environmental adaptation are substantial. In fact, to speak of the Lisu as a homogenous ethnic group is to do considerable damage to the notion of ethnicity. PRC demographers classify them as an official minority nationality, but there is relatively little unity among the Lisu subgroups. Although most Lisus are willing to acknowledge a certain cultural affinity and historical connection to one another, they tend to form their own ethnic identities more parochially, based on distinctive regional and linguistic factors. The rugged geography of Lisu country in Yunnan is characterized by mountains, gorges, deep valleys, and dense forests. Communication between different Lisu communities over the centuries has been difficult, which explains their division into so many distinctive subgroups. Among the more well-known Lisu subgroups are the Anung, Che-nung, Khae Lisaw, Khae Liso, Lasaw, Le Shu O-op'a, Lesuo, Leur Seur, Li, Lihsaw, Lip'a, Lipo, Lip'o, Lisaw, Li-shaw, Lishu, Liso, Loisu, Lusu, Lu-tzu, Shisham, Yaoyen, Yawyen, and Yeh-jen. In the PRC, Lisus have also been subdivided, by non-Lisu people at least, by their dress; for example, the White Lisus, the Black Lisus, and the Variegated Lisus.

The Lisu social structure is characterized by the existence of clans that overlap linguistic and regional differences. Among the more prominent of the Lisu clans are the Ngawzas, Jayzas, Heyzas, Nofa Lemas, Jailis, Lafufas, Fuches, Meches, and Dafulus. These Lisu clans, however, are somewhat unique because they do not insist on clan exogamy and possess no stratified hierarchy. Apparently, the clan names are associated with occupational roles in the ancient past.

Ethnolinguists classify the Lisu language as part of the Tibeto-Burman* language group. It is closely related to the Lahu,* Akha,* and Yi* languages. Although Christian missionaries and Chinese political and educational officials have worked to provide a written script for the Lisu language, it is used only by linguists and scholars to study the culture. The Lisus themselves have little use for the written language.

Lisu oral historians claim that their people originated long ago on the Tibetan* plains, primarily on the eastern plateau. Chinese scholars as far back as the seventh century discuss the Lisu, who were sometimes referred to as part of the so-called Southern Barbarian people. Over the years, there has been a schizophrenic relationship between Han* Chinese* and the Lisu. Han people recognize the Lisu as a branch of Han culture, albeit an inferior one. Trade, intermarriage, and cultural exchanges, as well as peaceful coexistence, have characterized their relationship during certain periods, but at other times, the Han and Lisu have engaged in warfare against each other as well as political kidnappings, banditry, and enslavement. Lisu have fought Han expansionism for more than two thousand years, and because their homeland consists of mountains, deep valleys, heavy forests, and generally rugged, precipitious terrain, they were able to control the mountain passes and inflict considerable damage on Han armies.

Mongol* armies conquered the Lisus in 1253, and Mongol soldiers settled permanently in the region and married Lisu women. The Mongol presence lasted for more than a century, but in 1368, an army under the control of the Ming dynasty invaded southwestern China and drove out the Mongols. At that point, Lisu people came under the Chinese civil service system and the system of county magistrates. The Chinese imperial court governed the Lisu people indirectly through the use of official Lisu leaders. Thousands of Han soldiers and administrators settled permanently in the region and took Lisu wives. The local culture remained far more Lisu than Han, but it was the beginning of a process of acculturation that continues today.

Even then, Lisus could be counted on to harass government officials and Han people. After the revolution of 1911, which led to the establishment of the Republic of China, military authority broke down in the region, and Lisu political and military strength increased dramatically. Traditional Lisu clans reasserted their authority, and the opium traffic, which generated cash for the Lisu economy, boomed. Lisu traders sold the opium in Chinese black markets. By the late 1920s, marauding groups of Lisu soldiers, now heavily armed with modern weapons, regularly raided the suburbs of Han Chinese settlements, where they robbed, pillaged, and took slaves.

After the Communist takeover in 1949 and the formation of the People's Republic of China, Han military and political officials were assigned to the Lisu, and the Nuchiang Lisu Autonomous Region was formed. The new government abolished all debts, outlawed slavery, implemented vigorous land reform schemes, and moved toward communal agriculture. Han agronomists tried to move the Lisu away from their traditional swidden agricultural techniques in favor of more efficient and productive practices, such as double cropping and the use of fertilizers, irrigation, and terracing. Opium production, long a source of cash to Lisu farmers, was suppressed. These economic changes constituted a form of assimilation, and the Lisus resisted, though unsuccessfully. During the Cultural Revolution years of the 1960s, when Han Chinese Communists tried to cleanse the entire country ideologically, the Lisu found themselves under new cultural pressures to abandon their language and any lingering sense of their ethnic nationalism. Nineteenth- and twentieth-century conflicts with Han oppression drove hundreds of thousands of Lisus out of Yunnan and into Myanmar, India, and Thailand.

Many Lisus in China have been assimilated into the larger polity and economy, but hundreds of thousands of others still live in traditional villages. Their villages are situated on the slopes of hills, just below the ridgeline. This placement enables them to gather water for crops and avoid attacks by ethnic rivals. Most Lisu villages are located between 3,500 and 10,000 feet in altitude. In China, Lisus are swidden farmers who raise maize, mountain rice, barley, and millet. Farther south in Thailand, they raise rice and opium. In recent years, they have abandoned the practice of raising cotton and hemp for clothing, preferring to purchase cloth commercially. They also raise pigs and chickens to augment their protein supply.

The Lisu social system is organized into patrilineal, exogamous clans. Different households form political alliances based on kinship ties. Families tend to be large and multigenerational. Those family loyalties extend in to the next world as well, because Lisu religion revolves around animistic themes as well as worship of the previous two deceased generations of relatives.

SUGGESTED READINGS: Alain Y. Dessant, ''Economic Organization of the Lisu of the Thai Highlands,'' Ph.D. diss., University of Hawaii, 1972, and ''Lisu,'' in Paul V. Hockings, ed., *Encyclopedia of World Cultures*, vol. 6, *East and Southeast Asia*, 1991; E. Paul Durrenberger, "The Ethnography of Lisu Curing," Ph.D. diss., University of Illinois, Champaigne-Urbana, 1971; *Life among the Minority Nationalities of Northwest Yunnan*, 1989; Asim Matra, *A Guide Book to Lisu Language*, 1988; Shi Zhiyi, "Bathing Festival of the Lisu People," *China Reconstructs* 37 (October 1988), 66–68; Xie Jun, "Lisu Nationality 'Sword Pole' Festival," *China Reconstructs* 38 (August 1989), 34–40.

LIUJIANG. The Liujiangs are a subgroup of the Zhuang* people of the People's Republic of China. The Liujiang language is classified as one of the Northern Zhuang* dialects, and most of its speakers live today in Liujiang, Northern Laibin, Yishan, Liucheng, and Xincheng counties in the Guangxi Zhuang Autonomous Region.

LLOBA. The Llobas are one of the officially recognized minority nationalities of the People's Republic of China. With a 1990 population of only 2,312 people, they are also one of the smallest minority nationalities; however, most PRC ethnolinguists believe that the 1990 census seriously underestimated the total Lloba population. Llobas can be found today in Mainling, Medog, Lhunze, Nangxian, and Luoyu counties in southeastern and eastern Tibet. The ethnonym "Lloba" means "southern savages" in Tibetan,* but they do not identify themselves as such. Lloba identity tends to revolve instead around patrilineal clans or the names of localities. Other Tibetans have long looked down upon Llobas as an inferior people and have confined them to certain regions and have outlawed intermarriage with them. They speak a language that is part of the Tibeto-Burman* group of the Sino-Tibetan linguistic family.

Actually, two barely mutually intelligible Lloba languages divide the Llobas into two very distinct groups of people, different enough to be considered independent ethnic entities, although the PRC government does not recognize either of them officially. The Bogar* (Bokar) language is spoken by approximately 3,000 people who live in Milin, Longzi, and Medog counties in the Tibetan Autonomous Region. The second major Lloba language is Yidu,* which is spoken by approximately 7,000 people living along the Danbajiang River in Chayu County of Changdu Prefecture of the Tibetan Autonomous Region.

Most Llobas function today in an agricultural economy where hunting is still an important source of protein. Their hunting distribution system reflects older economic times, when they cleared land by means of forest fires, planted seeds with sticks, and supplemented their diet with hunting. Even today, hunting is a group affair in which kills are evenly distributed to villagers. Lloba farmers raise maize, millet, rice, and buckwheat, and they trade animal hides, furs, bear paws, and musk to ethnic Tibetans for steel tools, fabrics, salt, wool, wheat, and tea. A typical Lloba meal consists of dried meat, cheese, and buckwheat bread.

Llobas in southwestern Tibet can be identified by their clothing. Most Lloba men wear a sleeveless tunic and a round bear skin or bamboo hat. They carry a sword, bow, and arrows with them at all times. Lloba women wear round-necked blouses and checked woolen skirts. Men wear their hair long, down past their shoulders; women bind their long hair into buns at the backs of their heads. Men wear bamboo earrings and bracelets, but Lloba women traditionally wear several pounds of ornaments, bracelets, necklaces, bells, chains, knives, and shells.

Lloba religion is animistic, and they regularly sacrifice chickens as a means of appeasing unseen gods and warding off evil. Every important human decision must be preceded by chicken sacrifices, and Llobas are known for sometimes sacrificing ten to twenty chickens a day. In recent years, elements of Tibetan Lamaist Buddhism have made modest inroads into Lloba culture. Improved public education, all but forced upon the Llobas by the Chinese government, has helped integrate the Llobas into the larger economy, a fact that is rapidly changing Lloba lifestyle.

SUGGESTED READINGS: Tiley Chodag, *Tibet: The Land and the People*, 1988; Paul V. Hockings, "Lloba," in Paul V. Hockings, ed., *The Encyclopedia of World Cultures*, vol. 6, *East and Southeast Asia*, 1991; S. A. Wurm, B. T'sou, D. Bradley, et al., eds., *Language Atlas of China*, 1987.

LOBA. Loba is the dialect of Uigur* spoken in the eastern region of Xinjiang Province in the People's Republic of China.

LOHEI. See **LAHU.**

LOI. See **LI.**

LOI. The Lois (Loilas) are considered by many ethnologists in the People's Republic of China to be a subgroup of the Wa,* an officially recognized minority nationality. Most Wa live in the southwestern reaches of Yunnan Province, primarily in Ximeng, Cangyuan, Menglian, Gengma, Lancang, Shuangjiang, Yongde, and Zhenkang counties. They are concentrated demographically in Ximeng and Cangyuan counties. Most Loi are farmers, but their techniques vary from village to village. Some farmers use traditional slash-and-burn methods, and others employ more modern, sophisticated techniques. They raise wet rice, dry rice, maize, millet, tubers, and wheat.

LOILA. See **LOI** and **WA.**

LOISU. The Loisus, a subgroup of the Lisu* people of Yunnan Province in the People's Republic of China, live primarily, with other Lisu people, between the Sawleen and Mekong rivers in western Yunnan Province. Their language, which is not mutually intelligible with most of the other Lisu tongues, is closely related to Akha,* Lahu,* and Yi.* Loisus are more likely to identify themselves as ethnic Loisus than as Lisus. Their social system revolves around a variety of patrilineal, exogamous clans which exercise great political power. Most Loisus live at higher elevations, usually in ridgeline villages between 3,500 and 10,000 feet in altitude. Swidden farmers, they raise maize, mountain rice, millet, and barley.

LOKUEI. See **YI**.

LOLO. See **YI**.

LOLOISH. See **YI**.

LOMAI. The Lomais are considered to be an ethnic subgroup of the Hani* people, an officially recognized minority nationality, who are located primarily in the far southwestern reaches of Yunnan Province in the People's Republic of China. Other Lomai live in northern Laos, northern Thailand, and east central Myanmar (Burma). Their economy is largely a subsistence one; farmers employ slash-and-burn techniques to raise maize, millet, tubers, and potatoes. For a cash crop they have produced tobacco for several decades, and more recently, farmers have turned to opium as a cash crop, which they sell to Han* traders in exchange for metal tools, cloth, and different types of food. Central government efforts to suppress the opium traffic, however, have in recent years reduced Lomai income. Foraging and hunting remain important economic and social activities. Indigenous Hani animism remains important to their religious beliefs.

LONGHORN MIAO. See **MIAO**.

LONGQU. The Longqu people are a linguistic subgroup of the Chuqu* people, who themselves are a dialect subgroup of the Wu*-speaking Han* people in the People's Republic of China. More than five million people speak the Longqu dialect, and most of them live in the Pucheng region of Fujian Province; the Shangrao, Yushan, Guangfeng, and Dexing regions of Jiangxi Province; and Longquan, Songyang, Suichang, Quzhou, Longyou, Kaihua, Changshan, Jiang-shan, and Qingyuan counties of Zhejiang Province. See **CHUZHOU**.

LONG-SKIRT MIAO. See **MIAO**.

LONGSLEEVED MIAO. See **MIAO**.

LOP. Lop, also known as Lopa and Loba, is one of the three dialects of the Uigur* people of the Xinjiang Uigur Autonomous Region in the People's Republic of China.

LOP NUR. Lop Nur is one of the vernacular subgroups of the Uigur* language spoken in Xinjiang Uigur Autonomous Region of the People's Republic of

China. Most speakers of Lop Nur live in and around the oasis community of Lop Nur.

LOPA. See **LLOBA.**

LOQUEI. The Loqueis are one of the subgroups of the Yi* people of the People's Republic of China. Although the Yi are an officially recognized minority nationality of more than seven million people, they are divided into a variety of subgroups whose sense of ethnic identity is quite parochial, based on region and dialects that usually are not mutually intelligible. Loqueis can be found living today in Yunnan Province, typically in autonomous political subdivisions established by the PRC government for the Yi. They descend from the ancient Tusan people native to the Kunming region of Yunnan and the Chengdu in Sichuan. The Loquei economy is overwhelmingly agricultural. At lower elevations, farmers produce maize, potatoes, buckwheat, and oats as staples. In the highlands, they raise cattle, sheep, goats, and horses. Chickens and pigs are ubiquitous in Yi villages. Poorer families supplement their diets by collecting acorns, roots, wild vegetables, and herbs, and by fishing and hunting. Most Loqueis live in mountain hamlets of fewer than twenty households.

LOUSHAO. The Loushao people are a subgroup of the Xiang*-speaking Han* Chinese* of the People's Republic of China. Most Loushaos live today in eighteen cities and counties of Hunan Province as well as in the Quanzhou, Ziyuan, Guanyang, and Xing'an regions of the Guangxi Zhuang Autonomous Region.

LOWER THREE VILLAGES RUKAI. The Lower Three Villages Rukai people speak one of the two Rukai* dialects and live today in the Touna, Maolin, and Mantong regions of Gaoxiang County in the People's Republic of China.

LOWER YANGTZE MANDARIN. See **EASTERN MANDARIN.**

LU. The Lus are one of the many subgroups of the Dai* people, an officially recognized minority nationality in the People's Republic of China. The vast majority of them live in Yunnan Province, particularly in the Dehong Dai and Jingpo Autonomous Prefecture and in the Xishuangbanna Dai Autonomous Prefecture. The Lu have been commercial farmers for more than a thousand years. They were also among the first rice cultivators in the region. More than 1,400 years ago, when most of the inhabitants of Yunnan were hunters and foragers, the Lu were wet-rice farmers who cultivated large paddy fields. They used elephants as draft animals to plow the fields. Today, most Lu farmland is employed in wet-rice farming. They also produce dry rice on terraced, hillside fields. Cash crops include tea, cotton, tobacco, camphor, sisal, sugarcane, coffee, bananas, mangoes, and rubber.

LUHSU. See **NAXI.**

LUHTU. Luhtu is one of the dialects of the Tsou* language spoken by indigenous peoples on the island of Taiwan in the Republic of China. Luhtu speakers can be found in Xinyi Township of Nantou County.

LUJIA. Lujia is one of the five mutually intelligible dialects of the Puyuma* language which is spoken by an indigenous people living on Taiwan in the Republic of China.

LUKHI. See **NAXI.**

LULIANG. The Luliangs are one of the linguistic subgroups of the more than 48 million Han* people who speak the Jin* Chinese* language. Luliang is further divided into two subgroups. The Fenzhou people live in Fenyang, Lishi, Fangshan, Zhongyang, Linxian, and Liulin counties in Shanxi Province and in Jiaxian, Wubu, and Qingjian counties in Shaanxi Province. The other Luliang subgroup—the Xingxis—live in Xingian, Lanxian, Jingle, Xixian, Jiakou, Shilou, Yonghe, and Daning counties in Shanxi Province.

LUOBA. See **LLOBA.**

LUOFU. The Luofu people live today primarily in Boluo and Zengcheng counties in Guangdong Province of the People's Republic of China. The Luofus are one of the two subgroups of the She* people.

LUOLUO. The Luoluos are an ethnic group in the People's Republic of China, although the central government has never extended to them formal recognition as a minority nationality. Official PRC publications classify them as a Yi* subgroup, and, indeed, they speak a Yi language. But Luoluo is not mutually intelligible with the vast majority of other Yi languages, and Luoluos give themselves a distinct, separate identity. They will acknowledge a certain cultural affinity with the Yi, but they insist that they are a separate people. Most Luoluos live today in Yunnan Province and work as farmers.

LUOLUO. Not to be confused with Luoluos,* a Yi* minority of Yunnan Province, the Luoluos are one of the many subgroups of the Li* people of Hainan Island in the People's Republic of China. Luoluo, one of three dialects of the Ha* dialect of Li, is spoken mainly in Ledong County and along the Changhua River in Dongfang County. Luoluo is considered to be the standard dialect of the Li language.

LUOPOHE MIAO. The Luopohe Miao are an ethnic group of approximately 40,000 people who live in Guizhou Province, particularly in Fuquan, Weng'an,

Guiding, Longli, Kaiyang, and Kaili counties, in the People's Republic of China (PRC). The Luopohe language is further divided into four mutually intelligible dialects. Although PRC demographers and ethnologists classify them as a Miao* subgroup, the Luopohes have a distinct sense of their own identity.

LUOYUE. See **SHUI.**

LUQUAN. The Luquans constitute an ethnic group in the People's Republic of China (PRC), although the central government has never extended to them formal recognition as a minority nationality. Official PRC publications classify them as a Yi* subgroup, and, indeed, they speak a Yi language. But Luquan is not mutually intelligible with the vast majority of other Yi languages, and the Luquans give themselves a distinct, separate identity. Although they acknowledge a certain cultural affinity with the Yi, they nevertheless insist that they are a separate people. The Luquan language is very closely related to Nasu.* Most Luquans live today in Yunnan Province, where they are concentrated in Luquan County, north of Kunming, the provincial capital. Farmers, they produce a variety of grains and livestock.

LUSU. The Lusus (Lu-tzus), a subgroup of the Lisu* people of Yunnan Province in the People's Republic of China, are found primarily, with other Lisu people, between the Sawleen and Mekong rivers in western Yunnan Province. Their language is not mutually intelligible with most of the other Lisu tongues, but it is closely related to Akha,* Lahu,* and Yi.* Lusus are more likely to identify themselves as ethnic Lusus than as Lisus. Their social system revolves around a variety of patrilineal, exogamous clans which exercise great political power. Most of them live at higher elevations, usually in ridgeline villages between 3,500 and 10,000 feet in altitude.

LUTZE. See **NU.**

LU-TZU. See **LISU and LUSU.**

LUTZU. See **NU.**

LUXI. See **NAXI.**

M _____

MACANESE. It is technically premature in 1997 to speak about the people of the island of Macao as an ethnic group in the People's Republic of China (PRC), but the more than 500,000 people now living in Macao are scheduled to revert to PRC sovereignty in 1999. When they become citizens of the PRC, they will constitute a unique ethnic group in the country. The total area of Macao comprises only six square miles of land at the end of the Pearl River estuary on the coast of the South China Sea, just across the bay from Hong Kong.

In 1557 Portugal established a permanent trading post on Macao. Hundreds of Portuguese* merchants and sailors settled in Macao and became the nucleus of the Portuguese ethnic community, an elite, Roman Catholic minority. Most of the other residents of Macao at the time were Yue*-speaking Han* Chinese.* In subsequent centuries, thousands of Hakka*-speaking Hans settled there as well.

Portugal hoped to use Macao as a staging area for the commercial exploitation of China and Japan, and they succeeded for several centuries. Macao became the commercial hub of an Asian trade empire that brought to China various European manufactured goods, pepper and seasonings from the Spice Islands, and cotton and muslin from India. Portuguese traders traded these commodities to China for silk, which they then carried to Japan and sold for silver.

Portugal was the first European nation to establish an overseas empire, and it was also the first of the empires to experience long-term decline. In 1640 Japan expelled the Portuguese from their trading post in Nagasaki, and the Dutch soon captured Malacca, which ended the Portuguese spice monopoly. When the British moved into China in the nineteenth century, Macao had long since been eclipsed as a commercial center. Great Britain occupied Macao for several years early in the nineteenth century, but they soon left, unhappy over the willingness of the Portuguese community to intermingle sexually with the local Han people. As the strength of Hong Kong grew in the nineteenth century, Macao declined in significance. Macao became known for specializing in gold, opium, and labor trafficking.

In 1887 China formally recognized Portuguese sovereignty over Macao, as long as the Portuguese agreed not to sell the territory to another European power. The Chinese correctly surmised that it would be much easier for them to manipulate Portugal than Great Britain. Macao's status remained just that until the 1960s, when the Cultural Revolution in the People's Republic of China sent a torrent of Han refugees into the territory. China forced Portugal to repatriate many of the refugees. Late in the 1960s and early in the 1970s, Portugal underwent a revolution of its own and faced rebellions in its African colonies. Macao lost its significance to Portugal. On March 26, 1987, China and Portugal signed an agreement that will turn sovereignty of Macao over to China on December 20, 1999. The agreement guarantees a fifty-year period for Macao to maintain its capitalist economy. On December 20, 1999, the residents of Macao, including the 8,500 Portuguese, will become citizens of the PRC.

Today, the nearly 500,000 people living on Macao come from diverse backgrounds. A total of 8,500 of them are ethnic Portuguese, and tens of thousands of other Macaoans are mixed-blood people, descendents of Portuguese-Han ancestry. The term "Macanese" can be a generic reference to all residents of Macao, but more specifically it refers to the more than 30,000 people of Portuguese-Han descent living in Macao. More than 90 percent of Macao's population, however, are Yue- and Hakka-speaking Chinese. Like their counterparts in Hong Kong, however, the Han people of Macao do not necessarily identify ethnically with the Mainland Han. While Mandarin* has been the official language of the People's Republic of China, Yue (Cantonese) has been the primary language of Macao. Even before the transfer of power, the Beijing government has not disguised its intention of increasing the teaching of Mandarin in Macao. It is believed that the ultimate cultural integration of Macao into mainland society cannot take place until Mandarin has made the necessary inroads into Macao.

It is not just language that has separated the people of Macao from the mainland. The vast majority of the Chinese citizens living in Kwangtung Province, just across the border with Macao, are also Yue speaking, but the Macanese do not identify ethnically with them due to the economic and cultural chasm that exists between the two societies. Ethnic identity is not just a function of race, religion, and language. It also possesses an economic and cultural dimension.

At the time of the transfer, more than half of the people of Chinese descent living in Macao will be native to the region. They have never lived under the authority of the Communist regime in Beijing or with its ideological purity and its attempts to direct the course of history bureaucratically. The Portuguese colony adopted a laissez-faire approach to economic development, and many economists argue that Macao enjoys one of the purest forms of capitalism in the world. Making money was the primary reason for being. Values were materialistic, the economy consumer oriented, and personal goals highly commercialized.

The people of Macao have been accustomed to freedom of religion, association, and expression. The government had long stayed out of their businesses and out of their bedrooms. They were used to the government's playing only a minimal role in their lives. In fact, among all the people of the developed world, the Hong Kongese and Macanese have experienced the least amount of government interference in their lives. Thousands of Eurasians—people of mixed Portuguese and Han Chinese ancestry—also live in Macao, and they consider themselves neither British nor Chinese.

SUGGESTED READINGS: C. R. Boxer, *Fidalgoes in the Far East, 1570–1750: Fact and Fancy in the History of Macao*, 1948, and *The Portuguese Seaborne Empire*, 1969; Nigel Cameron, *Hong Kong, The Cultured Pearl*, 1978; "Macao Waits Its Turn," *National Geographic* 191 (March 1997), 30–31; Ross Marlay, "Macao," in James S. Olson, ed., *Historical Dictionary of European Imperialism*, 1991; Wei Xiutang and Huan Huixian, "Macao Looks Toward 1999," *China Reconstructs* 36 (November 1987), 8–11.

MAEN. The Maens are considered by many ethnologists in the People's Republic of China to be a subgroup of the Wa,* an officially recognized minority nationality. Most Was live in the southwestern reaches of Yunnan Province, primarily in Ximeng, Canghyuan, Menglian, Gengma, Lancang, Shuangjiang, Yongde, and Zhenkang counties. Most Maens are farmers, but their techniques vary regionally; some use traditional slash-and-burn methods, and others employ more modern, sophisticated techniques. They raise wet rice, dry rice, maize, millet, tubers, and wheat.

Classifying the Maen as a subgroup of the Wa poses problems to ethnologists and ethnolinguists. The Maen dialect is not mutually intelligible with most of the other Wa dialects, and because of that reality, most Maens view themselves more as Maen than as Wa.

MAGPIE MIAO. See **MONMIN.**

MAINGTHA. See **ACHANG.**

MAK. The Mak people are an ethnic group in the People's Republic of China, although the central government has not yet extended to them recognition as an official minority nationality. Chinese officials classify them as a subgroup of the Bouyei.* They number in excess of 10,000 people and can be found living throughout Guizhou and northern Guangxi provinces, particularly in northwestern Libo County of Guizhou. Their language is part of the Dong-Shui* branch of the Zhuang-Dong group of Tai* languages. The Mak language is distinctive enough from the other Dong-Shui languages to convince ethnolinguists that they separated centuries ago. A written script for Mak is not in existence, but literate Maks can read and write Mandarin* Chinese.* Most people can speak a local Chinese dialect as well as their native Mak.

Mak country was independent of Han* authority until the thirteenth century, when Chinese armies and then political administrators occupied Guangxi. Beginning with the Qing dynasty in 1271, Mak farmers had to provide an annual tribute payment in grain to the Chinese imperial government. Over the centuries, the exact nature of Han imperial control has changed with succeeding dynasties and with the rise of Communists to power since 1949, but the reality of Han political and economic domination has not changed.

The Mak economy today is primarily agricultural. They prefer to locate their villages in valleys and in the lower hillsides, where they live in one-story mud-walled houses. Two-generation households is the norm, and young men prefer to marry one of their mother's brother's daughters. The social system is based on patrilineal descent. Maks tend to live in single-surname villages, which gives each community powerful family bonds. Farmers employ plow technology in raising rice, maize, wheat, and potatoes. They are also known to produce peanuts, melons, cotton, and a number of vegetables. Water buffalo, oxen, and horses serve as draft animals.

SUGGESTED READINGS: Ma Yin, ed., *China's Minority Nationalities*, 1989; S. Robert Ramsey, *The Languages of China*, 1987.

MAN. See **MANCHU.**

MAN. See **MIAO.**

MAN. See **YAO.**

MANCHIA. The Manchias constitute an ethnic group in the People's Republic of China (PRC), although the central government has never extended to them formal recognition as a minority nationality. Official PRC publications classify them as a Yi* subgroup, and, indeed, they speak a Yi language. But Manchia is not mutually intelligible with the vast majority of other Yi languages, and the Manchias give themselves a distinct, separate identity. Although they acknowledge a certain cultural affinity with the Yi, they nevertheless insist that they are a separate people. Manchias can be found in Guizhou and Yunnan provinces. The Manchia economy, which is primarily agricultural, revolves around the production of maize, potatoes, buckwheat, and oats, along with the raising of cattle, sheep, goats, poultry, swine, and horses in the highlands. Villages are quite small, more like hamlets, and their homes are constructed of wood and dirt. Their religious beliefs today remain an eclectic mix of Daoism, Buddhism, animism, and shamanism; a minority of Manchias practice Christianity.

MANCHU. The Manchus (Manchurians), who call themselves the Mandzhu, are an ethnic group of approximately ten million people who live in northeastern China, particularly in southern Manchuria. They have also been identified over the centuries as the Man, Jurchen, Quren, and Nuzhen. The 1990 census of the People's Republic of China (PRC) placed their population at 9,821,180 people. Most Manchus are concentrated today in Liaoning Province. Other substantial clusters of Manchus can be found in Jilin and Heilongjiang provinces, and there are scattered Manchu communities in Hebei, Gansu, Shandong, and Ningxia, as well as in the Inner Mongolian Autonomous Region. Such major Chinese cities as Beijing, Chengdu, Xian, and Guangzhou have significant Manchu ethnic communities.

Manchus are descendents of the ancient Tungus people who were present in Manchuria as early as the third century B.C. The Tungus represented a consolidation of such local tribes as the Sushen, Ilu, Wochu, Wuchi, and Moho, as well as a variety of neighboring Turkic and Mongol* tribes. By the early seventeenth century, the Manchus had become a self-conscious ethnic entity, and they were led by Emperor Nurhatsi, who established an imperial capital at Mukden. The name "Manchu" by that time referred to the people of the region. Later in the seventeenth century, the Manchus established the Qing dynasty after they conquered Korea, Mongolia, and China. They pushed into Dzungaria, Tibet, and other borderlands in the eighteenth century. The Qing imperial government then sent out Manchu administrators throughout the empire to manage its affairs, which accounts for the relatively wide distribution of Manchus in the PRC today.

But the expansion eventually diluted Manchu culture, and the language entered a period of steady decline as more and more Manchus adopted Chinese.* The Qing dynasty of the Manchus survived in China from 1644 to 1911, when Sun Yat-sen and the Republicans took over the country. Manchus enjoyed a temporary revival of political power in 1931, when Japan invaded Manchuria. Interested in exploiting the region's valuable natural resources, the Japanese established a puppet government, known as Manchukuo, and declared it an independent state. It was independent in name only. As the head of state, the Japanese installed Pu Yi Aisengoro, who happened to be the last of the Manchu emperors in China. When World War II ended in 1945, Chinese sovereignty over Manchuria was restored.

Ethnolinguists classify Manchu with the Manchu-Tungus branch of the Altaic* group in the Uralo-Altaic linguistic family. Early in the seventeenth century, Manchu scholars developed a script for the language based on Mongol forms. Today, both written and spoken Manchu are rapidly falling into disuse. One can most likely hear Manchu spoken by elderly people in the city of Sanjiazi in Fuyu County of Heilongjiang Province, and in the town of Dawujia in Aihui County, also in Heilongjiang. Manchu acculturation to Han* institutions and assimilation with Han people has reached an advanced state. In the People's Republic of China, the Manchu today work primarily as farmers raising grains, legumes, hemp, and vegetables, while a number of highland Manchus work in the lumber industry. Only a handful of people living in Siberian Russia are even aware of their roots as Manchu people, although approximately 20,000 people speak one of the Manchu languages: the Hezhen,* Orok, Orochen, Ulchi, and Udegei.

Today it is difficult really to speak of the Manchu people as a self-conscious ethnic group. Some linguists argue that they really ought to be called Chinese of Manchu ancestry. Their state of assimilation with Han Chinese is so extensive, and the remainders of any distinctly Manchu institutions so few, that they really cannot be called an ethnic group. Their language is all but extinct, and there is no region of the PRC that can be called Manchu. They enjoy lifestyles that are virtually indistinguishable from those of Han people, with whom they have lived and intermarried for centuries.

SUGGESTED READINGS: Aisin-Gioro Pu Jie, "China's Manchu Nationality," *China Reconstructs* 27 (November 1979), 28–31; Alice Bartels and Dennis Bartels, "Soviet Policy toward Siberian Native People," *Canadian Dimension* 19 (1985), 36–44; Mike Edwards, "Siberia: In from the Cold," *National Geographic* 177 (March 1990), 2–49; Jian Qun, "Reviving Ancient Languages," *China Today* 42 (August 1993), 41–43; Constantine Krypton, "Soviet Policy in the Northern National Regions after World War II," *Slavic Review* 13 (October 1954), 339–53; S. Robert Ramsey, *The Languages of China*, 1987; Harry G. Schwarz, *The Minorities of Northern China: A Survey*, 1984; Sun Qiuli, "A Manchu-Style Wedding," *China Reconstructs* 38 (April 1989), 53–56; Piers Vitebsky, "Perestroika among the Reindeer Herders," *Geographical Magazine* 61 (June 1989), 23–34.

MANCHU PEOPLE. The term Manchu People is a generic reference to members of those groups who speak one of the Manchu* languages in the Uralo-Altaic linguistic family. The primary groups are the Hezhen,* Orok, Orochen, Ulchi, and the Udegei.

SUGGESTED READING: Ronald Wixman, *The Peoples of the USSR: An Ethnographic Handbook*, 1984.

MANCHURIAN. See **MANCHU** and **MANCHU PEOPLE.**

MANDARIN. The term "Mandarin" is used here to describe the people of Han descent who speak the Mandarin language as their native tongue. Today, an estimated 800 million people in the People's Republic of China (PRC) and the Republic of China on Taiwan speak Mandarin. No other language in the world has so many speakers. Mandarin speakers dominate three-quarters of the People's Republic of China, and the Mandarin culture area extends from Heilongjiang, Jilin, and Liaoning provinces in the northeast, out to Gansu Province in the northwest, and then southeast into Sichuan and Yunnan provinces. Guizhou, Hubei, Hunan, Shaanxi, Shanxi, Ningxia, Anhui, Jingxia, Shandong, and Tianjin provinces are also predominantly Mandarin.

Discussing the structure of the Chinese language is not as simple matter as it might appear. The PRC government insists that there is only one Chinese language, but that it is divided into a number of dialects. Most linguists argue, however, that a dialect, by definition, means that it is mutually intelligible with other dialects of the same language. The Chinese government claims that eight dialects of the language exist within the national boundaries: Mandarin,* Jin,* Wu,* Gan,* Xiang,* Hakka,* Yue,* and Min.* The problem with that definition, of course, is that none of these so-called dialects is mutually intelligible with the other. The people who speak them may very well be united by their Han* descent and their shared eclectic mix of Buddhist, Daoist, and Confucianist religious beliefs, but they cannot understand one another's spoken languages, which should render them members of different ethnic groups. Complicating the issue even more is the fact that each of the eight Chinese languages possesses many dialects, and some of those dialects are not mutually intelligible to speakers of related dialects.

At the same time, however, they share an unusual linguistic similarity. The spoken Chinese languages cannot be mutually understood by different speakers, but they all employ the same written script, which can be read by all. Some linguists have begun employing the term "regionalect" to describe the eight Chinese languages. Whether or not Mandarin, Wu, Jin, Gan, Xian, Hakka, Yue, and Min are dialects, regionalects, or languages, they divide the more than 1.1 billion Han people into distinguishable, individual groups whose members share loyalty and a sense of identity with one another because of language.

Over the years, linguists have employed several classification systems for analyzing Mandarin, although there is general agreement that it is indeed a single language because its many dialects are mutually intelligible. In that sense, Mandarin is different from such other Chinese languages as Yue, Min, Hakka, and Gan. Because of the mutual intelligibility of the Mandarin dialects, Mandarin speakers are not divided into well-defined ethnic subgroups, either by official demographers in the People's Republic of China or by Western ethnologists.

Mandarin is divided into several branches. Northeastern Mandarin is spoken by more than 140 million people in Jilin, Liaoning, and Heilongjiang provinces and in the Inner Mongolian Autonomous Region (IMAR). Northeastern Mandarin is divided into three major dialects: Jishen, Hafu, and Heisong. For its part, Jishen is divided into the Jioning, Tongxi, and Yanji vernaculars. Hafu has two subdialects: Zhaofu and Changjin. Finally, the Heisong dialect of Northeastern Mandarin possesses three subdialects: Nenke, Jiafu, and Zhanhua.

Some linguists, but certainly not all, also include the Jialiao dialect of Mandarin in the Northeastern Mandarin group. Jialiao is spoken by approximately 10 million people, most of whom live in thirty cities and counties in Shangdong Province and fourteen cities and counties in Liaoning Province. Jiliao can be divided into three subdialects: Qingzhou, Denglian, and Gaihuan.

The second major Mandarin branch spoken in the People's Republic of China is known as the Beijing group. It is spoken by more than 25 million people in the city of Beijing and its surrounding area, the city of Tianjin and its surrounding area, Heibei Province and the bordering regions of Shaanxi and Liaoning provinces and the IMAR, and in western Shandong Province. The Beijing group is divided into three subdialects: Jingshi, Huaicheng, and Chaofeng. The PRC government considers the Beijing dialect to be the standard form of the language.

Closely related to the Beijing dialect group is the Beifang group, which is spoken by more than 120 million people in 165 cities and counties in Heibei and Shandong provinces and the IMAR. The Beifang dialect can be divided into the Baotang (and its Laifu, Dingba, Tianjin, Jizun, Fulong, and Luanchang vernaculars), Shiji (and its Zhaoshen, Xinghen, and Liaotai vernaculars), and Canghui (and its Huangle, Yangshou, Juzhao, and Zhanghuan vernaculars) subdialects.

Zongyuan Mandarin is another major Mandarin dialect. More than 130 million people speak one of the Zongyuan dialects, and most of them live in Henan, Hebei, Shandong, Anhui, and Jiangsu provinces. Zhongyuan Mandarin itself can be divided into nine dialects: Zhengcao, Cailu, Luoxu, Xinbeng, Fenhe, Guanzhong, Qinlong, Longzhong, and Nanjiang. The Fenhe dialect has three vernaculars: Pingyang, Jiangzhou, and Xiezhou.

The Jianghuai Mandarin group of dialects is spoken by approximately 65 million people in eighty-four cities and counties in Anhui, Jiangsu, and Hubei provinces. Jianghuai can itself be divided into three subgroups, or vernaculars: Hongchao, Tairu, and Huangxiao.

More than 9 million people in the People's Republic of China speak the Lanyin Mandarin dialect. Most of them live today in the Ningxia Hui Autonomous Region and Gansu Province, with some as well in Qinghai and Shaanxi provinces. Lanyin can be divided into four primary subdialects: Jincheng, Yinwu, Hexi, and Tami.

Chinese linguists disagree about whether to include the Jin dialects within the Mandarin group or to separate them out and classify them as an independent Chinese language or dialect, such as Gan, Min, Yue, Hakka, Wu, and Xiang.

Xinjiang Mandarin (also known as Northwestern Mandarin)—the group of Mandarin dialects spoken in the Xinjiang Uigur Autonomous Region—actually includes representatives from a number of other Mandarin dialects. Because of the central government's assimilationist goals, large numbers of Mandarin-speaking Han Chinese have relocated to Xinjiang during the previous two centuries. Today, there are more than 6 million Mandarin speakers in Xinjiang. The most prominent Mandarin representatives are Beijing Mandarin, Beifang Mandarin, Lanyin Mandarin, and Zhongyuan Mandarin.

Finally, Southwestern Mandarin is spoken in 517 cities and counties in Sichuan, Yunnan, Guizhou, Guangxi, Gansu, Jiangxi, and Hubei provinces. More than 240 million people speak a Southwestern Mandarin dialect: Chengyu, Dianxi, Qianbei, Kungui, Guanchi, Ebei, Wutian, Cenjiang, Qiannan, Xiangnan, and Guiliu. The Dianxi dialect can be subdivided into the Yaoli and Baolu vernaculars. The Guanchi dialect consists of the Minjiang, Renfu, Yamian, and Lichuan vernaculars.

SUGGESTED READINGS: S. Robert Ramsey, *The Languages of China*, 1987; S. A. Wurm, B. T'sou, D. Bradley, et al., eds., *Language Atlas of China*, 1987.

MANDJU. See **MANCHU** and **MANCHU PEOPLE.**

MANDJURI. See **MANCHU** and **MANCHU PEOPLE.**

MANDJURIAN. See **MANCHU** and **MANCHU PEOPLE.**

MANDJURY. See **MANCHU** and **MANCHU PEOPLE.**

MANDZHU. See **MANCHU.**

MANDZHURI. See **MANCHU** and **MANCHU PEOPLE.**

MANDZHURIAN. See **MANCHU** and **MANCHU PEOPLE.**

MANDZHURY. See **MANCHU** and **MANCHU PEOPLE.**

MAN-EATING MIAO. See **MANNAONEN.**

MANEGRY. See **EVENK.**

MANG. The Mang people, also known historically as the Mang-U and Mang-Tam, are a tiny ethnic group living today in far northern Myanmar (Burma), with a handful probably located across the border in the southern reaches of Yunnan Province of the People's Republic of China. The total Mang population numbers no more than 3,000 people, and the vast majority of them are on the Myanmar side of the Sino-Burmese frontier. They are primarily slash-and-burn agriculturalists who raise a variety of crops, including maize, millet, rice, tubers, goats, pigs, and chickens. The Mang religion is a syncretic mix of Buddhism and their indigenous animistic faith.

The Mang speak a Mon-Khmer* language in the Austroasiatic linguistic family. Some ethnolinguists have tried to classify the Mang people as a subgroup of the Wa,* but their languages, though related, are not mutually intelligible. Others believe that the Mangs are a subgroup of the Kmhmu* people. Because the Mang language is loaded with De'ang* cognates, some ethnolinguists wonder if they are not a subgroup of the De'ang. Still others postulate that Mang is a completely different branch within the Mon-Khmer group. The Mang language is divided into a number of mutually intelligible dialects, including Mang-Khmu, Mang-Muong, and Mang-Puok.

SUGGESTED READINGS: Robert Parkin, *A Guide to Austroasiatic Speakers and Their*

Languages, 1991; Wang Aihe, "Wa," in Paul V. Hockings, ed., *The Encyclopedia of World Cultures*, vol. 6, *East and Southeast Asia*, 1991; Wen Yiqun, "Women of the Highlands," *China Today* 44 (May 1995), 33–35.

MANG-KHMU. Mang-Khmu is one of the dialects of the Mang language of the Mang* people who live in Yunnan Province in the People's Republic of China.

MANG-MUONG. Mang-Muong is one of the dialects of the Mang language of the Mang* people who live in Yunnan Province in the People's Republic of China.

MANG-PUOK. Mang-Puok is one of the dialects of the Mang language of the Mang* people who live in Yunnan Province in the People's Republic of China.

MANG-U. See **MANG.**

MANTZU. The Mantzus are one of the subgroups of the Yi* people of the People's Republic of China (PRC). Although the Yi are an officially recognized minority nationality of more than seven million people, they are divided into a variety of subgroups whose sense of ethnic identity is quite parochial, based on region and dialects that are usually not mutually intelligible. Mantzus can be found living today in Guizhou and Yunnan provinces, usually in autonomous political subdivisions established by the PRC government for the Yi. They descend from the ancient Tusan people native to the Kunming region of Yunnan and the Chengdu in Sichuan. The Mantzu economy is overwhelmingly agricultural. At lower elevations, they produce maize, potatoes, buckwheat, and oats as staples. In the highlands, they raise cattle, sheep, goats, and horses. Chickens and pigs are ubiquitous in Mantzu villages. Poorer families supplement their diets by collecting acorns, roots, wild vegetables, and herbs, and by fishing and hunting. Most Mantzus live in mountain hamlets of fewer than twenty households.

MANZI. See **QIANG.**

MAONAN. The Maonans, who are also known regionally as the Anan, are an officially recognized minority nationality in the People's Republic of China (PRC). In their own language, Maonans refer to themselves as the Kungnung or Aik Nan people. Their population is approximately 75,000 to 80,000 people, most of whom live today in Huanjiang County and Hechi County in the Guangxi Zhuang Autonomous Region. They live in close proximity to the Shui,* who border them to the south, and they are closely related culturally to the Zhuang.* Maonans speak a language that is classified with the Dong-Shui* branch of the Zhuang-Dong group of the Sino-Tibetan linguistic family. They are demographically so compact that there are no dialect variations in the Maonan language.

Because their villages are scattered among those of Zhuang, Yao,* Miao,* and Han* people, Maonans are not only frequently bilingual but trilingual because they speak Chinese* and Zhuang as well.

Their ethnic origins are a matter of scholarly debate. Approximately 60,000 Maonans are of one family group, using the surname Tan and claiming origins centuries ago in Hunan Province. The remaining Maonans, named Lu, Meng, Yan, and Wei, trace their origins back to Fujian Province and Shandong Province. That is an intriguing claim in as much as Fujian and Shandong provinces are separated by approximately six hundred miles. Scholars have yet to sort out just how the Maonans became one ethnic group with origins as diverse as Hunan, Fujian, and Shandong.

Although most Maonans live in ethnically homogenous villages, they have become highly sinicized since the fourteenth century, when intermarriage with Han people became increasingly common. To a lesser extent, those Maonans living in close proximity to the Zhuang have taken on that culture. They worship such Daoist and Buddhist gods as Divine Mother and the Lord of Three Worlds, celebrate the Chinese New Year's Festival, and participate in ancestor worship. But they also fear and try to appease a malevolent god known as General Meng. Maonan ancester worship, unlike that of the Han, includes female ancestors on the altar. To calm the rest of the invisible world of benign and malignant gods, ghosts, and spirits, each family, at least on one occasion each generation, must sponsor an elaborate sacrificial ceremony involving the killing of thirty-six animals. The ceremony must include one ox and seven pigs. There are also several thousand Christian Maonans, who were converted before the Communist revolution.

Under the impact of government development policies, the Maonan economy has changed. Before the revolution in 1949, land tenure was almost feudal, with large numbers of Maonans working as farm tenants or laborers on large estates. The Communists collectivized Maonan agriculture, seizing property in the name of the state and organizing multicultural labor forces. Agricultural production suffered until the early 1980s, when economic reforms created more capitalist incentives for individual Maonan families. Today, Maonan farmers raise maize, wheat, sorghum, sweet potatoes, soybeans, tobacco, and wet rice.

SUGGESTED READINGS: Norma Diamond, ''Maonan,'' in Paul V. Hockings, ed., *The Encyclopedia of World Cultures*, vol. 6, *East and Southeast Asia*, 1991; Ma Yin, ed., *China's Minority Nationalities*, 1989.

MARU DANGBAU. The Maru Danbaus, who call themselves Lawngwaws, are one of the smaller of the Kachin*-speaking groups. The vast majority of them live today in the border areas of southwestern Yunnan Province in the People's Republic of China and in Kachin State in northern Myanmar (Burma). They prefer to live in valleys and small plains that are surrounded by mountains. Marus select their village sites at the foot of a mountain or at the edge of a plain. A typical village consists of several patrilineally related groups.

Chinese historians first make note of the Marus during the Tang dynasty more than a thousand years ago. They had originated to the north and to the east in what is today northern Myanmar and had settled in western Yunnan. Because of geographical isolation and indigenous economies, the region of far western Yunnan Province has never had a monoculture. Different ethnic groups live in close proximity to one another, even among one another in many pluralistic villages. Marus are surrounded by a variety of other ethnic groups in the region, including the Dai,* the Jingpo,* the Han,* the De'ang,* and the Wa.* Because they have adopted so much of the material culture of the surrounding groups, Marus are hardly distinguishable any more to outsiders as a distinct ethnic identity.

The Maru language is classified by ethnolinguists as one of the Kachin languages and part of the Tibeto-Burman* cluster in the Sino-Tibetan language family. It remains their primary language, although many Marus are also bilingual in Dai, Chinese,* Jingpo, Wa, or De'ang.

Historically, the Maru economy revolved around subsistence levels of wet-rice agriculture. They have adapted their planting and harvesting to the prevailing weather patterns, particularly the arrival of the monsoon season. Tobacco, sugarcane, and oil-producing plants have generated cash for the Maru economy. Textile production and silversmithing are also part of the local economy.

Since the Communist victory in 1949, the central government has become increasingly involved in Maru economic life. State programs to resettle Han people throughout the country as a means of encouraging assimilation have brought tens of thousands of immigrants to western Yunnan Province. The newcomers have succeeded in taking control—through outright seizure, legal purchase, or government condemnation—of large portions of Maru land. Instead of working as subsistence farmers on communal land, the Marus are rapidly becoming skilled workers, employed primarily by local businessmen. Since 1956 the Marus still engaged in agriculture have been forced by law to sell their produce to the central government at a fixed price.

Land tenure has also evolved over the years. For many years, land was controlled by Dai feudal lords or Maru chiefs. After the revolution, the landlords lost their land, although peasant families still had to pay rent to them. A brisk commerce in land sales took place among peasant households until 1956, when the central government mandated communal/state ownership of the land. They then experienced a steady, long-term decline in production, since the peasants could no longer keep the fruits of their labor. In 1982 Chinese officials reversed their policy and redivided the communal land among the peasants, a decision that has led to substantial increases in agricultural productivity.

The Maru social structure is based on a system of patrilineal descent, in which members of a village or several villages trace their ancestry back to a common male. Individuals must marry outside their patrilineal group, and marriages are generally arranged by parents for economic advantage. The fundamental family unit of Maru society is a patriarchal family that includes two or three generations.

Like other Kachin-speaking groups, the Marus maintain very eclectic religious beliefs. For many centuries now, they have been Buddhists, a religion given to them by surrounding Dai-speaking people. At the same time, traditional Maru animism survives. In the indigenous Maru religion, animals, plants, minerals, sun, moon, stars, and the earth are alive and are imbued with a measure of knowledge, individual consciousness, and awareness of things around them. Marus give names to every tree, animal, river, stream, meadow, mountain, hill, and valley, as well as to days, weeks, months, and seasons. All of creation has a spiritual essence, and there is a balance and solidarity to nature. Shamanism is present. Special religious practitioners function to bring good fortune to Marus and to prevent natural disasters.

MASHAN. The Mashan Miao are an ethnic group of approximately 100,000 people who live in Guizhou Province, particularly in Changshun, Luodian, Huishui, and Wangmo counties. The Mashan language is further divided into four mutually intelligible dialects. Although demographers and ethnologists in the People's Republic of China classify the Mashan as a Miao* subgroup, Mashans have a distinct sense of their own identity.

MECHE. The Meches are one of the most prominent clans of the Lisu* people of the People's Republic of China.

MEIFU. The Meifu (Moifau) people are one of the many subgroups of the Li* people of Hainan Province in the People's Republic of China. Like other Li groups, they have earned a reputation over the years for ferocious anti-Han* xenophobia, which has often taken the form of guerrilla warfare against Han immigrants to Hainan. Their hatred of the Nationalist government in the 1930s and 1940s also made them willing allies of Mao Zedong and the Communists, and when Mao triumphed, the Li were afforded recognition as heroes. Most Meifu today are farmers who raise coconuts, coffee, cocoa, sisal, rubber, cashews, pineapples, mangoes, and bananas. Rice is their staple, and because of the tropical climate of Hainan and its fertile soil, they are able to produce three rice crops a year. There are approximately 30,000 Meifus.

MEMPA. See **MOINBA.**

MENBA. See **MOINBA.**

MENG. See **MONGOL.**

MENGDA. The Mengdas are a subgroup of the Salar,* a Muslim minority in the People's Republic of China. The Mengda dialect is commonly heard among

Salar speakers in Mengda, Muchang, and Tashapo in Xunhua County of the Xinjiang Uigur Autonomous Region.

MENGSA. See **ACHANG.**

MENGSA-SHAN. See **ACHANG.**

MENPA. See **MOINBA.**

MEO. See **MIAO.**

MERGEN. The Mergens are one of the subdivisions of the Butha,* themselves a subgroup of the Daur* people of the People's Republic of China.

MEUNEU. Meuneu is one of the subdialects of the Lahuna* dialect of the Black Lahu* language in the People's Republic of China. See **LAHU.**

MIAN. Although the People's Republic of China classifies the Mian people as a subgroup of the Yao,* and for that reason does not extend to them official recognition as a minority nationality, the Mians actually constitute a self-conscious ethnic identity. Their language, though certainly in the Yao family, is not mutually intelligible with other Yao dialects. Mian possesses three primary dialects: Mianjin, Biaomin, and Zaomin. Biaomin can be subdivided into the Biaomin and Jiaogongmin subdialects. The Mian population of Yunnan Province today exceeds 135,000, of whom the vast majority live in Jinping, Funing, Guangnan, Malipo, Mengla, and Hekou Yao Autonomous counties.

Most Mians work as settled agriculturalists. A minority remain loyal to swidden, slash-and-burn techniques, but most of them use plowing techniques to cultivate rice. Where heavily forested regions border Mian farmlands, the people continue to hunt actively, often in carefully organized communal groups. The Mian social system revolves around patrilineal descent and patrilineal clans. Residence is patrilocal, and Mians prefer that all marriages be cross-cousin arrangements, in which young men marry their mother's brother's daughter.
SUGGESTED READING: S. A. Wurm, B. T'sou, D. Bradley, et al., eds., *Language Atlas of China*, 1987.

MIAO. The Miao people—also known as the Hmongs and Meos—are one of the largest officially recognized minority nationalities in the People's Republic of China (PRC). The 1990 national census placed their population at 7,398,677 people. Since they are one of the country's most rapidly growing ethnic groups, it is safe today to say that the Miao population is currently nearer to eight million people. They are very closely related to the Hmong people of Laos, Vietnam, and Thailand—all Miao people who continued their southern migration. Approximately 50 percent of the Chinese Miao live today in Guizhou Province.

Perhaps a third of the Miaos are equally divided between Sichuan and Guangxi provinces. The rest of the Miaos live in Guangdong Province and in Hainan Province. The Chinese government has established a number of autonomous political units for the Miao.

Any discussion of the Miao people as if they were a single ethnic group is frought with cultural and linguistic difficulties. Some scholars estimate that there are as many as seventy or eighty Miao subgroups scattered throughout the People's Republic of China, Laos, Thailand, Myanmar (Burma), and Vietnam. Others argue that the number of Miao subgroups in Southeast Asia numbers in the hundreds. Some of those groups have a strong sense of ethnicity; others have a less focused sense of group identity. On the other hand, nearly all of the Miao subgroups acknowledge their Miao heritage and understand the self-designation Hmong, but their actual ethnic focus is decidedly more local. Marriage is almost exclusively endogamous among the larger Miao peoples, but there is no stigma to marrying an individual from one of the other subgroups.

A key explanation for the internal diversity of the Miao people involves their history during the past four centuries, during what has been called the ''Miao'' diaspora. Between 1698 and 1855, the Chinese government conducted a series of brutal military campaigns against the rebellious Miao, who, in the process, scattered widely. The groups included today as the Black Miaos moved south into what is today Hunan and Guangxi provinces. The Red Miao moved slowly east into Hunan. White Miaos made their way northwest into what is today Suchuan Province. There are also Blue Miao and Flowery Miao.

The Miao people divide themselves into two general groupings based on cultural differences. Representatives from both groups can be found in China, Myanmar, Laos, Thailand, and Vietnam. The Monngua, also known as the Monlen, are the so-called Green Miao, which translates as the ''green,'' ''blue,'' or ''azure'' Miao. The term Blue Miao has been used synonymously with Green Miao. The Monklaw people constitute the second major Miao cluster. They are also known as White Miaos.

In addition to these two general clusters, a variety of other cultural, artistic, and linguistic factors have divided the Miao people into other subgroups. In the nineteenth and twentieth centuries, outside observers began to distinguish between various subgroups based on the clothing worn by Miao women, which varied from group to group and served as a culturally identifying characteristic to Miaos as well. The pleated skirts of Miao women are adorned by locally distinct, wax-resistant, dyed fabrics. The Monquamban, for example, are the Banded Sleeve Miao, named after the colorful vertical lines that appear on the sleeves of women's dresses. The Striped Miao, or Monyaochua people, are known for the telltale, colorful vertical stripes that run from the waistline to the hemline on women's dresses. The so-called Longhorn Miao are identified by the traditional headdress of women, in which the hair is wrapped around a device constructed from cattle horns. Other groups include the Short-Skirt Miao, Big-Board Miao, Cowrie-Shell Miao, Upside-Down Miao, Long-Skirt Miao, Shrimp

Miao, and Steep-Slope Miao. The so-called Miao people of Hainan Island are not Miao at all but ethnic Yaos* taken there by Han* military officers during the sixteenth century to assist in the pacification of the warlike Li* people.

Other Miao subdivisions are based on customs and rituals specific to that group which seem particularly notable to other Miao peoples. The Montuanu people, for example, are known as the Oxen-Killing Miao because of an annual, ceremonial sacrifice of oxen. The Montenkaus, or Amulet Miao, are named for their practice of wearing indigo-colored amulets. Many Miao groups trace their origins back to a mythical dog ancestor, and one group—the Monndaukles, or Dog-Mouth Miao—remember that ancestor ceremonially. The Monnaonens, or Man-Eating Miao, are still identified by their traditional ceremonial exogamous cannibalism, which is no longer practiced. The Pumpkin-Hole Miao, or Monqhaotaus, are another of these Miao subgroups. So are the Monmins, who are also known as the Miao-Min, Yu-Miao, and San-Miao. Their ethnonym translates into Engish as Magpie Miao.

The pace of acculturation with the larger commercial economy and Han society is another way of dividing Miao peoples into subgroups. The Monpw people, or Tame Miao, are named for their early rejection of violent reprisals and internecine warfare so common to mountain people in Southeast Asia. The Monsuas are the Sinicized Miaos who have traveled the farthest along the road toward Han acculturation. Many Han people also call them the Cooked Miao, as opposed to the Raw Miao, who have not assimilated much at all. The Monchis, or the White-Skinned Maio, are known for their relatively fair complexions.

Linguistic differences divide the Miao into dozens of distinct groups, making the idea of a single Miao ethnic community ludicrous. Ethnolinguists classify the various Miao dialects within the Miao branch of the Miao-Yao cluster of languages in the Sino-Tibetan language family. Miao is divided into three mutually unintelligible languages, each of which contains many mutually unintelligible dialects and subdialects. Western Hunan Miao is spoken by more than 800,000 people, perhaps one-quarter of the Miao people, who live in the western counties of Hunan Province and eastern Guizhou Province. It is also known as Xiang Xi or Eastern Miao. There are five primary Xiang Xi subdialects, each of which possesses several of its own vernaculars. The western local dialect is spoken by more than 700,000 people in Huayuan, Fenghuang, Jishou, Baojing, Guzhang, and Longshan counties in Hunan Province; Songtao and Tongren counties in Guizhou Province; and Hechi and Nandan counties in the Guangxi Zhuang Autonomous Region. The eastern local dialect is spoken by nearly 100,000 Miaos in the Luxi, Jishou, Guzhang, and Longshan counties in Hunan Province. Xiang Xi is distinct from Chuan Qing Dian and Qian Dong in that it possesses only six tones, instead of eight. Xiang Xi is not mutually intelligible with Chuan Qian Dian and Qian Dong.

The second major Miao language is Eastern Guizhou Miao, which is spoken by nearly 1.5 million people, more than one-third of all Miao people in China, most of whom live in Eastern Guizhou province. It is also known as Qian Dong or, to many linguists, Central Miao. Although most Qian Dongs are located in Guizhou Province, some Qian Dongs live in Guangxi Province and in Hunan Province. Qian Dong can be divided into three primary subdialects, and several distinct vernaculars can be identified in each of them. The northern local dialect can be heard among more than 900,000 people in Kaili, Huangping, Leishan, Taijianng, Jianhe, and Sandu counties in Guizhou Provinnce. The eastern local dialect is spoken by more than 200,000 people in Jinping and Liping counties in Guizhou Province and in Jingxian and Huitong counties in Hunan Province. More than 300,000 Miaos speak the southern dialect of the Eastern Guizhou language. It is commonly heard in Rongshui and Sanjiang counties in the Guangxi Zhuang Autonomous Region. Qian Dong possesses eight tones. Official Chinese ethnologists lump all Qian Dongs together with all Chuan Qian Dians as one ethnic group.

The third major language is known as Chuan Qian Dian Miao, also known to linguists as Sichuan-Guizhou-Yunnan Miao. The Chuan Qian Dian dialect is spoken by 1.7 million people in Sichuan, Guizhou, and Yunnan provinces. Chuan Qian Dian possesses seven subdialects, and those seven subdialects are themselves all divided into two or three distinct vernaculars. The primary dialect has two subdialects. Northeastern Yunnan Miao is spoken by 200,000 people in the cities of Yunming and Zhaotong and in Wuding, Luquan, Yiliang, Daguan, and Yongshan counties in Yunnan Province and in Weining and Hezhang counties in the Shuicheng Special Region of Guizhou Province. The Guiyang Miao dialect has four of its own subdialects. So does the Huishui Miao dialect, which is spoken in Huishui and Changshun counties in Guizhou. The Mashan dialect is spoken by more than 100,000 people in Changshun, Luodian, Huishui, Ziyun, and Wangmo counties in Guizhou Province. Mashan possesses four primary subdialects of its own. Luopohe Miao is spoken by nearly 50,000 people in Fuquan, Weng'an, Guiding, Longli, Kaili, and Kaiyang counties in Guizhou Province. Finally, nearly 50,000 Miaos speak the Chong'anjiang dialect and live in Huangping, Kaili, Qianxi, and Zhijin counties in Guizhou Province. Miao is a tonal language, and the Chuan Qian Dian dialect possesses eight tones. Because Chuan Qian Dian is not intelligible to other Miao speakers, some ethnologists insist on identifying Chuan Qian Dian people as a distinct ethnic group.

Because of the reality of these linguistic differences, describing the Miao as one people is difficult. Most of the subdialects of the three Miao languages are not mutually intelligible, which further subdivides them ethnically. In recent years, the Chinese government has begun to acknowledge this reality by extending official recognition to several of the Miao dialects and subdialects and by attempting to develop romanized written scripts for them, but the idea of trying to identify each of the Miao subgroups as a distinct ethnic group is too daunting.

In addition to these dialect differences within the Miao society, a variety of demographic considerations adds another layer that complicates the ethnic picture even more. Relatively few Miaos live in ethnically homogenous regions. On the contrary, most Miao villages are interspersed with those of other ethnic groups, and depending upon the concentrations of non-Miao people, the Miao language has picked up a substantial number of loan words, enough to distinguish them from other Miao groups. For example, Chuan Qing Dian speakers whose villages are surrounded by Han settlements will have picked up many Chinese* words, while Chuan Qing Dian speakers living among Zhuang* people will use many Zhuang words.

A number of Miao subgroups no longer speak their native language but nevertheless identify as ethnically distinct from the surrounding people whose languages they have adopted. Ethnolinguists today count more than 350,000 ethnic Miaos who speak Yao, Dong,* Tung, or Han Chinese languages as their native tongues. In Hunan, for example, more than 100,000 ethnic Miaos speak Chinese, although it is a Chinese language heavily mixed with Miao vocabulary. As many as 50,000 Dong-speaking Miaos can be found today in Hunan as well. Perhaps 15,000 Miaos in Guangdong Province speak a Yao language. Classifying these ethnically is difficult, particularly if linguistic loyalties are used as the defining factor of ethnicity. Nevertheless, they are included here as Miaos because of their own self-identity. Even if they speak Chinese as their primary language, surrounding ethnic Hans do not view them as Han. Nor do Dongs or Yaos when Miaos speak one of their languages. And the Miaos themselves, even when their native language has been abandoned, do not identify ethnically with the people whose languages they speak. There are also more than 40,000 Miaos who live on Hainan Island, where they speak various Miao, Li, and Chinese dialects.

Further complicating the Miao ethnic mosaic is the fact that the cultural subgroups and linguistic subgroups do not necessarily correspond. Over the course of many centuries of migration, Miao people have spread out over the Southeast Asian landscape. A group of Chuan Qian Dian speakers identified as Magpie Miao may have migrated and settled among a group of Cowrie-Shell Miao who speak a different dialect. The Magpies may acculturate to Cowrie-Shell Miao dress but retain their own dialect. In many instances, similar Miao cultural subgroupings do not speak the same dialect. Geographical boundaries do not regionally confine the Miao subgroups. Representatives of many of the cultural and linguistic subgroups can be found scattered throughout the Miao regions of Southeast Asia, living in different environmental settings. In the Ziyun region, where the Mashan Miao dialect is commonly found, there are also enclaves of Miao people who speak Chuan Qian Dian subdialects, which are not mutually intelligible with Mashan. And because Miaos have long been an animistic people whose religion is closely connected with specific ecological settings, unique religious beliefs and rituals have developed locally. Miao people from the same cultural group, and speaking the same dialect, may not share the same religious ceremonies, which becomes an ethnically distinguishing factor.

There are also a number of ethnic groups in Yunnan and Guizhou provinces who have at one time or another been classified as Miaos but who have vehemently denied such a grouping. Included in these groups are the Shuis,* Dongs, Tujias,* and Gelaos,* all of whom have recently received official recognition as separate minority nationalities. There are a number of other so-called Miao subgroups who would also appreciate such separate recognition.

Given this bewildering variety of cultural, linguistic, demographic, religious, and environmental factors, it is no wonder that Miao society is so ethnically complex. The number of possible ethnic permutations that stem from combining dozens of different linguistic, cultural, and geographic factors is huge. The Chinese government, in trying to make sense out of the country's ethnic complexity, chose to cluster all of these people into one category, but scholars and various Miao nationalists can easily disagree with the decision.

Miao society and political organization revolves around sixteen patrilineal clans. Within each Miao community, each clan is represented on a village council by a patriarch, who meets regularly with other clan headmen to make decisions concerning the entire community.

Chinese archaeologists and historians trace Miao origins back more than two millenia to the ancient San Miao Kingdom in central China. Tribal confederations of Miao migrated south from the regional plains between the Yellow River and the Yangtze River toward Dongting Lake, where they developed into the San Miao Kingdom. For the next millenium, the Miao continued their southeastern migration, pressured by the increasing size of the Han population and by the expansion of the imperial government during the Han and Song dynasties. The ancestors of contemporary Miaos put down roots in what is today western Hunan Province and Guizhou Province. Some Miao groups stayed on the move, heading south into what is today Guangxi Province and along the Wu River into Sichuan and Yunnan provinces. During the ensuing Yuan, Ming, and Qing dynasties, the migration continued, bringing Miao groups into what is today Laos, Vietnam, Myanmar, and Thailand.

The only way for the Miao to escape from Han pressure was to settle in highland areas unattractive to Han settlers. They employed slash-and-burn farming techniques to raise dry rice, wheat, buckwheat, and a variety of other products. In the late sixteenth and early seventeenth centuries, European traders introduced Irish potatoes into China, and Miao farmers readily adopted them. The potato was a perfect food—plentiful nutrients, adaptable to a variety of soils, extremely high yield per acre, and storable for long periods. They also adopted maize in the late sixteenth century. At the same time, Miao farmers began to produce such other high-altitude crops as barley, oats, and buckwheat. Miaos supplemented their diets by hunting and foraging.

During the past two centuries, Miaos have acquired the reputation of being a rebellious people. As the pressure of Han settlement increased and imperial Chinese political power descended on Miao communities, social and economic life changed. Landlordism increased, with Han people owning the land and Miaos having to work it. Tax burdens became heavier and heavier. Political corruption was extensive. Miaos frequently joined other ethnic minorities in rebelling against the imperial government. Miaos in western Hunan carried on an extended rebellion and guerrilla warfare against the Chinese from 1795 to 1806. In Guizhou Province, Miao rebellions erupted repeatedly between 1854 and 1872. In 1936 Miaos in western Hunan rebelled against the Chinese government's requirement that they work government land.

Chinese authorities over the years were alternatively enraged and perplexed over Miao intransigence. The government switched back and forth from assimilation to relocation to extermination and then back to assimilation. During the first half of the twentieth century—the so-called Republican period of Chinese history—the government promoted assimilation and suppressed Miao ethnicity. With the revolution in 1949, a policy shift occurred. The Communist government, on the surface at least, promoted Miao autonomy. In 1956 China established the Qiandongnan Miao-Dong Autonomous Prefecture and the Qianan Bouyei-Miao Autonomous Prefecture in Guizhou. They also organized Chengbu Miao Autonomous County in Hunan. In 1958 the central government established the Wenshan Zhuang-Miao Autonomous Prefecture of Yunnan. Altogether, there are ten other Miao autononomous political units in Guizhou, Yunnan, Sichuan, and Guangxi provinces. Large clusters of Miaos also live in the autonomous political units of other ethnic groups.

Miao settlements vary in size depending upon their elevation. At the higher altitudes, such as the plateau connecting Guizhou and Yunnan provinces, Miao villages are rarely larger than twenty households. At lower elevations, Miao settlements can be as large as one thousand households. The Miao economy also varies from region to region. Unlike many of the mountain peoples of southwestern China, the Miaos do not build their houses on elevated pilings. Most high-altitude villages support themselves through swidden farming techniques, raising buckwheat, oats, potatoes, corn, and hemp. When they are surrounded by Han farmers, Miaos use more sophisticated farming techniques, employing plows, fertilizers, and irrigation systems. Cowrie-Shell Miaos in Guizhou Province are settled agriculturalists who raise tobacco, millet, wheat, beans, vegetables, and wet-rice. Black Miaos in southeast Guizhou practice sophisticated, irrigated, terraced farming to raise rice.

Miao religious beliefs are equally complex and varied. Over the centuries, various Miao groups have adopted elements of folk Daoism and Buddhism, which they have added to their own traditional animism. Large numbers of White Miaos and Flowery Miaos converted to Christianity during the early decades of the twentieth century. As a result, Miao religion is quite eclectic. In traditional Miao animism, the world is seen as inhabited by a vast number of unseen ghosts, dragons, demons, angels, and spirits, which represent the afterlife of one's ancestors or the unseen spirits of trees, animals, bridges, rivers, mountains, heavenly bodies, wells, stones, and valleys. Guardian spirits watch over households and villages, but evil spirits can also interfere in human affairs, and people need the intervention of shamans to protect them.

Miao religion is preoccupied with fears of disease and sudden death. Over the millenia, the extremes of temperature they have faced in their mountain homelands have given them unusually high mortality rates, as has what many consider to be an inadequate diet. But there is also a phenomenon of "sudden death syndrome" that continues to afflict significant numbers of Miao, enough to raise the curiosity of epidemiologists around the world.

During the years of the Indochinese wars between 1954 and 1975, Miaos divided their loyalty among the forces of North Vietnam, the United States, and even the Khmer Rouge in Cambodia. Thousands of Miaos moved back and forth across the Laotian and Vietnamese Chinese border during the conflict. In 1975, when the Communists triumphed in Cambodia, Laos, and Vietnam, the pro-American Miaos found themselves in difficult political circumstances. Tens of thousands of Miao, or Hmong, people emigrated to the United States and Western Europe. The sudden death phenomenon followed them to the United States.

SUGGESTED READINGS: Bai Ziren, ed., *A Happy People*, 1988; Robert G. Cooper, *Resource Scarcity and the Hmong Response: Patterns of Settlement and Economy in Transition*, 1984; Chen Rinong, "Proud Miao Villagers Shake Off Poverty," *China Today* 42 (March 1993), 12–17; Norma Diamond, "The Miao and Poison: Interactions on China's Southwest Frontier," *Ethnology* 27 (1988), 1–25; R. A. D. Forest, *The Chinese Language*, 1965; W. R. Geddes, *Migrants of the Mountains: The Cultural Ecology of the Blue Miao (Hmong Njua) of Thailand*, 1976; André G. Haudicourt, "Introduction à la phonologie historique des langues Miao-Yao," *BEFEO* (1954), 564–65; Glenn L. Hendricks, Bruce T. Downing, and Amos S. Deinard, eds., *The Hmong in Transition*, 1986; Thomas Amis Lyman, *Grammar of Mong Njua (Green Miao): A Descriptive Study*, 1979; Margaret Mickey, *The Cowrie Shell Miao of Kweichow*, 1947; Ruey Yih-Fu, "The Magpie Miao of Southern Szechuan," in George Peter Murdock, ed., *Social Structure in Southeast Asia*, 1960; Louisa Schein, "The Dynamics of Cultural Revival among the Miao in Guizhou," in Chiao Chien and Nicholas Tapp, eds., *Ethnicity and Ethnic Groups in China*, 1989; Sun Chengdi, "The Grand, Traditional Miao People," *China Today* 44 (February 1995), 68–75; Nicholas Tapp, "Hmong," in Paul V. Hockings, ed., *The Encyclopedia of World Cultures*, vol. 6, *East and Southeast Asia*, 1991; Zeng Qingnan, "Celebrating with the Longhorn Miao," *China Today* 41 (January 1992), 68–74.

MIAO-YAO. In addition to referring to two distantly related peoples in Southeast Asia—the Miaos* (Hmongs) and the Yaos*—"Miao-Yao" is a term that is employed by ethnolinguists to describe a language group in the region. It consists of just two languages—Miao and Yao—which are different enough today to convince anthropologists that the two peoples separated centuries, perhaps even millenia, ago. The Miao-Yao languages stretch from just below the Yangtze River in Hubei Province of the People's Republic of China in the north to central Thailand in the south. Linguists cannot really speak of Miao or Yao as single languages, since each contains dozens of dialects that are not always mutually intelligible.

SUGGESTED READINGS: Herbert C. Purnell, ed., *Miao and Yao Linguistic Studies: Selected Articles in Chinese*, trans. by Chang Yu-hung and Chu Kuo-ray, 1972; S. Robert Ramsey, *The Languages of China*, 1987.

MIEN YAO. The Mien Yaos are currently considered by the People's Republic of China to be a subgroup of the Yao* people, who live in Guangxi, Hunan, Guangdong, Jiangxi, Guizhou, and Yunnan provinces. The problem with classifying Mien Yaos with the other so-called Yao peoples is language. The government argues that there are four subgroups of the Yao people—Byau Min Yao,* Kim Mun Yao,* Mien Yao, and Yao Min.* But these are not really dialects. Although all four are classified in the Miao-Yao linguistic family, they are not mutually intelligible. If the language spoken by Mien Yaos is not comprehensible to the other Yao subgroups, then the argument for separate and official ethnic status is a compelling one.

Demographers estimate that there are more than 1.3 million Mien Yao people. Their economies vary according to ecological setting, with agriculture, hunting, and foraging occupying the Mien. Their social system is based on patrilineal descent, and young people are expected to marry endogamously. Elders frown on someone who marries an individual from another Yao group. That stigma against exogamous marriage to any other people, including other Yaos, is more evidence that Mien Yaos constitute a distinct ethnic entity.

MIN. The term ''Min'' is used here to describe the people who speak the Min Chinese* language. Linguists estimate today that more than 50 million people speak Min, which has also been called Hokkien. Min speakers today can be found in southern China, primarily in Fujian, Hainan, Zhejiang, and Guangdong provinces in the People's Republic of China (PRC), as well as on Taiwan in the Republic of China. Traditionally, Min speakers were fishermen and seafarers, which gave them the opportunity to settle along coastal areas. Taiwan was settled by Min speakers from southern Fujian Province who crossed the Formosa Straits during the Ming dynasty.

Although PRC linguists insist that Min is simply a dialect of Chinese, it is not mutually intelligible with other Chinese dialects. For most linguists, mutual intelligibility is a requirement for a language to be classified as a dialect. The various Chinese dialects are not mutually intelligible. At the same time, however, they share an unusual linguistic similarity. The spoken Chinese languages cannot be mutually understood by different speakers, but they all read and write with the same script. Some linguists have begun employing the term ''regionalect'' to describe the eight Chinese languages. Whether or not Mandarin, Wu, Jin, Gan, Xiang, Hakka, Yue, and Min are dialects, regionalects, or languages, they divide the more than 1.1 billion Han people into distinguishable, individual groups whose members share loyalty and a sense of identity with one another because of language.

Among the Min-speaking peoples of southern China, ethnic divisions based on dialect are especially compelling, because so many of the dialects are not mutually intelligible. Linguist S. Robert Ramsey has stated that the Min dialects are ''the most heterogeneous in China.'' Some linguists have identified nine mutually unintelligible dialects in Fujian Province, several more in Guangdong

Province, and on Taiwan. Others claim that there are even more mutually un-intelligible dialects. A widely accepted classification system today claims that there are seven fundamental Min languages: Minnan, Puxian, Mindong, Minbei, Minzhong, Qiongwen, and Shaojiang. Each of them is mutually unintelligible. The Minnan, Mindong, and Qiongwen languages can also be divided into a variety of dialects, many of which are not mutually intelligible.
SUGGESTED READINGS: S. Robert Ramsey, *The Languages of China*, 1987; S. A. Wurm, B. T'sou, D. Bradley, et al., eds., *Language Atlas of China*, 1987.

MINBEI. Approximately 2.2 million people in the People's Republic of China speak Minbei, a dialect of the Min* Chinese* language. Minbei speakers can be found today in the Jian'ou, Jianyang, Chong'an, Songxi, Zhenghe, Nanping, Pucheng, and Shunchang regions of northern Fujian Province. See **HAN**.

MINCHIA. See **BAI**.

MINCHIA-TZU. See **BAI**.

MINDONG. Approximately 8 million people in the People's Republic of China speak Minnan, a dialect of the Min* Chinese* language. Mindong speakers can be found today in nineteen cities and counties of northeastern Fujian Province. Mindong can be divided into two dialects: Houguan and Funing. See **HAN**.

MINHE. The Minhes are one of the two primary subgroups of the Tu* people, who live in Qinghai Province in the People's Republic of China.

MINJIA. See **BAI**.

MINNAN. Approximately 36 million people in the People's Republic of China speak Minnan, a dialect of the Min* Chinese* language. Minnan speakers can be found today in fifty-three cities and counties of southern Fujian Province, eastern Guangdong Province, and Taiwan. Minnan can also be divided into three dialects: Quanzhang, Datian, and Chaoshan. See **HAN**.

MINZHONG. Approximately 750,000 people in the People's Republic of China speak Minzhong, a dialect of the Min* Chinese* language. Minzhong speakers can be found today in the Sanming, Yong'an, and Shaxian regions of central Fujian Province. See **HAN**.

MISABA. The Misabas are an ethnic group who live in the People's Republic of China (PRC), although the central government has never extended to them formal recognition as a minority nationality. Official PRC publications classify them as a Yi* subgroup, and, indeed, they speak a Yi language. But Misaba is not mutually intelligible with the vast majority of other Yi languages, and the

Misabas give themselves a distinct, separate identity. Although they acknowledge a certain cultural affinity with the Yi, they nevertheless insist that they are a separate people. Misabas can be found in Guizhou and Yunnan provinces. Their economy, which is primarily agricultural, revolves around the production of maize, potatoes, buckwheat, and oats, and they raise cattle, sheep, goats, poultry, swine, and horses in the highlands. Their villages are quite small, more like hamlets, and their homes are constructed of wood and dirt.

MITRO. See **DAI.**

MNGAHRIS. The Mngahris people are ethnic Tibetans* who speak the Mngahris vernacular of the Dbusgtsang* dialect. Most Mngahris speakers live today in Ngari Prefecture of the Tibetan Autonomous Region of the People's Republic of China.

MOAMIAMI. See **AMI.**

MOIFAU. See **MEIFU.**

MOINBA. The Moinbas—or Menbas, Monpas, Monbas, Moinpas, Menpas, and Dakpas—are one of the smallest officially recognized minority nationalities in the People's Republic of China (PRC). Other Moinbas can be found in India, primarily in the Kameng District of Arunachal Pradesh State. Because they live in Tibet, of course, Tibetan nationalists around the world reject the notion that the Moinbas are a Chinese nationality. Their population in the 1990 census totaled only 7,475 people, but that number vastly underestimates the number of people in the PRC who are aware of their Moinba heritage. Most Moinbas live in Medog, Nyingchi, and Cona counties in southern Tibet. They are surrounded by ethnic Tibetans,* with whom they have intermarried for decades. Moinbas speak a Tibeto-Burman* language, which is part of the Sino-Tibetan family. It is subdivided into dozens of dialects.

Two Moinba languages, which are barely mutually intelligible, divide the Moinbas into two very distinct groups of people, different enough to be considered independent ethnic entities, although the PRC government does not recognize either of them officially. The Cuona* language of Moinba is spoken by approximately 35,000 people, most of whom live in Lebu Prefecture in Cuona County and in Linzhi County in the Tibetan Autonomous Region. The other Moinba language, known as Motuo,* is spoken by approximately 5,000 people, most of whom live in Motuo and Linzhi counties of Dongjui Prefecture of the Tibetan Autonomous Region.

Moinba history in southeastern Tibet is relatively recent. Most historians and archaeologists believe that nearly three centuries ago, the Moinbas migrated across the Himalayas from the Moinnyu area to Mainling on the Yarlung Zangbo River, and then along the river to settle in Medog, Nyingchi, and Cuona coun-

ties. There they transplanted an agricultural, pastoral lifestyle. Because of persecution from ethnic Tibetans over the years, Moinbas live in isolated, forested,
mountainous, or deep gorge areas of southern Tibet. Their local climate is subtropical and the soil fertile. Moinba farmers cultivate rice, maize, millet, buckwheat, soybeans, and sesame seeds. Moinba pastoralists herd cattle and sheep,
and hunting remains important as a source of protein and male bonding. They
are also well-known regionally for their skills in manufacturing saddle bags,
carpets, and mats. Moinba dress separates them from surrounding Tibetans. In
the Lekpo region, Moinba women wear bright red gowns made of tweed. They
also wear red conical hats bordered by an orange stripe. White aprons are also
common among Moinba women. In the Medog region, Moinba women differentiate themselves from other Tibetans by wearing a multicolored, striped apron.

Although some elements of traditional Moinba animism survive in contemporary culture, most Moinbas are Lamaist Buddhists, just like their Tibetan
neighbors. Devoutly religious, they are committed to pursuing individual enlightenment, accept the idea of reincarnation, and believe that, after many cycles
of the recurrent process of life, death, and rebirth, the individual soul finds
enlightenment and enters nirvana. The major Moinba Lamaist monastery is located in Tawang. The sixth Dalai Lama, Tsangtang Gyatso, was a Moinba.

SUGGESTED READINGS: Tiley Chodag, *Tibet: The Land and Its Peoples*, 1988; Paul
V. Hockings, ''Moinba,'' in Paul V. Hockings, ed., *The Encyclopedia of World Cultures*,
vol. 6, *East and Southeast Asia*, 1991; Ma Yin, ed., *China's Minority Nationalities*, 1989;
S. A. Wurm, B. T'sou, D. Bradley, et al., eds., *Language Atlas of China*, 1987; Zhang
Jiannghua and Wu Congzhong, ''Tibet's Menba Nationality,'' *China Reconstructs* 28
(July 1979), 54–56.

MOINPA. See **MOINBA.**

MOK. The Moks are considered by many ethnologists in the People's Republic
of China to be a subgroup of the Wa,* an officially recognized minority nationality. Most Wa people live in the southwestern reaches of Yunnan Province,
primarily in Ximeng, Canghyuan, Menglian, Gengma, Lancang, Shuangjiang,
Yongde, and Zhenkang counties. Most Moks are farmers, but their techniques
vary from village to village; some use traditional slash-and-burn methods, and
others employ more modern, sophisticated techniques. They raise wet rice, dry
rice, maize, millet, tubers, and wheat. Classifying them as a subgroup of the Wa
poses problems to ethnologists and ethnolinguists because the Mok ''dialect''
is not mutually intelligible with most of the other Wa dialects.

MOKERTU. The Mokertus are a subgroup of the Hailar* people, who are themselves a subgroup of the Daur* ethnic group in the People's Republic of China.

MOLAO. See **MULAM.**

MOLO. See **MULAM.**

MONBA. See **MOINBA.**

MONCHI. The Monchis, a Miao* subgroup, are identified by their relatively fair complexions. The name Monchi is translated as "White-Skinned Miao." They live in Yunnan Province of the People's Republic of China.

MONGOL. See **TU.**

MONGOL. The Mongols are one of the officially recognized minority nationalities of the People's Republic of China (PRC), and Mongol people can also be found in Mongolia, Russia, Kazakstan, and Kirgizstan today. The Mongolian cultural region stretches from northeastern Manchuria into eastern Xinjiang. On a north-south axis, Mongol culture extends from the Ordos Desert in the south to Lake Baikal in Siberian Russia. In Mongolia, they constitute more than 90 percent of the country's population of 2 million; in the Inner Mongolian Autonomous Region (IMAR) of the People's Republic of China, where they account for only 14 percent of the population, they are vastly outnumbered by Han* and Hui* people. There are roughly 2.9 million Mongols living today in the IMAR. Other Chinese Mongols can be found in Qinghai Province and in the Xinjiang Uigur Autonomous Region. Throughout the PRC, the Mongol population today exceeds 5 million people. The 1990 national census counted 4,806,849 Mongols, but they have one of the highest birthrates of the minority groups.

Mongols in the People's Republic of China are divided into a great variety of subgroups based on dialect and historical circumstance. The Mongolian language is classified with the Mongolian branch of languages in the Altaic* linguistic family. It has strong affiliations with Daur,* Bonan,* Dongxiang,* Tu,* and Enger,* which is the eastern dialect of Yugur.* It is divided into dozens of mutually intelligible dialects. The Oirat* dialect, one of the two major Mongolian dialects of the Mongolian People's Republic, is spoken primarily there in the western reaches of the country. Oirat is also spoken in northwestern Xinjiang and in Qinghai Province. The Chakhar* dialect is spoken in the central region of the IMAR in the People's Republic of China; so is Shiliingol,* which is closely related to Chakhar. Both Chakhar and Shiliingol bear strong similarities to Khalkha, the major Mongolian dialect spoken in the Mongolian People's Republic. The Barga* (Bargu) Mongolian dialect, as well as Buryat,* is spoken primarily in the northeastern IMAR. The major Mongolian dialect spoken in southeastern IMAR is Korchin* (Jirem), while Alshaa* is the major dialect of the northwest. In southwestern IMAR, Ordos (see **ORDO**) is the key Mongolian dialect. All of the Mongolian dialects spoken in Xinjiang, Qinghai, and IMAR are mutually intelligible. The various Mongol dialects are also divided into a series of closely related yet distinct vernaculars. The Korchin dialect of southeastern Mongolia, for example, possesses a number of distinct vernaculars, several of which correspond to the country's southeastern political subdivisions: Subhaatar, East Govi, and South Govi. The Ordos dialect of southwestern Mongolia is divided into the Bayan-Hongor, Govi-Altay, and Hovd vernaculars. Each of the above-mentioned vernaculars is also spoken in the corresponding, cross-border regions of the IMAR. Other Mongol subgroups, whose identity is based on other historical circumstances, include the Khiangan, Juu Ud, and Tumed.

Until the early thirteenth century, Mongols were an unknown, insignificant tribal people native to north central Asia. Beginning in the mid-1200s, however, Mongol armies swept out of their homelands and became one of the most feared political forces in the world. Before the rise of the Mongol empire in the thirteenth century, the region that is contemporary Mongolia was inhabited by the warlike Xiongnu people, who may very well have been the same, or closely related, to the Huns who laid waste to much of Europe in the fourth and fifth centuries. Turkic-speaking people migrated into the region later, and out of a mixture of these groups and others emerged the Mongols. By the thirteenth century, they had evolved into thirty distinct tribes.

By 1206 the Mongol leader Temujen had put together a federation of many of those tribes, and he was installed as the Genghis Khan, or "strong ruler." Five years later, he led the Mongol armies on a crusade that brought much of the known world under his control. Within a decade, Genghis Khan's armies had conquered a region that stretched from what is today North Korea all the way west to the Mediterannean Sea in southern Europe. Later in the century, however, the Mongols began to disintegrate into what became a series of independent khanates.

After the Manchu* conquest in 1644, the new dynastic government divided the Mongolian cultural region into two districts—Outer Mongolia and Inner Mongolia. Each of those two districts was further subdivided into "banners," which were political subdivisions out of which individual Mongol communities could not migrate. The banner system was a Manchu attempt to cut down on Mongol nomadism. When the Manchu, or Qing, dynasty disintegrated in 1911, a power struggle between the Chinese and the Russians* began over who would control Outer Mongolia and Inner Mongolia. Outer Mongolia essentially became the Russian-controlled Mongolian People's Republic in 1924, and the Japanese established a puppet government in Inner Mongolia in 1937. Soviet troops entered the region when the Japanese troops withdrew in 1945. Inner Mongolian forces threw their support behind Mao Zedong during the Chinese civil war. As a result, the Inner Mongolian Autonomous Region remains a Chinese territory today.

Traditionally, the Mongol economy has reflected the local ecology. Although a diverse collection of mountains and steppes, Mongolia is a landlocked, arid part of the world. Summers are hot and winters dry and cold. For hundreds of years, nomadic pastoralism characterized Mongol economic life, as they raised and grazed horses, cattle, camels, sheep, and goats. In recent years, Mongol pastoralists have begun to emphasize sheep production, primarily because they can maximize their investment by selling wool and meat. But they have also been farmers for several centuries now, and today Mongol agriculturalists produce wheat, barley, buckwheat, millet, oats, corn, potatoes, and a variety of fruits and vegetables. Mongol society remains overwhelmingly rural.

Until the sixteenth century, when Lamaist Buddhism made its way into Mongolia, Mongol animism and shamanism governed the religious lives of most people. During the reign of the Manchus, Lamaist Buddhism thrived, although it was usually an eclectic mix of Buddhism and animism. Most of traditional Mongolian animism no longer survives in the Mongolian People's Republic, but it is still strong in the IMAR, where it is known as the *oboo* faith. Individual Mongol communities maintain *oboo* shrines, which they believe are inhabited by various ghosts, spirits, and gods. There are also several thousand Muslim Alshaa Mongols in the western IMAR.

For the Russians and the Chinese, Mongols have long posed a strategic concern. During the first half of the twentieth century, from the Russo-Japanese War of 1904–1905 through the end of World War II, Japan focused on Mongolia as a way of establishing its own political foothold in Siberia and East Asia. Japanese, and for that matter, Chinese political officials had long considered Siberia to be a ripe plum ready for the taking, a region rich in natural resources that Russia and later the Soviet Union could not govern from Moscow, thousands of miles to the west. Japanese agents have repeatedly tried to foment pan-Mongolian sentiments among the various Mongol peoples of Russia, Mongolia, and China. They fostered it during the Russo-Japanese War, again during the post-Bolshevik civil war in Russia between 1918 and 1922, after their invasions of Manchuria in 1931 and China in 1937, and throughout World War II. Cozy relationships between Mongol nationalists and the Japanese have periodically infuriated the Soviets, who took out their frustrations in genocidal attacks upon the Mongol people. Although it would certainly be a long shot, the political unification of Khalkhas, Oirats, Ordos, Buryats, Bargas, Chakhars, Shiliingols, Korchins, Alshaas, and even Daurs in north central Asia would create a new political force that would threaten Moscow's control of Siberia.

China has historically had similar difficulties with the Mongols. Like the Russians and Soviets, they too were troubled and frightened by repeated Japanese overtures to the Mongols during the twentieth century. After World War II, when the Soviet Union essentially made a satellite out of the Mongolian People's Republic, Chinese fears of pan-Mongolism lost their anti-Japanese flavor and took on an anti-Soviet flavor. Pan-Mongolism henceforth was seen as a Soviet subterfuge to strengthen its presence in central and East Asia. Dashi-Nima Dondupov, for example, a Russian Buryat nationalist and cultural elitist, has developed a following among other Buryats in the IMAR.

The Lamaist Buddhist beliefs of so many Mongols also pose a threat to the Chinese because of the religion's strong ties to Tibet. During the nineteenth and early twentieth centuries, military forces from British India frequently pushed their way into Tibet, and Chinese forces did the same from the north and north-east. For centuries, Chinese authorities had looked longingly at Tibet. The in-terlocking Karakorum, Ladak, and Himalayan mountain ranges protected China from India in the south and from European imperialists from the west, but China had long been obsessed with the possibility of a foreign power's colonizing Tibet. For British armies in Tibet, an invasion of China would be a relatively easy matter.

After losing tens of millions of people during World War II at the hand of Japanese occupation forces, China became even more paranoid about its fron-tiers. In 1950, a year after Mao Zedong's Communist victory, the new revolu-tionary government of the People's Republic of China decided to act on its fears. Chinese military forces invaded the Kham, U, and Tsang districts of Tibet and proclaimed political sovereignty there. In 1959 the Dalai Lama went into exile in India; nevertheless, he remains the religious leader of millions of Ti-betans and Mongols. Chinese officials worry that an independence movement in Tibet would inspire similar feelings among their own Mongol people. Today, China reacts immediately and oppressively to any expression of Tibetan or Mon-golian nationalism.

Politics today in the IMAR continue to reflect feelings of suspicion and hos-tility between Mongols and Han. Han Chinese now constitute more than 80 percent of the IMAR's population, and Mongols look upon them as usurpers, late arrivals who have gobbled up power for themselves. For their part, the Han Chinese resent recent PRC affirmative action programs that have favored the hiring of ethnic Mongols into positions of political and economic responsibility. They also resent the fact that the People's Republic of China exempts Mongols from its one-child state population policy.

By the early 1990s, the rivalry between Han Chinese and Mongols in the IMAR had spawned a dissident movement demanding reunification between Inner Mongolia and Mongolia. The collapse of the Soviet Union had allowed Mongolia to become a democratic republic, and, in the process, Mongolian cul-ture thrived. Mongolian language newspapers and radio and television broad-casts coming out of Mongolia reached Inner Mongolia, creating a sense of cultural unity that had not been there before. Dissident groups—such as the General Coordination Committee of Inner Mongolian Rejuvenation Move-ments—began to attract attention, demanding unification with Mongolia, a ban on any future Han immigration to Inner Mongolia, and freedom of speech and assembly. The PRC has banned all of the Mongol nationalist groups, and a number of Mongol dissidents, such as Uringkhai N. Tumen and Tsenglet, have relocated to Ulan Bator, the capital of Mongolia, to continue their campaign for freedom. Political restlessness in Mongolia is not as deep or widespread as it is among Tibetans and Xinjiang Muslims, but it is nevertheless a very real source of concern to PRC officials.

SUGGESTED READINGS: Cynthia Beall and Melvyn Goldstein, ''Mongolian Nomads,'' *National Geographic* 183 (May 1993), 127–38; Don Belt, ''The World's Great Lake,''

National Geographic 181 (June 1992), 2–40; Mike Edwards, "Lord of the Mongols: Genghis Khan," *National Geographic* 190 (December 1996), 2–37; *Great Soviet Encyclopedia*, 11:364–68, 1973; Sechin Jacchid and Paul Hyer, *Mongolia's Culture and Society*, 1979; William Jankowiak, "Mongols," in Paul V. Hockings, ed., *The Encyclopedia of World Cultures*, vol. 6, *East and Southeast Asia*, 1991; Jia Laikuan, "Ordos Wedding on the Grasslands," *China Today* 41 (November 1992), 49–51; Jian Qun, "Reviving Ancient Languages," *China Today* 42 (August 1993), 41–43; Walter Kolarz, *The Peoples of the Soviet Far East*, 1954; Ross Marlay, "Buryats," in James S. Olson, ed., *Ethnohistorical Dictionary of the Soviet Union*, 1993; William O. McCagg and Brian D. Silver, eds., *Soviet Asian Ethnic Frontiers*, 1979; "Mongol," *Current Digest* 41 (March 22, 1989): 22–23; *New York Times*, July 19, 1992; Robert Rupen, *How Mongolia Is Really Ruled*, 1979, and *Mongols of the Twentieth Century*, 1964; Sevyan Vainshtein, *Nomads of South Siberia*, 1979; K. V. Vyatkina, "The Buryats," in M. G. Levin and L. P. Potapov, eds., *The Peoples of Siberia*, 1964; Pyotr Zubkhov, "Buryatia: A Republic on Lake Baikal," *Soviet Life* 378 (1988), 41–46.

MONGOLIAN. See **MONGOL.**

MONGOLIAN HUIHUI. See **DONGXIANG.**

MONGSHA. See **ACHAN.**

MONGUOR. See **TU.**

MON-KHMER. Ethnolinguists employ the term "Mon-Khmer" to describe a linguistic family in Southeast Asia. The Mon people are a prominent ethnic group in southern Myanmar (Burma) and Thailand, and the Khmers* are the dominant group in Cambodia. Three Mon-Khmer languages are spoken in the People's Republic of China, all in the country's southwestern extremity of Yunnan Province: Blang,* De'ang,* and Wa.*
SUGGESTED READING: S. Robert Ramsey, *The Languages of China*, 1987.

MONKLAW. The Monklaws, also known as White Miaos, are one of the two major subgroupings of the Miao* people of Southeast Asia. There are also a number of Miao tribal groupings who identify themselves as Monklaws.

MONLEN. See **MONNGUA.**

MONMIN. The Monmins are one of the Miao* subgroups of the People's Republic of China. They are also known as the Miao-Min, Yu-Miao, and San-Miao. Their ethnonym translates into English as "Magpie Miao."

MONNAONEN. The Monnaonens, whose name translates as the "Man-Eating Miao," are one of the many subgroups of the Miao* people of the People's

Republic of China. The name is derived from their traditional, ceremonial exogamous cannibalism, which they no longer practice.

MONNDAUKLE. The Monndaukle people, also known as the Dog-Mouth Miao, are one of the subgroups of the Miao* people of the People's Republic of China.

MONNGUA. The Monngua people are one of the two major subgroupings of the Miao* people of Southeast Asia. They are also known as the Green Miao or the Blue Miao. There are also a number of Miao tribal groupings who identify themselves as Monngua.

MONPA. See **MOINBA.**

MONPW. The Monpw people are one of the subgroups of the Miao* people of the People's Republic of China. Their ethnonym translates as ''Tame Miao,'' which derives from their early rejection of retaliatory violence.

MONQHAOTAU. The Monqhaotaus, who are also known as the Pumpkin-Hole Miao, are one of the subgroups of the Miao* people of the People's Republic of China.

MONQUAMBAN. The Monquamban, which translates as ''Banded Sleeve Miao,'' are one of the Miao* cultural subgroups in the People's Republic of China.

MONSUA. The Monsuas are one of the subgroups of the Miao* people of the People's Republic of China. Their name translates as ''Sinicized Miao,'' which is based on their advanced state of acculturation with surrounding Han* institutions.

MONTENKAU. The Montenkaus are one of the subgroups of the Miao* people of the People's Republic of China. Their name translates as ''Amulet Miao.''

MONTUANU. The Montuanus are one of the subgroups of the Miao* people of the People's Repubic of China. Their name translates into English as ''Oxen-Killing Miao.''

MONYAOCHUA. The Monyaochua, which translates as ''Striped Miao,'' are one of the Miao* cultural subgroups in the People's Republic of China.

MONZHI. The Monzhis are a dialect subgroup of the Jingpo* branch of the Jingpo people of the People's Republic of China. They all live in Yunnan Province.

MO-QUAMI. See **AMI.**

MOSO. See **NAXI.**

MOSO MAN. See **NAXI.**

MOSU. The Mosus are an ethnic group in the People's Republic of China, although the central government has never extended to them formal recognition as a minority nationality. Official PRC publications classify them as a Yi* subgroup, and, indeed, they speak a Yi language. But Mosu is not mutually intelligible with the vast majority of other Yi languages, and the Mosus give themselves a distinct, separate identity. Although they acknowledge a certain cultural affinity with the Yi, they nevertheless insist that they are a separate people.

Most Mosus live today in Yunnan Province. Their economy is primarily agricultural. Mosu farmers at lower altitudes raise maize, potatoes, buckwheat, and oats; in the highlands, they raise cattle, sheep, goats, and horses. Poorer Mosu families still engage in foraging activities to supplement their diet. Mosu villages are quite small, more like hamlets, and their homes are constructed of wood and dirt. Their religious beliefs today remain an eclectic mix of Daoism, Buddhism, animism, and shamanism.

MOSUO. See **YI.**

MOSUO. The Mosuo people are an ethnic group in the People's Republic of China, although the central government has never extended to them formal recognition as a minority nationality. Official PRC publications classify the Mosuo people as a subgroup of the Naxi,* and, indeed, they speak a Naxi language. The Mosuo language, however, is not really mutually intelligible with Naxi, and Mosuos give themselves a distinct, separate identity. About 15,000 Mosuos live, at an altitude of more than 9,000 feet, around Lugu Lake in the Ninglang Yi Autonomous County of northern Yunnan Province. Here, they live amidst the Pumi* people.

Mosuo villages range in size from twenty to more than a thousand people. They build their homes in close proximity to one another, with vegetable gardens and fruit orchards nearby. Farther away, but within convenient walking distances, are their fields where staple crops are raised. Traditional Mosuo homes were made of logs and roof slats weighted down by heavy rocks, but in recent years Mosuos have begun to construct homes similar to those of their Han* and Pumi neighbors: wood frames, tiled roofs, and tamped earth or adobe walls.

Most Mosuos are farmers today, although the crops they harvest vary depending upon the altitude of their settlements. Mosuo farmers at lower elevations are most likely to raise wet rice, citrus, and vegetables. At higher elevations, they produce wheat, legumes, maize, apples, and pears. Because these crops do not thrive at higher altitudes, Musuo farmers there produce potatoes and turnips. At the higher elevations where forage is good, they are active pastoralists, raising goats, sheep, and cattle. Higher still, Musuo herders raise yaks and mixed cattle-yak breeds. Most Mosuo family compounds also abound in chickens, pigs, oxen, ducks, and water buffalo. They also harvest shrimp and carp from the lake.

Unlike most surrounding ethnic groups, the Mosuos are loyal to a matriarchal order. Descent is matrilineal and residence is matrilocal. In recent years, under the social pressures of the increasing number of Han people settling in the region, patriarchal institutions are making inroads into Mosuo society.

Mosuo religion is a reflection of their long history and the multiethnic setting of Yunnan Province. Their faith is an eclectic mix of traditional Mosuo animism along with Buddhist and Daoist beliefs. For centuries now, marriages and funerals have often been mixed ceremonies presided over by Mosuo religious specialists and Tibetan* and Chinese monks. The pantheon of Mosuo deities includes thousands of invisible beings who reside in heaven and in purgatory and throughout the natural world. Every plant, animal, and major geographical landmark has its own deity, and often the Mosuos believe such gods have demonic counterparts. Life, and the world itself, is one long struggle for power between good and evil, and the Mosuos rely on shamans known as *dobbaqs* to assist them in interpreting the events transpiring around them and in warding off the negative influences of evil spirits. Mosuos believe that after death, the soul of an individual can be reincarnated but that eventually it must travel the road of its ancestors and return home to the ''north.''

SUGGESTED READINGS: Mike Edwards, ''Our Man in China: Joseph Rock,'' *National Geographic* 191 (January 1997), 62–100; Anthony Jackson, *Na-khi Religion: An Appraisal of the Nakhi Ritual Texts*, 1979, and *Life among the Minority Nationalities of Northwest Yunnan*, 1989; Charles F. McKhan, ''Naxi,'' in Paul Hockings, ed., *The Encyclopedia of World Cultures*, vol. 6, *East and Southeast Asia*, 1991; Peng Jianqun, ''The Matriarchal Village of Lugu Lake,'' *China Today* 44 (March 1995), 10–12; Joseph Rock, *The Ancient Na-khi Kingdom of Southwest China*, 1947.

MOTUO. The Motuo people are a small ethnic group who live today in the Tibetan Autonomous Region of the People's Republic of China. Chinese demographers estimate their contemporary population at approximately 5,000 people. Motuos are classified as part of the officially recognized Moinba* minority nationality, but their language is not really mutually intelligible with the other major Moinba language, which is known as Cuona.* Although the central government of the PRC does not consider them to be a distinct ethnic entity, most Motuos identify themselves as Motuos rather than as Moinbas, although they certainly acknowledge Moinba kinship. The vast majority of the Motuo population today lives in Cuona County of Lebu Prefecture and Medog County in Dexing Prefecture of the Tibetan Autonomous Region.

Motuos speak a Tibeto-Burman* language, which is part of the Sino-Tibetan family, and it is divided into dozens of mutually intelligible dialects. Most Mutuo families are farmers and pastoralists. Because of persecution from ethnic Tibetans over the years, they live in isolated, forested, mountainous, or deep gorge areas of southern Tibet. Their local climate is subtropical and the soil fertile. Motuo farmers produce rice, maize, millet, buckwheat, soybeans, and sesame seeds. Motuo pastoralists herd cattle and sheep, and hunting remains important as a source of protein and male bonding.

SUGGESTED READINGS: Tiley Chodag, *Tibet: The Land and Its Peoples*, 1988; Paul V. Hockings, "Moinba," in Paul V. Hockings, ed., *The Encyclopedia of World Cultures*, vol. 6, *East and Southeast Asia*, 1991; Ma Yin, ed., *China's Minority Nationalities*, 1989; S. A. Wurm, B. T'sou, D. Bradley, et al., eds., *Language Atlas of China*, 1987.

MOUNTAIN SHOR. See SHOR.

MRASSA. See SHOR.

MUHSO. See LAHU.

MULAM. The Mulam people—also identified by the ethnonyms of Bendiren, Jin, Ling, Molao, Molo, Mulao, and Mulaozu—are one of the People's Republic of China's officially recognized minority nationalities. The 1990 national census placed their total population at 159,328 people, and today it is approaching 175,000 people. More than 155,000 Mulams live in the Luocheng Mulao Autonomous County of the Guangxi Zhuang Autonomous Region. The remaining Mulams are scattered throughout bordering counties, particularly Yishan, Liucheng, Du'an, Xincheng, Hechi, and Huanjiang counties.

Ethnolinguists consider the Mulams to be close relatives of the Dong* and the Maonan* people because of the structural similarities in their languages. They also possess a close cultural affiliation with the Zhuang.* The Mulam language is classified as part of the Dong-Shui* branch of the Zhuang-Dong cluster of languages in the Sino-Tibetan linguistic family. A written script for Mulam is not in existence, but literate Mulams can read and write Mandarin* Chinese.* Most people can speak a local Chinese dialect as well as their native Mulam.

Mulam country was independent of Han* authority until the thirteenth century, when Chinese armies and then political administrators occupied Guangxi. Beginning with the Qing dynasty in 1271, Mulam farmers had to provide an annual tribute payment in grain to the Chinese imperial government. Over the centuries, the exact nature of Han imperial control has changed with succeeding dynasties and with the rise of the Communists to power in 1949, but the reality of Han political and economic domination has not changed.

The Mulam economy today is primarily agricultural. Mulams, who prefer valleys and lower elevated hillsides for the placement of their villages, live in one-story mud-walled houses. Two-generation households is the norm, and young men prefer to marry one of their mother's brother's daughters. The social system is based on patrilineal descent. Mulams tend to live in single-surname villages, which gives each community powerful family bonds. Farmers use plows to raise rice, maize, wheat, and potatoes. They are also known to produce peanuts, melons, cotton, and a number of vegetables. Water buffalo, oxen, and horses serve as draft animals.

Indigenous Mulam animism still survives. They believe that a soul, which they call *yin*, is present in individuals, animals, plants, and natural phenomena. Male priests, known as *mubao*, and female shamans, known as *bayas*, assist the community in regulating the spiritual world and in preventing personal and natural disasters. Since the days of the Sung dynasty, Buddhism and Daoism have also found a home in Mulam culture, and Daoist priests and Buddhist monks also serve each village's spiritual needs.

SUGGESTED READINGS: Norma Diamond, "Mulam," in Paul V. Hockings, ed., *The Encyclopedia of World Cultures*, vol. 6, *East and Southeast Asia*, 1991; Ma Yin, ed., *China's Minority Nationalities*, 1989.

MULAO. See **MULAM.**

MULAOZU. See **MULAM.**

MUMIN. See **HUI.**

MUNGUN. The Mungun people are a subgroup of the Jingpo* people of Myanmar (Burma) and the People's Republic of China. The Jingpo themselves are one of the Kachin*-speaking people, a transnational ethnic group living today in Myanmar, China, and India.

MUNYA. The Munya people are a recently discovered minority nationality who live in the People's Republic of China (PRC). PRC social scientists are currently conducting ethnographic research into Munya origins, trying to determine how to classify them, and until that research is completed, the process of extending them official recognition will be postponed. The Munya language has not yet been classified. PRC demographers estimate the Munya population at approximately 15,000 people, the vast majority of whom live in the Ganzhi Tibetan Autonomous Prefecture in Sichuan Province. Most Munyas live in highland villages where they raise rice, maize, millet, pigs, poultry, and wheat.

SUGGESTED READING: S. A. Wurm, B. T'sou, D. Bradley, et al., eds., *Language Atlas of China*, 1987.

MUSSO. See **LAHU.**

MUSSUH. See **LAHU.**

MUSSUR. See **LAHU.**

MUSSUR KWI. See **LAHU.**

MUYA. The Muyas are one of the smaller subgroups of the Qiang* people of the People's Republic of China. Their language, one of the Qiang dialects, is part of the Qiang branch of the Sino-Tibetan language family. No written script exists for Qiang, and a Chinese* dialect is gradually becoming the native language of more and more Muyas. They are closely related to the neighboring Muyamis,* another Qiang subgroup. Muyas occupy the mountain pass that separates the Chinese lowlands in the east from the Tibetan* highlands to the west. Most Muyas reside in rugged mountain villages, and their homes consist of multistoried, flat-roofed houses constructed of stone. Subsistence farmers, they raise barley, buckwheat, maize, potatoes, and beans. Apples, walnuts, peppers, opium, firewood, and medicinal herbs are sold for cash. Most Myuas remain loyal to their ancestral animistic religion. The Muya population today is approximately 35,000 people.

MUYAMI. The Muyamis are a subgroup of the Qiang* people of the People's Republic of China. Their language, one of the Qiang dialects, is a member of the Qiang branch of the Sino-Tibetan language family. No written script exists for Qiang. The Muyamis live in the mountain corridor that links the Chinese lowlands in the east from the Tibetan* highlands to the west. They are very closely related culturally to their immediate neighbors, the Muyas,* who are also a Qiang subgroup. Muyamis, who live in mountain villages, are subsistence farmers who raise barley, maize, buckwheat, potatoes, and beans. They also sell apples, walnuts, peppers, opium, firewood, and medicinal herbs for cash. The current Muyami population is estimated at approximately 30,000 people.

MYEN. The Myens are the primary subgroup of the Yao* people of the People's Republic of China. The 1990 national census counted 2,134,000 Yao people in China, and given their birthrate, which is above the national average, it is safe to say that the Yao population is now approaching 2.4 million people. More than 1.5 million Yaos live today in Guangxi Province, usually in mountain villages, but another 900,000 Yaos can be found scattered throughout the border regions of surrounding Hunan Province, Guangdong Province, Jiangxi Province, Guizhou Province, and Yunnan Province. They are particularly concentrated demographically in the Guangxi Zhuang Autonomous Region. Myens constitute 44 percent of the total Yao population. Myen is considered to be the main Yao language, but it is divided into a number of dialects, some of which are mutually unintelligible.

N _____

NABAI. See **HEZHEN.**

NACHRI. See **NAXI.**

NAGA. The term ''Naga'' is used here to refer to a series of ethnically related tribes who live in the Nagaland region of far northeastern India. The Naga population today exceeds one million people, the vast majority of whom live in Nagaland State in India, although some elements survive across the border in northern Myanmar (Burma), and even smaller numbers can be found on the headwaters of the Mekong River near the frontier between Myanmar and Yunnan Province in the People's Republic of China (PRC).

Archaeologists and anthropologists trace Naga origins back to China, where they probably began their southern migration from the Yangtze River basin. They gradually uprooted themselves during a period of from two to three thousand years and relocated farther south in Southeast Asia. Early in the 1800s, British explorers, and then missionaries and soldiers, made contact with the Nagas in northeastern India, but the Nagas wanted nothing to do with Europeans. They fought a bitter guerrilla war against the British, and British retaliation often involved a scorched-earth policy in Naga communities. The British did not subdue the Nagas until late in the nineteenth century. Even some early French expeditions up the Mekong River encountered Naga resistance.

It is difficult, however, to talk about the so-called Naga people because they are divided into so many mutually unintelligible languages. The major Naga subgroups are the Kangami, Ao, Chang,* Kacha, Kalyo, Kengu, Konyak, Lhote, Rengma, Sangtam, Sema, Tangkhul, Lukomi, and Yachumi. The speakers of these subgroups do not understand one another's languages, but they have developed a pidgin language, known as Bodo or Nafamese, that serves as a lingua franca in the region. The Naga subgroups have traditionally constituted distinct ethnic entities, but during recent decades in India, American missionaries have successfully proselytized among the Nagas, which has generated a sense of identity among the Nagas that transcends the language groups.

Most Nagas today are subsistence farmers who raise rice, wheat, millet, and corn in terraced, hillside fields. They also produce a variety of vegetables and legumes, and they raise goats, sheep, cattle, pigs, and dogs for food. Hunting and fishing remain important sources of protein for them.

During the last forty years, the various Naga subgroups have slowly been transcending their subgroup identities to attain an identity as a larger group of people. Soon after India became independent in 1947, a number of Naga nationalists began demanding independence. Full-scale civil war developed in the region in 1956 when Naga nationalists declared their secession from India and the establishment of an independent Naga nation. The rebellion continued sporadically until 1963, when India established the state of Nagaland. A relative peace prevailed until 1972, when the chief minister of Nagaland was assassinated by an Indian. A new peace settlement was not reached until 1975. Although peace has prevailed since then, there are still Naga guerrilla groups operating out of Myanmar, and perhaps also out of Yunnan Province, who demand secession and independence.

SUGGESTED READINGS: *Nagas at Work*, 1996; M. M. Thomas, *Nagas toward A.D. 2000*, 1992.

NAHSI. See **NAXI.**

NAIMAN. The Naimans are a subgroup of the Kazak* people of the Xinjiang Uigur Autonomous Region, Gansu Province, and Qinghai Province in the People's Republic of China.

NA-KHI. See **NAXI.**

NAKHI. See **NAXI.**

NAMHPEHN. Namhpehn is one of the subdialects of Nu,* a dialect of the Black Lahu* language of the People's Republic of China. See **LAHU.**

NAMHSAN. The Namhsan people are one of the many subgroups of the De'ang* minority of the People's Republic of China. The Namhsan dialect is considered to be the standard De'ang language.

NAMUYI. The Namuyis are one of the smaller subgroups, in terms of population, of the Qiang* people of the People's Republic of China. The Namuyi population is approximately 5,000 people. Their language, one of the Qiang dialects, is part of the Qiang branch of the Sino-Tibetan language family. No written script exists for Qiang, and a Chinese* dialect is gradually becoming the native language of more and more Namuyis. They live in the mountain pass that separates the Chinese lowlands in the east from the Tibetan* highlands to the west. Most Namuyis reside in rugged mountain villages, and their homes consist of multistoried, flat-roofed houses constructed of stone. They are subsistence farmers who raise barley, buckwheat, potatoes, and beans, using both slash-and-burn hoe farming and double-team cattle plowing. In the Namuyi villages located below 7,000 feet in elevation, maize has become the staple product. As cash crops, they produce apples, walnuts, peppers, and opium, and they collect bundles of firewood and medicinal herbs for commercial sale. Most Namuyis remain loyal to their ancestral animistic religion.

Like other Qiang subgroups, many Namuyis consider themselves a distinct ethnic entity, not simply an extension or a subgroup of the Qiang people. Following the lead of Pumi* nationalists, who in 1960 secured official recognition for the Pumis as a minority nationality, Namuyi nationalists have made requests for a similar classification from the central government. With a population of as many as 35,000 people, they argue that their claim is as compelling as that of the Pumis. As of yet, the central government has not agreed with them.

NANAI. See **HEZHEN.**

NANCHANG. The Nanchang people speak a dialect of Gan,* one of the primary languages spoken by Han* Chinese* people in the People's Republic of China.

NANIAO. See **HEZHEN.**

NANSHI AMI. The Nanshi Amis are one of the five primary subgroups of the Ami* people of Taiwan in the Republic of China. Most Nanshi Amis live in the vicinity of Nanshi in Hualian County. They are also known as the Northern Ami.*

NANTUN. The Nantuns are a subgroup of the Hailar* people, who are themselves a subgroup of the Daur* ethnic group of the People's Republic of China.

NANWANG. See **BEINAN** and **PUYUMA.**

NARI. See **NAXI.**

NASHEE. See **NAXI.**

NASHI. See **NAXI.**

NASI. See **NAXI.**

NASU. The Nasus (Nosos, Nosus) are an ethnic group in the People's Republic of China (PRC), although the central government has never extended to them formal recognition as a minority nationality. Official PRC publications classify them as a Yi* subgroup, and, indeed, they speak a Yi language. But Nasu is not mutually intelligible with the vast majority of other Yi languages, and the Nosu identify themselves as a separate people, although they do acknowledge a certain kinship with the Yi. Most Nasus live today in Yunnan Province, primarily in the Hetaojing settlement outside of Kunming, the provincial capital, where they labor as farmers producing a variety of grains, livestock, and vegetables.

NATKI. See **HEZHEN.**

NAWEN. The Nawens are one of the subdivisions of the Butha,* who are themselves a subgroup of the Daur* people of the People's Republic of China.

NAXI. The Naxi people—also known as the Naxhi, Nashee, Lukhi, Luhsi, Luxi, Moso, Moso Man, Nachri, Nahsi, Nashi, Na-khi, Nakhi, Nari, Nasi, Nazo, Hli-khin, and Wuman—are a recognized national minority in the People's Republic of China (PRC). The 1990 national census counted 278,000 Naxi, and their population today is approaching 300,000 people. Most Naxis live in Lijiang Naxi Autonomous County in northwestern Yunnan Province, not far from the border with Myanmar (Burma). They can also be found in Weixi, Zhongdian, and Ninglang Yi Autonomous counties. Naxis regard the city of Lijiang as their cultural capital. A few Naxi communities are also located across the border in southern Sichuan Province. Their homeland is mountainous, and most Naxis live at an elevation of between 5,000 and 10,000 feet. Some Naxis also live in the deep gorge of the Golden Sand River. They boast that no mountain-climbing team has ever reached the summit of Snow Dragon Jade Mountain, the region's most conspicuous geographical landmark.

Ethnolinguists classify the Naxi language as part of the Tibeto-Burman* group of the Sino-Tibetan linguistic family. The language comprises two basic dialects—Western Naxi and Eastern Naxi—which divide Naxis into two recognizable subgroups. Because their homeland in Yunnan Province is very diverse ethnically, it is not at all uncommon to find Naxi speakers fluent in other languages, including Mandarin,* Yi,* Lisu,* Pumi,* and a variety of Tibetan* dialects. More than a thousand years ago, Naxi scholars invented a hieroglyphic writing system for their language, but today only a handful of people can read it.

Anthropologists tracing Naxi origins place them millenia ago to the north in what is today eastern Tibet, western Sichuan Province, or Qinghai Province. A good percentage of scholars link the Naxis with the Qiang* people who reside today in northwestern Sichuan. Throughout their history, the Naxis have found themselves forced to deal politically and culturally with their more numerous and militarily powerful Tibetan and Han* neighbors. From A.D. 500 to 1100, the Naxis were part of the Nanzhao and Dali empires, whose capital was near Lake Erhai, approximately ninety miles south of what is today the town of Liang. At the time of the Tang dynasty in China (618–906), the Nanzhao empire enjoyed political supremacy in western Yunnan, southern Sichuan, northern Myanmar, and western Tibet. But in 1252, Mongol troops under Kublai Khan conquered the Naxis.

Traditionally, China ruled the Naxis indirectly through hereditary ethnic Naxi chiefs, and because those chiefs welcomed Han merchants, scholars, administrators, and religious leaders to the region, the Han cultural influence in the region became overwhelming. Because of centuries of political domination by, and cultural interaction with, the Han people, the Naxis are one of the most sinicized minority nationalities in China. Although a substantial number of Naxis today live an urban lifestyle in the city of Lijiang, thousands remain in traditional village settings. Naxi villages range in size from twenty to more than a thousand people. They build their homes in close proximity to one another, with vegetable gardens and fruit orchards nearby. Farther away, but within convenient walking distances, are their fields, where staple crops are raised. Traditional Naxi homes were made of logs and roof slats weighted down by heavy rocks, but in recent years they have begun to construct homes that are similar to those of their Han and Bai* neighbors: wood frames, tiled roofs, and tamped earth or adobe walls.

Except for their compatriots living in the city of Lijiang, most Naxis are farmers today, although the crops they harvest vary depending upon the altitude of their settlements. Naxi farmers at lower elevations are most likely to raise wet rice, citrus, and vegetables. At higher elevations, they produce wheat, legumes, maize, apples, and pears. Since these crops do not thrive at higher altitudes, Naxi farmers there produce potatoes and turnips. At even higher elevations, where forage is good, the Naxis are active pastoralists who raise goats, sheep, and cattle. Higher still, Naxi herders raise yaks and mixed cattle-yak breeds. Most Naxi family compounds also abound in chickens, pigs, oxen, ducks, and water buffalo. Naxi horses and mules are well known regionally for their fine quality.

The 1949 victory of Mao Zedong and the Communists brought dramatic changes to the Naxi lifestyle. As part of a concerted effort to assimilate the minority nationalities, the central government encouraged Han settlement in Yunnan and Sichuan provinces. The system of land tenure also changed. Until 1949 land was owned by individual families, and upon the death of a father, the acreage was equally divided among his sons. Early in the 1950s, however, when the central government launched its ideological crusade to implement Marxism, all privately owned land reverted to the state. Local Communist party officials organized the Naxi into communal farming teams. The experiment was a failure, although the government did not acknowledge that until the 1980s. Collective farming arrangements gradually led to reduced productivity as peasant Naxis began to realize that there was no correlation between individual effort and individual rewards. Early in the 1980s, when the central government finally realized its folly, the collective farms were replaced by a new "household responsibility system," in which individual families work plots of land owned by the state. Those households that were most successful in meeting government-mandated production goals received appropriate financial rewards.

Different social systems divide the Naxis into two subgroups. The Lijiang Naxis, who live in and around the city of Lijiang, organize their families and society around a system of patrilineal descent. Lijiang Naxis also prefer patrilineal cross-cousin marriages, in which a man marries his father's sister's daughter. The Yongning Naxis, on the other hand, want nothing to do with patrilines. Their matrilineal social system revolves around matriclans. Ethnologists in China, therefore, have identified Lijiang Naxi society as patriarchal and Yongning society as matriarchal.

Naxi religion is a reflection of their long history and the multiethnic setting of Yunnan Province. Their faith is an eclectic mix of traditional Naxi animism along with Buddhist and Daoist beliefs. For centuries now, marriages and funerals have often been mixed ceremonies presided over by Naxi religious specialists as well as Tibetan and Chinese monks. Nearly three centuries ago, most Yongning Naxis converted to the Gelug-pa sect of Tibetan Buddhism.

The pantheon of Naxi deities includes thousands of invisible beings who reside in heaven and in purgatory and throughout the natural world. Every plant, animal, and major geographical landmark has its own deity, and the Naxis believe that such gods often have demonic counterparts. Life and the world is one long struggle for power between good and evil, and the Naxis rely on shamans to assist them in interpreting the events transpiring around them and in warding off the negative influences of evil spirits. Naxis believe that after death, the soul of an individual can be reincarnated but that eventually it must travel the road of its ancestors and return home to the "north."

There is a great deal of concern today about the survival of Naxi culture. Older Naxi women can still be seen wearing their traditional blue blouses and peaked caps and capes, but younger women find the outfit heavy and uncomfortable. Traditional music can still be heard in coffeehouses, although it is performed only by female students from a local music school and a few elderly musicians. Some Naxi shamans still practice religious rituals, but they are all quite elderly, since no new Naxi shamans have been trained since 1949. Occasionally a traditional Naxi cremation ceremony takes place for the dead, but Han funerary traditions are now common.

Naxi identity, however, remains quite distinct and intact. Memories of Han oppression are still quite vivid. During the excesses of the Cultural Revolution during the 1960s, Red Guard cadres, usually consisting of young Han zealots, entered Naxi villages, attacked local shamans, and defaced Naxi temples. Naxi musicians buried their traditional instruments out of fear that the Red Guards would destroy them. Most Naxis are well aware that the ethnic rivalries so common in past centuries with the Han have not permanently disappeared and may be bubbling just below the surface of contemporary Chinese cultural and political life.

SUGGESTED READINGS: Mike Edwards, "Our Man in China: Joseph Rock," *National Geographic* 191 (January 1997), 62–81; Peter Goullart, *Forgotten Kingdom*, 1955; *International Herald Tribune*, May 30, 1994; Anthony Jackson, *Na-khi Religion: An Appraisal of the Nakhi Ritual Texts*, 1979, and *Life among the Minority Nationalities of Northwest Yunnan*, 1989; Charles F. McKhan, "Naxi," in Paul V. Hockings, ed., *The Encyclopedia of World Cultures*, vol. 6, *East and Southeast Asia*, 1991; Joseph Rock, *The Ancient Na-khi Kingdom of Southwest China*, 1947; Wu Zelin, "From Pairing to Marriage—The Changing Marriage System of the Naxi Minority in Yongning," *China Reconstructs* 29 (July 1980), 59–61.

NAZO. See **NAXI.**

NEGIDAL. The Negidal—also known as the El'kan, Beyenin, Eleke Beye, Neidal, Iizhdal, and Negeden—are a subgroup of the Evenk,* an ethnic group of Russian Siberia and Heilongjiang Province and the Inner Mongolian Autonomous Region in the People's Republic of China. Today, the Negidals are not recognized as a distinct ethnic entity in the People's Republic of China, but are lumped together with other Evenks.

NEIDA. See **EVENK.**

NEIDAL. See **EVENK.**

NEIDEN. See **EVENK.**

NEISU. The Neisus (Nesu) are an ethnic group in the People's Republic of China (PRC), although the central government has never extended to them formal recognition as a minority nationality. Official PRC publications classify them as a Yi* subgroup, and, indeed, they speak a Yi language. But Neisu is not mutually intelligible with the vast majority of other Yi languages, and the Neisus give themselves a distinct, separate identity.

NEMOR. The Nemors are one of the subdivisions of the Butha,* who themselves are a subgroup of the Daur* people of the People's Republic of China.

NEPALESE. The term "Nepalese" is used here generically to refer to the more than 16 million people who live today in the Himalayan country of Nepal, which is bordered by Tibet in the People's Republic of China (PRC) to the north, and by India to the east, west, and south. Nepal sits at the crossroads between the Lamaist Buddhism religion of the north and the Hindu religion of the south. The official language of Nepal is Nepalese, an Indo-Aryan language, but more than two dozen other languages are spoken by different ethnic groups there.

Included among the Nepalese ethnic groups are Hindu Indians, Newars,* Gurungs,* Magars, Thakalis,* Nyinbas, Brahmans and Chhetris, Gurkhas, Sherpas,* Lepchas,* Tamangs, Rais,* Bhotias,* and Limbus.* Because of the proximity of Nepal to Tibetan and Himalayan trade routes, hundreds of Nepalese are living in Tibet at any given time.

On July 1, 1997, when Hong Kong reverted to the political sovereignty of the PRC, several thousand Nepalese came under Beijing's authority. The vast majority of this group of Nepalese are domestic workers, primarily single women, working in the homes of well-to-do Hong Kong families.
SUGGESTED READINGS: "Chinese Maids and Foreign Helpers in Hong Kong," *Modern China* 22 (October 1996), 448–79; Chandra K. Sharma, *Nepal and the Nepalese*, 1979.

NEPALI. See **NEPALESE.**

NESU. See **NEISU** and **YI.**

NEW XIANG. New Xiang is one of the two primary divisions of Xiang,* a Chinese* language. New Xiang is spoken primarily in northwestern Hunan Province and in cities and larger towns throughout the province in the People's Republic of China. New Xiang speakers cannot converse with speakers of Old Xiang,* but their language is mutually intelligible with the Southwestern Mandarin* language. For that reason, some linguists today classify New Xiang as a Mandarin dialect, not as a companion to Old Xiang.

NEWAR. The Newar people—also known as Newas and Newaris—are an ethnic group who live today primarily in Nepal. Just over half of all Newars still reside in the Kathmandu Valley, their traditional homeland, where they raise wheat, potatoes, rice, and maize. Newar craftsmen are also regionally famous for their bronze, brass, and copper works. Finally, Newars are well known regionally—inside and outside the Kathmandu Valley—for their mercantile skills. Historically, the Kathmandu Valley was the midpoint in a major Nepalese-Tibetan* trade route, and Newar merchants could be found all along that commercial corridor. The Newar population today exceeds 500,000 people. The Newars not living in the Kathmandu Valley can be found today in commercial and administrative centers in Sikkim and Bhutan. Because Sikkim dominates the historic Kalimpong-Llasa trade route, which regularly brought Tibetans, Indians, Nepalese,* and Sikkimese* into contact, there are Newar merchants today in the region. A handful of people in Llasa, Tibet, are also aware of their Newar heritage.

The Newar people speak a Tibeto-Burman* language that is divided into four basic dialects: Kathmandu, which is considered the standard dialect; Bhaktapur; Dolakha; and Pahari. Newar also contains many loan words from such Indic languages as Sanskrit, Maithili, and Nepalese. Their religion is a complicated, syncretic mix of traditional Newar animism, Lamaist Buddhism, and Hinduism. Their social structure is patrilineal. They are generally considered, in Nepal, to be an elite group.

SUGGESTED READINGS: Hiroshi Ishii, "Newar," in Paul V. Hockings, ed., *The Encyclopedia of World Cultures*, vol. 3, *South Asia*, 1991; Gopal Singh Nepali, *The Newars*, 1965; John Scofield, "Kathmandu's Remarkable Newars," *National Geographic* 155 (February 1979), 268–84; Mary Shepherd Slusser, *Nepal Mandala: A Cultural Study of the Kathmandu Valley*, 1982.

NEWARI. See **NEWAR.**

NGACHANG. See **ACHANG.**

NGAWZA. The Ngawzas are one of the most prominent clans of the Lisu* people of the People's Republic of China.

NGIAW. See **DAI.**

NGIO. See **DAI.**

NGOSU. The Ngosus—closely related to the neighboring Norsu* and Nasu* peoples—are an ethnic group in the People's Republic of China (PRC), although the central government has never extended to them formal recognition as a minority nationality. Official PRC publications classify them as a Yi* subgroup, and, indeed, they speak a Yi language. But Ngosu is not mutually intelligible with the vast majority of other Yi languages, and Ngosus identify themselves as a separate people.

NIANG. See **DE'ANG.**

NINGLONG. The Ninglong people are a linguistic subgroup of the Hakka*-speaking Han* people of the People's Republic of China (PRC). Ninglong speakers can be found today living in Ningdu, Xingguo, Shicheng, Ruijin, Huichang, Anyuan, Xunwu, Xinfeng, Dingnan, Longnan, Quannan, Guangcheng, and Yongfeng counties in Jianxi Province of the PRC.

N'KUNG. The N'kungs are a dialect subgroup of the Jingpo* branch of the Jingpo people of the People's Republic of China. They all live in Yunnan Province.

NO. See **YI.**

NO GELAO. The No Gelaos are one of the four linguistic subdivisions of the Gelao* people of the People's Republic of China.

NOFA LEMA. The Nofa Lemas are one of the most prominent clans of the Lisu* people of the People's Republic of China.

NOFU. The Nofus are one of the many subgroups of the Li* people of Hainan Province in the People's Republic of China. Like other Li groups, they have earned a reputation over the years for their ferocious anti-Han* xenophobia, which has often taken the form of guerrilla warfare against Han immigrants to Hainan. Their hatred of the Nationalist government in the 1930s and 1940s made them willing allies of Mao Zedong and the Communists, and when Mao triumphed, the Nofus, as well as most Lis, were afforded recognition as heroes. Most Nofus today are farmers.

NONGAN. See **ZHUANG.**

NORSU. The Norsus, who are closely related to the Nasus, are an ethnic group in the People's Republic of China (PRC), although the central government has never extended to them formal recognition as a minority nationality. Official PRC publications classify them as a Yi* subgroup, but Norsu is not mutually intelligible with the vast majority of other Yi languages, and Norsus identify themselves as a separate people. They do, however, acknowledge a certain cultural affinity with the Yi.

NORTHEAST XIBE. See **XIBE.**

NORTHEASTERN KAZAK. Northeastern Kazak is one of the two primary dialects of the Kazak* peoples of the People's Republic of China (PRC). Approximately 850,000 Kazaks speak the northeastern dialect, and the vast majority of them are scattered throughout the Xinjiang Uigur Autonomous Region of the PRC.

NORTHERN AMI. Northern Ami is one of the five primary dialects of the Ami* language, which is spoken by the Ami people, an indigenous group who live on Taiwan in the Republic of China. Northern Ami people are also known as the Nanshi Amis.*

NORTHERN DE'ANG. Ethnolinguists group the many De'ang* dialects in three clusters, one of which is known as Northern De'ang. Since so many of the De'ang dialects are not mutually intelligible, it might be more appropriate to describe them as separate languages.

NORTHERN KHAM. The Northern Kham* people are ethnic Tibetans* who speak the northern vernacular of the Kham* dialect. Most Northern Kham speakers live today in the Yushu Tibetan Autonomous Prefecture of Qinghai Province.

NORTHERN KIRGIZ. Northern Kirgiz is one of the two major divisions of the Kirgiz* language in the Xinjiang Uigur Autonomous Region. It is divided into a number of subdialects of its own. The northern dialect, spoken in the region north of the Kizilsu River, is divided into Heiziwei, Ulukqiat, and Toyun, which are spoken in Uqia County; Kalajun and Tugaimait, which are spoken in Akqi County; Jiamansu, which is spoken in Uqturpan County; Baozitong, which is spoken in Wensu County; Kuoketielik, which is spoken in Tekes County; and Shato, which is spoken in Monggolkure County. See **UIGUR.**

NORTHERN KMHMU. The Kmhmu* language of Laos, Thailand, and China is divided into two mutually intelligible, although quite distinct, dialect groups. The Northern Kmhmu dialects can be found in far northern Laos and in far southern Yunnan Province in the People's Republic of China.

NORTHERN MANDARIN. Chinese linguists identify four general clusters of Mandarin* dialects. One of them, Northern Mandarin, is spoken all over northeastern China. It includes Beijingese, a Northern Mandarin dialect. All of the Northern Mandarin dialects are mutually intelligible with one another and with most other Mandarin dialects as well.

NORTHERN SIASIYAT. The Northern Siasiyats are one of the primary subdivisions of the Siasiyat* people of Taiwan in the Republic of China. Most of them live today in the highlands of Hsinchu County.

NORTHERN TSOU. See **TSOU.**

NORTHERN ZHUANG. The Zhuang* people, who live in the Guangxi Autonomous Region, as well as in Gizhou and Yunnan provinces of the People's Republic of China, are divided into two large subgroups based on dialect. The Zhuangs living north of the Xiang River in southern Guangxi speak the Northern Zhuang dialect. Among the primary subdialects of Northern Zhuang are Yongbei, Youjiang, Guibian, Lujiang, Gubei, Hongshuihe, Qiubei, and Lianshan.

NORTHWESTERN MANDARIN. Chinese linguists identify four general groups of Mandarin* dialects, one of which is Northwestern Mandarin. Northwestern Mandarin dialects, which are all mutually intelligible, extend out to the northwest in the People's Republic of China, encompassing the Mandarin speakers of the Loess Plateau and farther west. Northwestern Mandarin speakers can be found today in Shanxi, Ningxia, and Gansu provinces.

NOS. The Nos are one of the subgroups of the Yi* people of the People's Republic of China. Although the Yi are an officially recognized minority nationality of more than seven million people, they are divided into a variety of subgroups whose sense of ethnic identity is quite parochial, based on region and dialects that are usually not mutually intelligible. Nos can be found living today in Yunnan Province. They descend from the ancient Tusan people native to the Kunming region of Yunnan and the Chengdu in Sichuan. The Nos economy is overwhelmingly agricultural. At lower elevations, Nos farmers produce maize, potatoes, buckwheat, and oats as staples. In the highlands, they raise cattle, sheep, goats, and horses.

NOSO. See **NASU** and **YI.**

NOSU. See **NASU** and **YI.**

NU. Nu is one of the major dialects of the Black Lahu* language in the People's Republic of China. Nu includes the Kaishin and Namhpehn subdialects. See **LAHU**.

NU. One of the People's Republic of China's (PRC) smaller officially recognized minority nationalities, the Nu people, who are also known as A Longs, A Nus, A Yias, Anus, Lutzus, Noutzus, Nutsus, Nutzus, Nusus, and Rourous, live in northwestern Yunnan Province, particularly in Bijiang, Fugong, and Gongshan counties of the Nujiang Lisu Autonomous Prefecture. Some Nu also live next door in the Deqen Tibetan Autonomous Prefecture. The Nu, or Salween, River drains their mountainous homeland. They dwell in the Salween Valley, which stretches from southeastern Tibet through Yunnan Province and into northern Myanmar (Burma). In 1990 official Chinese census takers counted just over 27,000 Nu people, and today that number is probably closer to 30,000. They are closely related culturally to the Tibetans.*

The Nu language is part of the Tibeto-Burman* cluster of languages in the Sino-Tibetan linguistic family. There are three mutually intelligible dialects of Nu, each one consistent with its residential location, that divide the Nus into ethnic subgroups. Bijiang Nu is the most distinct of the three, and Chinese linguists find its structure quite similar to the language of the Yi* people. Fugong Nu and Deqen Nu are the other two dialects. Although official Chinese ethnology classifications place Gongshan Nu as one of the Nu subgroups, there is considerable disagreement about that conclusion, since Gongshan Nu is not mutually intelligible with the Fugong, Bijiang, and Deqen dialects. In fact, it is mutually intelligible with Drung.* Because of this debate and the issue of intelligibility, the Gongshan Nus are treated as a distinct ethnic entity here.

The Nu people have a profound sense of ethnic identity and consider themselves to be culturally and even racially separate from surrounding peoples, although modern ethnologists would certainly disagree with that point of view. Not surprisingly, the Nu people believe that they are the original inhabitants of the region and have been there since the creation of the world, and that every other group is a later arrival and, by definition, an interloper.

Like the other longtime residents of northwestern Yunnan, the Nus fell under the authority of the Nanzhao Kingdom in the eighth and ninth centuries and the

Dali Kingdom in the tenth, eleventh, and twelfth centuries. Early in the thirteenth century, Naxi* armies seized control of the region, and the Nus were frequent victims of Lisu* slave raiding parties. Han* military authority and later hundreds of thousands of Han settlers came to Nu country, but the Nus did not possess the technology or the organization to resist Han imperialism. Periodically, they rebelled and fought guerrilla wars against Han officials, but the rebellions were always suppressed. The most recent rebellion occurred in 1935, when the Nus joined in a panethnic rebellion against Han administration in what was then known as the Guomindang Frontier Administration. Such a history has bequeathed to Nu culture a healthy suspicion toward ethnic outsiders. The People's Republic of China established the Nujiang Autonomous Prefecture in 1954, and Gongshan Autonomous County was created in 1956.

Most Nus live in relatively compact villages built at some distance from neighboring villages. Each village consists of perhaps 150 people who descend from the same patriline. Single-story wood plank houses are the norm. Nu villages are among the poorest in China, in spite of government efforts to encourage economic development. Although some Nu farmers employ plow technologies, most still use slash-and-burn techniques to raise buckwheat, rye, barley, oats, and maize. They grow hemp to supply their clothing. Nu farmers pasture cattle, sheep, pigs, and horses in commonly held unused fields. A few cottage industries supply most manufactured needs.

Before the Communist revolution, pastures, forests, and uncultivated highland land was communal property owned by patrilines or villages. Farm land was owned by individual households and could be bought and sold. Collectivization in the 1950s turned all land over to the state, and government officials encouraged multilineage and, where possible, multiethnic labor teams to work the land. It was not until the early 1980s that economic reforms restored a measure of economic power to individual households.

Nu religion reflects their multicultural history. Nu animism was so complex that quite different religious ceremonies characterized the dozen or so patriclans around which the society was organized. Shamans maintained the environmental balance and community well-being. Because Nu communities are located in far northwestern Yunnan, near the Tibetan border, and inside the Deqen Tibetan Autonomous Prefecture, Lamaist Buddhism also made its way into their religion. Many Nu young men became Lamaist priests. Beginning in the 1930s, Protestant and Catholic missionaries came to Nu country and experienced great success in converting thousands of Nus to Christianity. Many Nu villages today are primarily Christian.

SUGGESTED READINGS: Norma Diamond, ''Nu,'' in Paul V. Hockings, ed., *The Encyclopedia of World Cultures*, vol. 6, *East and Southeast Asia*, 1991; Ma Yin, ed., *China's Minority Nationalities*, 1989; Shen Che and Lu Xiaoya, *Life among the Minority Nationalities of Northwest Yunnan*, 1989.

NUA. The Nuas are one of the many subgroups of the Dai* people, an officially recognized minority nationality in the People's Republic of China. The vast majority of Nuas live in Yunnan Province, particularly in the Dehong Dai and Jingpo Autonomous Prefecture and in the Xishuangbanna Dai Autonomous Prefecture. Nuas have been commercial farmers for more than a thousand years. They are also among the first to cultivate rice in the region. At a time more than 1,400 years ago, when most of the inhabitants of Yunnan were hunters and foragers, the Nuas were wet-rice farmers using large paddy fields. Elephants were used as draft animals to plow the fields. Today, most Nua farmland is employed in wet-rice farming. They also produce dry rice on terraced, hillside fields. Cash crops include tea, cotton, tobacco, camphor, sisal, sugarcane, coffee, bananas, mangoes, and rubber.

NUNG. The Nung people are one of the larger minority groups of the Socialist Republic of Vietnam. There are more than 600,000 Nung people living in Vietnam, the vast majority of them in northeastern Vietnam, primarily in what used to be the Tay Bac Autonomous Region. Today the region is included in the three provinces of Lai Chau, Son La, and Hoang Lien Son. Several thousand Nung people can also be found today across the Sino-Vietnamese border in the southwestern portion of the Guangxi Zhuangzu Autonomous Region of the People's Republic of China.

Anthropologists believe that the Nungs are closely related culturally and linguistically to the Tay people and that they originated in China, south of the Yangtse River. From there, centuries ago, they migrated south into the mountainous region north of the Red River Delta in Vietnam. Most of the Nungs settled in the canyons and narrow river valleys of Vietnam just south of the Chinese border, although several thousand Nung can still be found living north of the border. The Nung people of Vietnam and China live in rural villages where they practice swidden agriculture to raise maize, buckwheat, watercress, sugarcane, manioc, and a variety of vegetables. They are also wet-rice farmers.

During the Vietnam War, the Nungs actively supported Ho Chi Minh and the Vietminh political organization. Nungs could also be counted on to join the Vietminh army in its battle against France between 1946 and 1954. During the years of the Vietnamese War against the United States, the Nungs were also recruited into the North Vietnamese Army. A number of Nung people reached prominent positions in the Communist party of Vietnam. Unlike South Vietnam, which tried to wipe out its indigenous cultures, North Vietnam worked to appease the tribal peoples of Vietnam, and their policy was a success.

SUGGESTED READINGS: John F. Embree, *Ethnic Groups of Northern Southeast Asia*, 1950; Paul V. Hockings, "Vietnamese," in Paul V. Hockings, ed., *Encyclopedia of World Cultures*, vol. 6, *East and Southeast Asia*, 1991; George McT. Kahin, "Minorities in the Democratic Republic of Vietnam," *Asian Survey* 12 (July 1972), 23–27; Peter Kunstadter, ed., *Southeast Asian Tribes, Minorities, and Nations*, 1967; Nguyen Khac Viet, ed., *Mountain Regions and National Minorities in the Democratic Republic of Vietnam*, 1968.

NUQUAY. The Nuquays are an ethnic subgroup of the Hani* people of the People's Republic of China (PRC). Scattered groups of Nuquays can also be found living in Thailand and Myanmar (Burma). The PRC Nuquays are located in the far southeastern corner of Yunnan Province, between the Mengle and the Ailao mountain ranges. Their society is patrilineal and patriarchal, and kinship relations are organized around patrilineal clans. Each clan consists of from thirty to forty households, and each clan maintains elaborate ancestral histories. Their sense of group identity is based more on a sense of being Nuquay than on being Hani. Most Nuquays remain tied to the agricultural economy, and a few still work in a traditional subsistence economy. They raise a variety of crops, including rice, maize, beans, buckwheat, millet, tea, peanuts, sugarcane, cotton, chili peppers, ginger, and indigo. Because of recent economic development programs in southwestern Yunnan, increasing numbers of Nuquay men can be found working in local factories and mines.

NUSU. See **NU.**

NUTSU. See **NU.**

NUTZU. See **NU.**

NUZHEN. See **MANCHU.**

NYO. The Nyo (Nya) are considered by many ethnologists in the People's Republic of China to be a subgroup of the Wa,* an officially recognized minority nationality. The Nyo live in the southwestern reaches of Yunnan Province, primarily in Shungjiang County, where most of them are farmers who raise maize, millet, wet and dry rice, tubers, chickens, and pigs. Classifying them as a subgroup of the Wa poses problems to ethnologists and ethnolinguists. Since their ''dialect'' is not mutually intelligible with most of the other Wa dialects, most Nyo view themselves more as Nyo than as Wa.

O _____

OIRAT. The Oirats—also known historically as Oyirats, Oletus, Kalmyks, Kalmuks, Kalmucks, and Sogpos—are a subgroup of the Mongol* people of the People's Republic of China (PRC). Their dialect, which is spoken primarily in the northwestern reaches of the Xinjiang Uigur Autonomous Region and in Qinghai Province, can be divided into two vernaculars: the Torgut vernacular is spoken by as many as 110,000 people, and the Kok Nur vernacular, by perhaps 35,000 people.

Most Oirats are farmers and herders who raise barley, wheat, oats, corn, millet, potatoes, buckwheat, sorghum, apples, and a variety of vegetables. Oirats also raise horses, cattle, camels, and goats, although their preferred livestock today is sheep.

At the end of the sixteenth century, to escape the political and economic pressures of Chinese,* Kazak,* and Mongol feudal lords, the Oirats, known then as Kalmyks, began migrating slowly to the west. They eventually settled in the lower Volga River basin, between the Don River and the Ural River. That region, formerly part of the Astrakhan Khanate, had been incorporated into Russia in 1556. By the late sixteenth century, the region known today as Kalmykia was under the authority of the Kalmyk Khanate. By the early 1600s, the Kalmyks were coming under more direct Russian* authority, a political development that protected them from the ravages of the larger and more aggressive khanates. During the years of the sixteenth and seventeenth centuries, they became even more loyal to the Lamaist tradition of Buddhism.

In 1771, however, the Kalmyks found themselves in a disastrous situation. Word reached the Kalmyks that the Oirats, their ethnic cousins still living in China, were undergoing intense persecution at the hands of the Chinese. The majority of Kalmyks decided to migrate back to China to come to their rescue, but the decision proved to be catastrophic. On their trip to Mongolia, the Kalmyks came under vicious attacks from Bashkirs and Kazaks, and when they reached Dzhungaria, they were attacked by the Chinese. Only a few thousand of the migrating Kalmyks survived the migration and reached China where they remained among the Oirats.

SUGGESTED READING: Baatr Kitinov, "Kalmyks in Tibetan History," *Tibet Journal*, 21 (Autumn 1996), 35–46.

OLD XIANG. Old Xiang, one of the two primary clusters of the Xiang* language, is spoken by millions of people in Hunan Province of the People's Republic of China, primarily in rural farming and mountainous areas. It is so different from the New Xiang* language that the two peoples cannot understand one another. The languages are not mutually intelligible. Speakers of New Xiang and Southwestern Mandarin,* however, do understand one another, leading some ethnolinguists to classify New Xiang as a dialect of Southwestern Mandarin. Consequently, it is impossible to classify New Xiang as part of the Xiang language family, as it is to cluster them with Old Xiang speakers as a single ethnic group.

OLETU. See **OIRAT.**

OLOSSU. See **RUSSIAN.**

ONGBE. See **LIMKOU.**

ORDO. The Ordos are a subgroup of the Mongol* people of the People's Republic of China. Their dialect is spoken primarily in the southwestern section of the Inner Mongolian Autonomous Region (IMAR). The Ordos dialect of southwestern Mongolia is divided into the Bayan-Hongor, Govi-Altay, and Hovd vernaculars. Each of these vernaculars is also spoken in the corresponding, cross-border regions of the IMAR. Most Ordos are farmers and herders who raise barley, wheat, oats, corn, millet, potatoes, buckwheat, sorghum, apples, and a variety of vegetables. Ordos also raise horses, cattle, camels, and goats, although their preferred livestock today is sheep.

SUGGESTED READING: Jia Laikuan, "Ordos Wedding on the Grasslands," *China Today* 41 (November 1992), 49–51.

OROQEN. The Oroqen people—also known as Chilins, Orochs, Orochels, Orochens, Orochons, Orochans, Oronchans, Orochens, Orochis, Oroquens, Solons, Soluns, and Suluns—are one of the smaller of the officially recognized minority nationalities existing in the People's Republic of China (PRC). In the 1990 national census, government demographers counted a total of 6,965 Oroqens, most of whom are located in Huma, Xunke, Aihui, and Jiayin counties in Heilongjiang Province and in the Hulun Buir League of the Inner Mongolian Autonomous Region (IMAR). Oroqens surround such settlements as Songling, Keyihe, Jiwen, Alihe, Jagdaqi, Nuomin, Tozhamin, and Dayangshu. In their language, which is part of the Tungus (see **TUNGUSIC PEOPLE**) branch of the Manchu-Tungus branch of the Altaic* linguistic family, "Oroqen" translates as "mountain people" or "reindeer herders." Many ethnolinguists consider Oroqen to be a dialect of Evenk.* Oroquen has many dialects, although the Gankui dialect, which is spoken by most Oroqens, is considered the standard. Many Oroqens still move back and forth during the winter and summer in the Greater and Lesser Hinggan Mountains. They are quite closely related to the Hezhens.*

Oroqens are descendents of the ancient Tungus people who were present in Manchuria as early as the third century B.C. The Tungus represented a consolidation of such local tribes as the Sushen, Ilu, Wochu, Wuchi, and Moho, as well as a variety of neighboring Turkic (see **TURKIC PEOPLE**) and Mongol* tribes. By the early seventeenth century, the Manchus* had become a self-conscious ethnic entity, and they were led by Emperor Nurhatsi, who established an imperial capital at Mukden. The name "Manchu" by that time referred to the people of the region. Later in the seventeenth century, the Manchus established the Qing dynasty by conquering Korea, Mongolia, and China. They pushed into Dzungaria, Tibet, and other borderlands in the eighteenth century.

There are more Oroqens living today in Russian Siberia than there are in the PRC. Russia's first annexations of Manchu land occurred in 1850, when Saint Petersburg annexed the Amur Delta. The first Russian* settlement was established in the same year at Nikolayevsk-na-Amure, at the mouth of the Amur River. Russia's eastward thrust occurred at the same time that Japan was extending its influence northward. Both powers eyed Sakhalin Island and, in 1855, a Russo-Japanese condominium was reached, establishing dual control of the 29,000-square-mile island. This agreement was dissolved in 1875 when Russia ceded the Kurile Islands to Japan. Sakhalin Island then became part of the Russian empire and was used primarily as a penal colony until 1905. After ceding southern Sakhalin to Japan following the Russo-Japanese War, the Romanovs tried to develop northern Sakhalin by encouraging Russian settlements.

A power vacuum, caused by the collapse of the czarist government and the Russian civil war, prompted local people in August 1918 to invite Japanese forces to occupy the region and thereby bolster the influence of the local Japanese minority who were opposed to the Bolshevists. Unrest between the Bolsheviks and the Japanese culminated in the infamous Nikolayevsk Massacre of March 11–15, 1920, when Red forces murdered countless "reactionaries," primarily the Japanese minority. Gradually, the Japanese presence was replaced by the Far Eastern Republic, a Leninist creation based in Chita. By 1922 this republic had annexed all the Manchu territories, and in the same year, the republic was merged into the Soviet Union. As part of the Soviet Union, the Manchu areas were reincorporated into Russia, now renamed the Russian Soviet Federated Socialist Republics (RSFSR).

The Chinese Oroqens first began migrating into what is today Heilongjiang Province and the Inner Mongolian Autonomous Region in the seventeenth century to avoid the increasingly obnoxious presence of czarist Russia. The Bolshevik revolution only introduced more instability, as did Communist collectivization campaigns in the 1920s and 1930s. As a result of these developments, more Russian Oroqens migrated into China. The People's Republic of China established the Oroqen Autonomous Banner in 1957.

The Japanese invasion of Manchuria in 1931 and coastal China in 1937 devastated the Oroqens. Japanese troops forcibly drafted Oroquen young men into the army during World War II, and they drove thousands of Oroqens deep into the forests. Large numbers of Oroqens were relocated into concentration camps, where they were forced into slave labor or service as human subjects in medical and weapons experiments. By 1945 the Oroqen population of China had fallen to less than 1,000 people. Since then, their population has recovered.

In terms of religion, the Oroqens retain many of their traditional animist, indigenous beliefs, although they have also incorporated elements of Russian Orthodoxy, Buddhism, and Confucianism into their faith. They believed in the god Sangi, ruler of the skies, who intervenes in human affairs to prevent sadness or to punish people for damaging the environment. Chinese education policies have served in recent decades to wean many Oroqens away from their traditional beliefs.

PRC economic policies have similarly altered the Oroqen way of life. Their traditional economy revolved around hunting sea mammals, but after the 1949 revolution and the collectivization of agriculture, they were gradually integrated into farming and animal husbandry. Soviet economic policies also disrupted Oroqen life. During the 1960s, 1970s, and 1980s, local oil refineries and pulp and paper mills badly polluted the Amur River, destroying much of the fish population and depriving many Oroqens in Russia and China of their livelihoods.

Some Oroqens are protesting what has happened to them over the last several decades. The Association of the Orochi is a lobbying group designed to protect the environment in which the surviving Oroqen live. Lyudmila Grishina, president of the Association of the Orochi in Khabarovsk Territory, claims that "over the past 20 years my people's numbers have steadily declined. The reason—being forced to resettle in other regions. We've already been moved five times from our ancestral lands. That's why we don't have any fishermen or hunters in our villages, and we are losing our native language and culture. Poor health services and unfit housing conditions have taken their toll too."

SUGGESTED READINGS: Alice Bartels and Dennis Bartels, "Soviet Policy toward Siberian Native People," *Canadian Dimension* 19 (1985), 36–44; Da Gen, "Three Oroqen Sisters," *China Today* 45 (March 1996), 25–27; Mike Edwards, "Siberia: In from the Cold," *National Geographic* 177 (March 1990), 2–49; He Chongyun, "The Oroqens: A Hunting People Settles Down," *China Reconstructs* 37 (July 1988), 58–60; Jia Laikuan, "The Oroqen—From Hunting Nomads to Settled Farmers," *China Today* 41 (May

1992), 57–59; Constantine Krypton, "Soviet Policy in the Northern National Regions after World War II," *Slavic Review* 13 (October 1954), 339–53; Ma Yin, *China's Minority Nationalities*, 1989; Paul V. Hockings, "Oroqens," in Paul V. Hockings, ed., *The Encyclopedia of World Cultures*, vol. 6, *East and Southeast Asia*, 1991; Henry G. Schwarz, *The Minorities of Northern China: A Survey*, 1984; Alexander Tropkin, "Congress of Hope," *Soviet Life* (December 1990), 10–15; Piers Vitebsky, "Perestroika among the Reindeer Herders," *Geographical Magazine* 61 (June 1989), 23–34; Xu Yixi, "Folk Arts of the Oroqen," *China Reconstructs* 31 (February 1982), 56–57.

OROQUEN. See **OROQEN.**

OUJIANG. The Oujiang people are a linguistic subgroup of Wu*-speaking Han* people in the People's Republic of China. Oujiang speakers total nearly 4.5 million people and live in Yongjia, Wenzhou, Ouhai, Ruian, Yueqing, Pingyang, Cangnan, Wencheng, Taishun, Dongtou, Yuhuan, and Qingtian counties in Zhejiang Province.

OWENK. See **EVENK.**

OWENKO. See **EVENK.**

OXEN-KILLING MIAO. See **MONTUANU.**

OYIRAT. See **OIRAT.**

P

PA RAUK. The Pa Rauks (Praoks) are considered by many ethnologists in the People's Republic of China to be a subgroup of the Wa,* an officially recognized minority nationality. Most Pa Rauks live in the southwestern reaches of Yunnan Province, primarily in Gengma County, where they support themselves as slash-and-burn farmers who raise maize, millet, wet and dry rice, tubers, chickens, and pigs. Their "dialect" is not mutually intelligible with most of the other Wa dialects, and most Pa Rauks view themselves more as Pa Rauk than as Wa.

PAGARAGORO. See **PAIWAN.**

PAHARI. The Paharis are one of the primary linguistic subgroups of the Newar* people of Nepal.

PAI. See **BAI.**

PAI-I. See **DAI.**

PAIJEN. See **BAI.**

PAIMAN. See **BAI.**

PAIWAN. The Paiwan, also known as the Tsarisen, are one of the indigenous peoples of Taiwan. Although Taiwanese government officials no longer keep count of the tribal populations of the indigenous people, demographers estimate that there are approximately 30,000 Paiwans today, most of whom are concentrated in the central Dawu mountain range of southeastern Taiwan. They can also be found in Laiyi, Mudan, and Neishe townships in Pingdong County and in Dawu and Damali townships in Taidong County. Roughly 55,000 Paiwans speak the language, which is Proto Austronesian in its classification and is closely related to other central and south Pacific languages. In fact, many ethnologists consider the Paiwans to be Polynesian in their ethnic origins. They are very closely related to the Rukai,* who border them to the north and whose lifestyle is quite similar to theirs.

Like most people in the world still engaged in a premodern lifestyle, the Paiwans live largely in a subsistence economy characterized by the slash-and-burn cultivation of millet, rice, sweet potatoes, and taro. They supplement their fundamentally agricultural diet by hunting deer and wild boar. Paiwans traditionally dressed themselves in clothing made of bark, but in recent years they have begun to choose instead commercially produced shirts, pants, and dresses. Paiwans live in closely settled villages of from between 100 and 1,000 people, which are usually located on hillsides. Walls composed of stone and bamboo surround each village, and the Paiwan regularly post roving guards outside the walls.

The Paiwans can be divided into two primary subgroups based on linguistic differences: the Raval and the Butaul. The Butauls can themselves be divided into four subgroups: the Paumaumaqs, Chaoboobols, Parilarilaos, and Pagarogaro. In recent years, Taiwanese government policy has worked to integrate the Paiwans into modern society and the modern economy by means of infrastructural improvements and public education. Although they are aware of their ethnic ancestry, the Paiwans are not likely to maintain that identity for much longer.
SUGGESTED READINGS: Raleigh Ferrel, *Taiwan Aboriginal Groups: Problems in Cultural and Linguistic Classification*, 1969; *The Republic of China Yearbook 1995*, 1996; Paul V. Hockings, ''Taiwan Aboriginal Peoples,'' in Paul V. Hockings, ed., *Encyclopedia of World Cultures*, vol. 6, *East and Southeast Asia*, 1991; Yvonne Yuan, ''Migrate, Assimilate, or Integrate?'' *Free China Review* 42 (June 1992), 4–15.

PAIWANIC. The term ''Paiwanic'' is a linguistic reference to a group of languages spoken by indigenous peoples on the island of Taiwan in the Republic of China. Included in the Paiwanic cluster are Paiwan,* Ami,* Bunun,* Rukai,* Puyuma,* Saisiyat,* and Yimi. The total number of Paiwanic speakers today exceeds 200,000 people.
SUGGESTED READING: S. A. Wurm, B. T'sou, D. Bradley, et al., eds., *Language Atlas of China*, 1987.

PAKHTUN. The Pakhtun—also known as Pashtos, Pathans, and Pushtuns—are one of the predominant ethnic groups of northern Pakistan and southern Afghanistan. They are renowned in the history of the British empire as one of the few ethnic groups on the subcontinent to defeat, again and again, the expansion of British authority into their homelands. They are especially powerful in the

North-West Frontier Province, where difficult geography has helped to isolate them. Small numbers of Pakhtuns can also be found scattered across the northern areas and just across the border in the People's Republic of China.

The exact numbers of Pakhtuns are not precisely known, since they are extremely suspicious of census takers who make invasive inquiries about their families, but it is doubtful that they number many more than several thousand people. The recent completion of the Karakoram Road through the Karakoram Range has made contact between Pakhtuns in China and their ethnic compatriots in Pakistan somewhat easier. There are as many as 20 million Pakhtuns in Pakistan and Afghanistan, but only a few thousand in China.

The Pakhtun people are devout Sunni Muslims, and their society is characterized by a virulent sense of egalitarianism. Their code of individual male conduct, known as *pakhtunwali*, is central to Pakhtuni ethnicity. It is an exaggerated sense of masculinity that includes a profound sense of honor, known as *nang*, and the principle of revenge, known as *badal*, to be exercised whenever honor is violated. Consequently, Pakhtun society is known for its internecine violence and vengeance feuds.

SUGGESTED READINGS: Akbar S. Ahmed, *Millenium and Charisma among the Pathans*, 1976, and *Pakistan Society: Ethnicity and Religious Identity*, 1986; Ali Banuazzi and Myron Weiner, eds., *The State, Religion, and Ethnic Politics: Afghanistan, Iran, and Pakistan*, 1986; Ernest Gellner, *Muslim Society*, 1983; James W. Spain, *Pathan Borderland*, 1963.

PALA. Classifying the Pala people of Yunnan Province in the People's Republic of China poses some interesting challenges. Like many other indigenous people in Yunnan, they are swidden farmers who raise rice, tubers, pigs, and a variety of vegetables. Their population numbers fewer than two thousand people. What is unusual about the Palas is that they are of Jingpo* extraction but speak the Pala language, a dialect of Zaiwa.*

PALAUNG. See **DE'ANG.**

PALONG. See **DE'ANG.**

PAMIR PEOPLE. The term Pamir people is an older, generic designation for the Shugnan, Rushan, Bartang, Yazgul, Ishkashim, Wakhan, Badzhui, and Khufi groups who live in the Pamir Mountain range that crosses the border of Afghanistan and the People's Republic of China (PRC) in the Xinjiang Uigur Autonomous Region. They have also been known as Mountain Tajiks (see **TAJIK**), Pamirian Tadjiks, and Golchas.

Although local tradition among the Pamirian people holds that they descend from the leaders of Alexander the Great's invading army, who reached the area in the fourth century B.C. and decided to live in the inaccessible mountain valleys, the Pamir people first appear historically in the second century A.D. when

Chinese chroniclers mentioned the Rushans, Shugnans, and Wakhans. Although they enjoyed brief periods of independence over the years, the Pamir people were usually under the political control of a foreign power. In the mid-eighteenth century, Ahmad Shah Durrani established an independent Afghan state, and by the late nineteenth century, during the reign of Abdur Rahman, most of the Pamir people were controlled politically from Kabul. The Emir of Bukhara, part of a Russian protectorate, was expanding to the south. At the same time, the British were expanding toward the Hindu Kush. In 1895, to prevent a collision, Britain and Russia agreed to place the border between Russia and Afghanistan at the Pjandzh River. The Emir of Bukhara controlled land on the northern side, while Afghanistan controlled the land to the south. Russia annexed all of the Pamir possessions of the Emir of Bukhara in 1904.

The Pamir people, who speak Iranian languages, live primarily in the western region of the Gorno-Badakhshan Autonomous Oblast in Tajikistan. As Muslims, they are Ismailis of the Nizarit rite, except for the Yazgulems and Vanchis, and some Bartangs, who are Sunnis of the Hanafi school. Russian and then Soviet ethnologists long viewed them as distinct people, but for the past sixty years they have been included as Tajik subgroups. The Shugnan dialect is the lingua franca for the Pamir people. PRC ethnologists also regard them as Tajik subgroups. In the early 1990s, the population of all of the Pamir groups is just below 100,000 people.

SUGGESTED READINGS: Shirin Akiner, *Islamic Peoples of the USSR*, 1983; Alexander Bennigsen and S. Enders Wimbush, *Muslims of the Soviet Empire: A Guide*, 1986; Ned Gillette, ''Adventure in Western China,'' *National Geographic* 159 (February 1981), 174–99; Yuri Kushko, ''The Pamirs,'' *Soviet Life* (June 1990), 28–35; Ronald Wixman, *The Peoples of the USSR: An Ethnographic Handbook*, 1984.

PAN. The Pans are one of the lineage subgroups of the She* people, who can be found scattered throughout sixty counties in Zhejiang, Fujian, Guangdong, Jiangxi, and Anhui provinces in the People's Republic of China. See **LAN.**

PANAI. Panai is one of the subdialects of the Lahuna* dialect of the Black Lahu* language in the People's Republic of China. See **LAHU.**

PANAKA. See **TIBETAN.**

PANAPANAYAN. See **PUYUMA.**

PANDIT. There may very well be a handful of Pandit people living today in the People's Republic of China (PRC), or at least in that part of Jammu and Kashmir claimed and occupied by the PRC. Pandits believe that they are the original inhabitants of the Valley of Kashmir and that their Kashmiri* dialect is the purest form of the Kashmir language. Their homeland is high in the Himalayas, near the junction of Russia, the People's Republic of China, and

Pakistan. Unlike most residents of the Kashmir Valley, the Pandits are Hindus, not Muslims. They are classified as upper-caste Brahmins in India, and over the years, Pandits have been prominent figures in Kashmiri finance, trade, administration, education, and land ownership.

When China seized control of portions of Jammu and Kashmir in 1959, it acquired sovereignty over several dozen Pandits who were living in the region at the time, most of whom were doing business. Today, there are probably several dozen Pandits still doing business in the region. India still claims them, although China controls them.

SUGGESTED READINGS: Sisir Gupta, *Kashmir: A Study in India-Pakistan Relations*, 1966; Trioki Madan, "Religious Ideology in a Plural Society: The Muslims and Hindus of Kashmir," *Contributions to Indian Sociology* 6 (1972), 106–41.

PANGHSE. See **HUI.**

PANGTASH. See **AMI.**

PANTHAY. See **HUI.**

PANTHE. See **HUI.**

PANTHEE. See **HUI.**

PAOAN. See **BONAN.**

PARILARILAO. See **PAIWAN.**

PASHTO. See **PAKHTUN.**

PASHTUN. See **PAKHTUN.**

PATHAN. See **PAKHTUN.**

PAUMAUMAQ. See **PAIWAN.**

PA-Y. See **DAI.**

PAY YAO. See **YAO.**

PAZEH. The Pazeh people are one of the indigenous ethnic groups who live on the island of Taiwan in the Republic of China. They are confined to the coastal area of far northwestern Taiwan, where they support themselves by slash-and-burn farming. The Pazeh people speak two dialects: Kahabu and Pazeh proper, which are mutually intelligible. The Pazeh language is all but extinct, spoken today by only a few dozen people. The chances that it will survive as a spoken language past the next generation are quite remote.

SUGGESTED READING: S. A. Wurm, B. T'sou, D. Bradley, et al., eds., *Language Atlas of China*, 1987.

PE. The Pe people are a recently discovered minority nationality in the People's Republic of China (PRC). PRC social scientists are currently conducting ethnographic research into Pe origins, trying to determine how to classify them, and until that research is completed, the process of extending them official recognition will be postponed. The Pe language has not yet been classified. PRC demographers estimate the Pe population at approximately 12,000 people, the vast majority of whom live in the Ganzhi Tibetan Autonomous Prefecture in Sichuan Province. Most Pe live in highland villages where they raise rice, maize, millet, pigs, poultry, and wheat.

SUGGESTED READING: S. A. Wurm, B. T'sou, D. Bradley, et al., eds., *Language Atlas of China*, 1987.

PEI. See **PEI-I** and **YI**.

PEI ER MI. See **PUMI**.

PEI-I. The Pei-Is are one of the subgroups of the Yi* people of the People's Republic of China (PRC). Although the Yi are an officially recognized minority nationality of more than seven million people, they are divided into a variety of subgroups whose sense of ethnic identity is quite parochial, based on region and dialects that are usually not mutually intelligible. Pei-Is can be found living today in Guizhou Province, usually in autonomous political subdivisions established by the PRC government for the Yi. They descend from the ancient Tusan people native to the Kunming region of Yunnan and Chengdu in Sichuan. Their economy is overwhelmingly agricultural. At lower elevations, farmers produce maize, potatoes, buckwheat, and oats as staples. In the highlands, they raise cattle, sheep, goats, and horses. Many Pei-I supplement their diets by collecting acorns, roots, wild vegetables, and herbs, and by fishing and hunting. Most Pei-Is live in mountain hamlets of fewer than twenty households.

PEIMI. See **PUMI**.

PEINAN. The Peinan Amis are one of the five primary subgroups of the Ami* people of Taiwan in the Republic of China. They are often considered by ethnologists to be part of the Southern Ami, which also includes the Hengchun* people. The Peinans are concentrated in north central Taitung County.

PELAM. See **PUYUMA**.

PENGLUNG. See **DE'ANG.**

PENGYU. See **DE'ANG.**

PENTI. See **BOUYEI.**

PERNUTU. See **BAI.**

PERTSU. See **BAI.**

PETSEN. See **BAI.**

PETSO. See **BAI.**

PETSU. See **BAI.**

PETSU SHUA BER NI. See **BAI.**

PHZOME. The Phzome (Phzomi) people are considered by ethnologists in the People's Republic of China to be a subgroup of the Pumi* people, an officially recognized minority nationality living today in Lijiang Naxi Autonomous County, Ninglang Yi Autonomous County, and Lanping County in Yunnan Province and in Jiulong, Yanyuan, and Muli Tibetan Autonomous counties in Sichuan Province. Most Phzomes live in high-elevation mountain villages where they work as farmers, raising corn, wheat, rice, buckwheat, barley, beans, and oats.

PIHSIEHK'A. See **TUJIA.**

PILAM. See **PUYUMA.**

PILING. The Piling people are a dialect subgroup of the Taihu* people, who are themselves a linguistic subgroup of the Wu*-speaking Han* people of the People's Republic of China. More than ten million people speak Piling, and they live in the Changzhou, Danyang, Liyang, Yixing, Wujin, Jintan, Jiangyin, Shazhou, Jingjiang, Nantong, Haimen, Qidong, and Gaochun regions of Jiangsu Province.

PISEKA. See **TUJIA.**

PLAO. See **WA.**

POBA. See **TIBETAN.**

POINTED MIAO. See **MIAO.**

PONAN. See **BONAN.**

PORTUGUESE. Today, approximately 8,500 people of Portuguese descent live in Macao, a six-square-mile peninsula on the coast of China, forty miles downriver from the city of Guangzhou (Canton). Included in Macao, which has been an overseas province of Portugal since the sixteenth century, are the tiny islands of Taipa and Kuoloane (Coloanne). Today, Macao is the last remaining territory of Portugal's once vast overseas empire. Another 1,500 or so Portuguese live in Hong Kong. In 1841, when the British began the process leading to the annexation of Hong Kong, they invited young Portuguese to relocate from Macao to Hong Kong to assist in the European administration of political affairs. Some Portuguese families, descended from those young administrators, are still living in Hong Kong and are aware of their Portuguese heritage. More recent Portuguese arrivals are connected to various Portuguse-owned commercial enterprises located on Macao and Hong Kong (see also **HONG KONGESE** and **MACANESE**).

In the mid-sixteenth century, Portugal decided to make money and Roman Catholic converts in Asia, and Macao became the heart and soul of its Far Eastern empire. In 1557 China allowed Portugal to establish permanent trading posts on Macao, although the foreigners were required to remain isolated behind a wall. Hundreds of Portuguese merchants and sailors settled in Macao and became the nucleus of the Portuguese ethnic community there. They became an elite, Roman Catholic minority on the island.

Portugal had hoped to use Macao as a staging area for the commercial exploitation of China and Japan, but it never really happened. Portugal was the first European nation to establish an overseas empire, but it was also the first to experience long-term decline. When the British moved into China in the nineteenth century, Portugal did not have the resources to resist. Great Britain occupied Macao for a few years early in the nineteenth century, but they soon left, unhappy over the willingness of the Portuguese community to intermingle sexually with the local Han* people. As the strength of Hong Kong grew in the nineteenth century, Macao declined in significance. Macao became known for specializing in gold, opium, and labor trafficking.

In 1887 China formally recognized Portuguese sovereignty over Macao, as long as the Portuguese agreed not to sell the territory to another European power. The Chinese correctly surmised that it would be much easier for them to manipulate Portugal than Great Britain. Macao's status remained just that until the 1960s, when the Cultural Revolution in the People's Republic of China sent a torrent of Han refugees into the territory. China forced Portugal to repatriate many of the refugees. Late in the 1960s and early in the 1970s, Portugal underwent a revolution of its own as well as rebellions in its African colonies. Macao lost its significance to Portugal, and on March 26, 1987, China and

Portugal signed an agreement that will turn sovereignty of Macao over to China on December 20, 1999. The agreement guarantees a fifty-year period for Macao to maintain its capitalist economy. On December 20, 1999, the residents of Macao, including the 8,500 Portuguese, will become citizens of the People's Republic of China.

SUGGESTED READINGS: C. R. Boxer, *Fidalgoes in the Far East, 1570–1750: Fact and Fancy in the History of Macao*, 1948, and *The Portuguese Seaborne Empire*, 1969; Nigel Cameron, *Hong Kong, The Cultured Pearl*, 1978; Ross Marlay, "Macao," in James S. Olson, ed., *Historical Dictionary of European Imperialism*, 1991.

POSDANTIELIK. The Posdantieliks are a subgroup of the Kirgiz* people. They speak a southern Kirgiz dialect and live primarily in Uqia County in the Xinjiang Uigur Autonomous Region of the People's Republic of China.

POUNANG K'UNG. See **BONAN.**

POUYEI. See **BOUYEI.**

POUYI. See **BOUYEI.**

PRAOK. See **PA RAUK** and **WA.**

PRIMI. See **PUMI.**

P'U NOI. The P'u Noi are a small ethnic group who live primarily in the highlands of northern Laos. Although census figures are notoriously unreliable, Laotian demographers estimate the P'u Noi population at perhaps 35,000 people, with several thousand more living across the border in China. Ethnolinguists, however, have found it extremely difficult to classify their language, since it is not understood by other groups. The P'u Noi live an indigenous lifestyle, maintaining a largely subsistence economy through swidden agriculture. Their most important crops are rice and corn. Because of the typography of their homeland and the backward state of the infrastructure, the P'u Noi have not generally been integrated into a commercial economy. Unlike many of the other indigenous peoples of Laos and China, however, the P'u Noi no longer practice an animistic, shamanistic religion. Practically all of the P'u Noi people are Buddhists.

SUGGESTED READINGS: Gerald C. Hickey, "P'u Noi," in Frank M. LeBar, Gerald C. Hickey, and John Musgrove, eds., *Ethnic Groups of Mainland Southeast Asia*, 1964; Karl Gustav Izikowitz, *Lamet: Hill Peasants in French Indochina*, 1951.

PUBIAU. The Pubiau people are a recently discovered minority nationality living in the People's Republic of China (PRC). PRC social scientists are currently conducting ethnographic research into Pubiau origins, trying to determine how to classify them, and until that research is completed, the process of extending them official recognition will be postponed. The Pubiau language has not yet been classified. PRC demographers estimate the Pubiau population at only a few thousand people, the vast majority of whom live in Malipo County of Yunnan Province. Most Pubiaus are swidden farmers who raise rice, tubers, pigs, and a variety of vegetables.

SUGGESTED READING: S. A. Wurm, B. T'sou, D. Bradley, et al., eds., *Language Atlas of China*, 1987.

PUHUI. See **BOUYEI**.

PUI. See **BOUYEI**.

PULAANG. See **DE'ANG**.

PULI. The Pulis are an ethnic subgroup of the Hani* people of the People's Republic of China (PRC). Scattered groups of Pulis can also be found living in Thailand and Myanmar (Burma). The PRC Pulis are located in the far south-eastern corner of Yunnan Province, between the Mengle and Ailao mountain ranges. Their society is patrilineal and patriarchal, with kinship relations organized around patrilineal clans. Each clan consists of from thirty to forty house-holds, and each clan maintains elaborate ancestral histories. Their sense of group identity is based more on a sense of being Puli than on being Hani. Most Pulis remain tied to the agricultural economy, and a few still work in a traditional subsistence economy. They raise a variety of crops, including rice, maize, beans, buckwheat, millet, tea, peanuts, sugarcane, cotton, chili peppers, ginger, and indigo. Because of recent economic development programs in southwestern Yunnan, increasing numbers of Puli men can be found working in local factories and mines.

P'U-MAN. The P'u-man are one of the officially unrecognized ethnic minorities of the People's Republic of China. Many ethnolinguists consider them to be a subgroup of the De'angs,* but P'u-man diversity is so extensive that they cannot be so easily classified. They number in the tens of thousands and can be found today living in Yunnan Province, especially in an area located between Paoshan, the Wuliang Hills, and down to Sumao, Lants'ang, Kengma, and Chenk'ang. Their language is part of the Mon-Khmer* group of the Austroasiatic linguistic family. It is divided into a number of mutually intelligible dialects.

But not all P'u-mans speak P'u-man as their native tongue. The P'u-mans living in the region between Chenk'ang and Yunhsien no longer speak P'u-man at all but have adopted Chinese* as their native language. Only a few remaining elderly people here still speak the indigenous language today. The P'u-mans north of the Chenk'ang-Yunhsien corridor, primarily along the Mekong River east of the road connecting Yunhsien and Nanchien, still speak P'u-man as their native tongue. Another group of P'u-mans, who live on the Red River, close to the border with Vietnam, speak a Kachin* dialect. Finally, some P'u-mans have adopted one of the Wa* dialects as their own. Because of these linguistic differences, it is difficult for social scientists to describe the P'u-mans as a single ethnic group.

P'u-mans prefer to locate their villages at higher altitudes, usually on hilltops or on the ridges between hills. Houses sit on stilts and villages are often surrounded by stockades. Livestock are kept beneath the house. P'u-mans are primarily farmers who produce rice, tobacco, hemp, beans, peas, maize, chilis, tomatoes, eggplants, bananas, sugarcane, mangoes, and jackfruit. They have traditionally also raised tea for consumption and for export. Some P'u-man groups also fish to supplement their diets with extra protein. Larger P'u-man villages have a monastery and a special house for Buddhist images, since their religion is a syncretic mix of traditional animism and Theravada Buddhism.

SUGGESTED READINGS: Joel M. Maring, ''Palaungs,'' in Paul V. Hockings, ed., *The Encyclopedia of World Cultures*, vol. 6, *East and Southeast Asia*, 1991; Joel M. Maring and Ester G. Maring, *Historical and Cultural Dictionary of Burma*, 1973; Mary Milne, *A Dictionary of English-Palaung and Palaung-English*, 1931, and *The Home of the Eastern Clan: A Study of the Palaungs of the Shan States*, 1924; Robert Parkin, *A Guide to Austroasiatic Speakers and Their Languages*, 1991.

PUMI. The Pumis, long considered to be a subgroup of the Qiang* people, are today one of the smaller of the officially recognized minority nationalities found in the People's Repubic of China (PRC). Historically, they have also been identified by the following ethnonyms: Pei Er Mi, Peimis, Primis, and Xifans. Today, the Pumi population is approximately 32,000 people, based on growth rates since the 1990 national census, which gave them a total of 29,657. Most of them live in northwestern Yunnan Province, particularly in Lijiang Naxi Autonomous County, Ninglang Yi Autonomous County, and Lanping County. Much smaller clusters of Pumis can be found across the border in Sichuan Province. The main settlements of Pumis in the PRC can be found between the Mekong and the Yangtze rivers. They are related linguistically and in terms of their material cultural with Tibetan* people. In fact, more than half of all Pumi speakers are of Tibetan ethnic ancestry.

The Pumi language is classified as one of the Tibeto-Burman* languages in the Sino-Tibetan linguistic family. It is divided into three dialects, and Pumi ethnic identity is related more to membership in a dialect group than to any generic Pumi membership. They identify themselves by dialect, not by being Pumi. In this sense, some ethnologists prefer to divide Pumis into three separate ethnic groups. The three Pumi languages are Phzomi, Phzome,* and Tshomi.*

Until the fairly recent past, the Pumis were a pastoral people who herded cattle and sheep throughout the Qinghai-Tibet Plateau. They lived in nomadic clusters and seasonally migrated to provide pasturage for their livestock. Gradually over the centuries, they migrated into the Hengduan Mountain region of Yunnan Province, where they settled permanently. As they left the flatlands and rolling elevations of the plateau, farming slowly replaced livestock as the primary focus of their economy. It remains so today.

The Pumis have become a mountain people; their villages are located at elevations reaching 9,000 feet. Villages, situated on gentle hillside slopes, are separated from one another by about 1,500 or so feet. Houses are two-story wood plank affairs, with the lower floor reserved for livestock. Corn is the Pumi staple, but they also produce rice, wheat, barley, beans, oats, buckwheat, and a variety of vegetables. They are known regionally for their cottage-industry woolen and bamboo goods. Under the influence of central government planners and agricultural extension agents, Pumi farmers have largely abandoned swidden agricultural techniques in favor of more sophisticated irrigation and terraced-field methods.

Pumi society is divided into dozens of patrilineal, exogamous clans, with marriages often arranged and cross-cousin relationships encouraged. Polygamy was traditionally popular among them, but since the Communist revolution in 1949 it has largely disappeared. Most Pumis are Lamaist Buddhists, although elements of traditional animism—particularly their belief in tutelary household spirits and ancestor ghosts—remain intact today.

SUGGESTED READINGS: Paul V. Hockings, "Pumi," in Paul V. Hockings, ed., *The Encyclopedia of World Cultures*, vol. 6, *East and Southeast Asia*, 1991; *Life among the Minority Nationalities of Northwest Yunnan*, 1989; Ma Yin, ed., *China's Minority Nationalities*, 1989.

PUMPKIN-HOLE MIAO. See **MONQHAOTAU.**

PUNJABI. The Punjab is a large region containing more than 80 million people on the subcontinent of South Asia, divided between Pakistan and India. The region is drained by the Jhelum, Chenab, Ravi, Beas, and Sutlej rivers, which all flow into the Indus River. Throughout history, because the Punjab sits just south of such mountain passes as the Khyber and the Kurram from Afghanistan, it has been the scene of repeated invasions from the west. In 1949, when the British empire extended independence to India and Pakistan, the Punjab was divided in two. Today, 98 percent of Punjabi-speaking Pakistanis are Muslims, while only 1 percent of Punjabi-speaking Indians are Muslims. The rest of the Indians are Hindis, Sikhs, and Christians. Punjabi Muslims are overwhelmingly Sunni Muslims of the Hanafi school. Only about 8 percent of them are Shiite Muslims, and most of them are of the Ithna Ashari branch.

In Pakistan, the Punjabis are a political and commercial elite. They tend to be well educated, multilingual, and accustomed to the rhythms of an urban, commercial society. Punjabis can be found dominating the Pakistani civil service, the educational system, the military, and the business communities. They are also very prominent in the mass media and entertainment industries. Punjabis have a similar, if not quite so dramatic, elite status in northwestern India.

Several thousand Punjabis are living today in the People's Republic of China, or at least in territory claimed by China. India would certainly dispute this claim. The region known as Jammu and Kashmir, which has been the source of intense, long-term hostility between Pakistan and India, is home to Pakhtuns,* Shinas, and Punjabis, as well as other ethnic groups. The Aksai Chin region of the Kashmir, which borders Tibet, was clearly under Indian, not Pakistani, control until 1959, when Chinese armies moved in and claimed the region. India protests the claim, but the matter has not yet been settled. When China claimed sovereignty over the Aksai Chin territory of Kashmir, a handful of Punjabis living there became a Chinese minority.

SUGGESTED READINGS: Makhdum Tassaduq Ahmad, *Systems of Social Stratification in India and Pakistan*, 1972; Saghir Ahmad, *Class and Power in a Punjabi Village*, 1977; Zekiya Eglar, *A Punjabi Village in Pakistan*, 1960.

PUNU. The Punus are a major subgroup of the Yao* people of the People's Republic of China. The 1990 national census counted 2,134,000 Yao people in China, and given their birthrate, which is above the national average, it is safe to say that the Yao population is now approaching 2.4 million people. More than 1.5 million Yaos live today in Guangxi Province, usually in mountain villages, but another 900,000 Yaos can be found scattered throughout the border regions of surrounding Hunan Province, Guangdong Province, Jiangxi Province, Guizhou Province, and Yunnan Province. They are particularly concentrated demographically in the Guangxi Zhuang Autonomous Region. Punus constitute 32 percent of the total Yao population. Punu is considered to be the main Yao language, but it is divided into a number of dialects, some of which are mutually unintelligible.

PUSHTUN. See **PAKHTUN.**

PUXIAN. Approximately three million people in the People's Republic of China speak Puxian, a dialect of the Min* Chinese* language. Puxian speakers can be found today in Xianyou County in eastern Fujian Province. See **HAN.**

PUYI. See **BOUYEI.**

PUYUEH. See **BOYUEI.**

PUYUMA. The Puyumas—also known regionally as Panapanayan, Pelam, Pilam, Piuma, and Pyuma—are one of the nine indigenous tribal peoples of Taiwan in the Republic of China. In terms of population, the Puyumas are one of the smallest indigenous groups, with fewer than 10,000 people, and the vast majority of them are concentrated in the flatlands of Taidong County in southeastern reaches of the island. Although still aware of their ancestral ethnic identity, the Puyumas have been all but assimilated by the surrounding Han* culture and society. There are five mutually intelligible dialects of the Puyuma language: Beinan, also known as Nanwang; Zhiben; Lujia; Beisijiu; and Taibaliujiu.

Until fairly recently, the Puyumas lived an exclusively subsistence economy, raising millet, taro, sweet potatoes, and beans planted in gardens cleared by means of slash-and-burn techniques. They typically dwelt in villages of roughly six hundred people, and each village was politically independent and endogamous. In terms of their social structure, the Puyumas were matrilineal and matrilocal. They also maintained elaborate moiety and age-group systems. A typical Puyuma man, for example, was raised by his nuclear family until he was eighteen years old. He then moved into a men's house or dormitory, where he was segregated from women for the next four years. At the age of twenty, he was allowed to marry, at which point he moved into his wife's household.

Traditional Puyuma religion was animistic in its belief that the environment was inhabited by a variety of spirit beings that could influence people's lives. They also believed that each human being has three souls—one in each shoulder and one in the head. Illness occurs when a soul leaves the shoulder, and women shamans restore health to the individual by returning the lost soul to him or her. Death occurs when the soul leaves the head. In recent years, Buddhist and Christian influences have made their way into Puyuma religion, which has resulted in a complicated, syncretic belief system.

More recently, the Puyumas have come under the cultural influence of the Paiwan* and Rukai* peoples. Social policies of the government of the Republic of China in recent years have been directed at expanding use of the Mandarin* language in Puyuma country through public education and by integrating the region into the larger commercial economy. Today, Puyumas are far more likely to speak Mandarin or even Ami* than Puyuma.

SUGGESTED READINGS: Raleigh Ferrel, *Taiwan Aboriginal Groups: Problems in Cultural and Linguistic Classification*, 1969; *The Republic of China Yearbook 1995*, 1996; Mei-chun Tang, "Han and Non-Han in Taiwan: A Case of Acculturation," *Bulletin of the Institute of Ethnology* (Taipei) 30 (1970), 6–12; Yvonne Yuan, "Migrate, Assimilate, or Integrate?" *Free China Review* 42 (June 1992), 4–15.

PUYUMA AMI. See **SOUTHERN AMI.**

PYIN. The Pyins are considered by many ethnologists in the People's Republic of China to be a subgroup of the Wa,* an officially recognized minority nationality. Most Wa live in the southwestern reaches of Yunnan Province, primarily in Ximeng, Canghyuan, Menglian, Gengma, Lancang, Shuangjiang, Yongde, and Zhenkang counties. Pyins are farmers whose techniques range from primitive swidden practices to sophisticated, scientific agriculture. Their sense of group identity is more Pyin than Wa.

PYUMA. See **PUYUMA.**

Q _____

QI. The Qis are one of the many subgroups of the Li* people of Hainan Province in the People's Republic of China. Most Qi speakers can be found living today in Baoting and Qiongzhong counties, which constitute the eastern half of the Li-Miao Autonomous Prefecture. Like other Li groups, they have earned a reputation over the years for their ferocious anti-Han* xenophobia. Most Qis today are farmers who raise coconuts, coffee, cocoa, sisal, rubber, cashews, pineapples, mangoes, and bananas. Rice is their staple, and because of the tropical climate of Hainan and its fertile soil, they are able to produce three rice crops a year. They are divided into three subgroups of their own, each based on differences in dialect. The Tongshi (Tongza) dialect of Qi is spoken primarily in the western and northwestern areas of Qiongzhong County, as well as in far western Baoting County. Tongshi speakers constitute more than 70 percent of the 195,000 Qi speakers. The other Qi dialects are Qiandui and Baocheng.*

QIAN DONG. Qian Dong, also known as Eastern Guizhou Miao and Central Miao, is one of the three major dialects of the Miao* language in the People's Republic of China. It is spoken by nearly 1.5 million people, most of whom live in Eastern Guizhou province. Eastern Guizhou Miao is divided into three subdialects. The northern local dialect can be heard among more than 900,000 people in Kaili, Huangping, Leishan, Taijianng, Jianhe, and Sandu counties in Guizhou Province. The eastern local dialect is spoken by more than 200,000 people in Jinping and Liping counties in Guizhou Province and in Jingxian and Huitong counties in Hunan Province. More than 300,000 Miaos speak the southern dialect of the Eastern Guizhou language. It is commonly heard in Rongshui and Sanjiang counties in the Guangxi Zhuang Autonomous Region.

QIANDUI. The Qianduis are a subgroup of the Qi people, who are themselves a subgroup of the Li* minority of Hainan Island in the People's Republic of China. Qiandui speakers constitute 16 percent of the Qi people. Most Qianduis live in eastern and southern Qiongzhong County.

QIANG. The Qiangs are the primary subgroup, in terms of population and dialect, of the Qiang* peoples of the People's Republic of China. Their language, one of the Qiang dialects, is part of the Qiang branch of the Sino-Tibetan language family. No written script currently exists for Qiang, and a Chinese* dialect is gradually becoming the native language of more and more Qiangs. Most Qiangs live in the mountain pass that separates the Chinese lowlands in the east from the Tibetan* highlands to the west. Qiangs are concentrated at the eastern edge of that mountain corridor. In the Maowen Xian region, Qiangs constitute nearly 80 percent of the population and are demographically concentrated. Most Qiangs reside in rugged mountain villages, and their homes consist of multistoried, flat-roofed houses constructed of stone. They are subsistence farmers who raise barley, buckwheat, potatoes, and beans, using both slash-and-burn hoe farming and double-team cattle plowing. In Qiang villages located below 7,000 feet in elevation, maize has become the staple product. As cash crops, Qiangs produce apples, walnuts, peppers, and opium, and they collect bundles of firewood and medicinal herbs for commercial sale. Most Qiangs remain loyal to their ancestral animistic religion.

QIANG. The Qiang (K'iangs) peoples are an officially recognized minority nationality in the People's Republic of China (PRC). Over the centuries, they have been identified by a number of different ethnonyms, including Chiang, Di, Juma, Jumei, Manzi, Rma, and Rong. "Rma" is their self-designation. The contemporary Qiang population stands just under 600,000 people, and their rate of population growth is one of the highest in the country.

The Qiang peoples live across a great arc stretching from Nanping in the northwest reaches of Sichuan Province to Lijiang in northern Yunnan Province. Their homeland is in the mountain corridor that connects the Tibetan* highlands in the west from the Chinese lowlands in the east. At one time they were a contiguous population there, but in the last century Han,* Tibetan, and Yi* people have settled among them. The region, part of the Central Asian plateau, is cut by deep river channels and is characterized by sharply rising mountains. At higher altitudes, rainfall is plentiful, but the region drys out, becoming semiarid on the lower slopes and dry enough in the valleys to require irrigation for successful commercial agriculture. Most of this region of southwestern China is covered by forests and high-elevation grasslands.

The Qiang languages constitute a separate branch of the Tibeto-Burman* cluster of languages in the Sino-Tibetan linguistic family. An intense scholarly and political debate surrounds the nature of the Qiang languages, primarily because of the complicated ethnic history of the region and the linguistic diversity found there. There are eight primary subgroups based on linguistic differences. The Qiang people proper, one of the subgroups, live on the eastern edge of the mountainous corridor. They are further subdivided into two groups based on dialect: the Heisuhui Qiang and the Boluozu Qiang. The combined population of the two Qiang subgroups is approximately 235,000 people. At the far western stretches of the mountainous corridor, near the Tibetan highlands, are the Jiarong, the second largest of the Qiang subgroups. They have a current population of approximately 195,000 people. In between the Jiarongs and the Qiangs are 40,000 Baimas, 30,000 Ersus, 35,000 Muyas, 30,000 Muyamis, and 35,000 Namuyis.

Ethnic identity among the Qiang subgroups is currently a hotly debated political issue in the People's Republic of China's central government. At the time of the Communist revolution in 1949, only the Qiang subgroup of the Qiang peoples had developed any real self-conscious identity, at least in terms of being able to express them collectively as a political entity. The other subgroups had not been able to coalesce much beyond an ability to recognize differences in dialect among the various groups. Over the years, however, the sense of ethnicity, or minzu as the Chinese call it, has gained momentum among the subgroups. In 1960 the Pumis,* long considered another Qiang subgroup, convinced the central government to award them separate status as an officially recognized minority nationality. Several of the other subgroups—particularly the Baimas, Ersus, Jiarongs, and Namiyus—have been for years requesting similar status, so that they too can enjoy the same political classification as the Qiangs and Pumis. So far, the central government has not seen fit to extend official recognition. The subgroups will no doubt continue to apply for recognition in the future.

Of all the subgroups of the Qiang peoples, the Qiangs proper are acculturating the most rapidly to Han institutions. Most Qiangs no longer speak Qiang as their native language, and virtually all Qiangs have adopted Han surnames. While marriage is relatively unimportant in traditional Qiang culture, modern Qiangs have adopted Han marriage patterns. They have even adopted Han patrilineal values, even though the traditional Qiang social ideology is decidedly matriarchal.

More than three thousand years ago, the Qiang peoples maintained close alliances with the Zhuangs.* Contact between Qiang and Han peoples also goes back three thousand years in Chinese history. At the time, the material cultures of lowlanders and highlanders in the region were quite similar; both groups engaged in hunting, foraging, and very limited agriculture. But in the sixth century B.C., Han culture underwent significant changes. Intensive agriculture made its appearance among them, and they prospered from surpluses of food and fiber. Many Qiangs, in order to escape Han influence and maintain their traditional lifestyle, began migrating west into the mountains. As nomadic herders, the Qiangs functioned on the fringe of Chinese civilization until the fourth century, when they emerged as one of the "Five Barbarians" and helped overrun much of northern China. In the eighth century, the Tibetan empire expanded

from the west, putting its own squeeze on Qiang society. When the Mongol*
armies showed up in the thirteenth century, Qiangs essentially became a conquered people. The *tusi* system was imposed upon them, in which the imperial
government ruled through Qiang agents. When the Mongol empire began to
contract a century later, Han power replaced it. By 1900 most Qiang country
was under the firm control of the Chinese government. Some Jiarong groups
held out longer, maintaining a quasi-independence until the revolution in 1949.

Qiang villages usually consist of close kinship relatives who live endogamously. They often claim descent from a single male or female ancestor. Traditionally, Qiang society was matriarchal, including each of the local political
systems, in which primary matriarchs functioned as village chiefs. Qiang society
also places a great value on egalitarianism, and even before the Communist
revolution in 1949, more than 90 percent of Qiangs were free farmers. The heart
and soul of each household is the mother and the children; men are considered
to be quite secondary in importance. Lineages are relatively insignificant in
Qiang society. Even after marriage, a man retains dual residence in the home
of his own parents and in the household of his wife. Polygamy does not exist.

Most people who speak a Qiang language live in flat-roofed, single-story
houses made of stone. Livestock occupy the ground floor, where compost is
stored. The second story serves as the household's living compound, and the
third floor functions as a meeting place and threshing floor. Qiang villages differ,
however, from Jiarong villages. Qiangs build their villages on mountainsides
with houses clustered closely together, which makes defensive operations easier.
Stone towers as high as 150 feet house watchmen who keep a close eye on
surrounding areas. Two or three Qiang villages may be clustered close together,
but other villages will be located about a mile away. Qiangs prefer to build
villages just below the treeline, leaving lower elevations for Han settlements.
Jiarong villages, on the other hand, are more widely dispersed, with individual
households more diffusely placed. They prefer higher elevations, often up to
11,000 feet, and villages frequently stretch from the bottom of the valleys
thousands of feet up the mountainsides.

Qiang farmers employ a variety of techniques to raise their crops. Most of
them are subsistence cultivators whose production is primarily for their own
household's consumption. Some Qiangs are swidden agriculturalists, using
slash-and-burn methods and a hoe. Others use plows drawn by double-oxen
teams. Farmers fertilize the land with compost and cattle manure. They raise
barley, buckwheat, potatoes, and beans, and below 7,000-foot elevations, they
also produce maize. To fulfill their needs for cash, Qiang farmers raise and
market rapeseed, apples, walnuts, peppers, and opium. Hunting and foraging
retain some importance in the Qiang economy, and the collection and marketing
of medicinal herbs is another source of cash. Qiangs can also still be found
living as nomadic pastoralists raising sheep, yaks, horses, and cattle.

Qiang religion is an eclectic mix of traditional animism, Daoism, and Buddhism. Throughout all Qiang villages, white stones can be seen adorning roof-

tops and altars. This "White Stone Religion" revolves around the conviction that such stones can ward off a host of evil and dangerous invisible spirits. Among large numbers of Qiangs, the belief is quite common that human beings descend from the sexual union of the daughter of the heaven god and some type of earthly primate, either a man or a monkey. Large numbers of Qiangs also follow the teachings of Lamaist Buddhism. Ancestor worship is also present in most Qiang villages.

SUGGESTED READINNGS: William Gill, *The River of Golden Sand*, 1880; David Graham, *The Customs and Religion of the Ch'iang*, 1957; Hu Baoyu and Huang Baoshan, *Snowy Mountains and Grassland*, 1990; Gerald A. Huntley, "Qiang," in Paul V. Hockings, ed., *The Encyclopedia of World Cultures*, vol. 6, *East and Southeast Asia*, 1991.

QIARLENG. The Qiarlengs are a subgroup of the Kirgiz* people. They speak a southern Kirgiz dialect and live primarily in Akto, Yengishar, and Guma counties in the Xinjiang Uigur Autonomous Region of the People's Republic of China.

QINGHAI BONAN. The Bonan people of Qinghai Province in the People's Republic of China are related linguistically to the larger group of Bonans* living in Gansu Province. The primary difference between the two groups is religion. While the Gansu Bonans are Muslims, most Qinghai Bonans are Lamaist Buddhists, although they are in an advanced state of assimilation with surrounding Tibetans.*

QINLIAN. The Qinlian people are a subgroup of Yue*-speaking Han* Chinese* in the People's Republic of China. Most Qinlians live in the Qinzhou, Beihai, Hepu, Pubei, Lingshan, and Fangcheng regions of the Guangxi Zhuang Autonomous Region.

QIONGSHAN. The Qiongshan people are subgroup of the Limkou* people of Hainan Island in the People's Republic of China. Most Qiongshans can be found living today around Haikou City and in Qiongshan County. More than 175,000 people speak Qiongshan.

QIONGWEN. Approximately 4.5 million people in the People's Republic of China speak Qiongwen, a dialect of the Min* Chinese* language. Qiongwen speakers can be found today in fourteen cities and counties of Hainan Province. Qiongwen can itself be divided into five dialects: Fucheng,* Wenchang,* Wanning,* Changgan,* and Yaxian.* See **HAN**.

QIQIHAR. The Qiqihars, a linguistic subgroup of the Daur* people, live primarily in the Molidawa Daur Autonomous Banner District of far northeastern China in the Inner Mongolian Autonomous Region and across the border in Heilongjiang Province. The remainder of the Daurs can be found on the other side of the country, living near the city of Qiqihar in the Xinjiang Uigur Autonomous Region. Approximately 40,000 Daurs speak the Qiqihar dialect, which can be heard in and around Qiqihar City, Fuyu County, Longjiang County, Araong Banner, and Vutha Banner. Qiqihar itself is divided into three distinct vernaculars: Jiangdong, which is spoken in Fuyu County, especially east of the Nonni River; Jiangxi, which is spoken in the area north of Meilisi and west of the Nonni River; and Fularji, the third Qiqihar vernacular.

QIREN. See **MANCHU.**

QIU. See **DRUNG.**

QIUBEI. The Qiubei people are a subgroup of the Zhuang* people of the People's Republic of China. The Qiubei language is classified as one of the Northern Zhuang* dialects, and most of its speakers live today in Qiubei County and Yanshan County in Yunnan Province.

QUA GELAO. The Qua Gelaos are one of the four linguistic subdivisions of the Gelao* people of the People's Republic of China.

QUANZHANG. The Quanzhang people are a subgroup of Minnan* people, who are themselves a linguistic subgroup of the Min* language of Chinese* in the People's Republic of China and the Republic of China on Taiwan. Quanzhang speakers can be found today in the Xiamen, Jinmen, Tong'an, Zhangzhou, Changtai, Hua'an, Longhai, Zhangpu, Yunxiao, Nanjing, Pinghe, Dongshan, Zhao'an, Zhangping, Longyan, Quanzhou, Jinjang, Nan'an, Anxi, Yongchun, Dehua, and Hui'an regions of Fujian Province and the Taipei, Jilong, Yilan, Zhanghua, Nantou, Taizhong, Yunlin, Jiayi, Tainan, Pingdong, Gaoxiong, Taidong, Hualian, and Penghu regions of Taiwan. See **HAN.**

QUMOL. Qumol is one of the vernacular subgroups of the Uigur* language spoken in the Xinjiang Uigur Autonomous Region of the People's Republic of China. Most speakers of Qumol live in and around the oasis community of Qumjol.

QYRGYZ. See **KIRGIZ.**

R

RA-ANG. See **DE'ANG.**

RAI. The Rai people are, along with Limbus, one of the two subgroups of the Kiranti* people of Nepal. The Rais are concentrated in eastern Nepal, with other clusters in India, Sikkim, and elsewhere in Nepal. For their own part, the Rais are further divided into two subgroups—the Khambus and the Yakhus. Rai religion is an eclectic mix of animism, Lamaist Buddhism, and Hinduism. Those Rais in Nepal and Bhutan can sometimes be found living in Tibet, where they work the commercial trade routes through the Himalayas. The Rais themselves are further divided into two subgroups: the Khambus and the Yakhus. See **BHU-TANESE.**

RAU. See **YANGUANG.**

RAVAL. See **PAIWAN.**

RAVET. The Ravets are considered by many ethnologists in the People's Republic of China to be a subgroup of the Wa,* an officially recognized minority nationality. Most Wa live in the southwestern reaches of Yunnan Province, primarily in Ximeng, Canghyuan, Menglian, Gengma, Lancang, Shuangjiang, Yongde, and Zhenkang counties. Ravets are farmers who raise wet rice, dry rice, maize, millet, tubers, and wheat. Because the Ravet language is not mutually intelligible to speakers of other Wa languages, it is difficult to classify them simply as a Wa subgroup. Ravets are more likely to identify themselves to outsiders as Ravet people than as Wa.

RAW MIAO. The term "Raw Miao" has been used over the years by Han* Chinese* to describe Miao* people who have not acculturated to Han institutions.

RAWANG. The Rawang people are an unrecognized minority nationality who live in northern Myanmar (Burma) and in the People's Republic of China, in southwestern Yunnan Province. The Rawangs are one of the subgroups of the larger Kachin* people of Myanmar, northeast China, and India; however, they are unique among the Kachin subgroups inasmuch as their language is closely related to that of the Nung.* They prefer to live in valleys and small plains that are surrounded by mountains. Rawangs select their village sites at the foot of a mountain or at the edge of a plain, and a typical village consists of several patrilineally related groups.

Chinese historians first make note of Rawangs during the Tang dynasty more than a thousand years ago. They had originated to the north and to the east in what is today northern Myanmar and had settled in western Yunnan. Because of geographical isolation and indigenous economies, the region of far western Yunnan Province has never had a monoculture. Different ethnic groups live in close proximity to one another, even among one another in many pluralistic villages. Rawangs are surrounded by a variety of other ethnic groups in the region, including the Dai,* the Jingpo,* the Han,* the De'ang.*

Historically, the Rawang economy revolved around subsistence levels of wet-rice agriculture. They have adapted their planting and harvesting to the prevailing weather patterns, particularly the arrival of the monsoon season. Tobacco, sugarcane, and oil-producing plants generated cash for the Rawang economy. Textile production and silversmithing were also part of the local economy.

Since the Communist victory in 1949, however, the central government has become increasingly involved in Rawang economic life. State programs to resettle Han people throughout the country as a means of encouraging assimilation have brought tens of thousands of immigrants to western Yunnan Province. The newcomers have succeeded in taking control—through outright seizure, legal purchase, or government condemnation—of large portions of Rawang land. Instead of working as subsistence farmers on communal land, the Rawangs are rapidly becoming skilled workers, employed primarily by Shan businessmen.

The Rawang social structure is based on a system of patrilineal descent, in which members of a village or several villages trace their ancestry back to a common male. Individuals must marry outside their patrilineal group, and marriages are generally arranged by parents for economic advantage. The fundamental family unit of Rawang society is a patriarchal family that includes two or three generations.

RED BENGLONG. See **DE'ANG.**

RED LAHU. See **LAHU.**

REPUBLICAN CHINESE. See **TAIWANESE.**

RMA. See **QIANG.**

RONG. See **QIANG.**

RONGBA. The Rongba people are ethnic Tibetans* who speak the Rongba vernacular of the Amdo* dialect. Most Rongba speakers live today in Hualong Hui Autonomous County, Xunhua Salar Autonomous County, and Ledu County in Qinghai Province. See **KHAM.**

RONGMAHBROGA. The Rongmahbroga people are ethnic Tibetans* who speak the Rongmahbroga vernacular of the Amdo* dialect. Most Rongmahbrogas live today in Tongren County of the Huangnan Tibetan Autonomous Prefecture in Qinghai Province and in Xiahe County of the Gannan Tibetan Autonomous Prefecture in Gansu Province. See **KHAM.**

ROUROU. See **NU.**

RTAHU. The Rtahu people are ethnic Tibetans* who speak the Rtahu vernacular of the Amdo* dialect. Most Rtahu speakers live today in Dawu and Lahu counties in the Garze Tibetan Autonomous Prefecture in Sichuan Province. See **KHAM.**

RUEN DAI. See **DAI.**

RUKAI. The Rukais, also known as the Tsarisen, are one of the indigenous peoples of Taiwan. Although Taiwanese* government officials no longer keep count of the tribal populations of the indigenous peoples, demographers estimate that there are approximately 10,000 Rukais today, most of whom are concentrated in southeastern Taiwan. The Rukais speak a Proto Austronesian language whose roots are in the South and Central Pacific. In fact, many ethnologists consider the Rukais to be Polynesian in their ethnic origins. They are closely related to the Paiwans,* who border them to the south. They are also bordered by the Bunun* people to the north and the Puyumas* to the east. There are two mutually intelligible Rukai dialects: the Lower Three Villages dialect, which is spoken in the Touna, Maolin, and Mantong regions of Gaoxiong County; and the Taromak-Vudai dialect, which is spoken is the Danan region of Taidong County and the Wutai (Vudai) region of Pingdong County. Once a matrilineal people, the Rukais today have a social system based on ambilineal kinship relationships. They are widely known for their wood and stone sculptures.

Like most people in the world still living a premodern lifestyle, the Rukais live largely in a subsistence economy characterized by the slash-and-burn cultivation of millet, rice, sweet potatoes, and taro. They supplement their fundamentally agricultural diet by hunting deer and wild boar. Rukais traditionally dressed themselves in clothing made of bark, but in recent years they have begun to wear commercially produced shirts, pants, and dresses. In recent years, Taiwanese government policy has worked to integrate the Rukais into modern society and into the modern economy by means of education and infrastructural improvements.

SUGGESTED READINGS: Raleigh Ferrel, *Taiwan Aboriginal Groups: Problems in Cultural and Linguistic Classification*, 1969; *The Republic of China Yearbook 1995*, 1996; Yvonne Yuan, "Migrate, Assimilate, or Integrate?," *Free China Review* 42 (June 1992), 4–15.

RUMAI. See **DE'ANG.**

RUSSIAN. Between 1918 and 1922, during and just after the civil war in Russia, several thousand Mensheviks, or White Russians, who opposed the triumphant Bolsheviks, fled to what is today the Xinjiang Uigur Autonomous Region of the People's Republic of China (PRC), particularly in Tacheng District and Altai District near the towns of Yining, Qoqek, Burqin, Qitai, and Urumqi where the borders of Russia, Mongolia, and China converge. Another group of White Russians settled in Hulunbuir League in Inner Mongolia and in Xunke County and Huma County in Heilongjiang Province. By the outbreak of World War II, the number of ethnic Russians in China had reached more than 15,000 people.

Because of the turmoil in China between the end of the war and Mao Zedong's triumph in 1949, several thousand of these Russians migrated to Hong Kong. The Russian population in China declined again after 1960, when the Sino-Soviet rivalry threatened to erupt in violence. The ethnic Russians living near the Soviet-Xinjiang border were viewed as a potential fifth column by the Chinese, and many of them moved back to Russia. Some returned to the Soviet Union. On July 1, 1997, when Hong Kong reverted to the People's Republic of China, several hundred Hong Kongese were aware of their Russian ancestry. Today, there is disagreement about the number of ethnic Russians living in the PRC. The 1957 Chinese census placed the number at 9,000, which had dropped to only 600 in the 1978 census. The 1982 census counted 2,935 ethnic Russians living in China, which increased to 13,504 according to the 1990 census.

SUGGESTED READING: Henry G. Schwarz, *The Minorities of Northern China: A Survey*, 1984.

S

SAAROA. The Saaroa are one of the primary linguistic subdivisions of the Tsouic*-speaking people of Taiwan in the Republic of China. The Saaroa language is spoken today by only several dozen people who live along the upper extension of the Laonongxi River. Most Saaroas are slash-and-burn agriculturalists. Demographers and ethnolinguists have little hope that the Saaroa language will survive for more than one or two more generations.
SUGGESTED READING: S. A. Wurm, B. T'sou, D. Bradley, et al., eds., *Language Atlas of China*, 1987.

SAIS. The Sais are one of the many subgroups of the Li* people of Hainan Province in the People's Republic of China. Like other Li groups, they have earned a reputation over the years for their ferocious anti-Han* xenophobia, which has often taken the form of guerrilla warfare against Han immigrants to Hainan. Most Sais today are farmers who raise coconuts, coffee, cocoa, sisal, rubber, cashews, pineapples, mangoes, and bananas. Rice is their staple, and because of the tropical climate of Hainan and its fertile soil, they are able to produce three rice crops a year.

SAISIYAT. The Saisiyats—also known regionally and in the scholarly literature as Saiset, Saisiat, and Saisirat—are one of the indigenous people living on Taiwan in the Republic of China. Although government census takers no longer calculate the populations of the indigenous groups, most demographers place the Saisiyat population at around 8,000 people. They are divided into two groups, one northern and the other southern. The northern Saisiyats occupy the mountainous highlands of Hsinchu County. Southern Saisiyats can be found in the highlands of Maioli County and are bordered to the east by Atayal* people, whose culture is having an increasingly significant impact on them. The two cities in Taiwan with the most Saisiyat influence are Maioli and Hsinchu. The Saisiyats are in an advanced state of acculturation and assimilation with neighboring Han* and Atayal people. Only a few thousand Saisiyats still speak their native language, and most of them are members of the older generation. The Saisiyat language is divided into two mutually intelligible dialects. Northern Saisiyat is spoken in the Da'ai, Wufeng, and Beipu regions of Xinzhu County, while Southern Saisiyat is spoken in the Donghe, Nanzhuang, and Shitan regions of Miaoli County.

The Saisiyats have long been known for their gentle, nonviolent culture, and they have historically often found themselves facing oppression from the more populous and aggressive Atayal. Today, their economy revolves around forestry and the agricultural production of millet, rice, sweet potatoes, and a variety of other crops. Saisiyats live in clusters of villages that share farmland and fishing waters. They were among the first of the indigenous peoples of Taiwan to begin the process of assimilation into Han culture.

SUGGESTED READINGS: Raleigh Ferrel, *Taiwan Aboriginal Groups: Problems in Cultural and Linguistic Classification*, 1969; *The Republic of China Yearbook 1995*, 1996; Mei-chun Tang, "Han and Non-Han in Taiwan: A Case of Acculturation," *Bulletin of the Institute of Ethnology* (Taipei) 30 (1970); Yvonne Yuan, "Migrate, Assimilate, or Integrate?" *Free China Review* 42 (June 1992), 4–15.

SAKA. See **YAKUT.**

SAKHA. See **YAKUT.**

SAKIZAYA. Sakizaya is one of the five primary dialects of the Ami* language, which is spoken by the Ami people, an indigenous group living on Taiwan in the Republic of China.

SALAR. The Salar people, also known today as Salors and Salas, are one of the Muslim ethnic minorities in the People's Republic of China (PRC). With a current population of approximately 90,000 people, they are concentrated in the Xunhua Salar Autonomous County of eastern Qinghai Province, particularly in and around the towns and cities of Hualong, Gandu, Jiezi, Jishi, Qingshui, Mengda, Tashapo, Dahejia, Muchang, Baizhhuang, and Linxia City. The special autonomous region for the Salars was established in 1954. Qinghai Province is located in north central China. Other Salars can be found in Hualong County and in Linxia County in Gansu Province. Relatively small numbers of Salars also live in the Xinjiang Uigur Autonomous Region.

Salar legend traces their origins back to immigrants who left the Samarkand region sometime between 1368 and 1644 during the Ming dynasty. Two brothers began the journey to find a new homeland because of Mongol* depradatons. They came with a white camel, Samarkand soil, Samarkand water, and a copy of the Koran. The two young men followed the Silk Road all the way to the Xunhua region of what is today eastern Qinghai Province. They settled in a hilly environmnent of little interest to other peoples, and from those two brothers descend the Salar peoples.

Ethnologists debate the origins of the Salars, but most think their ethnonym comes from the word "Salor," which is the name of a prominent Turkmen subgroup. Historical documents discussing the Salar people go back as far as the early eleventh century. Salar oral historians confirm that idea, claiming that the Salars split from the Turkmen in Samarkand in the fourteenth century and migrated to the Xunhua region. During that era, which was part of the Ming dynasty, the Salars enjoyed effective self-government in the area, controlling taxation, military affairs, and the legal system.

Beginning in the years of the Qing dynasty, however, the era of Salar independence slowly came to an end. Qing military forces gradually extended their authority over the Salars during the eighteenth century, even though the Salars were a troublesome charge, rebelling frequently against what they viewed as oppressive Qing policies.

It was at that time, in the late seventeenth and early eighteenth centuries, that the Salars adopted the Hanafi rite of Islam. A Muslim missionary named Muhammad Amin brought the Hanafi rite to the Gansu-Qinghai region, and the Salars readily accepted it. They had already been living in close proximity for many decades to neighboring Muslim peoples, particularly the Dongxiangs* and the Bonans.* The Salars also earned reputations for being particularly devout Muslims. Mosques dotted Salar communities, and mullahs were the primary powerbrokers. In 1958 Communist authorities began a concerted campaign against the Muslim clergy throughout the country, and Salars actively resisted the oppression. During the Cultural Revolution of the mid-1960s, Communist ideologues managed to suppress religious practices throughout the country, including Zunhua Salar Autonomous County, but as soon as the political pressure eased, Salar religious devotions sprouted up stronger than ever. Today, the Salars are by far the most devout of China's Muslim minorities.

Ethnolinguists classify the Salar language as one of the Oguz branch of the Turkic group (see **TURKIC PEOPLE**) within the larger Altaic* family of languages. It is an eclectic language that reflects Salar history and their interaction with other ethnic groups in the neighboring Xinjiang Uiger Autonomous Region. Salar consists mostly of Turkic words, although it is also loaded with words from Arabic, Farsi, Chinese,* Tibetan,* and Mongolian. Salar has no written script, although before 1949 a considerable number of Salars could read Arabic in order to study the Koran. A number of contemporary linguists consider Salar to be a dialect of Uigur,* and that the only real difference between the two peoples is geographic, since the Salars live in the eastern corner of Qinghai Province, far removed from the main body of Uigurs in Xinjiang. Today, literate Salars read only Chinese.

Salar is divided into two distinct but very similar and mutually intelligible dialects. The Jiezi dialect is spoken in Jiezi, Qingshui, and Baizhuang in Xunhua County, Gandu in Hualong County, Dahejia in Gansu County, and in Yining County. All of these are in Xinjiang. The Mengda dialect is commonly heard among Salar speakers in Mengda, Muchang, and Tashapo in Xunhua County.

The Salar economy is overwhelmingly agricultural. Most Salar farmers raise cattle, walnuts, winter melons, grapes, apricots, jujubes (a species of dates), and apples. Vegetable soup, steamed buns, and noodles constitute the basic Salar diet, and Salars keep sheep for wool and mutton. The local infrastructure is poorly developed and the industrial base limited mostly to shops where farm equipment is repaired. Many Salars today work as lumberjacks.

SUGGESTED READINGS: Suzanne Kakuk, "Sur la phonetique de la langue salare," *Acte Orientalia Hungaricai* 15 (1962), 161–72; Li Wei, "A Fairyland Valley in Qinghai Province," *China Reconstructs* 33 (February 1984), 47–49; Nicholas Poppe, "Remarks on the Salar Language," *Harvard Journal of Asiatic Studies* 16 (1953), 438–77; S. Robert Ramsey, *The Languages of China*, 1987; Henry G. Schwarz, *The Minorities of Northern China: A Survey*, 1984, and "Salars," in Richard V. Weekes, ed., *Muslim Peoples*, 1984; Zeng Qingnan, "The Sala Nationality," *China Reconstructs* 33 (1984), 66–68.

SALARE. See **SALAR.**

SALOR. See **SALAR.**

SAMTAU. The Samtau people—also known historically as the Bulangs, Tai Lois, and Wa Kuts—are considered by many ethnologists to be a subgroup of the Wa.* In the People's Republic of China (PRC), they do not enjoy official recognition as a minority nationality. The major dilemma with including Samtaus as a Wa subgroup is that their languages, although both Mon-Khmer* in their linguistic classification, are mutually unintelligible. Most Samtaus live today in the northeastern region of Kengtung State of Myanmar (Burma), but several thousand can also be found across the border in Yunnan Province of the PRC.

The Samtau language is closely related to De'ang* and to Bulang (see **ZHUANG**), which are spoken in Yunnan and Myanmar. They have a long, common history with De'angs. More than two thousand years ago, Han* expansion reached Samtau country. By the Tang dynasty of the seventh and eighth centuries, Samtaus had begun to distinguish themselves ethnically from surrounding peoples, acquiring a sense of group identity based on language and religion. During the centuries of the Tang dynasty, they found themselves under the political domination of the Nanzhao Kingdom. The Dali Kingdom controlled them during the Song dynasty from the tenth to the thirteenth centuries.

Until then, the Samtaus had consistently pursued a hunting and foraging lifestyle, with their social system based on matrilineal descent values. But changes came to their society during the Yuan and early Qing dynasties. Massive immigration of Han and Dai* people during these years stimulated a dramatic change in the Samtau economy, from hunting and foraging to agriculture, and the social system gradually changed from matrilineal to patrilineal descent. Farming became central to their economy, and hunting became secondary, although it retained its ritualistic, ceremonial, and social importance.

Today, Samtaus live in mountain villages that contain anywhere from one hundred to four hundred families. Houses are constructed of bamboo and elevated above the ground, with the ground underneath used for livestock. They are mountain farmers who use agricultural techniques consistent with different ecological settings. Some Samtau farmers still use thirteenth-century techniques of slash-and-burn, fertilizing land with ashes and using a stick to plant seeds. Others combine slash-and-burn methods with plowing and hand seeding. Crop rotation, mixed-crop planting, and leaving land periodically fallow preserve fertility. Wheat, dry rice, maize, millet, and tubers are the most common products. Other Samtau farmers cultivate rice paddies, but only where the land is level and access to water is relatively easy.

SUGGESTED READINGS: Fang Dong, "A Long Road Upward for the Wa Nationality," *China Reconstructs* 31 (March 1982), 10–17; Robert Parkin, *A Guide to Austroasiatic Speakers and Their Languages*, 1991; Peng Jianqun, "Bao Hongzhong, A Wa Headman," *China Today* 44 (July 1995), 56–58; Wang Aihe, "Wa," in Paul V. Hockings, ed., *The Encyclopedia of World Cultures*, vol. 6, *East and Southeast Asia*, 1991; Wen Yiqun, "Women of the Highlands," *China Today* 44 (May 1995), 33–35.

SANGLA. The Sanglas are an ethnic subgroup of the Bhutanese* people of Tibet. They live primarily in southern Bhutan and practice a Lamaist Buddhist religion.

SANI. The Sanis are one of the subgroups of the Yi* people of the People's Republic of China. Although the Yi are an officially recognized minority nationality of more than seven million people, they are divided into a variety of subgroups whose sense of ethnic identity is quite parochial, based on region and dialects that are usually not mutually intelligible. Sanis can be found living today in Yunnan Province, usually in autonomous political subdivisions established by the PRC government for the Yi. They are especially concentrated near Lunan, a town that is located southeast of the city of Kunming.

Ethnolinguists believe that Sani is more closely related to Hani* and Lisu* than to Yi. The Sanis descend from the ancient Tusan people native to the Kunming region of Yunnan and the Chengdu in Sichuan. The Sani economy is overwhelmingly agricultural. At lower elevations, Sani farmers produced maize, potatoes, buckwheat, and oats as staples. In the highlands, they raise cattle, sheep, goats, and horses. Chickens and pigs are ubiquitous in Yi villages. Poorer Sani families supplement their diets by collecting acorns, roots, wild vegetables, and herbs, and by fishing and hunting. Most Sanis live in mountain hamlets of less than twenty households. They continue to be devoted to an eclectic religion that has fused elements of Buddhism, Daoism, and their own indigenous animism, although a minority converted to Christianity in the 1920s and 1930s.

SANTA. See **DONGXIANG.**

SANTAISHAN. The Santaishan are one of the three subgroups of the De'ang* people of Yunnan Province in the People's Republic of China. They live today in the Santaishan region of Luxi County.

SARAOA. See **TSOU.**

SARIKOL. The Sarikols (Sarikol, Sarykoli, Saryqoli) are the larger of the two Tajik* groups of people living in the Xinjiang Uigur Autonomous Region of the People's Republic of China. They are concentrated in what is known as Tajik District. Demographers estimate the Sarikol population in China at approximately 25,000 people. They speak the Sarikol dialect of the Shugni language. Sarikols are divided into three subgroups based on the subdialects they speak: Tashqurghani, Vachani, and Byryugsoli. Sarikols are primarily seminomadic mountain farmers and pastoralists who raise wheat, barley, and peas in the spring. During the summer, they take herds of cattle, sheep, and goats to mountain pastures for grazing. Sarikols are loyal to the Ismaili sect of Islam.

SARKOLI. See **TAJIK.**

SART. See **TAJIK.**

SARYKOLI. See **SARIKOL** and **TAJIK.**

SARYQOLI. See **SARIKOL** and **TAJIK.**

SEDEG. The Sedegs, also known as Sedeqs, are one of the indigenous people of Taiwan in the Republic of China. Some ethnolinguists consider them to be one of the subgroups of the Atayal* people of Taiwan. Approximately 20,000 people speak Sedeg, most of whom live in northern Taiwan, southeast of Atayal settlements, particularly in the mountainous regions of Hualien and Nantou counties.
SUGGESTED READING: S. A. Wurm, B. T'sou, D. Bradley, et al., eds., *Language Atlas of China*, 1987.

SEDEQ. See **ATAYAL** and **SEDEG.**

SEGOLEG. The Segolegs, also known as Seqoleqs, are one of the primary subgroups of the Atayal* people of Taiwan in the Republic of China.

SELEKUR. See **TAJIK.**

SEQOLEQ. See **ATAYAL.**

SHAGAI. See **GELAO.**

SHAN. See **DAI.**

SHANDA. See **SHE.**

SHANGDANG. The Shangdangs are one of the linguistic subgroups of the more than 48 million Han* people who speak the Jin* Chinese* language. Most Shangdangs live today in fifteen cities and counties in southeastern Shanxi Province in the People's Republic of China.

SHANGHAIESE. The term "Shanghaiese" refers to the residents of the city of Shanghai and its surrounding culture area in the People's Republic of China (PRC). Shanghai, China's largest city, is located on the flatlands of the Shanghai Delta. The city is connected to the Yangtze River estuary by the Whangpoo River. Until the mid-nineteenth century, Shanghai was an insignificant fishing community, shadowed by the much larger, influential city of Soochow. But in the second half of the nineteenth century, as foreign penetration of China increased, Shanghai's fortunes changed. When the Chinese government granted concessions to foreign countries to conduct business along the Yangtze River corridor, an enormous amount of foreign capital found its way into Shanghai. Shanghai became a boomtown that attracted a large-scale in-migration from the surrounding countryside. Because of the presence of large numbers of foreigners, Shanghai acquired a reputation for diversity, and even today it remains the most cosmopolitan region, other than Hong Kong, in the PRC.

Today, more than eleven million people live in Shanghai. The vast majority of them are of Han* descent and speak Shanghaiese, a dialect of the Wu* Chinese* language. Shanghaiese is widely considered to be the standard Wu dialect. When asked to identify themselves, the residents of the city readily respond "Shanghaiese," whose connotations today reflect an attitude of superiority, confidence, and high self-esteem. With such a sense of special identity, the residents of Shanghai essentially constitute a distinct ethnic group in the People's Republic of China.

SUGGESTED READINGS: William S. Ellis, "Shanghai," *National Geographic* 185 (March 1994), 2–34; S. Robert Ramsey, *The Languages of China*, 1987; Michael Sherard, "Shangai Phonology," Ph.D. diss., Cornell University, 1972.

SHANHA. See **SHE.**

SHANTU REN. See **JINGPO.**

SHAOJIANG. Approximately 800,000 people in the People's Republic of China speak Shaojiang, a dialect of the Min* Chinese* language. Shaojiang speakers can be found today west of the Futunxi River in the Shaowu, Guangze, Jiangle, and Shunchang regions of Fujian Province. See **HAN**.

SHAONAN. The Shaonan people are a linguistic subgroup of the Yuetai* Hakka* people of the People's Republic of China. Shaonans today can be found living in the Meixian, Jiaoling, Pingyuan, Shaognan, Qujiang, and Yingde regions of Guangdong Province in the PRC. Approximately 1.1 million people speak Shaonan.

SHAOZHOU TUHUA. The Shaozhou Tuhua people are believed by Chinese* ethnologists to be one of the indigenous groups of people living in Guangdong Province in the People's Republic of China. They are closely related to the other indigenous, or "Gaoshan," people of Fujian Province, Hunan Province, and Taiwan in the Republic of China. The Shaozhou Tuhuas live in northern Guangdong, particularly in the Lianxian, Liannan, Lechang, Ruyuan, Qujiang, Shaoguan, Renhua, and Nanxiong regions. Most of them are farmers who raise millet, rice, sweet potatoes, and taro. They are rapidly being assimilated by Hakka*- and Yue*-speaking Han people.
SUGGESTED READINGS: *The Republic of China Yearbook*, 1995, 1996; S. A. Wurm, B. T'sou, D. Bradley, et al., eds., *Language Atlas of China*, 1987; Yvonne Yuan, "Migrate, Assimilate, or Integrate?" *Free China Review* 42 (June 1992): 4–15.

SHARPA. See **SHERPA**.

SHATO. The Shatos, a subgroup of the Kirgiz* people, speak a Northern Kirgiz* dialect and live primarily in Mongolkure County in the Xinjiang Uigur Autonomous Region of the People's Republic of China.

SHE. The She people—also known locally and by scholars as the Shandas, Shanhas, Sheds, Shemins, Sho, Dongliao, Dongman, and Yus—are one of the officially recognized minority nationalities of the People's Republic of China (PRC). They can be found today living near the coast of the East China Sea on both sides of the border between Fujian Province and Zhejiang Province in southeastern China. More scatttered settlements of She can also be found in Guangdong, Jiangxi, and Anhui provinces. Altogether, She people reside in sixty counties of the People's Republic of China. The 1990 national census listed the She population at approximately 630,000 people, but today it is almost certainly closer to 650,000. They prefer the highlands, and most She settlements are located between 1,500 and 3,500 feet in altitude. They live in ethnically homogenous, small, diffuse rural villages, which are situated on relatively steep slopes of mountains surrounding narrow valleys. Their traditional thatched bamboo houses are now giving way to wood framed homes with gray tile roofs.

The She language, which is part of the Sino-Tibetan linguistic family, is closely related to Hakka* Chinese.* In fact, most She people today speak Hakka as their native language. The few thousand She people who still speak their native language are largely confined to Buluo, Zengcheng, Huidong, and Haifeng counties in Guangdong Province. There are two mutually intelligible dialects of She: Luofu and Lianhua.

Historians and archaeologists disagree about She origins. According to one theory, the Shes migrated to an area bounded by Fujian, Guangdong, and Jiangxi provinces in the late sixth and early seventh centuries. Another school of thought claims that the Shes and the Yaos* both descend from a common group of ancestors native to Hunan Province. Some scholars contend that the Shes descend from Yao people in Guandgong and Guangxi provinces. Historians, however, are certain that, by the fourteenth century and perhaps as early as the seventh century, the Shes had settled in the highlands of what is today eastern Fujian Province, northeastern Jiangxi Province, and southern Zhejiang Province.

During the next several centuries, the Shes became culturally, economically, and politically acculturated to many of the institutions of their Han* neighbors, with whom they had become widely interspersed. Their language acquired its similarities with Hakka, and they began to use Mandarin* and the local Chinese language. There is no written She script. Although some elements of traditional animism survive, She religion is becoming increasingly difficult to differentiate from that of their Han neighbors. As the She economy becomes more integrated with the larger economy of southeastern China, the forces of acculturation will become even stronger.

Early in the twentieth century, She leaders threw in their lot with such reformers as Sun Yat-sen, who wanted to bring China into the modern political era. During World War II, She troops fought a bloody guerrilla war against Japanese invasion forces and played an important role in inflicting huge losses on the army of occupation. When the war was over, Shes sided overwhelmingly with Mao Zedong and the Chinese Communists against Jiang Jieshi (Chiang Kai-shek) and the Guomintang nationalists. When the Communists triumphed in 1949, She fighters were afforded the status of heroes in the new China.

That status has often proved politically useful for the Shes. The central government has created nine autonomous counties for them, where they enjoy a considerable degree of self-government. Perhaps the most significant concession the government has made to the Shes is in the area of family planning. In order to control its population growth, the People's Republic of China began implementing in the late 1970s a draconian family-planning policy, in which couples were confined to having only one child. Parents producing additional children were heavily taxed. The She people, however, are exempt from these family-planning dictates.

The She homeland is perfect for agriculture because of fertile soil, abundant rainfall, and the warm, humid weather provided by their proximity to the East China Sea. For several thousand years, the Shes were subsistence horticulturalists who employed slash-and-burn techniques to raise crops. Because of that planting system, they had to relocate their fields frequently and their villages every decade or so as well in order to have reasonably convenient access to fertile fields. Since the Communist revolution, however, She farmers have made the transition away from seminomadic swidden farming to fixed production and permanent residency. The use of fertilizers, crop rotation, and irrigation has changed She life. They have also begun to cut terraced, irrigated fields into hillsides near their villages, and their productivity has increased substantially. The major crops produced on She farms include rice, wheat, sweet potatoes, peanuts, and tea. She tea, which is called Huiming Tea, is famous in Chinese communities throughout the world. Fruit orchards of peaches, pears, and carambolas also dot the She countryside.

Because of their location in southeastern China near the coast and the central government's ambitious efforts to improve transportation and communications infrastructures there, the She economy is complex and diverse. Lumber production is an important source of cash, and Shes run a variety of rice mills, food-processing plants, and tea-processing factories. Tens of thousands of She men and women also labor as blue-collar workers in Hanrun factories and in coal, iron, gold, and copper mines. More accelerated development will no doubt continue to occur in She areas as the regions become integrated into the larger economy.

One element of the traditional She economy, however, still thrives, even though it no longer supplies the bulk of their dietary needs. Before they made the adjustment to swidden agriculture, the Shes were hunters and foragers, and even after farming became important to them, significant protein needs in the villages were supplied by hunting. Hunting today in She villages is usually confined to January and February, when the climate is not conducive to many agricultural endeavors. Groups of adult male hunters, accompanied by cheering throngs of women and children, go after deer and wild boar, with all of the kills divided equally among the villagers. Although the economic significance of hunting is declining, its social significance remains as important as ever.

She society is patrilineal in its descent rules, with males serving as the heads of all lineage groups and property being handed down from father to son. Marriage is surname exogamous, with young men and women required to marry an individual outside their surname group. That is sometimes difficult because only four surnames exist in She society—Pan, Lann, Lei, and Zhong. The names are compelling enough to divide Shes into surname subgroups, and each village contains a temple or ancestral hall for each lineage group. The standard She household is a nuclear family.

SUGGESTED READINGS: Stephen C. Averill, "The Shed People and the Opening of the Yangzi Highlands," *Modern China* 9 (1983), 84–126; Fu Liangji, "Wedding Rites of the She People," *China Reconstructs* 37 (September 1988), 48–50; Lan Zhougen, "The She People of the Green Mountains," *China Reconstructs* 33 (1984), 53–56; Liu Cheng, "The She Nationality," *Women of China* (December 1984), 35–37; Jordan I.

Pollack, "She," in Paul V. Hockings, ed., *The Encyclopedia of World Cultures*, vol. 6, *East and Southeast Asia*, 1991.

SHED. See **SHE.**

SHEHLEH. Shehleh is one of the major dialects of the Black Lahu* language in the People's Republic of China. Shehleh includes the Laho Aleh subdialect. See **LAHU.**

SHEMIN. See **SHE.**

SHERPA. The Sherpas, or Sharpas, are one of the so-called Bhotia* peoples, a series of Tibetan* groups living in Nepal (see **NEPALESE**). The major group of Sherpas today lives in the Solu-Khumbu region in the northern section of Sagarmatha District in eastern Nepal, particularly in Khumbu, Pharak, Shorong, Arun, and Rolwaling valleys. Other Sherpa settlements can be found in Kathmandu, the capital city of Nepal, and in the towns of Darjeeling, Kalimpong, and Siliguri in India. The total Sherpa population today exceeds 25,000 people.

Several thousand Sherpas also live in Tibet, primarily in the Kham District of southeastern Tibet. Many archaeologists and historians trace Sherpa origins back to the Kham.* The ancestors of today's Sherpas migrated across the Himalayas from Tibet to Nepal in the sixteenth century. They made their living by farming and herding yaks, cows, and mixed cow-yak breeds. Today, the staple of the Sherpa diet is the potato, which was introduced to Nepal in the nineteenth century. Barley, wheat, and millet are also raised. During the years of British* domination of the subcontinent in the nineteenth century, Sherpas became middlemen near Nana Pa La, the "Inside Pass" through the Himalayas between Tibet and Nepal. More recently, they have earned reputations as tourist guides for mountaineering groups, labor contractors, and trans-Himalayan commercial entrepreneurs.

Sherpa society is divided into a series of patrilineal, exogamous clans. The clans themselves are then divided into lineages, through which Sherpas trace their origins back to the first founding families. The single-resident nuclear family is the typical Sherpa domestic arrangement. Egalitarian values and a respect for individual autonomy characterize Sherpa culture. Their religion revolves around the Tibetan version of Mahayana Buddhism. Celibate monasticism is especially popular among the Sherpas. In addition to the Buddhist divinities, Sherpas also concern themselves with lesser deities and a host of local ghosts, demons, and spirits who influence day-to-day affairs.

SUGGESTED READINGS: Christoph von Furer-Haimendorf, *The Sherpas of Nepal: Buddhist Highlanders*, 1964; Luther G. Jerstad, *Mani-Rimdu, Sherpa Dance Drama*, 1969; Sherry B. Ortner, *Sherpas through Their Rituals*, 1978; Robert A. Paul, "Sherpas," in Paul V. Hockings, ed., *The Encyclopedia of World Cultures*, vol. 3, *South Asia*, 1991, and *The Tibetan Symbolic World: Psychoanalytic Explorations*, 1982; Tian Di, "Zhangmu—Tibetan Border Town," *China Reconstructs* 34 (March 1985), 598–99.

SHIDONG. See **JINGPO.**

SHIHING. The Shihing people are a recently discovered minority nationality who live in the People's Republic of China (PRC). PRC social scientists are currently conducting ethnographic research into Shihing origins, trying to determine how to classify them, and until that research is completed, the process of extending them official recognition will be postponed. They could be of Miao,* Yao,* or Yi* extraction, or some combination of those groups with Han* Chinese* immigrants. PRC demographers estimate the Shihing population at approximately 2,000 people, the vast majority of whom live in the Liangshan Yi Autonomous Prefecture of Sichuan Province. Most Shihings live in highland villages where they raise rice, maize, millet, pigs, poultry, and wheat and maintain a social system characterized by patrilineal descent and patrilocal residence. SUGGESTED READING: S. A. Wurm, B. T'sou, D. Bradley, et al., eds., *Language Atlas of China*, 1987.

SHILIINGOL. The Shiliingols are a subgroup of the Mongol* people of the People's Republic of China (PRC). Their dialect is spoken primarily in the central section of the Inner Mongolian Autonomous Region and is closely related to the Chakhar* dialect. Both Chakhar and Shiliingol bear a close resemblance to Khalkha, the primary dialect of the Mongolian People's Republic. Most Shiliingols are farmers and herders who raise barley, wheat, oats, corn, millet, potatoes, buckwheat, sorghum, apples, and a variety of vegetables. Shiliingols also raise horses, cattle, camels, and goats, although their preferred livestock today is sheep.

SHINAN. More than 100,000 Shinan people live in the Gilgat region of northern Pakistan, and a few thousand more live today in the northeastern-most region of Afghanistan and in the far western reaches of the Xinjiang Uigur Autonomous Region in the People's Republic of China. Until the twelfth century, most Shinans were Buddhists, but they then began to convert to the Sunni Islam faith. That process was barely complete by the late fifteenth century when Shiite Muslims working out of Persia began winning over the Shinans. By the end of the sixteenth century, the vast majority of Shinans were Shiites. They remain so today. They speak a language that ethnolinguists classify as part of the Dardic branch of the Indo-Iranian family. It is divided into a number of distinct dialects. Since Shinan is unwritten, Urdu serves as their written script. Their homeland is a rugged, mountainous region where they have managed effectively to isolate themselves for centuries. Most Shinan farmers raise wheat, maize, millet, and a variety of vegetables. They also raise sheep and goats.

SUGGESTED READING: Iurii V. Gankovskii, *The Peoples of Pakistan: An Ethnic History*, 1971.

SHIRONGOL MONGOL. See DONGXIANG.

SHISHAM. The Shishams are a subgroup of the Lisu* people of Yunnan Province in the People's Republic of China. Along with other Lisu people, most Shishams are concentrated between the Sawleen River and the Mekong River in western Yunnan Province. The Shisham language is not mutually intelligible with most of the other Lisu tongues but is closely related to Akha,* Lahu,* and Yi.* They are more likely to identify themselves as ethnic Shishams than as Lisus. Their social system revolves around a variety of patrilineal, exogamous clans that exercise great political power. Most Shishams live at higher elevations, usually in ridgeline villages between 3,500 and 10,000 feet in altitude. Swidden farmers, they cultivate maize, mountain rice, millet, and barley.

SHIVE. See XIBE.

SHO. See SHE.

SHOR. Several thousand people living in the Xinjiang Uigur Autonomous Region of the People's Republic of China (PRC) are aware of their Shor ethnic origins. The Shor—also known historically as the Mountain Shor, Mrassa, Kondoma, Aba (Abin), Chysh, and Kuznets Tatars—are a small Turkic-speaking people who live in the south of Kuznetsk Basin in southern Russian Siberia. The Shor are the product of a long-term process of ethnogenesis which brought together various tribes of Samoyedic, Kettic, and Turkified Ugrian peoples who were living in south central Siberia. Their language is part of the Old Uigur* subgroup of the eastern division of the Turkic branch of the larger Altaic* language family. It is divided into two basic dialects, one spoken in the region of Mrass and Tomsk and the other in Kondoma and the Lower Tom' region. The first sustained contact between Shors and Russians* began in the seventeenth century, when Russian settlers began arriving in large numbers and the tsarist government established its political authority there. At the time, the Shor economy revolved around hunting, fishing, and cedar-nut gathering. The arrival of the Russians gradually brought the Shors into a larger commercial economy, and they traded pelts and cedar nuts with Russians in order to earn the cash they needed for trade goods.

When the Russians first arrived in the seventeenth century, the Shor religion was similiar to the shamanistic-animistic beliefs of the other indigenous people of Siberia. For the Shor, religion and their own geographical environment were inseparable. The world was inhabited by invisible spirit beings of all sorts whose interaction with human beings was constant and whose control over the elements was absolute. No natural phenomenon was accidental or coincidental. Everything from disease and sickness to natural disasters could be attributed to the invisible powers of the universe, and human beings were obligated to treat those forces with respect and submission. Shamans were central figures in Shor culture because they propitiated those invisible forces. Missionaries from the Russian Orthodox Church began working actively among the Shor in the eighteenth century, and they made superficial progress, but what ultimately emerged was an eclectic fusion of Shor folk beliefs and Christian doctrine.

The Bolshevik revolution and its subsequent full-scale economic development of the Shor homeland had a dramatic, and ultimately devastating, impact on Shor ethnicity. The Kuznetsk Basin contains some of the world's richest iron ore deposits, which Soviet industry desperately needed. At first, the new Soviet government worked hard at paying due respect to Shor culture. They established the Mountain Shor (Gorno-Shorskiy) National Rayon in 1929 and developed a literary language for the Shor using a Cyrillic alphabet. At the time there were approximately 12,600 Shorian people living there, and they constituted the majority of the population. In 1930 Soviet authorities ordered the use of a Latin alphabet for the Shor literary language.

By that time, however, there were already problems between the Shor and the government. For centuries Shor hunters had known of the iron ore deposits in their homeland; they called it the "red stone." But in the late 1920s they refused to cooperate with Soviet geologists in locating the deposits, fearing the impact that economic development would have on their lifestyle. Their fears were well founded. When the iron ore deposits were located, the Soviet government began importing thousands of Russian and Ukrainian miners to extract the ore. By 1931 the Shor constituted only 40 percent of the population of the Mountain Shor National Rayon, and by 1938 their percentage had dropped to 13 percent. In 1939 the Soviet government dissolved the Mountain Shor National Rayon and required any Shor publications to employ the Cyrillic alphabet. Because of the arrival of so many Russians during the 1920s and 1930s, a number of Shor people emigrated from Russia into China. They settled in the region just south of the Russian Siberian border where the borders of Russia, China, and Mongolia meet. Such towns as Habahe, Altay, and Burgin and the surrounding areas of northernmost Xinjiang have Shor people living there today. They are not acknowledged as a minority nationality by the Chinese government.

SUGGESTED READING: Walter Kolarz, *The Peoples of the Soviet Far East*, 1969.

SHORT-SKIRT MIAO. See **MIAO.**

SHRIMP MIAO. See **MIAO.**

SHTAFARI. Shtafari is one of the two dialects of the Thao* people, who live today on Taiwan in the Republic of China.

SHUI. With a contemporary population of approximately 340,000 people, the Shui (Sui, Shui-chia) are one of the officially recognized minority natonalities of the People's Republic of China (PRC). They refer to themselves as the "Ai Sui," which means "water people," a curious ethnonym given the fact that as a people they are landlocked. The vast majority of Shuis live along the upper reaches of the Long River and the Duliu River. Others can be found in Nandang and Rongshui counties in western Guangxi Zhuang Autonomous Region and in Rongjiang, Libo, Dushan, Duyun, and Liping counties in southern Guizhou Province. About 60 percent of the Shuis are concentrated in Sandu Shui Autonomous County of the Guizhou Bouyei-Miao Autonomous Prefecture. Their language is classified as one of the Zhuang-Dong cluster in the Sino-Tibetan family. There is no written Shui script, except for an ancient language used only in formal religious ceremonies, and even it consists of a number of symbols that are employed in divination and geomancy. The Shui written script contains, at most, only 150 symbols. Most Shuis can read and write Mandarin,* and they speak the Chinese* dialect used by Han* people in southern Guizhou Province. In fact, many older Shuis worry about the eventual disappearance of their language because most young Shuis no longer speak it as their native tongue. They have already made the transition to Chinese.

Historians, archaeologists, and ethnolinguists believe that Shuis descend from the Louyue (Liao) people. They trace their roots to the Xiou, a branch of the ancient Baiyue people. Sometime during the Ming dynasty in the thirteenth and fourteenth centuries, the Shuis took on the ethnonym "Shui" and distinguished themselves ethhnically from surrounding peoples. At that time they also made the transition from dry-field slash-and-burn agriculture to wet-rice paddy farming, which they had learned from neighboring Han people. Today Shui farmers raise wet rice, wheat, rapeseeds, ramie, oranges, lemons, limes, and a variety of other fruits. In ancient times, land was controlled by Han feudal lords, who rented it out to tenant farmers or allowed it to be worked by sharecroppers. Some Shuis labored as peasants on large manorial estates.

That land tenure pattern changed after the Communist revolution in 1949. The central government immediately nationalized all of the land, although tenant farmers still had to pay rent to the former landlords. In 1956, however, the central government collectivized agriculture in southern Guizhou Province. Large-scale agricultural production worked by multicultural and multihousehold labor teams replaced older, traditional systems of family farming. Shui farmers now worked for the state, not for themselves, and the agricultural economy suffered. Although gross production increased as more land was put into production, yields per acre entered a long period of decline. That trend was not reversed until the early 1980s, when the central government, anxious to bring the country back from the economic and political disasters of the Cultural Revolution, established the "household-responsibility" system among Shui farmers. Farmers were required to pay a grain tax to the state and sell an established annual quota of crops to the state at artificially low prices, but after meeting

those requirements, they could sell the surplus at market prices and keep whatever profits they had earned. Fishing was traditionally an important source of
protein in the Shui diet.

Although Protestant and Roman Catholic missionaries made some headway
in winning Christian converts during the late nineteenth and early twentieth
centuries, only a few thousand Shuis are Christians today. Most of them practice
an eclectic mix of Buddhism, Daoism, and traditional Shui animism, which is
polytheistic and shamanistic. Unseen spirits cause misfortune and illness, Shuis
believe, and shamans are necessary to restore balance in the world.

SUGGESTED READINGS: Lu Xinglun and Wu Zhixian, ''Homeland of the Shui,'' *China
Reconstructs* 36 (December 1987), 53–56; Paul V. Hockings, ''Shui,'' in Paul V. Hock-
ings, ed., *The Encyclopedia of World Cultures*, vol. 6, *East and Southeast Asia*, 1991;
Ma Yin, ed., *China's Minority Nationalities*, 1989; Zeng Qingnan, ''The Landlocked
'Water' People,'' *China Today* 41 (June 1992), 52–55.

SHUI BAIYI. See **DAI.**

SHUI DAI. See **DAI.**

SHUI-CHIA. See **SHUI.**

SHUIHU. See **BOUYEI.**

SHUIT. The Shuitians constitute a relatively small ethnic group of several thousand people who live in the mountainous highlands along the border between
Yunnan and Sichuan provinces in the People's Republic of China. Most Shuitian
people are slash-and-burn and plow agriculturalists who raise dry rice, wheat,
buckwheat, maize, and millet. Although state ethnologists have classified the
Shuitians as a subgroup of the Yi* people, the Shuitians reject the classification.
They do share geographic, demographic, and even cultural similarities with Yi
people, and their language is in the same family as Yi, but the languages are
not mutually intelligible and neither the Shuitians nor the Yi agree that they are
members of the same group. Even Han* neighbors living along the Sichuan-
Yunnan frontier know that Shuitians are different, but in spite of a number of
Shuitian applications for official recognition as a minority nationality, the government has never agreed.

SHUIZU. See **SHUI.**

SIAM. See **DAI.**

SIBE. See **XIBE.**

SIJIAJI. The Sijiajis are one of the subgroups of the Dongxiang* people, a Muslim ethnic group living in Dongxiang Autonomous County in Gansu Province of the People's Republic of China. The subdivision is based on minor, though mutually intelligible, language differences. About 20 percent of Dongxiangs speak Sijiaji, primarily in the townships of Sijia, Tangang, and Kaole, as well as in Yongjing County.

SIKKIMESE. The term "Sikkimese" is a generic reference to the residents of the Himalayan Kingdom of Sikkim. Sikkim is bordered by Tibet, Nepal, India, and Bhutan. Located in the Himalayan highlands, the population of Sikkim numbers approximately 375,000 people. The term Sikkimese is not strictly an ethnic reference, since people of Indian, Nepalese,* Bhutanese,* and Lepcha* extraction live there. Most Sikkimese are small farmers who raise rice, corn, cardamom, apples, and potatoes. Although Lamaist Buddhism is the official state religion, practiced by approximately one-quarter of the population, most Sikkimese are Hindus.

Historically, there has been a great deal of contact between Tibetans* and Sikkimese because of the Himalayan passes into Tibet's Chumbi Valley. Sikkim also dominated the historic Kalimpong-Llasa trade route, which regularly brought Tibetans, Indians, Nepalese, and Sikkimese into contact. During the years of the British* control of the subcontinent, Sikkim was considered the avenue of access to Central Asia. Today, because of that historical commercial relationship and because of their current proximity to the Tibetan border and Himalayan trade routes, it is likely that at any given time there are hundreds of Sikkimese living in the People's Republic of China.

SUGGESTED READING: Pradyumna Karan and William M. Jenkins, *The Himalayan Kingdoms: Bhutan, Sikkim, and Nepal*, 1963.

SINGHPO. See **JINGPO** and **KACHIN.**

SINICIZED MIAO. See **MONSUA.**

SINLI. The Sinli people are a subgroup of the Jingpo* people of Myanmar (Burma) and the People's Republic of China, and the Sinli language is considered to be the standard Jingpo dialect by Chinese authorities. The Jingpo themselves are one of the Kachin*-speaking people, a transnational ethnic group living today in Myanmar, China, and India.

SIYI. The Siyi people are a dialect subgroup of Yue*-speaking Han* Chinese.* Approximately 3.6 million people speak Siyi, and most of them live in the Heshan, Xinhui, Jiangmen, Doumen, Enping, Kaiping, and Taishan regions of Guangdong Province.

S'LAI. See **LI.**

SOGPO. See **OIRAT.**

SOLON. See **EWENK.**

SOLON. See **OROQEN.**

SOLUN. See **EWENK.**

SOLUN. See **OROQEN.**

SON. The Son people are a tiny ethnic group who live today in far northern Myanmar (Burma); a handful of Son also probably live across the border in the southern reaches of Yunnan Province in the People's Republic of China. The total Son population numbers no more than 1,500 people, and the vast majority of them are on the Myanmar side of the Sino-Burmese frontier. They speak a Mon-Khmer* language in the Austroasiatic linguistic family. Some ethnolinguists have tried to classify the Son people as a subgroup of the Wa,* but their languages, though related, are not mutually intelligible. Son are closely related to the neighboring En* people. They are primarily slash-and-burn agriculturalists who raise a variety of crops, including maize, millet, rice, tubers, goats, pigs, and chickens. The Son religion is a syncretic mix of Buddhism and their own indigenous animistic faith.
SUGGESTED READINGS: Robert Parkin, *A Guide to Austroasiatic Speakers and Their Languages*, 1991; Wang Aihe, "Wa," in Paul V. Hockings, ed., *The Encyclopedia of World Cultures*, vol. 6, *East and Southeast Asia*, 1991; Wen Yiqun, "Women of the Highlands," *China Today* 44 (May 1995), 33–35.

SONI. The Sonis are an ethnic subgroup of the Hani* people of the People's Republic of China (PRC). Scattered groups of Sonis can also be found living in Thailand and Myanmar (Burma). The PRC Sonis are located in the far southeastern corner of Yunnan Province, between the Mengle and the Ailao mountain ranges. Their society is patrilineal and patriarchal, with kinship relations organized around patrilineal clans. Each clan consists of from thirty to forty households. Most Sonis remain tied to the agricultural economy, and a few still work in a traditional subsistence economy. They raise a variety of crops, including rice, maize, beans, buckwheat, millet, tea, peanuts, sugarcane, cotton, chili peppers, ginger, and indigo. Because of recent economic development programs in southwestern Yunnan, increasing numbers of Soni men can be found working in local factories and mines.

SONOBA. The Sonobas are one of the three subgroups of the Dongxiang* people, a Muslim group living in the People's Republic of China. The subdivision is based on minor, though mutually intelligible, language differences. The

Sonoba dialect, spoken by approximately 50 percent of Dongxiangs, can be heard in Sonan, Chuntai, Pingzhuang, Mianguchi, Dashu, Yanling, Dabankong, Dongyuan, and Baihe in Dongxiang Autonomous County of Gansu Province. Sonoba is also spoken in portions of Linxia County and Hezheng County.

SOU. See **BAI.**

SOUTH GOVI. South Govi is a vernacular of the Korchin* dialect of Mongolian. Most people who speak South Govi live in the South Govi subdivision of Mongolia and across the border in the corresponding region of the Inner Mongolian Autonomous Region in the People's Republic of China. See **MONGOL.**

SOUTHERN AMI. The Southern Ami people, also known as Puyuma Amis and Hengchun Amis, are one of the five subgroups of the Ami* people of Taiwan in the Republic of China.

SOUTHERN KHAM. The Southern Kham people are ethnic Tibetans* who speak the southern vernacular of the Kham* dialect. Speakers of Southern Kham live today in the Diqing Tibetan Autonomous Prefecture of Yunnan Province and in the Muli Tibetan Autonomous County of Sichuan Province.

SOUTHERN KIRGIZ. Southern Kirgiz is one of the two major divisions of the Kirgiz* language in the Xinjiang Uigur Autonomous Region. It is divided into a number of subdialects of its own, including Posdantielik of Uqia County; and Kalakqik, Zhulukbash, Subash, Bulongkol, Kiziltao, and Qiarleng of Atko, Yengishar, and Guma counties.

SOUTHERN KMHMU. See **KMHMU.**

SOUTHERN SAISIYAT. The Southern Saisiyats are one of the primary subdivisions of the Saisiyat* people of Taiwan in the Republic of China. Most of them live in the highlands of Maioli County.

SOUTHERN ZHUANG. The Zhuang* people, who live in the Guangxi Autonomous Region, as well as in Gizhou and Yunnan provinces in the People's Republic of China, are divided into two large subgroups based on dialect. The Zhuangs living south of the Xiang River in southern Guangxi speak the Southern Zhuang dialect. Southern Zhuang has the following subdialects: Yongnan, Zuojiang, Dejing, Yanguang, and Wenma.

SOUTHWESTERN KAZAK. Southwestern Kazak is one of the two primary dialects of the Kazak* people of the People's Republic of China. Approximately 75,000 Kazaks speak the southwestern dialect, and most of them can be found today living in Qapqal, Tekes, and Tokkuztara counties of the Ili Kazak Autonomous Prefecture of the Xinjiang Uigur Autonomous Region.

SOUTHWESTERN MANDARIN. Some linguists classify the Mandarin* language into four mutually intelligible clusters of dialects. One of those clusters is Southwestern Mandarin. The southwestern group of Mandarin dialects is predominant in Sichuan Province and in the border areas of Guizhou, Qinghai, and Shaanxi provinces in the People's Republic of China.

STAIS. The Stais are one of the many subgroups of the Li* people of Hainan Province in the People's Republic of China. Like other Li groups, they have earned a reputation over the years for their ferocious anti-Han* xenophobia, which has often taken the form of guerrilla warfare against Han immigrants to Hainan. Most Stais today are farmers who raise coconuts, coffee, cocoa, sisal, rubber, cashews, pineapples, mangoes, and bananas. Rice is their staple, and because of the tropical climate of Hainan and its fertile soil, they are able to produce three rice crops a year.

STEEP-SLOPE MIAO. See **MIAO.**

STRIPED MIAO. See **MIAO.**

SUBASH. The Subashes are a subgroup of the Kirgiz* people. They speak a Southern Kirgiz dialect and live primarily in Akto, Yengishar, and Guma counties in the Xinjiang Uigur Autonomous Region of the People's Republic of China.

SUBHAATAR. Subhaatar is a vernacular of the Korchin* dialect of Mongolian. Most people who speak Subhaatar live in the Subhaatar subdivision of Mongolia and across the border in the corresponding regions of the Inner Mongolian Autonomous Region in the People's Republic of China. See **MONGOL.**

SUHUJIA. The Suhujia people are a dialect subgroup of the Taihu* people, who are themselves a linguistic subgroup of the Wu*-speaking Han* people of the People's Republic of China. More than 25 million people speak the Suhujia language, and they can be found today in the Changshu, Wuxi, Suzhou, Wujiang, Kunshan, Taicang, Nantong, Rudong, Qidong, Haimen, and Shazhou regions of Jiangsu Province; in the Jiaxing, Jiashan, Tongxiang, Pinghu, Haiyan, and Haining regions of Zhejiang Province; and in and around the city of Shanghai. See **HAN** and **SHANGHAIESE.**

SUI. See **SHUI.**

SULUN. See **OROQEN.**

SUSHEN. See **HEZHEN.**

SUWAN. The Suwans are a subgroup of the Kazak* people of the Xinjiang Uigur Autonomous Region, Gansu Province, and Qinghai Province in the People's Republic of China.

T

TA-ANG. See **DE'ANG.**

TABUNUT. The Tabunut people are an identifiable subgroup of the Buryats,*
a Mongol* people of Siberian Russia and the Inner Mongolian Autonomous
Region in the People's Republic of China.

T'ACHIK'O. See **TAJIK.**

TADZHIK. See **TAJIK.**

TADZIK. See **TAJIK.**

TAHUERH. See **DAUR.**

T'AI. The T'ais are one of the many subgroups of the Li* people of Hainan
Province in the People's Republic of China. Like other Li groups, T'ais maintain
hostile feelings toward Han* Chinese. They work as farmers, raising coconuts,
coffee, cocoa, sisal, rubber, cashews, pineapples, mangoes, and bananas. Rice
is their staple, and because of the tropical climate of Hainan and its fertile soil,
they are able to produce three rice crops a year.

TAI. The term "Tai" is used by ethnolinguists to refer to a language family
that exists today in southeast Asia. It is also a generic reference to all of the
people who speak one of the many Tai languages. Thai, the official language
of Thailand, is the most prominent of the Tai languages. More than twenty-two
million people speak Thai. In the People's Republic of China, the Tai languages

are known as the Zhuang-Dong group of languages. The Zhuang-Dong group is itself divided into three primary clusters. The Zhuang-Dai* cluster is composed of the Zhuang,* Buyi, and Dai* languages. The Dong-Shui* (Kam-Sui) cluster includes Dong,* Shui,* Mulam,* and Maonan.* Li,* the language spoken on Hainan Island, is the third branch of Tai languages.

Anthropologists and historians have found evidence of Tai people living in China as early as the first millenium B.C., when they were cultivating rice in the Yangtze Valley. The early Wu Kingdom, near what is today Shanghai, and the Yue Kingdom, along the southeastern coast of China, were probably Tai states. Some ethnologists believe that as many as 60 percent of Yue-speaking Han* people have elements of Tai ancestry. As the Han people expanded into southern China, the Tais were either sinicized and assimilated or driven farther south. Thailand and Laos, populated by the descendents of those early migrants, are modern Tai states. Most of the Tai people of the People's Republic of China live a lifestyle closely resembling that of nearby Han people. They usually speak the local Chinese* language as well as their own Tai language, and they dress and farm in the same way as the Han. Except for the use of their own language, they are all but indistinguishable from local Han people.

SUGGESTED READINGS: Paul K. Benedict, *Austro-Thai Language and Culture*, 1975; Fang-Kuei Li, *A Handbook of Comparative Tai*, 1977; S. Robert Ramsey, *The Languages of China*, 1987.

TAI LO. See **TAME WA** and **WA.**

TAIBALIUJIU. Taibaliujiu is one of the five mutually intelligible dialects of the Puyuma* language spoken by an indigenous people living on Taiwan in the Republic of China.

TAIHU. The Taihu people are a linguistic subgroup of Wu*-speaking Han* people in the People's Republic of China. Taihu speakers, who total nearly fifty million people, can be found living primarily in Jiangsu and Zhejiang provinces and in the city of Shanghai. Taihu itself can be divided into six distinctive dialects: Piling,* Suhujia,* Tiaoxi,* Hangzhou,* Linshao,* and Hongjiang.

TAILI. See **DAI.**

TAILOY. See **WA.**

TAILY. See **DAI.**

TAINA. See **DAI.**

TAINI. See **DAI**

TAINING. The Taining people are a linguistic subgroup of Gan*-speaking Han* Chinese.* Most Tainings live in Taining County in northwestern Fujian Province of the People's Republic of China.

TAIPENG. See **DAI.**

TAIWANESE. The term "Taiwanese" has a number of different references depending upon one's perspective, and it is difficult to speak of the Taiwanese as a single ethnic community. To some people, it means all of the residents today of the Republic of China, which occupies the island of Taiwan, formerly known as Formosa. In that sense, there exists a political sense of identity among the Taiwanese as members of the Republic of China. Taiwan is located north of the Philippines and east of Fukien Province in the South China Sea. Its 1991 population exceeded 20.4 million people. With only 36,179 square kilometers of land, Taiwan is one of the most densely populated regions in the world. More than 98 percent of Taiwan's population is Chinese.* The economy is engaged in a rapid process of industrialization.

For other people, the word Taiwanese carries more specific connotations. To some, it is a reference to all of the aboriginal people of Taiwan who occupied the island before the arrival of the Han* people. Of those indigenous people, only twelve groups survive today as conscious, identifiable ethnic entities: the Ami,* the Atayal,* the Bunun,* the Tsou,* the Puyuma,* the Paiwan,* the Rukai,* the Saisiyat,* the Yami,* the Thao,* the Kavalan,* and the Pazeh.* Among some people in the Republic of China and outside scholars, the term Taiwanese is a generic reference to the Ami people who, with a population exceeding 130,000, are the largest and most identifiable of the indigenous peoples of the island. They are also the only one of the surviving indigenous peoples who still speak their native language.

But the indigenous Taiwanese are dwarfed in numbers today by descendents of mainland people who migrated to the island. In the early sixteenth century, Chinese pirates of Han extraction established bases on Taiwan, and over the course of the next four centuries waves of other Han immigrants came to the island. The vast majority of these arrivals spoke the Min,* or Hokkien, version of Chinese. Eventually, they drove most of the indigenous peoples into the mountainous highlands. Hakka*-speaking immigrants also migrated to the island. Today, when people speak of the "native" Taiwanese language, they are referring to the Min dialect, not to one of the aboriginal languages.

The Netherlands established a colony in Taiwan in 1624 when they founded the town of Taipei. China formally annexed Taiwan in 1683, but over the years they had a difficult time maintaining control of the island. After Mao Zedong and the Communists seized control of mainland China in 1949, the followers of Jiang Jie-shi (Chiang Kai-shek) brought several million Mandarin* and Yue* speakers to Taiwan. Xiang,* Jin,* Gan,* and Wu* speakers were also among the refugees from Mao Zedong's revolution. Residents of Taiwan consider themselves citizens of the Republic of China, an independent nation, but in Beijing, the capital city of the People's Republic of China, Taiwan is considered to be a part of China, albeit currently in rebellion.

SUGGESTED READINGS: Paul V. Hockings, "Taiwanese," in Paul V. Hockings, ed., *The Encyclopedia of World Cultures*, vol. 6, *East and Southeast Asia*, 1991; George Stafford, "Good Sons and Virtuous Mothers: Kinship and Chinese Nationalism in Taiwan," *Man* (June 1992), 363–78; Margery Wolf, *The House of Lim: A Study of a Chinese Farm Family*, 1968.

TAIYA. See DAI.

TAIYAL. See ATAYAL.

TAIZHOU. The Taizhou people are a linguistic subgroup of Wu*-speaking Han* people in the People's Republic of China. The nearly five million Taihu speakers live in Linhai, Sanmen, Tiantai, Xianju, Huangyan, Jiaojiang, Wenling, Yuhuan, Yueqing, and Ninghai counties in Zhejiang Province.

TAJIK. The Tajiks, also sometimes called Sarts or Sarkolis, are a Central Asian, Farsi-speaking people whose country, the Republic of Tajikistan, is surrounded by Uzbekistan, Afghanistan, Kirgizstan, and the Xinjiang Uigur Autonomous Region of the People's Republic of China (PRC). The more than 13 million Tajiks in the world live in the Republic of Tajikistan, Afghanistan, Uzbekistan, Kirgizstan, Iran, Pakistan, and the PRC. Most of the Tajik people of China can be found in the Taxkorgan Tajik Autonomous County of the Xinjiang Uigur Autonomous Region. They are concentrated in the eastern Pamir mountains. PRC Tajiks have a contemporary population of just over 35,000 people.

The Tajik language is part of the southwest division of the Iranian cluster of Indo-European languages. It is closely related to Persian, a factor that sets Tajiks apart from other Turkic-speaking Central Asian people. Tajik is divided into a variety of dialects. The two dialects spoken by Chinese Tajiks are Sarikol* and Wakhan.* The differences between the dialects are mainly phonetic.

Until the eighth century, Tajiks were devoted to Buddhism, Nestorianism, Zoroastrianism, and Manichaeanism. But the Arab conquests of the eighth century brought Islam to them, particularly the Sunni Sect of the Hanafi school of Shariah law. Most Tajiks living in the southern reaches of the Pamir mountains, however, became Ismaili Muslims, and that group includes the Wakhan and Sarikols of the Xinjiang Uigur Autonomous Region.

With the breakup of the Soviet Union in 1991, Chinese Communist party officials became increasingly concerned about ethnic nationalism among the Xinjiang Muslims. PRC officials had long taken a cautious approach to governing the Tajiks. In 1954 they established Taxkorgan Tajik Autonomous County in Xinjiang Uigur Autonomous Region. In the early 1990s, militant uprisings among the Uigurs* in Xinjiang were ruthlessly crushed by troops from the

People's Liberation Army. PRC officials probably do not have to worry a great deal about Tajik separatism. The Tajik population in the Xinjiang Uigur Autonomous Region is very small, not nearly as large as that of the Uigurs and Kazaks.* Second, Tajiks speak an Iranian, not Turkic, language and feel little kinship with Turkic-speaking Uzbeks, Uigurs, Kirgiz,* and Kazaks. Finally, PRC Tajiks are geographically separated from the Republic of Tajikistan.

SUGGESTED READINGS: Shirin Akiner, *Islamic Peoples of the Soviet Union*, 1983; Edward Allworth, ed., *Central Asia: A Century of Russian Rule*, 1967; Michael Dillon, *China's Muslims*, 1996; Ned Gillette, "Adventure in Western China," *National Geographic* 159 (February 1981), 174–99; Rick Gore, "Journey to China's Far West," *National Geographic* 157 (March 1980), 292–332; René Grousset, *The Empire of the Steppes: A History of Central Asia*, 1970; Ma Yin, ed., *China's Minority Nationalities*, 1989; Lee Pappas, "Tajik," in James S. Olson, ed., *An Ethnohistorical Dictionary of the Russian and Soviet Empires*, 1993; Peng Jianqun, "An Apricot Village Deep in the Mountains of Xinjiang," *China Today* 39 (November 1990), 52–55; Barry M. Rosen, "An Awareness of Traditional Tadzhik Identity in Central Asia," in Edward Allworth, ed., *The Nationality Question in Soviet Central Asia*, 1973; Wong How-Man, "Peoples of China's Far Provinces," *National Geographic* 165 (March 1984), 283–377.

TAKANERH. See **DAUR.**

TAKBANUATH. The Takbanuaths are one of the primary subgroups of the Bunun* people of Taiwan in the Republic of China.

TAKEBAKA. The Takebakas are one of the primary subgroups of the Bunun* people of Taiwan in the Republic of China.

TAKETODO. The Taketodos are one of the primary subgroups of the Bunun* people of Taiwan in the Republic of China.

TAKEVATAN. The Takevatans are one of the primary subgroups of the Bunun* people of Taiwan in the Republic of China.

TAKOPULAN. The Takopulans are one of the primary subgroups of the Bunun* people of Taiwan in the Republic of China. Today, however, the Takopulans have been completely assimilated by the surrounding Bunun groups, and only a handful of people recognize themselves as part of the Takopulan culture.

TAKUANERH. See **DAUR.**

TAME MIAO. See **MONPW.**

TAME WA. The term "Tame Wa," though widely used during the twentieth century in Burma and China, is hardly a ethnographic reference. Instead, it tends to refer to various Wa* groups of people who had long ago abandoned the practice of headhunting and acculturated themselves to a settled economy. The term "Tame Wa" was used in contradiction to the "Wild Wa," who maintained ritualistic headhunting well into the twentieth century. Other ethnonyms for the Tame Wa include Kut Wa, K'ala, Kawa, Tai Lo, Hsap Tai, and Guangpyat.

TANGAM. The Tangams are one of the ethnic subdivisions of the Adi* people, most of whom live in the Arunachal Pradesh region of far northeastern India. Adis can also be found scattered across the border in southeastern Tibet, northern Myanmar (Burma), and the far northwestern corner of Yunnan Province in the People's Republic of China. In India, where most Adis live, they can be found primarily on the banks of the Siang River and the Yamne River. Like other Adi people, the Tangams were part of the southern migration which brought them, centuries ago, out of Tibet and across the Himilayan mountains into the Assam Valley of India. During the ensuing centuries after their arrival, to avoid political and economic domination by other Assamese* groups, they relocated out of the valley into the highlands, where they currently reside. They locate their villages with defense in mind. Tangams prefer to live on hilltops, with access to a river via a sloping incline, with a very steep decline on the opposite side of the village. Houses are then constructed on elevated platforms, with the rear of the home facing the hillside. Like the other Adi subgroups, they still function in a largely subsistence economy based on slash-and-burn agriculture, fishing, foraging, and hunting.

TANGIN. Along with the Bokars, Boris, Padams, Minyongs, Pangis, Shimongs, Ashings, Pasis, Karkos, Ramos, Pailibos, Milans, Tangams,* and Gallongs, the Tangins are one of the subgroups of the Adi* people. The Adis can be found today living primarily in the Assam Valley of the Arunachal Pradish region of India. They are also located in southeastern Tibet, northeastern Myanmar (Burma), and far northwestern Yunnan Province in the People's Republic of China. They migrated centuries ago from Tibet on the other side of the Himalayan range, settled in the Assam Valley, and subsequently moved into villages built on the hillsides of the valley. Tangin is a dialect of Adi, a language that is part of the Tibeto-Burman* branch of the Sino-Tibetan family. Most Tangin farmers continue to work the land using swidden techniques to raise rice, millet, maize, vegetables, and a variety of fruits. They also produce cotton. Their indigenous religion is still intact, as is their traditional social structure.

TANGUT. See **TIBETAN.**

TAPANGU. Tapangu is one of the dialects of the Tsou* language spoken on Taiwan in the Republic of China. Tapangu speakers can be found today in the villages of Dabang, Lijia, Shanmei, and Xinmei in Wufeng Township in Jiayi County.

TARANG. Tarang is one of the two primary linguistic divisions of the Deng* people of the Tibetan Autonomous Region in the People's Republic of China. Approximately 6,000 people speak the Tarang language.

TAROMAK-VUDAI. The Taromak-Vudai people speak one of the two dialects of Rukai,* an indigenous language spoken on the island of Taiwan in the Republic of China.

TARTAR. See **TATAR.**

TASHQURGHANI. The Tashqurghanis are a subgroup of the Sarikol* people, who are themselves a subgroup of the Tajiks* in the People's Republic of China.

TATAR. The Tatar people, also known as Turks and more anciently as Tartars, constitute only a tiny percentage of the population of the People's Republic of China (PRC) and less than 1 percent of the total Tatar population worldwide. The 1990 national census in China counted only 4,837 Tatars, most of whom lived in the cities of Yining, Qoqek, and Urumqi in the Xinjiang Uiger Autonomous Region. Each of those cities is located near the border with the former Soviet Union. A few hundred Tatars could be found living outside Xinjiang in 1990. Their language is part of the Turkic branch of the Altaic* linguistic family. Tatar possesses no written script, but literate Tatars in China read and write Uigur,* Kazak,* or Chinese.* During the early twentieth century, Republic of China officials used the term ''Tatar'' generically to refer to all people using one of the Turkic languages.

The term Tatar has been used in a variety of ways over the years in Russia, the Soviet Union, the Commonwealth of Independent States, and the PRC. For centuries it was a generic reference to anybody of Muslim or Turkic descent. Sometimes Russians* used it to describe anybody of Asian descent. More specifically, however, the term Tatar describes the descendents of the Kypchak and other Turkic tribes who migrated west out of southern Siberia between the tenth and the thirteenth centuries. Much of the Mongol* armies in the thirteenth century were composed of these Turkic-speaking peoples. These people tended to mix with indigenous groups wherever they settled—with Finnic, Slavic, and Bolgar peoples in the Volga River Valley and in the Crimea, with Caucasic people in the eastern reaches of the North Caucasus, with various Siberian people in West Siberia, and with various minority groups in Yunnan and Sichuan provinces. Modern Tatars descend primarily from intermarriage between Boyar, Kipchak, and Mongol peoples.

During that process of ethnogenesis, the people who retained their Kypchak dialects and converted to Islam—the Hanafi rite of the Sunni faith—became more particularly known as Tatars. By the 1500s the Golden Horde had fallen under the control of its Turkic elements, and the terms Tatar and Golden Horde had become essentially synonymous. When the Golden Horde disintegrated, several new Tatar states emerged, such as the Astrakhan Khanate and the Kazan Khanate. Russia conquered Kazan in 1552 and Astrakhan in 1556. Eventually, the Tatars had spread from the Polish border in the west to Siberia in the east, and in the process became divided into a variety of tribal and territorial groups. The Volga Tatars, or Kazan Tatars, were considered the main group of Tatars, but there were the Astrakhan Tatars, which included the Kundrov Tatars and the Karagash Tatars; the West Siberian Tatars, which included the Baraba Tatars, the Tam Tatars, the Tara Tatars, the Tobol Tatars, and the T'jumen Tatars; and the Belarusian Tatars, Chulym Tatars, Crimean Tatars, Glazov Tatars, Kara Tatars, Kasimov Tatars, Kryashen Tatars, Lithuanian Tatars, and Mishar Tatars.

Chinese historical documents record the Tatars as the "Dadans," who were part of the Turkic Khanate until its collapse in the eighth century. Most of the Tatars in China today descend from Tatar ancestors who fled the Volga and Kama regions of Central Asia when ethnic Russians moved in there in the nineteenth century. Relatively few of the Tatars were settled farmers. An urban people, they make their living in commerce and industry. Some Tatar pastoralists herd cattle.

Although geographical and political reality dictate against the idea, a number of educated Chinese Tatars have closely followed the Tatar nationalist movement in the former Soviet Union. Groups such as the Mardzhani Society, Tugan Yak (Our Father's Land), Bulgar el dzhadid (New Bulgar), Society of Cultural Ecology, Tatar Public Center, the Ittifak (Alliance) National Independence Party, and the Suverenitet (Sovereignty) Committee appeared. The most radical Tatar leaders, such as Fauzia Bairamova, called in 1991 for an independent Tatar Republic. They also wanted to expand Tatar political reach well beyond the boundaries of the Tatar Autonomous Republic to include all lands ever controlled historically by Tatars—more than half of Russia. But only half of the Tatar Autonomous Republic in 1990 was ethnic Tatar; the others were primarily ethnic Russians who controlled the cities and opposed Tatar independence.

Tatarstan began taking formal steps toward independence in August 1990 when its supreme soviet adopted the Declaration on the State Sovereignty of the Republic of Tatarstan. In February 1992 Tatarstan stopped sending tax revenues to Russia, and in March 1992, leaders of Tatarstan held a referendum on sovereignty. More than 61 percent of the 2,132,000 people who voted approved the resolution for state sovereignty and absolute control of natural resources, especially the huge oil and natural gas reserves in the Tatar Autonomous Republic. Mintimer Sharimiyev, president of Tatarstan, also refused to sign Mikhail Gorbachev's union treaty in 1992. To do so, he argued, would be tantamount to denying the Tatar right to sovereignty. The supreme soviet of Tatarstan also began debating secession from Russia, primarily because they resented the loss of thirty million tons of their own oil to Russia each year. Russian President Boris Yeltsin denounced all plans for an independent Tatarstan, since the loss of the region to Russia would be a strategic and economic disaster.

There are some minority pan-Tatar political sentiments among the Tatars of the PRC. In 1996 and early in 1997, they sympathized with the outbreak of Uigur nationalism in Xinjiang Province. PRC officials were, of course, very concerned about Uigur nationalism, but they did not have to pay any special attention to Tatar nationalism in Xinjiang because the PRC Tatar population was too small and because they did not enjoy any territorial contiguity with the Tatars in Tatarstan.

SUGGESTED READINGS: *Current Digest* 41 (February 22, 1989), 1–2, 43 (December 25, 1991), 1–6, 44 (April 15, 1992), 24–25, and (April 22, 1992), 6–8; Alan W. Fisher, *The Crimean Tatars*, 1987; Ned Gillette, "Adventure in Western China," *National Geographic* 159 (February 1981), 174–99; Rick Gore, "Journey to China's Far West," *National Geographic* 157 (March 1980), 292–332; Chantal Lemercier-Quelquejay, "The Crimean Tatars: A Retrospective Summary," *Central Asian Review* 16 (1968), 15–25; Ma Yin, ed., *China's National Minorities*, 1989; Azade-Ayse Rorlich, *The Volga Tatars: A Profile in National Resilience*, 1986; Henry G. Schwarz, *The Minorities of Northern China: A Survey*, 1984; Ann Sheehy, *The Crimean Tatars and Volga Germans: Soviet Treatment of Two National Minorities*, 1971; Wong How-Man, "Peoples of China's Far Provinces," *National Geographic* 165 (March 1984), 283–377.

T'AT'AREH. See **TATAR.**

TAVALONG-VATAAN. Tavalong-Vataan is one of the five primary dialects of the Ami* language, which is spoken by the Ami people, an indigenous group living on Taiwan in the Republic of China.

TAY. The Tay people are one of the larger minority groups of the Socialist Republic of Vietnam. They have also been referred to as the Tho and Thu people, although they consider both references to be pejorative. They are closely related to the Nung* people, another tribal group in Vietnam that originated in China and has remnants still there. There are more than 1.2 million Tay people living in Vietnam, the vast majority of them concentrated in northeastern Vietnam, primarily in what used to be the Tay Bac Autonomous Region. Today the region is included in the three provinces of Lai Chau, Son La, and Hoang Lien Son. Several thousand Tay people can also be found today across the Sino-Vietnamese border in the southwestern portion of the Guangxi Zhuangzu Autonomous Region of the People's Republic of China, primarily in the highlands between Pingxiang and Qinzhou.

Anthropologists believe that the Tay people, who are closely related culturally and linguistically to the Thai,* originated in China, south of the Yangtse River. From there, centuries ago, they migrated south into the mountainous region north of the Red River Delta in Vietnam. The Tay people of Vietnam and China live in rural villages where they practice swidden agriculture, raising maize, buckwheat, watercress, sugarcane, manioc, and a variety of vegetables. They are also rice farmers. The Tay enjoy reputations in Vietnam and south China for being astute merchants and traders.

During the Vietnam War, Tay people actively supported Ho Chi Minh and the Vietminh political organization. A number of Tay people reached prominent positions in the Communist party of Vietnam. Today, most of the Tay people are in an advanced state of assimilation in Vietnam.

SUGGESTED READINGS: John F. Embree, *Ethnic Groups of Northern Southeast Asia*, 1950; "Tai," Paul Hockings, ed., *Encyclopedia of World Cultures*, vol. 6, *East and Southeast Asia*, 1991; George McT. Kahin, "Minorities in the Democratic Republic of Vietnam," *Asian Survey* 12 (July 1972), 163–75; Peter Kunstadter, ed., *Southeast Asian Tribes, Minorities, and Nations*, 1967; Nguyen Khac Viet, ed., *Mountain Regions and National Minorities in the Democratic Republic of Vietnam*, 1968.

TAYAL. See **ATAYAL.**

TEHUNG TAI. See **DAI.**

TEN. See **YANGUANG.**

TENG. See **DENG.**

TENGPA. See **DENG.**

TFUEA. Tfuea is one of the dialects of the Tsou* language of Taiwan in the Republic of China. Tfuea speakers can be found today in Leye and Laiji villages, as well as several other villages in Wufeng Township of Jiayi County.

THAI. On July 1, 1997, when Hong Kong reverted to the sovereignty of the People's Republic of China, approximately 5,000 ethnic Thais became a new ethnic group in the PRC. The vast majority of these people are Thai women who work as domestic help in prosperous homes of Hakka*- and Yue*-speaking Han* people on the island. Thais can also be found in the domestic employment of British* families in Hong Kong. See **HONG KONGESE.**

SUGGESTED READING: "Chinese Maids and Foreign Helpers in Hong Kong," *Modern China* 22 (October 1996): 448–79.

THAI. See **DAI.**

THAKALI. The Thakali people, who are also known as the Tamus and Tamangs, are a Nepalese* ethnic group who live primarily today in the Jomson District of central Nepal. They are a small ethnic group, with a population of no more than 5,000 people. Thakalis are of Mongol* extraction and speak a Tibeto-Burman* language. Thakali roots reach back to Tibet. During the nineteenth and twentieth centuries, Thakali merchants played an influential role in the Nepalese-Tibetan trade routes. After the Chinese conquest of Tibet, most Thakalis then living in Tibet migrated south into Nepal and even northern India. Nev-

ertheless, there are likely still a handful of people in Tibet who are aware of their Thakali heritage.
SUGGESTED READING: Shigeru Iijima, *Himalayan Traders*, 1975.

THAO. Thao is an all but extinct language spoken by an indigenous people in Taiwan in the Republic of China. Thao speakers, who today number no more than a few dozen people, live in central Taiwan, primarily in Buju Township south of Sun Moon Lake. They are slash-and-burn farmers. There are two mutually intelligible dialects of Thao: Brawbaw and Shtafari. There is little hope that Thao will survive for more than another generation.
SUGGESTED READING: S. A. Wurm, B. T'sou, D. Bradley, et al., eds., *Language Atlas of China*, 1987.

THEINBAW. See KACHIN.

THEN. The Then people are an ethnic group in the People's Republic of China, although the central government has not yet extended to them recognition as an official minority nationality. They number in the tens of thousands and can be found living throughout Guizhou and northern Guangxi provinces. Their language is part of the Dong-Shui* branch of the Zhuang-Dong group of Tai* languages. Then is distinctive enough from the other Dong-Shui languages to convince ethnolinguists that they separated ethnically centuries ago. A written script does not exist, but literate Thens can read and write Mandarin* Chinese.* Most people can speak a local Chinese dialect as well as their native Then.

Then country was independent of Han* authority until the thirteenth century, when Chinese armies and then political administrators occupied Guangxi. Beginning with the Qing dynasty in 1271, Then farmers had to provide an annual tribute payment in grain to the Chinese imperial government. Over the centuries, the exact nature of Han imperial control has changed with succeeding dynasties and with the rise of Communists to power since 1949, but the reality of Han political and economic domination has not changed.

The Then economy today is primarily agricultural. They prefer valleys and lower elevated hillsides for village placement, and they live in one-story mud-walled houses. The two-generation household is the norm, and young men prefer to marry one of their mother's brother's daughters. The social system is based on patrilineal descent. Thens tend to live in single-surname villages, which give each community powerful family bonds. Farmers employ plow technology to raise rice, maize, wheat, and potatoes. They are also known to produce peanuts, melons, cotton, and a number of vegetables. Water buffalo, oxen, and horses serve as draft animals.

Indigenous Then animism still survives in their belief that a soul, which they call *yin*, is present in individuals, animals, plants, and natural phenomena. Male priests and female shamans assist the community in regulating the spiritual world and in preventing personal and natural disasters. Since the days of the

Sung dynasty, Buddhism and Daoism have also found a home in Then culture, and Daoist priests and Buddhist monks also serve each village's spiritual needs. SUGGESTED READINGS: Ma Yin, ed., *China's Minority Nationalities*, 1989; S. Robert Ramsey, *The Languages of China*, 1987.

THI. See **GELAO.**

THO. See **TAI.**

THO. See **ZHUANG.**

THU. See **GELAO.**

THU. See **TAI.**

TIAOXI. The Tiaoxis are a dialect subgroup of the Taihu* people, who are themselves a linguistic subgroup of the Wu*-speaking Han* people of the People's Republic of China. More than three million people speak the Tiaoxi language, and the vast majority of them live in the Huzhou, Deqing, Yuhang, Anji, and Changxing regions of Zhejiang Province.

TIBETAN. Including Tibetans in an ethnic description of China is a politically perilous act. To Tibetan nationalists, China is an oppressive interloper determined to destroy their way of life. To the People's Republic of China (PRC), Tibet is not an independent state but is actually the Xizang Autonomous Region, a strategically critical political subdivision buffering China from the subcontinent. The Chinese government claims to have "liberated" Tibet by occupying the kingdom, although large numbers of Tibetans have no idea what they were being liberated from. Nevertheless, the reality is that China is firmly in control of Tibet and therefore Tibetans are included in this dictionary.

Tibet, known as the "Land of Snow," is one of the most unique geographical regions of the world. Criss-crossed by mountain systems running from the northwest to the southeast, Tibet is surrounded by the greatest mountain ranges in the world. Running across the entire southern boundary of Tibet are the Himalayas. In the far west, the Ladakh mountain range cuts into Tibet from the Baltistan region to the southeast. Just north of the Ladakh range are the Karakoram mountains. The Kunlun mountains constitute the northern flank of Tibet. Just south of the Kunlun range is the vast Taklimakan Desert. The Kunluns themselves are composed of two ranges—the Astin Tagh mountains and the Altyn Tagh mountains. The Tangkula mountains border Tibet to the east. Much of northwestern Tibet is uninhabitable; the mountains are so rugged that frontier boundaries with Pakistan are indeterminate. South of the Kunlun mountain range are the vast tablelands of Tibet, home of nomadic pastoralists.

The term "Tibetan" does not provide an exact reference to a single ethnic group, and the people themselves usually call themselves the Pobas. The two main ethnic groups in Tibet are the Bopas,* who pursue a settled, agricultural or commercial lifestyle, and the Drokpas* (Drukpas, Dards), who are nomadic pastoralists who raise cattle, horses, sheep, and goats. The Bopas and the Drokpas are further subdivided among themselves by dialect and regional identities. Other ethnic groups living in Tibet include Sherpas,* Moinbas,* Llobas,* Khams,* and Dengs.*

The country is divided into four districts: the Tsang and U districts constitute central Tibet; the Kham District is eastern Tibet; and the Nga-Ri District is western Tibet. The Tsang and U districts are the cradle of Tibetan civilization, home to the capital city of Llasa and the most prominent Lamaist Buddhist temples and monasteries in the country. The region is drained by the Tsangpo River, which traverses Tibet from west to east and constitutes the country's commercial lifeline. The river runs eight hundred miles before it enters India. Tsang and U are also drained by the Chi-Ch'u and Nyang-Ch'u rivers. The town of Gyantse in southern Tibet has long served as the northern terminus of the Indo-Tibetan trade route. One hundred kilometers southwest of Gyantse is the town of Pha-Ri, which serves as the primary entry point from Sikkim and Nepal into Tibet.

In the Kham District, or far eastern Tibet, the population density is much higher than it is in the rest of Tibet, primarily because the soil is more fertile and rainfall more plentiful. Trade routes from Kham connect Tibet with Yunnan and Sichuan provinces. Silk and tea from China enter Tibet in Kham and are distributed throughout the rest of the country. Tibetan medicinal herbs, furs, skins, and incense enter Yunnan and Sichuan from Kham.

The Nga-Ri District in far western Tibet could not be more different. Sparsely populated and characterized by poor soil, Nga-Ri borders Ladakh, Jammu, and Kashmir. The Indus and Sutlej rivers descend from the Nga-Ri highlands. The northern reaches of Nga-Ri consists of the Chang Tang highlands, which run all the way to the Dang-La mountains and constitute much of northwestern and north central Tibet. With an average altitude of 15,000 feet, Chang Tang is a windswept region home to hunters, fur trappers, nomadic pastoralists, and a few farmers.

Tibetans can also be found outside Tibet proper (the Xizang Autonomous Region). More than two million people who consider themselves ethnic Tibetans live today in the western reaches of Qinghai Province. In 1950, in fact, Tibetans were by far the largest ethnic group in Qinghai Province, but today, because of the central government's assimilation policies and the resulting arrival of millions of Han* settlers, Tibetans now constitute less than 20 percent of the Qinghai population.

The Tibetan language, a member of the Tibeto-Burman* cluster of the Sino-Tibetan linguistic family, is known as Bodish. It actually is composed of three languages: Dbusgtsang,* Kham,* and Amdo.* Dbusgtsang and Amdo are mutually unintelligible, and Kham is a transitional language between them. Under most circumstances, such differences would divide Tibetans into distinct ethnic clusters and mitigate against their being considered a single group. But in Tibet, the overwhelming political and cultural influence of Lamaist Buddhism, as well as the struggle for self-determination and independence vis-à-vis the PRC, have given Tibetans a powerful sense of national identity. Of the total population of ethnic Tibetans in the PRC, 86 percent of them speak either Dbusgtsang, Kham, or Amdo as their native language. The remainder speak either Chinese* or other languages. The Dbusgtsang dialect, spoken widely throughout the Tibetan Autonomous Region, can be divided into four primary dialects, all of which are mutually intelligible: Dbus, Gtsang, Mngahris, and Sharpa. The Kham dialect is spoken in the Changdu region of the Tibetan Autonomous Region; the Ganzi Tibetan Autonomous Prefecture in Sichuan Province; the Diqing Tibetan Autonomous Prefecture in Yunnan Province; the Yushu Tibetan Autonomous Prefecture in Qinghai Province; and in the Gannan Tibetan Autonomous Prefecture in Gansu Province. Speakers of the Amdo dialect are located in several autonomous prefectures in Gansu and Qinghai provinces; in Hualong Hui Autonomous County, Xunhua Salar Autonomous County, and Ledu County in Qinghai Province; and in the Aba Tibetan Autonomous Prefecture of Sichuan Province.

Most archaeologists and ethnolinguists believe that the ancestors of modern Tibetans migrated into the plateau more than 13,000 years ago, coming from points to the northeast. They settled along the Tsangpo River, and from there Tibetan civilization began to emerge. By A.D. 400, along the Tsangpo River watershed, the first Tibetan political kingdom had developed. In 632 the Tibetan empire expanded well into central Asia to the northwest and into northern China and Mongolia in the northeast. Buddhism, which came to Tibet during the imperial period, evolved into the central feature of Tibetan ethnicity. In the mid-ninth century, the Tibetan empire began to disintegrate into a great variety of smaller political entities.

During the thirteenth century, Tibet was controlled politically by a Buddhist theocracy, which gave way to three secular dynasties between 1354 and 1642. At that time, the Yellow Hat, or Gelugspa, Buddhist sect, a Mongolian group led by the Dalai Lama, took control of the central Tibetan plateau. The Dalai Lama and his hereditary successors maintained political control of Tibet for the next three centuries.

That power, however, was always threatened from the south and the east. During the nineteenth and early twentieth centuries, military forces from British India frequently pushed their way into Tibet, and Chinese forces did the same from the north and northeast. For centuries, Chinese authorities had looked longingly on Tibet. The interlocking Karakorum, Ladakh, and Himalayan mountain ranges protected China from India in the south and European imperialists from the west, but China had long been obsessed with the possibility of a foreign power's colonizing Tibet. For British armies located in Tibet, an invasion of China would be a relatively easy matter.

After losing tens of millions of people during World War II at the hand of

Japanese occupation forces, China became even more paranoid about its frontiers. In 1950, a year after Mao Zedong's Communist victory, the new revolutionary government of the People's Republic of China decided to act on its fears. Chinese military forces invaded the Kham, U, and Tsang districts of Tibet and proclaimed political sovereignty there. At the time, the Chinese left the Dalai Lama in place, hoping to employ him as a modern-day *tusi* administrator, a figurehead leader thoroughly under their control.

Extraordinarily religious and blessed with a long historical tradition, Tibetans wanted nothing to do with the People's Republic of China, especially because of the antireligious nature of Marxist theory. Tibetan guerrilla forces continually harassed Chinese troops for nearly a decade, and in 1959 a general uprising against China was brutally oppressed. During the 1950s, because of emigration and war, Tibet lost more than one million people. The central government also implemented new political and economic arrangements to undermine the Lamaist hierarchy of Tibet. For centuries, large monasteries had been supported by peasant farmers, but Chinese officials considered the system little more than a form of religious feudalism, and they abolished it.

In 1959, when he realized that Chinese Communist officials were destroying the economic infrastructure upon which Lamaist Buddhism rested in Tibet, the Dalai Lama fled Tibet and established a government in exile in Dharamsala, India. Hundreds of thousands of Tibetans also went into exile abroad. China established the Tibet (Xizang) Autonomous Region and a number of autonomous prefectures and counties in neighboring areas of Qinghai, Gansu, Sichuan, and Yunnan provinces where ethnic Tibetans lived. In the 1990 national census, China claimed a total of 4.5 million Tibetans, half of them located in the Tibet Autonomous Region and half in Qinghai, Gansu, Sichuan, and Yunnan.

After the Chinese takeover, Han people were encouraged to relocate to Tibet, and today they consititute the majority group in the three largest Tibetan cities. In addition to Han settlers, the Tibetan government was staffed by Han cadres who had little respect for Tibetan traditions. During the years of the Cultural Revolution in the late 1960s and early 1970s, those cadres made life miserable for Tibetan monks and their monasteries. Tibetan patriots became increasingly resentful of Han oppression and the exile of the Dalai Lama. They also resented PRC laws that prohibited the display of photographs of the Dalai Lama. Late in the 1980s and early in the 1990s, violent anti-Han and anti-PRC demonstrations erupted repeatedly in Llasa, the Tibetan capital, and People's Liberation Army soldiers were deployed to crush the rebellions, which they did with relish. More than one thousand Tibetans died in the fighting. PRC officials were also quick to suppress any expression of Tibetan nationalism in Qinghai Province.

But while PRC authorities were employing force to quell Tibetan nationalism, they were also becoming more sensitive to nationalism's demands. Chinese Communist party leaders watched with alarm the disintegration of the Soviet Union in the late 1980s and early 1990s, and they became particularly concerned about the desire of ethnic minorities for national independence. Such sentiments had destroyed the Soviet Union, and Chinese officials decided to become somewhat more careful in their approach to local government. Throughout the late 1980s and 1990s, the number of Han people in Tibet's government positions steadily declined as they were replaced by ethnic Tibetans. Whether the new Chinese policies will help subdue the forces of Tibetan nationalism remain to be seen.

The Tibetan economy varies from region to region. The northern plain is almost uninhabited, except for occasional incursions by nomadic herders. The Tsangpo River Valley in southern Tibet is the counry's agricultural breadbasket. There farmers raise high-altitude barley, wheat, buckwheat, peas, mustard, potatoes, and other vegetables. Farming is also the central economic activity in the southeast, where a subtropical climate prevails. In the high-altitude, rolling grasslands of the Central Tibetan plateau, nomadic pastoralists raise yaks and a mixed-breed cow-yak, which can tolerate the cold winters, and sheep. At lower elevations, they raise goats and cattle. The third major Tibetan occupation, in addition to farming and herding, is monkhood, which attracts hundreds of thousands of Tibetan males.

Tibetans are among the most devoutly religious people in the world. Only such devotion could support so many religious professionals. Although there is a tiny Muslim minority in Tibet, the vast majority are Tibetan Buddhists. Tibetan Buddhism is a syncretic mix of Indian Buddhism, Tantrism, and local animism, which historically was polytheistic and shamanistic. Tibetan priests, known as lamas, manage the religion through large monasteries and temples. Before 1950 some demographers estimated that anywhere from one-sixth to one-fourth of all Tibetan males were Lamaist monks. That number has declined under Chinese control, but large numbers of Tibetans still feel an obligation to support the monasteries through contributions of money, labor, and their sons.

In doing so, individuals earn merit and move along the path toward enlightenment, the ultimate goal of all Buddhists. After death, Tibetans believe that the deceased spends forty-nine days in limbo before being reincarnated in a new body. Depending upon how one lived, that reincarnation can come in the form of a human being, an animal, a god, or even an evil spirit. Individuals go through the cycle of life, death, and reincarnation many times before enlightenment is finally achieved, at which point the spirit loses its individual consciousness and merges with nirvana.

SUGGESTED READINGS: Barbara Aziz, *Tibetan Frontier Families*, 1978; Tiley Chodag, *Tibet: The Land and the People*, 1988; Dalai Lama, *My Land and My People*, 1962; Mike Edwards, "Our Man in China: Joseph Rock," *National Geographic* 191 (January 1997), 62–100; Rebecca French, *The Golden Yoke: The Legal System of Buddhist Tibet*, 1994; Lauran R. Hartley, "The Role of Regional Factors in the Standardization of Spoken Tibet," *Tibet Journal* 21 (Winter 1996), 30–57; Yasheng Huang, "China's Cadre Transfer Policy Toward Tibet in the 1980s," *Modern China* 21 (April 1995), 184–204; H. A. Jaschke, *A Tibetan-English Dictionary: With Special Reference to the Prevailing Dialects*, 1881 and 1980; Hollis S. Liao, "The Recruitment and Training of Ethnic Minority

Cadres in Tibet,'' *Issues & Studies* 31 (December 1995), 55–67; *New York Times*, September 9, 1991; Tsung-Lien Shen and Shen-Chi Liu, *Tibet and the Tibetans*, 1953; David Snelgrove and Hugh Richardson, *A Cultural History of Tibet*, 1980.

TIBETO-BURMAN. Ethnolinguists use the term ''Tibeto-Burman'' to describe the largest group of languages in Southeast Asia, which includes the languages of more than two hundred distinct ethnic groups. In that sense, Tibeto-Burman enjoys a linguistic complexity similar to that of the Indo-European languages. Tibeto-Burman is divided into four branches of its own: Tibetan,* Yi,* Jingpo,* and Qiang.* The following languages spoken in China are part of the Tibeto-Burman family: Tibetan, Moinba,* Yi, Lisu,* Hani,* Lahu,* Jino,* Naxi,* Jingpo, Drung,* Qiang, Pumi,* Lloba,* Nu,* Achang,* and Bai.*
SUGGESTED READINGS: Paul Benedict, *Sino-Tibetan*, 1972; Roy Andrew Miller, ''The Tibeto-Burman Languages of South Asia,'' in Thomas A. Sebeok, ed., *Current Trends in Linguistics*, vol. 5, *South Asia*, 1969; S. Robert Ramsey, *The Languages of China*, 1987.

TINGZHOU. The Tingzhou people are a linguistic subgroup of the Hakka*-speaking Han* people of the People's Republic of China (PRC). Tingzhou speakers can be found today living in Changting, Yongding, Shanghang, Wuping, Ninghua, Qingliu, Mingxi, and Liancheng counties in western Fujian Province of the PRC.

TIOL. The Tiol people, who have also been known as the Kiorrs, are a very small, officially unrecognized ethnic group living in far southern Yunnan Province in the People's Republic of China. Many ethnolinguists classify them a Kmhmu* subgroup, but the two languages, though both in the Mon-Khmer* branch of the Austroasiatic family, are not mutually intelligible. The number of Tiols living in southern Yunnan and northern Laos may today be no more than a few dozen people. During the mid-eighteenth century, the expansion of Tai*-speaking people from the south and west into Laos pushed the Kmhmuic groups into northern Laos and southern Yunnan. Tiols were among this displaced group.

   The traditional Tiol village is located in tropical rain forests at lower elevations on mountain ridges. Their villages typically contain from fifteen to one hundred households, with anywhere from 150 to 1,200 people. They dwell in bamboo and wooden houses built on stilts, which permit the people to remain dry during the monsoon rainy season. Most Tiol farmers raise dry rice on mountain slopes using slash-and-burn agricultural techniques. Fields are usually planted for one or two years and then left fallow for as long as ten years. They plant seeds using planting sticks, not plows, and their major crops in addition to dry rice are maize, legumes, chilies, taro, and yams. To boost their sources of protein, most Tiol villages raise pigs, chickens, ducks, goats, and water buffalo. During lean periods, when food supplies are diminished and the harvest is still weeks or months away, Tiol people revert to ancient hunting and foraging activities, collecting wild plants, berries, and small game animals.

SUGGESTED READINGS: Kristina Lindell, Hakan Lundstrom, Jan-Olof Svantesson, and Damrong Tayanin, *The Kammu Year: Its Lore and Music*, 1982; Kristina Lindell, Jan-Ojvind Swahn, and Damrong Tayanin, *Folk Tales from Kammu*, 4 vols., 1977–1989; Robert Parkin, *A Guide to Austroasiatic Speakers and Their Languages*, 1991; Frank Proschan, "Kmhmu," in Paul V. Hockings, ed., *Encyclopedia of World Cultures*, vol. 6, *East and Southeast Asia*, 1991; Dang Nghiem Van, "The Khmu in Vietnam," *Vietnamese Studies* 36 (1973), 17–27.

TLHAI. The Tlhais are one of the many subgroups of the Li* people of Hainan Province in the People's Republic of China. Like other Li groups, they have earned a reputation over the years for their ferocious anti-Han* xenophobia, which has often taken the form of guerrilla warfare against Han immigrants to Hainan. Their hatred of the Nationalist government in the 1930s and 1940s also made them willing allies of Mao Zedong and the Communists, and when Mao triumphed, the Tlhais were afforded recognition as heroes. Most Tlhais today are farmers who raise coconuts, coffee, cocoa, sisal, rubber, cashews, pineapples, mangoes, and bananas. Rice is their staple.

TONG. See **DONG.**

TONG-CHIA. See **DONG.**

TONGGU. The Tonggu people are a linguistic subgroup of the Hakka*-speaking Han* people of the People's Republic of China (PRC). Tonggu speakers can be found today living in Tonggu, Xiushui, Wuning, Jing'an, Fengxin, Gao'an, Yifeng, and Wanzai counties in Jiangxi Province and Kiuyang and Pingjiang counties in Hunan Province of the PRC.

TONGHSIANG. See **DONGXIANG.**

TONGREN. The Tongrens are the smaller of the two subdivisions of the Bonan* people. Tongrens, who are primarily Buddhists, live in Tongren County of Qinghai Province of the People's Republic of China.

TONGSHI. The Tongshi (Tongza) people are a subgroup of the Qi* people, who are themselves a subgroup of the Li* minority of Hainan Island in the People's Republic of China. Tongshi speakers constitute 70 percent of the Qi people. Most Tongshis live in western and northwestern Qiongzhong County and in western Baoting County.

TONGUS. See **EVENK.**

TONGZA. See **TONGSHI.**

TONGZU. See **DONG.**

TORGUT. Torgut is one of the vernaculars of the Oirat* language of the People's Republic of China.

TOUS. The Tous are an ethnic group in the People's Republic of China (PRC), although the central government has never extended to them formal recognition as a minority nationality. Official PRC publications classify them as a Yi* subgroup, and, indeed, they speak a Yi language. But Tous is not mutually intelligible with the vast majority of other Yi languages, and the Tous give themselves a distinct, separate identity. Although they acknowledge a certain cultural affinity with the Yi, they nevertheless insist that they are a separate people. Most Tous live today in Yunnan Province.

The traditional Tous economy is primarily agricultural. Tous farmers living at lower altitudes raise maize, potatoes, buckwheat, and oats; cattle, sheep, goats, and horses are raised in the highlands. Poorer Tous families still engage in foraging activities to supplement their diet. Tous villages are quite small, more like hamlets, and their homes are constructed of wood and dirt. Their religious beliefs today remain an eclectic mix of Daoism, Buddhism, animism, and shamanism; a few thousand Tous practice Christianity.

TSAI. The Tsais are one of the many subgroups of the Li* people of Hainan Province in the People's Republic of China. Most Tsais today are farmers who raise rice as their staple as well as coconuts, coffee, cocoa, sisal, rubber, cashews, pineapples, mangoes, and bananas.

TSARISEN. See **PAIWAN** and **RUKAI.**

TSEOLE. The Tseoles, also known as Tse'ole', are one of the primary subgroups of the Atayal* people of Taiwan in the Republic of China.

TSHOMI. The Tshomi people are considered by ethnologists in the People's Republic of China (PRC) to be a subgroup of the Pumi* people, an officially recognized minority nationality living today in Lijiang Naxi Autonomous County, Ninglang Yi Autonomous County, and Lanping County in Yunnan Province and in Jiulong, Yanyuan, and Muli Tibetan Autonomous counties in Sichuan Province. Most Tshomis live in high-elevation mountain villages and work as farmers, raising corn, wheat, rice, buckwheat, barley, beans, and oats.

TSOU. The Tsou—also known regionally and by ethnologists as Alishan, Arisan, Northern Tsou, Tsu'u, Tsuou, and Tzu—are one of the indigenous peoples of Taiwan. Although Taiwanese government officials no longer keep count of the tribal populations of the indigenous people, demographers estimate that approximately 20,000 people speak the Tsou language today. Their original homeland was in the western central mountains near Mount Ali, Wufeng Township in Jiayi County, and in Xinyi township in Nantou County. There are three Tsou dialects: Luhtu is spoken in Xinyi Township of Nantou County; Tfuea is spoken in Leye and Laiji villages, as well as several other villages, in Wufeng Township of Jiayi County; and Tapangu is spoken in the villages of Dabang, Lijia, Shanmei, Xinmei in Wufeng Township—all in the highlands of south central Taiwan. Their most immediate indigenous neighbors are the Bununs,* who live south, east, and north of the Tsous.

To sustain themselves, the Tsou engage in mountain-slope agriculture, hunting, and fishing. Like most people in the world who still live a premodern lifestyle, the Tsou live largely in a subsistence economy characterized by the slash-and-burn cultivation of millet, rice, sweet potatoes, and taro. Many also engage in wet-rice farming. They supplement their fundamentally agricultural diet by hunting deer and wild boar. The Tsou traditionally dressed themselves in leather clothing, but in recent years they have begun to purchase and wear commercially produced shirts, pants, and dresses. Also in recent years, they have largely given up the traditional ironsmithing techniques they used to produce spears, knives, and axes in favor of buying stronger, commercially manufactured steel tools.

The Tsou have long been loyal to their indigenous animistic faith, in which their Taiwanese environment is alive with spirits, ghosts, and unseen forces, and in which tribal shamans must appease those forces through ritualistic ceremonies. They speak a Proto Austronesian language whose roots are in the South and Central Pacific. There are three Tsou subdivisions based primarily on linguisic differences: Tsou, Kanakanabu,* and Saaroa.* The Tsou dialects are quite separate from the other Taiwanese languages, which indicates differences in origins based on area, time, or both.

SUGGESTED READINGS: Raleigh Ferrel, *Taiwan Aboriginal Groups: Problems in Cultural and Linguistic Classification*, 1969; *The Republic of China Yearbook, 1995*, 1996; Mei-chun Tang, "Han and Non-Han in Taiwan: A Case of Acculturation," *Bulletin of the Institute of Ethnology* (Taipei) 30 (1970), 7–13; Yvonne Yuan, "Migrate, Assimilate, or Integrate?" *Free China Review* 42 (June 1992), 4–15.

TSOUIC. The term "Tsouic" is a linguistic reference to a group of languages spoken by the indigenous Tsou* people on the island of Taiwan in the Republic of China. Included in the Tsouic group are Tsou, Kanakanabu,* and Saaroa.*

SUGGESTED READING: S. A. Wurm, B. T'sou, D. Bradley, et al., eds., *Language Atlas of China*, 1987.

TSUOU. See **TSOU.**

TSU'U. See **TSOU.**

T'U. See **ZHUANG.**

TU. The Tu people—who are also known by such ethnonyms as Huzhus, Guantings, Mongols,* Monggors, Monguors, Turens, and White Mongols—are an officially recognized minority nationality of the People's Republic of China (PRC). Their population in the 1990 Chinese census was listed at 191,624 people, and simple extrapolations from that number would indicate a current population approaching 200,000. Some Chinese* demographers place the Tu population at nearly 350,000 people. The vast majority of Tu people live along the Huang River, the Yellow River, and the Datong River in the Huzhu Tu Autonomous County of Qinghai Province, near the border with Gansu Province. The primary Tu settlements are located in the vicinity of Minhe, Ldu, Yongdeng, Huzhu, Datong, Menyuan, and Tianzhu. The can be found approximately one hundred miles northwest of the major Salar* and Dongxiang* settlements in the PRC. Han* Chinese often refer to them as ''Turen,'' which translates as ''local people,'' ''aboriginal people,'' or ''indigenous people.'' The Tu were well established in Qinghai before Han immigrants began arriving from the east.

The Tu speak a Mongolian language in the Altaic* linguistic family. It is a close relative of Bonan,* Dongxiang, and Mongolian. There are two primary Tu dialects. The Huzhu dialect is spoken in the northern reaches of Tu country, and the Minhe dialect is spoken in the south, in the Tu settlements on the Huang and Yellow rivers. In Datong County, Tu people no longer speak their native language at all. Chinese has replaced it.

The Tu refer to themselves as Mongols or White Mongols. A process of ethnogenesis began to create the Tu people in 1227 when Mongol armies invaded their region of Qinghai, which at the time was occupied by the Tibetan,* Uigur,* and Shato* ethnic groups. Mongol soldiers, who were on permanent assignments without the opportunity to return home, married Tibetan, Uigur, and Shato women. Their children were the ancestors of the Tu people, who began to emerge as a distinct ethnic group in the fifteenth century. It is no wonder the Tu refer to themselves as Mongolians. Scholars feel that the Tu are descendents of an ethnogenesis from the mixing of Han, Mongol, Turkish (see **TURKIC PEOPLE**), Qiang,* and Tibetan peoples. Their religion is a unique mix of Yellow Sect Buddhism, Daoism, and animism.

The Tibetan connection is also important in Tu culture. For centuries, Tus lived among Tibetans who had descended from the older Xixia Kingdom. The Tu social system gradually evolved into a close approximation of Tibetan society, and Lamaist Buddhism became the primary Tu religion. When the Tu received an education, it was usually constructed along Tibetan models. Because of that, it was not at all unusual for Tu men to become Lamaist monks. Tu and Tibetan people regularly intermarried, creating a hybrid culture. The Tu even adopted many Tibetan legends, festivals, songs, and fairy tales and claimed them as their own.

Today, the Tu homeland has also been settled by Han* and Hui* people, making the regional population a diverse collection of Tus, Uigurs, Mongols, Tibetans, Huis, and Hans. The Tus, however, are quite distinct from the others and can easily be identified by their traditional dress, which is characterized by women's heavy brocaded shoes and the rainbow-colored sleeves on their dresses. Both Tu men and Tu women wear elaborate white felt hats during the winter months.

Until the years of the Ming dynasty, virtually all Tus were pastoralists who grazed sheep and goats in plateau grasslands. Some Tus changed to agriculture during the Ming years, and since then they have produced rice, wheat, maize, millet, and a variety of vegetables and fruits. Although most Tus continue to be farmers today, increasing numbers of them are wage laborers in local mines, factories, food-processing plants, construction projects, and manufacturing facilities.

During the 1920s and 1930s, Roman Catholic misssionaries worked diligently in Qinghai Province where they estabished churches and schools among the Tu. But Christianity was only a thin veneer covering the indigenous Tu culture. Because the original Tibetan women who intermarried with the Mongol soldiers were Lamaist Buddhists, they taught the religion to their children, and it became the core of Tu religious values. Four Lamaist monasteries have been located in Tu country for centuries, and most families with two sons sent one of them to a monastery. The monasteries owned huge amounts of property, leased farmland out to tenant farmers, exacted taxes from peasants, and acted as bankers to Tu farmers.

So many Tu young men entered Lamaist monasteries that marriage customs came to reflect the shortage of eligible males. Women unable to find husbands remain in their natal nuclear families but are allowed to take lovers. The community considers such women to be married to heaven. Any children borne automatically become members of her patrilineal family and take the surname of her father. That pattern continues today in Tu communities because an inordinately large number of young men still enter Lamaist monasteries.

Buddhism still competes, however, with Tu animism, which remains alive and well in Tu culture. Shamans play a key role in Tu folk religion. Like other animists, the Tus are convinced that an invisible world of spirits, ghosts, gods, and demons directly influences human affairs. Each Tu village possesses a "white shaman" who is capable of curing people from illness and a "black shaman" who specializes in revenge, against other individuals as well as against the beings of the unseen world.

SUGGESTED READINGS: Paul V. Hockings, "Tu," in Paul V. Hockings, ed., *The Encyclopedia of World Cultures*, vol. 6, *East and Southeast Asia*, 1991; Ma Yin, ed., *China's Minority Nationalities*, 1989; S. Robert Ramsey, *The Languages of China*, 1987; Henry G. Schwarz, *The Minorities of Northern China: A Survey*, 1984; Kevin Stuart and Hu Jun, "A Tu Nationality Festival," *China Reconstructs* 38 (April 1989), 29–31; Xie

Jun, "Visit to a Tu Nationality Village," *China Today* 39 (August 1990), 29–31; Xie Shengcai, "The Tu People of the Qinghai Plateau," *China Reconstructs* 30 (January 1981), 29–31.

TUBALAR. The Tubalars are one of the primary subgroups of the Altais,* a minority ethnic group living today in far northern Xinjiang Province in the People's Republic of China.

T'UCHIA. See TUJIA.

TUCHIA. See TUJIA.

TUDING. See TUJIA.

TUGAIMAIT. The Tugaimaits are a subgroup of the Kirgiz* peoples. They speak a Northern Kirgiz* dialect and live primarily in Akqi County in the Xinjiang Uigur Autonomous Region of the People's Republic of China.

T'UJEN. See ZHUANG.

TUJIA. The Tujia people are an officially recognized minority nationality in the People's Republic of China (PRC). Other ethnonyms that have identified them in the past are Bizika, Bizka, Tuchia, Piseka (Pihsiehk'a), Tuding, Tujen, and Tumin. They can be found today living in three south central provinces: 1 million live in Xiangxi Tujia-Miao Autonomous Prefecture in Hunan Province; 1.5 million, in southwestern Hubei Province; and 620,000, in eastern Sichuan Province. Almost all Tujias live south of the Yangtze River in the Wulang mountains, usually at between 1,300 feet and 5,000 feet in elevation. Tujia country is heavily forested and subject to abundant rainfall.

The size of the Tujia population has been somewhat controversial. In the 1982 national census, government officials claimed that 2.83 million people in China claimed to be Tujias. But acccording to the 1990 census, there were 5,704,223 Tujias living in the PRC. Most demographers explain the discrepancy politically. During the years of the Cultural Revolution in the late 1960s and much of the 1970s, the central government went to great lengths to purify Chinese society ideologically. They wanted to eradicate every semblance of bourgeois capitalism. In the hands of young Red Guard cadres, who were overwhelmingly Han* in ethnic composition, the crusade often took the shape of Han ethnocentrism as the cadres tried to crush any expression of minority values. Even though the Cultural Revolution petered out late in the 1970s, in 1980, when Han census takers went through Tujia villages asking questions, many people denied their Tujia heritage.

It was not difficult to deny it. Ethnologists still debate about Tujian origins, arguing about whether they came from Sichuan or Guizhou or Jiangxi, or whether they were indigenous to western Hunan and southwestern Hubei. The latter point of view is most commonly held today. The Tujias were already there when Han, Mongol,* and Miao* settlers arrived, and they acculturated to these external forces. According to many ethnolinguists, Tujia is probably a member of the Tibeto-Burman* branch of the Sino-Tibetan linguistic family, but that is the subject of some debate since so few scholarly examinations of Tujian have ever been completed. The language, which is closely related to Yi,* is spoken by relatively few Tujias, although Tujian can still be heard in Longshan County in the Xiangsi Autonomous Prefecture. Most Tujians today speak Han or Miao as their primary language. Since intermarriage between Hans and Tujias has occurred for centuries, census takers could not determine otherwise in the early 1980s when an ethnic Tujian claimed Han ancestry.

Because of the extent of Tujian intermarriage with Hans and Miaos, the Chinese government did not initially recognize the Tujias as a distinct nationality. That recognition did not come until 1956. In 1957 the government formally declared the establishhment of the Xiangxi Tujia-Miao Autonomous Prefecture in western Hunan Province. Twenty-three years later, in 1980, Hefeng Autonomous County was established, as was Laifeng Autonomous County in Hubei Province. In 1983 the government created the Exi Tujia-Miao Autonomous Prefecture in Hubei Province. Several other autonomous Tujian counties have recently been formed in Sichuan Province.

Tujia settlements range in size from barely one hundred people to more than 1,500 people. Villages are almost always located on lower slopes or valley floors near a river, lake, or stream so that access to water is readily available. They live in homes much like those of their Han neighbors: wood and stone construction with tile roofs. The two-story houses reserve the ground floor for family living and the upper floor for family meetings and a residence for the spirits of dead ancestors. Most Tujias farm fields in the valleys and terraced fields on mountain slopes. Their most important staple is wet rice, but they also raise potatoes, peppers, turnips, eggplants, sunflowers, and oranges. Pigs and chickens are raised commercially, as are cotton, beets, and tea. Tujians are also known for their loyalty to hunting and fishing. Contemporary anthropologists consider the Tujians to be a highly sinicized minority group.

Traditional Tujian society was patrilineal and patrilocal in residence. Cross-cousin marriages were preferred, and unions had to be lineage exogamous, although that became more and more difficult when so many Tujians took Han surnames, particularly Peng, Tian, and Xiang. Nuclear families constitute the most common Tujian household. Polygamy is not recognized. Tujian religion is an eclectic mix of animism, Daoism, Buddhism, and ancestor worship.

SUGGESTED READINGS: Lin Yueh-Hwa (Lin Yaohua) and Zhang Haiyang, ''Tujia,'' in Paul V. Hockings, ed., *The Encyclopedia of World Cultures*, vol. 6, *East and Southeast Asia*, 1991; Ma Yin, ed., *China's Minority Nationalities*, 1989; Peng Bo and Peng Xiumo, *Special Issue on Tujia Ethnicity*, 1981.

TUJIAZU. See **TUJIA.**

TULONG. See **DRUNG.**

TULUNG. See **DRUNG.**

TUMED. The Tumeds are one of the subgroups of the Mongol* people of the Inner Mongolian Autonomous Region in the People's Republic of China.

TUMIN. See **TUJIA.**

TUNBAO. The Tunbao people are one of the more curious ethnic groups who live today in the People's Republic of China (PRC), although PRC government demographers have not awarded formal recognition to the Tunbao as a minority nationality. Most of them can be found in the vicinity of Mount Yunjiu, about forty miles west of the city of Guiyang in Yunnan Province. Although they are primarily of Han* Chinese* descent, they maintain a distinct sense of identity. They first arrived in Yunnan in 1381. At that time, there was a political uprising against the Ming dynasty, and the Ming emperor deployed more than 300,000 troops to the region. The vast majority of the soldiers were Han Chinese.

After suppressing the rebellion, thousands of the soldiers decided to remain in the area. Most of them married women of Han, Miao,* and Yao* descent, and over time they began calling themselves ''Tunbao,'' which means ''old Chinese.'' When large numbers of Han Chinese immigrated into Yunnan Province in the sixteenth, seventeenth, and eighteenth centuries, the Tunbaos continued to distinguish themselves as a separate group of ''Chinese.'' Their sense of ethnicity even included feelings of superiority over other peoples.

Today, most Tunbaos work as farmers and continue to practice their own religion, which is an amalgam of Buddhism, Daoism, and Miao and Yao animism. In more than twenty local temples, Tunbaos carry out their religious worship. Tunbao women today can be identified by their knee-length, plain cotton gowns, white or blue silk belt around the waist, and black aprons. They coil their hair into a bun with a hairpin and handerchief holding it in place.
SUGGESTED READING: Chi Qian, ''The Tunbao: Ethnic Minority or Forgotten Chinese?,'' *China Today* 45 (December 1996), 35–41.

TUNG. See **DONG.**

TUNG VA WA. The Tung Va Was are considered by many ethnologists in the People's Republic of China to be a subgroup of the Wa,* an officially recognized minority nationality. Most Wa live in the southwestern reaches of Yunnan Province, primarily in Ximeng, Canghyuan, Menglian, Gengma, Lancang, Shuangjiang, Yongde, and Zhenkang counties. Tung Va Was are farmers, but their techniques vary from region to region, with some people using traditional slash-

and-burn methods and others employing more modern, sophisticated techniques. They raise wet rice, dry rice, maize, millet, tubers, and wheat. Classifying them as a subgroup of the Wa poses problems to ethnologists and ethnolinguists. The Tung Va Wa "dialect" is not mutually intelligible with most of the other Wa dialects, and because of that reality, most of the Tung Va Wa view themselves more as Tung Va Wa than as Wa. The process of ethnogenesis, which would enable them to see themselves primarily as Wa people, is not yet complete.

TUNG-AN. See **HUI.**

TUNGCHIA. See **DONG.**

TUNGHSIANG. See **DONGXIANG.**

TUNGJEN. See **DONG.**

TUNGUS. See **EVENK.**

TUNGUS. See **YAKUT.**

TUNGUSIC PEOPLE. The term Tungusic People is an older, linguistic reference to those indigenous people in the People's Republic of China and Siberian Russia who speak a language belonging to the Tungusic branch of the Tunguso-Manchu group within the Uralo-Altaic language family. It includes the Evens, Evenks,* and Negidals.*
SUGGESTED READING: Ivan A. Lopatin, "The Tungus Languages," *Anthropos* 53 (1958), 427–40.

TUREN. See **TU.**

TURFANLIK. See **UIGUR.**

TURK. See **TATAR.**

TURKIC PEOPLE. The term Turkic People is a term widely used in what used to be the Soviet Union and in the People's Republic of China to describe the indigenous peoples of those countries who speak a Turkic language. Included in this large group of people are the Bashkirs, Tatars,* Kumyks, Karachais, Balkars, Kazaks,* Kirgiz,* Karakalpaks, Nogais, Altais,* Gagauz, Azerbaijanis, Chuvashes, Khakass, Tuvinians, Tofalars, Yakuts,* Turkmen, Uigur,* Turks, Karaims, Dolgans, Shors,* and Uzbeks.* Most scholars believe that the Turkic people originated in Mongolia and then fanned out across Asia and into Europe. They first appear historically as an identifiable group in the sixth century. Their arrival in what was once the Soviet Union came in three stages. They had appeared in Central Asia and Siberia by the sixth century, in Transcaucasia in the eleventh century, and west of the Volga River in the thirteenth century. For the most part, the Turkic people became ethnically dominant in the areas they conquered, and the Turkic language spread widely.

The Turkic presence in Central Asia was signified by the rise of the Gokturk empire or "khaganate" in the sixth century when nomadic Semirech'e tribes consolidated politically. It survived until the eighth century when the Uigurs seized control; they eventually succumbed politically to the Kirgiz. By that time, various Turkic-speaking people had penetrated southern Siberia. In the eleventh century, the Seljuk-Oghuz tribes established an empire which reached from the Amu-Darya River in the east to the Euphrates River in the west. Turkic speakers spread throughout Transcaucasia. The Mongol* invasions of the thirteenth century constituted the final stage in the Turkic penetration of Central Asia.
SUGGESTED READINGS: Shirin Akiner, *Islamic Peoples of the Soviet Union*, 1983; Michael Dillon, *China's Muslims*, 1996; Ronald Wixman, *The Peoples of the USSR: An Ethnographic Handbook*, 1984.

TUYON. The Tuyons are a subgroup of the Kirgiz* people. They speak a Northern Kirgiz* dialect and can be found living today in Uqia County in the Xingiang Uigur Autonomous Region of the People's Republic of China.

TYITSO. The Tyitso people are an ethnic subgroup of the Hani* people, who are located primarily in the far southwestern reaches of Yunnan Province in the People's Republic of China. Other Tyitso communities exist in northern Laos, northern Thailand, and east central Myanmar (Burma). The Tyitso economy is largely a subsistence one, in which Tyitso farmers employ slash-and-burn techniques to raise maize, millet, tubers, and potatoes. For a cash crop they have produced tobacco for several decades, and more recently, Tyitso farmers have turned to opium as a cash crop, which they sell to Han* traders in exchange for metal tools, cloth, and different types of food. Foraging and hunting remain important economic and social activities. Indigenous Hani animism remains important to their religious beliefs.

TZU. See **TSOU.**

U

U. The U people speak a dialect of the Central Tibetan language and live in south central and southeastern Tibet in the People's Republic of China. The U dialect is itself divided into a number of regional subdialects and vernaculars. See **TIBETAN**.

UIGUR. The Uigur—also known as Aksulik, Kashgarlik, Uighur, Uyghur, Uighar, and Turfanlik—are a Turkic people who today are concentrated in the Xinjiang Uigur Autonomous Region of the People's Republic of China (PRC). Uigurs in Xinjiang can be found primarily in the Hotan, Kashgar, Turfan, Aksu, and Korla districts. They tend to live on land bordering the Taklamakan Desert and the Tarim Basin. The PRC census counted 7,215,000 Uigurs in 1990, but the Uigurs are experiencing a rapid population growth, so it is safe to say today that their population exceeds 7.5 million people. Another 2 million Uigurs can be found living today outside Xinjiang in Uzbekistan, Kazakstan, Kirgizstan, India, Pakistan, Afghanistan, and Turkmenistan. Uigurs constitute 80 percent of the population of the Xinjiang Province, where their language is recognized as the official one and Uigurs have been integrated into the region's political infrastructure.

The so-called Yellow Uigurs* are a Uigur constituency who really can no longer be considered a subgroup of the Uigur people of the PRC. In the ninth century, the Yellow Uigurs splintered off from the main Uigur community in the Xinjiang region and migrated to what is today Gansu Province. Over the years, the Yellow Uigur language has evolved quite differently from the other Uigur dialects, and it has adopted a wealth of Mongol* and Chinese* loan words. Today, Yellow Uigur is no longer intelligible to speakers of the other Uigur dialects. Yellow Uigurs are also religiously distinct from their Xinjiang brethren. Because they split in the ninth century, before the Uigur conversion to Islam, Yellow Uigurs remain faithful to their traditional Buddhist faith.

Along with Uzbek,* Uigur is a member of the Karluk division of the Turkic family of the Uralo-Altaic languages. Today, the Uigurs of the former Soviet Union are divided into two basic cultural groups based on differences in dialect and history. The southern Uigurs, or Fergana Uigurs, live in the Fergana Valley of Uzbekistan. Most of these Uigurs are in a state of advanced assimilation with the larger body of Uzbeks, and their dialect of Uigur, when they speak it, is laced with Uzbek words. The northern Uigurs, or Semirechie Uigurs, live in the Semirechie Region of Kazakstan. They have maintained a strong sense of Uigur identity, retaining their language and their culture and marrying endogamously.

In the Xinjiang Uigur Autonomous Region of the PRC, there are two primary Uigur dialects and a number of vernaculars. Hotan is the Uigur dialect spoken in southern Xinjiang, and Lop is the dialect spoken in eastern Xinjiang. The primary vernaculars of these two dialects are Kashgar, Aksu, Yarkant, Qomul, Lop Nur, Urumqi, Korla, Bugur, Kuqa, Kargalik, Guma, and Ili. Most Chinese Uigurs tend to identify themselves ethnically by the oasis town near which they live. Each oasis uses its own Uigur vernacular. All of the Uigur dialects and vernaculars employ an Arabic script.

The Uigurs are one of the oldest of the Turkic-speaking peoples of Central Asia. They originated with the nomadic tribes of eastern Turkestan in the third and fourth centuries, and until the eighth century they were part of the Juan-Juan Khanate. They then became part of the Turkic Khanate, but when it disintegrated in the eighth century, the Uigur underwent a process of ethnic consolidation and formed a Uigur state on the Orkhon River. That made them the rulers of the Mongol steppes. The Yenesei Kirgiz* overran the Uigurs in 840, expelling them from Mongolia, which precipitated a migration of some Uigurs to eastern Turkestan and Kansu, where they formed two independent states. Both of those Uigur states later fell victim to the Tanguts, Karakitais, and Mongols. During the era of Mongol domination, the Uigur language was a lingua franca in the area. By the fourteenth century, the term Uigur had fallen into disuse, and the Uigurs identified themselves by their place of residence, such as the Kashgarlik, or people of Kashgar, or by their occupations, such as the Taranchi, meaning "farmers."

In the mid-eighteenth century, the Manchus* of China established control over the Uigurs, and a long period of oppression and exploitation began. In the mid-1700s, the Chinese resettled approximately 6,000 Uigur families in the Ili Valley. Most of them were farmers—the Taranchis. Russia seized the Ili Valley in 1871, and when it was returned to China in 1882, most of the Taranchis moved farther west to remain under Russian* control. The Uigurs rebelled several times against Manchu domination in the eighteenth and nineteenth centuries.

The relatively few southern Uigurs were settled by Russian authorities in the Fergana Valley among the local Uzbeks and Kirgiz. Much smaller numbers of them were settled in Tajikistan and Turkmenistan. The northern Uigurs, who finally settled in the Semirechie region, came primarily from the Ili Valley in Xinjiang. Between 1881 and 1883, nearly 50,000 Ili Uigurs, escaping their abortive Muslim revolt against the Manchus, came to Russia, and Russian authorities settled them in isolated regions where they maintained their distinct identity. In 1884 the Xinjiang Uigurs, the Qing dynasty of the Han imperial government, took control of the province.

The Uigurs often migrated as whole villages, and as a result, they retained that decentralized identity. The Aksulak came from the village of Aksu, while the Kashgarlik migrated from the town of Kashgar in Chinese Turkestan. The Turpanlik, or Turfanlik, came from the town of Turfan. The Yarkenlik (Yarkendlik) traced their roots back to the town of Yarkend in Chinese Turkestan. After the victory of Mao Zedong in China in 1949, a second wave of Uigur emigrants settled in the Soviet Union to escape the political turmoil at home.

The eighteenth-century migration from Chinese Turkestan to Semirechie and the Fergana Valley led to dramatic changes in the Uigur lifestyle. For centuries they had practiced a pastoral nomadism which kept them on the move from oasis to oasis, but after the great migration they began to make the transition to settled agriculture. Uigur farmers settled permanently around the oases and worked small farms, raising melons, cotton, maize, peaches, plums, and wheat. In the cities and towns of the region, they became shopkeepers, merchants, and craftsmen. The more settled lifestyle also helped produce a more sophisticated Uigur literature. Such poets as Shair Akhun, Khislat Kashgari, Turdy Garibi, and Abduraim Nizari rose to prominence, and Uigur writers, in protest of the years of Manchu and Chinese oppression, developed a literature of social protest.

Over the centuries, the Uigurs have undergone a series of religious transformations, from their indigenous animistic shamanism to Buddhism to Manicheanism. But beginning around the tenth century, when Islam penetrated Central Asia and Turkestan, the Uigur began a conversion process which was complete by the fourteenth century. They were, and are today, Sunni Muslims of the Hanafi rite, and like so many other Muslim groups of Central Asia, the Uigurs have been heavily influenced by the Sufi orders. The eighteenth- and nineteenth-century migrations to Uzbekistan and Kyrgyzia intensified the Muslim devotion of the Uigur people.

The Bolshevik revolution had a dramatic impact on Uigur identity. Because of their location on the border between the Soviet Union and China, and the interest both countries had in maintaining the political loyalties of their border minorities, the Soviet Union encouraged, rather than discouraged, the development of Uigur national identity. They were not given an autonomous region, but at the All-Uigur Congress held in Tashkent in 1921, the Soviet Union allowed them to use the term Uigur to identify themselves. That was surprising, given the fact that many Uigurs had joined in the 1916 Kazak* rebellion against Russian authority. When the Uigurs were forced to adopt collectivization of farming in the 1920s and 1930s, several thousand of them fled to China to escape those political and economic pressures.

During World War II and in the years immediately following the war, Uigur nationalists—with the cooperation of a number of Kazak, Uzbek, and Kirgiz nationalists—managed to establish the Republic of East Turkestan. In 1944 the new nation claimed boundaries that included much of present-day Xinjiang as well as the eastern frontiers of Uzbekistan, Kazakstan, and Kirgizstan. The Soviet Union and China, of course, refused to recognize the new nation, but there was little they could do about it. For the Soviets, fighting the Germans on the western front was more important and immediate to national survival than whatever was taking place in Central Asia. China, of course, was preoccupied with fighting the Japanese occupation forces in Manchuria, eastern China, and southeastern China.

But with the defeat of Germany and Japan in the spring and summer of 1945, the Soviet Union and China began to reassert control over East Turkestan. The Russians moved in first. Soviet troops were dispatched to the Uzbek, Kazak, and Kirgiz Soviet Socialist Republics to secure the border with Xinjiang. At that point, the Republic of East Turkestan became an exclusively Xinjiang reality. China could do little about the republic's existence, beyond issuing formal protests, because of the civil war raging between Mao Zedong's Communists and the Kuomintang. But with Mao's triumph in 1949, the new People's Republic of China moved quickly to suppress the Xinjiang nationalist movement. The Republic of East Turkestsan ceased to exist in 1949.

Today, most Xinjiang Uigurs no longer engage in their traditional pastoral lifestyle. Centuries ago they made the transition to agriculture, and today they are sophisticated farmers, raising cotton, grains, and fruits on irrigated farms. They also raise sheep. In recent decades, large numbers of Uigurs have found their way into manufacturing, construction, and commerce. Their economy today is quite diversified.

Like so many other Central Asian groups, the Uigurs have been dramatically affected by the centrifugal forces of nationalism and political disintegration, although not so directly as several other groups. During the 1989 and 1990 ethnic violence and rebellion in the Fergana Valley of the former Soviet Union, many Uigurs joined Uzbeks, with whom they are rapidly assimilating, in their attacks on the Meskhetians and ethnic Russians. Unemployment and inflation in the region were severe, and economic hopelessness became a breeding ground for social unrest. The more northern Uigurs, whose sense of ethnic identity has always been more pronounced, revived the idea of an All-Uigur movement in the late 1980s and began trying to make contact with Uigur groups scattered throughout Tajikistan, Kazakstan, Kirgizstan, and Uzbekistan, as well as with the much larger Uigur community of the People's Republic of China.

Late in 1996, a spontaneous Uigur insurgency appeared for the first time in many years in Xinjiang. Tensions between Han* Chinese and the Turkic Uigurs had been mounting for several years. The revival of Islamic fundamentalism throughout Central Asia and the Middle East in the 1980s affected Uigur Muslims as well, creating in many of them a desire to see the Uigurs achieve in

Xinjiang what the Kazaks, Uzbeks, Kirgiz, and Tajiks* had achieved in the former Soviet Union: political independence. Some Uigurs also nurtured pan-Islamic feelings, hoping to create a single Islamic state in Central Asia that included Kazaks, Kirgiz, Tajiks, Tatars,* and Uzbeks. Most Uigurs also resent the ubiquitous statues of Mao Zedong erected by the PRC. To Muslims, such statues are offensive graven images. Given the linguistic, political, economic, and social differences between those peoples, to say nothing of the geopolitical implications of the rise of such an Islamic state, a Central Asian Islamic state is highly unlikely, but Chinese officials in Beijing are keeping a close watch on political and religious developments in Xinjiang.

Uigur nationalists have also been worried about what they considered to be the central government's concerted effort to assimilate them. Many Uigur leaders still fume over the treatment of Muslims during the years of the Cultural Revolution, and they feel that current policies, although less heavy-handed, are nevertheless still committed to the eventual disappearance of the Uigur people. For several decades, Beijing had implemented social and economic programs designed to encourage the settlement of Han people in western China, and they had arrived by the millions, steadily reducing the Uigur percentage of the total population of Xinjiang.

During the 1990s, the frustrations of Uigur nationalists erupted in Xinjiang. A series of bombings, kidnappings, and assassinations occurred, usually targeted at pro-Beijing figures in Xinjiang. Terrorist attacks on randomly selected Han Chinese people also escalated. In early February 1997, more than one thousand Muslim separatists rioted in the town of Yining, which is located in far western Xinjiang, just thirty miles from the border of Kazakstan. Government security forces crushed the rebellion, but not before ten people had been killed, more than one hundred injured, and five hundred arrested. The rioting was triggered by the attempt of a Han Chinese policeman to arrest a Uigur criminal suspect. When the Uigur resisted arrest, he was beaten. A crowd, which formed to witness the confrontation, soon turned into a mob and attacked several government buildings.

More trouble erupted later in the month. A series of bombings and terrorist attacks occurred in the city of Urumqi. Bombings of buses carrying Han people in other Chinese cities were also attributed by PRC officials to Uigur terrorists. Azat Akimbeck, a Uigur leader whose father was a leader in the establishment of the Republic of East Turkestan in 1944, told reporters, ''Uigurs will fight for our liberty and independence and we want to be as free as the other Asian republics of the old Soviet Union.'' For Akimbeck, only independence could resolve the problems of police brutality against Uigurs and anti-Islamic political pressures from the central government.

PRC officials reacted violently to the emergence of Uigur nationalism. The number of People's Liberation Army troops deployed to northwestern Xinjiang increased, as did the force with which demonstrators were attacked. PRC officials deported foreign journalists from the region to reduce the flow of information. Babur Makhsut, a former Communist turned Uigur nationalist, bitterly characterized government policies: "Their strategy," he claimed, "is to keep all Uigurs from enjoying their most fundamental human rights to practice their religion without persecution and to hold office in their own local governments. Their policy is to leave the Uigurs barefooted and so poor that they cannot even buy pants to wear."

Many Central Asian political scientists consider it quite unlikely, however, that Uigur nationalism will ever find political expression in real statehood. The southern Uigur in the Fergana Valley, for example, are too far along the road to assimilation with the Uzbeks, whereas the northern Uigur in Semirechie, although more overtly aware of their identity, have neither the historical experience nor the political infrastructure necessary for independence. The much larger body of Uigurs in the People's Republic of China do possess such an infrastructure, but the PRC would never acquiesce to a revival of the Republic of East Turkestan, at least not without a bloody fight. The PRC considers Xinjiang critically important to the security of China's western frontier; furthermore, foreign oil companies have recently located huge reserves of oil and natural gas in the region, and Chinese Communist party officials, given their economic development plans for the country, are not about to surrender the region or its resources to Uigur Muslim separatists.

SUGGESTED READINGS: Elizabeth E. Bacon, *Central Asia under Russian Rule*, 1966; Alexandre Bennigsen and S. Enders Wimbush, *Muslims of the Soviet Empire: A Guide*, 1986; *Current Digest* 41 (July 5, 1989); 16–18; Michael Dillon, *China's Muslim Nationalities*, 1996; Ned Gillette, "Adventure in Western China," *National Geographic* 159 (February 1981), 174–99; Dru Gladney, "The Ethnogenesis of the Uighur," *Central Asian Survey* 9 (1990), 1–27; Rick Gore, "Journey to China's Far West," *National Geographic* 157 (March 1980), 292–332; *Great Soviet Encyclopedia* 26:553–54, 1973; Li Chaochen, "Uygur Crafts and Customs in Old Kashgar," *China Reconstructs* 32 (April 1983), 18–21; David Lu, *Moslems in China Today*, 1964; Ma Yin, ed., *China's Minority Nationalities*, 1989; Colin Mackerras, ed., *The Uighur Empire according to the T'ang Dynastic Histories: A Study in Sino-Uighur Relations*, 1973; *New York Times*, June 15, 1983, and February 28, 1997; Peng Jianqun, "Uygur Craftsman Solves the Riddle of the 'Huxitar'," *China Today* 39 (June 1990), 44–46; S. Robert Ramsey, *The Languages of China*, 1987; Henry G. Schwarz, *The Minorities of Northern China: A Survey*, 1984; *Washington Post*, February 11, 1997; H. H. Wiens, "Change in the Ethnography and Land Use of the Ili Valley and Region, Chinese Turkestan," *Annals of the Association of American Geographers* 59 (1969), 753–75; Wong How-Man, "Peoples of China's Far Provinces," *National Geographic* 165 (March 1984), 283–377; I-fan Yang, *Islam in China*, 1957.

UIGURY. See **BURYAT.**

ULUKQIAT. The Ulukqiats, a subgroup of the Kirgiz* people, speak a Northern Kirgiz* dialect and can be found living today in Uqia County in the Xinjiang Uigur Autonomous Region of the People's Republic of China.

UPSIDE DOWN MIAO. See **MIAO.**

URANGKHAI SAKHA. See **YAKUT.**

URUMQI. Urumqi, one of the vernacular subgroups of the Uigur* language, is spoken in the Xinjiang Uigur Autonomous Region of the People's Republic of China. Most speakers of Urumqi live in and around the oasis community of Urumqi.

UYGUR. See **UIGUR.**

UZBEK. The Uzbeks, also known as Uzbeqs, are one of the tiniest recognized minority nationalities in the People's Republic of China (PRC). The 1990 Chinese national census counted only 14,592 Uzbeks, most of whom live in the cities of Yining, Qoqek (Tacheng), Kashgar, Urumqi, Yarkant, and Kargilik (Yecheng) in Xinjiang Province. Those cities are all located near the Xinjiang border with the new nation of Uzbekistan. The Uzbek population there exceeds fourteen million people today. Most PRC Uzbeks live at high elevations on the eastern slopes of the Pamir mountain range. There they can be found in close proximity to ethnic Tajiks.* Uzbek settlements can also be found today in Kazakstan, Kirgizstan, Turkmenistan, and Afghanistan. Most Uzbeks in Xinjiang also speak Uigur,* a similar language and one spoken by their ethnic neighbors, and many Uzbeks are in a state of advanced acculturation with Uigurs. In fact, it is extremely difficult for outsiders to distinguish Uzbeks from Uigurs in regions they mutually inhabit.

Uzbek is a Turkic (see **TURKIC PEOPLE**) language belonging to the large Altaic* linguistic family. But among the Uzbeks of the People's Republic of China, the language is changing rapidly. Because of the close association between Tajiks and Uzbeks in Xinjiang, the Uzbek language there has recently become closer and closer to Tajik, which is an Iranian language. The former nine-vowel system of traditional Uzbek has now become a six-vowel system identical to Tajik. The number of Tajik words that have made their way into Uzbek is today in the thousands.

Xinjiang Uzbeks, like other Uzbeks, are Muslims. In Central Asia, Islam has served as the social cement bringing together various tribes and clans. It was in the eighth century that Islam first reached the region known today as Uzbekistan. Conquering Arab armies brought the religion with them. They conquered Khiva in 711, and the surrounding regions soon fell in rapid succession, victims of Arab military skill and their own internal political rivalries.

In 1512 Uzbek tribes captured Samarkand, and their armies then radiated out and conquered most of what is modern Uzbekistan. The territory was then divided into three states ruled by Uzbek emirs or khans: Bukhara, Khiva, and Kokland. Powerful commercial relationships were soon established with Muscovy to the northwest, and over the next three centuries, the Uzbek states served as conduits for the exchange of goods between Russia and China. The contemporary Uzbek residents of China descend primarily from those traders. In the nineteenth century, however, the expansion of the Russian* empire into Central Asia accelerated, and by the 1860s the conquest of the Uzbeki states was complete.

Uzbeks resented the Russian expansion, and in 1898, Uzbeks in the Ferghana Valley rebelled. Their leader, Muhammed Ali Khalfa, a charismatic Sufi, launched a holy war, or jihad, against the Russian infidels. Russian troops crushed the rebellion, but in the process the Uzbeks earned a reputation for ferocious intransigence. Another jihad erupted in 1916 when tsarist officials tried to draft Uzbek men into the Russian army. This time, rebellion spread out from the Fergana Valley to other regions of Turkestan.

Uzbeks were also hostile to the Communist regimes that appeared in the Soviet Union and the People's Republic of China in the twentieth century. Both countries were officially atheistic and periodically engaged in intense persecution of their Muslim minorities. They outlawed the hajj—Muslims must make at least one pilgrimage to Mecca during their lifetimes—and prohibited the giving of alms, an obligation of well-to-do Muslims to assist their poorer compatriots. Communists insisted that the giving of alms was not necessary in Marxist society because poverty no longer existed. Mosques were often closed and mullahs persecuted.

Although the PRC government made great pretenses of allowing relative political autonomy to its religious minorities in the 1950s, the Cultural Revolution from 1966 to 1975 proved to Chinese Uzbeks that Chinese communism was no better than Russian communism. Red Guard cadres composed of fanatical Han* ideologues, went after every expression of religious sentiment in the country, and Muslims were targeted for intense persecution. In Xinjiang, the Uzbeks saw mosques closed, mullahs beaten, and Moslems forced to eat pork. Fasting during Ramadan earned Muslims lengthy prison sentences.

As a result of such persecution over the years, Uzbeks developed a strong sense of ''folk Islam.'' With their mosques closed, Korans unavailable, Muslim teachers in prison, and religious schools shut down, many Uzbeks reverted to a form of Islam that did not depend on formal instiutions. Their belief in Allah remained intact, but many adapted a type of animism to Islam, awarding spiritual significance to the graves of dead mullahs or to prominent geographical features.

Uzbeki nationalism in China has recently been greatly affected by the events taking place in the former Soviet Union. The disintegration of the Soviet Union accelerated in June 1990, when Uzbekistan declared its independence. After decades of suppression under Soviet rule, Uzbek culture underwent a renaissance. The Islamic Renaissance Party (IRP) steadily gained power, and Uzbek intellectuals intensified their demands for a revival of Uzbek culture.

Events in Uzbekistan had an impact in Xinjiang as well. The drive to establish Uzbek as the official language of Uzbekistan found much sympathy in Xinjiang, as did the desire to replace the Latin or Arabic script. Chinese authorities are playing their political hand carefully because they do not want to antagonize their Muslim minorities and generate Muslim rebellions on their western frontiers. Chinese political officials have been quick to respond militarily to the smallest sign of political insurgency among Uzbeks. They have also recently negotiated diplomatic agreements with Uzbekistan to protect the PRC-Uzbekistan border. To prevent Uzbeki nationalists from moving back and forth across the frontier, the agreement provides for PRC-Uzbekistan police cooperation in searching travelers for guns, explosives, currency, and propaganda literature.

Although a few Uzbeks in China are pastoralists who herd livestock in the northern reaches of Xinjiang, where they live among the Kazaks,* most are city dwellers who labor as merchants, factory workers, professionals, and craftsmen. They are readily identifiable by their distinctive dress. Uzbek men wear a turban cap, a long cotton skirt, baggy pants, and boots. Women are adorned with a red and white *chadar* (head shawl) and dresses with high yokes and long skirts. Uzbek intermarriage in Xinjiang with Uigurs and Kazaks is extensive today, giving rise to fears among some Uzbeks that their culture cannot long survive in the People's Republic of China.

SUGGESTED READINGS: Edward Allworth, *The Modern Uzbeks*, 1990; Wilfrid Blunt, *The Golden Road to Samarkand*, 1973; James Crithlow, *Nationalism in Uzbekistan: A Soviet Republic's Road to Sovereignty*, 1991; Ned Gillette, "Adventure in Western China," *National Geographic* 159 (February 1981), 174–99; Rick Gore, "Journey to China's Far West," *National Geographic* 157 (March 1980), 292–332; René Grousset, *The Empire of the Steppes: A History of Central Asia*, 1970; Ma Yin, ed., *China's Minority Nationalities*, 1989; Karl H. Menges, "People, Languages and Migrations," in Edward Allworth, ed., *Central Asia: 120 Years of Russian Rule*, 1989; *New York Times*, February 28, 1997; Michael Rywkin, *Moscow's Muslim Challenge*, rev. ed., 1990; Denis Sinor, ed., *The Cambridge History of Early Inner Asia*, 1990; Paul D. Steeves, *Keeping the Faiths: Religion and Ideology in the Soviet Union*, 1989; *Washington Post*, February 11, 1997; Wong How-Man, "Peoples of China's Far Provinces," *National Geographic* 165 (March 1984), 283–377.

UZBEQ. See **UZBEK.**

V

VA. See WA.

VACHANI. The Vachanis are a subgroup of the Sarikol* people, who are themselves a subgroup of the Tajiks* in the People's Republic of China.

VAKHAN. See WAKHAN.

VAKHI. See WAKHAN.

VANG. The Vangs are considered by many ethnologists in the People's Republic
of China to be a subgroup of the Wa,* an officially recognized minority nationality. Most Wa live in the southwestern reaches of Yunnan Province, primarily in Ximeng, Canghyuan, Menglian, Gengma, Lancang, Shuangjiang,
Yongde, and Zhenkang counties. Vangs are a farming people, but their techniques vary from village to village; some farmers use traditional slash-and-burn
methods, and others employ more modern, sophisticated techniques. They raise
wet rice, dry rice, maize, millet, tubers, and wheat. Classifying them as a subgroup of the Wa poses problems to ethnologists and ethnolinguists. The Vang
"dialect" is not mutually intelligible with most of the other Wa dialects, and
because of that reality, most Vangs tend to view themselves more as Vangs than
as Was. The process of ethnogenesis, by which they may come to regard themselves primarily as Wa people, is not yet complete.

VIETNAMESE. The Vietnamese are one of the smaller, though certainly not
the smallest, ethnic group in the People's Republic of China (PRC). There are
three distinct groups of Vietnamese living today in the PRC. Several thousand

ethnic Vietnamese can be found living in southern China along the coast of the South China Sea, primarily in the Shiwan Dashan region of the Guangxi Autonomous Region, just north of the Sino-Vietnamese border. Most of them are rice farmers who live in the vicinity of the Chinese city of Dongxing. They are simply the northernmost extension of Vietnamese society. The second group of ethnic Vietnamese are the Jings,* who live on three islands off the coast of Vietnam: Jiangwei, Wutou, and Shanxin. They first settled the islands in the fifteenth century as fishermen. Fishing has changed in recent years from small boats and bamboo rafts to motorized technologies. Jing culture reflects that maritime background. None of their pots or pans are ever placed upside down because it signifies a capsized ship. They never use the word "oil" because it resembles "swim" in Chinese, and the only Jing who ever swim are those whose ships have capsized. A third group of ethnic Vietnamese today live in Hong Kong, which on July 1, 1997, became part of the People's Republic of China.

Ethnographers believe that the Vietnamese people originated in southern China and over the course of the last several thousand years moved south to assume control over the eastern South China Sea coast of the Indochinese peninsula. During the last two millenia, the Vietnamese have developed a strong sense of rivalry with Han* Chinese,* primarily because of China's repeated inclination to invade Vietnam. Over the centuries, the Vietnamese frequently had to fight guerrilla wars to expel the Chinese. That battle became a central dynamic in Vietnamese history. An ancient Vietnamese proverb captured that dynamic: "Vietnam is too far from heaven and too close to China."

Although the vast majority of Vietnamese are Buddhists, the French empire, which lasted in Vietnam from the 1850s to 1954, imposed a veneer of Roman Catholicism on the country. Educated Vietnamese who interacted closely with French imperial authorities converted to Roman Catholicism. By 1954, when the Vietminh Communists defeated the French at the Battle of Dienbienphu and then managed, in the Geneva Accords, to expel France from Indochina, approximately 10 percent of the Vietnamese were Roman Catholics. The Geneva Accords divided Vietnam at roughly the seventeenth parallel. North Vietnam, officially called the Democratic Republic of Vietnam, was a Communist state with its capital in Hanoi. South Vietnam, officially named the Republic of Vietnam, was an anticommunist state with its capital in Saigon.

Between 1954 and 1973, the United States entered the Indochinese conflict on the side of South Vietnamese anticommunists and against Ho Chi Minh, North Vietnam, and South Vietnam. During the years of the American intervention in Vietnam, the South Vietnamese elite—often French-educated, Roman Catholic, and intensely anticommunist—associated closely with the United States military and civil administration. For a generation, American officials implemented U.S. military and political policies in South Vietnam through this South Vietnamese elite. South Vietnam had long been the enterprising, capitalist heart of Indochina, and the presence of the United States for twenty years in South Vietnam only reinforced those values.

In April 1975, when South Vietnam fell to the North Vietnamese army, that South Vietnamese elite found itself in a difficult position. Their pro-American pro-capitalist history made them vulnerable to ideological reprisals from the Vietcong and the North Vietnamese. Millions of Vietnamese had been killed and wounded during the conflict, and more than a few Vietnamese Communists held the South Vietnamese elite responsible. Almost as soon as North Vietnamese troops broke into the U.S. embassy grounds in Saigon on April 30, 1975, the refugee flight from South Vietnam began. American television viewers received a close-up look at the desperation of these South Vietnamese when they tried to get aboard the helicopters fleeing Vietnam from the roof of the U.S. embassy.

That refugee flight took place over the course of the next twenty years. Frightened South Vietnamese, most of them Roman Catholics, boarded flimsy boats and tried to make their way across the South China Sea to the Philippines and to Hong Kong (see **HONG KONGESE**). Hundreds of thousands of them died at the hands of pirates, bad weather, and starvation. Between 1975 and 1995, more than 400,000 Vietnamese refugees reached Hong Kong. British authorities there had signed agreements with the United States providing for the settlement of the refugees in America, Canada, and Western Europe.

By the 1980s, however, it had become obvious that most of the Vietnamese refugees who were reaching Hong Kong were fleeing from economic privation, not political persecution. Vietnamese were arriving faster than Hong Kong could resettle them. In 1989 Hong Kong announced a screening program to separate political refugees from economic immigrants, the goal being to resettle the political refugees and repatriate the economic immigrants. By 1995 the wave of Vietnamese immigrants became so heavy that authorities in Hong Kong announced a new policy refusing to accept any more boat people. Most of the Vietnamese were eventually resettled, but more than 10,000 remained living in Hong Kong.

The ultimate irony of their lives, of course, occurred on July 1, 1997, when Hong Kong reverted to the People's Republic of China. The Vietnamese had risked life and limb to make their way to freedom in Hong Kong, only to find themselves once again under the authority of a Communist regime. By that time, Hong Kong authorities had repatriated all but 2,000 ethnic Vietnamese and sent them back to Vietnam.

SUGGESTED READINGS: Nigel Cameron, *Hong Kong, The Cultured Pearl*, 1978; Peng Jianqun, ''Adding Tourism and Trade to an Old Tradition,'' *China Today* 42 (June 1993), 60 62.

VO. See **VU.**

VO LIMKOU. See **LIMKOU.**

VONUM. See **BUNUN.**

VU. The Vu (Vo) people are considered by many ethnologists in the People's Republic of China to be a subgroup of the Wa,* an officially recognized minority nationality. Most Vu live in the southwestern reaches of Yunnan Province, primarily in Gengma County, where they support themselves as slash-and-burn farmers who raise maize, millet, wet and dry rice, tubers, chickens, and pigs. Their ''dialect'' is not mutually intelligible with most of the other Wa dialects, and most Vus regard themselves more as Vu than as Wa.

VUNUN. See **BUNUN.**

W _____

WA. The Wa people are an officially recognized minority nationality in the People's Republic of China (PRC). They refer to themselves as the Va people, the Pa Rauk people, and the A Va people, as well as the Brao and Plao, all of which translate roughly as "people who live in the mountains." Their homeland, A Wa Shan, which means Mount A Wa, is located in the southern reaches of the Nu Shan mountains, which lie between Lancang Jiang and Nu Jiang. It is rugged country, with steep mountains reaching more than 9,000 feet in elevation.

Most Wa live in the southwestern reaches of Yunnan Province, primarily in Ximeng, Cangyuan, Menglian, Gengma, Lancang, Shuangjiang, Yongde, and Zhenkang counties. They are concentrated demographically in Ximeng and Cangyuan counties, where today they constitute more than 80 percent of the population. The Wa population ranges from 10 to 20 percent of the population in the counties of Menglian, Gengma, Lancang, Shuangjiang, Yongde, and Zhenkang. The other ethnic groups living among the Wa in these counties include the Dai,* the Lahu,* and the Han.* Other Wa groups can be found in the Baoshan, Dehong, and Xishuangbanna regions of Yunnan Province and across the border in Myanmar (Burma) and Thailand. Chinese demographers estimate a current Wa population of approximately 375,000 people.

The Wa people speak a language that is classified as part of the Mon-Khmer* branch of the Austroasiatic linguistic family. It is closely related to De'ang* and to Bulang,* which are spoken in Yunnan and Myanmar. They have a long-term, common history with De'angs and Bulangs. More than two thousand years ago, Han expansion reached Wa country. By the Tang dynasty of the seventh and eighth centuries, the Wa had begun to distinguish themselves ethnically from surrounding peoples, acquiring a sense of group identity based on language and religion. During the centuries of the Tang dynasty, they found themselves under the political domination of the Nanzhao Kingdom. The Dali Kingdom controlled them during the Song dynasty from the tenth to the thirteenth centuries.

Until then, the Wa people had consistently pursued a hunting and foraging lifestyle, with their social system based on matrilineal descent values. But changes came to Wa society during the Yuan and early Qing dynasties from the thirteenth through the eighteenth centuries. Massive in-migration of Han and Dai peoples during these years stimulated a dramatic change in the Wa economy, from hunting and foraging to agriculture, and the social system gradually changed from matrilineal to patrilineal descent. Farming became central to their economy and hunting became secondary, although it retained its ritualistic, ceremonial, and social importance. Those Wa groups that made the transition to settled agriculture earliest became known as "Tame Wa," while those who continued to hunt, forage, and practice headhunting were known as the "Wild Wa."

But there were other major distinctions among the Wa peoples. In fact, it is still difficult to speak of the Wa as a homogenous ethnic identity because they remain divided into so many linguistic subgroups. PRC officials continue to classify them as differences in dialect, but most Western linguists insist that, by definition, a dialect must be mutually intelligible with all of the other dialects of a language. If a dialect is not mutually intelligible with others, it actually constitutes a separate language, and if language constitutes the primary definition of ethnicity, then a dialect group should not be classified as a subgroup of another group whose language it cannot understand. Among the many so-called Wa subgroups of the PRC are the A Va, A Vo, A Wa, Amok, Benren, Da Ka Va, Hkawa, Hkun, Hkun Loi, Hsen, Hsensum, Kála, Ka Va, La, Lave, Lawa, Le Va, Lem, Loi, Loila, Maen, Mang Tam, Mok, Nya, Nyo, Pa Rauk, Praok, Pyin, Ravet, Tai Loi, Tung Va Wa, Va, Vu, Vo, Vang, Wu, and Xiao Ka Va.

In the nineteenth century, the process of ethogenesis among the various Wa peoples began to reach a new plateau. Until that time, individual Wa tribal groups had commanded more ethnic loyalty than the group as a whole. But political consolidation and ethnic consciousness reached a new level when seventeen Wa tribes came together militarily and politically to resist Great Britain's concerted attempt to extend their imperial authority from India and Burma into southwestern China. The Wa also became much more active in regional commerical markets, acquiring iron tools, cloth, tea, and weapons.

By the time of the Communist revolution in 1949, Wa society differed from region to region. In central A Wa Shan, more than 80 percent of all farmland was owned by private families. Remaining land was the common property of the village. In other Wa communities farther away from A Wa Shan, all land and forest animals belonged to hereditary princes and was rented out to Wa tenants or worked by farm laborers. Huge amounts of opium were produced on that land and sold for cash.

The Communist revolution introduced major economic, political, and social changes to Wa communities. In 1950 the central government outlawed opium production, an economic blow to Wa landlords and Wa peasants. Beginning in 1954, in a move to bring about a purely Marxist society, the central government abolished private property, collectivized agriculture, and organized all of the Was into so-called People's communes. The government nationalized all property, forced everybody to work for the commune and share economic resources, and required the sale of crop surpluses to the state at below-market prices. The government established the Menglian Dai, Lahu, and Wa Autonomous County in 1954 and the Gengma Dai and Wa Autonomous County in 1955. In 1964 and 1965, the government established new Wa autonomous counties in Ximeng and Cangyuan.

Today, the Wa people live in mountain villages that contain anywhere from one hundred to four hundred families. Houses are constructed of bamboo and elevated above the ground; the ground underneath is used for livestock. They are mountain farmers who use agricultural techniques consistent with different ecological settings. Some Wa farmers still use thirteenth-century slash-and-burn techniques and fertilize land with ashes and use a stick to plant seeds. Others combine slash-and-burn methods with plowing and hand seeding. Crop rotation, mixed-crop planting, and leaving land periodically fallow preserve fertility. Wheat, dry rice, maize, millet, and tubers are the most common products. Other Wa farmers cultivate rice paddies, but only where the land is level and access to water is relatively easy.

The social structure in Wa villages is based on patrilineal descent and clan membership. The nuclear family is the basic unit of society. The Wa can trace their ancestors back twenty to thirty generations because of a unique surname system. Each son's surname is a combination of his own given name and his father's surname, which also happens to be a combination of the father's and grandfather's names. Marriages are strictly exogamous by clan, and cross-cousin marriages are preferred. Property is passed from father to son.

Wa women can be identified by the clothing they wear. They dress themselves in dark blue, sleeveless, collarless blouses and skirts patterned in black, red, purple, blue, and yellow. The headdress is a collection of silver bands combined with a black headscarf or a woman's own hair coiled into a braid. They also wear a great deal of silver jewelry.

Wa spirituality continues to revolve around the indigenous faith. They maintain a unique creation story. According to Wa theology, the Wa people, who were the first people on the earth, originated in a cave on Mount A Wa. After they emerged from the cave, other people followed, including the Han, De'ang, Dai, Lahu, and Bulang. In fact, Was believe that all the people of the earth eventually followed them out of the cave on Mount A Wa. They are animists who believe that the environment is replete with unseen ghosts and spirits connected with animals, plants, heavenly objects, weather systems, and geographical landmarks. Those spirits are capable of interfering beneficially or malignantly with human affairs and influencing natural events. They also believe that the spirits of dead ancestors, if revered properly, can bless the lives of the living and protect them from the hostile acts of unseen spirits.

Two of the most memorable religious ceremonies of the Wa have been out-lawed since the Communist revolution. They were known for centuries through-out southwestern Yunnan Province for their headhunting proclivities. Wa religion demanded the heads of enemies to propitiate the grain god and guar-antee good harvests. They also believed that stacking human skulls into piles at the entrances of their villages would ward off evil spirits and bring good fortune to the Wa. Soon after the revolution in 1949, Chinese officials banned both practices. During the Cultural Revolution's ideological crusades of the late 1960s and 1970s, Red Guard cadres forced the Wa to abandon as superstitious their "cutting the tail of the oxen" ceremony, in which Wa villagers would spend seventeen days cutting the flesh off of dozens of live oxen. During those years, Wa religious leaders, known as *mobas*, were persecuted intensely, and they were unable to train a younger generation of *mobas*. As a result, many other traditional ceremonies and rituals have been lost.

SUGGESTED READINGS: Fang Dong, "A Long Road Upward for the Wa Nationality," *China Reconstructs* 31 (March 1982), 10–17; Peng Jianqun, "Bao Hongzhong, A Wa Headman," *China Today* 44 (July 1995), 56–58; Wang Aihe, "Wa," in Paul V. Hock-ings, ed., *The Encyclopedia of World Cultures*, vol. 6, *East and Southeast Asia*, 1991; Wen Yiqun, "Women of the Highlands," *China Today* 44 (May 1995), 33–35.

WA LON. The Wa Lons are one of the two subgroups of the so-called Wild Wa* people of Yunnan province in the People's Republic of China. See **WA** and **WILD WA.**

WA PWI. The Wa Pwis are one of the two subgroups of the so-called Wild Wa* people of Yunnan province in the People's Republic of China. See **WA.**

WAKHAN. The Wakhan people are the smaller of the two Tajik* subgroups, most of whom can be found living today in the Mountain Badakhshan Auton-omous Region of Tajikistan, Wakhan District in Afghanistan, the Chitral, Gilgit, and Hunza regions of northern Pakistan, and the far western reaches of the Xinjiang Uigur Autonomous Region of the People's Republic of China. Their numbers today are approaching 25,000 people, of whom approximately 3,500 are Chinese citizens. They speak a language that is classified as part of the Pamiri division of the southeastern group of Iranian languages. Beginning in the eleventh century, the Wakhans began to convert to the Ismaili sect of Islam. They remain Ismailis today.

WAKHI. See **WAKHAN.**

WANGJIAJI. The Wangjiajis are one of the subgroups of the Dongxiang* people, a Muslim group in the People's Republic of China. Their subdivision is based on minor, though mutually intelligible, language differences. The Wangjiaji dialect is spoken in the townships of Guoyan, Nalesi, and Daban in Dongxiang Autonomous County. About 30 percent of Dongxiangs speak Wangjiaji.

WANNING. The Wanning people are a subgroup of the Qiongwen* people, who are themselves a linguistic subgroup of the Min* language of Chinese* in the People's Republic of China and the Republic of China on Taiwan. Wanning speakers can be found today in Wanning and Lingshui counties in Hainan Province. See **HAN** and **MINNAN**.

WEIUR. See **UIGUR**.

WEIWUERH. See **UIGUR**.

WENCHANG. The Wenchang people are a subgroup of the Qiongwen* people, who are themselves a linguistic subgroup of the Min* language of Chinese* in the People's Republic of China and the Republic of China on Taiwan. Wenchang speakers can be found today in Wenchang and Qionghai counties in Hainan Province. See **HAN** and **MINNAN**.

WENMA. The Wenma people are a subgroup of the Zhuang* people of the People's Republic of China. The Wenma language is classified as one of the Southern Zhuang* dialects, and most of its speakers live today in Wenshan, Malipo, Maguan, and Kaiyuan counties in Yunnan Province.

WESTERN KHAM. The Western Kham people are ethnic Tibetans* who speak the western vernacular of the Kham* dialect. Speakers of Western Kham live in Gerze, Bangoin, Nyainrong, Xainza, Amdo, and Nagqu in the Tibetan Autonomous Region of the People's Republic of China.

WESTERN NAXI. See **NAXI**.

WHITE HORSE PEOPLE. See **BAIMA** and **QIANG**.

WHITE LAHU. See **LAHU**.

WHITE MIAO. See **MONKLAW**.

WHITE MONGOL. See **TU**.

WHITE-SKINNED MIAO. See **MONCHI**.

WHITE YI. See **YI**.

WILD NUCHEN. See **HEZHEN.**

WILD WA. The term Wild Wa, though widely used during the twentieth century in Burma and China, is hardly an ethnographic reference. Instead, it refers to various Wa* groups of people who continued the practice of headhunting well into the twentieth century. The term "Wild Wa" was used in contradiction to the "Tame Wa," who long ago abandoned ritualistic headhunting. The Wild Was divide themselves into two groups—the Wa Pwi and the Wa Lon.

WONI. See **HANI.**

WU. Not to be confused with the Han* people who speak the Wu* language of Chinese,* the Wus are considered by many ethnologists in the People's Republic of China to be a subgroup of the Wa,* an officially recognized minority nationality. Most Wus live in the southwestern reaches of Yunnan Province, primarily in Yongde County. They are slash-and-burn farmers who raise maize, millet, wet and dry rice, tubers, chickens, and pigs. Classifying them as a subgroup of the Wa poses problems to ethnologists and ethnolinguists. Their "dialect" is not mutually intelligible with most of the other Wa dialects, and most Wus view themselves more as Wu than as Wa.

WU. The term "Wu" is used here to describe people of Han* descent who speak the Wu Chinese* language as their native tongue. The Wu language is spoken by more than 85 million people, the vast majority of whom live along the Yangtze Delta and in and around the city of Shanghai. Jiangsu and Zhejiang provinces in the People's Republic of China are the areas where most Wu speakers can be found today.

Discussing the structure of the Chinese language is not as simple a matter as it might appear, primarily because the government of the People's Republic of China insists on maintaining the fiction that there is only one Chinese dialect, and that it is divided into a series of dialects. To argue otherwise would require government officials to recognize major ethnic divisions within the dominant Han people, something Chinese officials have been extremely reluctant to do.

Most linguists in the West, however, argue that the definition of "dialect" means that it is mutually intelligible with other dialects of the same language. The Chinese government claims that eight dialects of the language exist within the national boundaries: Mandarin,* Jin,* Wu, Gan,* Xiang,* Hakka,* Yue,* and Min.* The problem with that definition, of course, is that none of these so-called dialects is mutually intelligible with any other. The people who speak them may very well be united by their Han descent and their shared eclectic mix of Buddhist, Daoist, and Confucian religious beliefs, but they cannot understand one another's spoken languages, which should render them members of different ethnic groups. Complicating the issue even more is the fact that each of the eight Chinese languages possesses many dialects, and some of those dialects are not mutually intelligible to speakers of related dialects.

At the same time, however, they share an unusual linguistic similarity. The spoken Chinese languages cannot be mutually understood by different speakers, but they all employ the same written script, which is mutually readable. Some linguists have begun to use the term "regionalect" to describe the eight Chinese languages. Whether or not Mandarin, Jin, Wu, Gan, Xiang, Hakka, Yue, and Min are dialects, regionalects, or languages, they divide the more than 1.1 billion Han people into distinguishable, individual groups whose members share loyalty and a sense of identity with one another because of language. There are a number of Wu dialects, although the dialect of the city of Shanghai is considered the standard, the measure by which all other Wu dialects are measured.

Contemporary ethnolinguists break down the Wu language into a variety of dialects and subdialects, some of which are not mutually intelligible to one another. A widely accepted classification system divides Wu into six major subcategories: Taihu, Taizhou, Oujiang, Wuzhou, Chuqu, and Xuanzhou. The Taihu dialect possesses six subdialects: Piling, Suhujia, Tiaoxi, Hangzhou, Linshao, and Yongjiang. Chuqu has two subdialects: Chuzhou and Longqu.
SUGGESTED READINGS: William L. Ballard, "Phonological History of Wu," Ph.D. diss., University of California, Berkeley, 1969; S. Robert Ramsey, *The Languages of China*, 1987; S. A. Wurm, B. T'sou, D. Bradley, et al., eds., *Language Atlas of China*, 1987.

WUHUA. The Wuhua people are a dialect subgroup of Yue*-speaking Han* Chinese.* Approximately 1.1 million people speak Wuhua, and most of them live in the Wuchuan, Huazhou, and Zhanjiang regions of Guangdong Province. See **HAN** and **YUE**.

WUMAN. See **NAXI**.

WUMAN. See **NAXI**.

WUMING. See **ZHUANG**.

WUNAI. Wunai is a subdialect of the Bunu* language, which is part of the larger Yao* cluster of languages in the People's Republic of China.

WUTAI. The Wutai people are a subgroup of the Jin*-speaking Han* Chinese.* Most Wutais live today in thirty cities, counties, and banners of northern Shanxi Province and northern Shaanxi Province, as well as in the Houtao Prefecture in the Inner Mongolian Autonomous Region of the People's Republic of China.

WU'TZUPIEHK'O. See **UZBEK**.

WUZHOU. The Wuzhou people are a linguistic subgroup of Wu*-speaking Han* people in the People's Republic of China. Wuzhu speakers total more than four million people and live in the Jinhua, Lanxi, Pujiang, Yiwu, Dongyang, Pan'an, Yongkang, Wuyi, and Jiande regions of Zhejiang Province. See **WU** and **HAN**.

X

XA CAO. See **KMHMU.**

XAN LAO. See **GELAO.**

XIANG. The term "Xiang" is often used today to refer to people of Han*
descent who speak the Xiang Chinese* language. Discussing the structure of
the Chinese language is not as simple a matter as it might appear, primarily
because the government of the People's Republic of China insists on maintaining
the fiction that there is only one Chinese dialect, and that it is divided into a
series of dialects. To argue otherwise would require government officials to
recognize major ethnic divisions within the dominant Han people, something
Chinese officials have been extremely reluctant to do.

Most linguists argue, however, that the definition of "dialect" means that it
is mutually intelligible with other dialects of the same language. The Chinese
government claims that eight dialects of the language exist within the national
boundaries: Mandarin,* Wu,* Jin,* Gan,* Xiang, Hakka,* Yue,* and Min.* The
problem with that definition, of course, is that none of these so-called dialects
is mutually intelligible with any other. The people who speak them may very
well be united by their Han descent and their shared eclectic mix of Buddhist,
Daoist, and Confucian religious beliefs, but they cannot understand one another's spoken languages, which should render them members of different ethic
groups. Complicating the issue even more is the fact that each of the eight
Chinese languages possesses many dialects, and some of those dialects are not
mutually intelligible to speakers of related dialects. There is also a great variety
of vernaculars.

At the same time, however, they share an unusual linguistic similarity. The spoken Chinese languages cannot be mutually understood by different speakers, but they all employ the same written script, which is mutually readable. Some linguists have begun to use the term ''regionalect'' to describe the eight Chinese languages. Whether or not Mandarin, Wu, Gan, Xiang, Hakka, Jin, Yue, and Min are dialects, regionalects, or languages, they divide the more than 1.1 billion Han people into distinguishable, individual groups whose members share loyalty and a sense of identity with one another because of language.

Xiang, one of the eight recognized Chinese languages, is spoken by more than 50 million people—approximately 4.8 percent of all speakers of Chinese. Hunan Province is home to most of the contemporary Xiang speakers. The region is surrounded on the north, west, and southwest by Mandarin speakers. Like Gan, Xiang is considered a transitional tongue between the northern and southern Chinese languages. Different Xiang dialects exist all along the Gan River drainage system in Jiangxi, although most of them are mutually intelligible, at least on a fundamental level. Ethnolinguists divide Xiang into two so-called dialect groups, although the two are not readily understandable to one another. New Xiang* is the dominant language in northwestern Hunan Province, and it is also the most common language in Hunan's cities, large towns, trade routes, and markets. Old Xiang,* which is spoken primarily in rural areas, is quite different from New Xiang. In fact, the two peoples cannot readily understand one another. Speakers of New Xiang and Southwestern Mandarin,* however, do understand one another, leading some ethnolinguists to classify New Xiang as a dialect of Southwestern Mandarin. Consequently, classifying New Xiang speakers as part of the Xiang language family is quite impossible, as is clustering them together with Old Xiang speakers as a single ethnic group. There are three major Xiang dialects in Hunan Province and in the Guangxi Zhuang Autonomous region: Changyi, Loushao, and Jixu.

SUGGESTED READING: S. Robert Ramsey, *The Languages of China*, 1987.

XIANG XI. Xiang Xi is one of the primary dialects of the Miao* language of the People's Republic of China. Also known as Western Hunan Miao, it is spoken by more than 800,000 people in western Hunan Province and eastern Guizhou Province. Xiang Xi is divided into two dialects: western and eastern. The western local dialect is spoken in Huayuan, Fenghuang, Jishou, Baojing, Guzhang, and Longshan counties in Hunan Province; Songtao and Tongren counties in Guizhou Province; and Hechi and Nandan counties in the Guangxi Zhuang Autonomous Region. The eastern local dialect is spoken by nearly 100,000 Miaos in Luxi, Jishou, Guzhang, and Longshan counties in Hunan Province.

XIAO KA VA. The Xiao Ka Vas are considered by many ethnologists in the People's Republic of China to be a subgroup of the Wa,* an officially recognized minority nationality. Most Wa people live in the southwestern reaches of Yunnan Province, primarily in Ximeng, Cangyuan, Menglian, Gengma, Lancang, Shuangjiang, Yongde, and Zhenkang counties. They are concentrated demographically in Ximeng and Cangyuan counties. Most Xiao Ka Vas are farmers, but their techniques vary from village to village; some farmers use traditional slash-and-burn methods, and others employ more modern, sophisticated techniques. They raise wet rice, dry rice, maize, millet, tubers, and wheat. Classifying them as a subgroup of the Wa poses problems to ethnologists and ethnolinguists. The Xiao Ka Va "dialect" is not mutually intelligible with most of the other Wa dialects, and because of that reality, most Xiao Ka Vas view themselves more as Xiao Ka Va than as Wa. The process of ethnogenesis, which would enable them to see themselves primarily as Wa people, is not yet complete.

XIAOSHAN. See JINGPO.

XIBE. The Xibes (Xibos), or Sibes (Shives), are an officially recognized minority nationality in the People's Republic of China (PRC). National census takers counted 172,847 Xibes in 1990, but today that number probably exceeds 185,000 people. They can be found today in Liaoning Province and on the banks of the Ili River in the Xinjiang Uigur Autonomous Region. They also reside along the Tekes River and in and around the towns of Qapchal, Gongliu, Tekes, and Zhaosu. They speak a language that is classified in the Manchu* cluster of the Manchu-Tungus branch of the Altaic* linguistic family. In fact, many linguists consider Xibe to be a dialect of Manchu. There is no original writing system for Xibe, but they have adapted a Manchu written script to their own use.

Xibes trace their origins back to the Xibe people, an ancient hunting, fishing, and foraging group in Liaoning Province, which today borders North Korea and Inner Mongolia in far northeastern China. They came under Mongol* domination in the thirteenth century and Manchu control in the late sixteenth century. The Manchu leader at the time was a man named Nurhachi, who imposed political order on the Xibes and forced them into permanent agricultural settlements. The Manchus certainly recognized Xibes as cultural kinsmen, but they also feared the Xibe warrior spirit. In the 1690s, the Manchu government distributed Xibe soldiers throughout the country, from Beijing to Xinjiang. That relocation process continued throughout much of the eighteenth century. Over the centuries, these relocated Xibes came under increasing Han* control as the Chinese imperial government resettled ethnic Hans in Liaoning Province. Inevitably, they began to acculturate to many Han institutions.

Late in the seventeenth century, during the Qing dynasty, Chinese imperial officials began relocating Xibe military leaders and some civilian administrators to frontier areas, as well as to Beijing and to large cities in Liaoning. That process accelerated in the mid-eighteenth century, when 5,000 Xibe soldiers relocated across the country to Xinjiang Province in northwestern China. Their assignment was to provide political and military control over recently conquered peoples, who were known collectively as the Jungars.

That mid-eighteenth century process of resettlement explains why today the Xibes are divided into two subgroups and separated by thousands of miles of territory in northern China. The Liaoning, or Northwestern, Xibes today are in a state of increasingly advanced acculturation and assimilation to Han values, since they have been surrounded by a majority Han Chinese population for so long. The Xinjiang Xibes, on the other hand, are more conservative, less acculturated to Han institutions, and less likely to speak a Chinese* dialect.

The two groups of Xibes live somewhat different lifestyles. In Xinjiang, the Xibes live in walled villages that contain anywhere from one hundred to two hundred houses. They are farmers who raise wheat, wet rice, cotton, sesame, and a variety of fruits and vegetables. Given their more isolated location in the far west, Xinjiang Xibes remain quite loyal to hunting. In the northeast, where the Liaoning Xibes live, villages are larger and hunting as an economic activity is a thing of the past. Liaoning Xibe society is far more integrated into the regional and national economy than that of the Xinjiang Xibes.

Because of the rapid pace of acculturation and assimilation now occurring, the Xibe language is spoken as a native tongue only among 20,000 or so people who live in the Xibo Autonomous County, which is located in the Ili River Valley near the western edge of Xinjiang. These Xibe poeple are direct descendents of Manchu soldiers stationed in the region.

Not surprisingly, the indigenous Xibe religion remains active among the Xinjiang Xibes but has all but disappeared among Liaoning Xibes, who have adopted Daoism, Buddhism, and Chinese ancestor worship. A few Xibes are devout Lamaist Buddhists. Many Xinjiang Xibes still maintain devotion to a polytheistic theology, in which the most prominent positions are occupied by the Insect King, the Earth Spirit, the Dragon Spirit, the god Xilimama, who is responsible for domestic tranquility, and the god Hairkan, whose primary responsibility is the protection of livestock. The Smallpox Spirit long held a prominent position in the Xibe pantheon, but the World Health Organization's successful global campaign against the disease has eliminated such fears and the need for such a deity.

SUGGESTED READINGS: Paul V. Hockings, "Xibe," in Paul V. Hockings, ed., *The Encyclopedia of World Cultures*, vol. 6, *East and Southeast Asia*, 1991; Long Shan, "The Xibo People—'Guardians of the Frontier,' " *China Reconstructs* 34 (February 1985), 24–26; Ma Yin, ed., *China's Minority Nationalities*, 1989; Henry G. Schwarz, *The Minorities of Northern China: A Survey*, 1984.

XIFAN. See PUMI.

XIN. The Xins are one of the many subgroups of the Li* people of Hainan Province in the People's Republic of China. Like other Li groups, they have earned a reputation over the years for their ferocious anti-Han* xenophobia, which has often taken the form of guerrilla warfare against Han immigrants to Hainan. Their hatred of the Nationalist government in the 1930s and 1940s also made them willing allies of Mao Zedong and the Communists, and when Mao triumphed, the Lis were afforded recognition as heroes. Most Xins today are farmers who raise coconuts, coffee, cocoa, sisal, rubber, cashews, pineapples, mangoes, and bananas. Rice is their staple.

XINGAN. The Xingan people speak a dialect of Gan,* one of the primary languages spoken by Han* Chinese* people in the People's Republic of China. Most Xingan speakers live in southern Jiangxi Province.

XINGHUA. The Xinghua people are a linguistic subgroup of the Yuetai Hakka* people of the People's Republic of China (PRC). Xinghuas today can be found living in the Xingning, Wuhua, Dabu, Fengshun, and Zijin regions of Guangdong Province in the PRC. Approximately 3.4 million people speak Xinghua.

XINHUI. The Xinhui people are a linguistic subgroup of the Yuetai* Hakka* people of the People's Republic of China (PRC). Xinhuis today can be found living in the Xinfeng, Huiyang, Huidong, Bao'an, Longmen, Fogang, Qingyuan, Conghua, Zengcheng, Haifeng, Lufeng, and Dongguan regions of Guangdong Province in the PRC. Approximately 2.4 million people speak Xinhui.

XINJIANG XIBE. The Xinjiang Xibes consist of Xibe* people who live in the Xinjiang Uigur Autonomous Region. They constitute a subgroup of the Xibes and are known for a conservative loyalty to indigenous traditions.

XINPING DAI. Xinping Dai is one of the six written versions of the Dai* language of southwestern China and the northern reaches of southeast Asia. People who read and write the language are sometimes referred to as Xinping Dai.

XISHUANGBANNA DAI. Xishuangbanna Dai is one of the six written versions of the Dai* language today. Of all the Dai written scripts, Xishuangbanna is probably the most widely used. It is especially prominent in the Xishuangbanna region of Yunnan Province in southwestern China.

XIUGULUAN AMI. The term Xiuguluan Ami is used to refer to the so-called Central Ami or Coastal Ami* living on the island of Taiwan in the Republic of China. See **AMI**.

XUNXHUAN. See **ACHANG**.

Y

YAKHU. The Yakhus are a subgroup of the Rai* people, who are themselves one of the two subgroups of the Kiranti* people of Nepal. See **NEPALESE.**

YAKUT. The Yakuts (Iakuts), who call themselves the Sakha (Saka), have also been known historically as the Tungus, Jekos, and Urangkhai Sakha. They are numerically the largest of the ethnic groups in Russian Siberia. The Yakut population has increased from 296,244 people in 1970 to 328,018 in 1979 to more than 400,000 in 1997. Most Yakuts live in what used to be the Yakut Autonomous Soviet Socialist Republic and in immediately adjacent areas.

Their language is part of the northeastern branch of the Turkic languages (see **TURKIC PEOPLE**), although its vocabulary is laced with Mongol* and Tungusian words. Such Yakut clan names as Osekuji, Ontuls, Kokui, Kiriks, Kyrgydays, and Orgots indicate their Siberian origins; other clan names reveal Turkish beginnings. Within that Turkic language branch, however, Yakut is somewhat isolated and is not highly subdivided into different dialects. Its distinctiveness is the natural result of their demographic isolation from other Turkic speakers since the fourteenth century. There are relatively few regional differences in Yakut dialects. All of them are mutually intelligible and quite similar to one another. Most Russian* ethnographers suspect the Yakuts have descended from a mix of people from the area of Lake Baikal, Turkish tribes from the steppe and Altai mountains, and indigenous people of Siberia, particularly the Evens and Evenks.*

The Yakuts themselves are divided into two primary groups based on geography and economics. Agriculture was possible only in the southern areas along the middle stretches of the Lena River, although the Yakuts did not make the transition to sedentary farming until the nineteenth century. The Yakut groups living farther north in what was once the Yakut Autonomous Soviet Socialist Republic are seminomadic hunters, fishermen, and reindeer breeders like so many of the other northern people of Siberia. They have traditionally been poorer than their southern neighbors. Yakut fisherman caught carp, mundu, muksun, and salmon in the rivers and lakes of the region, while Yakut hunters took squirrels, hares, elk, foxes, bear, deer, ermine, partridge, geese, wild reindeer, and ducks. They smoked the meat and transformed the hides into pelts, which they used for clothing or as trade items. The reindeer-breeding Yakuts used the animals primarily for transportation, milk products, and sale.

Farther to the south, where temperatures were slightly more moderate, the Yakuts were pastoralists who raised horses and cattle. Their livestock pursuits have traditionally distinguished these Yakuts from the other ethnic groups of Siberia. They were seminomadic and used horses and cattle for hides, meat, milk, and transportation. During the late eighteenth and early nineteenth centuries, the Yakut pastoralists went through a transition when cattle raising became more economically important than horse breeding. Some of these Yakuts also engaged in reindeer breeding. The Yakuts working in animal husbandry were also familiar with the range grasses of Siberia and harvested them with scythes in order to feed their animals during the long winter months. Because of their skills in working with horses, these southern Yakuts also developed sophisticated blacksmithing skills, extracting iron ore and smelting it in primitive forges.

When ethnic Russians first arrived in the region of Yakutia in the 1620s, the Yakuts were living between the Lena and Amga rivers, the lower Viliui and Olekma rivers, and the upper Iana River. They functioned in a seminomadic, subsistence economy, moving their cattle herds twice yearly between summer and winter pastures. The more northern Yakut groups were engaged primarily in hunting, fishing, and reindeer breeding. When the Russians first arrived, the Yakuts were divided into about eighty patriarchal clans, with strong nuclear families the focus of social life. Even at that point, however, the clan-tribal loyalties were beginning to break down, and the Yakuts were acquiring a broader sense of ethnic identity. That broader sense of identity led to the creation of the *toyon* class, an elite group of Yakuts who controlled large amounts of land and cattle and horse herds and who held other Yakuts in slavery or other forms of bondage. Much of Yakutia was in an essentially feudal state when the Russians began arriving.

Russia annexed Yakutia in the 1620s and imposed a fur tax on the Yakuts. Soldiers and merchants poured into the area to crush any Yakut resistance. The tribute taxes, which the Yakuts paid in sable and fox furs, were oppressive, requiring the Yakuts to ignore their cattle herds in order to secure enough pelts for the tax. The Yakuts rose up in rebellion against Russians several times between 1634 and 1642, but in each case they were crushed. The violence, along with the introduction of a variety of European diseases, took its toll on the Yakut population. Large numbers of Yakuts tried to escape Russian influence by migration. That became more common as the fur resources of the region became depleted in the eighteenth century. By the end of the eighteenth century, there were new Yakut settlements on the Kolyma, Indigirika, Olenek, and Anabar rivers.

During the eighteenth century, as Russia annexed territories to the east— Kamchatka, the Chukchi Peninsula, the Aleutian Islands, and Alaska—Yakutia became a thoroughfare between eastern and western Siberia. More ethnic Russians settled in the area, and the Yakuts were increasingly incorporated into the regional cash economy. The completion of the mail route in 1773 brought more Russians in, as did the construction of convict camps to which the tsars sent their political opponents. In 1846 gold was discovered in Yakutia, and the discovery brought a new deluge of Russian settlers. Construction of the Siberian Railroad in the 1880s and 1890s, as well as the development of commercial shipping on the Lena River, accelerated the commercialization of the region. Southern Yakuts made the transition to sedentary agriculture, maintaining cattle herds but also turning to the production of oats, rye, barley, potatoes, and vegetables.

The Bolshevik revolution had a dramatic impact on Yakut life. Yakuts had developed a strong sense of ethnic nationalism before the Bolshevik revolution. Yakut written literature began to appear in the late 1800s and early 1900s from the pens of such people as A. E. Kulakovskii, A. I. Sofronov, and N. D. Neustroev. Yakut nationalists formed the Yakut Union in 1906 and demanded that all Yakut lands seized by the state, the Russian Orthodox Church, and ethnic Russians be returned to the Yakut people. The new Soviet government issued the Declaration of the Rights of the Peoples of Russia in 1917, which guaranteed the "equality and sovereignty of the peoples of Russia; the right of self-determination, including separation and the formation of independent states; abolition of all national and national-religious privileges or restrictions; and free development of national minorities and ethnic groups inhabiting the territory of Russia." Because the Yakuts were by far the largest of the northern peoples, there was little doubt that at least the appearance of ethnic autonomy would be extended to them. In 1922 the Soviet Union established the Yakut Autonomous Soviet Socialist Republic (ASSR), with 3,103,200 square miles carved out of the Russian Republic.

But disaster struck the Yakuts in 1928, when Joseph Stalin launched the collectivization campaign against Yakut pastoralists, breeders, and hunters, and the Yakuts violently resisted the loss of their property and the imposition of new lifestyles. The Soviet government ruthlessly implemented the decree, and tens of thousands of Yakuts disappeared. In 1926, on the eve of the campaigns, there were 240,709 ethnic Yakuts in the Soviet Union. Demographers do not know exactly how many Yakuts Stalin eliminated, but as late as 1963 the Yakut population had not recovered to its precollectivization level. It was an enormous purge, a bloodletting from which the Yakuts did not recover for decades. In 1928 the Central Committee of the All-Union Communist party purged the local

Yakut leaders of the Yakut ASSR, dissolved all ethnic Yakut organizations, and prohibited Yakut publications. Subsequent purges during the 1930s wiped out another level of Yakut leadership.

During the collectivization crusade and the purges, thousands of ethnic Yakuts fled Russian Siberia for Heilongjiang Province in northwestern China, where they remain today. The People's Republic of China does not recognize the Yakuts as an official minority nationality, but they exist nonetheless. At the time of their migration in the 1920s and 1930s, Yakuts often settled among existing Evenk communities, and Chinese demographers and ethnologists, rather than trying to distinguish between the various groups of seminomadic pastoralists, chose to lump the Yakuts together with the Evenks and call them all Evenks. That classification continues today, even though most Northeast Asian anthropologists know that the Yakuts outnumber the Evenks in terms of their population. As many as five thousand Yakuts may be currently classified as Evenks.

SUGGESTED READINGS: Alice Bartels and Dennis Bartels, "Soviet Policy toward Siberian Native People," *Canadian Dimension* 19 (1985), 36–44; Mike Edwards, "Siberia: In from the Cold," *National Geographic* 177 (March 1990), 2–49; Péter Hajdú, *Samoyed Peoples and Languages*, 1962; F. George Heine, "Reindeer Breeders in China," in Thomas Heberer, ed., *Ethnic Minorities in China: Tradition and Transformation*, 1984; Constantine Krypton, "Soviet Policy in the Northern National Regions after World War II," *Slavic Review* 13 (October 1954), 339–53; Walter Kolarz, *The Peoples of the Soviet Far East*, 1969; Peng Jianqun, "A New Life for the Yao of the Dayao Mountains," *China Today* 41 (August 1992), 60–62; Piers Vitebsky, "Perestroika among the Reindeer Herders," *Geographical Magazine* 61 (June 1989), 23–34.

YAMI. The Yamis are one of the nine tribal indigenous peoples in the Republic of China. With a population of less than 5,000 people, they are also the smallest of the indigenous groups. They speak an agglutinative, Austroasiatic language whose origins are in the central and south Pacific. In fact, many ethnologists consider the Yami people to be of Melanesian descent, related closely to other people of the east central Pacific. Their language is mutually intelligible with Ivatan, a dialect of the Batan peoples of the Batan Islands in the Philippines.

The vast majority of Yamis live on Orchid (Lanyu) Island, which is located about forty-four miles off the southeastern coast of Taiwan. Yami also possesses some similarities to the language spoken by the Paiwan* people of Taiwan (see **TAIWANESE**), even though the Paiwans are of Polynesian origins and the Yamis are Melanesian.

The Yami economy and political organization revolve around fishing. They form fishing and distribution cooperatives based on kinship bonds within villages. The Yamis are also subsistence farmers who raise sweet potatoes, yams, and millet. They live in nuclear families and have patrilocal and patrilineal social systems. The Yami religion is an animistic one in which the fear of evil, malignant ghosts is endemic. Yamis are convinced that ghosts exercise real power over their lives, and although shamanism does not exist among them, they nevertheless manipulate magic amulets to ward off evil influences. Unlike the other indigenous peoples of the Republic of China, the Yami have never practiced headhunting.

SUGGESTED READINGS: Raleigh Ferrel, *Taiwan Aboriginal Groups: Problems in Cultural and Linguistic Classification,* 1969; *The Republic of China Yearbook* 1995, 1996; Te-hsuing Yao, *Formosan Aboriginal Culture Village,* 1988; Yvonne Yuan, "Migrate, Assimilate, or Integrate?" *Free China Review* 42 (June 1992), 4–15.

YANGUANG. The Yanguang (Yanghuang) people, also known as Raus and Tens, are a subgroup of the Zhuang* people of the People's Republic of China (PRC). The Yanguang language is classified as one of the Southern Zhuang* dialects, and most of its speakers live today in Yanshan, Guangnan, Malipo, Maguan, and Wenshan counties in Yunnan Province and in Pingtang, Huishui, and Dushan counties in Guizhou Province. Their current population is approximately 25,000 people. The Yanguang language is part of the Dong-Shui* branch of the Zhuang-Dong group of Tai* languages. It is distinctive enough from the other Dong-Shui languages to convince ethnolinguists that they separated ethnically centuries ago. A written script for Yanguang is not in existence, but literate Yanguangs can read and write Mandarin Chinese.* Most people can also speak a local Chinese dialect.

Yanguang country was independent of Han* authority until the thirteenth century, when Chinese armies and then political administrators occupied Guangxi. Beginning with the Qing dynasty in 1271, Yanguang farmers had to provide an annual tribute payment in grain to the Chinese imperial government. Over the centuries, the exact nature of Han imperial control has changed with succeeding dynasties and with the rise of Communists to power since 1949, but the reality of Han political and economic domination has not changed.

The Yanguang economy today is primarily agricultural. They prefer valleys and lower elevated hillsides for village placement, and they live in one-story mud-walled houses. Two-generation households are the norm, and young men prefer to marry one of their mother's brother's daughters. The social system is based on patrilineal descent. Yanguangs tend to live in single-surname villages, which gives each community powerful family bonds. Farmers employ plow technology to raise rice, maize, wheat, and potatoes. They are also known to produce peanuts, melons, cotton, and a number of vegetables. Water buffalo, oxen, and horses serve as draft animals.

SUGGESTED READINGS: Ma Yin, ed., *China's Minority Nationalities,* 1989; S. Robert Ramsey, *The Languages of China,* 1987; S. A. Wurm, B. T'sou, D. Bradley, et al., eds., *Language Atlas of China,* 1987.

YAO. The People's Republic of China (PRC) today recognizes the Yao people, also known as Pai Yao, as one of its official minority nationalities. The 1990 national census counted 2,134,000 Yao people in China, and given their birthrate, which is above the national average, it is safe today to say that the Yao population is approaching 2.4 million people. More than 1.5 million Yaos live today in Guangxi Province, usually in mountain villages, but another 900,000 Yaos can be found scattered throughout the border regions of surrounding Hunan Province, Guangdong Province, Jiangxi Province, Guizhou Province, and Yunnan Province. They are particularly concentrated demographically in the Guangxi Zhuang Autonomous Region.

The various Yao languages are classified in the Miao-Yao* linguistic family. Thousands of Yao people, mistakenly called Miaos,* live in Hainan. Their ancestors were brought to the island in the sixteenth century by Han* Chinese in order to assist in the pacification of the rebellious Li* people. Perhaps a fifth of all Yao people also speak another language, most commonly Zhuang,* Dong,* Miao, or Chinese.* Other ethnonyms which have been used to describe the Yao are as follows: Iu Mien, Kim Mien, Kim Mun, Lingnan Yao, Man, and Yu Mien. Actually, there are more than three hundred names describing Yao people, primarily because their own ethnonyms and sense of identity vary greatly from region to region. There are three main Yao languages. Myens constitute 44 percent of the total Yao population. Myen is considered to be the main Yao language, but it is divided into a number of dialects, some of which are mutually unintelligible. The Punu language is spoken by about one-third of all Yaos, and it too is divided into a number of dialects, some of which are unintelligible. Many ethnolinguists believe that Punu is actually more Miao than Yao. Finally, perhaps 25,000 people speak Lakkya, which some ethnolinguists classify with Kham,* a Tibetan language.

Yao folk culture claims that the Yao people descend from a five-colored dog named P'an Hu, who brought the Chinese emperor the severed head of a political rival and made an expensive military expedition unnecessary. Contemporary scholars have a much less spectacular explanation. Chinese historians and archaeologists believe that the Yao people emerged from a process of ethnogenesis that included centuries of widespread intermarriage among Han, Zhuang, Dong, and various Miao peoples. During the Tang dynasty, Han imperial administrators first identified them as "Mo Yao" people because they had adopted the ethnonym of "Yao" to refer to themselves.

For more than a thousand years, Yaos have worked as settled agriculturalists. A minority of Yao farmers remain loyal to swidden, slash-and-burn techniques, but most of them employ plowing techniques to produce rice. Where heavily forested regions border Yao farmlands, the people continue to hunt actively, often in carefully organized communal groups. Foraging as a significant economic activity no longer exists among Yao people.

The Yao social system is based on patrilineal descent, with inheritance going from father to son. Patrilineal clans are the most important governing institutions in Yao society, and residence is patrilocal. Yaos prefer that all marriages be cross-cousin arrangements, with young men marrying their mother's brother's daughter.

Whether or not the Yaos are even a single ethnic group, however, remains a source of political and academic controversy in the PRC. There are four so-called Yao subgroups—the Byau Min Yaos,* the Kim Mun Yaos,* the Mien Yaos,* and the Yao Mins.* Although all four of those groups refer to themselves as Yaos and share similar social institutions, their languages are not mutually intelligible. Linguists usually insist that dialects of one language must be mutually intelligible. If the Byau Min Yao, Kim Mun Yao, Mien Yao, and Yao Min languages were mutually intelligible, then they could be considered dialects of a single language. Each of these groups could then clearly be considered a subgroup of the single Yao people.

The complexity of Yao ethnicity can be illustrated by looking at two of the many so-called Yao subgroups. The Bunus* are a subgroup of the Yaos. Demographers place the Bunu population at nearly 500,000 people, most of whom live in remote mountainous regions of the Guangxi Zhuang Autonomous Region and in Guizhou, Hunan, and Yunnan provinces. The Bunu language is divided into five mutually intelligible dialects: Bunao, Baheng, Wunai, Jiongnai, and Younuo. The Bunao dialect itself can then be broken down into five subdialects: Dongnu, Nunu, Bunuo, Naogelao, and Numao. The Mians are another Yao subgroup. Mians can be found living today primarily on Hainan Island; in the Guangxi Zhuang Autonomous Region; and in Hunan, Yunnan, Guangdong, Guizhou, and Jiangxi provinces. The Mian language possesses three primary dialects: Mianjin, Biaomin, and Zaomin. Mianjin possesses three distinct vernaculars: Youmian, Biaoman, and Jinmen (Kimmun). Biaomin can then be subdivided into the Biaomin and Jiaogongmin subdialects. Each of these subgroups possesses a distinct sense of ethnic identity. Similarly complex subidentities characterize many of the other Yao people.

SUGGESTED READINGS: Paul V. Hockings, "Yao," in Paul V. Hockings, ed., *The Encyclopedia of World Cultures*, vol. 6, *East and Southeast Asia*, 1991; Jacques Lemoine and Chiao Chien, eds., *The Yao of South China: Recent International Studies*, 1991; Ma Yin, ed., *China's Minority Nationalities*, 1989; S. A. Wurm, B. T'sou, D. Bradley, et al., eds., *Language Atlas of China*, 1987; S. Robert Ramsey, *The Languages of China*, 1987; Zeng Qingnan, "The Yao of Guizhou Province," *China Today* 44 (July 1995), 52–55.

YAO MIN. The Yao Mins, currently considered by the People's Republic of China to be a subgroup of the Yao* people, live in Guangxi, Hunan, Guangdong, Jiangxi, Guizhou, and Yunnan provinces. The problem with classifying them with the other so-called Yao peoples is language. The government argues that there are four subgroups of the Yao people—Byau Min Yaos,* Kim Mun Yaos,* Mien Yaos,* and Yao Mins. But these are not really dialects. Although all four are classified in the Miao-Yao* linguistic family, they are not mutually intelligible. If the language spoken by Yao Mins is not comprehensible to the other Yao subgroups, then the argument for separate and official ethnic status is a compelling one.

Demographers estimate that there are more than 500,000 Yao Min people. Their economies vary according to ecological setting, with agriculture, hunting, and foraging occupying them. Their social system is based on patrilineal descent, and young people are expected to marry endogamously. Elders frown on an individual who marries someone from another Yao group. That stigma against exogamous marriage to any other people, including other Yaos, is more evidence that Yao Mins constitute a distinct ethnic entity.

YARKANT. Yarkant is one of the vernaculars of the Uigur* language spoken in Xinjiang Uigur Autonomous Region of the People's Republic of China.

YAWYEN. See LISU.

YAWYIN. See LISU.

YAWYIN. The Yawyins are one of the Kachin* peoples of Myanmar (Burma), China, and India. They are actually speakers of the Lisu* language who became associated over time with Kachin groups. Most Yawyins live in Myanmar, but they also have a presence in southwestern Yunnan Province in the People's Republic of China. Yawyins prefer to live in valleys and small plains that are surrounded by mountains. They select their village sites at the foot of a mountain or at the edge of a plain, and a typical village consists of several patrilineally related groups.

The Yawyin language is classified by ethnolinguists as one of the Kachin languages and part of the Tibeto-Burman* cluster in the Sino-Tibetan language family. It remains their primary language, although many Yawyins are also bilingual in Dai,* Chinese,* Jingpo,* Wa,* or De'ang.*

Historically, the Yawyin economy revolved around subsistence levels of wet-rice agriculture. They have adapted their planting and harvesting to the prevailing weather patterns, particularly the arrival of the monsoon season. Tobacco, sugarcane, and oil-producing plants generates cash for the Yawyin economy. Their social structure is based on a system of patrilineal descent, in which members of a village or several villages trace their ancestry back to a common male. Individuals must marry outside their patrilineal group, and marriages are generally arranged by parents for economic advantage. The fundamental family unit of Yawyin society is a patriarchal family that includes two or three generations.

YAXIAN. The Yaxian people are a subgroup of the Qiongwen* people, who are themselves a linguistic subgroup of the Min* language of Chinese* in the People's Republic of China and the Republic of China on Taiwan. Yaxian speakers can be found today in Yaxian and Ledong counties in Hainan Province. See **HAN** and **MINNAN**.

YE REN. See JINGPO.

YEH-JEN. See **LISU.**

YELLOW KUCONG. See **LAHU.**

YELLOW LAHU. Yellow Lahu is one of the two major Lahu* languages in the People's Republic of China. One of its major dialects is Lahu, and Lahu has one subdialect of its own spoken in China: Bankeo. Lahoshi is another Yellow Lahu dialect, and its two dialects are Banlan and Nankeo.

YELLOW UIGUR. The so-called Yellow Uigurs are a Uigur constituency who really can no longer be considered a subgroup of the Uigur* people of the People's Republic of China. In the ninth century, the Yellow Uigurs splintered off from the main Uigur community in the Xinjiang region and migrated to what is today Gansu Province. At the time they were fleeing bloody, genocidal depradations by Kirgiz* imperial soldiers. Over the centuries, the Yellow Uigur language has evolved quite differently from the other Uigur dialects, and it has adopted a wealth of Mongol* and Chinese* loan words. Today, Yellow Uigur is no longer intelligible to speakers of the other Uigur dialects. Another important linguistic development among many Yellow Uigurs was their adoption of Mongolian. During the thirteenth-century expansion of Genghis Khan, Yellow Uigur territory became subject to Mongol political control. In the process, those Yellow Uigurs who remained for long periods in the presence of Mongol troops slowly abandoned their own Turkic language (see **TURKIC PEOPLE**) for a Mongol tongue, or slipped into an eclectic, transitional language that combined Turkic and Mongol elements.

Yellow Uigurs are also religiously distinct from their Xinjiang brethren. Because they split off in the ninth century, before the Uigur conversion to Islam, Yellow Uigurs remain faithful to their traditional Buddhist faith, which also combines elements of an indigenous animism and shamanism. Unlike their Uigur counterparts to the north and west, the Yellow Uigurs also have maintained use of the traditional Uigur literary language and written script. Because of these profound religious and linguistic differences, many ethnologists, as well as many Yellow Uigur leaders, would like to see them recognized as an official minority nationality. To date, the Chinese government has not agreed with their point of view.

SUGGESTED READINGS: Elizabeth E. Bacon, *Central Asia under Russian Rule*, 1966; Michael Dillon, *China's Muslim Nationalities*, 1996; Ned Gillette, "Adventure in Western China," *National Geographic* 159 (February 1981), 174–99; Dru Gladney, "The Ethnogenesis of the Uighur," *Central Asian Survey* 9 (1990), 1–27; Rick Gore, "Journey to China's Far West," *National Geographic* 157 (March 1980), 292–332; *Great Soviet Encyclopedia*, 26:553–54, 1973; David Lu, *Moslems in China Today*, 1964; Ma Yin, ed., *China's Minority Nationalities*, 1989; Colin Mackerras, ed., *The Uighur Empire according to the T'ang Dynastic Histories: A Study in Sino-Uighur Relations*, 1973; Peng Jianqun, "Uygur Craftsman Solves the Riddle of the 'Huxitar,' " *China Today* 39 (June

1990), 44–46; Henry G. Schwarz, *The Minorities of Northern China: A Survey*, 1984; *Washington Post*, February 11, 1997; H. H. Wiens, "Change in the Ethnography and Land Use of the Ili Valley and Region, Chinese Turkestan," *Annals of the Association of American Geographers* 59 (1969), 753–75; Wong How-Man, "Peoples of China's Far Provinces," *National Geographic* 165 (March 1984), 283–377.

YI. The Yi people, with a current population approaching 7 million, are one of the largest officially recognized minority nationalities in the People's Republic of China (PRC). They have traditionally been called the Lolos, but it is a designation that they have rejected. Most Yis live in villages on the slopes and in the valleys of the Greater and Lesser Liangshan mountain ranges, especially south of the Dadu River. Many of them are settled on the banks of the Anning River. Of the nearly 7 million Yis, 1.4 million of them are located in the Liangshan Yi Autonomous Prefecture of Sichuan Province. More than 3 million Yis live in Yunnan Province, particularly in the Chuxiong Yi Autonomous Prefecture. There are several other autonomous counties for the Yi in Yunnan. Nearly 600,000 Yi live today in Guizhou Province. A relatively small group of perhaps 5,000 Yis have moved to the Guangxi Zhuang Autonomous Region, which represents the most eastern extension of Yi people.

It is difficult, if not impossible, to speak of the Yi people as a distinct ethnic identity. They speak a Tibeto-Burman* language that is part of the Sino-Tibetan linguistic family. Yi is subdivided, however, into a variety of mutually unintelligible dialects, or languages, and the Yi people themselves are more likely to identify themselves by dialect and region than by any generic sense of Yi peoplehood. They live widely scattered among Miao,* Lisu,* Hui,* Hani,* Zhuang,* Han,* and Tibetan* peoples, and intermarriage with those groups has set in motion a complex ethnogenesis that all but defies simple classification. Included among the Yi subgroups are the Ahis,* Axis,* Hei-Is,* Hei-Kus,* Ichias,* Is,* Ku Tous,* Leisus,* Lokqueis, Lolos, Luoluos,* Luquans,* Manchias,* Mantzus,* Misabas,* Mosus,* Nasus,* Neisus,* Ngosus,* Nos,* Norsus,* Nosus, Pei-Is,* Sanis,* and Tous.*

A unique social structure, which transcended dialect, regional, and language differences, characterized Yi society. Yi society was divided into three basic groups. At the top of the social structure were the Black Yi, also known as the Black Bone Yi, who constituted the Yi aristocracy and dominated social, political, and economic life. In the middle were the White Yis, who outnumbered the Black Yis by more than ten to one. White Yis were essentially of Han Chinese extraction, the descendents of Han Chinese people taken in Yi slave raids. Over the centuries, however, they acquired certain property rights and transcended their status as slaves. At the bottom of the social structure were former slaves—Han people and their children who had only recently been forced into slavery. One of the first laws implemented by the new PRC government in 1949 was freedom for all of the slaves in China. Although the PRC officially

abolished the Yi Castes after the revolution, most Yis remain aware today of
their caste origins.

Today, outsiders can identify both Black Yi and White Yi by their characteristic large felt capes that serving as clothing and bedding. Black and White
Yi men also wear large turbans on their heads, usually colored black, white, or
blue. More often than not, a large braid of hair protrudes from an opening in
the turban.

Like the Bai,* Naxi,* Lahu,* and Lisu peoples of Yunnan Province and the
Dai* and Qiang* peoples of western Sichuan Province, the Yis descend from
the ancient Tusan people native to the Kunming region of Yunnan and the
Chengdu in Sichuan. By the third century A.D., the Yi forerunners extended
from northeastern and southern Yunnan to northwestern Guizhou and Guangxi.
The Yi people appeared soon after. In the seventh century, six Yi tribes coa-
lesced politically and formed the Nanchao Kingdom, which survived for more
than six hundred years. Since then, Yi history has been one of continuous interaction with Han culture, much of it violent. Yis have fought Han expansionism for more than two thousand years, and because their homeland—60,000
square miles of territory surrounding Cool (Liangshan) Mountain—consists of
mountains, deep valleys, heavy forests, and generally rugged, precipitious terrain, they were able to control the mountain passes and inflict considerable
damage on Ham armies.

Mongol* armies conquered the Yi in 1253, and Mongol soldiers settled permanently in the region and married Yi women. The Mongol presence lasted for
more than a century, but in 1368, an army under the control of the Ming dynasty
invaded southwestern China and drove out the Mongols. At that point, Yi people
came under the Chinese civil service system and the system of county magistrates. The Chinese imperial court governed the Yi people indirectly through the
use of official Yi leaders. Thousands of Han soldiers and administrators settled
permanently in the region and took Yi wives. The local culture remained far
more Yi than Han, but it was the beginning of a process of acculturation that
continues today.

Even then, the Yi could be counted on to harass government officials and
Han people. After the Revolution of 1911, which led to the establishment of
the Republic of China, military authority broke down in the region and Yi
political and military strength increased dramatically. Traditional Yi clans reasserted their authority, and the opium traffic, which supplied cash to the Yi
economy, boomed. Yi traders sold the opium in Chinese black markets. By the
late 1920s, marauding groups of Yi soldiers, now heavily armed with modern
weaponry, regularly raided the suburbs of Han Chinese settlements, where they
robbed, pillaged, and took slaves. During the 1930s and the years of World War
II, Yi military parties controlled much of southern Sichuan Province.

Before the Communist revolution in 1949, less than 20 percent of the Yi
population owned 75 percent of the land; most Yis worked as peasant farmers,
tenant farmers, or farm laborers. In the mid-1950s, the central government na-

tionalized all of the land and forced Yi farmers into collectives. The program alienated Yi elites, who lost much of their wealth but had relatively little impact on most tenant farmers and laborers. Since then, Yi farmers have seen land tenure systems evolve according to changing government policies. Since the early 1980s, in order to boost agricultural productivity, the central government has turned back to individual and family production systems and away from collective entities.

The traditional Yi economy was overwhelmingly agricultural. At lower elevations, Yi farmers produced maize, potatoes, buckwheat, and oats as staples. They also raised cattle, sheep, goats, and horses in the highlands of the Liangshang mountains. Chickens and pigs are ubiquitous in Yi villages. Poorer Yi families supplemented their diets by collecting acorns, roots, wild vegetables, and herbs, and by fishing and hunting. Opium was an important cash crop. The Chinese government outlawed its production late in the 1930s, and the Communist government has continued the prohibition; nevertheless, many Yi farmers still produce opium illegally and sell it on the black market.

After Mao Zedong's victory in 1949, traffic along the Burma Road slowed to a standstill. Government policies, which discouraged anything resembling free enterprise capitalism, rendered southwestern China a very inhospitable place for capital investment or commerce. During the 1960s and 1970s, the Cultural Revolution, with its ideological zealotry, only made things worse. The Yi economy, as well as that of much of China, reverted practically to subsistence levels of production. In 1979, however, to lift the country out of the morass into which it had fallen, the central government began to implement economic reforms. Market economy instruments and personal profit were no longer considered evil, and an economic revival came to southeastern China in the 1980s and 1990s.

Most Yis live today in mountain hamlets that cannot even be considered villages. They usually average no more than twenty households. Yi homes are single-story constructions of wood and dirt. There are no windows in Yi houses. Cattle and sheep sleep indoors with family members. In recent years, more and more Yi families are building brick and tile houses similar to those used by neighboring Han families.

An eclectic mix of Daoism, Buddhism, and traditional ancestor worship characterizes Yi religious beliefs in Yunnan, Guizhou, and Guangxi provinces. In the Liangshan region, an indigenous animism—in which the world is filled with invisible ghosts, spirits, and deities who regularly interfere in human affairs and natural phenomena—exists. Yi shamans, known as *bimos* and *suyas*, preside over religious rituals, including animal sacrifice, designed to appease the powers of the unseen world. Thousands of Yis are also Christians today, descendents of Yi people who listened to Christian missionaries in the 1920s and 1930s.

SUGGESTED READINGS: Mike Edwards, "Our Man in China: Joseph Rock," *National Geographic* 191 (January 1997), 62–100; Li Ming, "Liang Mountains: Home of the Yi People," *China Today* 39 (July 1990), 34–39; Lin Yueh-Hwa (Lin Yaohua) and Naranbilik, "Yi," in Paul V. Hockings, ed., *The Encyclopedia of World Cultures*, vol. 6,

East and Southeast Asia, 1991; Ma Yin, ed., *China's National Minorities: A Survey*, 1989; S. Robert Ramsey, *The Languages of China*, 1987; Xie Jun, "Celebrating with the Yi Nationality," *China Today* 42 (April 1993), 10–12, and "Costumes Fit for a Festival," *China Today* 42 (November 1993), 10–11.

YI. In addition to describing millions of people who live in Yunnan Province in the People's Republic of China (PRC), the term "Yi" is employed by ethnolinguists to describe a branch of the Tibeto-Burman* language family, although they are more closely related to Burman than to Tibetan. "Yi" is synonymous with the term "Loloish." In the PRC, the following languages are included in the Yi branch: Yi,* Lisu,* Hani,* Lahu,* Jino,* and Naxi.*
SUGGESTED READINGS: David Bradley, *Lahu Dialects*, 1979, and *Proto-Loloish*, 1978; Lin Yueh-hua, *The Lolo of Liang Shan*, 1961; S. Robert Ramsey, *The Languages of China*, 1987.

YIDU. The Yidu people are a small ethnic group of approximately 7,000 people who live today along the Danbajiang River in Chayu County of Changdu Prefecture in the Tibetan Autonomous Region. Although the government of the People's Republic of China classifies them as part of the Lloba* minority nationality, the Yidus are more likely to identify themselves as Yidus than as Llobas. They have difficulty understanding the other so-called Lloba language, which is known as Bogar. Yidus were part of the southern migration which brought them, centuries ago, out of central Tibet into southern Tibet. During the ensuing centuries after their arrival, to avoid political and economic domination by other groups, they settled in mountainous highlands, where they currently reside. They locate their villages with defense in mind. Yidus prefer to live on hilltops, with access to a river via a sloping incline, with a very steep decline on the opposite side of the village. Houses are then constructed on elevated platforms, with the rear of the home facing the hillside. They still function in a largely subsistence economy based on slash-and-burn agriculture, fishing, foraging, and hunting.
SUGGESTED READINGS: Tiley Chodag, *Tibet: The Land and the People*, 1988; Paul V. Hockings, "Lloba," in Paul V. Hockings, ed., *The Encyclopedia of World Cultures*, vol. 6; *East and Southeast Asia*, 1991; S. A. Wurm, B. T'sou, D. Bradley, et al. eds., *Language Atlas of China*, 1987.

YILIU. The Yiliu people are a subgroup of the Gan*-speaking Han* Chinese* of the People's Republic of China. Most Yiliu speakers can be found today in the city of Liling and in Liuyang County in Hunan Province and in the Xichun, Yifeng, Shanggao, Qingjiang, Xin'gan, Xinyu, Fenyi, Pingxiang, Fengcheng, and Wanzai regions of Jiangxi Province.

YINGYI. The Yingyi people are a subgroup of the Gan*-speaking Han* Chinese* of the People's Republic of China. Most Yingyis today live in Jiangxi

Province, primarily in the Yingtan, Guixi, Yujiang, Wannian, Leping, Jingde-zhen, Yugan, Boyang, Pengze, Hengfeng, Yiyang, and Yanshan regions.

YOHUR. The Yohurs (Yohuers) are a subgroup of the Yugur* people of the People's Republic of China. They live in the western region of Sunan Yugur Autonomous County in Gansu Province. The question of whether they should be considered an independent ethnic group in their own right is a controversial one in China. Yohur roots are the same as those of the other Yugur subgroup—the Engers*—but their languages are distinctly different. Yohur belongs to the Turkic (see **TURKIC PEOPLE**) branch of the Altaic* linguistic family; Enger is classified with the Mongolian branch of the Altaic family. While Yohur is closely related to Uigur* and Salar,* Engers is more closely tied to Bonan,* Tu,* and Mongolian (see **MONGOL**). Neither Yohur nor Enger has a written script.

The Yohurs and Engers, as the Yugur people, descend from a group of Uigurs who, in the ninth century, fled Mongolia after a series of genocidal attacks perpetrated by Kirgiz* armies. The Uigurs who settled in Dunhuang, Zhangye, and Wuwei slowly evolved a distinct ethnic identity of their own and became known as the Hexi Quigurs. That ethnonym later evolved into Yugur. Today they are a pastoral people. Yohurs living at higher elevations raise oxen, sheep, goats, and horses; those at lower altitudes raise oxen, sheep, camels, and goats. SUGGESTED READING: Chen Xin, ''Some Customs of the Yugur People,'' *China Reconstructs* 38 (May 1989), 44–46.

YONGBEI. The Yongbei people are a subgroup of the Zhuang* people of the People's Republic of China. The Yongbei language is classified as one of the Northern Zhuang* dialects, and most of its speakers live today in Wuming, Northern Yongning, Hengxian, Binyang, and Pingguo counties in the Guangxi Zhuang Autonomous Region.

YONGJIANG. The Yongjiang are a dialect subgroup of the Taihu* people, who are themselves a linguistic subgroup of the Wu*-speaking Han* people of the People's Republic of China. More than four million people speak the Yongjiang language, and the vast majority of them live in the Ningbo, Yinxian, Fenghua, Xiangshan, Zhenhai, Dinghai, Putuo, Daishan, Shengsi, and Ninghai regions of Zhejiang Province.

YONGNAN. The Yongnans are a subgroup of the Zhuang* people of the People's Republic of China. The Yongnan language is classified as one of the Southern Zhuang* dialects, and most of its speakers live today in Long'an, Fusui, Shangsi, and Qinzhou counties in the Guangxi Zhuang Autonomous Region.

YONGNING NAXI. The Yongning Naxis are one of the primary subgroups of the Naxi* people of Yunnan and Sichuan provinces in the People's Republic of

China. They are distinguished from the Lijiang Naxis* by their social system, which is based on matrilineal descent arrangements. The Lijiang Naxi social system is patrilineal. Yongning Naxis are also more likely to be converts to the Gelug-pa sect of Tibetan Buddhism.

YONGXUN. The Yongxun people are a dialect subgroup of Yue*-speaking Han* Chinese.* Approximately five million people speak Yongxun, and most of them live in the Nanning, Liuzhou, Yongning, Chongzuo, Ningming, Hengxian, Guiping, and Pingnan regions of the Guangxi Zhuang Autonomous Region in the People's Republic of China.

YOUJIANG. The Youjiang people are a subgroup of the Zhuang* of the People's Republic of China. The Youjiang language is classified as one of the Northern Zhuang* dialects, and most of its speakers live today in Tiandong, Tianyang, and Bose counties in the Guangxi Zhuang Autonomous Region. Yongxun is divided into several of its own subdialects.

YOUNUO. Younuo is a subdialect of the Bunu* language, which is part of the larger Yao* cluster of languages in the People's Republic of China.

YSU GELAO. The Ysu Gelaos are one of the four linguistic subdivisions of the Gelao* people of the People's Republic of China.

YU. See **SHE.**

YU MIEN. See **MIAO.**

YUAN ZHYN. See **HUE.**

YUANMEN. Yuanmens are a subgroup of the Bendi* peoples, who are themselves a subgroup of the Li* ethnic group of Hainan Island in the People's Republic of China. The Yuanmen dialect can be heard today in southeastern Baisha County, where it is spoken by nearly 9,000 people.

YUE. The term ''Yue'' is used here to describe the speakers of the Yue Chinese language. Yue is also called Cantonese. More than 80 million people speak Yue; the vast majority of them live in Guangdong Province and in southern Guanxi Province. Yue is also widely spoken in Hong Kong and in the overseas Chinese communities. Most Chinese immigrants to the United States came from the Taishan region of Guangdong Province, a rural area about sixty miles southwest of the city of Guangzhou (Canton).

Although Chinese linguists describe Yue as a ''dialect'' of Chinese,* it is not mutually intelligible with other Chinese dialects. Most linguists argue, however, that the definition of ''dialect'' means that it is mutually intelligible with other dialects of the same language. The Chinese government claims that eight dialects of the language exist within the national boundaries: Mandarin,* Wu,* Gan,* Xiang,* Hakka,* Jin,* Yue, and Min.* The problem with that definition, of course, is that none of these so-called dialects is mutually intelligible with any other. The people who speak them may very well be united by their Han* descent and their shared eclectic mix of Buddhist, Daoist, and Confucian religious beliefs, but they cannot understand one another's spoken languages, which should render them members of different ethnic groups. Complicating the issue even more is the fact that each of the eight Chinese languages possesses many dialects, and some of those dialects are not mutually intelligible to speakers of related dialects.

At the same time, however, they share an unusual linguistic similarity. The spoken Chinese languages cannot be mutually understood by different speakers, but they all employ the same written script, which is mutually readable. Some linguists have begun employing the term "regionalect" to describe the eight Chinese languages. Whether or not Mandarin, Wu, Gan, Xiang, Hakka, Yue, Jin, and Min are dialects, regionalects, or languages, they divide the more than 1.1 billion Han people into distinguishable, individual groups whose members share loyalty and a sense of identity with one another because of language.

There are a number of Yue dialects, although the dialect of the city of Guangzhou is considered the standard, the measure by which all other Cantonese dialects are measured. In Guangdong Province, there are five primary Yue dialects: Guangfu,* Siyi,* Gaoyang,* Goulou,* and Wuhua.* The major Yue dialects spoken in the Guangxi Zhuang Autonomous Region are Guangfu, Yongxun,* Goulou,* and Qinlian.* The Han Chinese who speak Yue, regardless of their dialect, possess a powerful sense of Cantonese identity, one which revolves around language. For Yue speakers, the city of Canton is the center of the world, and Cantonese culture is superior to all others. The Cantonese dialect of Yue became prominent in southeastern China during the Ming dynasty, when the city of Canton and the Pearl River had become the economic and cultural heart of southern China.

Yue is also distinct from most of the other Chinese languages because it developed its own vernacular literature with a series of nontraditional characters for colloquial words and expressions. Only Mandarin enjoys such a distinction; Gan, Xiang, Jin, Hakka, Min, and Wu do not. Government officials in the People's Republic of China discourage publications using the Yue vernacular characters, but they still appear everyday, especially in Hong Kong. Whether or not the People's Republic of China will crack down on written Yue after July 1, 1997, remains to be seen.

SUGGESTED READINGS: O'kan Yue Hashimoto, *Studies in Yue Dialects*, vol. 1, *Phonology of Cantonese*, 1972; S. Robert Ramsey, *The Languages of China*, 1987.

YUEBAI. The Yuebai people are a linguistic subgroup of the Hakka*-speaking Han* people of the People's Republic of China (PRC). Yuebai speakers can be found today living in Shixing, Nanxiong, Wengyuan, Yingde, Ruyuan, Renhua, Liannan, Lianxian, Yangshan, and Lechang counties in northern Guangdong Province of the PRC.

YUETAI. The Yuetai people are a subgroup of the Hakka*-speaking Han* people of the People's Republic of China and the Republic of China. They can be found living today in twenty cities and counties of eastern Guangdong Province, three counties of northeastern Taiwan, and two counties of southern Taiwan. Yuetai Hakka is itself divided into four subdialects: Jiaying,* Xinghua,* Xinhui,* and Shaonan.*

YUEZHONG. The Yuezhong people are a linguistic subgroup of the Hakka*-speaking Han* people of the People's Republic of China (PRC). Yuezhong speakers can be found today living in Heiping, Lianping, Longchuan, Boluo, and Heyuan counties in central Guangdong Province of the PRC.

YUEZI. See **JING.**

YUGUI. The Yugui people are a linguistic subgroup of the Hakka*-speaking Han* people of the People's Republic of China (PRC). Yugui speakers can be found today living in Yudu, Ganxian, Nankang, Dayu, Chongyi, Shangyou, Ninggang, Jinggangshan, Yongxin, Ji'an, Suichuan, Wan'an, and Taihe counties in Jianxi Province and in Rucheng, Guidong, Lingxian, Chaling, and Youxian counties in Hunan Province of the PRC.

YUGUR. The Yugurs (Yogurs) are one of the smallest officially recognized minority nationalities in the People's Republic of China (PRC). The 1990 national census put their population at 12,297 people, but it is probably closer to 13,000 today. Approximately 90 perent of the Yugurs live in Sunan Yugur Autonomous County, a political division of Gansu Province. The county sits in the Hexi Corridor of Gansu, where pastoral pursuits constitute the economic activities of most people.

Historians and archaeologists trace Yugur origins back to the Uigur* people, from who they separated in the ninth century. At the time, one group of Uigurs had been repeatedly attacked by Kirgiz* armies moving down from the north, and thousands of Uigurs died in the assaults. To save themselves, the surviving Uigurs fled their homeland in Mongolia and settled in the regions now known as Dunhuang, Zhangye, and Wuwei in Gansu Province—trading Kirgiz genocide for Tibetan* domination. During the course of the next several centuries, they became known as Hexi Ouigurs and had to accommodate themselves to a variety of imperial powers—the Tufan kingdom, the Xixia Tangut state, the Mongol empire, and the domination of Hans during the Ming and Qing dynasties.

The slow process of ethnogenesis gradually created a sense of Yugur identity among them. During the fourteenth and fifteenth centuries, thousands of Yugurs migrated outside the Great Wall to the west, where they confronted a variety of new ethnic groups and herded their oxen and sheep. By the early sixteenth century, however, the Yugurs found themselves facing increasingly hostile attacks from the Tufan people, and in response, the Yugurs moved back east, behind the protection of the Great Wall but also back under the influence of Han society. The Yugurs who settled in the Huangnibao region soon made the transition to a settled, agricultural existence; the Yugurs in Sunan continued, even today, to live as migratory pastoralists. The Sunan Yugurs living at higher elevations raise sheep, goats, horses, and Tibetan oxen; those at lower elevations raise oxen, camels, sheep, and goats.

Their migrations and repeated resettlements have created two primary Yugur subgroups, whose differences are based primarily on language. The language spoken by Yugurs living in the western reaches of the Sunan Yugur Autonomous County is called Yohur,* a language that is classified in the Turkic (see **TURKIC PEOPLE**) branch of the Altaic* linguistic family. Yugurs residing in eastern Sunan Yugur Autonomous County—particularly in and around Kangle, Hongziao, and Qinglong—speak Enger,* which ethnolinguists place in the Mongolian branch of the Altaic family. While Yohur is closely related to Uigur and Salar,* Enger's closest relatives are Mongolian (see **MONGOL**), Bonan,* and Tu.* Enger and Yohur are not mutually intelligible and therefore cannot be considered dialects of Yugur.

That distinction, of course, has created a political controversy over ethnicity in the People's Republic of China. Beginning in the 1950s, when government officials invited various ethnic groups to apply for official recognition, both the Yohurs and the Engers made such an application. Their most important argument against being a single Yugur people, of course, was linguistic; Yohur and Enger are not mutually intelligible. But because their population was so small, and because more than 90 percent of Engers and Yohurs lived in what became the Sunan Yugur Autonomous County, and because their pastoral lifestyle was so visible, the government refused to recognize Engers and Yohurs as officially distinct ethnic entities. Today, both Enger and Yohur leaders continue to request official recognition as distinct minority nationalities.

Back in the ninth century, before their migration east to flee from maurauding bands of Kirgiz, Yugurs were primarily animists who believed in an emperor of heaven, named Han Tengri, who governed and controlled an invisible world of spirits capable of interfering in human affairs. A few poor, uneducated Yugurs continue to worship Han Tengri today. In the eighth century, a small minority of Yugurs converted to a Gnostic Christian denomination. When they migrated east and came under the political control of the Tibetan kingdom, however, most Yugurs converted to Lamaist Buddhism, which is their primary religious loyalty today.

SUGGESTED READINGS: Paul V. Hockings, "Yugur," in Paul V. Hockings, ed., *The Encyclopedia of World Cultures*, vol. 6; *East and Southeast Asia*, 1991; C. G. E. Mannerheim, "A Visit to the Saro and Shera Yogurs," *Journal de la Société Finno-Ougrienne* 27 (1913), 161–79; Ma Yin, ed., *China's Minority Nationalities*, 1989; Henry G. Schwarz, *The Minorities of Northern China: A Survey*, 1984.

YUKAGIR. The Yukagir (Yukaghir, Jukagir, Jukaghir), who call themselves the Odul or Detkil', are one of the smallest identifiable ethnic groups in Russia, and there are a few Yukagirs among the Evenks* in the People's Republic of China, primarily in Heilongjiang Province. At one time, the Yukagirs wandered across a wide swath of tundra and steppes in northeastern Siberia, but in the past two centuries their numbers have dwindled dramatically, although they have recovered somewhat in the last several decades. The 1926 census of the Soviet Union listed the Yukagir population at 443 people, and it increased to 615 people in 1970 and to 835 in 1979. Although reliable census information was not available concerning the Yukagir, estimates place the population at approximately 850 people in the early 1990s. In Russia, they are being assimilated by Yakuts* and Evenks. The number of people in China who identify themselves as Yukagirs cannot be more than one hundred. Yukagir is a Paleoasiatic language with close ties to the Uralic and Altaic* languages, indicating a considerable linguistic mixing over the centuries. Yukagir is also loaded with Russian,* Evenk, Yakut, and Nenet words.

Historically, the Yukagir economy was primarily a nomadic hunting and fishing one; relative few Yukagirs tended reindeer herds. Those who did were the Tundra Yukagirs. The Yukagirs, widely scattered throughout northeastern Siberia, numbered in the thousands of people. They were especially concentrated from the Lena River to the mouth of the Anadyr' River. Although they spoke a similar language, the Yukagir did not have a sense of common ethnic identity since their matrilineal clan loyalties were so powerful.

Ethnic Russians first encountered the Yukagirs in the mid-seventeenth century. Commercial traders, fur trappers, and hunters then established permanent contact with the Yukagirs. Systematic Russian contact brought a wave of epidemic diseases—influenza, mumps, smallpox, chicken pox, and so on—and the Yukagir underwent a rapid population decline, from approximately 10,000 people in 1700 to 2,350 in 1859. Moscow authorized the granting of citizenship to any native who converted to Christianity—a process that led to forced baptisms and enserfment by local rulers, who then used their native serfs to increase fur trapping. But as the numbers of fur-bearing animals decreased, Moscow lost interest in the area and the well-being of its natives. The Yukagirs, along with many other Siberian peoples, were part of this entire administrative process. By the mid-eighteenth century, the Russians and Yukagirs were increasingly drawn together in a commercialized economy. They began holding annual fairs in which the Yukagirs would trade reindeer hides and furs for alcohol, iron tools, firearms, ammunition, and tobacco. In the nineteenth century, as increasing numbers of ethnic Russians settled in the region, the economic contacts strengthened.

Completion of the Trans-Siberian Railroad in 1905 further expanded those economic contacts.

Because of their integration into the larger commercial economy, many Yukagirs assimilated into Russian society. Those Yukagirs who remained committed to a hunting economy declined dramatically in numbers during the twentieth century, primarily because of disease and economic dislocation. Many of them threw in their lot with the Evenks and Yakuts and began assimilating among them as well. When many Evenks and Yakuts fled into China during the 1920s and 1930s to avoid Soviet collectivization schemes, there were Yukagirs among them. The handful of people in the People's Republic of China today who are aware of their Yukagir heritage are the descendents of these people.

YUPIBO. See **HEZHEN.**

Z

ZAIWA. The Zaiwa people—also known historically as the Atsas, Atsis, Atzis, Atzas, or Azis—are not one of the officially recognized minority nationalities of the People's Republic of China (PRC). Instead, they have been classified, probably inappropriately, as a subgroup of the Jingpo* people of Yunnan Province in southeastern China. They are part of the much larger Kachin* group, a transnational Southeast Asian ethnic group numbering as many as 700,000 people. Virtually all of the Chinese Zaiwas live in Yunnan Province, most of them in the Dehong Dai and Jingpo Autonomous Prefecture in the far western reaches of Yunnan. There are perhaps 550,000 Zaiwas living in Myanmar (Burma), and a few thousand more in the Assam region of India, where they are identified as the Singhpos. The Chinese Zaiwa population in the 1990 national census was placed at approximately 119,209, but that number included not only the Zaiwas but also the closely related Lachis and Langwos,* whose language is not mutually intelligible with Zaiwa. The number of Zaiwas proper is approximately 75,000 people.

The Zaiwa language is a complex one that has created problems for ethnolinguists studying it. Most agree that it is part of the large Tibeto-Burman* branch of the Sino-Tibetan language family. In the People's Republic of China, there are three major Zaiwa subgroups, each of which is based on dialect differences. These include the Lachis, Langwos, and Bulas.* A major scholarly controversy exists in China over whether or not the Zaiwa people of Yunnan Province are a distinct ethnic group in their own right or merely a subgroup of the Jingpos. They are officially classified for political purposes as a Jingpo subgroup, but Zaiwa is not really mutually intelligible with Jingpo. In fact, some ethnolinguists classify them into different branches of the Tibeto-Burman language family. Because language is a defining characteristic of ethnic identity, Zaiwas are treated as a separate group in this dictionary.

Given the linguistic debate over the Zaiwas, it is hardly surprising to find archaeologists and historians disagreeing over their origins. Most scholars, however, believe that the ancestors of the Zaiwas originated near the headwaters of the Irrawaddy River in Tibet and then began moving south some 1,500 years ago. They entered the Dehong area in the fifteenth century. The region was already occupied by Dai,* De'ang,* and Han* peoples, and the Chinese *tusi* system, an administrative structure in which the Chinese imperial government ruled the region through local, hereditary ethnic leaders, was already in place when the Zaiwas arrived. At first they found themselves under Dai control, but Zaiwa militarism soon made them a valuable, and eventually independent, political force.

Most Zaiwa villages, which are relatively small and contain only from twenty to thirty households, are located on the hillside slopes of the Gaoligong mountains. Zaiwas prefer the higher elevations; most of their villages can be found between 4,500 feet and 7,000 feet in altitude. Zaiwa country catches the Indian Ocean monsoons, which guarantee abundant summer rainfall. The climate is semitropical.

Until a century ago, most Zaiwas were slash-and-burn cultivators who were forced to relocate their villages every few years. Many Zaiwa farmers still raise rice through these swidden techniques, but others have made the transition to the sedentary, terraced cultivation of rice, and they live in permanent villages. Other crops include dry rice, maize, millet, soybeans, kidney beans, potatoes, chili peppers, ginger, garlic, cucumbers, pumpkins, and sugarcane. Livestock are also important in the Zaiwa economy; water buffalo, cattle, and pigs are the most popular animals. Zaiwas also earn cash by collecting and then selling mushrooms, wild vegetables, timber, firewood, and herbal medicines. They have, as well, a long history of producing opium.

At the time of Mao Zedong's Communist revolution in 1949, most Zaiwas enjoyed limited private ownership of property. Rice paddy fields could be bought, sold, leased, and bequeathed, although only to members of the village. Forest lands were generally considered to be communal property. In 1957, the central government tried to take a step toward realizing the goal of a completely socialist economy and collectivized Zaiwa agriculture. All land was owned either by the state or by agricultural cooperatives. Production plummeted, and no amount of government tinkering could fix the problem until 1981, when central economic planners established the household contract-responsibility system. Under this arrangement, individual Zaiwa families could contract for a certain portion of paddy land and make their own decisions about resource allocation. They had to pay a tax in rice to the state and sell a set quota of their harvest at state prices, which happened to be 40 percent below market prices. But those families with surpluses after the rice tax and the quota sale could keep the proceeds of the extra production.

Zaiwa society is patrilineal and clan based. Families are based upon the principles of lineage exogamy, assymetrical matrilateral cross-cousin marriages, strict class endogamy between aristocrats and commoners, and occasional polygyny. With the advent of the Communist victory in 1949, prohibitions against class exogamy were eliminated. The necessity of matrilateral cross-cousin marriage is also easing, although most Zaiwa men still marry their mother's brother's daughter. Lineage exogamy, however, remains strictly enforced in Zaiwa society.

Although some elements of Han Confucianism and Dai Buddhism have made their way into the Zaiwa religion, most Zaiwas remain loyal to their indigenous, animist faith. It is a dualist theology in which reality is occupied by an ongoing struggle between good and evil spirits. Zaiwas believe that all unseen spirits were once human beings. Upon death, every individual becomes a supernatural, invisible spirit, some capable of evil and others of good. Those spirits do not leave the world but occupy it, interjecting themselves constantly into the daily lives of the living. Zaiwas call these spirits *nats*. Because all human beings eventually become *nats*, Zaiwa theology finds an infinite number of *nats* everywhere throughout the natural world, all of whom are responsible for sickness and health, good fortune and bad luck, drought and abundant harvests, fertility, natural disasters, and human destiny. *Nats* also have an edge to them and are easily offended. Human beings must appease them through prayer, worship, reverence, animal sacrifices, and the intervention of shamans known as *dumsas*.
SUGGESTED READINGS: Edmund R. Leach, *Political Systems of Highland Burma*, 1954; F. K. Lehman, "Kachin Social Categories and Methodological Sins," in W. McCormack and S. Wurm, eds., *Language and Thought: Anthropological Issues*, 1977; LaRaw Maran, "Towards a Basis for Understanding the Minorities of Burma: The Kachin Example," in Peter Kunstadter, ed., *Southeast Asian Tribes, Minorities, and Nations*, vol. 1, 125–46, 1967; David Nugent, "Closed Systems and Contradictions: The Kachin in and out of History," *Man* 17 (1982), 508–27; Wang Zhusheng, "Jingpo," in Paul V. Hockings, ed., *The Encyclopedia of World Cultures*, vol. 6, *East and Southeast Asia*, 1991.

ZHANGHU. The Zhanghu people are one of the linguistic subgroups of the more than 48 million Han* people who speak the Jin* Chinese* language. Most Zhanghus live today in twenty-seven cities and counties of northwestern Hebei Province and in the central region of the Inner Mongolian Autonomous Region in the People's Republic of China.

ZHIBEN. Zhiben is one of the five mutually intelligible dialects of the Puyuma* language which is spoken by an indigenous people living on Taiwan in the Republic of China.

ZHONG. See **SHE.**

ZHONGJIA. See **BOUYEI.**

ZHONGYUAN-REN. See **HUI.**

ZHUANG. The Zhuang people are the largest officially recognized minority nationality in the People's Republic of China (PRC). They have also been identified as Buban, Budai, Budong, Buman, Bumin, Buna, Bunong, Bupian, Bushuang, Butus, Bulangs, and Bulongs. Between the 1982 national census and its 1990 counterpart, the Zhuang population grew from 13,378,000 to 15,489,000. Conservative estimates of the Zhuang population today project a total of perhaps as many as 16.5 million people. Approximately 90 percent of all Zhuangs live in the Guangxi Autonomous Region, and most of them are concentrated in the western two-thirds of the area. Another 1 million Zhuangs can be found across the Guangxi border in the Wenshan Zhuang-Miao Autonomous Prefecture of Yunnan Province. Perhaps as many as 400,000 Zhuangs live in the Lianshan region of Guangdong Province. As many as 150,000 Zhuangs reside today in Hunan Province.

Ethnolinguists place Zhuang in the Zhuang-Dai* branch of the Tai* language family. It is very closely related to Bouyei,* Maonan,* and Mulam.* The language is tonal, based on an eight-tone system, and is closely related to the Yue Chinese* language spoken in Guangdong and Guangxi provinces. There are two major Zhuang dialects. Zhuang people living north of the Xiang River in southern Guangxi Province speak Northern Zhuang,* while those south of the river speak Southern Zhuang.* Northern Zhuang, which is spoken more widely, is more unified with fewer distinct dialects, and the Chinese central government today is pushing Northern Zhuang as the official Zhuang language. The Northern Zhuang vernacular spoken in Wuming County is officially considered to be the purest form of the language. Northern Zhuang is divided into eight subdialects: Yongbei, Youjiang, Guibian, Lujiang, Gubei, Hongshuihe, Qiubei, and Lianshan. Southern Zhuang has the following subdialects: Yongnan, Zuojiang, Dejing, Yanguang, and Wenma. In 1957 the government developed a romanized written script for Zhuang, which today appears in newspapers, books, magazines, and government documents. Reflecting their long history of interaction with other ethnic groups, both Zhuang dialects include a wealth of loan words from other languages.

In 211 B.C., when the Chinese imperial government first penetrated the region of Lingnan—what is today Guangdong and Guangxi provinces—their arrival inspired guerrilla warfare against Han* soldiers and the formation of what evolved into the Nan-Yue Kingdom, which eventually expanded into what is today northern Vietnam. In 111 B.C., China formally proclaimed sovereignty over Lingnan, but effective imperial control was not a reality for another seven centuries. During the Tang dynasty in the seventh century, increasing numbers of Han people settled among the Tai-speaking people of Guangxi, and a major Zhuang guerrilla uprising was crushed by imperial troops. The arrival of so many Han settlers steadily pushed native Tai speakers into the highlands or into western territories, while Hans staked out control of the river valleys and flatlands.

The incoming Han settlers launched a process of sinicization among the Zhuang people that continues today. Han settlers weaned Zhuangs away from swidden farming techniques in favor of plow agriculture using fertilizers, crop rotation, triple rice-cropping, and irrigation. The use of the Yue* Chinese language became more and more common among Zhuangs, and Mandarin Chinese slowly became the written Zhuang language. Zhuang animism and Chinese folk religion fused into beliefs in such deities as Tudigong, who protects villages; She Shen, the tutelary spirit of villages; Mountain Spirit, which protects certain upland forests from farming; Long Wang, the dragon king; and a host of other ghost, spirits, demons, and deities who occupy the natural world. Zhuang ancestor worship, however, still differs from that of the Han in that it includes mythical ancestral heroes.

In spite of the growing similarities with Han culture, Zhuang ethnic identity has remained intact, not just because of linguistic and religious differences but also because of the nature of the economy. Beginning with the Tang dynasty in the seventh century, a feudal system condoned by the Chinese imperial court developed, which reduced most Zhuangs to the status of farm tenancy and serfdom. Zhuangs chafed under such economic and political oppression, and during the 1850s they played a central role in the bloody Taipeng Rebellion. Zhuangs supplied large numbers of troops and military leaders to rebel forces. By the 1920s, Zhuang-dominated regions converted to communism and provided Mao Zedong and other revolutionary leaders with a great deal of support.

After Mao Zedong's revolutionary triumph in 1949, the Chinese Communist party worked to revive Zhuang ethnicity, even though most Zhuangs were so sinicized that they actually opposed the awarding of official recognition as a minority nationality. The zealousness with which Communist party officials approached the issue grew out of their desire to prove that the former nationalist Chinese government had persecuted the Zhuangs. In the early 1950s, most Zhuangs actually claimed to be of Han descent. Denying Zhuang origins was not all uncommon among Zhuang people. In 1952 the new government proclaimed establishment of a Zhuang Autonomous Region in western Guangxi Province. Six years later, the government declared all of Guangxi Province to be an autonomous region even though Han,* Miao,* Maonan, Dong,* Mulam, Jing,* and Hui* peoples also lived there. The government launched Zhuang-speaking radio stations, created a specialized romanized script for Zhuang, and dubbed films in movie houses into Zhuang. They even went so far as to declare Zhuang—along with Uigur,* Tibetan,* Mongolian, and Korean*—as one of China's premier minority languages. In 1960 the central government proclaimed the Zhuang-Miao Autonomous Prefecture in southeastern Yunnan Province and the Lianshan Zhuang-Yao Autonomous County in Guangdong Province.

Zhuang villages are located primarily in mountainous areas. In Guangxi, most communities are homogenous Zhuang; in Yunnan, Guangdong, and Hunan, they live in more multicultural settings. Village size ranges from hamlets of only twenty people to small towns of more than two thousand people. Some marketing centers are considerably larger. Zhuangs prefer villages to sit on mountain slopes, always facing a river. Their traditional two-story houses, constructed of wood pilings, can still be seen, although the one-story tile-roofed brick homes typical of Han people are becoming more common.

The Zhuang economy today is all but indistinguishable from that of the Han people. Zhuangs practice paddy-rice farming and dry-rice highland farming, and they also raise maize and yams. Because of the soil and climate, which is wet and humid, they are able to double-crop and triple-crop in most areas. Oranges, pineapples, bananas, litchis, mangoes, and sugarcane are widely grown as well. Zhuang men still hunt, but hunting supplies only a tiny amount of community food needs. The older foraging economy no longer exists, but collecting mushrooms and medicinal herbs for cash is common. Some Zhuang areas also produce tea, tung oil, cinnamon, and ginseng.

SUGGESTED READINGS: Lin Yueh-Hwa and Norma Diamond, ''Zhuang,'' in Paul V. Hockings, ed., *The Encyclopedia of World Cultures*, vol. 6, *East and Southeast Asia*, 1991; Ma Yin, ed., *China's Minority Nationalities*, 1989.

ZHUANG-DAI. The term ''Zhuang-Dai'' is employed by ethnolinguists to refer to a branch of the Tai* languages spoken in southwestern China. Included in the Zhuang-Dai cluster are Zhuang,* Bouyei,* and Dai.* These languages are closely related to the Lao* language spoken in Laos and to Thai* in Thailand.

SUGGESTED READING: S. Robert Ramsey, *The Languages of China*, 1987.

ZHULUKBASH. The Zhulukbashes are a subgroup of the Kirgiz* people. They speak a Southern Kirgiz* dialect and live primarily in Akto, Yengishar, and Guma counties in the Xinjiang Uigur Autonomous Region of the People's Republic of China.

ZIN. The Zins are one of the many subgroups of the Li* people of Hainan Province in the People's Republic of China. Most Zins are farmers who raise coconuts, coffee, cocoa, sisal, rubber, cashews, pineapples, mangoes, and bananas. Rice is their staple.

ZODI DAI. See **DAI**.

ZUOJIANG. The Zuojiang people are a subgroup of the Zhuang* people of the People's Republic of China. The Zuojiang language is classified as one of the Southern Zhuang* dialects, and most of its speakers live today in Longzhou, Ningming, Pingxiang, Chongzuo, Daxin, and Tiandeng counties in the Guangxi Zhuang Autonomous Region.

1990 Populations of Officially Recognized Nationalities in the People's Republic of China

Han	1,042,482,187
Bouyei	25,445,059
Zhuang	15,489,630
Manchu	9,821,180
Hui	8,602,978
Miao	7,398,035
Uigur	7,214,431
Yi	6,572,173
Tujia	5,704,228
Mongol	4,806,849
Tibetan	4,593,330
Dong	2,514,014
Yao	2,134,013
Korean	1,920,597
Bai	1,594,827
Hani	1,252,952
Kazak	1,111,718
Li	1,110,900
Dai	1,025,128
She	630,378
Lisu	574,856
Gelao	437,997

Lahu	411,476
Dongxiang	373,872
Wa	351,974
Shui	345,993
Naxi	278,009
Qiang	198,252
Tu	191,624
Xibe	172,847
Mulam	159,328
Kirgiz	141,549
Daur	121,357
Jingpo	119,209
Salar	87,697
Blang	82,280
Maonan	71,968
Tajik	(Est.) 31,000
Pumi	29,657
Achang	27,708
Nu	27,123
Evenk	26,315
Jing	18,915
Jino	18,021
De'ang	(Est.) 15,000
Uzbek	14,502
Russian	13,504
Yugur	12,297
Bonan	12,212
Moinba	7,475
Oroqen	6,965
Drung	5,816
Tatar	4,873
Hezhen	4,245
Lloba	2,312
Gaoshan	(Est.) 300

APPENDIX B

A Chronology of Chinese History

c. 2100 B.C.

The Xia dynasty begins its domination of China.

c. 1600 B.C.

The Xia dynasty disintegrates politically and its five-century rule of China comes to an end.

The Shang dynasty replaces the Xia dynasty and begins its political control of China.

1027 B.C.

The Shang dynasty ends in China.

The centuries of the Western Zhou dynasty begin.

771 B.C.

The Western Zhou dynasty gives way to the Eastern Zhou dynasty.

221 B.C.

After nearly five centuries, the Eastern Zhou dynasty collapses and gives way to what is known today as the "Spring and Autumn Era" of Chinese history. Simultaneously, the "Warring States Era," which began in 475 B.C., comes to an end.

The shortlived Qin dynasty begins.

207 B.C.

The Qin dynasty gives way to the Han dynasty.

A.D. 220

After more than four centuries, the Han dynasty ends.

The Era of the Three Kingdoms begins.

239

The Chinese emperor sends an exploratory force to Taiwan.

265

The rise of the Western and Eastern Jin dynasty begins.

280

The Era of the Three Kingdoms begins to disintegrate.

420

The Western and Eastern Jin dynasty ends.
The Northern and Southern dynasty begins.

581

The rise of the Sui dynasty begins.

589

The end of the Northern and Southern dynasty officially occurs.

600

Hakka-speaking Chinese begin settling Taiwan.

618

The Sui dynasty collapses.
The Tang dynasty begins.

907

The Tang dynasty ends.
The Era of the Five dynasties begins.

960

The Era of the Five Dynasties ends.
The Song dynasty begins.

1115

The steady rise to power of the Jin dynasty begins.

1207

Genghis Khan and his Mongol armies begin establishing a political empire that reaches from China and Korea west through Tibet and all the way to Europe.

1234

The Jin dynasty ends.

1271

The Song dynasty officially collapses.

The Yuan dynasty begins.

1368

The Yuan dynasty ends.

The Ming dynasty begins.

1624

The Dutch negotiate the right to establish settlements in Taiwan.

1626

Spanish forces seize control of northern Taiwan.

1642

Dutch forces defeat the Spanish and take control of all of Taiwan.

1644

The Ming dynasty ends.

The Qing dynasty begins.

1662

The Cheng family seizes control of Taiwan and expels the Dutch.

1788

Nepal invades Tibet.

1839

The Opium War erupts between China and Great Britain.

1842

The Opium War ends with the signing of the Treaty of Nanking.

1851

The Taipeng Rebellion begins in China.

1855

The Muslim, or Panthay, Rebellion erupts in Yunnan Province.

1856

The Arrow War is fought by China and Great Britain.

1858

The Treaty of Tientsin is signed.

1862

The Muslim, or Tungan, Rebellion breaks out in western China.

1864

The Taipeng Rebellion ends.

1871

Russian troops occupy the Ili Valley in Xinjiang Province.

1873

The Muslim, or Panthay, Rebellion in Yunnan Province comes to an end.

1874

The Muslim, or Tungan, Rebellion ends.

1881

Russia and China sign the Treaty of Saint Petersburg, which returns the Ili Valley to Chinese control.

1883

War erupts between France and China over Vietnam.

1885

The Sino-Franco War over Vietnam ends.

Korea becomes a coprotectorate of China and Japan.

1886

Burma ceases to become a Chinese tributary state and becomes a British colony.

1887

Taiwan is made a province of China.

1894

The Sino-Japanese War begins.

1895

With the Treaty of Shimonoseki ending the Sino-Japanese War, China cedes Taiwan to Japan.

The Canton Rebellion, led by Sun Yat-sen, fails.

1896

A secret alliance is concluded between Russia and China. Russia agrees to protect China from Japanese aggression, and China agrees to the construction of the Chinese Eastern Railway.

1897

Germany occupies and seizes Kiaochow Bay in Shantung.

Russia occupies Port Arthur and Darien.

1898

Great Britain requests the Yangtze Valley be declared its special sphere of influence, which leads to China's decision to lease Weihaiwei and Kowloon to the British.

France requests that Guangdong, Guangxi, and Yunnan provinces be declared a French sphere of influence.

Japan requests that Fukien Province be declared a Japanese sphere of influence.

1899

The United States declares the Open Door policy in China—to leave the entire country open to the commerce of all nations.

1900

The Boxer Rebellion begins in China.

Russia invades Manchuria.

1904

War breaks out between Russia and Japan.

1910

The Canton Uprising occurs.

1911

The Qing dynasty ends.

Outer Mongolia secedes from China.

1912

The Republic of China era begins. Sun Yat-sen is installed as president.

Tibet expels all Han Chinese from the country.

The thirteenth Dalai Lama proclaims Tibetan independence.

1914

World War I breaks out in Europe.

Japan invades Shantung, ending German sovereignty there.

1915

Japan delivers the Twenty-One Demands to China.

1918

World War I ends.

1919

The Treaty of Versailles is signed.

1921

The First Congress of the Chinese Communist Party is held in Shanghai.

1924

The First National Congress of the Kuomintang is held in Canton.

1927

Mao Zedong leads the Autumn Harvest Uprising in Hunan.
The Communist party's Canton Uprising fails.

1931

Japan invades Manchuria.

1932

The Japanese army invades Shanghai.

1934

The Long March of Mao Zedong and the Chinese Communists begins.

1937

Japan invades at a number of points along the southeastern coast of China.

1941

Japan attacks Pearl Harbor.
Japanese forces attack and occupy Guam, Wake, Hong Kong, and Formosa.

1945

At the Yalta Conference, President Franklin D. Roosevelt of the United States agrees to Russian sovereignty over Manchuria if the Soviet Union will join the war against Japan. The Soviet Union agrees, and Soviet troops march into Manchuria.

1947

The Inner Mongolian Autonomous Region is established.

1949

The Republic of China ends, and Mao Zedong and the Chinese Communist party establish the People's Republic of China.

1950

Chiang Kai-shek takes over the presidency of the Republic of China on Taiwan.
The Sino-Soviet Treaty of Friendship, Alliance, and Mutual Assistance is signed.
The Korean War breaks out when North Korean troops invade South Korea.

People's Liberation Army troops invade Tibet.

Ganzi Tibetan Autonomous Prefecture is established.

Tianzhu Tibetan Autonomous County is established.

North Gansu Mongolian Autonomous County is established.

Dongxiang Autonomous County is established.

1951

Longsheng Multinational Autonomous County is established.

Eshan Yi Autonomous County is established.

Oroqen Autonomous Banner is established.

Ewenki Autonomous Banner is established.

Yushu Tibetan Autonomous Prefecture is established.

1952

Yanbian Korean Autonomous Prefecture is established.

Liangshan Yi Autonomous Prefecture is established.

Jinxiu Yao Autonomous County is established.

Rongshui Miao Autonomous County is established.

Sanjiang Dong Autonomous County is established.

1953

Ngawa Tibetan Autonomous Prefecture is established.

Xishuangbanna Dai Autonomous Prefecture is established.

Dehong-Dai-Jingpo Autonomous Prefecture is established.

South Gansu Tibetan Autonomous Prefecture is established.

South Qinghai Tibetan Autonomous Prefecture is established.

Huangnan Tibetan Autonomous Prefecture is established.

North Qinghai Tibetan Autonomous Prefecture is established.

Liannan Yao Autonomous County is established.

Longlin Multinational Autonomous County is established.

Muli Tibetan Autonomous County is established.

Lancang Lahu Autonomous County is established.

Menyuan Hui Autonomous County is established.

Zhangjiachuan Hui Autonomous County is established.

A cease-fire is signed ending the hostilities of the Korean War.

1954

Nujiang Lisu Autonomous Prefecture is established.

Guoluo Tibetan Autonomous Prefecture is established.

West Qinghai Mongolian-Tibetan Autonomous Prefecture is established.

Bayingolin Mongolian Autonomous Prefecture is established.

Bortala Mongolian Autonommous Prefecture is established.

Kizilsu Kirghiz Autonomous Prefecture is established.

Changji Hui Autonomous Prefecture is established.

Ili Kazakh Autonomous Prefecture is established.

Jiangcheng Hani-Yi Autonomous County is established.

Menglian Dai-Lahu-Va Autonomous County is established.

South Gansu Yugur Autonomous County is established.

Aksay Kazak Autonomous County is established.

Huzhu Tu Autonomous County is established.

Hualong Hui Autonomous County is established.

Xunhua Salar Autonomous County is established.

Henan Mongolian Autonomous County is established.

Yanqi Hui Autonomous County is established.

Qapqai Xibe Autonomous County is established.

Mori Kazakh Autonomous County is established.

Hoboksar Mongolian Autonomous County is established.

Taxkorgan Tajik Autonomous County is established.

Barkol Kazakh Autonomous County is established.

Tongdao Dong Autonomous County is established.

Weining Yi-Hui-Miao Autonomous County is established.

1955

Xinjiang Uigur Autonomous Region is established.

Mengcun Hui Autonomous County is established.

Dachang Hui Autonomous County is established.

Jianghua Yao Autonomous County is established.

Chengbu Miao Autonomous County is established.

Du'an Yao Autonomous County is established.

Gengma Dai-Va Autonomous County is established.

1956

Southeast Guizhou Miao-Dong Autonomous Prefecture is established.

South Guizhou Bouyei-Miao Autonomous Prefecture is established.

Dali Bai Autonomous Prefecture is established.

Linxia Hui Autonomous Prefecture is established.

Qian Gorlos Mongolian Autonomous County is established.

Dorbod Mongolian Autonomous County is established.

Xinhuang Dong Autonomous County is established.

Bama Yao Autonomous County is established.

Songtao Miao Autonomous County is established.

Ninglang Yi Autonomous County is established.

Gongshan Drung-Nu Autonomous County is established.

Weishan-Yi-Hui Autonomous County is established.

Lunan Yi Autonomous County is established.

1957

Xiangxi Tujia-Miao Autonomous Prefecture is established.

Hainan Li-Miao Autonomous Prefecture is established.

Diqing Tibetan Autonomous Prefecture is established.

Honghe Han-Yi Autonomous Prefecture is established.

Sandu Shui Autonomous County is established.

1958

International tensions escalate when the People's Republic of China forces fire on the islands of Quemoy and Matsu, over which the Republic of China claims sovereignty.

Guangxi Zhuang Autonomous Region is established.

Ningxia Hui Autonomous Region is established.

Wenshan Zhuang-Miao Autonomous Prefecture is established.

Chuxiong Yi Autonomous Prefecture is established.

Harqin Left Wing Mongolian Autonomous County is established.

Fuxin Mongolian Autonomous County is established.

Changbai Korean Autonomous County is established.

Fangcheng Multinational Autonomous County is established.

Maowen Qiang Autonomous County is established.

Morin Dawa Daur Autonomous Banner is established.

1959

Tibet rebels against Chinese control, and the Dalai Lama goes into exile. Thousands of Tibetan nationalists are killed when Chinese troops brutally suppress the rebellion.

1960

People's Republic of China forces bombard Quemoy.

The Sino-Soviet rivalry begins anew when the Soviet Union recalls all Soviet technical advisors from China.

1961

Lijiang Naxi Autonomous County is established.

1962

Lianshan Zhuang and Yao Autonomous County is established.

1963

Ruyuan Yao Autonomous County is established.

Zhenning Bouyei-Miao Autonomous County is established.

Pingbian Miao Autonomous County is established.

Hekou Yao Autonomous County is established.

1964

Cangyuan Va Autonomous County is established.

1965

Tibetan Autonomous Region is established.

Nanjian Yi Autonomous County is established.

Ximeng Va Autonomous County is established.

1966

Ziyun Miao-Bouyei Autonomous County is established.

The Cultural Revolution begins in China. Red Guard cadres loot Tibetan temples and place thousands of Lamaist Buddhist monks in labor camps. Similar attacks begin on Muslim mosques throughout the country.

1969

Sino-Soviet border clashes occur.

1971

The People's Republic of China is admitted to the United Nations and assumes the seat formerly occupied by the Republic of China.

1972

President Richard Nixon visits China.

1975

Chiang Kai-shek dies.

1976

Zhou Enlai dies.

Mao Zedong dies.

1979

Mojiang Hani Autonomous County is established.

Xundian Hui-Yi Autonomous County is established.

1980

Yuanjiang Hani-Hi Autonomous County is established.

Xinping Yi-Dai Autonomous County is established.

1981

Guanling Bouyei-Miao Autonomous County is established.

Jishi Shan Bonan-Dongxiang Autonomous County is established.

1982

Southwest Guizhou Bouyei-Miao Autonomous Prefecture is established.

1983

Exi Tujia-Miao Autonomous Prefecture is established.

Xiushan Tujia-Miao Autonomous County is established.

Xiyang Tujia-Miao Autonomous County is established.

1984

Changyang Tujia Autonomous County is established.

Wufeng Tujia Autonomous County is established.

Fuchuan Yao Autonomous County is established.

Luocheng Mulam Autonomous County is established.

Ebian Yi Autonomous County is established.

Mabian Yi Autonomous County is established.

Pengshui Miao-Tujia Autonomous County is established.

Qianjiang Tujia-Miao Autonomous County is established.

Shizhu Tujia Autonomous County is established.

Yuping Dong Autonomous County is established.

1985

Jingning She Autonomous County is established.

Shuangjiang Lahu-Va-Blang-Dai Autonomous County is established.

Weixi Lisu Autonomous County is established.

Jingdong Yi Autonomous County is established.

Jinggu-Dai-Yi Autonomous County is established.

Puer Hani-Hi Autonomous County is established.

Yangbi Yi Autonomous County is established.

Luquan Yi-Miao Autonomous County is established.

Jinping Miao-Yao Autonomous County is established.

1987

Chinese soldiers crush Tibetan nationalist demonstrations held in Llasa.

1988

Anti-Chinese protest demonstrations continue to take place in Llasa, Tibet.

1989

The student rebellion at Tiananmen Square in Beijing is crushed by People's Liberation Army troops. More than 1,000 Chinese students die in the fighting.

Widespread anti-Chinese rioting erupts in Llasa, Tibet. China sends in People's Liberation Army troops to quell the rebellion. More than 300 demonstrators are killed.

1993

Large-scale demonstrations erupt in Llasa, Tibet, when Tibetan natonalists demand independence from China.

1997

Deng Xiaopeng dies.

Muslim unrest erupts in the Xinjiang Uigur Autonomous Region.

Hong Kong reverts to the sovereignty of the People's Republic of China.

1999 (tentative)

Macao reverts to the sovereignty of the People's Republic of China.

SOURCES: John F. Cooper, *Historical Dictionary of Taiwan*, 1993; Michael Dillon, *China's Muslims*, 1996; Pierre-Antoine Donnet, *Tibet: Survival in Question*, 1994; Colin Mackerras and Amanda Yorke, *The Cambridge Handbook of Contemporary China*, 1990.

APPENDIX C

Autonomous Ethnic Political Units in the People's Republic of China

Autonomous Regions	Province	Capital
Inner Mongolian Autonomous Region		Hohhot
Xinjiang Uigur Autonomous Region		Urumqi
Guangxi Zhuang Autonomous Region		Nanning
Ningxia Hui Autonomous Region		Yinchuan
Tibetan Autonomous Region		Llasa

Autonomous Prefectures	Province	Capital
Yanbian Korean Autonomous Prefecture	Jilin	Yanji
Exi Tujia-Miao Autonomous Prefecture	Hubei	Enshi
Xiangxi Tujia-Miao Autonomous Prefecture	Hunan	Jishou
Hainan Li-Miao Autonomous Prefecture	Hainan	Tongshen
Ganzi Tibetan Autonomous Prefecture	Sichuan	Kangding
Liangshan Yi Autonomous Prefecture	Sichuan	Xichang
Ngawa Tibetan Autonomous Prefecture	Sichuan	Maerkang
Southeast Guizhou Miao-Dong Autonomous Prefecture	Guizhou	Kaili
South Guizhou Bouyei-Miao Autonomous Prefecture	Guizhou	Duyun

Autonomous Regions	Province	Capital
Southwest Guizhou Bouyei-Miao Autonomous Prefecture	Guizhou	Xingyi
Xishuangbanna Dai Autonomous Prefecture	Yunnan	Jinghong
Dehong-Dai-Jingpo Autonomous Prefecture	Yunnan	Luxi
Nujiang Lisu Autonomous Prefecture	Yunnan	Liuku
Dali Bai Autonomous Prefecture	Yunnan	Dali
Diqing Tibetan Autonomous Prefecture	Yunnan	Zhongdian
Honghe Han-Yi Autonomous Prefecture	Yunnan	Gejiu
Wenshan Zhuang-Miao Autonomous Prefecture	Yunnan	Wenshan
Chuxiong Yi Autonomous Prefecture	Yunnan	Chuxiong
South Gansu Tibetan Autonomous Prefecture	Gansu	Hezuo
Linxia Hui Autonomous Prefecture	Gansu	Linxia
Yushu Tibetan Autonomous Prefecture	Qinghai	Yushu
South Qinghai Tibetan Autonomous Prefecture	Qinghai	Gonghe
Huangnan Tibetan Autonomous Prefecture	Qinghai	Tongren
North Qinghai Tibetan Autonomous Prefecture	Qinghai	Menyuan
Guoluo Tibetan Autonomous Prefecture	Qinghai	Maqen
West Qinghai Mongolian-Tibetan Autonomous Prefecture	Qinghai	Delingha
Bayingolin Mongolian Autonomous Prefecture	Xinjiang	Korla
Bortala Mongolian Autonomous Prefecture	Xinjiang	Bole
Kizilsu Kirgiz Autonomous Prefecture	Xinjiang	Artux
Changji Hui Autonomous Prefecture	Xinjiang	Changji
Ili Kazak Autonomous Prefecture	Xinjiang	Gulja

Autonomous Banners	Banner	
Oroqen Autonomous Banner	Inner Mongolia	

Autonomous Banners	Banner
Ewenki Autonomous Banner	Inner Mongolia
Morin Dawa Daur Autonomous Banner	Inner Mongolia

Autonomous Counties	Province
Mengcun Hui Autonomous County	Hebei
Dachang Hui Autonomous County	Hebei
Harqin Left Wing Mongolian Autonomous County	Liaoning
Fuxin Mongolian Autonomous County	Liaoning
Qian Gorlos Mongolian Autonomous County	Jilin
Changbai Korean Autonomous County	Jilin
Dorbod Mongolian Autonomous County	Heilongjiang
Jingning She Autonomous County	Zhejiang
Changyang Tujia Autonomous County	Hubei
Wufeng Tujia Autonomous County	Hubei
Tongdao Dong Autonomous County	Hunan
Jianghua Yao Autonomous County	Hunan
Chengbu Miao Autonomous County	Hunan
Xinhuang Dong Autonomous County	Hunan
Liannan Yao Autonomous County	Guangdong
Lianshan Zhuang and Yao Autonomous County	Guangdong
Ruyuan Yao Autonomous County	Guangdong
Longsheng Multinational Autonomous County	Guangxi
Jinxiu Yao Autonomous County	Guangxi
Rongshui Miao Autonomous County	Guangxi
Sanjiang Dong Autonomous County	Guangxi
Du'an Yao Autonomous County	Guangxi
Bama Yao Autonomous County	Guangxi
Fangcheng Multinational Autonomous County	Guangxi
Longlin Multinational Autonomous County	Guangxi

Autonomous Counties	Province
Fuchuan Yao Autonomous County	Guangxi
Luocheng Mulam Autonomous County	Guangxi
Muli Tibetan Autonomous County	Guangxi
Maowen Qiang Autonomous County	Sichuan
Xiushan Tujia-Miao Autonomous County	Sichuan
Xiyang Tujia-Miao Autonomous County	Sichuan
Ebian Yi Autonomous County	Sichuan
Mabian Yi Autonomous County	Sichuan
Pengshui Miao-Tujia Autonomous County	Sichuan
Qianjiang Tujia-Miao Autonomous County	Sichuan
Shizhu Tujia Autonomous County	Sichuan
Weining Yi-Hui-Miao Autonomous County	Guizhou
Songtao Miao Autonomous County	Guizhou
Sandu Shui Autonomous County	Guizhou
Zhenning Bouyei-Miao Autonomous County	Guizhou
Ziyun Miao-Bouyei Autonomous County	Guizhou
Guanling Bouyei-Miao Autonomous County	Guizhou
Yuping Dong Autonomous County	Yunnan
Eshan Yi Autonomous County	Yunnan
Lancang Lahu Autonomous County	Yunnan
Jiangcheng Hani-Yi Autonomous County	Yunnan
Menglian Dai-Lahu-Va Autonomous County	Yunnan
Gengma Dai-Va Autonomous County	Yunnan
Ninglang Yi Autonomous County	Yunnan
Gongshan Drung-Nu Autonomous County	Yunnan
Weishan-Yi-Hui Autonomous County	Yunnan
Lunan Yi Autonomous County	Yunnan

Autonomous Counties	Province
Lijiang Naxi Autonomous County	Yunnan
Pingbian Miao Autonomous County	Yunnan
Hekou Yao Autonomous County	Yunnan
Cangyuan Va Autonomous County	Yunnan
Shuangjiang Lahu-Va-Blang-Dai Autonomous County	Yunnan
Weixi Lisu Autonomous County	Yunnan
Jingdong Yi Autonomous County	Yunnan
Jinggu-Dai-Yi Autonomous County	Yunnan
Puer Hani-Hi Autonomous County	Yunnan
Yangbi Yi Autonomous County	Yunnan
Luquan Yi-Miao Autonomous County	Yunnan
Jinping Miao-Yao Autonomous County	Yunnan
Ximeng Va Autonomous County	Yunnan
Nanjian Yi Autonomous County	Yunnan
Mojiang Hani Autonomous County	Yunnan
Xundian Hui-Yi Autonomous County	Yunnan
Yuanjiang Hani-Hi Autonomous County	Yunnan
Xinping Yi-Dai Autonomous County	Yunnan
Tianzhu Tibetan Autonomous County	Gansu
North Gansu Mongolian Autonomous County	Gansu
Dongxiang Autonomous County	Gansu
Zhangjiachuan Hui Autonomous County	Gansu
South Gansu Yugur Autonomous County	Gansu
Aksay Kazakh Autonomous County	Gansu
Jishi Shan Bonan-Dongxiang Autonomous County	Gansu
Menyuan Hui Autonomous County	Qinghai
Huzhu Tu Autonomous County	Qinghai
Hualong Hui Autonomous County	Qinghai
Xunhua Salar Autonomous County	Qinghai

Autonomous Counties	Province
Henan Mongolian Autonomous County	Qinghai
Yanqi Hui Autonomous County	Xinjiang
Qapqai Xibe Autonomous County	Xinjiang
Mori Kazak Autonomous County	Xinjiang
Hoboksar Mongolian Autonomous County	Xinjiang
Taxkorgan Tajik Autonomous County	Xinjiang
Barkol Kazak Autonomous County	Xinjiang

SOURCE: Colin Mackerras and Amanda Yorke, *The Cambridge Handbook of Contemporary China*, 1990.

Selected Bibliography of English Titles

Aijmer, Goran. *The Religion of Taiwan Chinese in an Anthropological Perspective.* 1976.

Akiner, Shirim. *Islamic Peoples of the Soviet Union.* 1986.

Allworth, Edward, ed. *The Nationality Question in Soviet Central Asia.* 1973.

Atlas of Man. 1978.

Aziz, Barbara. *Tibetan Frontier Families.* 1978.

Bai Ziran, ed. *A Happy People: The Miaos.* 1988.

Bailey, Paul John. *China in the Twentieth Century.* 1988.

Ballard, William L. "Phonological History of Wu." Ph.D. diss., University of California, Berkeley. 1969.

Bannister, Judith. *China: A Country Study.* 1981.

Barnett, A. Doak. *China's Far West: Four Decades of Change.* 1993.

Barth, Frederick. "The Guru and the Conjurer: Transactions in Knowledge and the Shaping of Culture in Southeast Asia and Melanesia." *Man* 27 (June 1992), 640–57.

Baum, Richard. *Prelude to Revolution: Mao, the Party, and the Peasant Question.* 1975.

Baum, Richard, and Louise B. Bennett, eds. *China in Ferment: Perspectives on the Cultural Revolution.* 1971.

Benedict, Paul K. *Austro-Thai Language and Culture.* 1975.

———. *Sino-Tibetan: A Conspectus.* 1972.

Bennigsen, Alexandre, and Wimbush S. Enders. *Muslims of the Soviet Empire: A Guide.* 1986.

Bianco, Lucien. *Origins of the Chinese Revolution, 1915–1949.* 1971.

Bloom, Alfred H. "The Impact of Chinese Linguistic Structure on Cognitive Style." *Current Anthropology* 20 (September 1979), 585–601.

Bonavia, David. *The Chinese.* 1980.

Bradley, David. *Lahu Dialects.* 1979.

Cameron, Meribeth E. *The Reform Movement in China, 1898–1912.* 1931.

Chaio Chien and Nicholas Tapp, eds. *Ethnicity and Ethnic Groups in China.* 1989.

Chen, Chi-lu. *Material Culture of the Formosan Aborigines.* 1968.

Ch'en, Jerome. *Mao and the Chinese Revolution*. 1965.

Ch'en, Kenneth K. S. *Buddhism in China: A Historical Survey*. 1964.

Chen Leqi. "Xinjiang's Rich Song and Dance Tradition." *China Reconstructs* 38 (October 1989), 50–53.

Chen Rinong. "Yunnan: A Family of Many Nationalities." *China Today* 43 (December 1994), 10–14.

Ch'en, Yung-fa. *Making Revolution: The Communist Movement in Eastern and Central China, 1937–1945*. 1986.

Chesneaux, Jean. *China: The People's Republic, 1949–1976*. 1979.

Ch'i Hsi-sheng. *Nationalist China at War: Military Defeat and National Collapse, 1937–45*. 1982.

Chi Wen-shun. *Ideological Conflicts in Modern China: Democracy and Authoritarianism*. 1986.

Chien-min Chao. "The Procedure for Local Legislation in Mainland China and Legislation in National Autonomous Areas." *Issues and Studies* 30 (September 1994), 95–116.

"China's National Minorities." *Beijing Review* 27 (1983), 19–20.

"China's National Minorities." *China Today* 45 (April 1996), 15.

Chodag, Tiley. *Tibet: The Land and the People*. 1988.

Clarke, Samuel R. *Among the Tribes in Southwest China*. 1911.

Clubb, O. Edmund. *Twentieth Century China*. 1978.

Cohen, Myron L. "The Hakka or 'Guest People': Dialect as a Sociocultural Variable in Southeastern China." *Ethnology* 15 (1968), 237–92.

Comrie, Bernard. *The Languages of the Soviet Union*. 1983.

Constable, Nicole. *Christian Souls and Chinese Spirits: A Hakka Community in Hong Kong*. 1994.

Cooper, John F. *Historical Dictionary of Taiwan*. 1993.

Cremer, R. D., ed. *Macau: City of Commerce and Culture*. 1987.

DeFrancis, John. *Nationalism and Language Reform in China*. 1950.

Detrich, Craig. *People's China: A Brief History*. 1986.

DeYoung, Louise P. "Americans Visit South China's Minority Nationalities." *China Reconstructs* 34 (June 1985), 58–59.

Diamond, Norma. "The Miao and Poison: Interactions on China's Southwest Frontier." *Ethnology* 27 (1988), 1–25.

Dillon, Michael. *China's Muslims*. 1996.

Dittmer, Lowell. *China's Continuous Revolution: The Post-Liberation Epoch, 1949–1981*. 1986.

Dobby, Ernest. *Southeast Asia*. 1973.

Doolin, Dennis, and Robert C. North. *The Chinese People's Republic*. 1966.

Dreyer, June Teufel. *China's Forty Millions: Minority Nationalities and National Integration in the People's Republic of China*. 1976.

Durrenberger, E. Paul. "Law and Authority in a Lisu Village." *Journal of Anthropological Research* 32 (1976), 301–23.

Eastman, Lloyd E. *The Abortive Revolution: China under Nationalist Rule, 1927–1949*. 1984.

———. *The Nationalist Era in China, 1927–1949*. 1990.

Eberhard, Wolfram. *China's Minorities: Yesterday and Today*. 1982.

———. *The Local Cultures of South and East China*. 1968.

Ebrey, Patricia Buckley. *Chinese Civilization and Society: A Sourcebook.* 1981.

Edwards, Mike. "Hong Kong: Countdown to China." *National Geographic* 191 (March 1997), 32–39.

———. "Our Man in China: Joseph Rock." *National Geographic* 191 (January 1997), 62–100.

Ellis, William S. "Shanghai." *National Geographic* 185 (March 1994), 2–34.

Esherick, Joseph W. *The Origins of the Boxer Uprising.* 1987.

Fei, Hsiuao Tung (Xiaotong). *Ethnic Identification in China: Toward a People's Anthropology.* 1981.

Ferrell, Raleigh J. *Taiwan Aboriginal Groups: The Problems in Cultural and Linguistic Classification.* 1969.

Fisher, Charles. *Southeast Asia: A Social, Economic, and Political Geography.* 1966.

Fitzgerald, C. P. *The Southern Expansion of the Chinese People: Southern Fields and Southern Ocean.* 1972.

Forster, Keith. *Rebellion and Factionalism in a Chinese Province: Zhejiang, 1966–1976.* 1990.

French, Rebecca. *The Golden Yoke: The Legal System of Buddhist Tibet.* 1993.

Friedman, Jonathan. *System, Structure, and Contradiction.* 1979.

Gallin, Bernard. "Cousin Marriage in China." *Ethnology* 2 (1963), 104–8.

Gasster, Michael. *China's Struggle to Modernize.* 1972.

Geddes, W. R. *Migrants of the Mountains: The Cultural Ecology of the Blue Miao (Hmong Njua) of Thailand.* 1976.

Gill, Linda Hoyle. *Portraits of China.* 1990.

Gillette, Ned. "Adventure in Western China." *National Geographic* 159 (February 1981), 174–99.

Gittings, John. *China Changes Face: The Road from Revolution, 1949–1989.* 1989.

Gladney, Dru C. "The Ethnogenesis of the Uighur." *Central Asian Survey* 9 (1990), 1–27.

———. *Muslim Chinese: Ethnic Nationalism in the People's Republic.* 1991.

Goldman, Merle. *Sowing the Seeds of Democracy in China: Political Reform in the Deng Xiaoping Era.* 1994.

Goldstein, Melvin, and Cynthia M. Beall. *The Changing World of Mongolia's Nomads.* 1994.

Gore, Rick. "Journey to China's West." *National Geographic* 157 (March 1980), 292–332.

Gray, Jack. *Rebellions and Revolutions: China from the 1800s to the 1980s.* 1990.

Grunfeld, A. T. "In Search of Equality: Relations between China's Ethnic Minorities and the Majority Han." *Bulletin of Concerned Asian Scholars* 17 (1985), 54–67.

———. *The Making of Modern Tibet.* 1987.

Guillen-Nunez, Cesar. *Macau.* 1984.

Guldin, Gregory Eliyu. "The Anthropological Study Tour in China: A Call for Cultural Guides." *Human Organization* 48 (Summer 1989), 126–34.

———. "Chinese Anthropologies." *Chinese Anthropology and Sociology* 20 (1988), 3–32.

Hanks, Lucien M. *Rice and Man.* 1972.

Hashimoto, Mantaro J. *The Hakka Dialect: A Linguistic Study of Its Phonology, Syntax, and Lexicon.* 1973.

Hashimoto, Oi-kan Yue. *Studies in Yue Dialects*, vol. 1, *Phonology of Cantonese.* 1972.

Hawkins, John N. "Educational Policy and National Minorities in the People's Republic of China: The Politics of Intergroup Relations." In J. N. Hawkins, ed., *Education and Society Change in the People's Republic of China*. 1983.

Heberer, Thomas, ed. *Ethnic Minorities in China: Tradition and Transformation*, 1984.

Hefner, Robert W. "Politics and Social Identity: Introduction." *Journal of Asian Studies* 46 (1987), 491–93.

Hendricks, Glenn L., Bruce T. Downing, and Amos S. Deinard, eds. *The Hmong in Transition*. 1986.

Ho Ping-ti. *Studies in the Population of China, 1368–1953*. 1953.

Hofheinz, Roy, Jr. *The Broken Wave: The Chinese Communist Peasant Movement, 1922–1928*. 1977.

Hsiao Kung-chuan. *Rural China: Imperial Control in the Nineteenth Century*. 1960.

Hsieh, Jiann. "China's Nationality Policy: Its Development and Problems." *Anthropos* 81 (1986), 1–20.

Hsiung, James, ed. *The Taiwan Experience, 1950–1980*. 1981.

Hsu, Immanuel C. Y. *The Rise of Modern China*. 1990.

Hsu Ying and J. Marvin Brown. *Speaking Chinese in China*. 1983.

Hu Sheng. *Imperialism and Chinese Politics*. 1981.

Huang Shu-min. *The Spiral Road: Changes in a Chinese Village through the Eyes of a Communist Party Leader*. 1989.

Hung Chang-tai. *Going to the People: Chinese Intellectuals and Folk Literature, 1918–1937*. 1986.

Israeli, Raphael, and Anthony H. Johns, eds. *Islam in Asia*. 1984.

Jacchid, Sechin, and Paul Hyer. *Mongolia's Culture and Society*. 1979.

Jen Yu-wen. *The Taiping Revolutionary Movement*. 1973.

Johnson, Chalmers A., ed. *The Taiping Revolutionary Movement*. 1973.

Johnson, Kay A. *Women, the Family, and Peasant Revolution in China*. 1985.

Kiang, Clyde. *The Hakka Odyssey and Their Taiwan Homeland*. 1994.

———. *The Hakka Search for a Homeland*. 1991.

Kim, Choong Soon. *Faithful Endurance: An Ethnography of Korean Family Dispersal*. 1988.

Kolarz, Walter. *The Peoples of the Soviet Far East*. 1954.

Kozlov, Viktor. *The Peoples of the Soviet Union*. 1946.

Kratochvil, Paul. *The Chinese Language Today*. 1968.

Kuhn, Philip. *Rebellion and Its Enemies in Late Imperial China: Militarization and Social Structure, 1796–1864*. 1980.

Kunstadter, Peter, ed. *Southeast Asian Tribes, Minorities, and Nations*. 1967.

Lary, Diana. *Warlord Soldiers: Chinese Common Soldiers, 1911–1935*. 1985.

LeBar, Frank M., Gerald C. Hickey, and John K. Musgrave. *Ethnic Groups of Mainland Southeast Asia*. 1964.

Lee, Chong-sik. *Revolutionary Struggle in Manchuria: Chinese Communism and Soviet Interest, 1922–1945*. 1983.

Lee, Hung Yung. *The Politics of the Chinese Cultural Revolution*. 1978.

Lehmann, Winfred P., ed. *Language and Linguistics in the People's Republic of China*. 1975.

Lemoine, Jacques, and Chiao Chien, eds. *The Yao of South China: Recent International Studies*. 1991.

Leung, Edwin Pak-wah. *Ethnic Compartmentalization and Regional Autonomy in the People's Republic of China. Chinese Law and Government.* 1982.

————. "Regional Autonomy versus Central Authority: The Inner Mongolian Autonomous Movement and the Chinese Response, 1925–1947." *Journal of Oriental Studies* 25 (1987), 49–62.

Levy, Marion Joseph. *The Family Revolution in Modern China.* 1949.

Lewis, Charlton M. *Prologue to the Chinese Revolution: The Transformation of Ideas and Institutions in Hunan Province, 1891–1907.* 1976.

Lewis, Paul, and Elaine Lewis. *Peoples of the Golden Triangle.* 1984.

Li Fugen. "A Living Encyclopedia of Chinese Ethnic Groups." *China Today* 44 (January 1995), 10–12.

Li Yushan. "Ethnic Songs and Dances, A Major Force in China's Culture." *China Today* 43 (October 1994), 35–41.

Lindbeck, John M. H., ed. *China: Management of a Revolutionary Society.* 1971.

Lipman, Jonathan. "Hui-Hui: An Ethnohistory of the Chinese-Speaking Muslims." *Journal of South Asian and Middle Eastern Studies* 11 (1987), 112–30.

Liu Guokai. *A Brief Analysis of the Cultural Revolution.* 1984.

Liu Hong. "When Minority Nationalities Marry." *China Today* 41 (January 1992), 43–45.

Liu Zhongpo. "China's Smallest Minority." *China Reconstructs* 29 (1980), 22–23.

Lopatin, Ivan A. "The Tungus Languages." *Anthropos* 53 (1958), 427–40.

Ma Yin, ed. *China's Minority Nationalities.* 1989.

"Macao Waits Its Turn." *National Geographic* 191 (March 1997), 30–31.

Mackerras, Colin, ed. *China: The Impact of Revolution: A Survey of Twentieth Century China.* 1976.

————. "Folksongs and Dances of China's Minority Nationalities: Policy, Tradition, and Professionalization." *Modern China* 10 (April 1984), 187–226.

Mackerras, Colin, and Amanda Yorke. *The Cambridge Handbook of Contemporary China.* 1990.

Mangrai, Sao Saimong. *The Shan States and the British Annexation.* 1965.

McCormack, William, and Stefan Wurm, eds. *Language and Thought: Anthropological Issues.* 1977.

McCreery, John L. "Women's Property Rights and Dowry in China and South Asia." *Ethnology* 15 (1976), 163–74.

Meisner, Maurice. *Mao's China and After.* 1986.

Melby, John F. *The Mandate of Heaven: A Record of Civil War in China, 1945–1949.* 1968.

Menges, Karl Heinrich. *The Turkic Languages and Peoples.* 1968.

Moise, Edwin E. *Modern China: A History.* 1986.

Moseley, George. *A Sino-Soviet Cultural Frontier: The Ili Kazakh Autonomous Chou.* 1966.

Moser, Leo J. *The Chinese Mosaic: The Peoples and Provinces of China.* 1984.

Naquin, Susan, and Evelyn Rawski. *Chinese Society in the Eighteenth Century.* 1987.

Nathan, Andrew J. *China's Crisis: Dilemmas of Reform and Prospects for Democracy.* 1990.

National Minorities Questions Editorial Panel. *Questions and Answers about China's Minorities.* 1985.

Newnham, Richard. *About Chinese.* 1971.

Norman, Jerry. "A Characterization of the Min Dialects." *Unicorn* 6 (1970), 19–34.
————. *Chinese*. 1988.
Nugent, David. "Closed Systems and Contradictions: The Kachin in and out of History." *Man* 17 (1982), 508–27.
O'Connor, Richard. "Agricultural Change and Ethnic Succession in Southeast Asian States: A Case for Regional Anthropology." *Journal of Asian Studies* 54 (November 1995), 968–96.
Olson, James S. *Ethnohistorical Dictionary of the Russian and Soviet Empires*. 1994.
Paksoy, H. B., ed. *Central Asia Reader: The Rediscovery of History*. 1994.
Pak-Wah Leung, Edwin. *Historical Dictionary of Revolutionary China, 1839–1976*. 1992.
Parkin, Robert. *A Guide to Austroasiatic Speakers and Their Languages*. 1991.
Pasternak, Burton, and Janet W. Salaff. *Cowboys and Cultivators: The Chinese of Inner Mongolia*. 1993.
Pedersen, Holger. *In Search of Old Shanghai*. 1983.
Peng Jianqun. "In the Mountains of the Gelos." *China Reconstructs* 36 (1987), 66–69.
Pepper, Suzanne. *Civil War in China: The Political Struggle, 1945–1949*. 1978.
Perry, Elizabeth. *Rebels and Revolutionaries in North China, 1845–1945*. 1980.
Pong, David, and Edmund S. K. Fung, eds. *Ideal and Reality: Social and Political Change in Modern China*. 1985.
Poppe, Nicholas. *Introduction to Altaic Linguistics*. 1965.
Potter, Jack M. *Thai Peasant Social Structure*. 1976.
Powell, Ralph L. *The Rise of Chinese Military Power, 1890–1912*. 1955.
Praybook, George. "Ethnology in China." *Current Anthropology* (April 1980), 264–80.
Price, Don C. *Russia and the Roots of the Chinese Revolution, 1896–1911*. 1974.
Pye, Lucian W. "China: Ethnic Minorities and National Security." In Nathan Glazer and Daniel P. Moynihan, eds. *Ethnicity: Theory and Practice*. 1975.
Ramsey, S. Robert. *The Languages of China*. 1987.
Roberts, John M., Chien Chiao, and Triloki N. Pandey. "Meaningful God Sets from a Chinese Personal Pantheon and a Hindu Personal Pantheon." *Ethnology* 14 (1975), 121–48.
Robinson, Thomas W., ed. *The Cultural Revolution in China*. 1971.
Rosenberg, William G., and Marilyn B. Young. *Transforming Russia and China: Revolutonary Struggle in the Twentieth Century*. 1982.
Rupen, Robert. *How Mongolia Is Really Ruled*. 1979.
Russell, Susan, ed. *Ritual, Power, and Economy: Upland-Lowland Contrasts in Mainland Southeast Asia*. 1989.
Schiffrin, Harold Z. *Sun Yat-sen and the Origins of the Chinese Revolution*. 1968.
Schwarz, Henry G. "Language Policies Toward Ethnic Minorities." *The China Quarterly* 16 (1962), 170–82.
————. *The Northern Minorities of China: A Survey*. 1984.
Scofield, John. "Kathmandu's Remarkable Newars." *National Geographic* 155 (February 1979), 268–84.
Seagrave, Sterling. *The Soong Dynasty*. 1986.
Shahrani, M. Nazil Mohib. *The Kirghiz and Wakhi of Afghanistan*. 1979.

Shen Che, and Lu Xiaoya. *Life among the Minority Nationalities of Northwest Yunnan.* 1989.

Sherard, Michael. *Shanghai Phonology.* 1972.

Sheridan, James E. *China in Disintegration: The Republican Era in Chinese History, 1912–1949.* 1975.

Snellgrove, David, and Hugh Richardson. *A Cultural History of Tibet.* 1980.

Snow, Edgar. *Red Star over China.* 1968.

Solomon, Richard H. *Mao's Revolution and the Chinese Political Culture.* 1971.

Spence, Jonathan D. *The Search for Modern China.* 1990.

Stafford, George. "Good Sons and Virtuous Mothers: Kinship and Chinese Nationalism in Taiwan," *Man* 27 (June 1992), 363–78.

Stafford, P. Steven. "Dialectics of Alienation: Individuals and Collectivities in Chinese Religion." *Man* 27 (June 1992), 378–92.

Stimson, Hugh. "Mandarin Dialects: A Problem in Classification." *Journal of the Chinese Language Teachers' Association* 1 (1966), 92–98.

Strong, Anna. *China's Millions: The Revolutionary Struggles from 1927–1935.* 1973.

Tan Manni. "A Land of Festivals." *China Today* 41 (January 1992), 33–36.

———. "Urumqi—Multinational City in China's Far West." *China Reconstructs* 30 (January 1981), 32–39.

Teiser, Stephen F. "Popular Religion." *Journal of Asian Studies* 54 (May 1995), 378–95.

Theroux, Paul. "China Passage." *National Geographic* 173 (March 1988), 296–328.

Thorton, Richard C. *China: A Political History.* 1981.

Thurston, Anne F. *Enemies of the People: The Ordeal of Intellectuals in China's Great Cultural Revolution.* 1988.

Tien Hung-mao. *Government and Politics in Kuomintang China, 1927–1937.* 1972.

———. *The Great Transition: Political and Social Change in the Republic of China.* 1989.

T'ien Ju'k'ang. *Religious Cults of the Pai-I along the Burma-Yunnan Border.* 1985.

Tsou Tang. *The Cultural Revolution and Post-Mao Reforms: A Historical Perspective.* 1986.

Tucker, Nancy Bernkopf. *Taiwan, Hong Kong, and the United States, 1945–1992.* 1994.

Vainshtein, Sevyan. *Nomads of South Siberia.* 1979.

Wachman, Alan M. *Taiwan: National Identity and Democratization.* 1994.

Wakeman, Frederic E., Jr. *The Fall of Imperial China.* 1975.

Walker, Anthony R., ed. *Farmers in the Hills.* 1986.

Wang, Y. C. *Chinese Intellectuals and the West, 1872–1949.* 1966.

Watson, James L. "Chattel Slavery in Chinese Peasant Society: A Comparative Analysis." *Ethnology* 15 (1976), 361–75.

Welch, Holmes. *The Practice of Chinese Buddhism, 1910–1950.* 1967.

Weller, Robert P. "Affines, Ambiguity, and Meaning in Hokkien Kin Terms." *Ethnology* 20 (1981), 15–29.

———. *Resistance, Chaos and Control in China: Taiping Rebels, Taiwanese Ghosts and Tiananmen.* 1994.

Weston, Anthony. *The Chinese Revolution.* 1980.

Wheeler, Geoffrey. *The Peoples of Soviet Central Asia.* 1966.

Wiens, Harold J. *China's March to the Tropics.* 1954.

Wilson, Dick. *Mao Tse-tung in the Scales of History.* 1977.

Wixman, Ronald. *The Peoples of the USSR: An Ethnographic Handbook.* 1984.

Wong How-Man. "Peoples of China's Far Provinces." *National Geographic* 165 (March 1984), 283–333.

Wu, David Y. H. "Chinese Minority Policy and the Meaning of Minority Culture: The Example of Bai in Yunnan, China." *Human Organization* 49 (Spring 1990), 1–13.

Wu Tien-wei. *Lin Biao and the Gang of Four: Contra-Confucianism in Historical and Intellectual Perspective.* 1983.

Yang, Martin C. "Peoples and Societies in Yunnan (Part I)." *Journal of Ethnology and Sociology* (Taipei) 16 (1978), 21–112.

Yi Xu. "Costumes and Ornaments of Minority Nationalities." *China Reconstructs* 32 (September 1983), 58–64.

You-ping Cheng. "The Interaction of Ethnicity and Party Politics in Taiwan." *Issues and Studies* 31 (November 1995), 1–15.

Yuen-fong Woon. "The Non-Localized Descent Group in Traditional China." *Ethnology* 18 (1979), 17–24.

Zarrow, Peter. *Anarchism and Chinese Political Culture.* 1990.

Zhang, Shifu, and David Y. H. Wu. "Ethnic Conflict and Unity: Examples of Conflict Management in Four Minority Groups in Yunnan, China." In J. D. Boucher, D. Landis, and K. Arnold, eds., *Inter-Ethnic Conflict: An International Perspective.* 1987.

Index

Boldface page numbers indicate location of main entries.

A Wa, **1**
Achang, **2–4**, 78, 166, 203
Adi, **4–6**, 321
Aga Khan, 36
Ahi, **6**
Aieng, 5
Aihui, **6**, 38
Aka, 4
Akabirting, 36
Akayev, Askar, 182
Akha, **6–8**
Akho, **8**, 135
Akimbeck, Azat, 347
Aksu, **8**
Alban, **8**
Alexander the Great, 36, 273
Ali Khalfa, Muhammad, 350
All-Uigur Congress, 345
Alshaa, **8**
Altai, **9–11**, 42, 188, 338
Altaic, **12**
Altai Kizhi, 9
Amdo, **12**, 293, 328
Ami, **12–13**, 40, 47, 81, 140, 148, 253, 260, 276, 296, 313, 324, 368
Amin, Mohammed, 297

Amok, **14**
Amulet Miao, 230
Anuchin, B. I., 10
Anung, **14**, 207
Ao, 251
Apa Tani, **14–15**
Ashing, 4
Asiluma, **15**, 135
Assamese, **15**, 81
Association of the Orochi, 269
Astrakhan Khanate, 266
Atayal, **15–16**, 81, 295–96, 300, 334
Atayalic, **16**
Axi, **16–17**

Baheng, **18**, 35
Bai, **18–21**
Baihong, 135
Baima, **21–22**, 287
Baisha, **22**, 25
Baiyi, **22**, 52
Baizhhung sect, 54
Baldakuyo, 36
Banded Sleeve Miao, 229
Bankeo, **23**, 190
Banlan, **23**

Baocheng, **23**, 285
Baoxian, **23**
Baozitong, **23**
Bar, 36
Baratilang, **23**, 36
Bare, 36
Barga, **23**
Bargat, 240
baya, 249
Bayan-Hongor, **23–24**
Beijingese, **24**
Beinan, **24**
Beisijiu, **24**
Bendi, 22, **25**, 202, 383
Benji Bama, 5
Benren, **25**
Bericho, 36
Bhaktapur, **25**, 258
Bhotia, **25–26**
Bhutanese, **26**, 299
Big-Board Miao, 229
Bijiang Nu, 262
Bi-Kaw, **27**, 135
Bingzhou, **27**
Biyue, **27**, 135
Black Lahu, **28**, 190, 262
Black Lisu, 207
Black Miao, 229
Black Pottery Culture, 98
Blang, **28–29**
Blue Miao, 229
Bo, Kingdom of, 19
Boat people, **29**
Bogar, **29–30**, 209
Bokar, 4
Bolshevik Revolution, 10, 37, 75, 141,
    172, 345
Boluozu Qiang, **30**
Bomo-Janbo, 5
Bon, 26, **30**
Bonan, **30–32**, 50, 80, 289, 333
Bopa, **32**
Bori, 4–5
Bouyei, **32–33**, 217–18
Boxer Rebellion, 75, 119
Brabaw, **33**
British, **33**

Buddhism, 3–4, 28–29, 53–54, 60, 81,
    108–11, 137, 305, 328–32
Bugalat, **34**, 37
Bugur, **34**
Bula, **34**
Bulgar el dzhadid, 323
Bulongkol, **34**
Bunao, **34**
Bunu, **34–35**, 81, 163, 362, 375, 383
Bunun, **35–36**, 154, 320
Burkhanism, 10–11
Burma Road, 19–20, 28, 380
Buroong, **36**
Burusho, 23, **36–37**, 55, 62, 179
Buryat, 34, **37–38**, 71, 178, 240, 316
Butha, **38**, 56, 228, 254, 257
Byau Min Yao, **39**
Byryugsoli, **39**

Canglo Moinba, **40**
Central Ami, 13, **40**
Central De'ang, **40–41**
Chagatai Khanate, 65
Chakhar, **41**, 240
Cham, **41**
Chang, **41**, 251
Changgan, **41**
Changjing, **41–42**, 80
Changyi, **42**
Chaoshan, **42**
Chelkan, 11, **42**
Chelpanov, Chot, 10
Che-nung, **42**, 207
Chinese Islamic Association, 66
Chinese (language), 24, **43–44**, 49, 79–
    80, 91–94, 145–46, 157–58, 220–23,
    236–37, 258, 361–62, 364–65, 383–84
Chi'ng Empire, 141
Chon, **44–45**
Chong'anjiang Miao, **45**
Christian, 19–20, 28, **45–46**, 69, 76, 159,
    195, 310
Chuan Qian Dian, **46**, 231–32
Chu Di, 130
Chuqu, **46–47**, 211
Chuzhou, **47**
Coastal Ami, **47**
Communist Party, 124–35, 181, 255–56

Confucianism, 21, 100, 102–3, 105–6, 110, 391
Confucius, 102–3
Constituent Congress of the High Altai, 10
Cooked Miao, **47**, 230
Cowrie-Shell Miao, 229, 232, 234
Cultural Revolution, 17, 20–21, 32, 53, 64, 66, 83–84, 127, 149–50, 208, 256–57, 278–79, 297, 338–39, 359
Cun, **47**
Cuona, 40, **47–48**, 238

Da Ka Va, **49**
Dabao, **49**
Dafla, **49–50**
Dafulu, **50**
Dahejia, **50**
Dai, 22, **50–54**, 60, 163, 168, 212, 263, 368
Daija, 52, **54**
Dailu, 52, **54**
daimong, 53
Daina, 52, **54**
Daina Daipeng, **54**
Dalai Lama, 37, 243, 327–32
Dali Kingdom, 19, 85, 168, 263, 298
Daoism, 17, 21, 81, 104
Dao Yin Mong, 53
Dard, **55**
Datian, **55**
Datong, **55**, 80
Daur, 38, **55–58**, 78, 91, 154, 253, 289–90
Dbu, **59**
Dbusgtsang, 12, **59**, 328
De'ang, **59–60**, 163, 205, 223, 252, 260, 280, 300
Declaration on the State Sovereignty of the Republic of Tatarstan, 323
dehanins, 35
Dehong Dai, **60**
Dejing, **60–61**
Deng, **61–62**, 169, 322
Deng Xiaoping, 94, 131–33
Deori, **62**
Deqen Nu, 262
Diramiting, 36, **62**

Divergent Lahu, **62**, 190
Divine Mother, 225
Dog-Mouth Miao, 230
Dolakha, **62**, 258
Dolie sect, 54
Dondupov, Dashi-Nima, 38, 242
Dong, **62–64**
Dong-shui, **64**
Dongsui, **64**, 80
Dongxiang, **64–66**, 311, 312–13, 359–60
Doni, **66–67**, 135
Draba, **67**
Drung, **67–69**
Du Wenxiu, 19

East Govi, **70**
East Turkestan, 347–48
Eastern Guizhou Miao, 230–31
Eastern Kham, **70**
Eastern Mandarin, **70**
Eastern Naxi, 254
Ekhirit, 37, **71**
Emu, **71**, 135
En, **71**
Enger, **71–72**
Eni, **72**, 135
Epom, 5
Ergong, **72**
Ersu, **72–73**, 287
Eurasian, **73**
Evenk, **73–76**, 91, 257

Far Eastern Republic, 141, 268
Filipino, **77**
Flowery Miao, 229, 234
Fuche, **77**
Fucheng, **78**
Fugong Nu, 262
Fuguang, **78**, 80
Fularji, **78**
Funing, **78**
Fusa, **78**

Gallong, 4
Gan, 24, 41, 43, 55, 64, 78, **79–80**, 148, 156, 157, 253, 259, 318, 368, 381
Gang of Four, 130–31
Gankui, **80**

Gansu Bonan, **80**
Gao'an, **80**
Gaori, **80**, 159
Gaoshan, **80–81**
Gaoyang, **81**
Garia, **81**
Gautama Siddhartha, 108–9
Ge, **81–82**
Gejia, **82**
Gelao, **82–84**, 91
Genghis Khan, 31, 114, 171–72
Getsuo, **84**, 135
glasnost, 133–34
Gokturk Empire, 342
Gongshan, **84–86**
Gorbachev, Mikhail, 133–34, 323
Goulou, **86**
Govi-Altay, **86**
Great Leap Forward, 126, 130, 181
Greater Altaian State, 11
Greater Oirotia State, 11
Green Miao, 229
Grishina, Lyudmila, 269
Gtsang, 59, **86**
Guangfu, **86**
Guangzhouese, **87**
Guari, **87**, 166
Gubei, **87**
Guibian, **87–88**
Guichong, **88**
G'uisha, 192
Guma, **88**
gunghengchao, 53
Guomindang, 120–26, 144–45, 303–4
Guozhou, **88**
Gurun, 26
Gurung, **88**
Guyiang Miao, **89**
Gyarung, **89**

Ha, 23, **90**, 138, 202
Ha-Ai, **90–91**, 135
Hailar, 56, **91**, 239, 253
Hainan Yao, **91**
Hakei Gelao, 83, **91**
Hakka, 24, 29, 43, 79, **91–94**, 144, 152, 157, 259, 302–3, 318, 332–33, 368, 384–85

hala, 57
Han, 10, 19, 24, 27, 32–36, 43–44, 47, 51, 85, 90, **94–134**, 150, 186–87, 201–3, 208, 255–57, 263, 266–67, 287–88, 301, 329–32, 338–39, 353–54, 373, 379–80, 393–94
Han Dynasty, 196
Hangzhou, **134–35**
Hani, 15, 27, 66, 71–72, 84, 90–91, **135–37**, 155, 167, 198, 265, 280, 312, 342
hanidos, 35
Han Tengri, 386
Hanxin, **138**
Hao-Bai, 135, **138**
Haoni, 135, **138**
Hayan, **138**
Hbrogpa, **138**
Hbrugchu, **139**
Hei-i, **139**
Hei-ku, **139**
Heisuhui Qiang, **139**
Heiziwei, **140**
Hengchun, **140**
Heyza, **140**
Hezhen, **140–42**
Hinayana Buddhism, 53–54, 57
Hkaku, **143**, 166
Hkawa, **143**
Hkun, **143**
Hong Kong, 91–94, 144–45, 278–79
Hong Kongese, **144–46**, 354
Hongshuihe, **146–47**
Hong Xiuquang, 117
Hotan, **147**, 344
Houguan, **147**
Hovd, **147**
hrmaal, 185
hrooy, 185
Hsen, **147**
Hsiukuluan, **148**
Hteu La, 135, **148**
Huaiyue, 80, **148**
Huangdi, 94
Hui, 19, 127, **148–51**
Huishui, **152**
Huizhou, 92, **152**
Hu Shi, 121

Huzhu, **152**
Hyin, **152**

Ichia, **153**
Ili, 56, **154**
Independent Yi, **154**
Is, **154**
Isibukun, 35, **154**
Islam, 30–32, 64–66, 148–51, 171–74,
    178–79, 282–83, 296–97, 322–23, 349–
    51
Islamic fundamentalism, 133, 346–50
Islamic Renaissance Party, 350
Ismaili Muslims, 36–37
Ittifak National Independence Party, 323

Jaizi, **155**
Jali, **155**
Jamtsarano, 37
Jen G'we, 135, **155**
Jesuits, 45
Jiamansu, **155**
Jiamao, **156**, 202
Jiangdong, **156**
Jiang Jieshi, 122–25, 144, 303
Jiang Jingkuo, 125
Jiangxi, **156**
Jianning, **156**
Jiarong, **156–57**, 287
Jiaying, **157**
Jicha, 80, **157**
Jiezi, **157**, 298
Jilian, **157**
Jin, 24, 27, 43, 49, 79, 138, **157–58**, 213,
    301, 362, 391
Jing, **158–59**, 353
Jingpo, 2, 80, 87, 142, **159–61**, 165, 249,
    259, 311
Jino, **162–63**
Jinping Dai, **163**
Jiongnai, 35, **163**
Jixu, **163**
Jone, **163**
Juan-Juan Khanate, 344
Junnong, **163**
Juu Ud, **164**

Ka Va, **165**
Kacha, 251
kachao, 53
Kachin, 159, **165–67**, 196–97, 225–27,
    292, 376, 389–90
Kaduo, **167–68**
Kahabu, **168**, 275
Kaishin, 28, **168**
K'ala, **168–69**
Kalajun, **169**
Kalakqik, **169**
Kalmyk, 266–67
Kalmyk Khanate, 266
Kalya, 251
Kaman, 61, **169**
Kanakanabu, **169–70**, 335
Kangami, 251
Kangzi, 116
Kanzychakov, Sary-Sen, 11
Karakoram Highway, 37
Kargalik, **170**
Karko, 4
Kashgar, **170**
Kashmiri, **170–71**
Kathmandu, **171**, 258
Kavalan, **171**
Kazak, 8, **171–74**, 252, 260, 313–15
Kazan Khanate, 323
kebang, 5
ke'eng, 68
Kengo, 251
Kerei, **174**
Kezei, **174**
Khae Lisaw, **175**, 207
Khae Liso, 207
Kham, 12, 26, 62, 139, **175**, 192, 260–
    61, 313, 328, 360
Khambu, **175**, 179, 291
Khampa, **175–76**
Kharachin, **176**
Khiangan, **176**
Khmer, **176–77**
Khmer Rouge, 177, 235
Kho, **177–78**
Khongodor, 37, **178**
Khora, 37, **178**
Khorchin, **178**
Khoton, **178–79**

Khurukut, 36, **179**
Kim Mun Yao, 39, **179**
Kiranti, **179**, 291
Kirgiz, 23, 34, 140, 155, 169, **180–83**,
    188, 261, 279, 289, 302, 313, 314,
    338, 342, 348, 394
Kiziltao, **183**
Kmhmu, **183–85**, 194, 223, 261
Kocambi Kingdom, 51
Kok Nur, **185**
Konkeu, **185–86**
Konyak, 251
Korchin, 70, 178, **186**, 314
Korean, 107, 133, **186–87**
Korean War, 129, 187
Korla, **187**
Ku Tous, **187–88**
Kulakovskii, A. E., 371
Kumandin, 11, **188**
Kuoketielik, **188**
Kuqa, **188**

La, **189**
Lafufa, **189**
Laho Aleh, 28, **190**
Lahoshi, 23, **190**
Lahu, 23, 28, 62, 88, **190–92**, 262, 274,
    377
Lahu Hpu, 190, **192**
Lahu Na, 190, **192**
Lahu She Leh, 190, **192**
Lahu Shi, 190, **192**
Lahul, **192**
Lahuna, 28, **193**, 228, 274
Lai, **193**
Lakkya, **193–94**, 374
Lamaist Buddhism, 26, 57–58, 76, 89,
    200, 210, 239, 242–43, 263, 327–32,
    336, 386
Lamet, **194–95**
Lan, **195**
Langwo, **195**
Lanna Kingdom, 51
Lao, **195–96**
Lasaw, 207
Lashi, 166, **196–98**
Lau, 135, **198**

Law on Regional Autonomy for Minori-
    ties, 131
Le Shu O-op'a, **199**, 207
Le Va, **199**
Lee Dengui, 125
Lee Kwan Yew, 94
Lee Teng-hui, 94
Lei, **199**
Leisu, **199–200**
Leizi, 80, **200**
Lem, **200**
Lepcha, **200–201**
Lesuo, 207
Leur Seur, **201**, 207
Lhai, **201**
Lhote, 251
Li, 22, 23, 25, 90, 138, 152, 156, **201–3**,
    207, 227, 260, 285, 295, 314, 316, 333–
    34, 367
Lianghe, **203**
Lianhua, **204**
Lianshan, **204**
Liaoning Xibe, **204**
Lijiang Naxi, **204**
Limbu, 26, **204**
Limkou, **204–5**, 289
Lincang, **205**
Lincheng, **205**
Linshao, **205**
Lip'a, **205–6**
Lisaw, **206**
Lishu, **206**, 207
Liso, 207, 210
Lisu, 14, 42, 50, 77, 85, 140, 175, 189,
    199, 201, **206–9**, 214, 227, 259–60,
    307
Liu Shaoqi, 126
Liujiang, **209**
Lloba, 29, **209–10**
Loba, **210**
Loi, **210**
Loisu, 207, **210–11**
Lomai, 135, **211**
Longhorn Miao, 229
Lon Nol, 177
Longqu, **211**
Long-Skirt Miao, 229

Lop, **211**, 344
Lop Nur, **211–12**
Loquei, **212**
Lord of the Three Worlds, 225
Lord Shang, 195
Loushao, **212**
Lower Three Villages Rukai, **212**
Lu, 52, **212**
Lu Meibei, 136
Luhtu, **213**
Lujia, **213**
Lukomi, 251
lulangdaopa, 53
Luliang, **213**
Luofu, **213**
Luohuo, 202
Luoluo, **213**
Luopohe Miao, **213–14**
Luquan, **214**
Lusu, 207, **214**
Lu-tzu, 207

Macanese, **215–17**
Macao, 215–17, 278–79
Maen, **217**
Mahayana Buddhism, 3–4, 109, 305
Mak, **217–18**
Manchia, **218**
Manchu, 56–57, 92, 114–19, 132, 140–41, **219–20**, 241–42, 268, 366–67
Manchu People, **220**
Mandarin, 24, 43, 79, **220–23**, 261, 314
Man-Eating Miao, 230
Mang, **223–24**
Mang-Khmu, **224**
Mang-Muong, **224**
Mang-Puok, **224**
Mantzu, **224**
Mao Zedong, 17, 20, 24, 32, 44–45, 75–76, 83, 90, 124–30, 144, 149, 172, 181, 202, 255, 318, 390, 393
Maonan, **224–25**
Mardzhani Society, 323
Maru Dangbau, **225–27**
Mashan, **227**
May Fourth Movement, 121–22
Meche, **227**
Meifu, 202, **227**

Melo, 5
Mengda, **227–28**, 298
Mensheviks, 10
Menzi, 103
Mergen, 38, **228**
Meuneu, 28, 190, **228**
Mian, **228**
Miao, 45–47, 63, 81, 89, 128, 152, 193–94, 227, **228–35**, 240, 285, 292, 365
Miao-Yao, **235**
Mien Yao, 39, **236**
Milang, 4–5
Mimat, 4–5
Min, 24, 41, 42–43, 55, 78, 79, 80–81, 147, **236–37**, 283, 289, 290, 318, 376
Minbe, **237**
Mindong, 78, 147, **237**
Ming Dynasty, 114–15, 296, 309, 340
Minhe, **237**
Minnan, 42, 55, **237**, 290
Minyong, 4–5
Minzhong, **237**
Misaba, **237–38**
Mngahris, 59, **238**
Moinba, 40, 48, 89, **238–39**, 247–48
Mok, **239**
mokan, 57
Mokertu, **239**
Mon, 200
Monchi, **240**
mong, 53
Mong Mao Kingdom, 51
Mongol, 8, 9–11, 19, 23, 31, 41, 64–66, 113–15, 149, 164, 176, 178, 186, 207–8, **240–44**, 266–67, 287, 306, 322–23, 336–38, 340
Mon-Khmer, **244**
Monklaw, 229, **244**
Monmin, 230, **244**
Monnaonen, 230, **244–45**
Monndaukle, 230, **245**
Monngua, 229, **245**
Monpw, **245**
Monqhaotau, 230, **245**
Monquaban, 229, **245**
Monsua, **245**
Montenkau, 230, **245**
Montuanau, **245**

Monyaochua, **245**
Monzhhi, 159, **245**
Mosu, **246**
Mosuo, **246–47**
Motuo, 40, 238, **247–48**
mubao, 249
Mudur, 142
Mulam, **248–49**
Mungun, 165, **249**
Munya, **249**
Muya, **250**, 287
Muyami, **250**, 287
Myen, **250**, 374

Naga, 41, **251–52**
Naiman, 252
Namhpehn, 28, **252**
Namhsan, 252
Namuyi, **252–53**, 287
Nanai, 140–42
Nanchang, 253
Nanjing, Treaty of, 118
Nanshi Ami, 253
Nantun, 253
Nan-Yue Kingdom, 392
Nanzhao Kingdom, 85, 136, 298
Nasu, **254**
Nationalist Party. *See* Guomindang
National People's Congress, 132
nats, 161, 167, 391
Nawen, 38, **254**
Naxi, 85, 204, 246–47, **254–57**, 382–83
Negidal, 73, **257**
Neisu, **257**
Nemor, 38, **257**
Neo-Confucianism, 112–13
Nepalese, 88, **257–58**
Neustroev, N. D., 371
New Xiang, **258**, 267, 365
Newar, 25, 62, 171, **258–59**, 271
New Culture Movement, 121
Ngawza, **259**
Ngosu, **259**
Nikolayevsk Massacre, 141, 268
nile, 68
Ninlong, 92, **259**
N'kung, 159, **259**
No, 83

No Gelao, **259**
Nofa Lema, **260**
Nofu, **260**
Norsu, **260**
Northeastern Kazak, **260**
Northern Altai, 9
Northern Ami, 12–13, **260**
Northern De'ang, **260**
Northern Kham, **260**
Northern Kirgiz, 180, **261**
Northern Kmhmu, 184, **261**
Northern Mandarin, 24, **261**
Northern Siasiyat, **261**
Northern Zhuang, 87–88, **261**
Northwestern Mandarin, **261**
Nos, **261–62**
Nu, 28, 85–86, 190, 252, **262–63**
Nua, 52, **263–64**
Nung, **264**
Nuquay, 135, **265**
Nurhatsi, Emperor, 140, 219, 268
Nyo, **265**

Oirat, 240, **266–67**, 334
Oirot Khan, 10
Oirot Republic, 10
Old Xiang, **267**, 365
Open Door Notes, 119
Opium War, 118
Ordo, 23–24, 86, 147, 240–41, **267**
Oroqen, 80, **267–70**
Oujiang, **270**
Oxen-Killing Miao, 230

Pa Rauk, **271**
Padam, 4
Pahari, 258, **271**
Pailibo, 4
Painted Pottery Culture, 97–98
Paiwan, 81, **271–72**
Paiwanic, **272**
Pakhtun, **272–73**
Pala, **273**
Pamir people, **273–74**
Pan, **274**
Panai, 28, 190, **274**
Pandit, **274–75**
Pangi, 4–5

Pan-Mongolism, 37–38, 242–43
Pasi, 4–5
Pathet Lao, 184, 195–96
Pazeh, **275–76**
Pe, **276**
Pei-i, **276**
Peinan, **276**
Peking Man, 96
Phzome, **277**, 281
Piling, **277**
Pol Pot, 177
Portuguese, 215–17, **278–79**
Posdantielik, **279**
P'u Noi, **279**
Pubiau, **279–80**
Puli, 135, **280**
P'u-man, **280–81**
Pumi, 22, 156, 277, **281–82**, 334
Pumpkin-Hole Miao, 230
Punjabi, **282–83**
Punu, **283**, 374
Puxian, **283**
Puyuma, 24, 81, **283–84**, 317, 391
Pyin, **284**

Qi, 23, **285**, 286
Qian Dong, **285**
Qiandui, **286**
Qiang, 22, 30, 72–73, 139, 156–57, 250, 252, 253, 254, **286–88**
Qianglong, 116
Qiarleng, **289**
Qin Dynasty, 104–6
Qing Dynasty, 19, 59, 114–19, 168, 219–20, 241, 248, 298, 366
Qinghai Bonan, **289**
Qinlian, **289**
Qiongshan, **289**
Qiongwen, 41, 78, **289**, 360, 376
Qiqihar, 56, 78, 156, **289–90**
Qiubei, **290**
Qua, 83
Qua Gelao, **290**
Quanzhang, **290**
Qumol, **290**

Rai, 26, 175, **291**, 369
Ramo, 4

Ravet, **291**
Raw Miao, 230, **292**
Rawang, 166, **292**
Red Guards, 21, 32, 66, 127, 256, 338
Red Hat Kargyupa sect, 26
Red Miao, 229
Rengma, 251
Revolution of 1911, 208
Revolutionary League, 119
Rice Mother, 7
Robo, 5
Rongba, **293**
Rongmahbroga, **293**
Rtahu, **293**
Ruen sect, 54
Rukai, 81, 212, **293–94**, 322
Russian, 10–11, 56, 74–76, 240–44, 266–68, **294**, 307–8, 344–45, 322–24, 370–72, 387–88
Russo-Japanese War, 10, 37, 141, 242

Saaroa, **295**, 335
Sais, **295**
Saisiyat, 81, 261, **295–96**
Sakizaya, 12–13, **296**
Salar, 31, 157, 227–28, **296–98**
Samtau, **298–99**
Sangla, 26, **299**
Sangtam, 251
San Miao Kingdom, 233
Sani, **299–300**
Santaishan, **300**
Sarikol, 39, **300**, 319, 322, 352
Sedeg, 15, **300**
Segoleg, 15, **300**
Sema, 251
Seti, 5
Shan, 3
Shangdang, **301**
Shang Dynasty, 95, 98–100
Shanghaiese, **301**
Shaojiang, **302**
Shaonan, **302**
Shaozhou Tuhua, **302**
Sharimiye, Mintimer, 323
Sharpa, 59
Shato, **302**
She, 195, 199, 204, 213, 274, **302–5**

Shehleh, 28, **305**
Sherpa, **305–6**
Shihing, **306**
Shiite Muslims, 66
Shiliingol, **306**
Shimong, 4–5
Shinan, **306–7**
Shisham, 207, **307**
Shor, **307–8**
Short-Skirt Miao, 229
Shrimp Miao, 229–30
Shtafari, **308**
Shui, **309–10**
Shuit, **310**
Sihhanouk, Norodom, 176
Sijiaji, 65, **311**
Sikkimese, **311**
Sinli, 165, **311**
Sino-Japanese War, 118
Siping, Duan, 19
Siyi, **311**
Society of Cultural Ecology, 323
Sofranov, A. I., 371
Son, **312**
Song Dynasty, 19, 111–13
Soni, **312**
Sonoba, 65, **312–13**
South Govi, **313**
Southern Altai, 9
Southern Ami, 13, **313**
Southern Kham, **313**
Southern Kirgiz, 180, **313**
Southern Kmhmu, 184
Southern Saisiyat, **313**
Southern Song Dynasty, 92
Southern Zhuang, **313**
Southwestern Kazak, **313–14**
Southwestern Mandarin, **314**
Stais, **314**
Stalin, Joseph, 38, 127–28, 371
Steep-Slope Miao, 230
Subash, **314**
Subhaatar, **314**
Suhujia, **314**
Sui Empire, 109–10
Sunni Muslims, 66, 148–49, 180, 282, 322
Sun Yat-sen, 119–23

Suverenitet Committee, 323
Suwan, **315**

Tabunut, 37, **316**
T'ai, **316**
Tai, 6–7, 32, 44, 50, 63, 192, **316–17**
Taibaliujiu, **317**
Taihu, 205, 277, 314, **317**, 327, 382
Taining, **318**
Taipeng Rebellion, 93, 117, 136
Taiwanese, **318–19**
Taizhou, **319**
Tajik, 39, 300, **319–20**, 359
Takbanuath, 35, **320**
Takebaka, 35, **320**
Taketodo, 35, **320**
Takevatan, 35, **320**
Takopulan, 35, **320**
Tamang, 88
Tame Wa, **320–21**
Tang Dynasty, 2, 109–10, 148, 168, 298, 392
Tangam, 4, **321**
Tangin, 4, **321**
Tangkhul, 251
Tapangu, **321**
Tarang, 61, **322**
Taromak-Vudai, **322**
Tashqurghani, **322**
Tatar, **322–24**
Tatar Public cener, 323
Tavalong-Vataan, 13, **324**
Tay, **324–25**
Telengit, 9
Telesy, 9
Teleut, 9
Temujen, 31, 114, 171–72
tenger, 58
Tfuea, **325**
Thai, **325**
Thakali, 88, **325–26**
Thamo, 36
Thao, 33, 308, **326**
Thatcher, Margaret, 145
Then, **326–27**
Theravada Buddhism, 3–4, 28–29, 281
Tiananmen Square, 132–33
Tiaoxi, **327**

Tibetan, 12, 26, 30, 32, 59, 61–62, 70, 86, 88, 89, 129–30, 138–39, 163, 175, 193, 201–2, 204, 209, 238, 260, 293, 311, **327–32**, 343, 360
Tibeto-Burman, **332**
Tingzhou, 92, **332**
Tiol, **332–33**
Tlhai, **333**
Tonggu, 92, **333**
Tongren, **333**
Tongshi, 285, **333**
Torgut, **334**
Tous, **334**
Tsai, **334**
Tsenglet, 243
Tseole, 15, **334**
Tshomi, 281, **334**
Tsilgalasho, 36
Tsou, 213, 321, 325, **334–35**
Tsouic, **335**
Tu, 152, 237, **336–38**
Tubalar, 9, 11, **338**
Tugaimait, **338**
Tugan Yak, 323
Tujia, 132, **338–39**
Tumed, **340**
Tumen, Uringkhai, 243
Tunbao, **340**
Tung Va Wa, **340–41**
Tungusic People, 74, **341**
Turkic Khanate, 323, 344
Turkic People, **341–42**
tusi, 51–52, 166, 287
Tuyon, **342**
Twenty-One Demands, 121
Tyitso, 135, **342**

U, **343**
Uigur, 34, 71–72, 88, 147, 154, 170, 187, 188, 210, 211, 290, **343–48**, 377–78
Ulukqiat, **348**
United Front, 122
United Hakka Association, 94
Urumqi, **349**
Uyongko, 36
Uzbek, **349–51**

Vachani, **352**
Vang, **352**

Variegated Lisu, 207
Vietnamese, 43–44, 107, **352–54**
Vietnamese War, 176–77, 184, 195–96, 235, 264, 325, **353–54**
Vu, **355**

Wa, 1, 14, 25, 49, 71, 143, 147, 165, 189, 199, 200, 210, 217, 239, 265, 271, 287, 291, 298, 320, 340, 352, **356–59**, 365
Wahhaabiyaa sect, 66
Wakhan, 319, **359**
Wa Lon, **359**
Wa Pwi, **359**
Wakhan, **359**
Wang Guoxing, 202
Wangjiaji, 65, **359–60**
Wang Mang, 108
Wanning, **360**
Warring States Period, 103–4
Wenchang, **360**
Wenma, **360**
Western Hunan Miao, 230
Western Kham, **360**
Western Naxi, 254
White Faith, 10–11
White Horse People, 21–22, 287
White Lisu, 207
White Lotus Society, 117
White Miao, 229, 234
White-Skinned Miao, 230
White Stone Religion, 289
Wild Wa, 359, **361**
World War II, 20, 29, 38, 144–45, 346
Wu, **361**
Wu, 24, 43, 46–47, 79, 211, 270, 317, 319, 327, **361–62**, 363
Wu Di, 107, 134–35, 277
Wuhua, **362**
Wunai, 35, **362**
wung, 53
Wutai, **362**
Wuzhou, **363**

Xia Dynasty, 99–100
Xiang, 24, 42–43, 79, 163, 212, 267, **364–65**
Xiang Xi, **365**

Xian Incident, 124
Xiao Ka Va, **365–66**
Xibe, 204, **366–67**, 368
Xin, **367–68**
Xingan, **368**
Xinghua, **368**
Xinhui, **368**
Xinjiang Xibe, **368**
Xinping Dai, **368**
Xishuangbanna Dai, **368**
Xiuguluan Ami, **368**
Xun, 99

Yakhu, 179, 291, **369**
Yakut, 73, **369–72**
Yakut Union, 371
Yami, 81, **372–73**
Yanguang, **373**
Yao, 18, 34–35, 39, 91, 179, 193, 228,
    236, 250, 282, **373–75**
Yao Min, 39, **375–76**
Yaoyen, 207
Yarkant, **376**
Yawyin, 166, 207, **376**
Yaxian, **376**
Yeh-jen, 207
Yelang Kingdom, 83
Yellow Hat sect, 329, 336
Yellow Lahu, 23, 190, **377**
Yellow Uigur, 343–44, **377–78**
Yeltsin, Boris, 323
Yi, 16, 139, 153, 187–88, 199, 212–14,
    218, 224, 237, 246, 254, 257, 259–62,
    276, 299–300, 310, 334, **378–81**
Yidu, 30, 209, **381**
Yiliu, 80, **381**
yin, 249
Yingyi, 80, **381–82**
Yohur, **382**
Yonaga Kingdom, 51
Yongbei, **382**

Yongjiang, **382**
Yongnan, **382**
Yongning Naxi, **382–83**
Yongxun, **383**
Yongzheng, 116–17
Youjiang, **383**
Younuo, 35, **383**
Ysu Gelao, 83, **383**
Yu, 98
Yuanmen, 25, **383**
Yuan Dynasty, 31, 113–14
Yuan Shikai, 120
Yue, 24, 29, 43, 79, 81, 86–87, 145–46,
    289, 311, 362, **383–84**
Yuebai, 92, **384–85**
Yue Fei, 113
Yue Kingdom, 107
Yuetai, 92, **385**
Yuezhong, 92, **385**
Yugui, 92, **385**
Yugur, 71–72, 382, **385–87**
Yukagir, 74, **387–88**

Zaiwa, 34, 160, 166, 273, **389–91**
Zhanghu, **391**
Zhao Kuangyin, 111
Zhau, Ziyang, 145
Zhiben, **391**
Zhou Dynasty, 100–102
Zhou Enlai, 127, 130
Zhu Geliang, 108
Zhu Xi, 112
Zhuang, 32, 51, 60–61, 87–88, 132, 146,
    204, 209, 261, 290, 360, 373, 382–83,
    392–94
Zhuang-Dai, **394**
Zhulukbash, **394**
Zhu Yuanzhang, 114
Zia Dynasty, 98–99
Zin, **394**
Zodi sect, 54
Zuojiang, **394**

About the Author and Contributor

JAMES S. OLSON is Distinguished Professor of History and Chair of the Department of History at Sam Houston State University. He is the author of more than 25 books on U.S. and world history, including his most recent *Historical Dictionary of the British Empire* (Greenwood, 1996) and *The Peoples of Africa*: *An Ethnohistorical Dictionary* (Greenwood, 1996).

TRACY STEELE earned her undergraduate degree from Georgetown University and her Ph.D. from the London School of Economics. She is an Assistant Professor of History at Sam Houston State University.

ISBN 0-313-28853-4

HARDCOVER BAR CODE

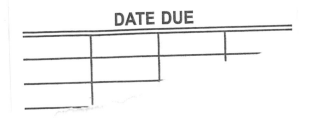